READING INSTRUCTION THAT WORKS

SOLVING PROBLEMS IN THE TEACHING OF LITERACY

Cathy Collins Block, *Series Editor*

RECENT VOLUMES

Reading Instruction That Works

The Case for Balanced Teaching

Third Edition

MICHAEL PRESSLEY

THE GUILFORD PRESS
New York   London

©2006 Michael Pressley
Published by The Guilford Press
A Division of Guilford Publications, Inc.
72 Spring Street, New York, NY 10012
www.guilford.com

Printed in the United States of America

This book is printed on acid-free paper.

Last digit is print number: 9 8 7 6 5 4 3

Library of Congress Cataloging-in-Publication Data

Pressley, Michael.
    Reading instruction that works : the case for balanced teaching / Michael Pressley.— 3rd
ed.
        p. cm. — (Solving problems in the teaching of literacy)
    Includes bibliographical references and index.
    ISBN 1-59385-229-0 (hardcover : alk. paper) — ISBN 1-59385-228-2 (pbk. : alk. paper)
    1. Reading (Elementary) I. Title. II. Series.
    LB1573.P72 2006
    372.41—dc22

                                                                                        2005022680

A few years ago, while I was conducting research in a classroom that included the publishing of student-written books, I overheard a little boy, DJ, reflect, "Why doesn't anyone ever dedicate their book to me?" I told him, "I'll see what I can do." I'll never forget DJ. This one's for you . . . and for other unforgettable DJs, too.

About the Author

Michael Pressley, PhD, is University Distinguished Professor in Teacher Education, as well as Counseling, Educational Psychology, and Special Education, at Michigan State University. With more than 300 publications, he has made numerous research contributions to the fields of memory development, metacognition, and reading. His reading research has focused on vocabulary instruction, comprehension strategies, and the nature of effective literacy instruction. Dr. Pressley is currently editor of *Scientific Studies of Reading,* the flagship archive of the Society for the Scientific Study of Reading, which will begin with the 2007 volume. He has received major awards from the International Reading Association, the National Reading Conference, the American Psychological Association, and the American Educational Research Association. His most recent recognition was as the 2004 recipient of the Thorndike Award for distinguished contributions to educational psychology.

Contents

Introduction

This is a book about effective elementary literacy instruction, intended for the many constituencies who have a need to know about what works to develop readers in elementary school. It is intended especially for those who want to form research-based opinions about effective elementary literacy instruction, including reading educators and specialists, staff developers and in-service professionals who focus on reading, teacher educators, graduate students, policymakers concerned with reading and elementary education, and parents who feel a need to know more about the reading instruction that is occurring and could occur in schools. In short, this volume is aimed at a broad audience who want an accessible and reader-friendly review of the research evidence pertaining to beginning reading, one that doesn't require them to have technical background knowledge in reading research.

I make the case in this book for a balanced perspective on reading instruction, rather than stressing either a whole-language or skills-first instructional orientation. Balanced-literacy teachers combine the strengths of whole-language and skills instruction, and in so doing create instruction that is more than the sum of its parts. The case for balanced instruction is most forcefully and completely made in the latter half of the book, because it is much more convincing following coverage of whole language, reviewed in Chapter 1, the nature of skilled reading, reviewed in Chapter 2, and potential difficulties in beginning reading. When the first edition of this book was written in the mid-1990s, taking a balanced approach to literacy instruction was definitely countercultural. There were many who identified strongly with the skills approach or with whole language. Proposing that better instruction entailed both skills instruction and holistic reading and writing experiences irritated both of these warring camps. I have often heard the accusation that the balanced approach is simply whole language in disguise, a criticism offered by some skills enthusiasts. I have just as often heard that the balanced approach is a camouflage for skills instruction, a complaint from some whole-language proponents. Of course, my view is that both of these criticisms distort my position, which is that balanced literacy instruction entails both skills teaching and holistic opportunities. As such, it requires that the well-informed teacher know much about teaching of skills and much about how to structure holistic reading and writing experiences.

Unfortunately, there are now many more ways a consumer can become misinformed about the nature of balanced literacy instruction than when I wrote the first edition of this book. Look at any Internet data base of books in print for books on balanced literacy instruction, and many titles will appear. My reading of most of these books—and I have read quite a few of them—is that they often are dedicated to either a skills or holistic perspective more than to balance. There has been something of a self-fulfilling prophecy: The claims I heard that balance is a smokescreen for either a skills perspective or whole language seem to have stimulated some authors to construct such smokescreens for their positions. In contrast, I emphasize here that skills and holistic instruction are best when they occur in tandem, with my envisionment of that tandem much better informed as I write in 2005 than when I wrote the first edition 8 years ago or the second edition 4 years ago.

Before you dive into this book, let me offer some advice. Following the first and second editions, I have interacted with many educators who have massively tabbed the book, who have reported to me that they have studied the volume, reading and rereading, and finding new meaning with each pass through the text. Although the big message of balance comes through loudly and clearly, there are many smaller messages embedded in the text, with my intent to stimulate thinking with respect to a broad range of issues in reading education and research. Based on those previous encounters, be prepared for the possibility that the binding on your copy of the book will give out before you are done studying the volume. I am heartened that it is difficult to find a "clean, tight" copy of the book on any of the used bookseller sites on the web.

Perhaps the most common advice to writers is to "write what you know about." This book is about what I know and believe, based on my interpretation of research on reading and reading instruction, but also my lived experience as a reader and a student as well as by my own research on reading and reading instruction. I overview that life in this Introduction because I think it will help you to understand better the ideas favored in this book.

MY LIFE AS A DEVELOPING READER

Many of the conclusions offered in this book align with the facts of my own life as a student learning to read. I grew up in a home filled with what are now referred to as "emergent literacy experiences," with the early years at my house consistent with the best preschool literacy development practices, covered in Chapter 4 of this volume.

I met Dick, Jane, and Sally as a first-grade student in the fall of 1957. From the earliest days of grade 1, I was learning whole words, consistent with the approach used in the reading series featuring the three children who have become cultural icons representing all that was good and bad about America in the mid-20th century (Kismaric & Heiferman, 1996). In a 1995 letter, my former first-grade teacher, Miss Lindley McKinney, confided to me that she did follow the whole-word approach with a lot of phonics added to the instruction. Her memory jibes well with my own recall of her lessons, in which there was much sounding out of words and much reflection on the sounds in words. I have learned from personal experience that effective instruction need not be entirely consistent with any one perspective but rather can be a blending of perspectives, a major conclusion of this book.

Although learning to read in the sense of decoding went well for me in grade 1 and after that, I made less certain progress in becoming a good comprehender. For example, in junior high school, my strategy with high school textbook assignments was to read them again and again, which I now know to be a strategy of choice for many high school students (Wood, Motz, & Willoughby, 1998), continuing in many cases into college (Cordón & Day, 1996). That strategy works poorly and demands a great deal of time. As a result, I became exceptionally anxious about school, grades, and exams as a junior high school and senior high school student. For example, during junior year, I was required to read a book a week in the college preparatory English section in which I was enrolled. I always read my book, but I must admit I always had a great deal of fear that I would be quizzed on books read, for I was having difficulty in understanding and remembering much of what was in them.

I was exposed to some comprehension strategies instruction during junior and senior high school through the SQ3R (Survey, Question, Read, Recite, Review) approach (Robinson, 1961), which involves skimming a text first; asking questions about it based on the title, headers, and pictures; and then reading, reciting, and reviewing. It seemed difficult to execute and certainly did not improve my comprehension and memory noticeably. I knew even then that there had to be better strategies. There are, and they will be covered in Chapter 9 of this book.

In college, I learned the value of prior knowledge. My first year at

Northwestern University was exceptionally demanding. There was no hope of keeping up with many classmates in some of the subjects I was taking, for they had better background knowledge than I did in those subjects. I was not entirely left out of the prior-knowledge-advantaged club, however, for through some enrichment opportunities in high school I knew a great deal about chemistry, and thus freshman college chemistry was much easier for me than for other students. By the end of freshman year, I understood very well that background knowledge was critical to understanding and learning, both from when I was disadvantaged in prior knowledge relative to others and when I was advantaged. There will be much about the importance of background knowledge contributing to reading comprehension in the pages of this book.

I started to use reading and study strategies very extensively during college, generally picking them up from classmates. By the late undergraduate years, I was on my way to becoming a strategic reader. It took a while to get to the level of strategy use now evident in my reading, however. At middle age, I can read books very quickly in subject areas in which I possess a great deal of prior knowledge. I have learned to overview books and to skim in order to avoid detailed reading of parts of texts covering material I already know. I attempt to relate what I am reading to my prior knowledge and beliefs, explicitly looking for points of similarity and dissimilarity with other conceptions I have encountered. I pay special attention to and read very carefully those sections of texts that are likely to be useful to me later, sections I want to understand well and remember. At midlife and midcareer, I am a skilled reader who can communicate with confidence the ideas encountered in books. As a scholar studying reading, I also have come to understand that exceptionally strategic reading is rare in college students, requiring years of reading experience to develop. That work is taken up in Chapter 2.

DEVELOPMENT AS A SCHOLAR OF READING AND READING INSTRUCTION

My scholarly experiences had profound effects on the ideas in this book. Specifically, my thinking was influenced by my background in psychology, especially developmental and educational psychologies. This disciplinary preparation in psychology prepared me for conducting experimental analyses of reading and reading instruction, but also to adapt my skills and outlooks as new issues in reading have come to the fore. Work from a number of disciplines is reviewed in this book, as is research carried out with a variety of methodologies, consistent with the diversity in my own research.

Education as a Research Psychologist

I majored in psychology at Northwestern between 1969 and 1973. While at Northwestern, I undertook a senior honor's thesis that placed me in a number of schools in Evanston, Illinois, for much of my senior year. There was much innovation going on in the Evanston schools at the time, informed by research and a variety of scholarly perspectives on education. My time spent in the Evanston schools did much to stimulate my career-long interest in how research can inform the education of children.

In August 1973, I drove to Minneapolis to begin a PhD in child psychology at the University of Minnesota. Thanks to a cooperative agreement within the Big Ten, I was able to take some of my doctoral work in the Department of Educational Psychology at the University of Wisconsin–Madison and carried out research there for the concluding 2 years of my graduate program. I emerged in 1977 with a PhD. Since then, I have been involved in a series of interrelated scholarly efforts that prepared me for the task of writing this book.

Research on Human Development and Instruction

During graduate school and the years immediately following completion of the PhD, I conducted much research on natural strategy development and strategy instruction. A major conclusion that followed from this work was that sophisticated intellectual strategies develop over many years. However, I also became aware of much other work supporting the conclusion that even children in the early elementary grades can be taught strategies they would naturally acquire only many years later, if at all. That is, I discovered early in my research career that natural development is often slow and uncertain relative to development via instruction. Since the second edition of this book, I have had a chance to review that work formally (Pressley & Hilden, 2006).

Research on Skilled Reading

Excellent developmental researchers understand that to know development it is essential to know about what is developing. Studies of highly skilled performances can be very informative about factors that should be encouraged during development. In the early 1990s, my students and I carried out a study of exceptionally skilled reading, having university professors think aloud as they read articles in their areas of expertise (Wyatt et al., 1993). The outcomes in that study were consistent with the outcomes in other think-aloud studies that Peter Afflerbach and I reviewed in *Verbal Protocols of Reading: The Nature of Constructively Responsive Reading* (Pressley

& Afflerbach, 1995). The case made in that book and reviewed in Chapter 2 of this volume is that exceptionally skilled reading is very active reading, from before reading begins to after it is concluded. Much of the activity can be described as strategic responses articulated with prior knowledge related to the topical content of what is being read. Pressley and Afflerbach (1995) refer to excellent reading as constructively responsive reading, because good readers are continuously attempting to construct meaning. Their meaning-construction activities are consistently in response to ideas encountered in the text, with the responses very much influenced by the reader's prior knowledge that can be related to the text.

This book takes the position that the development of constructively responsive reading is an appropriate goal for reading educators, and one that can begin in the elementary years, in particular, through comprehension strategies instruction (Chapter 9). I came to this position—that comprehension strategies can and should be taught to children—largely through my research on reading instruction. That work has also informed my thinking about beginning reading instruction, including teaching about decoding.

Research on Elementary Reading Instruction

One of my best-known works in reading focused on the development of comprehension skills through strategies instruction. The main research tactic was to study schools where such instruction was making a big impact and to understand the nature of such effective instruction. Many of the insights about comprehension instruction covered in Chapter 9 were developed in this program of research.

This work on comprehension strategies instruction was followed by studies of instruction in primary-level classrooms known to produce high literacy achievement. The work at the primary level is being complemented by research at the middle school level as this revision is being prepared. The research to date on effective primary-grade and middle school teaching goes far in informing Chapter 8, which takes up effective teaching in detail.

When I began my studies of excellent teaching, I went in with an open mind. What I have emerged with as a function of those interactions is a well-informed mind about what instruction can look like when it is done well. I am much in admiration of excellent teachers, and I am very grateful that some of them have admitted me into their classroom communities to observe what they do. When I think of my work in excellent classrooms, I am reminded of the motto of Northwestern University, my undergraduate alma mater: "Whatsoever is true, whatsoever is honorable, whatsoever is just, whatsoever is pure, whatsoever is pleasing, whatsoever is commendable, if there is any excellence or anything worthy of praise, think about these things" (Philippians 4:8). That is good advice, especially with respect to the study of teaching. Much more can be learned about teaching by studying good teaching than by lamenting bad teaching. I have done the former, and that goes far in explaining my perspectives on instruction that are detailed in this book.

When reading the descriptions of excellent teaching covered here, give the teachers the credit rather than me. I was privileged to showcase their work with my efforts in collaboration with many graduate students. In particular, Pamela El-Dinary, Rachel Brown, Ruth Wharton-McDonald, Alysia Roehrig, Lisa Raphael, Kristen Bogner, and Sara Dolezal were important colleagues in these research efforts. Together, the outstanding teachers who were studied and these graduate students helped me to shape a more complete perspective on the nature of balanced elementary literacy instruction than existed previously. As effortful as it was to do it, my students and I always found this work interesting and fun, and we were honored that some of the outstanding teachers we observed became our coauthors and friends. I have been privileged to have great people working with me throughout my career.

Integrative Scholarship on Reading Instruction

I have never been a researcher who has carried out his work unaware of related research (Kiewra, Cresswell, & Wadkins, 1997). Throughout my involvement in reading research, I have studied carefully the major conceptual and empirical works related to reading and reading instruction (e.g., Pressley with McCormick, 1995; Pressley, Woloshyn, & Associates, 1995). Those efforts went far in defining the conclusions advanced in the chapters that follow.

Participation in Development of a Reading Instruction Series

In addition to my research and scholarly writing, in 1991 I became part of the author team of an elementary reading program. My interactions with my coauthors, including then Marilyn Adams and still Carl Bereiter, did much to increase my understanding of the nature of reading instruction that makes sense. In particular, this experience sensitized me to many of the issues surrounding decoding instruction, including the tensions that constitute the whole-language versus phonics debate.

HISTORY AND PURPOSE OF THIS BOOK

Much of this book is an expansion of a series of lectures that I gave to many audiences across North America between 1994 and 2004. This was part of my role as a principal investigator at the National Reading Research Center (NRRC) from 1992 through 1997 and the National Center for English Language Arts Achievement (CELA) from 1997 through 2000. The U.S. Department of Education, Office of Educational Research and Improvement (OERI), funded both centers, and I am grateful to OERI for its financial support of my research. I am also grateful to the University of Maryland at College Park (1989–1993) and the University at Albany, State University of New York (1993–1997), the universities at which I was appointed when this book was first conceived and written. The second edition was possible because of the generous support I received from Notre Dame, where I hung my professional hat from 1997 to 2002. Since moving to Michigan State University in 2002, I and my colleagues landed support from the university to fund a Literacy Achievement Research Center (LARC), which hosts me during this second revision effort.

Since this book's first appearance in 1998, many readers have let me know that they found what was in this volume to be credible and helpful. Beyond listening to the praise, however, I have also listened carefully to reservations that were expressed about what I said in the 1998 and 2002 editions and concerns about issues not addressed in those versions. My rethinking of those issues in light of the feedback received is reflected in the chapters that follow. I wish that I could have interacted with more people over prior editions, but contending with serious illness prevented me from spending as much time with readers of the book as I would have liked. More personally, their enthusiasm for the balanced perspective intensified my understanding that putting up a fight to remain alive was worthwhile, that I did have a message worth imparting, one that might make an important difference in the literacy education of students. As I pen this third draft, I am enduring treatment for a fourth primary cancer, with the expectation that I will once again survive. I am looking forward to many future exchanges with educators about the ideas in this version of the book.

A positive by-product of being ill is that there is increased opportunity to sit with new books and articles and reflect on them. There have been a lot of papers and articles published about literacy research since the 2002 edition appeared. Thus, there is important updating contained in this edition. One of the more important developments since I wrote the preceding edition was the expanding success of the journal *Scientific Studies of Reading*. Much of my reading of research that enters this edition was in its pages as well as in the pages of the *Journal of Educational Psychology*. As the editor of the latter publication from 1997 to 2002, I was pleased that literacy research increased in prominence during my tenure. Literacy continues to remain a prominent concern under current editor Karen R. Harris.

In short, a lot of good scholarship in literacy education has become available since the 2002 edition was written, and this book continues to be strongly evidence-based, including the most recent evidence on literacy and literacy education. Thus, every chapter is updated based on the research published during the past 4–5 years as well as some additional reflection on the research included in the previous editions. Even so, my envisionment of balanced literacy instruction is not something that can be grown only in a university R&D hothouse, but rather something that any teacher could decide to do. Alternatively, any school or school district could decide to promote a balanced approach. The teachers featured in this book all constructed their own balanced instructional worlds, although it is clear that excellent balanced-literacy teachers often go to great lengths to inform themselves about what is research-based best practice in literacy education. Since balanced-literacy instruction is the construction of individual teachers, it is not an instructional package that can be imported, such as many school/classroom reforms that are offered in the marketplace. That said, I am not opposed to widespread reform efforts or even commercial efforts to develop ways to stimulate balanced instruction. Indeed, I am impressed that with every passing year there is additional evidence that some of the most prominent national reform efforts, in fact, are having a positive impact on American students—for example, Reading Recovery, the Perry Preschool Project, the Abecedarian Project, high-quality versions of Head Start and Title 1 early intervention initiatives, and Success for All (e.g., Arnold & Doctoroff, 2003; Borman & Hewes, 2002; D'Agostino & Murphy, 2004; Datnow, Borman, Stringfield, Overman, & Castellano, 2003; Reynolds, Ou, & Topitzes, 2004; Reynolds, Temple, Robertson, & Mann, 2002; Zigler & Styfco, 2004). Often the effects of such programs are smaller and more variable that proponents would like, but on the whole there appear to be more positive than negative outcomes for the national reforms that have been in the public eye for some time.

While on the topic of national whole-school efforts, I should mention that since the latest version of this volume I have continued to coauthor a national basal reading series. At every turn I have done everything possible to encourage users of basals to balance skills instruction and holistic literacy experiences for their students. I urge everyone involved in the development of educational materials and resources to do the same—to do everything they can do to encourage balanced teaching as conceived in this book! Balanced literacy instruction is something that terrific literacy teachers do, but it is also something that terrific curriculum developers and school reformers can promote through their efforts.

A very important direction since the 2002 version of this volume has been the scholarly analyses of the National Reading Panel (2000) report as well as the legislated curricular directions it stimulated (namely, Reading First as part of the No Child Left Behind legislation). The National Reading Panel was narrow methodologically and conceptually. By favoring only true experiments and quasi experiments, a great deal of excellent literacy scholarship was excluded from its coverage. Even more disturbing was the decision to review instructional research on phonemic awareness, phonics, fluency, vocabulary, and comprehension to the exclusion of many other topics (e.g., writing and its effects on reading; use of literature in reading instruction; and motivation and reading). The result is a national agenda favoring a narrow range of reading skills to the exclusion of much else. Excellent scholars have offered a trenchant critique of these shortcomings of the Panel and the Reading First conceptualization of beginning reading instruction (e.g., Allington, 2003; Cunningham, 2001; Pressley, 2002; Pressley, Duke, & Boling, 2004). Reading First as a program is increasingly recognized as the narrow envisionment of a small clique of policymakers rather than the result of deliberate and admirable reflection on what should be emphasized in beginning literacy instruction (Miskel & Song, 2004). Still, the prominence of the National Reading Panel and Reading First forced a change in this book, one that is favorable: The preceding volume covered phonemic awareness, phonics, and comprehension well. This edition now includes chapters dedicated to the two aspects of Reading First not covered extensively in prior editions: Chapter 6 takes up fluency and Chapter 7 vocabulary. To make the point that a balanced discussion of elementary literacy must include commentary on writing, there is also a new chapter on writing (i.e., Chapter 10). With these additions, this volume should make sense in many professional development efforts, ranging from those in response to Reading First to conceptually broader undertakings.

Because this book started out as a series of talks and I have talked about the book as often as I could in recent years, the ideas have been tried out on many audiences. I think of the book as being like a Marx Brothers movie. Their zany comedies were funny because they were first tried out on the road as plays. The brothers benefited from audience reactions, only keeping the good stuff in the final film versions. Similarly, I have tried out many ideas about reading and reading instruction on my audiences, who have made very clear which arguments have been more credible to them. Those are the arguments that made it into this book. My goal was to write a book as informative and compelling about reading and reading instruction as Marx Brothers' films were entertaining. I leave it to you, the reader, to decide whether I succeeded.

This book can be read alone but will be more useful as a gateway to the literature on reading and reading instruction. There will be some who complain that the parenthetical references in the body of the text interrupt reading and hence distract the reader. I have opted for this approach, however, for I find that alternative referencing systems—for example, using footnotes—do not make as clear who did and claimed what. I have erred on the side of providing more references rather than fewer because my experience is that those interested in elementary reading want a great deal of information, and specifically they want to know where they can go to get more information about points that they consider critical. Thus, I have provided references for each chapter because I am aware that some readers are much more interested in some topics than in others. Each chapter is intended to contribute to the overall book as well as to serve as a stand-alone reference for readers who want information on any of the topics covered in the individual chapters. In closing this Introduction, I want to point out that in the chapters that follow much will be said about reading achievement as defined by objective measures, because that is the benchmark of effective instruction for many policymakers and educational administrators. For me, however, there is another way to think about such instruction, a way that brings it to life much better than focusing only on the test scores.

My colleagues and I have been impressed that effective literacy education environments, in which children are learning how to do difficult things and in fact do them well, are also *happy* environments. Most striking, good teachers have far fewer disciplinary encounters with children than do teachers whose literacy instruction is ineffective. Thus, one of the reasons to love effective literacy instruction is the engagement it produces (see Chapter 11), which leads to more harmonious classroom relations. My associates and I frequently have found ourselves wishing that many more children could experience the kinds of classrooms that we have been privileged to study, not simply because the classrooms are good for children's academic development but also because such classrooms are warm, wonderful places. When instructors become excellent literacy teachers, they also seem to become agents of peace in children's lives.

If you find what follows to be compelling, I'll be pleased. Never forget, however, as you read, that much work remains before the ideas detailed in this book are translated as completely as they might be into literacy instruction in elementary schools. There is much more research that can be done and much implementation that needs to occur. More commitment to refine implementation through continuing inquiry also is needed. I expect to revise this book again, perhaps in 5 years or so, and I pray that much revision will then be in order because progress will have been made in the scholarly analysis and dissemination of effective reading instruction, as well as continuing reflective evaluation of literacy development through state-of-the-art teaching.

REFERENCES

Allington, R. L. (2003b). *Big brother and the national reading curriculum: How ideology trumped evidence.* Portsmouth, NH: Heinemann.
Arnold, D. H., & Doctoroff, G. L. (2003). The early education of socioeconomically disadvantaged children. *Annual Review of Psychology, 54,* 517–545.

Borman, G. D., & Hewes, G. M. (2002). The long-term effects and cost-effectiveness of Success for All. *Educational Evaluation and Policy Analysis, 24,* 243–266.

Cordón, L. A., & Day, J. D. (1996). Strategy use on standardized reading comprehension tests. *Journal of Educational Psychology, 88,* 288–295.

Cunningham, J. (2001). Essay book review: *The National Reading Panel Report. Reading Research Quarterly, 36,* 326–335.

D'Agostinio, J. V., & Murphy, J. A. (2004). A meta-analysis of Reading Recovery in United States schools. *Educational Evaluation and Policy Analysis, 26,* 23–38.

Datnow, A., Borman, G. D., Stringfield, S., Overman, L. T., & Castellano, M. (2003). Comprehensive school reform in culturally and linguistically diverse contexts: Implementation and outcomes from a four-year study. *Educational Evaluation and Policy Analysis, 25,* 143–170.

Kiewra, K. A., Cresswell, J., & Wadkins, T. (1997, March). *Biographical sketches of prolific researchers: R. Anderson, R. Mayer, and M. Pressley.* Paper presented at the annual meeting of the American Educational Research Association, Chicago.

Kismaric, C., & Heiferman, M. (1996). *Growing up with Dick and Jane: Learning and living the American dream.* New York: Scott Foresman.

Miskel, C., & Song, M. (2004). Passing Reading First: Prominence and processes in an elite policy network. *Educational Evaluation and Policy Analysis, 26,* 89–109.

National Reading Panel. (2000). *Teaching children to read: An evidence-based assessment of the scientific research literature on reading and its implications for reading instruction: Reports of the subgroups.* Washington, DC: National Institute of Child Health and Human Development.

Pressley, M. (2002). Effective beginning reading instruction: A paper commissioned by the National Reading Conference. *Journal of Literacy Research, 34,* 165–188.

Pressley, M., & Afflerbach, P. (1995). *Verbal protocols of reading: The nature of constructively responsive reading.* Hillsdale, NJ: Erlbaum.

Pressley, M., Duke, N. K., & Boling, E. C. (2004). The educational science and scientifically-based instruction we need: Lessons from reading research and policy making. *Harvard Educational Review, 74,* 30–61.

Pressley, M., & Hilden, K. R. (2006). Cognitive strategies. In D. Kuhn & R. Siegler (Eds.), W. Damon & R. Lerner (Series Editors), *Handbook of child psychology: Vol. 2. Cognition, perception, and language* (6th ed.). Hoboken, NJ: Wiley.

Pressley, M., with McCormick, C. B. (1995). *Advanced educational psychology for educators, researchers, and policymakers.* New York: HarperCollins.

Pressley, M., Woloshyn, V. E., & Associates. (1995). *Cognitive strategy instruction that really works with children* (2nd ed.). Cambridge, MA: Brookline Books.

Reynolds, A. J., Ou, S.-R., & Topitzes, J. W. (2004). Paths of effects of early childhood intervention on educational attainment and delinquency: A confirmatory analysis of the Chicago child–parent centers. *Child Development, 75,* 1299–1328.

Reynolds, A. J., Temple, J. A., Robertson, D. L., & Mann, E. A. (2002). Age 21 cost-benefit analysis of the Title I Chicago child–parent centers. *Educational Evaluation and Policy Analysis, 24,* 267–303.

Robinson, F. P. (1961). *Effective study* (2nd ed.). New York: Harper & Row.

Wood, E., Motz, M., & Willoughby, T. (1998). Examining students' retrospective memories of strategy development. *Journal of Educational Psychology, 90,* 698–704.

Wyatt, D., Pressley, M., El-Dinary, P. B., Stein, S., Evans, P., & Brown, R. (1993). Comprehension strategies, worth and credibility monitoring, and evaluations: Cold and hot cognition when experts read professional articles that are important to them. *Learning and Individual Differences, 5,* 49–72.

Zigler, E., & Styfco, S. J. (2004). *The Head Start debates.* Baltimore: Brookes.

CHAPTER 1

Whole Language

Elementary reading instruction is a topic that has commanded a great deal of attention in recent years. One reason is that learning to read is painfully difficult for some children. There are students in every school in the nation who are experiencing difficulties becoming readers. A second is that, in the eyes of many parents, there is an obvious culprit when their child does not learn to read in school. They believe that their son or daughter is the victim of the reading instructional approach their child experienced. In the 1990s, that approach often was based entirely on whole-language principles, with such principles continuing to affect reading instruction across the nation in the early 21st century.

Whole language is an approach to literacy education that emphasizes natural development of literacy competence. Immersion in real literature and daily writing is favored over explicit teaching of basic reading skills. Skills instruction occurs in wholly committed whole-language classrooms on an as-needed basis only, and then only in the context of reading and writing rather than as a focal point of instruction. Many suspect that the reading problems of many students are more pronounced than those of previous generations because of whole language and that students who might be at risk for reading failure are at even greater risk in wholly committed whole-language classrooms than in environments in which instruction is more explicit (Pressley & Rankin, 1994).

I emphasize that this is not a book about the whole-language versus skills-instruction debate. My view is that the whole-language philosophy has had some profound and very positive effects on elementary literacy instruction and that many whole-language practices should be in elementary literacy programs. However, other practices should be there as well, and much space in the chapters that follow is devoted to making a case for a balance of decoding and comprehension skills instruction with elements of whole language to create an effective and attractive elementary literacy curriculum. I am opposed to wholly committed whole-language instruction, but I find attractive many of the elements of instruction promoted by whole language.

Getting to a balance of whole language and skills instruction requires understanding of whole language, which can be challenging. Those most strongly identified with whole language have often resisted attempting to define it precisely in terms of curricular practices, arguing that an approach that is whole cannot be easily reduced to parts. Even so, for many others, including the author of this book, it is helpful to think in terms of particular instructional practices associated with an educational philosophy. One scholar, in particular, did much to clarify the nature of whole language in terms of practice. Bette S. Bergeron's (1990) article on the subject captured a great deal of attention when it first appeared in the *Journal of Reading Behavior* and continues to be referred to by scholars and practitioners interested in the nature of whole language.

BERGERON'S DEFINITION OF WHOLE LANGUAGE

Bergeron (1990) lamented in the introduction to her article that the term "whole language" was being used too loosely. She believed that this had the potential to undermine the credibility of whole language as an instructional approach as well as lead to misuses of it.

Methodology

Bergeron's approach to defining whole language has a lot of credibility. First of all, she analyzed journal articles, which tend to contain the most up-to-date information as well as the most carefully thought-out ideas. Bergeron exhaustively searched for and reviewed all journal articles on whole language published between 1979 and 1989, the period of time during which wholly committed whole language was conceived and shaped. The articles reviewed included ones by such important figures in whole-language education as Kenneth S. Goodman, Jerome Harste, Sharon Rich, and Bill Harp.

Bergeron's (1990) analysis began with an initial list of characteristics and practices that she expected might be reported as part of whole language. As the study proceeded, however, the list of practices expanded, informed by what was in the articles, with the final list of practices then used to score all of the studies.

Findings

Bergeron's (1990) analysis produced a great deal of information about various issues pertaining to the definition and practice of whole language.

Definition

Bergeron (1990) found that two-thirds of the manuscripts she reviewed contained definitions of whole language—all different. Although the majority of articles provided information about the roles of constructing meaning and functional language in whole language, there was less agreement that whole language was pupil-centered (44% of articles), involved empowerment (42%), was communication-oriented (38%), integrated language arts (36%), encouraged risk taking (30%), included both reading and writing (17%), involved both oral and written language (16%), or was based on a cuing system for reading (i.e., use of semantic, syntactic, and letter-level cues to recognize words rather than relying primarily on letter-level cues; 14% of articles). In short, there was little agreement among the contributors to the whole-language literature about the basic definition of the approach.

Whole-Language Instructional Techniques and Strategies

Just as there was little agreement with respect to definition, there was little agreement about the instructional techniques and strategies used in whole language. Yes, 81% of the articles specified literature as important in whole language, and 64% identified process writing as part of whole language. About 65% of the articles discussed the cooperative nature of students in whole-language classrooms. A little more than half (56%) talked about the affective dimension as part of whole-language teaching. There was less agreement about other practices, however, with a little more than 40% of articles endorsing sharing, invented spelling, independent reading as part of whole language, thematic units, child-centered teaching, learning of skills in the context of real reading and writing, and student choice with respect to literacy activities. More than 40% of articles also specified that whole-language teachers were interactive with their students, with the teachers viewed as learners as well. A little more than 30% of the articles specified student writing of journals, reading aloud, and reading independently as part of whole language. Dramatics, choral reading, predictable books, a reading corner, student dictation of stories, learning centers, teacher modeling, teacher analysis of reading miscues (i.e., teacher analysis of student reading errors to discern student reading strategies), daily reading, daily writing, kidwatching (i.e., for assessment), and teacher–student conferences all garnered fewer mentions in the articles. Bergeron's (1990) interpretation of her outcomes was that the diversity in instructional recommendations probably reflected the diversity of practices in whole-language classrooms.

Bergeron (1990) also notes some instructional elements and practices that are inconsistent with whole language: the whole-word approach— which was the approach used in the Dick-and-Jane era, with students introduced to words to learn by sight—and phonics, with few of those writing the articles analyzed by Bergeron expressing any concern whatsoever that phonics be taught. Whole language also did not involve the teaching of skills out of the natural context of reading and writing, according to the frameworks Bergeron reviewed. Worksheets are not part of whole language, nor is teacher concern with accuracy during decoding. Ability grouping is viewed as conflicting with whole language.

A few years after publication of Bergeron (1990), an analysis using a similar approach was published—that is, involving the careful analysis of articles published in carefully reviewed journals relating to whole language. Moorman, Blanton, and McLaughlin (1994) came to conclusions generally consistent with the ones drawn by Bergeron. However, they also came up with a telling way of organizing their findings in terms of oppositional metaphors capturing what whole language is and what it is not. They argued that the authors of the various articles they reviewed emphasized naturalness and personal ownership of teaching and learning as characteristic of whole-language environments, but they found that whole-language classrooms do not include artificial instruction (i.e., experiences that are not real reading and writing, such as isolated skills instruction), which is controlled by authorities outside of the classroom (e.g., basal publishers). What may be surprising to readers is that, despite the murkiness in definition and in the descriptions of whole-language practices in the journal articles, there have been many volumes written about the nature of whole language, albeit with the more detailed ones coming after Bergeron (1990). It is worthwhile to spend some time reflecting on those volumes, because they are very revealing about the nature of whole language, especially as practiced in wholly committed whole-language classrooms.

VOLUMES ABOUT WHOLE LANGUAGE

There is much that can be read by anyone interested in learning about whole language. I could not possibly cover the many books on the topic, but will instead highlight some of the especially important authors in this section.

Frank Smith and Kenneth S. Goodman

There are a few volumes, continually cited whenever whole language is discussed, in which the case was originally made for making meaning construction the primary goal in learning to read from the very start. In these classics, there is deemphasis of the letter- and word-level processes that are involved in decoding of text in favor of higher-order meaning construction as the driving force in reading. Moreover, meaning construction during good reading is depicted as much more affected by the prior knowledge of the reader rather than determined by the information in the text.

An edited quotation from the second chapter of Canadian Frank Smith's (1979) *Reading without Nonsense* provides the flavor of this line of thinking (see also Smith, 2003, 2004), including clear antagonism for any conception of reading that focuses on letter- and word-level skills:

> One essential skill of reading that no reader is ever taught is to depend upon the eyes as little as possible. . . . [U]ndue concern with marks on the printed page can only make reading more difficult. . . . [V]isual information is not enough for reading. . . . The more you know in advance about a book, the easier it is to read. . . . Readers have nonvisual information about the choices available to an author, and make full use of their knowledge to reduce their own uncertainty about what successive words might be. . . . In other words, the reader knows so much that for every letter the author supplies, the reader can provide the next himself, without even looking. (pp. 12–30)

Among his many complaints about reading instruction, Smith (1979) objected to phonics, making the case that good readers routinely recognize words without sounding them out and that often a word cannot be recognized until its meaning has been comprehended. For those beginning readers who encounter words they do not know, Smith offered the following advice:

> The first alternative and preference is—to skip over the puzzling word. The second alternative is to guess what the unknown word might be. And the final and least preferred alternative is to sound the word out. Phonics, in other words, comes last. (p. 66)

In the concluding chapter of his 1979 book, a chapter concerned with the teaching of reading, Smith continued his attack on the teaching of letter- and word-level skills (which accelerated in the more recent volumes!). Indeed, his list of ways to interfere with learning to read includes the following: "Ensure that phonics skills are learned and used" and "Identify and treat problem readers as early as possible" (p. 138). As will become clear as this book proceeds, it would be hard to imagine advice less consistent with the scientific data on reading and reading instruction produced in the last 25 years. What is so striking in reading Smith's writing, however, is the certainty of his claims. If you reread the quotes I provided, you see no hesitancy, no tentativeness about the thinking, and, if anything, the certainty has increased in the recent volumes, which could have been informed by the voluminous data reviewed in this book. Smith is not advancing hypotheses but rather conclusions, implying as he does that any other conclusions simply are not supportable.

Although the emphases and specifics vary, Frank Smith (1971, 1975, 1979, 2003, 2004) as well as Kenneth S. Goodman (1986, 1996) produced many reiterations of the theme that learning to read is more about learning to guess words well, based on the meaning cues in the text and the prior knowledge brought to the text, with letter- and word-level cues definitely less important in word recognition. Goodman is no less assertive than Smith in his writing. Thus, despite quite a bit of evidence to the contrary at the time of his writing, Goodman (1996) concludes his Chapter 4, "How Proficient Reading Works," with the following:

> In these experiments [i.e., thought experiments that Goodman led readers through in the chapter] you studied your own reading process. You discovered how you achieve *effectiveness* (by successfully constructing meaning) while also being *efficient* (getting to meaning with the least amount of time, energy and visual input). You saw that reading was a far more efficient process than successively recognizing letters in words could ever be. And you discovered how active your mind could be in making sense of print. (p. 52; emphases in original)

If there be any doubt from that summary that Goodman holds no respect for the bottom-up processes involved in decoding text (i.e., translation of visual letter cues into sounds), the summary at the end of his next chapter, "How Developing Reading Works," leaves little doubt: "In the pre-Copernican world of understanding reading we thought accurate, rapid letter and/or word recognition was the center of the process and somehow comprehension followed. But now we know that reading is making sense of print" (p. 61).

By the end of Chapter 7, "The Reading Process: Cycles and Strategies," there is no doubt, with this conclusion offered:

> By calling reading a psycholinguistic guessing game, I wanted to emphasize the active role of the reader in making sense of written language as a new key element in our understanding of the reading process. I wanted people to take distance from the view that reading is the accurate, sequential recogni-

tion of letters and words. I wanted them to understand that, in order to make sense (construct meaning), readers:

- make continuous use of minimal information selected from a complex but incomplete and ambiguous text;
- draw on their knowledge of language and the world;
- use strategies for predicting and inferring where the text is going.

In short, I wanted them to understand that readers engage in informed guessing as they read. (pp. 115–116)

As it turns out, Smith and Goodman are correct that prior knowledge plays important roles in reading; that will be considered in detail in the chapters that follow. Where they are wrong, which will also be considered in detail, is in their belief that semantic cues and meaning cues in text should have priority in word recognition. The scientific evidence is simply overwhelming that letter–sound cues are more important in recognizing words (i.e., reading the words) than either semantic or syntactic cues (see especially Chapter 5 of this volume), despite the assertions to the contrary by Smith and Goodman.

Although the writings of Smith and Goodman did much to inspire the whole-language movement, these works were not very helpful with respect to implementation of whole language. To the extent that they deal with implementation, Smith and Goodman both are more anti-instruction than proinstruction, believing that learning to read depends much more on whole-reading and writing experiences than on teaching about the parts of words and how those parts can be combined (i.e., phonics instruction). Goodman (e.g., 1993), in particular, argued that learning to read is analogous to first-language acquisition, that it is a natural by-product of immersion in print experiences:

What we've learned from the study of language development, both oral and written, is that language is easy to learn when we deal with the whole of it as we use it functionally to make sense. Little children are understanding and making themselves understood in oral language long before they fully control the sound system. That's because they learn language in the context of its use. Children learn written language in the same way. They may learn the names of letters as they're learning to read, and even have some sense of how they relate to sounds. But they can learn the abstract phonics system only in the context of trying to make sense of meaningful print. They're good at learning language when it is in authentic, meaningful context. They're not very good at learning abstractions out of context. (p. 109)

Goodman (1993) concluded his book *Phonics Phacts* with a list of reasons not to teach letter–sound relationships out of the context of actual reading and writing, including (among others) the following:

- Such instruction turns reading from a process of making sense into one of saying sounds for letters.
- It ignores the meaning and structure of language. Phonics instruction distorts children's processing of language by taking instruction out of the language context.
- It begins with abstractions instead of functional, meaningful language that's easy to learn.

In summary, the most important fact about phonics, according to Goodman (1993), is that it should not be taught—because it does not *need* to be taught. Children can discover letter–sound regularities from experiencing actual print and doing real writing. As will become clear in the course of this volume, however, that is too sanguine a view about children's abilities to discover phonics regularities.

Constance Weaver

In my mind, the gold standard with respect to presenting whole-language theory to teachers in a coherent way is Constance Weaver's *Understanding Whole Language* (1994), although her more recent 2002 volume is also very helpful. Weaver does a very credible job of presenting the case that Smith, Goodman, and others began—that meaning making should take priority in reading at all times, including while children are learning to read. Better than Smith and Goodman, however, Weaver presents more contemporary theory and research pertaining to meaning-construction processes.

For example, she emphasizes schema theory, which was the driving force in much of reading research in the 1980s. Weaver leads her readers through the restaurant schema. Most Western adults understand what happens at a restaurant, from prior to arrival at the restaurant until departure (i.e., making reservations, arriving, being seated, getting the food, eating, paying). But the restaurant schema is more complicated than that. Adults recognize how each of the events in going to a restaurant plays out differently in specific restaurants, such as truck stops, fast-food restaurants, cafeterias, ethnic restaurants, family restaurants, cocktail restaurants, and expensive restaurants. Even within these categories, adults have very well differentiated knowledge; thus, many adults know what differences to expect at a variety of ethnic restaurants, such as Greek, Italian, Mexican, Chinese, and Thai establishments. This schematic knowledge is very important in getting through the restaurant event, with our expectations about what will happen leading us through a visit to a restaurant. Thus, while no one who knows about fancy Hungarian restaurants is surprised when a violinist shows up at the table, imagine the surprise if that were to occur at a McDonald's or Pizza Hut.

More pertinent here, when a child enters a McDonald's and encounters a menu, the child's reading of the menu is going to be colored by expectations based on prior knowledge of the restaurant. Thus, in McDonald's, a 6-year-old, when asked to read the top line on the menu over the counter, might say "Big Mac" immediately. In contrast, if the words *Big Mac* were presented to the child at home on a piece of paper, the child might not be able to read them. The context cues that trigger schematic knowledge are very important in reading, according to the whole-language perspective. Indeed, in the tradition of Smith and Goodman, Weaver (1994) makes a strong case that context cues and the schemata they trigger are prime players in reading. Because whole-language educators believe that schemata play a large role in comprehension, their approach is often thought of as a top-down approach. That is, the reader first gets the top level, big ideas, which inform his or her understanding of parts of the text. In contrast is the bottom-up approach, which involves analyzing individual letters to produce individual words that are combined to construct the meaning of the text.

There is little of the bottom-up approach in Weaver's view of reading and much of the top-down. She sums it up early in her book (Weaver, 1994) in the following way:

1. In isolation, most words do not have a single meaning but rather a range of possible meanings.
2. Words take on specific meanings as they transact with one another in sentence, text, social, and situational contexts.
3. Meaning is not in the text, nor will the meaning intended by the writer ever be perceived (or rather, constructed) exactly the same by a reader.
4. Readers make sense of texts by bringing to bear their schemata—their entire lifetime of knowledge, experiences, and feelings.
5. Meaning emerges as readers transact with text in a specific situational context.
6. Thus, the process of reading is to a considerable degree whole to part, top to bottom, deep to surface, inside out. (p. 43)

As part of learning to read this way, Weaver goes on in her volume to specify how every component cited by Bergeron (1990) can play a role in whole-language classrooms. There is much in Weaver's book about immersing children in literature and encouraging them to write. According to Weaver, both play a critical role in learning to read, including learning to recognize words.

Weaver portrays written-word recognition as involving analyses of multiple cues: semantic cues, syntactic cues, and graphemic–phonemic cues. Consider the following sentence, which has one word missing: *Mike is writing a* _____. *Could the word be goat?* No, *goat* makes no sense in this context. How about *lied?* Well, no, because *lied* is a verb, and knowledge of syntactic constraints rules a verb out in favor of a noun. How about *book?* That's more like it, for it is a noun that makes sense in context. With a little more processing of the graphemic–phonemic (e.g., visual) cues—that is, looking at the other letters—it might become obvious that the word was *book*. But what if the first letter was *p* (i.e., *p* _____)? In that case, *book* would not be thought of because you would process the first-letter cue of *p* and thus not think of a word starting with a *b*. *Poem* would make sense in that context, however.

For their conclusion that word recognition involves the use of these semantic, syntactic, and graphemic–phonemic cues, whole-language-oriented scholars cite as evidence the fact that when a reader misreads a word, the misreading typically can be explained as semantically related to the actual word (e.g., for the sample sentence in the last paragraph, if the reader read *play*), syntactically sensible (e.g., for the sample sentence, if the reader said a noun rather than a verb), or graphophonemically related to the target word (e.g., for the sample sentence, if the reader read *boom* instead of *book*; Goodman, 1993). Of course, the problem with such miscue data is that they represent reading when it is flawed rather than reading when it is done competently. Although it is completely illogical to argue that processing during errorful reading is like processing during competent reading, whole-language theorists consistently make this argument. Moreover, the patterns of miscues observed during flawed reading are such that the whole-language enthusiasts have concluded that semantic and syntactic cues take priority over graphemic–phonemic cues in reading, with processing of semantic and syntactic cues permitting more efficient use of visual cues. (Kenneth Goodman wrote a whole book about it in 1973, with a half-dozen how-to-do-it volumes on the topic now available in the marketplace.) As Weaver (1994) put it:

1. Highly effective readers use preceding syntactic and semantic context to predict what is coming next (that is, to reduce the number of reasonable alternatives). On the one hand, their reliance on prior knowledge and context makes their use of visual cues more efficient. On the other hand, it also generates predictions resulting in miscues, but ones that typically fit with the grammar and meaning of the preceding context.
2. Highly effective readers use the following syntactic and semantic context to confirm their prediction, or as an impetus to reread and try to correct.
3. Moderately effective readers use preceding syntactic and semantic context to predict, but they are less successful in noticing where

grammar or meaning has gone awry, and thus, less successful in using following context to correct what doesn't fit.
4. Somewhat effective readers use preceding syntactic context to predict, but they are not as successful at using preceding semantic context to predict. (p. 142)

Given Weaver's belief that good readers use semantic and syntactic
cues to a much greater extent than letter-level cues to recognize words—
especially words they know from hearing them but have not seen before—it
is sensible to play down the teaching of phonics and the analyses of letter-
level cues to recognize words. To say that Weaver plays down the teaching
of phonics is to put it very mildly. Indeed, Weaver (1994) leaves absolutely
no doubt where she stands with respect to the systematic teaching of
phonics:

> *It's not necessary.* Just as they learn the patterns of oral language, so most
> children will unconsciously learn common phonics patterns, given ample
> opportunity to read environmental print and predictable and enjoyable
> materials, and ample opportunity to write with invented (constructive)
> spelling. (p. 197; emphasis in original)

There it is in a nutshell, the classic whole-language philosophy with respect
to the development of word recognition skills: Do not teach decoding
directly. Rather, immerse children in print experiences and opportunities to
write with invented spelling, and they will learn to read.

Weaver (1994, pp. 197–199) goes on to list many reasons for not
teaching decoding systematically, among them her view that visual processing is just one of the cuing systems that should be used, with semantic and
syntactic cues reducing the need to process the visual characteristics of
words. Weaver worries that phonics instruction will lead children to
"sound out" words too much, with not enough attention paid to meaning.
That phonics is very difficult for young children because it involves analytical and abstract learning is a consistent claim of whole-language theorists,
as expressed, for example, by Goodman (1993):

> The phonic relationships in English . . . are . . . abstract: when we deal with
> phonics, we're dealing not with the relationship of language to meaning or
> to things, we're dealing with relationships between two abstract systems,
> oral and written language. (p. 106)

When all is said and done, Weaver comes to the conclusion that there
are many reasons to develop children's knowledge of letter–sound relations
and patterns through authentic reading and writing rather than through

isolated skills instruction. Much of the book you are now reading is about making the case that Weaver (1994)—and other whole-language theorists such as Goodman (1993)—had it about half-right with respect to the development of reading skills. Yes, authentic reading and writing are important in the development of literacy, but systematic instruction in skills is also very important.

Regie Routman

Regie Routman is a teacher who works in a school district that moved from conventional literacy instruction to whole language. As part of that, Routman became exceptionally well informed about the theoretical background supporting the whole-language approach as well as specific practices that can be used in whole-language classrooms. She has recorded her accumulated wisdom in her books, which include, among others, *Transitions: From Literature to Literacy* (1988); *Invitations: Changing as Teachers and Learners K–12* (1991); *Conversations: Strategies for Teaching, Learning, and Evaluating* (1999); and *Reading Essentials: The Specifics You Need to Teach Reading Well* (2002).

Whole-language practice in North America has been very much influenced by literacy instructional approaches in Australia, as defined, for example, by Brian Cambourne (1988, 1990, 1995), and in New Zealand, as described, for example, by Don Holdaway (e.g., 1984). Routman's writing reflects thorough familiarity with the work of these authors but also reflects her complete understanding of how whole language is being accomplished in North America. I am genuinely impressed with the set of beliefs she has come to as a function of her reflection on whole-language theory and living whole-language practice. As will become obvious as this book proceeds, I concur with most of them. The various tenets of her beliefs include the following:

- The developmental level of the learner must be respected.
- All students and teachers can learn.
- Focusing on the strengths must come first when looking at learners.
- We teachers need to demonstrate ourselves as "joyfully literate."
- Learners need many opportunities for "languaging."
- The learning process is highly valued.
- Evaluation is ongoing.
- The goal of education is independence.
- Learning is lifelong and requires thoughtfulness.
- The teacher is facilitator and colearner.
- Curriculum is negotiated, and learners have choices.
- "Demonstrations" are necessary for learning.

- Sharing is an important part of learning.
- Sufficient time is needed for optimal learning.
- Collaboration and social interaction foster literacy development. (Routman, 1991, p. 14)

Routman believes that literacy instruction should involve these key components: children reading and writing aloud, student sharing of reading and writing, teacher-guided reading and writing, and independent reading and writing (Routman, 1991, p. 31). Her books are filled with specific practices that teachers can incorporate into their classrooms. The books also include many insights about how literature can be incorporated into classrooms, students can be taught to respond to literature, spelling instruction can be accomplished so that it is consistent with whole language, content instruction can be integrated with language arts, and classroom management can foster whole language. Both books include "blue pages," which provide annotated bibliographies of references that might be helpful to teachers attempting to understand and implement whole language. The blue pages also provide lists of pieces of literature that are appropriate in whole-language classrooms (e.g., books that invite readers into print, books that are particularly good for readers just learning how to make sense of text, books that fit well into instruction in grades 1–6, books that invite writing, etc.), as well as appendices that can support various aspects of life in whole-language classrooms. Routman's books are invaluable resources for elementary teachers.

There are disturbing aspects of her perspectives, however, with the most saliently troubling being her stance on instruction in word recognition for beginning readers. Routman advocates a problem-solving approach when beginning readers encounter words in print that they do not recognize visually, with the reader making choices between a number of strategies for identifying a word:

- Skip the difficult word.
    Read on to the end of sentence or paragraph.
    Go back to the beginning of the sentence and try again.
- Read on. Reread, inserting the beginning sound of the unknown word.
- Substitute a word that makes sense.
- Look for a known chunk or small word.
    Use finger to cover part of the word.
- Read the word using only beginning and ending sounds.
    Read the word without vowels.
- Look for picture cues.
- Link to prior knowledge.

- Predict and anticipate what could come next.
- Cross check.
    "Does it sound right?"
    "Does it make sense?"
    "Does it look right?"
- Self-correct and self-monitor.
- Write words you can't figure out and need to know on Post-Its.
- Read passage several times for fluency and meaning. (1991, p. 226b)

What is wrong with this list of choices? For one, as will become apparent in the chapters that follow, sounding out a word is the preferred strategy of good readers and one associated with strong reading, in general, and yet it does not appear on this list. Second, although there is growing evidence that recognizing words through known parts of words (e.g., recognizing the -*ail* in *pail* from knowing *sail*) is an effective decoding strategy, it is buried in a long list of strategies based on orientation to semantic context cues. What this egalitarian list of word recognition strategies represents is Routman's complete commitment to use of multiple cues for word recognition—semantic, syntactic, and graphemic–phonemic—the approach favored in whole language.

In summary, I am certain that Routman is a very good whole-language teacher. Consistent with my belief that the practices and perspectives of excellent literacy teachers can be very informative about how literacy instruction should be carried out everywhere, I greatly admire much of what she has to say. I find myself most troubled, however, by her stance on the teaching of word identification, which is not in synchrony with a great deal of research data.

Even so, Routman is more balanced than some other whole-language advocates. For example, Routman makes clear in her 1996 book *Literacy at the Crossroads: Critical Talk about Reading, Writing, and Other Teaching Dilemmas* that at least some students, ones who have a great deal of difficulty in learning to read, really need intensive phonics instruction (pp. 99–100). Their problem is that they have not received systematic teaching of letter–sound relationships. This contrasts with other whole-language enthusiasts who actually contend that the source of difficulties for students who are very slow to read is that they have been taught phonics (e.g., Goodman, 1993, pp. 110–112; Weaver, 1994, p. 198)! In addition, Routman (1996) very soundly recommends that the aspiring whole-language teacher not throw out the spelling workbooks and basals until he or she is confident in teaching spelling using the contextual approach, a recommendation flying in the face of many whole-language opinions. Similarly, she dismisses the frequent recommendation by proponents of whole language not to teach handwriting. In general, there is a lot of reality in

Routman (1996) that I have not found in other texts pertaining to whole language. She recognizes limits of whole-language thinking that others identified with the movement do not.

IS WHOLE LANGUAGE SUPPORTED BY RESEARCH?

In this section I summarize evidence of the value of whole language in contemporary elementary instruction. Even so, whole language does not effectively promote all of the competencies that are required of skilled readers.

Stahl's Reviews

Steven A. Stahl did more than almost anyone else to summarize the effects of whole language on standardized measures of reading achievement. Perhaps the most visible article ever published pertaining to research and whole language was Stahl and Miller's (1989) paper in the prestigious *Review of Educational Research*. The authors reviewed all of the comparisons they could find of conventional reading instruction using a published reading series (i.e., basal instruction) and whole language or a precursor approach to whole language, the language experience approach.

Based on their review of the evidence, Stahl and Miller (1989) contended that the whole-language and language experience approaches are more effective in kindergarten than in grade 1. Since the Stahl and Miller review, when I have seen striking differences favoring whole language over alternatives—especially with disadvantaged children—the outcomes have typically been obtained at the kindergarten level (e.g., Sacks & Mergendoller, 1997). Stahl and Miller (1989) also concluded that whole language is effective in conveying some very general understandings about reading and writing but that it is not particularly effective in developing word recognition skills (i.e., decoding), which is essential if students are to learn to read with good comprehension. The basis for this conclusion is that in 33 comparisons at the kindergarten level involving measures of reading readiness, whole language proved superior to basal approaches, with basal approaches faring better than whole language in only 2 of the 33 comparisons. In contrast, at the grade-1 level, 65 comparisons of whole-language/language experience and basal instruction were available, with 13 clearly favoring the basal instruction, 9 favoring whole-language/language experience instruction, and 43 indeterminate.

A particularly important finding in the Stahl and Miller (1989) study, and one that has gotten a great deal of attention (Pressley & Rankin, 1994), is that positive whole-language effects are much less likely with weaker students and students at risk because of low socioeconomic status than with more advantaged students. Doubts about the effects of whole language with at-risk students have been confirmed in subsequent studies (Jeynes & Littell, 2000; Juel & Minden-Cupp, 2000). Especially striking were the outcomes pertaining to beginning reading (rather than reading readiness): For those 24 comparisons, the basal approach was favored in 9 of them and the whole-language/language-experience approaches were favored in none. An intriguing finding was that, despite the orientation in whole-language/language-experience approaches toward comprehension, if anything, these approaches have had more of an effect on word recognition measures than comprehension. In neither case is the effect dramatic, however, with a modest effect in favor of whole-language/language-experience approaches on word recognition and a slightly larger negative effect of whole-language/language-experience approaches on comprehension.

Stahl, McKenna, and Pagnucco (1994) revisited and updated the Stahl and Miller (1989) conclusions, based on a number of new comparisons of whole language with other forms of instruction. Again, whole language seemed to produce better outcomes with respect to some measures of reading readiness, although Stahl et al. (1994) alluded to some evidence that important readiness competencies, such as awareness that words are composed of sounds (i.e., phonemic awareness; see Chapter 5 of this volume), are not developed well by conventional whole language (e.g., Byrne & Fielding-Barnsley, 1993). What Stahl et al. (1994) found at grades 1 and 2 was a very modest positive effect of whole language on comprehension and a modest negative effect on students' decoding abilities. In general, Stahl and his associates found some support for whole language as a kindergarten approach. They found nothing to favor whole language after kindergarten.

An Overview of Documented Positive Associations between Whole-Language Experiences and Literacy Outcomes

Although the effects of whole language on standardized tests have not been as positive as might have been hoped for by whole-language proponents, there is, nonetheless, quite a bit of evidence that children benefit from experiencing whole-language education. Some of the most important findings are the following:

• One of the most striking and consistent findings in the research literature pertaining to whole language is that immersion in literature and writing increases children's understanding about the nature of reading and writing and stimulates children to do things that are literate (e.g., Graham & Harris, 1994; Morrow, 1990, 1991; Neuman & Roskos, 1990, 1992; Rowe, 1989). For example, there is a growing database supporting the conclusion that when literature drives instruction, there are positive effects on students' autonomous use of literature and attitudes toward reading (e.g., Morrow, 1992; Morrow, O'Connor, & Smith, 1990; Rosenhouse, Feitelson, Kita, & Goldstein, 1997).

• Consistent experiences with high-quality literature foster growth in understanding of the structure of stories, which improves both comprehension and writing, as well as the sophistication of children's language (e.g., Feitelson, Kita, & Goldstein, 1986; Morrow, 1992; Rosenhouse et al., 1997). For example, when teachers and children share books, which is a frequent type of interaction in whole-language environments, the children learn how to interpret stories and go beyond the literal information in the text to draw appropriate inferences (e.g., Cochran-Smith, 1984; Reutzel, Hollingsworth, & Eldredge, 1994).

• Just as broad reading expands the knowledge of adults (Stanovich & Cunningham, 1993), extensive experiences with stories expand children's knowledge of the world, as reflected, for example, by breadth of vocabulary (e.g., Elley, 1989; Robbins & Ehri, 1994; Rosenhouse et al., 1997). Having students read literature that deals with science themes increases the elementary students' understanding of science concepts (e.g., Morrow, Pressley, Smith, & Smith, 1997).

• Despite concerns that practices such as invented spelling might interfere with development of conventional spelling and reading skills, the effects seem to be just the opposite: Good invented spelling is associated with skill in learning to read (e.g., Richgels, 1995).

It should be apparent from this brief survey of outcomes that whole language practices are associated with positive achievements in literacy. Anyone who wishes to argue based on standardized test scores alone that whole language does not have positive effects must confront these data and explain them away. I, for one, do not believe that these data can be explained away, but rather that they provide the impetus for thinking very hard about how the advantages produced by whole language can be replicated in many more classrooms. If more convincing is needed, however, the work of one Ohio-based research team (discussed next) is especially worthy of attention.

Dahl and Freppon's (1995) Study

Although many researchers have offered evidence of whole language's effects on children's literacy development, two researchers are mentioned particularly often as fostering in-depth understanding about the impact of whole-language versus more conventional skills-oriented instruction: Karin L. Dahl of Ohio State University and Penny A. Freppon of the University of Cincinnati. Some discussion of one of their best-known studies will make clear that there is much substance to their work.

Dahl and Freppon (1995) focused on how kindergarten and grade-1 students in whole-language and skills-based classrooms interpret reading and writing and the instruction they are receiving. One aspect of the study that is impressive is its duration, with students studied for 2 years and each classroom in the study (four classrooms total, each year of the study) visited twice weekly. Within each classroom, 12 students in particular were selected for intensive study. All of these focal students were from socioeconomically disadvantaged homes, approximately equally divided between African American students and Appalachian whites.

What were the skills-oriented classrooms like? There was a traditional reading readiness focus with a great deal of attention to letter–sound relations. Grade 1 involved a basal reading program and associated workbooks and skill sheets. Phonics instruction occurred out of the context of actual reading, through skills and drills, with little discussion of how to apply phonics skills during actual reading. Although there was occasional journal writing, there was also copying from the board and writing workbooks. Round-robin reading was a daily occurrence in grade 1, although students also read trade books from the classroom library when their other work was completed. There was some choral reading. When there was storybook reading, the discussion of stories was usually limited to asking students to recall information in the stories. In short, Dahl and Freppon (1995) succeeded in finding prototypical skills-based primary classrooms, which are a far-from-extinct species in North America despite the widespread dissemination of whole language.

What were the whole-language classrooms like? There were long periods of independent reading and writing. The teachers sometimes worked with small groups of readers and writers, and sometimes worked with individuals. The students read fine children's literature, much of it from well-stocked classroom libraries. Teachers often demonstrated reading strategies and skills, for example, in the context of storybook reading. There was a lot of shared reading in these classrooms, with teachers and students engaging in real dialogue about a story as it was being read. Writing was often in response to stories read by the children, with children being taught writing strategies and conferring with teachers about how they might revise their rough drafts. The writing cycle culminated in publication of student writing, consistent with the Writer's Workshop approach so often encountered in whole-language classrooms. Writing was an everyday thing, including journals and opportunities to share writing with others. One means of sharing was that students read one another's published books. Also, an important part of writing involved reflection on phonics, with students encouraged to use letter–sound relations to figure out how to write the words they wanted to use. In summary, Dahl and Freppon (1995) succeeded in identifying prototypical whole-language classrooms.

One strength of the study is that the extensive observation permitted the researchers to ensure that the classrooms they were studying were in fact consistently either skills-based or whole-language. Beyond the extensive observations of instruction, however, there was also extensive measurement of students in order to understand how they understood reading and writing and reacted to the instruction they were receiving. All focal students were assessed with respect to the following:

- Students were presented a printed sentence and were asked if there was anything on the paper. The responses to this probe were revealing about whether students understood written language as a system with accessible meaning.
- Major concepts of books and print were measured (e.g., reading is left to right, front to back).
- Knowledge of letter–sound relations was tapped by, for example, asking students to write 10 spelling words or asking them to write anything they could, then telling about the writing.
- Children were asked to recall a story read to them and to tell a story with a puppet. This was intended to reveal students' knowledge of story structure.
- Children were asked to read a picture book to a doll and encouraged to make it sound like a real story. How they performed this task was compared with how they told about a family event, such as a birthday party. By comparing these tellings, the authors were able to gain understanding about what the students knew about the syntactic and word-level features in books.
- By asking the child to talk about her or his own writing, it was possible for the authors to make inferences about children's concepts of writing.

These measures, which were administered early in the kindergarten year and then late in the grade-1 year, along with the 2 years of actual classroom observations, permitted the authors to come to a number of conclusions about how progress in literacy development differed in the two types of classrooms. I review their results in some detail here.

Concern with Accuracy

An important tenet of whole-language theorists is that mistakes are a natural part of learning. Thus, the message in whole-language classrooms should be that it is OK to take risks; accuracy is not a paramount concern, according to the philosophy. Interestingly, however, students in both the skills-oriented and whole-language classrooms were concerned with accuracy.

Phonics

There was more evidence of skill in application of phonics knowledge in the students in the whole-language classrooms. For example, students' writing in whole-language classrooms often included approximations to words that included salient letters in the words, but this pattern was not observed in the students from skills-based classrooms. When they did not know words, the whole-language students were more likely to use credible invented spellings (i.e., ones reflecting knowledge of letter–sound relations) than were the skills-based students. Another disturbing finding with respect to the skills-based classroom students was that when they sounded out a word incorrectly when reading, they were less likely to notice that the word did not make sense and more likely to accept the misreading.

Response to Literature

The whole-language students made many more sophisticated responses to literature than did the students in the skills-based classrooms. When whole-language students told stories and talked about them, there was evidence of greater knowledge about characters, story events, and plot structuring. In telling and talking about stories, whole-language students were more likely to relate accurate information from well-known children's literature. It was clear that the whole-language students had learned more about literature as literature from their 2 years of immersion in whole language. The whole-language students were appropriately critical as well, expressing ideas about how authors might have varied stories.

Coping Strategies

Dahl and Freppon (1995) observed much more coping in whole-language classrooms when students experienced difficulties; in contrast, they observed more avoidance of challenging tasks in the skills-based classrooms. One reason for this difference in coping was that the whole-language classrooms were more social-collaborative settings, so that it was acceptable and appropriate to work with friends when the going got tough. That is not to say that everything was wonderful in the whole-language classrooms with respect to coping. For example, the least capable writers in the whole-language classrooms often socialized to avoid writing and often elected the nonwriting role in collaborations with other students (e.g., illustrating the story).

Sense of Self as Reader/Writer

The whole-language students more frequently viewed themselves as readers and writers. Only the best readers and writers in the skills-based classrooms seemed to be comparably aware of themselves as developing literates.

Engagement

Persistent engagement in reading and writing was striking in the whole-language classrooms, compared to the skills-based classrooms. The students in the skills-based classrooms certainly did not seem to be interested in reading as an elective activity, compared to the students in the whole-language classrooms.

Knowledge of Written Language Characteristics

In general, students had more similarities than differences in their understanding of concepts of print, knowledge of story structure, and concepts of writing, as well as other indicators of knowledge about written language. The one exception was that, by the end of grade 1, the whole-language students knew more about how the syntax and wording of stories differ from natural speech than did the students in the skills-based classes.

Word Recognition Strategies

The whole-language emphasis on use of context cues came through when students' reading was analyzed in the Dahl and Frippon (1995) study. When encountering an unfamiliar word, whole-language students were more likely to use picture cues, skip unknown words, reread and self-correct, and comment about the story than were students from skills-based classrooms. The skills-based students relied more exclusively on letter–sound relationships to recognize unknown words.

Summary

There were plenty of positives favoring the whole-language classrooms over the skills-based classrooms in Dahl and Freppon (1995), and the outcomes in their study are broadly consistent with the list of advantages compiled across a number of studies summarized earlier in this section. Dahl and Freppon have published some other analyses of the classrooms analyzed in the 1995 report, which also favor the whole-language classrooms. For example, Freppon (1991) reported that students in whole-language classrooms understood much better than skills-based students that reading is about getting the meaning rather than simply reading the words. Dahl (1993) analyzed the comments that the whole-language students made while they wrote. The students engaged in a great deal of self-regulated reflection on letter–sound relations as they wrote, with lots of attention to patterns in letters and words.

For all that was positive, there was an important difference between the classrooms that is telling from the perspective of many researchers studying reading. Although the whole-language students seem to have been learning much about letter–sound relations and how to use them, they seem not to have used them with as much certainty as students in skills-based classrooms. The whole-language students were much more likely than the skills-based students to rely on picture and semantic context cues. In the chapters that follow, the case will be made that this is a disastrous strategy—and that it points to a great weakness in whole-language instruction that does not include extensive, systematic coverage of word recognition in terms of consistent letter–sound and orthographic analysis of unfamiliar words.

Dahl, Scharer, Lawson, and Grogan (1999)

Dahl, Scharer, Lawson, and Grogan (1999) provided an extremely important follow-up to the Dahl and Freppon (1995) investigation. They studied eight grade-1 classrooms that were definitely consistent with whole-language philosophy. They specifically focused on the phonics instruction that occurred in these classrooms, with extensive observations from November to May of one school year. What they found was that there was a great deal of phonics instruction occurring in the context of reading literature and composing, largely in response to literature. That is, they found much phonics instruction occurring in the context of whole-language activities. Students received much encouragement and instruction to use phonics to decode words they were reading, with minilessons inserted on various aspects of sounding out as students read. During writing, teachers encouraged students extensively to spell words the way they sound. An important observation was that the instruction in these classrooms was very much tailored to the needs of particular students, very much in reaction to problems the students encountered as they read and wrote.

Such instruction seemed to make a difference, with clear increases in phonics knowledge (i.e., both ability to read words and spell them) over the course of the study on four different measures. Most impressively, the increases were observed with readers who were initially strong, those who were initially weak, and those in the middle.

Of course, we do not know how students in skills-oriented classrooms would have done with respect to phonics over a comparable period of time. In addition, the teachers were selected because they were very good whole-language teachers. The case will be made clear in Chapter 8 of this volume that only a minority of primary-grade teachers are excellent teachers, who are also the ones producing achievement most certainly. So, Dahl et al.'s results are an existence proof that there are good whole-language grade-1 classrooms where students make progress in their phonics knowledge. Moreover, no one could read this study and emerge without being impressed that there was much attractive about the instruction occurring in the classrooms studied by Dahl et al. We emphasize that point because many of the characteristics of the classrooms studied by Dahl et al. (1999) are the ones encountered in outstanding and effective primary-grade classrooms (see Chapter 8). This study is important enough that I will have more to say about it in Chapter 5, focusing there on the look of instruction that balances phonics and whole-language approaches.

Commentary

Some who are reading this book are probably wondering how whole language, which has enjoyed widespread dissemination, could have been studied so little. One side of the answer is that those most strongly identified with whole language are very little interested in studying it, comfortable in their philosophically and theoretically based convictions about whole language's effectiveness. The other side is that those same whole-language proponents have been aggressive in challenging reading researchers who want to study whole language. Indeed, a few years ago, when three researchers (McKenna, Robinson, & Miller, 1990) proposed in an even-handed, statesmanlike way that more research on whole language might be desirable, they were blasted in print in one of the most widely circulated educational research journals by whole-language advocate Carol Edelsky (1990). Here is a sample of Edelsky's comments to McKenna and colleagues' (1990) mere suggestion that whole language might be studied, which she viewed as inconsistent with her worldview and that of whole-language educators in general:

> They [McKenna et al.] don't know from *gornischt* (from nuthin') but they sure have *chutzpah* (unmitigated gall)!! . . . It is not necessary and often not in their interests for whites, Christians, and men [McKenna and his coauthors were all three] to appreciate that there might be a coherent perspective that drastically contradicts their own. . . . Between their paradigm blindness and their conceptual errors, it is no wonder that [their] proposed research agenda is off base. . . . Whole language objects to relative effectiveness studies because, with their typical reliance on test score data, they promote test-driven curricula. Such curricula and such studies weaken teachers and students and subvert whole language goals; that is, they feed into mechanisms for stratifying society. . . . After acting as self-appointed statesmen who can broker two conflicting points of view because they themselves supposedly are eclectic, after distorting or outright obliterating

whole language assumptions, arguments, definitions, and research agendas with an imposed agenda that doesn't acknowledge its own paradigmatic bias, McKenna et al. then deliver the crowning blow—they call on whole language proponents to collaborate in all this. Gei gezundt (lotsa luck to 'em). (Edelsky, 1990, pp. 7–10)

Fortunately, some very good scientists ignored such advisement (and other blistering attacks). Hence, there is a growing body of data addressing what whole language can do and what it does not do.

To review, we now know that there are many general points of understanding about reading and writing that are promoted by whole language. Moreover, literature and writing immersion promote the development of important content knowledge and ability in writing. At least in excellent whole-language classrooms, phonics is taught and phonics skills develop. Based on existing comparisons between skills-based and whole-language instruction, however, concerns remain, especially with respect to at-risk students, that learning to read words may not be as certain in whole-language as compared to skills-oriented classrooms. This is one reason that whole-language philosophy has not been embraced wholeheartedly by many concerned with early reading. Another reason is that, like Edelsky (1990), whole-language proponents often have packaged their ideas about curriculum as political perspectives—political perspectives unlikely to persuade many literacy educators.

POLITICS OF BEGINNING READING INSTRUCTION (AT LEAST ACCORDING TO SOME WHOLE-LANGUAGE LEADERS)

No one who has had any contact with recent discussions regarding elementary reading instruction could have missed the political tone of the whole-language leadership. I offer here a sampler of their political thinking.

Kenneth S. Goodman

One of the most important early documents in the great debates surrounding reading was *Becoming a Nation of Readers*, which was prepared largely by a group at the Center for the Study of Reading, University of Illinois, headed by Richard C. Anderson (Anderson, Hiebert, Scott, & Wilkinson, 1985). The Center and the writing of the document itself were supported by grants from the U.S. Department of Education. Consistent with substantial research that phonics instruction should be part of beginning reading programs, the report includes recommendations for systematic teaching of decoding. The Center would also oversee the writing of Marilyn Adams's (1990) *Beginning to Read: Thinking and Learning about Print*, which summarized the evidence supportive of decoding-skills instruction.

Goodman (1993), in a chapter titled "The Politics of Phonics," characterized Anderson and associates' *Becoming a Nation of Readers* as a tool of the "phonics-first lobby" (p. 103) and Adams's conclusions in *Beginning to Read* as "determined in advance by a federal government agency acting on the instructions of the Congress" (pp. 103–104). He concluded, "Some people further their own [conservative] political purposes by using phonics to frighten and politicize rural and working-class parents" (p. 98). Similar sentiments appeared in Goodman (1996).

Constance Weaver

Weaver's (1994) textbook includes an entire chapter (Chap. 7), "Phonics and Whole Language: From Politics to Research," largely dedicated to the proposition that skills instruction is part of the archconservative political agenda. Here are Weaver's words on the topic:

> There is substantial evidence that advocacy for heavy phonics instruction is coming particularly from certain individuals and organizations within the Far Right. For instance, the ultraright National Association of Christian Educators (NACE) and its action group Citizens for Excellence in Education (CEE) urge their Christian followers to insist upon the teaching of phonics in the school. . . . A publication of the Heritage Foundation, a conservative think tank in Washington, extols phonics as "the very first tenet of the back-to-basics approach," which is advocated as the best approach to the illiteracy problem. . . . A great deal of the force behind such advocacy seems to be the desire to promote a religious agenda and/or to maintain the socioeconomic status quo. (p. 295)
>
> Members of the Far Right who emphasize getting the words "right" and value so-called literal recall rather than construction of meaning also tend to insist upon the extensive and intensive teaching of phonics. Having children do extensive and intensive work with phonics suits their worldview. . . . Intensive phonics instruction is necessary because only the ability to sound out unfamiliar words will guarantee word-perfect reading. . . . [Quoting James A. Chapman, whom Weaver presents as a member of the Christian Right], "whenever initial emphasis is placed upon meaning instead of identifying the exact words that are on the page, a student is implicitly learning that individual words are not important. . . . [T]he emphasis upon individual words has always been of paramount importance to Christian educators, who believe in the verbal inspiration of the Scriptures and in quality education. Orthodox Christians believe that God gave every word of the Scripture, not just the thoughts." (p. 296)

> Teaching intensive phonics is . . . a way of keeping children's attention on doing what they're told and keeping them from reading or thinking for themselves. (p. 296)

Weaver continues elaborating the case that phonics instruction is part of a plan to maintain a stratified society, one in which those who are now lower-class spawn future generations of the lower class. According to Weaver (1994, p. 299), who was very much influenced in her thinking on this subject by postmodernist critics of education (e.g., Giroux, 1983; Shannon, 1992), this occurs because lower-class children arrive at school already far behind other children, because of, for example, restricted language experiences during the preschool years (see Chapter 4 of the present volume). Such children are assigned to lower reading groups and are subjected to more skills instruction (e.g., phonics) than are other children, because they are deemed to need it. As the first step in a long downward spiral, among other negatives, such boring instruction kills these students' motivation, perhaps eventuating in their dropping out of school. This dooms them to continue in the lower class, where they spawn children who begin the cycle again.

According to Weaver, the blame for membership in the lower class falls in part on the shoulders of scholars who document the efficacy of including skills instruction as part of early reading instruction. As she summed it up:

> Unfortunately, this vicious cycle is all too likely to be encouraged by . . . Marilyn Adams's book *Beginning to Read: Thinking and Learning About Print* . . . cited approvingly by Far Right advocates even before it was published. . . . It seems likely that such heavy phonics instruction will serve to perpetuate the nonmainstream status of many of these students through the overt curriculum, which keeps them busy with skills work instead of real reading. (pp. 301–302)

Regie Routman

Much of Routman's 1996 book *Literacy at the Crossroads: Crucial Talk about Reading, Writing, and Other Teaching Dilemmas* is concerned with politics. She makes the case that to some extent political leaders and policymakers have scapegoated educators and that the literacy crisis is not nearly as pronounced as many policymakers make it out to be. This point is reasonably credible, consistent with the conclusions of a thorough analysis published by Berliner and Biddle (1995), which influenced much of Routman's theory. Routman is also aware that educational change will be resisted by many (see her Chap. 4) and offers many suggestions as to how educators can work in their settings to overcome political resistance. Indeed, the entire 1996 book is a political document, specifically about how to make whole language more palatable to many stakeholders and thus more likely to be the language-arts approach of choice. For example, Routman (1996) revises the whole-language story, stating early in the book, "*The reality is and has always been that phonics is part of whole language*" (p. 9; emphasis in original). That is, according to Routman (1996), whole-language teachers have always been in favor of teaching phonics to students on an as-needed basis and have always believed that phonics knowledge develops during authentic reading and writing.

In part, Routman's point is to defend whole language against its political critics, but it is also aimed at teachers who misinterpreted whole language to mean no skills instruction. Routman is blatantly honest about the existence of such teachers, as in, for example, a section of her Chapter 3 titled "I'm Whole Language—I Don't Teach Phonics." My only point of difference with Routman is that I do not believe that such teachers seriously misunderstood whole language as it was portrayed to them, for I have read the books they would have read, and it is easy to leave those books feeling that to teach skills is inconsistent with whole language. That Dahl and her colleagues found whole-language teachers who teach skills probably reflects that they came to their position through some other means than buying the whole-language philosophy lock, stock, and barrel as portrayed in a number of volumes that depict whole language as not involving explicit skills instruction.

Are the Political Perspectives of Whole-Language Leaders Realistic?

To many, the highly politicized perspectives of whole-language leaders seem out of touch with reality. Clearly they do not take into account the concerns of many teachers who work very hard to develop literacy competencies in children. To the extent that such political perspectives have been addressed in formal studies, they have not proven accurate. Consider, for example, research relating to the perspectives of curriculum theorist Michael W. Apple (1982, 1986), who is sympathetic to whole language.

Apple argues that basal reading programs not only limit teachers' freedom but, more than that, actually de-skill them. The specific argument is that, rather than choosing among their various teaching skills to plan a reading curriculum, teachers who rely on a basal program surrender control to an outside authority. According to Apple, this leads to an atrophying of teaching planning skills—hence, the term "de-skilling" (Apple, 1986, p. 209). The problem with this argument is that it just does not square with the data. In fact, according to several investigations involving very different methodologies (Barr & Sadow, 1989; Baumann & Heubach, 1994; Hoffman et al., 1995), teachers do not just follow the basal manuals but rather are highly creative, carefully choosing and adapting parts of the basal program that make sense in their reading instruction. Of course, that basals do *not* de-skill teachers is just one of several data-based research conclusions that differ from what wholly committed whole-language and like-thinking curriculum theorists would have teachers believe.

In closing this section, I want to point out that my main intent in covering the political side of whole language is to make clear to readers why some whole-language proponents are so adamantly opposed to skills instruction: They believe that skills instruction serves political agendas not consistent with the best interests of many children.

I can understand their passions, given their perceptions and convictions about the world. Admittedly, politically conservative individuals do more closely identify themselves with skills instruction, especially phonics, than do politically liberal individuals (Paterson, 2003). I simply do not agree with whole-language theorists' tendency to politicize this question, and I cannot make a conscionable case based on political considerations for not teaching children literacy skills. Indeed, my own view is that one part of any strategy to prevent disadvantaged children from being upwardly mobile would be to deny them effective literacy instruction. Rather, I advocate employing the most convincing scientific analyses available to determine effectiveness. I sincerely believe that those who would deny such instruction to children for whatever reason are, in fact, working on behalf of those who might prefer to prevent the disadvantaged from becoming more advantaged.

I'll close by noting one peculiar omission in the concerns of the whole language theorists. They seem unconcerned about the brighter and more able students. One possibility is that the skills instruction they oppose should be opposed—at least in very high doses—for such children, because they are capable of learning to read and write when taught holistically. There are at least some suggestive data that overemphasis on skills instruction might not be in the best interests of children who enter grade 1 at the top of the class (Connor, Morrison, & Katch, 2004; Juel & Minden-Cupp, 2000; Leppänen, Niemi, Aunola, & Nurmi, 2004). This possibility deserves a great deal of attention in the years ahead.

SUMMARY AND CONCLUDING REFLECTIONS

1. Whole language was been a dominating force in contemporary elementary-level literacy instruction for more than a decade, perhaps diminishing slightly since the turn of the century, but still a potent force in elementary language arts. Dick, Jane, and Sally have been replaced by immersion in real literature, and there is a great deal more student writing

today than there was during the mid-20th century. These practices have improved students' knowledge and their composing skills, as well as positively affected their attitudes toward reading.

2. Frank Smith and like-minded psycholinguistically oriented scholars formulated a top-down view of reading. According to their perspective, readers have hypotheses based on prior knowledge and ideas already encountered about which words might be coming up in the text that they are reading. Their hypotheses are also affected by knowledge of English syntax and the lexical constraints imposed by syntax, so that the good reader does not expect a noun in a part of a sentence that takes a verb. Finally, the letters and letter chunks in words (i.e., graphemic–phonemic cues) are noted and processed. The proof that word recognition involves use of multiple cues in this fashion is in the reading errors that are sometimes made. Particularly important, misreadings often are related semantically to words misread, which whole-language enthusiasts take as evidence of the primacy of semantic cues over graphemic–phonemic cues.

3. Educators committed to whole language have been assisted in implementing their efforts by the writings of Constance Weaver, Regie Routman, and others. Weaver's conception of language-arts education seems entirely consistent with the thinking of Frank Smith, Kenneth S. Goodman, and whole-language educational theorists from New Zealand and Britain. It is filled with recommendations to immerse students in print and writing. Teachers are to expect much of young learners as they give them the time and opportunities they need to practice real literacy; they also must permit them to make the mistakes that are part of learning to read and write. The teacher's role is largely to provide timely and appropriate feedback when such mistakes occur, according to Weaver: to prompt students to reflect on their errors and in doing so construct new understandings about reading and writing.

Regie Routman's thinking seems to be less bound to whole-language principles than is Weaver's, reflecting her complete grounding in actual schooling. Even so, with respect to word recognition, Routman's prescriptions are much more consistent with Smith, Goodman, and other whole-language advocates than with the research-based perspective on word recognition that is outlined in the chapters that follow.

4. Although whole language is comprehensive with respect to language-arts education, and many specific whole-language practices have been identified for encouraging development of reading and writing competencies, one issue seems to be more important than all others in differentiating the whole-language perspective from others: Whole-language theorists and educators have a perspective on word recognition that contrasts with the positions of many others who are concerned with reading, especially beginning reading.

In addition, a point not much emphasized so far in this chapter, the whole-language approach to development of comprehension skills is read, read, and read. This is an old model of comprehension development. As will become evident in Chapter 9, there is much more that can be done to stimulate mature comprehension. Thus, my view is that whole language is an incomplete model of literacy development. By the end of this book, the case will be made that what is good in whole language should be combined with more explicit instruction of decoding and comprehension. To be certain, some whole-language teachers, such as those studied by Dahl and her associates, have made great progress down the road to balanced literacy instruction, but, based on my experience in observing a broad range of primary-grade classrooms, many wholly committed whole-language teachers are anything but balanced in their approach.

5. Whole language is a politically charged philosophy of curriculum. Whole-language advocates have claimed repeatedly that skills instruction is a tool of conservatives, a tool used to maintain current socioeconomic and political stratifications. Those perspectives provide important insights into why opposition to skills instruction is so intense within the whole-language education community.

Even so, students already at risk for school failure because of low socioeconomic status do not fare well with whole language when evaluated with standardized measures (e.g., Jeynes & Littell, 2000). This fact motivates much of the opposition of political conservatives to whole language. So does the mounting evidence that whole-language instructional practices do not affect some word-level reading competencies that are valued by political conservatives: Whole language does not promote spelling skills as well as alternatives (e.g., Graham, 2000), and reading of predictable texts does not develop word recognition skills as reliably as alternatives (e.g., Johnston, 2000) and does not produce as certain vocabulary growth (Swanborn & De Glopper, 1999). These are good reasons for politically liberal individuals who worry greatly about the education and welfare of disadvantaged children to be concerned about whole language as a pedagogical approach.

REFERENCES

Adams, M. (1990). *Beginning to read: Thinking and learning about print.* Cambridge, MA: MIT Press.

Anderson, R. C., Hiebert, E. H., Scott, J. A., & Wilkinson, I. A. G. (1985). *Becoming a nation of readers.* Washington, DC: National Institute of Education.

Apple, M. W. (1982). *Education and power.* New York: Ark Paperbacks.

Apple, M. W. (1986). *Teachers and texts: A political economy of class and gender relations in education.* New York: Routledge.

Barr, R., & Sadow, M. W. (1989). Influence of basal programs on fourth-grade reading instruction. *Reading Research Quarterly, 24,* 44–71.

Baumann, J. F., & Heubach, K. M. (1994). *Do basal readers deskill teachers?* (Reading Research Report No. 26). Athens, GA, and College Park, MD: National Reading Research Center.

Bergeron, B. S. (1990). What does the term whole language mean? Constructing a definition from the literature. *Journal of Reading Behavior, 22,* 301–330.

Berliner, D. C., & Biddle, B. J. (1995). *The manufactured crisis: Myths, fraud, and the attack on America's public schools.* Reading, MA: Addison-Wesley.

Byrne, B., & Fielding-Barnsley, R. (1993). Evaluation of a program to teach phonemic awareness to young children: A 1-year follow-up. *Journal of Educational Psychology, 85,* 104–111.

Cambourne, B. (1988). *The whole story: Natural learning and the acquisition of literacy in the classroom.* Auckland, New Zealand: Scholastic.

Cambourne, B. (1990). *Read and retell: A strategy for the whole language/natural learning classroom.* Portsmouth, NH: Heinemann.

Cambourne, B. (1995). Toward an educationally relevant theory of literacy learning: Twenty years of inquiry. *Reading Teacher, 49*(3), 182–190.

Cochran-Smith, M. (1984). *The making of a reader.* Norwood, NJ: Ablex.

Connor, C. D., Morrison, F. J., & Katch, L. E. (2004). Beyond the reading wars: Exploring the effect of child-intruction interactions on growth in early reading. *Scientific Studies in Reading, 8,* 305–336.

Dahl, K. L. (1993). Children's spontaneous utterances during early reading and writing instruction in whole-language classrooms. *Journal of Reading Behavior, 25,* 279–294.

Dahl, K. L., & Freppon, P. A. (1995). A comparison of inner-city children's interpretations of reading and writing instruction in the early grades in skills-based and whole language classrooms. *Reading Research Quarterly, 30,* 50–74.

Dahl, K. L., Scharer, P. L., Lawson, L. L., & Grogan, P. R. (1999). Phonics instruction and student achievement in whole language first-grade classrooms. *Reading Research Quarterly, 34,* 312–341.

Edelsky, C. (1990). Whose agenda is this anyway?: A response to McKenna, Robinson, and Miller. *Educational Researcher, 19*(8), 7–11.

Elley, W. B. (1989). Vocabulary acquisition from listening to stories. *Reading Research Quarterly, 24,* 174–187.

Feitelson, D., Kita, B., & Goldstein, Z. (1986). Effects of listening to series stories on first graders' comprehension and use of language. *Research in the Teaching of English, 20,* 339–356.

Freppon, P. A. (1991). Children's concepts of the nature and purpose of reading in different instructional settings. *Journal of Reading Behavior, 23,* 139–163.

Giroux, H. A. (1983). *Theory and resistance in education: A pedagogy for the opposition.* Granby, MA: Bergin & Garvey.

Goodman, K. S. (1973). *Miscue analysis: Applications to reading instruction.* Urbana, IL: National Council of Teachers of English.

Goodman, K. S. (1986). *What's whole in whole language?* Richmond Hill, Ontario, Canada: Scholastic. (Distributed in the United States by Heinemann)

Goodman, K. S. (1993). *Phonics phacts.* Portsmouth, NH: Heinemann.

Goodman, K. S. (1996). *On reading.* Portsmouth, NH: Heinemann.

Graham, S. (2000). Should the natural learning approach replace spelling instruction? *Journal of Educational Psychology, 92,* 235–247.

Graham, S., & Harris, K. R. (1994). The effects of whole language on children's writing: A review of literature. *Educational Psychologist, 29,* 187–192.

Hoffman, J. V., McCarthey, S. J., Bayles, D., Price, D., Elliott, B., Dressman, M., & Abbott, J. (1995). *Reading instruction in first-grade classrooms: Do basals control teachers?* (Reading Research Report No. 43). Athens, GA, and College Park, MD: National Reading Research Center.

Holdaway, D. (1984). *The foundation of literacy.* Sydney, New South Wales, Australia: Ashton Scholastic. (Distributed in the United States by Heinemann)

Jeynes, W. H., & Littell, S. W. (2000). A meta-analysis of studies examining the effect of whole language instruction on the literacy of low-SES students. *Elementary School Journal, 101,* 21–33.

Johnston, F. R. (2000). Word learning in predictable texts. *Journal of Educational Psychology, 92,* 248–255.

Juel, C., & Minden-Cupp, C. (2000). Learning to read words: Linguistic units and instructional strategies. *Reading Research Quarterly, 35,* 458–492.

Leppänen, U., Niemi, P., Aunola, K., & Nurmi, J.-E. (2004). Development of reading skills among preschool and primary school pupils. *Reading Research Quarterly, 39,* 72–93.

McKenna, M. C., Robinson, R. D., & Miller, J. W. (1990). Whole language: A research agenda for the nineties. *Educational Researcher, 19*(8), 3–6.

Moorman, G. B., Blanton, W. E., & McLaughlin, T. (1994). The rhetoric of whole language. *Reading Research Quarterly, 29,* 309–329.

Morrow, L. M. (1990). Preparing the classroom environment to promote literacy during play. *Early Childhood Research Quarterly, 5,* 537–554.

Morrow, L. M. (1991). Relationships among physical designs of play centers, teachers' emphasis on literacy in play, and children's literacy behaviors during play. In J. Zutell & S. McCormick (Eds.), *Learner factors/teacher factors: Issues in literacy research and instruction—fortieth yearbook of the National Reading Conference* (pp. 127–140). Chicago: National Reading Conference.

Morrow, L. M. (1992). The impact of a literature-based program on literacy achievement, use of literature, and attitudes of children from minority backgrounds. *Reading Research Quarterly, 27,* 251–275.

Morrow, L. M., O'Connor, E. M., & Smith, J. K. (1990). Effects of a story reading program on the literacy development of at-risk kindergarten children. *Journal of Reading Behavior, 22,* 255–275.

Morrow, L. M., Pressley, M., Smith, J. K., & Smith, M. (1997). The effect of a literature-based program integrated into literacy and science instruction. *Reading Research Quarterly, 32,* 54–76.

Neuman, S. B., & Roskos, K. (1990). The influence of literacy-enriched play settings on preschoolers' engagement with written language. In J. Zutell & S. McCormick (Eds.), *Literacy theory and research: Analyses from multiple paradigms* (pp. 179–188). Chicago: National Reading Conference.

Neuman, S. B., & Roskos, K. (1992). Literacy objects as cultural tools: Effects on children's literacy behaviors in play. *Reading Research Quarterly, 27,* 203–225.

Paterson, F. R. A. (2003). The politics of phonics. In R. L. Allington (Ed.), *Big brother and the national reading curriculum* (pp. 157–194). Portsmouth, NH: Heinemann.

Pressley, M., & Rankin, J. (1994). More about whole language methods of reading instruction for students at risk for early reading failure. *Learning Disabilities Research and Practice*, 9, 156–167.

Reutzel, D. R., Hollingsworth, P. M., & Eldredge, J. L. (1994). Oral reading instruction: The impact on student reading development. *Reading Research Quarterly*, 29, 40–59.

Richgels, D. J. (1995). Invented spelling ability and printed word learning in kindergarten. *Reading Research Quarterly*, 30, 96–109.

Robbins, C., & Ehri, L. C. (1994). Reading storybooks to kindergartners helps them learn new vocabulary words. *Journal of Educational Psychology*, 86, 54–64.

Rosenhouse, J., Feitelson, D., Kita, B., & Goldstein, Z. (1997). Interactive reading aloud to Israeli first graders: Its contribution to literacy development. *Reading Research Quarterly*, 32, 168–183.

Routman, R. (1988). *Transitions: From literature to literacy.* Portsmouth, NH: Heinemann.

Routman, R. (1991). *Invitations: Changing as teachers and learners K–12.* Portsmouth, NH: Heinemann.

Routman, R. (1996). *Literacy at the crossroads: Critical talk about reading, writing, and other teaching dilemmas.* Portsmouth, NH: Heinemann.

Routman, R. (1999). *Conversations: Strategies for teaching, learning, and evaluating.* Portsmouth, NH: Heinemann.

Routman, R. (2002). *Reading essentials: The specifics you need to teach reading well.* Portsmouth, NH: Heinemann.

Rowe, D. W. (1989). Author/audience interaction in the preschool: The role of social interaction in literacy lessons. *Journal of Reading Behavior: A Journal of Literacy*, 21, 311–349.

Sacks, C. H., & Mergendoller, J. R. (1997). The relationship between teachers' theoretical orientation toward reading and students outcomes in kindergarten children with different initial reading abilities. *American Educational Research Journal*, 34, 721–739.

Shannon, P. (Ed.). (1992). *Becoming political: Readings and writings in the politics of literacy education.* Portsmouth, NH: Heinemann.

Smith, F. (1971). *Understanding reading.* Hillsdale, NJ: Erlbaum.

Smith, F. (1975). *Comprehension and learning: A conceptual framework for teachers.* Katonah, NY: Owen.

Smith, F. (1979). *Reading without nonsense.* New York: Teachers College Press.

Smith, F. (2003). *Inspeakable acts, unnatural practices: Flaws and fallacies in scientific reading instruction.* Portsmouth, NH: Heinemann.

Smith, F. (2004). *Understanding reading: A psycholinguistic analysis of reading and learning to read.* Mahwah, NJ: Erlbaum.

Stahl, S. A., McKenna, M. C., & Pagnucco, J. R. (1994). The effects of whole language instruction: An update and reappraisal. *Educational Psychologist*, 29, 175–186.

Stahl, S. A., & Miller, P. D. (1989). Whole language and language experience approaches for beginning reading: A quantitative research synthesis. *Review of Educational Research, 59,* 87–116.

Stanovich, K. E., & Cunningham, A. E. (1993). Where does knowledge come from?: Specific associations between print exposure and information acquisition. *Journal of Educational Psychology, 85,* 211–229.

Swanborn, M. S. L., & De Glopper, K. (1999). Incidental word learning while reading: A meta-analysis. *Review of Educational Research, 69,* 261–285.

Weaver, C. (1994). *Understanding whole language: From principles to practice* (2nd ed.). Portsmouth, NH: Heinemann.

Weaver, C. (2002). *Reading process and practice.* Portsmouth, NH: Heinemann.

CHAPTER 2

Skilled Reading

Understanding the nature of skilled reading permits insights about what should be the goal of reading instruction. The analyses summarized in this chapter are among the most important influences on current efforts to develop powerful elementary reading instruction. The information in this chapter is essential for those who wish to understand why many researchers and reading educators are determined to increase the amount of decoding and comprehension strategies instruction in the elementary curriculum.

LETTER- AND WORD-LEVEL PROCESSES

Researchers have used a variety of methods to understand how good readers process letters and words. These are discussed in the following subsections.

Eye Movements

During the past half-century, a number of researchers have studied reading at the letter and word levels by studying the eye movements of readers as they process text (Carver, 1990; Just & Carpenter, 1980; Rayner, 1992; Ygge & Lennerstrand, 1994). Much is now known about how eyes move during reading. Eye movements can be thought of as involving *fixations* when the eye is stopped briefly, looking at something, and *saccades* when the eye is jumping to the next fixation. Sometimes the eye will jump back to examine an earlier word in a sentence or paragraph; this is referred to as a

49

regression. How does the eye know where to jump next? When reading in languages printed left to right, such as English, a reader processes the material a little to the right of the current point of fixation. More often than not, there is not enough processing of the material in the right periphery for the reader to know what the word is before it is fixated, but there is enough processing to permit the eye to make a jump to something informative— that is, to permit the eye to land on a word rather than a space between words.

When reading at a rate of 200–300 words per minute, good readers appear to process every single letter of the text. One piece of evidence consistent with this point is that the longer a word is, the longer it takes a reader who is reading aloud to begin to pronounce it from the onset of perception of the word. In fact, every additional letter results in about a 10- to 20-millisecond delay in the onset of reading of the word (Samuels, 1994). Another telling piece of evidence about how readers process individual letters is that if text is altered so that individual letters from words are deleted, reading is much slower (Rayner, Inhoff, Morrison, Slowiaczek, & Bertera, 1981). If you do not believe that single letters can make a difference, try reading an uncorrected letter typed by a pretty good typist in contrast to an uncorrected letter typed by an excellent typist. Mistyped and missing leters are vary distracting and slow reeding quite a bit, dn't they?

Why might it be important to process every single letter during reading? It is important because letter-level cues are the primary means of recognizing words. This conclusion, based on eye-movement and related analyses, clashes with the whole-language theory of word recognition. Whole-language theorists contend that reading a previously unfamiliar word often involves making a guess based on the meaning of the text that has been encountered prior to the new word. From this perspective, reading is very much a psycholinguistic guessing game (Goodman, 1967; Smith, 1971, 2004). However, this point of view simply is not supported by outcomes from eye-movement research. For example, if it were true, then good readers should have a pretty good idea of what the next word in the text is going to be—that is, the word to the right of the word just read. They don't. When adult readers are reading a text on a computer screen that suddenly goes blank, they can report the last fixated word reliably (McConkie & Hogaboam, 1985) but have a great deal of difficulty guessing the next word in the text, being correct about a quarter of the time. A skilled adult reader reading a text with content words missing has a very tough time guessing the missing words, doing so correctly with only 10% accuracy (Gough, 1983). Need convincing? Try guessing the correct word that is missing from this sentence: *The lanky ballplayer reached down to pick up a* _____ *that had jumped onto the field.* Do you now think that skilled readers guess words on the basis of context cues? If you do, reflect for a moment how much easier it is to read this: *The lanky ballplayer reached down to pick up a frog that had jumped onto the field.*

Thus, one problem with relying heavily on semantic context cues is that many words will be read incorrectly. That is, the psycholinguistic guesses will be wrong because any of a number of words could fit into the context. Relying heavily on semantic context cues is a weak strategy—the preferred strategy of weak readers only—as a number of investigators (e.g., Share & Stanovich, 1995) have concluded. This point is taken up in greater detail in Chapter 5.

With skilled readers, reading speed varies with the type of reading. Thus, during skimming, reading is faster because many words are skipped by the reader. In contrast, when a reader is attempting to learn what is in the text, reading is a word-by-word affair, with fixations on most of the individual words. For a skilled adult reader who is reading material carefully, each word is typically fixated for about a quarter of a second. That translates to about 200 words per minute when readers are reading to learn material (McConkie, Zola, Blanchard, & Wolverton, 1982). The less the reader is concentrating on learning the ideas in the text, the faster the reading rate. Reading at a relaxed pace typically occurs at a rate of between 250 and 300 words per minute, and thus more relaxed reading also is more word-by-word reading than anything else. Despite claims by speed reading programs, the fastest that humans can read and comprehend is about 600 words per minute (Carver, 1990, Chap. 21).

Decontextualized Word Recognition

The ability to read words even when there are no semantic context cues (e.g., on a flash card with only the to-be-read word) is almost a defining characteristic of the good reader (Share & Stanovich, 1995). A great deal of research effort has been devoted to determining how good readers recognize words as well as they do. Of course, for good readers, many words are sight words—well known from many past encounters. Recognition of sight words is said to be automatized, for reading these words requires little or no effort and is highly reliable (LaBerge & Samuels, 1974).

Much more telling about the skill of good readers, however, is that they typically can read words they have never seen before, even words that are really nonsense words or pseudowords, such as *swackle*, *preflob*, and *plithing*. They can do that because they can readily associate letters with their sounds and blend the sounds to pronounce a word. Sounding out is something that good readers do well (Share & Stanovich, 1995).

Recognition of the common letter combinations in one's native language is also automatized in the skilled reader. Good readers can recognize common English-letter combinations, such as *-kle*, *pre-*, and *-ing*, presumably because they have encountered these combinations many times during reading. This permits much more rapid decoding than occurs when an unknown word does not contain familiar letter combinations. Try reading these two words: *retuckable* and *ekuteracbl*. They both contain the same letters, but the first is easier than the second because it is composed of three familiar English-letter combinations whereas the second word's combinations are less familiar.

That readers rely more on letter-level cues than semantic–contextual cues to read a word does not mean that semantic–contextual cues are not important in processing words. In fact, they can be very important, *after the word has been recognized*. Read the following sentence: The duck could not be stopped from biting the boy, so his mother grabbed the bill! Now, read this sentence: *The boy could not be stopped from using his money to buy the duck, so his mother grabbed the bill*. How the word *bill* is interpreted depends heavily on semantic–contextual cues in this example (Phillip B. Gough, personal communication, June 1996). Although context does little to facilitate reading a word, it does much to facilitate understanding the meaning of the word once read.

One criticism of much of the work on letter-level and word-level processes is that such analyses do not put the focus on the reader as a meaning-maker. That criticism is valid to some extent, as will be made clear as this chapter proceeds, for much of skilled reading is getting meaning from sentences and paragraphs. Even if we keep in mind the caveat that reading is more than word recognition, however, the active processing of sentences and paragraphs cannot occur unless the reader can recognize individual words reliably and efficiently. That is why learning to decode is so important.

GETTING THE GIST

Every text has many ideas in it (e.g., Clark & Clark, 1977; Kintsch, 1974). Consider the sentence "John carefully nailed down the loose shingles on the roof" (Kintsch, 1982). There are four ideas in it: *John nails shingles*; *nailing is being done carefully*; *shingles are on the roof*; and *shingles are loose*. When good readers read such a sentence, they understand all of these ideas, although later they may remember only the main idea expressed in the sentence, namely, "John nailed shingles."

Unless they have exerted great effort to memorize a text verbatim, people do not remember everything from a text they read. What people remember is the gist, which comprises the main ideas in the text (Kintsch & van Dijk, 1978; van Dijk & Kintsch, 1983). In long discourse, such as is found in a book, there are layers of main ideas: At the top level, there is an overall summary of the book; then, each chapter in the book has main ideas, as does each paragraph in each chapter. The lower-level main ideas (e.g., paragraph-level) are integrated by the skilled reader to create the higher-level summaries (e.g., at the chapter and then book level; van Dijk & Kintsch, 1983, e.g., Chap. 2; Kintsch, 1988).

For example, suppose that a reader is beginning a paragraph-long text. The first sentence contains a number of ideas, with the reader coding the main idea of the sentence. This idea is held in active memory as the next sentence in the paragraph is read. Attempts are made to link the main idea from the first sentence to the ideas of the second sentence, with another main idea emerging from this synthesis, integrating the meanings expressed in the first two sentences of the paragraph.

Sometimes there will be a need for bridging inferences that reconcile the meaning of the previous sentence with the ideas in a new sentence—that is, to produce coherence between the sentence currently being read and the text read up until this point. These bridging inferences are derived largely from word knowledge the reader possesses. For instance, if a text about a worker pounding nails never mentions a hammer, the reader may infer "hammer" when the sentence "The head slipped off" is encountered. Perhaps the resulting main idea would be "The hammer broke while being used." By the end of the paragraph, good readers have implicitly generated a summary capturing the gist of the entire paragraph. (I emphasize *implicitly* at this point, for this process occurs automatically and unconsciously in the skilled reader.) Later, if the reader has to recall the paragraph, the most important ideas will be recalled (e.g., Kintsch & Keenan, 1973). The longer the retention interval between reading and recall, the fewer the details that are remembered (e.g., Kintsch & van Dijk, 1978). The recall data will reflect bridging inferences made during the original reading as well as some inferences made when the text is recalled.

Such inferences, again, are based on what the reader already knows; that is, memory for text typically reflects information in the text and the reader's knowledge of the world. For example, when I told my son the story of Charles Dickens's *A Christmas Carol*, I told the entire book-length story in about 5 minutes, remembering just about everything I could in that period of time. What I remembered were the main ideas of the story rather than what specific villagers said, or even the words of the four night visitors. During my telling of the tale, however, I mentioned that Tiny Tim had polio. I had to explain to my 9-year-old what polio was, since the disease is almost never encountered in contemporary America. Later, when he read the story, he pointed out to me that the story actually contained no information about the affliction that put Tiny Tim on crutches. What had occurred was that I had inferred at some point, probably during my original reading of the story or during one of the productions of the play that I have seen, that Tiny Tim was a polio victim. Memory of text is very personal, because the reader's background knowledge plays a large role in determining the meaning constructed by him or her.

Good readers do not make inferences willy-nilly, however. They do not make associations to prior knowledge that is completely remote from the ideas in the current text. Instead, they make inferences that are needed to understand the text (McKoon & Ratcliff, 1992; van den Broek, 1994). Nonetheless, as good readers read a story, they often create an elaborate understanding of the world in which the story is taking place (e.g., Fletcher, 1994; Kintsch, 1998). One of the important roles of prior knowledge is that it allows people to have a very good understanding of a very large situation, given relatively little information. Even in long novels, the author can describe in writing only the most important features of the story's setting and the most salient characteristics of the characters' personalities, and those readers with extensive prior knowledge are better able to fill in the gaps than those without such knowledge.

In summary, during normal beginning-to-end reading of a text, such as a story, the reader processes the individual ideas but remembers the gist. In processing the text and constructing the gist, prior knowledge plays an important role, permitting the generation of inferences required to understand the text. In some cases the inferences are elaborate, specifying complex situations. Although the model of reading discussed in this subsection has been studied most extensively with respect to narrative texts (i.e., stories), many of its main points apply to various types of expository texts as well (i.e., factual texts, such as articles concerned with a particular topic; e.g., Britton, 1994).

One of the reasons that people read is to know more—and indeed, people who read extensively are more knowledgeable than people who read less (Stanovich & Cunningham, 1993). The psycholinguists interested in how people learn from a text have established how general knowledge of the world changes as a function of reading (e.g., Graesser, 1981; Graesser, Hoffman, & Clark, 1980; Kintsch, 1974; Kintsch & Keenan, 1973; Kintsch, Kozminsky, Streby, McKoon, & Keenan, 1975). The gist of what has been read is integrated with what the reader knew before reading the text (i.e., prior knowledge) to create new knowledge (e.g., Anderson & Bower, 1973). Thus, if you read a magazine article about the literacy crisis in America, you might implicitly construct a summary that includes the main ideas covered in the article. At a party tomorrow, you could rely on this summary alone to guide partial retelling of the article to a friend who might be interested in the literacy crisis. More importantly, however, your long-term knowledge of literacy might be changed by reading the article. Thus, 6 months from now, when someone makes a claim about literacy that conflicts with what was in the article, you can respond, "But I thought . . . ," going on to relate a general point from the article, perhaps no longer aware of where the information was acquired.

CONSCIOUS COMPREHENSION: VERBAL PROTOCOLS OF READING

Skilled readers tend to know a lot more about things in general than do unskilled readers, for skilled reading results in the development of extensive knowledge. Much of this knowledge creation occurs automatically as a function of reading and "gistifying" text. It can also involve more conscious processes, for meaning making during reading is not just automatic, implicit processing of text—it also involves much conscious, controlled processing.

Much has been learned about conscious, active comprehension processes by having good adult readers think aloud as they read. That is, researchers have asked adults to read text, interrupting them every so often to have them tell exactly what they are thinking and what they are doing as they read. Conscious decision making during reading is more obvious when readers read demanding, difficult texts. Thus, the texts read in verbal protocol studies often have been very demanding, requiring a good deal of thought for readers to understand the messages in them.

Wyatt et al.'s (1993) Study

Because my students and I carried out an ambitious study of skilled reading using verbal protocol methods, I have some firsthand experience in this area (Wyatt et al., 1993). In that investigation, 15 professors from the University of Maryland thought aloud as they read articles that they had selected within their areas of expertise. Although each professor read a different article, and the professors and articles spanned a number of academic disciplines, there were important similarities that could be identified in their reading.

First, all of the readers were exceptionally active as they read:

- Based on information in the article being read and their prior knowledge of the topic of the article, the professors anticipated what might be said later in the article. They were very aware of when their predictions were on target versus when their predictions were in error.
- They looked for information that was relevant to their personal interests and personal goals in reading the article. Thus, the professor who was reading the article in preparation for writing a paper looked for information that might be helpful in preparing her or his own paper. Informa-

tion that was relevant to the professor's personal goal in reading the text was read more slowly than information considered not as important.

• Although the professors generally read the articles from the first page to last, they also jumped ahead sometimes to look for information that they thought might be in the article, and sometimes they looked back for additional clarification about a point that seemed confusing at first. Thus, if a sentence that was just read made little sense, they might reread it, and they might look back a few paragraphs to find information (i.e., a critical point they must have missed previously) that might render the sentence sensible.

• The professors explained the ideas in the text to themselves, constructing summaries and reasoning about why what was stated in the text made sense or, in some cases, did not make sense.

• The professors monitored their reading a great deal. That is, they were very aware of how difficult or easy the text was to read. They were aware of whether they already knew the ideas stated in the text or the text was covering new territory for them. And, as discussed previously, they were aware of just which portions of the text were most pertinent to their reading goals.

Second, and even more striking than all the activity that occurred during reading, the readers were extremely passionate as they read. They constantly evaluated what they were reading. This was possible because of their extensive prior knowledge. Thus, when the text included ideas near and dear to their hearts, they reacted positively, saying things like "Right on" or "She's got it!" In contrast were those occasions when text contained ideas that clashed with the reader's thinking. Such ideas were sometimes greeted with exclamations of disgust (including profanity) or nonverbal reactions, such as giving the article "the raspberry." Throughout reading, the readers reported when they were interested and when they were bored. It was very clear that reading was anything but an affectively neutral experience for these readers.

Pressley and Afflerbach's (1995) Analysis of Skilled Reading

This think-aloud study that my colleagues and I conducted is one of more than 60 think-aloud studies that have been published in scientific journals. The exact types of activities reported by readers as they read have varied from study to study, probably reflecting variation in the directions given to participants in different studies as well as the variety of texts read in the various investigations.

Despite the variability across studies in procedures and materials read, when Peter Afflerbach and I reviewed all the studies that were published up until 1994, we were able to construct a summary of good reading that cut across the various investigations (Pressley & Afflerbach, 1995). The readers that my students and I studied were not unusual. Active reading is apparent in virtually every verbal protocol study in the research literature. Yes, there is evidence that some readers are much more active than others, but in general consciously active reading seems to be common, especially among individuals who are known to be good readers. Moreover, as mature readers become more experienced with a particular type of reading, they often become more sophisticated in how they read the text (Strømsø, Bråten, & Samuelstuen, 2003). Even, so, in general, the conscious processing that is excellent reading begins before reading, continues during reading, and persists after reading is completed.

Before reading, good readers make certain that they know why they are reading the text and are clear about what they want to get from it (e.g., information about the role of the Native Americans in the French and Indian War, an understanding of what the professor who wrote this article is doing in her or his current research). Rather than simply diving into a text and beginning to read a piece from front to back, good readers often overview a text. During the overview, they are sensitive to the structure of the text, especially noting parts of the text that might contain information that is particularly relevant to their reading goal. Good readers make a reading plan in light of the information they obtain during the overview. The information gained during this overview permits the good reader to gauge which parts of the text should be read first, which parts of the text should be read more carefully than others, and which ones should not be read at all. The good reader begins to relate what is in the text to prior knowledge and to get a summary idea of what is in the text. Sometimes, the overview reveals that the text is entirely irrelevant to the reader's goals (e.g., there seems to be nothing new in it about the role of the Native Americans in the French and Indian War). In that case, a good reader might decide not to read the text further.

If the reader does think the text is worthwhile based on the overview, he or she begins to read from front to back, varying reading speed from section to section of the text, sometimes skimming and sometimes skipping sections. Sometimes the reader stops and rereads a segment or pauses to think about what was just said. The reader gives greater attention to information that is important relative to her or his reason for reading the text. Earlier predictions based on the overview are updated because of information encountered in the text. New predictions about upcoming content are also made continuously as the text is processed. That is, the good reader draws conclusions throughout reading, although the conclusions remain tentative, subject to change as reading continues.

Throughout reading, the good reader is making conscious inferences as well as inferences that are unconscious and automatic. Good readers try to fill in information gaps in the text, attempt to determine the meaning of unknown words, and relate ideas in the text to their prior knowledge (e.g., "That's just like . . ."). They make inferences about the author, such as her or his intentions in writing the text, or the particular sources that the author used. Fiction readers are always making inferences about the intentions of characters in the story. Good readers consciously attempt to integrate ideas encountered in different parts of a text (e.g., how the actions of characters in a story are related to the larger story). When beginning a work of fiction, they think about the setting and how new characters relate to the setting. The setting is kept in mind as the action proceeds. Readers look for cause-and-effect connections between different parts of the text (e.g., how one character's actions early in a story motivated another character's responses later in the story). In integrating ideas across the text, a reader may review previous text or jump ahead.

Good readers make many interpretations as they read. Sometimes this is apparent in paraphrases (e.g., "So this myth is like the Exodus story . . ."). They form personal images of the events described in a text. If reading an expository text, they come up with summary comments (e.g., "What the author really wants to say in this chapter is . . ."). In making interpretations, prior knowledge plays a big role. Thus, a gender-stereotyped story written in the early 20th century gets a more sympathetic reading from an ardent feminist reader than a gender-stereotyped story written for the most recent issue of *The New Yorker*.

Processing of text does not conclude when the final word of an article, chapter, or book is read. Rather, the good reader sometimes rereads sections or reskims parts that seemed especially important. The good reader might try to restate important ideas or construct a summary of the text to make certain the ideas in the text can be recalled later. Sometimes good readers make notes. They often continue to reflect on a text and what it might mean long after reading is concluded.

The monitoring processes that my students and I witnessed in our study of college professors reading articles (Wyatt et al., 1993) were also apparent in many other verbal protocol studies. Readers are consciously aware of many characteristics of the text, from the author's style to the tone of the messages in the text. They are especially aware of whether they are understanding the text and whether such understanding is easy or requires considerable effort. When good readers detect problems, whether it is in understanding overall meanings in a text or knowing the meaning of a particular word in it, they do what they can to solve the problem.

Finally, just as evaluations were salient in the verbal protocols collected by Wyatt et al. (1993), they were salient in many other verbal protocol studies. Readers express feelings as they read. They consciously accept or reject the style of the text (e.g., quality of the writing) as well as the ideas expressed in the text.

CONCLUDING REFLECTIONS

There is a broad base of agreement among researchers that reading is about constructing meaning from the text. After that agreement, there are differences of opinion about the nature of reading, although the differences can be resolved.

Bottom-Up versus Top-Down Processing

Some who have thought about meaning making during reading seem to think that meaning making occurs from the bottom up. For them, reading is about the processing of letters and words. Meaning making is sounding out the words, which are listened to by the mind. Indeed, there is a long history of distinguished research establishing that even when good readers read silently, there is something of a speech process involved. Sometimes, there is even silent speech (i.e., the reader literally says the words to her- or himself quietly). Sometimes the speech processes are not so complete, but, as words are read, information about the sounds of the words is activated in the mind, which seems to help the reader hold in memory the last few words that were read so that their meanings can be integrated to permit comprehension of the text (Carver, 1990, Chap. 4; Perfetti, 1985). The idea that reading involves decoding and listening comprehension, with readers listening to what they have decoded in order to understand the meanings conveyed by the text (Gough, 1984), is a simple view of reading.

Others who think about meaning making during reading think that it occurs from the top down. That is, based on world knowledge, people have hypotheses about what the text is going to say, and this prior knowledge goes far in explaining comprehension (Anderson & Pearson, 1984). There is plenty of evidence that what a text means varies from reader to reader, because text meaning is a joint product of the message the author intended to convey through the words placed in the text and the reader's prior knowledge (e.g., Beach & Hynds, 1991; Flower, 1994; Rosenblatt, 1978). An important point is that good readers do not let their prior knowledge processing get out of control (e.g., Williams, 1993): Their understanding of a story is never so completely personal that a retelling would be unrecognizable by someone else reading the same story. Yes, the listener might have a different perspective on some of what happened in the story, but the essential story that both readers understood would be the same.

Between the bottom-up approach to reading and the top-down model, there is an intermediate position, which is that both bottom-up and top-down processes are involved in constructing meaning from a text. Without a doubt, that is the most sensible conclusion that can be derived from the evidence reviewed in this chapter and when all of the evidence on comprehension of text is considered (e.g., Clifton & Duffy, 2001). The case that has been made here is that good readers may process every single letter using efficient eye movements that involve fixation on most words. The case has also been made that the reader's mind is very active in constructing hypotheses about what a text might mean, generating inferences, based on prior knowledge, that are necessary in making meaning, and initiating strategies to locate portions of the text that are especially likely to be informative. Bottom-up and top-down processing clearly interact as part of skilled reading. There cannot be one without the other if good reading is to occur (Kintsch, 1998; Rumelhart, 1994). They are in balance.

Does that mean that it will do no good to target educational efforts at either bottom-up or top-down processing alone? Not necessarily. In fact, there will be quite a bit of evidence considered in subsequent chapters that makes clear that targeting letter- and word-level processes sometimes can improve reading achievement, as can targeting comprehension strategies. Instruction of particular components can help on the road to excellent reading, which involves bottom-up and top-down thinking in interaction.

Analyses of Expert Reading That Leads to Ineffective Educational Interventions

I emphasize at this point that some conspicuous instructional intervention failures have resulted from past conceptions that compared expert reading to weaker reading. (I mention them at this juncture if for no other reason than to get them behind us.) For example, the eye movements of poor readers often differ from the eye movements of good readers, with left-to-right saccadic movement less apparent in poor readers and with poor readers less likely to fixate on words than on spaces between words. This deficiency in poor readers has inspired efforts to inculcate more efficient eye movements in poor readers, which sometimes have been successful in modifying fixations and saccades but generally have been unsuccessful in affecting reading. A general conclusion emerging from research on the modification of eye movements is that dysfunctional eye movements do not cause poor reading but rather are a symptom of poor reading (see Gaddes, 1985, Chap. 8, and Rayner & Pollatsek, 1989, Chap. 11, for reviews).

A second example of ineffective instruction based on a flawed conception of expert reading is speed reading instruction. There is no doubt that many readers can be taught to skim rather than read, and this is what speed reading courses do. The problem is that when readers skim, their comprehension goes down, although not always on the tests used in speed reading courses to prove to clients that they are comprehending. The tests often are very easy, involving questions that could have been answered correctly even without reading the passage. Consider the following sample question (provided by Carver, 1990, p. 372):

> Which one of the following least represents a folk society?
>
> 1. A group of people of similar ethnic backgrounds living close together in a city.
> 2. A group of survivors from a ship who land on a desert island.
> 3. The Aborigine[s] of Australia.
> 4. The Pueblo Indians of the Southwestern United States.

Although you did not read the passage, I am confident that you selected the correct answer, number 2. Many who run speed reading programs would have you believe that being able to answer such a question after reading a passage about folk societies tells you something about your reading comprehension, when in fact what it tells about is prior knowledge. In short, there is no credible scientific evidence that teaching people to read quickly can succeed when comprehension is tested with demanding test items (Carver, 1990, Chap. 18). This does not negate, however, the point made earlier in this chapter that a state of high prior knowledge often enables skimming with high comprehension and efficient selective reading of text. That is, learning to be a skimmer can be a good thing when there is a need to cover a great deal of material related to areas of high prior knowledge.

As the discussion proceeds in these pages, there will be no more consideration of eye-movement training or the development of reading speeds of thousands of words per minute. There will be evidence presented, however, that improving some letter- and word-level decoding processes can improve reading, as can instruction in comprehension strategies that are matched to the comprehension processes involved in skilled reading.

SUMMARY AND CONCLUDING REFLECTIONS

1. Skilled reading is a coordination of higher-order processes (e.g., comprehension) and lower-order processes (e.g., decoding). Getting meaning from a text very much depends on efficient lower-order processing: Good readers automatically recognize many words and efficiently decode unfamiliar words they encounter. Good readers process most words in the texts they read. Indeed, they seem to process most of the individual letters within words. The primary cues used to decode text are the letters and

words, not the meaning of the text in which the words are embedded or the syntactic context in which an unfamiliar word is embedded.

2. When skilled readers read, they abstract the gist from text, getting the big ideas even though many details may not be recallable. Comprehension involves processing the ideas in the text in light of one's own prior knowledge, with prior knowledge permitting readers to make many inferences as they proceed. One's knowledge, however, often changes as a function of reading.

3. Although much comprehension occurs implicitly, unconsciously, and almost automatically, much of comprehension involves conscious, active processing of the text. The good reader can be active before reading (e.g., overviewing the text and making predictions), during reading (e.g., updating predictions, constructing mental images), and after reading (e.g., constructing summaries, thinking about which ideas in the text might be useful later). Good readers are both interpretive and evaluative, often reacting to the validity of ideas in the text.

4. Understanding the nature of skilled reading provides perspectives on what reading instruction should accomplish. That expert readers are so proficient at word-level processes provides motivation for instruction that focuses on development of decoding. That excellent reading involves conscious comprehension processes motivates instruction that develops active comprehension habits.

5. That good readers do not seem to depend on meaning cues to decode words provides good reason to reject whole-language arguments that decoding instruction should emphasize orientation to meaning cues. By the conclusion of this book, it will be clear that advising children to attend first and foremost to meaning cues (e.g., to look at picture cues) to decode words is instructional advice that belongs on the same scrap heap as eye-movement training. Meaning cues are critical, however, in appraising whether decoding was done properly: If the decoding makes no sense given the context, the good reader knows to go back and look at the word again. Context cues also help the skilled reader to zero in on the intended meaning of words that have more than one definition.

6. Those who wish to teach reading well need to understand just what good reading is. Sound teaching of reading is aimed at developing readers who read as described in this chapter.

REFERENCES

Anderson, J. R., & Bower, G. H. (1973). *Human associative memory*. New York: Wiley.

Anderson, R. C., & Pearson, P. D. (1984). A schema-theoretic view of basic processes in reading. In P. D. Pearson (Ed.), *Handbook of reading research* (pp. 255–291). New York: Longman.

Beach, R., & Hynds, S. (1991). Research on response to literature. In R. Barr, M. L. Kamil, P. Mosenthal, & P. D. Pearson (Eds.), *Handbook of reading research* (Vol. 2, pp. 453–489). White Plains, NY: Longman.

Britton, B. K. (1994). Understanding expository text: Building mental structures to induce insights. In M. A. Gernsbacher (Ed.), *Handbook of psycholinguistics* (pp. 641–674). San Diego: Academic Press.

Carver, R. P. (1990). *Reading rate: A review of research and theory.* San Diego: Academic Press.

Clark, H. H., & Clark, E. V. (1977). *Psychology and language.* New York: Harcourt Brace Jovanovich.

Clifton, C., Jr., & Duffy, S. A. (2001). Sentence and text comprehension: Roles of linguistic structure. *Annual Review of Psychology, 52,* 167–196.

Fletcher, C. R. (1994). Levels of representation in memory for discourse. In M. A. Gernsbacher (Ed.), *Handbook of psycholinguistics* (pp. 589–607). San Diego: Academic Press.

Flower, L. S. (1994). *The construction of negotiated meaning: A social cognitive theory of writing.* Carbondale: Southern Illinois University Press.

Gaddes, W. H. (1985). *Learning disabilities and brain function* (2nd ed.). New York: Springer-Verlag.

Goodman, K. S. (1967). Reading: A psycholinguistic guessing game. *Journal of the Reading Specialist, 6,* 126–135.

Gough, P. B. (1983). Context, form, and interaction. In K. Rayner (Ed.), *Eye movements in reading* (pp. 203–211). New York: Academic Press.

Gough, P. B. (1984). Word recognition. In P. D. Pearson (Ed.), *Handbook of reading research* (pp. 225–254). New York: Longman.

Graesser, A. C. (1981). *Prose comprehension beyond the word.* New York: Springer-Verlag.

Graesser, A. C., Hoffman, N. L., & Clark, L. F. (1980). Structural components of reading time. *Journal of Verbal Learning and Verbal Behavior, 19,* 135–151.

Just, M. A., & Carpenter, P. A. (1980). A theory of reading: From eye fixations to comprehension. *Psychological Review, 87,* 329–354.

Kintsch, W. (1974). *The representation of meaning in memory.* Hillsdale, NJ: Erlbaum.

Kintsch, W. (1982). Text representations. In W. Otto & S. White (Eds.), *Reading expository material* (pp. 87–102). New York: Academic Press.

Kintsch, W. (1988). The role of knowledge in discourse comprehension: A construction–integration model. *Psychological Review, 95,* 163–182.

Kintsch, W. (1998). *Comprehension: A paradigm for cognition.* Cambridge, UK: Cambridge University Press.

Kintsch, W., & Keenan, J. M. (1973). Reading rate and retention as a function of the number of propositions in the base structure of sentences. *Cognitive Psychology, 5,* 257–279.

Kintsch, W., Kozminsky, E., Streby, W. J., McKoon, G., & Keenan, J. M. (1975). Comprehension and recall as a function of content variables. *Journal of Verbal Learning and Verbal Behavior, 14,* 196–214.

Kintsch, W., & van Dijk, T. A. (1978). Toward a model of discourse comprehension and production. *Psychological Review, 85,* 363–394.

LaBerge, D., & Samuels, S. J. (1974). Toward a theory of automatic information processing in reading. *Cognitive Psychology, 6,* 293–323.

McConkie, G. W., & Hogaboam, T. W. (1985). Eye position and word identification during reading. In R. Groner, G. W. McConkie, & C. Menz (Eds.), *Eye movements and information processing* (pp. 159–192). Amsterdam: Elsevier/North-Holland.

McConkie, G. W., Zola, D., Blanchard, H. E., & Wolverton, G. S. (1982). Perceiving words during reading: Lack of facilitation from prior peripheral exposure. *Perception and Psychophysics, 32,* 271–281.

McKoon, G., & Ratcliff, R. (1992). Inference during reading. *Psychological Review, 99,* 440–466.

Perfetti, C. A. (1985). *Reading ability.* New York: Oxford University Press.

Pressley, M., & Afflerbach, P. (1995). *Verbal protocols of reading: The nature of constructively responsive reading.* Hillsdale, NJ: Erlbaum.

Rayner, K. (Ed.). (1992). *Eye movements and visual cognition: Scene perception and reading.* New York: Springer-Verlag.

Rayner, K., Inhoff, A. W., Morrison, R. E., Slowiaczek, M. L., & Bertera, J. H. (1981). Masking of foveal and parafoveal vision during eye fixations in reading. *Journal of Experimental Psychology: Human Perception and Performance, 7,* 167–179.

Rayner, K., & Pollatsek, A. (1989). *The psychology of reading.* Englewood Cliffs, NJ: Prentice-Hall.

Rosenblatt, L. M. (1978). *The reader, the text, the poem: The transactional theory of the literary work.* Carbondale: Southern Illinois University Press.

Rumelhart, D. E. (1994). Toward an interactive model of reading. In R. B. Ruddell, M. R. Ruddell, & H. Singer (Eds.), *Theoretical models and processes of reading* (4th ed., pp. 864–894). Newark, DE: International Reading Association.

Samuels, S. J. (1994). Word recognition. In R. B. Ruddell, M. R. Ruddell, & H. Singer (Eds.), *Theoretical models and processes of reading* (pp. 359–380). Newark, DE: International Reading Association.

Share, D. L., & Stanovich, K. E. (1995). Cognitive processes in early reading development: Accommodating individual differences into a model of acquisition. *Issues in Education: Contributions from Educational Psychology, 1,* 1–57.

Smith, F. (1971). *Understanding reading: A psycholinguistic analysis of reading and learning to read.* New York: Holt, Rinehart & Winston.

Smith, F. (2004). *Understanding reading: A psycholinguistic analysis of reading and learning to read.* Mahwah, NJ: Erlbaum.

Stanovich, K. E., & Cunningham, A. E. (1993). Where does knowledge come from? Associations between print exposure and information acquisition. *Journal of Educational Psychology, 85,* 211–229.

Strømsø, H. I., Bräten, I., & Samuelstuen, M. S. (2003). Students' strategic use of multiple sources during expository text reading: A longitudinal think-aloud study. *Cognition and Instruction, 21,* 113–147.

van den Broek, P. (1994). Comprehension and memory of narrative texts: Inferences and coherence. In M. A. Gernsbacher (Ed.), *Handbook of psycho-linguistics* (pp. 539–588). San Diego: Academic Press.

van Dijk, T. A., & Kintsch, W. (1983). *Strategies of discourse comprehension.* New York: Academic Press.

Williams, J. P. (1993). Comprehension of students with and without learning disabilities: Identification of narrative themes and idiosyncratic text representations. *Journal of Educational Psychology, 85,* 631–641.

Wyatt, D., Pressley, M., El-Dinary, P. B., Stein, S., Evans, P., & Brown, R. (1993). Comprehension strategies, worth and credibility monitoring, and evaluations: Cold and hot cognition when experts read professional articles that are important to them. *Learning and Individual Differences, 5,* 49–72.

Ygge, J., & Lennerstrand, G. (Eds.). (1994). *Eye movements in reading.* Tarrytown, NY: Pergamon Press.

CHAPTER 3

Children Who Experience Problems in Learning to Read

Some primary-grade students of normal intelligence experience difficulty in learning to read. Moreover, primary-grade difficulties in learning to read predict to some extent continuing reading difficulties throughout schooling (e.g., Francis, Shaywitz, Stuebing, & Fletcher, 1994; Phillips, Norris, Osmond, & Maynard, 2002; Satz, Taylor, Friel, & Fletcher, 1978; Spreen, 1978) and into adulthood (Bruck, 1990, 1992; Finucci, Gottfredson, & Childs, 1985; Frauenheim & Heckerl, 1983; McNulty, 2003; Ransby & Swanson, 2003; Schonhaut & Satz, 1983; S. E. Shaywitz et al., 1996; Spreen, 1988).

The most salient problem in learning to read is learning to decode, to recognize words, initially by sounding out words. This is probably rooted in other language problems. For example, children with reading disabilities and those at risk for becoming poor readers do not discriminate speech sounds as well as other children (Bertucci, Hook, Haynes, Macaruso, & Bickley, 2003; Breier, Fletcher, Denton, & Gray, 2004; Chiappe, Chiappe, & Siegel, 2001; Espy, Molfese, Molfese, & Modglin, 2004; Guttorm, Leppanen, Richardson, & Lyytinen, 2001; Molfese et al., 2002; Molfese, Molfese, & Modgline, 2001; Serniclaes, Van Heghe, Mousty, Carré, & Sprenger-Charolles, 2004). Poor readers and those at risk for becoming poor readers also do not segment words into their constituent sounds as well as other children. They experience a great deal of difficulty hearing and/or saying the sounds represented by the constituent letters of the word and blending the sounds to produce the word. *There are many analyses producing outcomes consistent with these conclusions* (e.g., Booth, Perfetti, & MacWhinney, 1999; Brady & Shankweiler, 1991; Brady, Shankweiler, & Mann, 1983; Bruck, 1990, 1992; de Jong & van der Leij, 2003; Fletcher et al., 1994; Foorman, Francis, Fletcher, & Lynn, 1996; Goswami & Bryant, 1990; Gottardo, Stanovich, & Siegel, 1996; Gough, Ehri, & Treiman, 1992; Greenberg, Ehri, & Perin, 2002; Hammill, Mather, Allen, & Roberts, 2002; Liberman, Shankweiler, Fischer, & Carter, 1974; Manis, Custodio, & Szeszulski, 1993; Mann, Liberman, & Shankweiler, 1980; McCandliss, Beck, Sandak, & Perfetti, 2003; Metsala, 1997; Morris et al., 1998; Penney, 2002; Rack, Hulme, Snowling, & Wightman, 1994; Shankweiler et al., 1995; Shankweiler, Liberman, Mark, Fowler, & Fischer, 1979; Share, 1995; Share & Stanovich, 1995; Snowling, 2002; Snowling, Goulandris, & Defty, 1996; Sprenger-Charolles, Siegel, Bechennec, & Serniclaes, 2003; Stanovich, 1986, 1988; Stanovich & Siegel, 1994; Stone & Brady, 1995; Thompkins & Binder, 2003; Troia, 2004; Vellutino & Scanlon, 1982, 1987a, 1987b; Vellutino et al., 1996; Vellutino, Scanlon, Small, & Tanzman, 1991; Vellutino, Scanlon, & Tanzman, 1994; Wimmer, Mayringer, & Landerl, 1998; Ziegler, Perry, Ma-Wyatt, Ladner, & Schulte-Korne, 2003).

If struggling readers do not sound out words and blend the sounds specified by letters to produce words, what do such readers do instead? Weaker readers often rely much more on semantic–contextual cues to identify words than do skilled readers. That is, rather than trying to sound out an unfamiliar word, poorer readers rely on textual and picture cues and clues to make a guess about a word's meaning (Corley, 1988; Goldsmith-Phillips, 1989; Kim & Goetz, 1994; Nicholson, 1991; Nicholson, Bailey, & McArthur, 1991; Nicholson, Lillas, & Rzoska, 1988; Perfetti, Goldman, & Hogaboam, 1979; Perfetti & Roth, 1981; Schwantes, 1981, 1991; Simpson, Lorsbach, & Whitehouse, 1983; Stanovich, West, & Freeman, 1981; Tunmer & Chapman, 2004; West & Stanovich, 1978). Although such students might process the letters somewhat and use some letter-level information in making their guesses (e.g., limiting guesses to words beginning with *p*, since the word begins with *p*), their processing of the letter cues is much less complete than it could be, with the picture and semantic–contextual cues given priority.

Strong beginning readers certainly could make use of context cues with respect to decoding, but they do not do so exclusively. For anyone who can analyze words into their sounds and blend them, it makes little sense to rely on the semantic–contextual approach alone for word recognition, since there are a number of problems with relying on semantic–contextual cues. One is that the semantic–contextual approach is much less certain to produce accurate decoding than is sounding out words: A lot of guesses will be in error. A second problem is that when readers "read" words based on picture and other semantic–contextual cues, they are much less likely to make progress in transforming an unknown word into a sight word (e.g., Samuels, 1970). Thus, use of the semantic–contextual strategy negatively affects future reading by undermining the development of automatic word recognition. A third problem with relying on the semantic–contextual approach to decoding is that it is slow and thus consumes a great deal of short-term cognitive capacity. For the average person, about seven chunks of information can be held in consciousness at any one time (Miller, 1956). Slow decoding eats up much of this short-term capacity in contrast to automatic decoding, which requires relatively little short-term capacity. When a great deal of capacity is required to decode, little is left over for comprehension, and thus comprehension suffers (LaBerge & Samuels, 1974).

The reason for reading is not to decode but to get meaning from text. Comprehension, however, depends on word recognition skills, and thus, this discussion of comprehension begins with word-level comprehension failures in poor readers.

WORD-LEVEL COMPREHENSION FAILURES

Beyond being able to decode words by sounding them out, good readers can read many words without sounding them out. That is, although good readers can sound out unfamiliar words, with additional exposures unfamiliar words become sight words, ones recognized automatically without the need to analyze and blend component sounds. Such automaticity is crucial for children if they are to develop into skilled readers (Ehri & Snowling, 2004).

Why does automaticity matter? As discussed earlier, decoding does take place in short-term memory—that very limited capacity which is consciousness. In fact, decoding and comprehension compete for the available short-term capacity (LaBerge & Samuels, 1974). When a reader slowly analyzes a word into component sounds and blends them, a great deal of capacity is consumed, with relatively little left over for comprehension of the word, let alone understanding the overall meaning of the sentence containing the word and the paragraph containing the sentence. In contrast, automatic word recognition (i.e., recognizing a word as a sight word) consumes very little capacity and thus frees short-term capacity for the task of comprehending the word and integrating the meaning of the word with the overall meaning of the sentence, paragraph, and text. Consistent with this analysis, uncertain decoders comprehend less than do more rapid, certain decoders (see Perfetti, 1985; Perfetti & Hogaboam, 1975; Perfetti & Lesgold, 1977, 1979). (See Chapter 6 for much more extensive discussion of automaticity at the word level.)

Good readers are adept at word-level processing in ways other than rapid and accurate decoding. When a good reader reads a word that has multiple meanings, she or he more quickly zeroes in on the correct meaning of the word in the given context than do weak readers. This is, in part, because good readers more efficiently suppress context-irrelevant meanings than do poor readers (Gernsbacher, 1990; Gernsbacher & Faust, 1990; Gernsbacher, Varner, & Faust, 1990; Merrill, Sperber, & McCauley, 1981). That is, at the level of meaning, they do use semantic context cues to read the words in the text (Tunmer & Chapman, 2004). For example, the word *rock* differs in meaning depending on the context in which it occurs. When a good reader processes the sentence, *The thief lifted the rock from the jewelry case,* he or she understands quickly that *rock* refers to a precious stone rather than other types of rocks, or rock music. In contrast, weaker readers are more likely to think about the irrelevant meanings of *rock* when they encounter the word in the sentence. The failure of weaker readers to suppress irrelevant meanings of words is consistent with a more general inability of some struggling readers to suppress tangential (often bizarre) associations to material they are reading (McCormick, 1992; Purcell-Gates, 1991; Williams, 1993). The activation of irrelevant information interferes with processing, consuming the limited short-term cognitive capacity. That is, meaning-suppression failures create additional disadvantage for already disadvantaged readers.

FAILURES OF COMPREHENSION
ABOVE THE WORD LEVEL

Once poor readers can decode well enough to read texts, their problems often continue. Poor readers are less likely than good readers to make inferences linking ideas presented in text. Thus, Yuill and Oakhill (1991, Chap. 4) presented skilled and not-so-skilled 7- to 8-year-old readers such passages as the following:

> John had got up early to learn his spellings. He was very tired and decided to take a break. When he opened his eyes again the first thing he noticed was the clock on the chair. It was an hour later and nearly time for school. He picked up his two books, and put them in a bag. He started pedalling to school as fast as he could. However, John ran over some broken bottles and had to walk the rest of the way. By the time he had crossed the bridge and arrived at class, the test was over. (p. 71)

The most important finding in Yuill and Oakhill's work was that unskilled readers were much less likely to be able to answer inferential questions about such passages than skilled readers, even when the passages remained in front of them so that remembering the information was not a problem. Unskilled readers had more problems with questions such as these: "How did John travel to school?"; "What did John do when he decided to take a break?"; "Why did John have to walk some of the way to school?"; and "How do you know that John was late for school?" Yuill and Oakhill (1991; see also Cain & Oakhill, 2004; Oakhill & Cain, 2004) reported a number of outcomes consistent with the conclusion that unskilled and skilled child readers differ in their abilities to make inferences.

There are a number of factors contributing to such inferential failures (Cain & Oakhill, 2004; Oakhill & Cain, 2004). For example, inferential skills depend in part on the possession of prior knowledge related to text. Poor readers are often very deficient in their knowledge of the world relative to good readers—as reflected, for example, in vocabulary differences between good and poor readers (e.g., Ruddell, 1994). Good readers know more, in part, because they read more, and they get more out of each bit of reading they do (Cipielewski & Stanovich, 1992; Stanovich, 1986).

Inferential comprehension also depends, however, on knowing strategies and knowing when to use comprehension strategies (i.e., possessing metacognition about strategies; e.g., Cain, 1999; Cain & Oakhill, 2004; Oakhill & Cain, 2004). With respect to the latter, good child readers know more about how to read than do weaker child readers. For example, weak child readers are less likely than good child readers to recognize that they can reread, skim, selectively attend to the text as they read, or test themselves over reading, depending on their purpose (e.g., Forrest-Pressley & Waller, 1984; Garner & Kraus, 1981/82; Paris & Myers, 1981). Poor readers are less likely than good readers to recognize factors that can undermine their reading comprehension, such as inattention during reading or distraction (Paris & Myers, 1981). Children who are weak readers do not monitor their comprehension as well as do good readers; thus, they are less aware of when they understand and when they do not—and in a worse position than good readers to make decisions about when additional efforts to comprehend are required (e.g., Garner, 1980).

These differences in metacognition are related to strategic differences between weak and strong child readers. For example, Owings, Petersen, Bransford, Morris, and Stein (1980) observed that weak grade-5 readers were less certain to vary their reading with difficulty of material than good grade-5 readers. Also, weak middle school readers were less likely than good readers to look back in the text for answers to questions that they did not know (Garner & Reis, 1981). In Phillips's (1988) think-aloud study of grade-6 reading, low-proficiency readers were less likely to shift strategies when difficulty in comprehension was encountered, less likely to attempt to verify their emerging interpretations of text meaning, and less likely to empathize with messages in the text. That is, Phillips observed that weak readers are *less active* when they read, leading to reduced comprehension of the material.

In conclusion, metacognitive theorists have noted differences among child readers in long-term knowledge about reading and how reading can be carried out, in monitoring of comprehension, and in active, strategic adjustments during reading. Metacognitive theorists explicitly believe that the differences in long-term metacognition and monitoring are causal factors in the use of strategies (Flavell, Miller, & Miller, 1993) and thus in comprehension.

SUMMARY OF WORD-LEVEL DIFFICULTIES

In summary, the most typical difficulty experienced by beginning readers is in learning to recognize words—to decode. Poor readers are more likely than good readers to attempt to "read" words by looking at pictures for cues or making a guess based on the meaning of the text. The result is many errors in reading. In addition, poor readers make less certain and rapid progress in developing automatic word recognition skills. They also are less likely to understand individual words because they use capacity-demanding strategies for decoding (e.g., analyzing semantic–contextual cues, sounding out words that are sight words for same-age good readers). Often poor readers fail to orient to the most contextually relevant meaning of a multiple-definition word.

The inability to decode also interferes with strategic functioning above the word level, because use of active comprehension strategies requires a great deal of short-term memory capacity. Because reading is difficult and comprehension uncertain for poor decoders, their knowledge base does not expand as dependably through reading as does the knowledge base of good readers. That is, there are strong associations between decoding skills and the knowledge gained through the reading of a text (e.g., Cipielewski & Stanovich, 1992; Stanovich, 1986; Stanovich & Cunningham, 1993). Not learning much content from reading, of course, undermines future comprehension, for facility in comprehension very much depends on prior knowledge—developed, in part, through prior reading.

BIOLOGICAL DYSLEXIA

When a child experiences difficulties in learning to read, it is often tempting to explain it as a biological problem. Are there normally intelligent children who have biological differences that make it more difficult or impossible for them to learn to read, even in the context of intensive instruction that would be effective with most students of normal or above-average intelligence?

Biologically Determined Dyslexia versus Other Forms of Poor Reading

If a child of normal or superior intelligence receives intensive, high-quality instruction and still fails to learn to read, there is reason to suspect developmental dyslexia—biologically determined reading disorder (e.g., Harris & Hodges, 1981). (There is another type of dyslexia, acquired dyslexia, which refers to difficulty in reading following a brain injury.) One hallmark of developmental dyslexia is that the affected individuals experience much more profound problems with reading and closely related language functions than with other academic and cognitive tasks.

Although most of the relevant analyses of biological dyslexia have been carried out with children, there is a growing body of evidence that for many weak adult readers of normal intelligence there are language problems, with the most salient difficulties associated with decoding print into sound (Bell & Perfetti, 1994; Elbro, Nielsen, & Petersen, 1994; Greenberg, Ehri, & Perin, 1997; Swanson, Mink, & Bocian, 1999). What is particularly important to emphasize in these analyses is that language difficulties related to reading problems at the word level have emerged as a key factor in developmental dyslexia and reading difficulties over a number of other possibilities, including impairments in short-term (working) memory, semantic processing, and syntactic processing skills (Lyon, 1995). That said, I think we should expect that there will be more written on this issue. For example, de Jong (1998; see also Swanson & Alexander, 1997) provided a compelling demonstration that reading-disabled children really do seem to have less working memory capacity than do normal readers—that is, less ability to process multiple pieces of information concurrently. Since then, there have been multiple analyses substantiating impaired working memory in children and adults with reading disability as compared to normal readers and among inefficient readers in general (Cain, Oakhill, & Bryant, 2004; Kibby, Marks, Morgan, & Long, 2004; Linderholm & van den Broek, 2002; Swanson, 2003; Swanson & Sachse-Lee, 2001; Walczyk, Marsiglia, Bryan, & Naquin, 2001). Also, as important as decoding is in reading, the more the concern is with reading problems above the word level (e.g., miscomprehension), the more factors like working memory and language difficulties other than phonological problems figure into data-based explanations of reading problems (e.g. Cain & Oakhill, 2004; Hatcher & Hulme, 1999; Nation, Adams, Bowyer-Crane, & Snowling, 1999; Oakhill & Cain, 2004; Swanson, 1999b). Swanson's (1999a) analyses provide particularly compelling support for the hypothesis that high-order reading problems (e.g., comprehension) are determined by a variety of deficiencies, not just phonological processing deficiencies. Regardless of how important basic word recognition is in determining comprehension, it is only one of several factors affecting how well the child understands what is being read (e.g., Zinar, 2000).

It is common for students experiencing severe problems learning to read to manifest a variety of problems in language functions, from basic perception of language to memory of language to development of syntax to comprehension skills, with these language deficiencies often apparent from early childhood (see Catts, 1989; Catts, Fey, Zhang, & Tomblin, 1999; Elbro & Scarborough, 2004; Katz, Shankweiler, & Liberman, 1981; Liberman, Mann, Shankweiler, & Werfelman, 1982; Mann & Brady, 1988; Olson, Kliegl, Davidson, & Foltz, 1985; Sawyer & Butler, 1991; Stanovich, 1986; Vellutino, 1979). Preschoolers who will later experience severe reading difficulties manifest more differences in their use of language as compared to those who will be normal readers: Their utterances are shorter and not as syntactically sophisticated; their pronunciations are not as good; and they understand fewer words. It is harder for the eventually developmentally dyslexic child to label common objects than it is for the eventually normally achieving reader (e.g., Elbro & Scarborough, 2004; Scarborough, 1990).

In contrast to the dyslexic reader is the garden-variety poor reader, whose difficulties in learning to read are consistent with other academic difficulties because of his or her generally low intelligence (Stanovich, 1988). The use of the term "garden-variety" emphasizes that poor reading due to generally low intelligence is more prevalent than developmental dyslexia. For Caucasians, about 16% of the population has an IQ less than 85, with many such children experiencing reading difficulties because of low intelligence.

Dyslexia and garden-variety poor reading contrast with poor reading by children of normal intelligence and intact biology who are victims of poor instruction or educational neglect. However, it is often difficult or impossible to determine whether a student is developmentally dyslexic, a garden-variety poor reader, or a victim of poor teaching. Nonetheless, classification as dyslexic should occur only if it is known that general intelligence is at least average and a variety of approaches to teaching reading have been attempted with the student.

Prevalence of Dyslexia

Experts differ in their estimates of the prevalence of biological dyslexia. The highest estimate that I have encountered is 20% (i.e., 20% of the population suffers from a biological difference that impairs reading; e.g., Shaywitz, 1996). Most experts, however, cite much lower figures, with many claiming that 1% or less of normally intelligent children are biologically impaired, with most informed estimates not exceeding 5% of the population (Hynd & Hynd, 1984; Stevenson, 2004). After a lot of reflection, my answer when I am asked for prevalence is this: "It is closer to 1% than 20%. Many with well-informed opinions would be surprised if it were as high as 2% of the population and certainly not more than 5%." Yes, 20–30% of normally intelligent children experience some difficulties in learning to read words, but only a small fraction of them have biological differences that prevent them from learning to read words when given systematic instruction.

An analysis by Frank R. Vellutino and his associates (Vellutino et al., 1996; see also Vellutino & Scanlon, 2001) is one of the best bases for making an estimate of prevalence that I have encountered. From a total school population of 827 students in a suburban school district, the 9% who were falling behind the most during the grade-1 year but who were of normal or superior intelligence (i.e., an IQ greater than 90) were enrolled in a daily tutoring program for 30 minutes a day. The tutoring consisted mostly of intensive phonics instruction. After one semester of remediation, only 3% of the original sample continued below the 30th percentile on a nationally normed test and only 1.5% of the original sample remained below the 15th percentile. That is, it was a very small percentage of students who could not learn to read given intense decoding instruction. (Vellutino and associates' study, which contained carefully designed control conditions, is but the first of the studies taken up in this book that demonstrate that many children who experience difficulties in learning to read in school can overcome them if given intensive tutoring; see Chapter 5.)

There is a very, very important message in Vellutino et al. (1996): Until there is an intensive effort to teach a child to read words using a systematic approach, it is a huge mistake to assume that the child cannot learn to read because of biological differences. This message is especially telling in the context of a nation in which beginning reading instruction often is anything but systematic or intensive with respect to word recognition skills. Vellutino and colleagues' message is that most of the 20–30% of normally intelligent children who experience serious problems with word recognition can be helped with systematic instruction in decoding. That's an optimistic message— much more so than assuming that these children have a biologically based problem that is causing their difficulties with word recognition. Vellutino and colleagues' perspective is a solidly environmental one: The instructional environment counts for plenty, with the reading achievement of students very much affected by the teaching they experience.

It should not be missed, however, that the instruction that worked in Vellutino et al. (1996) was daily one-to-one tutoring for a semester or more, consistent with tutorial approaches used with struggling readers in studies that will be cited in the chapters ahead. Such intensity permits careful monitoring of specific difficulties and tailored instruction. That the control in the study was small-group instruction consistent with the school district's normal approach to remediation makes clear that instruction short of intensive one-to-one tutoring is just not as effective. At several points in this book, I'll make reference to one-to-one tutoring resources, with a main motivation for doing so being demonstrations like that of Vellutino et al. (1996) that such tutoring can turn struggling readers around. Since the publication of the first edition of this book, much has been happening with respect to the development of one-to-one tutoring for struggling beginning readers (see Invernizzi, 2001).

Individual Differences in the Word Recognition Problems of Readers with Dyslexia

There are a variety of specific word recognition problems that can underlie developmental dyslexia. Some with dyslexia experience difficulties in learning to decode rapidly, whereas others experience difficulties in decoding at any speed.

When students with dyslexia experience difficulties in recognizing words at all, even when permitted as much time as needed to decode, they are classified as decoding-accuracy-disabled (e.g., Lovett, 1984). The most certain indicator of the decoding-accuracy deficit is the inability of children who have received intensive instruction in decoding to read phonologically regular pseudowords (e.g., *maglum, croleb*; Rack, Snowling, & Olson, 1992). Decoding pseudowords requires much knowledge of letter–sound relationships (Hogaboam & Perfetti, 1978). Its advantage as an indicator of decoding ability over the reading of actual words is that pseudowords could never have been encountered by the child before and hence must be decoded by sounding them out. They cannot be recognized as sight words.

In contrast to decoding-accuracy-disabled readers, some readers with dyslexia, often referred to as rate-disabled decoders, can accurately decode but are very slow at it relative to classmates (e.g., Hogaboam & Perfetti, 1978; also Bowers & Swanson, 1991; Lovett, 1984). Maryanne Wolf and her colleagues (e.g., Wolf & Bowers, 1999; Wolf, Pfeil, Lotz, & Biddle, 1994), in particular, have argued that rate disability in decoding reflects a more general disability involving the speed of retrieval of linguistic information, as reflected, for example, in the relative slowness of some children to retrieve the names of things when presented pictures of them (Wolf, 1986, 1991; also see Denckla, 1972; Denckla & Rudel, 1976). In contrast, good readers respond quickly to the verbal symbols that constitute reading (Perfetti, 1985). Such slowness in verbal processing, predictive of extreme difficulties in learning to read (Levy, Bourassa, & Horn, 1999), can be detected in the early preschool years (e.g., McDougall, Hulme, Ellis, & Monk, 1994; Torgesen & Davis, 1996; Vellutino, Scanlon, & Spearing,

1995). In short, some dyslexic readers can barely decode at all. Others can learn to decode with intensive instruction, but their decoding is very slow, consistent with a speed deficit in linguistic retrieval abilities. Documenting the relative role of phonological processes and speed of processing in normal and troubled reading is an active area of research (Cardoso-Martins & Pennington, 2004; Catts, Gillispie, Leonard, Kail, & Miller, 2002; Kirby, Parrila, & Pfeiffer, 2003; Parrila, Kirby, & McQuarrie, 2004; Schatschneider, Fletcher, Francis, Carlson, & Foorman, 2004; Sunseth & Bowers, 2002).

The Genetic Basis of Developmental Dyslexia

When a child experiences difficulties in learning to read, a family history of reading problems, unaccompanied by evidence of a family history of low intelligence, may be one reason to suspect developmental dyslexia. Clinicians have suspected for years that there is a genetic basis to developmental dyslexia. Recent research has succeeded in substantiating the hypothesis that developmental dyslexia can be inherited.

If a characteristic is genetically determined, its co-occurrence in identical twins should be more likely than its co-occurrence in fraternal twins, since the former share 100% of genes and the latter share only 50%. That, in fact, is the case with respect to reading difficulties (e.g., Bakwin, 1973; Decker & Vandenberg, 1985; DeFries, Fulker, & LaBuda, 1987), and especially with respect to the ability to read unfamiliar words (Olson, 1994). If genetics determines reading ability, there also should be a higher correlation between the reading abilities of adopted children and their biological parents than between adopted children and adopting parents: That is the case as well (Cardon, DiLalla, Plomin, DeFries, & Fulker, 1990). In general, with each passing year, there is more and more evidence of a genetic basis for at least some reading disabilities, in particular, the most severe of reading problems (Byrne et al., 2002; Davis, Knopik, Olson, Wadsworth, & DeFries, 2001; Gayan & Olson, 2003; Gilger & Wise, 2004; Hohnen & Stevenson, 1999; Olson & Gayan, 2001; Stevenson, 2004; Thomson & Raskind, 2003; Tunick & Pennington, 2002).

Functional and Structural Differences in the Brains of Normal and Developmentally Dyslexic Readers

In general, the left cerebral hemisphere plays a larger role in language processing than does the right hemisphere. Modern imaging techniques, permitting detailed images of brain structures as well as dynamic images and records of brain activity during performance of tasks (e.g., reading), have provided a great deal of evidence of left-hemisphere differences in structure and function between some poor readers and normal readers (Conners, 1971; Duffy & McAnulty, 1990; Fiez et al., 1995; Flowers, Wood, & Naylor, 1991; Galaburda, Sherman, Rosen, Aboitz, & Geschwind, 1985; Galin, 1989; Gross-Glenn et al., 1988; Harter, 1991; Hier, LeMay, Rosenberger, & Perlo, 1978; Jernigan, Hesselink, Sowell, & Tallal, 1991; Johnson & Myklebust, 1967; Larsen, Hoien, Lundberg, & Odegaard, 1990; Mody, 2004; Rumsey, 1996; Rumsey, Nace, & Andreason, 1995; Shaywitz et al., 2000; Shaywitz & Shaywitz, 2003; Wood, Felton, Flowers, & Naylor, 1991). For example, some regions of the brain involved in reading tend to be smaller in reading-disabled readers (Hynd & Semrud-Clikeman, 1989). In addition, the patterns of brain activity differ as dyslexics and normal readers read. In short, there are real anatomical and physiological differences between good and some poor readers. (There is more detailed coverage of brain differences in skilled and less skilled readers in Chapter 6.)

One of the most important conclusions produced by neuroscientists interested in reading is that functional differences between normal and dyslexic readers are most often found in regions of the brain implicated in phonological processing (Mody, 2004; Shaywitz et al., 2000). This is powerful evidence in favor of theories of reading problems at the word level that emphasize phonological processing rather than other aspects of information processing, such as the visual system. Such work is not yet far enough along to be revealing about the brain regions mediating higher-order reading problems, such as difficulties in comprehension, however.

Are There Visual–Perceptual Problems That Cause Word Recognition Disabilities?

Vellutino (1979), in particular, made the first exceptionally strong case that dyslexia was the result of language deficits much more than visual–perceptual deficits. Vellutino's position was supported by many failed attempts to establish clear differences between learning-disabled and nondisabled students with respect to many aspects of visual processing. Until recently, Vellutino's (1979) strong statement on the primacy of language difficulties in students with dyslexia has been unchallenged in most of the serious reading research community.

Even so, some researchers who study eye movements during reading responded to Vellutino's (1979) book by continuing to reflect on unusual eye-movement patterns displayed by some dyslexic subjects during reading (see Lovegrove, 1992). When normal readers read in a word-by-word fashion (see Chapter 2), there is rapid eye movement, with jumps (saccades), typically about six to nine characters in length, and fixations, typically about a quarter of a second in duration (Rayner & McConkie, 1976). When someone is reading English, the normal saccadic movement is generally left to right, although there are also occasional right-to-left regressions. At the end of a line of normal reading, there is a smooth return, sweeping from right to left to the beginning of the next line of text.

In contrast to normal reading, which is more left to right than right to left, many dyslexic readers display what is referred to as the reverse-staircase pattern in their reading. It has been known since the early 20th century (Gray, 1917; Schmidt, 1917) that the return sweeps of some disabled readers are interrupted rather than smooth. Dyslexic readers also have been reported to make more and longer fixations during reading, more regressions (i.e., looking back) within a line of text, and more visual fixation regressions within individual words than do normal readers (Pirozzolo, 1979).

Though visual-processing differences between dyslexic readers and normal readers can be detected, the best-informed researchers typically have not viewed them as the cause of dyslexia. If they were the cause, then successful efforts to modify eye movements should result in improved reading, but they do not (Pirozzolo, 1979, 1983). Rather than being the *cause* of poor reading, it seems that the difference in eye movements may be a *result* of poor reading: Failures to decode and understand text cause regressions.

Even so, an important hypothesis in recent years has been that differences in visual-processing abilities between some dyslexic readers and normal readers really do reflect differences in fundamental spatial abilities. In particular, there are suspicions about differences between normal readers and some dyslexic readers in the visual abilities responsible for the rapid pickup of information about the general shape of words (coarse perceptual information). Such processing occurs in peripheral vision and can affect saccadic movement (Fischer, 1992; Lovegrove, 1992). That is, some dyslexic readers have difficulty in processing rapidly presented visual information, particularly information embedded in rapid sequences of information (e.g., Gaddes, 1982; Galaburda & Livingstone, 1993; Lovegrove, Garzia, & Nicholson, 1990; Martin & Lovegrove, 1987). If reading is anything, it is rapid processing of sequences of information. Whether this perceptual difference is a cause or effect of dyslexia is not known at this time.

Another important new hypothesis about a fundamental physiological cause of some reading disabilities is emerging from the complicated pattern of data now in the literature pertaining to eye movement and rapid sequential processing. Livingstone, Rosen, Drislane, and Galaburda (1991; also Galaburda & Livingstone, 1993) believe that some people with dyslexia may have atypical neural pathways linking the various parts of the visual system.

Additional research on these hypotheses about perceptual differences between normal readers and individuals with dyslexia promises to shed light on the possibility that dyslexia may not be just a language disorder.

Perhaps it is caused by a mix of language and visual–perceptual problems—or, alternatively, it is more a language disorder for some people with dyslexia and more a visual–perceptual disorder for other people with dyslexia. Moreover, there are other related possibilities, including that individuals with dyslexia might suffer from general difficulties (i.e., across a number of modalities rather than just in the visual modality) in rapid sequential processing of information (Farmer & Klein, 1995; Tallal, Miller, & Fitch, 1993) or general difficulties in making rapid discriminations between similar stimuli such as letters (Studdert-Kennedy & Mody, 1995). Thus, it may be that there are a variety of processing deficits that can result in dyslexia. This possibility has gained respectability (Martin, 1995), especially with the recognition that some of the possible causes of dyslexia (e.g., problems in rapid sequential processing of information) are much rarer than other deficiencies (e.g., language deficits; Rayner, Pollatsek, & Bilsky, 1995).

Summary

Some children who experience failures in learning to read do so because of generally low intelligence. Such failures are not puzzling to the research or education community; what is puzzling is when an otherwise normally intelligent or even very intelligent child fails to learn to read even after intensive efforts to teach him or her. That is developmental dyslexia.

A variety of biological pieces to the puzzle that is developmental dyslexia are now available. There is evidence of genetic determination of developmental dyslexia (Gilger & Wise, 2004; Smith, Kimberling, & Pennington, 1991). There are certainly neurological differences between some people with reading difficulties and normal readers, especially with respect to parts of the brain implicated in the processing of language that are consistent with language differences between reading-disabled and normal readers. Even as the evidence continues to accumulate that developmental dyslexia typically involves verbal–phonological processing problems, there are new hypotheses emerging about the role of perception, and in particular visual perception, in reading disabilities.

It is a tragic mistake to assume that initially poor reading necessarily implies a biological problem. A diagnosis of biologically caused dyslexia should be reached only after environmental deprivation has been ruled out (i.e., only after it is ensured that the child was provided instruction about how to decode, something that is not certain in many contemporary classrooms). The most compelling evidence on this point comes from studies such as Vellutino and associates' (1996) investigation, in which children who were experiencing difficulties in learning to read with normal classroom instruction came up to grade level once intensive tutoring began.

There will be reference to and discussion of other such investigations in the chapters that follow.

Most children experiencing initial reading problems are not biologically dyslexic. For many, their problem is that they have not been taught how to decode text and/or how to construct meaning from text in ways that are efficient and effective. By the end of this book, I hope to have you convinced that with most children of normal intelligence both decoding and comprehension are very teachable processes.

LATE-ONSET READING DIFFICULTIES

What cannot be missed is that reading difficulties that are apparent in the primary grades garner more attention from researchers than reading problems that become apparent at other age levels. This is so despite the fact that there is a widespread perception that at least some children experience a "fourth-grade slump," exhibiting reading difficulties for the first time at about the fourth-grade level. Because reading demands change at fourth grade—comprehension is emphasized more, while the difficulty of texts increases—there are definitely valid reasons to suspect there might be something to the possibility that some children experience reading difficulties for the first time at fourth grade.

In an important analysis, Leach, Scorborough, and Rescorla (2003) explored this possibility. They studied fourth graders from Philadelphia-area schools, examining their performances in the middle elementary grades and analyzing their reading achievement records before that. The students were drawn from schools serving affluent suburbs as well as more diverse neighborhoods.

There were a number of fascinating findings. First, about 31% of the full sample were identified as both having problems in the primary grades and having those problems persist into grade 3. By contrast, only 8% of the full sample were identified as having problems in the primary grades but with remedial services discontinued before third grade—presumably because those students were now reading at an acceptable level. What that means is that for every student who responded well to ameliorative efforts, four did not respond well enough to discontinue the intervention. This is a sobering statistic. Getting back on track in the public schools is not easy once a reading disability is manifest. Quite honestly, as I contemplate this Leach et al. (2003) statistic through my years of experience around schools, I feel that these researchers' data are accurate: Most troubled readers in the primary grades continue to need support *after* the primary grades.

Considering those students who at grade 4 had a reading disability, which was about *41%* of the students studied, there were roughly equal numbers of boys and girls. Of those experiencing difficulties, 42% had a word reading disability only and 18% had a reading comprehension disability only, while *39% had both word-level and comprehension problems.* If it is safe to worry only about word-level problems in the primary grades, that is definitely not the case by the middle elementary grades—in this sample, at the fourth-grade level, more than half the troubled readers had word-level problems and more than half had comprehension problems.

One of the most important statistics in the analyses, however, was that 47% of those experiencing difficulties in the middle elementary grades did not have difficulties in the primary grades. Notably, these figures are roughly consistent with the proportions of late and early identified problem readers in previous research (Badian, 1999; Shaywitz, Escobar, Shaywitz, Fletcher, & Makuch, 1992). Reading problems definitely emerge in the middle elementary grades for some children. Yes, there were some indications that the late identified troubled readers were not as impaired as the early identified—for example, they read words faster than early identified disabled readers, but still they read more slowly than normally achieving readers.

Leach et al. (2003) dramatically made the point that there has been too little study of the problems experienced after grade 3. This is an area that needs a great deal of additional study. There needs to be serious efforts to determine what can be done at the fourth-grade level and beyond to get the newly problematic readers back on track as well as move those with persistent reading problems as far as they can go. There is no excuse for a national reading agenda targeted only at the primary grades, such as the Reading First provisions of the No Child Left Behind legislation, for there remains much reason to remediate reading in the middle elementary grades and beyond. Some struggling primary-grades students will improve; some won't; some who did not struggle in the primary grades will do so in the middle and later grades; and some who did not struggle early will continue to do well (see Phillips et al., 2002, for additional supportive data on this point). The nation needs reading agendas that serve all such students well.

SUMMARY AND CONCLUDING REFLECTIONS

1. The most salient problem for many poor readers is that they do not decode well. In Chapter 5, more evidence is presented that many children who have experienced difficulties in learning to read nonetheless benefit from systematic, intensive instruction in decoding, letter–sound associations, and the blending of such sounds to produce words. For many poor readers, their problem may be that they have never received such instruction or have received it in a watered-down fashion.

2. Poor readers often rely on semantic–contextual cues in an attempt to decode text. This reliance on semantic cues results in inaccurate decodings. It is also an approach that requires great effort, and hence consumes much short-term memory capacity, leaving little capacity for comprehension of words once they are decoded. Even when struggling readers succeed in decoding a word, they often fail to zero in on the one of its several definitions that would make sense in the semantic context in which the word occurs. Poor readers often are confused by irrelevant meanings of words they have decoded.

3. Poor readers often do not use efficient comprehension strategies to derive the appropriate meanings from text. They are less likely to possess prior knowledge that can be related to text content, and when they do possess it, they are less likely to use it appropriately to understand fully the ideas presented in the text. When decoding is poor, students do not learn as much from texts as they would if their decoding were more comprehensive.

4. In some cases, an inability to read is caused by biological factors, with the two most conspicuous examples being people with low general intelligence and those suffering from developmental dyslexia. However, biology probably does not account for anything like the majority of individuals of normal intelligence who have word recognition difficulties. With a normally intelligent child, dyslexia should not be assumed as an explanation of reading failure until great efforts have been made to teach that student to read. If the student is of normal intelligence, the odds are very great that difficulties in learning to read are not the result of developmental dyslexia but rather of an environmental failure. One possibility is that the child has not experienced reading instruction that is systematic enough for him or her to learn how to read. Other possible environmental failures, however, will be considered in the next chapter, which takes up development during the preschool years. What happens during the preschool years affects children's subsequent success in learning to read in the primary years.

5. Reading difficulties are not restricted to the primary grades. Some children who experienced difficulties in the primary grades continue to have difficulties. Some children experience difficulties for the first time *after* the primary grades. And, of course, going back to the opening paragraph of this chapter, for some, reading difficulties persist into adulthood. Unfortunately, although there will be much to say about interventions in the elementary years, especially the early elementary years, in the pages ahead, there is disturbingly little intervention work beyond the elementary years. What there is would be for another book, since this book is about elementary instruction, but it would be a short book. Just as I encourage much more support for intervention research in the middle and later elementary school years, I also encourage much more intervention research beyond that.

REFERENCES

Badian, N. A. (1999). Reading disability defined as a discrepancy between listening and reading comprehension: A longitudinal study of stability, gender differences, and prevalence. *Journal of Learning Disabilities, 32,* 138–148.

Bakwin, H. (1973). Reading disability in twins. *Developmental Medicine and Child Neurology, 15,* 184–187.

Bell, L. C., & Perfetti, C. A. (1994). Reading skill: Some adult comparisons. *Journal of Educational Psychology, 86,* 344–355.

Bertucci, C., Hook, P., Haynes, C. Macaruso, P., & Bickley, C. (2003). Vowel perception and production in adolescents with reading disabilities. *Annals of Dyslexia, 53,* 174–200.

Booth, J. R., Perfetti, C. A., & MacWhinney, B. (1999). Quick, automatic, and general activation of orthographic and phonological representations in young readers. *Developmental Psychology, 35,* 3–19.

Bowers, P. G., & Swanson, L. B. (1991). Naming speed deficits in reading disability: Multiple measures of a single process. *Journal of Experimental Child Psychology, 51,* 195–219.

Brady, S., & Shankweiler, D. (Eds.). (1991). *Phonological processes in literacy.* Hillsdale, NJ: Erlbaum.

Brady, S., Shankweiler, D., & Mann, V. (1983). Speech perception and memory coding in relation to reading ability. *Journal of Experimental Child Psychology, 35,* 345–367.

Breier, J. I., Fletcher, J. M., Denton, C., & Gray, L. C. (2004). Categorical perception of speech stimuli in children at risk for reading difficulty. *Journal of Experimental Child Psychology, 88,* 152–170.

Bruck, M. (1990). Word-recognition skills of adults with childhood diagnoses of dyslexia. *Developmental Psychology, 26,* 439–454.

Bruck, M. (1992). Persistence of dyslexics' phonological awareness deficits. *Developmental Psychology, 28,* 874–886.

Byrne, B., Delaland, C., Fielding-Barnsley, R., Quain, P., Samuelsson, S., Høien, T., Corley, R., DeFries, J. C., Wadsworth, S., Willcutt, E., & Olson, R. K. (2002). Longitudinal twin study of early reading development in three countries: Preliminary results. *Annals of Dyslexia, 52,* 49–73.

Cain, K. (1999). Ways of reading: How knowledge and use of strategies are related to reading comprehension. *British Journal of Developmental Psychology, 17,* 292–312.

Cain, K., & Oakhill, J. (2004). Reading comprehension difficulties. In T. Nunes & P. Bryant (Eds.), *Handbook of children's literacy* (pp. 313–338). Dordrecht, The Netherlands: Kluwer Academic.

Cain, K., Oakhill, J., & Bryant, P. (2004). Children's reading comprehension ability: Concurrent prediction by working memory, verbal ability, and component skills. *Journal of Educational Psychology, 96,* 31–42.

Cardon, L. R., DiLalla, L. F., Plomin, R., DeFries, J. C., & Fulker, D. W. (1990). Genetic correlations between reading performance and IQ in the Colorado adoption project. *Intelligence, 14,* 245–257.

Cardoso-Martins, C., & Pennington, B. F. (2004). The relationship between phoneme awareness and rapid serial naming skills and literacy acquisition: The role of developmental period and reading ability. *Scientific Studies of Reading, 8,* 27–52.

Catts, H. (1989). Defining dyslexia as a developmental language disorder. *Annals of Dyslexia, 39,* 50–64.

Catts, H., Fey, M. E., Zhang, X., & Tomblin, J. B. (1999). Language basis of reading and reading disabilities: Evidence from a longitudinal investigation. *Scientific Studies of Reading, 3,* 331–361.

Catts, H. W., Gillispie, M., Leonard, L. B., Kail, R. V., & Miller, C. A. (2002). The role of speed of processing, rapid naming, and phonological awareness in reading achievement. *Journal of Learning Disabilities, 35,* 509–524.

Chiappe, P., Chiappe, D. L., & Siegel, L. S. (2001). Speech perception, lexicality, and reading skill. *Journal of Experimental Child Psychology, 80,* 58–74.

Cipielewski, J., & Stanovich, K. E. (1992). Predicting growth in reading ability from children's exposure to print. *Journal of Experimental Child Psychology, 54,* 74–89.

Conners, C. K. (1971). Cortical visual evoked response in children with learning disorders. *Psychophysiology, 7,* 418–428.

Corley, P. J. (1988). A developmental analysis of sentence comprehension abilities in good and poor readers. *Educational Psychologist, 23,* 57–75.

Davis, C. J., Knopik, V. S., Olson, R. K., Wadsworth, S. J., & DeFries, J. C. (2001). Genetic and environmental influences on rapid naming and reading: A twin study. *Annals of Dyslexia, 51,* 231–247.

Decker, S. N., & Vandenberg, S. G. (1985). Colorado twin study of reading disability. In D. B. Gray & J. Kavanaugh (Eds.), *Biobehavioral measures of dyslexia* (pp. 123–135). Baltimore: York Press.

DeFries, J. C., Fulker, D. W., & LaBuda, M. C. (1987). Evidence for a genetic aetiology in reading disability of twins. *Nature, 329,* 537–539.

de Jong, P. F. (1998). Working memory deficits of reading disabled children. *Journal of Experimental Child Psychology, 70,* 75–96.

de Jong, P. F., & van der Leij, A. (2003). Developmental changes in the manifestations of a phonological deficit in dyslexic children learning to read a regular orthography. *Journal of Educational Psychology, 95,* 22–40.

Denckla, M. B. (1972). Color naming deficits in dyslexic boys. *Cortex, 8,* 164–176.

Denckla, M. B., & Rudel, R. G. (1976). Rapid automatized naming (R.A.N.): Dyslexia differentiated from other learning disabilities. *Neuropsychologica, 14,* 471–476.

Duffy, F. H., & McAnulty, G. (1990). Neuropsychological heterogeneity and the definition of dyslexia: Preliminary evidence for plasticity. *Neuropsychologica, 28,* 96–103.

Ehri, L. C., & Snowling, M. J. (2004). Developmental variation in word recognition. In C. A. Stone, E. R. Silliman, B. J. Ehren, & K. Apel (Eds.), *Handbook of language and literacy: Development and disorders* (pp. 433–460). New York: Guilford Press.

Elbro, C., Nielsen, I., & Petersen, D. K. (1994). Dyslexia in adults: Evidence for deficits in non-word reading and in the phonological representation of lexical items. *Annals of Dyslexia, 44,* 205–226.

Elbro, C., & Scarborough, H. S. (2004). Early identification. In T. Nunes & P. Bryant (Eds.), *Handbook of children's literacy* (pp. 339–359). Dordrecht, The Netherlands: Kluwer Academic.

Espy, K. A., Molfese, D. L., Molfese, V. J., & Modglin, A. (2004). Development of auditory event-related potentials in young children and relations to word-level reading abilities at 8 years. *Annals of Dyslexia, 54,* 9–38.

Farmer, M. E., & Klein, R. M. (1995). The evidence for a temporal processing deficit linked to dyslexia: A review. *Psychological Bulletin and Review, 2,* 460–493.

Fiez, J. A., Tallal, P., Raichle, M. E., Katz, W. F., Miezin, F. M., & Petersen, S. E. (1995). PET studies of auditory and phonological processing: Effects of stimulus type and task condition. *Journal of Cognitive Neuroscience, 7,* 357–375.

Finucci, J. M., Gottfredson, L. S., & Childs, B. (1985). A follow-up study of dyslexic boys. *Annals of Dyslexia, 35,* 117–136.

Fischer, B. (1992). Saccadic reaction time: Implications for reading, dyslexia, and visual cognition. In K. Rayner (Ed.), *Eye movements and visual cognition: Scene perception and reading* (pp. 31–45). New York: Springer-Verlag.

Flavell, J. R., Miller, P., & Miller, S. (1993). *Cognitive development* (3rd ed.). Englewood Cliffs, NJ: Prentice-Hall.

Fletcher, J. M., Shaywitz, S. E., Shankweiler, D. P., Katz, L., Liberman, I. Y., Stuebing, K. K., Francis, D. J., Fowler, A. E., & Shaywitz, B. A. (1994). Cognitive profiles of reading disability: Comparisons of discrepancy and low achievement definitions. *Journal of Educational Psychology, 86,* 6–23.

Flowers, D. L., Wood, F. B., & Naylor, C. E. (1991). Regional cerebral bloodflow correlates of language processes in reading disability. *Archives of Neurology, 48,* 637–643.

Foorman, B. R., Francis, D. J., Fletcher, J. M., & Lynn, A. (1996). Relation of phonological and orthographic processing to early reading: Comparing two approaches to regression-based, reading-level-matched designs. *Journal of Educational Psychology, 88,* 639–652.

Forrest-Pressley, D. L., & Waller, T. G. (1984). *Cognition, metacognition, and reading.* New York: Springer-Verlag.

Francis, D. J., Shaywitz, S. E., Stuebing, K. K., & Fletcher, J. M. (1994). The measurement of change: Assessing behavior over time and within a developmental context. In G. R. Lyon (Ed.), *Frames of reference for the assessment of learning disabilities: New views on measurement issues* (pp. 29–58). Baltimore: Brookes.

Frauenheim, J. G., & Heckerl, J. R. (1983). A longitudinal study of psychological and achievement test performance in severe dyslexic adults. *Journal of Learning Disabilities, 16,* 339–347.

Gaddes, W. H. (1982). Serial order behavior: To understand it, a scientific challenge, an educational necessity. In W. M. Cruickshank & J. W. Lerner (Eds.), *Coming of age: Vol. 3. The best of ACLD* (pp. 87–107). Syracuse, NY: Syracuse University Press.

Galaburda, A., & Livingstone, M. (1993). Evidence for a magnocellular defect in developmental dyslexia. *Annals of the New York Academy of Sciences, 682,* 70–82.

Galaburda, A. M., Sherman, G. F., Rosen, G. D., Aboitz, F., & Geschwind, N. (1985). Developmental dyslexia: Four consecutive patients with cortical anomalies. *Archives of Neurology, 35,* 812–817.

Galin, D. (1989). EEG studies in dyslexia. In D. J. Bakker & H. van der Vlugt (Eds.), *Learning disabilities: Vol. 1. Neuropsychological correlates and treatment.* Amsterdam: Swets.

Garner, R. (1980). Monitoring of understanding: An investigation of good and poor readers' awareness of induced miscomprehension of text. *Journal of Reading Behavior, 12,* 55–64.

Garner, R., & Kraus, C. (1981/82). Good and poor comprehenders differences in knowing and regulating reading behaviors. *Educational Research Quarterly, 6,* 5–12.

Garner, R., & Reis, R. (1981). Monitoring and resolving comprehension obstacles: An investigation of spontaneous text lookbacks among upper-grade good and poor comprehenders. *Reading Research Quarterly, 16,* 569–582.

Gayan, J., & Olson, R. K. (2003). Genetic and environmental influences on individual differences in printed word recognition. *Journal of Experimental Child Psychology, 84,* 97–123.

Gernsbacher, M. A. (1990). *Language comprehension as structure building.* Hillsdale, NJ: Erlbaum.

Gernsbacher, M. A., & Faust, M. E. (1990). The role of suppression in sentence comprehension. In G. B. Simpson (Ed.), *Understanding word and sentence* (pp. 97–128). Amsterdam: North-Holland.

Gernsbacher, M. A., Varner, K. R., & Faust, M. E. (1990). Investigating differences in general comprehension skill. *Journal of Experimental Psychology: Learning, Memory, and Cognition, 16,* 430–445.

Gilger, J. W., & Wise, S. E. (2004). Genetic correlates of language and literacy impairments. In C. A. Stone, E. R. Silliman, B. J. Ehren, & K. Apel (Eds.), *Handbook of language and literacy: Development and disorders* (pp. 25–48). New York: Guilford Press.

Goldsmith-Phillips, J. (1989). Word and context in reading development: A test of the interactive–compensatory hypothesis. *Journal of Educational Psychology, 81,* 299–305.

Goswami, U., & Bryant, P. (1990). *Phonological skills and learning to read.* London: Erlbaum.

Gottardo, A., Stanovich, K. E., & Siegel, L. S. (1996). The relationships between phonological sensitivity, syntactic processing, and verbal working memory in the reading performance of third-grade children. *Journal of Experimental Child Psychology, 63,* 563–582.

Gough, P. B., Ehri, L., & Treiman, R. (Eds.). (1992). *Reading acquisition.* Hillsdale, NJ: Erlbaum.

Gray, C. T. (1917). Types of reading ability as exhibited through tests and laboratory experiments. *Supplementary Educational Monographs, 1*(5), 1–191.

Greenberg, D., Ehri, L. C., & Perin, D. (1997). Are word reading processes the same or different in adult literacy students and 3rd–5th graders matched for reading level? *Journal of Educational Psychology, 89,* 262–275.

Greenberg, D., Ehri, L. C., & Perin, D. (2002). Do adult literacy students make the same word-reading and spelling errors as children matched for word-reading age? *Scientific Studies of Reading, 6,* 221–243.

Gross-Glenn, K., Duara, R., Yoshii, F., Barker, W. W., Chen, J. Y., Apicella, A., Boothe,

T., & Lubs, H. A. (1988). PET-scan reading studies of familial dyslexics [Abstract]. *Journal of Clinical and Experimental Neuropsychology, 10*, 34–35.

Guttorm, T. K., Leppanen, P. H. T., Richardson, U., & Lyytinen, H. (2001). Event-related potentials and consonant differentiation in newborns with familial risk for dyslexia. *Journal of Learning Disabilities, 34*, 534–544.

Hammill, D. D., Mather, N., Allen, E. A., & Roberts, R. (2002). Using semantics, grammar, phonology, and rapid naming tasks to predict word identification. *Journal of Learning Disabilities, 35*, 121–136.

Harris, T. L., & Hodges, R. W. (Eds.). (1981). *A dictionary of reading and related terms*. Newark, DE: International Reading Association.

Harter, M. R. (1991). Event-related potential indices: Learning disabilities and visual processing. In J. E. Obrzut & G. W. Hynd (Eds.), *Neuropsychological foundations of learning disabilities: A handbook of issues, methods, and practice* (pp. 437–473). San Diego: Academic Press.

Hatcher, P. J., & Hulme, C. (1999). Phonemes, rhymes, and intelligence as predictors of children's responsiveness to remedial reading instruction: Evidence from a longitudinal intervention study. *Journal of Experimental Child Psychology, 72*, 130–153.

Hier, D. B., LeMay, M., Rosenberger, P. B., & Perlo, V. P. (1978). Developmental dyslexia: Evidence for a subgroup with a reversal of cerebral asymmetry. *Archives of Neurology, 35*, 90–92.

Hogaboam, T. W., & Perfetti, C. A. (1978). Reading skill and the role of verbal experience in decoding. *Journal of Educational Psychology, 70*, 717–729.

Hohnen, B., & Stevenson, J. (1999). The structure of genetic influences on general cognitive, language, phonological, and reading abilities. *Developmental Psychology, 35*, 590–603.

Hynd, G. W., & Hynd, C. R. (1984). Dyslexia: Neuroanatomical/neurolinguistic perspectives. *Reading Research Quarterly, 19*, 482–498.

Hynd, G. W., & Semrud-Clikeman, M. (1989). Dyslexia and brain morphology. *Psychological Bulletin, 106*, 447–482.

Invernizzi, M. A. (2001). The complex world of one-to-one tutoring. In S. B. Neuman & D. K. Dickinson (Eds.), *Handbook of early literacy research* (pp. 459–470). New York: Guilford Press.

Jernigan, T. L., Hesselink, J. R., Sowell, E., & Tallal, P. A. (1991). Cerebral structure on magnetic resonance imaging in language- and learning-impaired children. *Archives of Neurology, 48*, 539–545.

Johnson, D., & Myklebust, H. R. (1967). *Learning disabilities: Educational principles and practice*. New York: Grune & Stratton.

Katz, R. B., Shankweiler, D., & Liberman, I. Y. (1981). Memory for item order and phonetic recoding in the beginning reader. *Journal of Experimental Child Psychology, 32*, 474–484.

Kibby, M. Y., Marks, W., Morgan, S., & Long, C. J. (2004). Specific impairment in developmental reading disabilities: A working memory approach. *Journal of Learning Disabilities, 37*, 349–363.

Kim, Y. H., & Goetz, E. T. (1994). Context effects on word recognition and reading comprehension of poor and good readers: A test of the interactive–compensatory hypothesis. *Reading Research Quarterly, 29*, 178–188.

Kirby, J. R., Parrila, R. K., & Pfeiffer, S. L. (2003). Naming speed and phonological awareness as predictors of reading development. *Journal of Educational Psychology*, *95*, 453–464.

LaBerge, D., & Samuels, S. J. (1974). Toward a theory of automatic information processing in reading. *Cognitive Psychology*, *6*, 293–323.

Larsen, J. P., Hoien, T., Lundberg, I., & Odegaard, S. (1990). MRI evaluation of the size and symmetry of the planum temporale in adolescents with developmental dyslexia. *Brain and Language*, *39*, 289–301.

Leach, J. M., Scarborough, H. S., & Rescorla, L. (2003). Late-emerging reading disabilities. *Journal of Educational Psychology*, *95*, 211–224.

Levy, B. A., Bourassa, D. C., & Horn, C. (1999). Fast and slow namers: Benefits of segmentation and whole word training. *Journal of Experimental Child Psychology*, *73*, 115–138.

Liberman, I. Y., Mann, V. A., Shankweiler, D., & Werfelman, M. (1982). Children's memory for recurring linguistic and nonlinguistic material in relation to reading ability. *Cortex*, *18*, 367–375.

Liberman, I. Y., Shankweiler, D., Fischer, F. W., & Carter, B. (1974). Explicit syllable and phoneme segmentation in the young child. *Journal of Experimental Child Psychology*, *18*, 201–212.

Linderholm, T., & van den Broek, P. (2002). The effects of reading purpose and working memory capacity on the processing of expository texts. *Journal of Educational Psychology*, *94*, 778–784.

Livingstone, M. S., Rosen, G. D., Drislane, F. W., & Galaburda, A. M. (1991). Physiological and anatomical evidence for a magnocellular deficit in developmental dyslexia. *Proceedings of the National Academy of Sciences, USA*, *88*, 7943–7947.

Lovegrove, W. J. (1992). The visual deficit hypothesis. In N. N. Singh & I. L. Beale (Eds.), *Learning disabilities: Nature, theory, and treatment* (pp. 246–269). New York: Springer-Verlag.

Lovegrove, W. J., Garzia, R. P., & Nicholson, S. B. (1990). Experimental evidence for a transient system deficit in specific reading disability. *Journal of the American Optometric Association*, *61*, 137–146.

Lovett, M. W. (1984). A developmental perspective on reading dysfunction: Accuracy and rate criteria in the subtyping of dyslexic children. *Brain and Language*, *22*, 67–91.

Lyon, G. R. (1995). Toward a definition of dyslexia. *Annals of Dyslexia*, *45*, 3–27.

Manis, F. R., Custodio, R., & Szeszulski, P. A. (1993). Development of phonological and orthographic skill: A 2-year longitudinal study of dyslexic children. *Journal of Experimental Child Psychology*, *56*, 64–86.

Mann, V. A., & Brady, S. (1988). Reading disability: The role of language deficiencies. *Journal of Consulting and Clinical Psychology*, *56*, 811–816.

Mann, V. A., Liberman, I. Y., & Shankweiler, D. (1980). Children's memory for sentences and word storage in relation to reading ability. *Memory and Cognition*, *8*, 329–335.

Martin, F., & Lovegrove, W. (1987). Flicker contrast sensitivity in normal and specifically disabled readers. *Perception*, *17*, 203–214.

Martin, R. C. (1995). Heterogeneity of deficits in developmental dyslexia and implications for methodology. *Psychonomic Bulletin and Review, 2*, 494–500.

McCandliss, B., Beck, I. L., Sandak, R., & Perfetti, C. (2003). Focusing attention on decoding for children with poor reading skills: Design and preliminary tests of the word building intervention. *Scientific Studies of Reading, 7*, 75–104.

McCormick, S. (1992). Disabled readers' erroneous responses to inferential comprehension questions: Description and analysis. *Reading Research Quarterly, 27*, 156–176.

McDougall, S., Hulme, C., Ellis, A., & Monk, A. (1994). Learning to read: The role of short-term memory and phonological skills. *Journal of Experimental Child Psychology, 58*, 112–133.

McNulty, M. A. (2003). Dyslexia and the life course. *Journal of Learning Disabilities, 36*, 363–381.

Merrill, E. C., Sperber, R. D., & McCauley, C. (1981). Differences in semantic encoding as a function of reading comprehension skill. *Memory and Cognition, 9*, 618–624.

Metsala, J. L. (1997). Spoken word recognition in reading disabled children. *Journal of Educational Psychology, 89*, 159–169.

Miller, G. A. (1956). The magical number seven, plus-or-minus two: Some limits on our capacity for processing information. *Psychological Review, 63*, 81–97.

Mody, M. (2004). Neurobiological correlates of language and reading impairments. In C. A. Stone, E. R. Silliman, B. J. Ehren, & K. Apel (Eds.), *Handbook of language and literacy: Development and disorders* (pp. 49–72)). New York: Guilford Press.

Molfese, D. L., Molfese, V. J., Key, S., Modglin, A., Kelley, S., & Terrell, S. (2002). Reading and cognitive abilities: Longitudinal studies of brain and behavior changes in young children. *Annals of Dyslexia, 52*, 99–119.

Molfese, V. J., Molfese, D. L., & Modgline, A. A. (2001). Newborn and preschool predictors of second-grade reading scores: An evaluation of categorical and continuous scores. *Journal of Learning Disabilities, 34*, 545–554.

Morris, R. D., Stuebing, K. K., Fletcher, J. M., Shaywitz, S. E., Lyon, G. R., Shankweiler, D. P., Katz, L., Francis, D. J., & Shaywitz, B. A. (1998). Subtypes of reading disability: Variability around a phonological core. *Journal of Educational Psychology, 90*, 347–373.

Nation, K., Adams, J. W., Bowyer-Crane, C. A., & Snowling, M. J. (1999). Working memory deficits in poor comprehenders reflect underlying language impairments. *Journal of Experimental Child Psychology, 73*, 139–158.

Nicholson, T. (1991). Do children read words better in context or in lists? A classic study revisited. *Journal of Educational Psychology, 83*, 444–450.

Nicholson, T., Bailey, J., & McArthur, J. (1991). Context cues in reading: The gap between research and popular opinion. *Journal of Reading: Writing and Learning Disabilities, 7*, 33–41.

Nicholson, T., Lillas, C., & Rzoska, A. (1988). Have we been misled by miscues? *Reading Teacher, 42*, 6–10.

Oakhill, J. V., & Cain, K. (2004). The development of comprehension skills. In T. Nunes & P. Bryant (Eds.), *Handbook of children's literacy* (pp. 155–180). Dordrecht, The Netherlands: Kluwer Academic.

Olson, R. K. (1994). Language deficits in "specific" reading disability. In M. A. Gernsbacher (Ed.), *Handbook of psycholinguistics* (pp. 895–916). San Diego: Academic Press.

Olson, R. K., & Gayan, J. (2001). Brains, genes, and environment in reading development. In S. B. Neuman & D. K. Dickinson (Eds.), *Handbook of early literacy research* (pp. 81–94). New York: Guilford Press.

Olson, R. K., Kliegl, R., Davidson, B. J., & Foltz, G. (1985). Individual and developmental differences in reading disability. In G. E. MacKinnon & T. G. Waller (Eds.), *Reading research: Advances in theory and practice* (Vol. 4, pp. 1–64). Orlando, FL: Academic Press.

Owings, R. A., Petersen, G. A., Bransford, J. D., Morris, C. D., & Stein, B. S. (1980). Spontaneous monitoring and regulation of learning: A comparison of successful and less successful fifth graders. *Journal of Educational Psychology, 72,* 250–256.

Paris, S. G., & Myers, M. (1981). Comprehension monitoring, memory, and study strategies of good and poor readers. *Journal of Reading Behavior, 13,* 5–22.

Parrila, R., Kirby, J. R., & McQuarrie, L. (2004). Articulation rate, naming speed, verbal short-term memory, and phonological awareness: Longitudinal predictors of early reading development? *Scientific Studies of Reading, 8,* 3–26.

Penney, C. G. (2002). Teaching decoding skills to poor readers in high school. *Journal of Literacy Research, 34,* 99–118.

Perfetti, C. A. (1985). *Reading ability.* New York: Oxford University Press.

Perfetti, C. A., Goldman, S. R., & Hogaboam, T. W. (1979). Reading skill and the identification of words in discourse context. *Memory and Cognition, 7,* 273–282.

Perfetti, C. A., & Hogaboam, T. (1975). The relationship between single word decoding and reading comprehension skill. *Journal of Educational Psychology, 67,* 461–469.

Perfetti, C. A., & Lesgold, A. M. (1977). Discourse comprehension and sources of individual differences. In M. A. Just & P. A. Carpenter (Eds.), *Cognitive processes in comprehension* (pp. 141–183). Hillsdale, NJ: Erlbaum.

Perfetti, C. A., & Lesgold, A. M. (1979). Coding and comprehension in skilled reading: Implications for reading instruction. In L. B. Resnick & P. Weaver (Eds.), *Theory and practice of early reading* (Vol. 1, pp. 57–84). Hillsdale, NJ: Erlbaum.

Perfetti, C. A., & Roth, S. F. (1981). Some of the interactive processes in reading and their role in reading skill. In A. M. Lesgold & C. A. Perfetti (Eds.), *Interactive processes in reading* (pp. 269–297). Hillsdale, NJ: Erlbaum.

Phillips, L. M. (1988). Young readers' inference strategies in reading comprehension. *Cognition and Instruction, 5,* 193–222.

Phillips, L. M., Norris, S. P., Osmond, W. C., & Maynard, A, M. (2002). Relative reading achievement: A longitudinal study of 187 children from first through sixth grades. *Journal of Educational Psychology, 94,* 3–13.

Pirozzolo, F. J. (1979). *The neuropsychology of developmental reading disorders.* New York: Praeger.

Pirozzolo, F. J. (1983). Eye movements and reading disability. In K. Rayner (Ed.), *Eye movements in reading: Perceptual and language processes* (pp. 499–510). New York: Academic Press.

Purcell-Gates, V. (1991). On the outside looking in: A study of remedial readers' meaning-making while reading literature. *Journal of Reading Behavior, 23,* 235–253.

Rack, J., Hulme, C., Snowling, M., & Wightman, J. (1994). The role of phonology in young children learning to read words: The direct mapping hypothesis. *Journal of Experimental Child Psychology, 57,* 42–71.

Rack, J. P., Snowling, M. J., & Olson, R. K. (1992). The nonword reading deficit in developmental dyslexia: A review. *Reading Research Quarterly, 27,* 28–53.

Ransby, M. J., & Swanson, H. L. (2003). Reading comprehension skills of young adults with childhood diagnoses of dyslexia. *Journal of Learning Disabilities, 36,* 538–555.

Rayner, K., & McConkie, G. W. (1976). What guides a reader's eye movements? *Vision Research, 16,* 829–837.

Rayner, K., Pollatsek, A., & Bilsky, A. B. (1995). Can a temporal processing deficit account for dyslexia? *Psychonomic Bulletin and Review, 2,* 501–507.

Ruddell, M. R. (1994). Vocabulary knowledge and comprehension: A comprehension-process view of complex literacy relationships. In R. B. Ruddell, M. R. Ruddell, & H. Singer (Eds.), *Theoretical models and processes of reading* (4th ed., pp. 414–447). Newark, DE: International Reading Association.

Rumsey, J. M. (1996). Neuroimaging in developmental dyslexia: A review and conceptualization. In G. R. Lyon & J. M. Rumsey (Eds.), *Neuroimaging: A window on the neurological foundations of learning and behavior in children* (pp. 57–77). Baltimore: Brookes.

Rumsey, J. M., Nace, K., & Andreason, P. (1995). Phonologic and orthographic components of reading imaged with PET. *Journal of the International Neuropsychological Society, 1,* 180.

Samuels, S. J. (1970). Effects of pictures on learning to read, comprehension, and attitudes. *Review of Educational Research, 40,* 397–407.

Satz, P., Taylor, H. G., Friel, J., & Fletcher, J. M. (1978). Some developmental and predictive precursors of reading disabilities: A six-year followup. In A. L. Benton & D. Pearl (Eds.), *Dyslexia: An appraisal of current knowledge* (pp. 457–501). New York: Oxford University Press.

Sawyer, D. J., & Butler, K. (1991). Early language intervention: A deterrent to reading disability. *Annals of Dyslexia, 41,* 55–79.

Scarborough, H. S. (1990). Very early language deficits in dyslexic children. *Child Development, 61,* 1728–1743.

Schatschneider, C., Fletcher, J. M., Francis, D. J., Carlson, C. D., & Foorman, B. R. (2004). Kindergarten prediction of reading skills: A longitudinal comparative analysis. *Journal of Educational Psychology, 96,* 265–282.

Schmidt, W. A. (1917). An experimental study in the psychology of reading. *Supplemental Educational Monographs, 1*(2), 1–123.

Schonhaut, S., & Satz, P. (1983). Prognosis for children with learning disabilities: A review of follow-up studies. In M. Rutter (Ed.), *Developmental neuropsychiatry* (pp. 542–563). New York: Guilford Press.

Schwantes, F. M. (1981). Locus of the context effect in children's word recognition. *Child Development, 52,* 895–903.

Schwantes, F. M. (1991). Children's use of semantic and syntactic information for word recognition and determination of sentence meaningfulness. *Journal of Reading Behavior, 23,* 335–350.

Serniclaes, W., Van Heghe, A., Mousty, P., Carré, R., & Sprenger-Charolles, L. (2004). Allophonic mode of speech perception in dyslexia. *Journal of Experimental Child Psychology, 87,* 336–361.

Shankweiler, D., Crain, S., Katz, L., Fowler, A., Liberman, A., Brady, S., Thornton, R., Lundquist, E., Dreyer, L., Fletcher, J., Stuebing, K., Shaywitz, S., & Shaywitz, B. (1995). Cognitive profiles of reading-disabled children: Comparison of language skills in phonology, morphology, and syntax. *Psychological Science, 6,* 149–156.

Shankweiler, D., Liberman, I. Y., Mark, L. S., Fowler, C. A., & Fischer, F. W. (1979). The speech code and learning to read. *Journal of Experimental Psychology: Human Learning and Memory, 5,* 531–545.

Share, D. L. (1995). Phonological recoding and self-teaching: Sine qua non of reading acquisition. *Cognition, 55,* 151–218.

Share, D. L., & Stanovich, K. E. (1995). Cognitive processes in early reading development: Accommodating individual differences into a model of acquisition. *Issues in Education: Contributions from Educational Psychology, 1,* 1–57.

Shaywitz, B. A., Pugh, K. R., Jenner, A. R., Fulbright, R. K., Fletcher, J. M., Gore, J. C., & Shaywitz, S. E. (2000). The neurobiology of reading and reading disability (dyslexia). In M. L. Kamil, P. B., Mosenthal, P. D. Pearson, & R. Barr (Eds.), *Handbook of reading research* (Vol. 3, pp. 229–249). Mahwah, NJ: Erlbaum.

Shaywitz, S. E. (1996). Dyslexia. *Scientific American, 275*(5), 98–104.

Shaywitz, S. E., Escobar, M. D., Shaywitz, B. A., Fletcher, J. M., & Makuch, R. (1992). Evidence that dyslexia may represent the lower tail of a normal distribution of reading ability. *New England Journal of Medicine, 326,* 145–150.

Shaywitz, S. E., & Shaywitz, B. A. (2003). Neurological indices of dyslexia. In H. L. Swanson, K. R. Harris, & S. Graham (Eds.), *Handbook of learning disabilities* (pp. 514–531). New York: Guilford Press.

Shaywitz, S. E., Shaywitz, B. A., Pugh, K. R., Skudlarski, P., Fulbright, R. K., Constable, R. T., Bronen, R. A., Fletcher, J. M., Liberman, A. M., Shankweiler, D. P., Katz, L., Lacadie, C., Marchione, K. E., & Gore, J. C. (1996). The neurobiology of developmental dyslexia as viewed through the lens of functional magnetic resonance imaging technology. In G. R. Lyon & J. M. Rumsey (Eds.), *Neuroimaging: A window on the neurological foundations of learning and behavior in children* (pp. 79–94). Baltimore: Brookes.

Simpson, G., Lorsbach, T., & Whitehouse, D. (1983). Encoding contextual components of word recognition in good and poor readers. *Journal of Experimental Child Psychology, 35,* 161–171.

Smith, S. D., Kimberling, W. J., & Pennington, B. F. (1991). Screening for multiple genes influencing dyslexia. *Reading and Writing: An Interdisciplinary Journal, 3,* 285–298.

Snowling, M. J. (2002). Reading development and dyslexia. In U. Goswami (Ed.), *Blackwell handbook of childhood cognitive development* (pp. 394–411). Malden MA: Blackwell.

Snowling, M. J., Goulandris, N., & Defty, N. (1996). A longitudinal study of reading development in dyslexic students. *Journal of Educational Psychology, 88,* 653–669.

Spreen, O. (1978). *Prediction of school achievement from kindergarten to grade five: Review and report of a follow-up study* (Research Monograph No. 33). Victoria, British Columbia, Canada: University of Victoria, Department of Psychology.

Spreen, O. (1988). *Learning disabled children growing up: A follow-up into adulthood.* New York: Oxford University Press.

Sprenger-Charolles, L., Siegel, L. S., Bechennec, D., & Serniclaes, W. (2003). Development of phonological and orthographic processing in reading aloud, in silent reading, and in spelling: A four-year longitudinal study. *Journal of Experimental Child Psychology, 84,* 194–217.

Stanovich, K. [E.] (1986). Matthew effects in reading: Some consequences of individual differences in the acquisition of literacy. *Reading Research Quarterly, 21,* 360–407.

Stanovich, K. E. (1988). Explaining the differences between the dyslexic and the garden-variety poor reader: The phonological-core variable-difference model. *Journal of Learning Disabilities, 21,* 590–604.

Stanovich, K. E., & Cunningham, A. E. (1993). Where does knowledge come from?: Specific associations between print exposure and information acquisition. *Journal of Educational Psychology, 85,* 211–229.

Stanovich, K. E., & Siegel, L. S. (1994). Phenotypic performance profile of children with reading disabilities: A regression-based test of the phonological-core variable-difference model. *Journal of Educational Psychology, 86,* 24–53.

Stanovich, K. E., West, R. F., & Freeman, D. J. (1981). A longitudinal study of sentence context effects in second-grade children: Tests of an interactive–compensatory model. *Journal of Experimental Child Psychology, 32,* 185–199.

Stevenson, J. (2004). Epidemiology: Genetic and social influences on reading ability. In T. Nunes & P. Bryant (Eds.), *Handbook of children's literacy* (pp. 293–311). Dordrecht, The Netherlands: Kluwer Academic.

Stone, B., & Brady, S. (1995). Evidence for phonological processing deficits in less-skilled readers. *Annals of Dyslexia, 45,* 51–78.

Studdert-Kennedy, M., & Mody, M. (1995). Auditory temporal perception deficits in the reading-impaired: A critical review of the evidence. *Psychonomic Bulletin and Review, 2,* 508–514.

Sunseth, K., & Bowers, P. G. (2002). Rapid naming and phonemic awareness: Contributions to reading, spelling, and orthographic knowledge. *Scientific Studies of Reading, 6,* 401–429.

Swanson, H. L. (1999a). *Interventions for students with learning disabilities: A meta-analysis of treatment outcomes.* New York: Guilford Press.

Swanson, H. L. (1999b). Reading comprehension and working memory in learning-disabled readers: Is the phonological loop more important than the executive system? *Journal of Experimental Child Psychology, 72,* 1–31.

Swanson, H. L. (2003). Age-related differences in learning disabled and skilled readers' working memory. *Journal of Experimental Child Psychology, 85,* 1–31.

Swanson, H. L., & Alexander, J. E. (1997). Cognitive processes as predictors of word recognition and reading comprehension in learning-disabled and skilled readers: Revisiting the specificity hypothesis. *Journal of Educational Psychology, 89,* 128–158.

Swanson, H. L., Mink, J., & Bocian, K. M. (1999). Cognitive processing deficits in poor readers with symptoms of reading disabilities and ADHD: More alike than different? *Journal of Educational Psychology, 91,* 321–333.

Swanson, H. L., & Sachse-Lee, C. (2001). A subgroup analysis of working memory in children with reading disabilities: Domain-general or domain-specific deficiency? *Journal of Learning Disabilities, 34,* 249–263.

Tallal, P., Miller, S., & Fitch, R. H. (1993). Neurobiological basis of the case for the preeminence of temporal processing. In P. Tallal, A. M. Galaburda, R. R. Linas, & C. von Euler (Eds.), *Temporal information processing in the nervous system: Special reference to dyslexia and dysphasia* (pp. 27–47). New York: New York Academy of Sciences.

Thompkins, A. C., & Binder, K. S. (2003). A comparison of the factors affecting reading performance of functionally illiterate adults and children matched by reading level. *Reading Research Quarterly, 38,* 236–258.

Thomson, J. B., & Raskind, W. H. (2003). Genetic influences on reading and writing disabilities. In H. L. Swanson, K. R. Harris, & S. Graham (Eds.), *Handbook of learning disabilities* (pp. 256–270). New York: Guilford Press.

Torgesen, J. K., & Davis, C. (1996). Individual difference variables that predict response to training in phonological awareness. *Journal of Experimental Child Psychology, 63,* 1–21.

Troia, G. (2004). Phonological processing and its influence on literacy learning. In C. A. Stone, E. R. Silliman, B. J. Ehren, & K. Apel (Eds.), *Handbook of language and literacy: Development and disorders* (pp. 271–301). New York: Guilford Press.

Tunick, R. A., & Pennington, B. F. (2002). The etiological relationship between reading disability and phonological disorder. *Annals of Dyslexia, 52,* 75–97.

Tunmer, W. E., & Chapman, J. W. (2004). The use of context in learning to read. In T. Nunes & P. Bryant (Eds.), *Handbook of children's literacy* (pp. 199–212). Dordrecht, The Netherlands: Kluwer Academic.

Vellutino, F. R. (1979). *Dyslexia: Theory and research.* Cambridge, MA: MIT Press.

Vellutino, F. R., & Scanlon, D. M. (1982). Verbal processing in poor and normal readers. In C. J. Brainerd & M. Pressley (Eds.), *Verbal processes in children* (pp. 189–264). New York: Springer-Verlag.

Vellutino, F. R., & Scanlon, D. M. (1987a). Linguistic coding and reading ability. In S. Rosenberg (Ed.), *Advances in applied psycholinguistics* (Vol. 2, pp. 1–69). New York: Cambridge University Press.

Vellutino, F. R., & Scanlon, D. M. (1987b). Phonological coding, phonological awareness, and reading ability: Evidence from a longitudinal, experimental study. *Merrill–Palmer Quarterly, 33,* 321–363.

Vellutino, F. R., & Scanlon, D. M. (2001). Emergent literacy skills, early instruction, and individual differences as determinants of difficulties in learning to read: The case for early intervention. In S. B. Neuman & D. K. Dickinson (Eds.), *Handbook of early literacy research* (pp. 295–321). New York: Guilford Press.

Vellutino, F. R., Scanlon, D. M., Sipay, E. R., Small, S. G., Pratt, A., Chen, R., & Denckla, M. B. (1996). Cognitive profiles of difficult-to-remediate and readily remediated poor readers: Early intervention as a vehicle for distinguishing between cognitive and experiential deficits as a basic cause of specific reading disability. *Journal of Educational Psychology, 88,* 601–638.

Vellutino, F. R., Scanlon, D. M., Small, S. G., & Tanzman, M. S. (1991). The linguistic basis of reading ability: Converting written to oral language. *Text, 11*, 99–133.

Vellutino, F. R., Scanlon, D. M., & Spearing, D. (1995). Semantic and phonological coding in poor and normal readers. *Journal of Experimental Child Psychology, 59*, 76–123.

Vellutino, F. R., Scanlon, D. M., & Tanzman, M. S. (1994). Components of reading ability: Issues and problems in operationalizing word identification, phonological coding, and orthographic coding. In G. R. Lyon (Ed.), *Frames of reference for the assessment of learning disabilities: New views on measurement issues* (pp. 279–324). Baltimore: Brookes.

Walczyk, J. J., Marsiglia, C. S., Bryan, K. S., & Naquin, P. J. (2001). Overcoming inefficient reading skills. *Journal of Educational Psychology, 93*, 750–757.

West, R. F., & Stanovich, K. E. (1978). Automatic contextual facilitation in readers of three ages. *Child Development, 49*, 717–727.

Williams, J. P. (1993). Comprehension of students with and without learning disabilities: Identification of narrative themes and idiosyncratic text representations. *Journal of Educational Psychology, 85*, 631–641.

Wimmer, H., Mayringer, H., & Landerl, K. (1998). Poor reading: A deficit in skill-automatization or a phonological deficit? *Scientific Studies of Reading, 2*, 321–340.

Wolf, M. (1986). Rapid alternating stimulus naming in developmental dyslexias. *Brain and Language, 27*, 360–379.

Wolf, M. (1991). The word-retrieval deficit hypothesis and developmental dyslexia. *Learning and Individual Differences, 3*, 205–223.

Wolf, M., & Bowers, P. G. (1999). The double-deficit hypothesis for the developmental dyslexias. *Journal of Educational Psychology, 91*, 415–438.

Wolf, M., Pfeil, C., Lotz, R., & Biddle, K. (1994). Towards a more universal understanding of the developmental dyslexias: The contribution of orthographic factors. In V. W. Berninger (Ed.), *The varieties of orthographic knowledge: Vol. I. Theoretical and developmental issues* (pp. 137–171). Dordrecht, The Netherlands: Kluwer Academic.

Wood, F., Felton, R., Flowers, L., & Naylor, C. (1991). Neurobehavioral definitions of dyslexia. In D. D. Duane & D. B. Gray (Eds.), *The reading brain: Biological basis of dyslexia* (pp. 1–25). Parkton, MD: York Press.

Yuill, N. M., & Oakhill, J. V. (1991). *Children's problems in text comprehension: An experimental investigation.* Cambridge, UK: Cambridge University Press.

Ziegler, J. C., Perry, C., Ma-Wyatt, A., Ladner, D., & Schulte-Korne, G. (2003). Developmental dyslexia in different languages: Language-specific or universal? *Journal of Experimental Child Psychology, 86*, 169–193.

Zinar, S. (2000). The relative contributions of word identification skill and comprehension-monitoring behavior to reading comprehension ability. *Contemporary Educational Psychology, 25*, 363–377.

CHAPTER 4

Before Reading
Words Begins

Much that is relevant to the development of literacy occurs before a child first passes through the schoolhouse door. Among literacy researchers, it has become something of a truism to assert that literacy development begins at birth, with many opportunities for events in the home life of preschoolers that have implications for literacy development. That is, there are many opportunities for emergent literacy (Saada-Robert, 2004; Tolchinsky, 2004). These include game and play activities; interactions during meals; media viewed by children and their parents (e.g., watching of educational shows); outings (e.g., to the library); and reading, writing, and drawing (Baker, Sonnenschein, Serpell, Fernandez-Fein, & Scher, 1994). Such activities can go far in stimulating the development of a child's language, which is critical for subsequent development of reading and writing skills (e.g., Frijters, Barron, & Brunello, 2000; Leseman & de Jong, 1998). They can also increase a child's knowledge about the conventions of print, for example, understanding that reading in English is from left to right and top to bottom as well as awareness of the difference between pictures and print. Preschool interactions with adults can result in knowledge of the alphabet. In short, the child who experiences rich linguistic interactions with adults during the preschool years is massively advantaged with respect to literacy development relative to the child who has less rich interactions (e.g., Whitehurst & Lonigan, 1998, 2001). What should be emphasized is that the healthiest environments for the development of literacy during the preschool years are ones in which literate interactions are part of the natural fun of home life. That is, the home that fosters preschooler emergent literacy is not school-like but rather playful, verbal, and stimulating in ways that are interesting to preschoolers (Sonnenschein et al., 1996). There are responsive relationships with adults. It is widely accepted by literacy researchers that the environment the preschool child experiences is a critical determinant of reading and writing abilities once formal schooling begins.

Literacy researchers studying the preschool years have been very much influenced by developmental psychology. The first section of this chapter takes up John Bowlby's theory of attachment and how the development of a secure attachment is critical to productive cognitive interactions between parents and children. The second section reviews briefly the theory of development proposed by Lev S. Vygotsky, who believed that many of the skills a child acquires reflect internalization of thinking first carried out by the child and adults in interaction. Then, the third section considers the emergent literacy skills, which have been studied closely by literacy researchers who are interested in the preschool years. The chapter concludes with coverage of the development of a skill that seems to be especially important with respect to the development of beginning reading competence—namely, the awareness that words are composed of sounds blended together (i.e., phonemic awareness).

A SECURE ATTACHMENT RELATIONSHIP
AS A CONTEXT FOR LITERACY DEVELOPMENT

When parent–infant interactions go well, babies form strong emotional ties with their caregivers. The attached baby interacts extensively with the primary caregivers, who become the primary adult attachment objects. Once attachment occurs, a baby does what it can to maintain proximity to primary caregivers, including crawling toward them, crying when they are out of sight, and clinging hard to them. John Bowlby (1969) provided a comprehensive theory about both the course of attachment and the biological and social mechanisms that account for attachment. The developmental course of infant–caregiver attachment has been studied extensively in the quarter-century since Bowlby's book first appeared, with Bowlby's perspective now enjoying a great deal of research support (e.g., Sroufe, 1996).

Perhaps the most important finding in the attachment literature is that the more responsive the adult—or, rather, the more the adult is there to help when the baby needs help—the more secure the emerging attachment between the infant and the adult. When researchers have measured both parental sensitivity early in the first year of a baby's life and security of attachment later in the first year, they have found a clear association between them (Sroufe, 1996, Chap. 10). That is important with respect to other aspects of development, for the more secure the attachment, the more effective the parent is in helping the child to explore the world (Ainsworth, 1967; Schaffer & Emerson, 1964).

Security of Attachment and Later Development

Bowlby (1969) contended that secure attachment was a precursor of good mental health—that securely attached infants are more likely to be well adjusted and sociable when they are older. One possible interpretation of a secure attachment during infancy is that it reflects the development of basic trust whereas an insecure attachment reflects basic mistrust (e.g., Erikson, 1968). Basic trust in infancy is linked to later security and trust in interacting with others, which affects the quality of the interactions the child has. If social interactions matter in cognitive development, as I think they do, then the child who has experienced secure attachment is going to benefit cognitively.

Particularly relevant here is the correlation between secure attachment during infancy and subsequent cognitive interactions with parents. For example, in a well-known study, Matas, Arend, and Sroufe (1978) demonstrated that secure attachment during infancy predicted the quality of problem solving undertaken by 2-year-olds and their mothers working together. The children, in interaction with their mothers, figured out how to get a lure from a long tube by using two sticks. They also figured out how to weigh down the end of a lever with a block to raise candy through a hole in a Plexiglas box. How did this occur? The mothers of 2-year-olds with securely attached infants offered higher-quality support to their 2-year-olds during the problem-solving tasks. Problem solving was happier for the securely attached children as compared to the less securely attached children, who more often rejected their mothers' suggestions, even aggressing against them when suggestions were offered. Others have replicated this result (Frankel & Bates, 1990), and Moss and St. Laurent (2001) have documented that secure attachment at school entry (i.e., age 6) predicts higher academic performance in the primary grades. In general, when there is a secure attachment, parental directions and support are more likely to be at an appropriate level, neither too little nor too much (Fagot & Kavanaugh, 1993). That is, in emotionally secure parent–child dyads, parents provide support as needed but back off and permit the child to go it alone when that is possible (Borkowski & Dukewich, 1996; Moss, 1992). Such preparation for going it alone seems to serve children's academic development well (Moss & St. Laurent, 2001).

Security of Attachment and Emergent Literacy Experiences

The quality of a child's socioemotional relationship with its primary caregiver very much affects the quality of parent–preschooler literacy interactions. In particular, mother–child attachment security is related to the quality of mother–child emergent literacy experiences (Bus, 2001). Dutch researchers Adriana G. Bus and Marinus H. van IJzendoorn (1988) observed 1-year-olds, 3-year-olds, and 5-year-olds and their mothers as they watched *Sesame Street*, read a picture book together, and went through an alphabet book—all prototypical emergent literacy contexts. They also measured attachment as it is usually measured, by watching the interactions of infants when they are reunited with the mother after a brief separation (Main, Kaplan, & Cassidy, 1985), with more securely attached infants happier on the mother's return than less securely attached infants. Consistently, the interactions during emergent literacy tasks were more positive for securely attached compared to less securely attached children. Securely attached children were more attentive and less easily distracted during emergent literacy interactions. Particularly critical with respect to the development of emergent literacy, secure dyads were more oriented to reading and reading-related skills during their interactions. The mothers of the securely attached children demanded more of their children, and the children met the demands.

Bus and van IJzendoorn (1995) studied a group of 3-year-olds who varied in the security of their attachments to their mothers. One important finding was that the frequency of reading that mothers reported doing with their children was related to security of attachment, with more securely attached children and mothers doing more reading together than less securely attached child–mother dyads. During the study, the researchers observed children and their mothers as they engaged in storybook reading. There was less engagement during reading when insecure dyads read than when securely attached children and mothers read with each other. The greater the insecurity, the more the children were inattentive and the more the discussion digressed from the story. The less secure the attachment, the harder it seemed for the children to get the message of the text.

In short, security in attachment predicts healthy interactions as parents and children tackle intellectual challenges together, including reading with one another. Security of attachment fosters book reading together as a routine mother and child activity, with the child more likely to learn from encounters with text when the mother–child attachment is secure (Bus, 2001; Bus, Leseman, & Keultjes, 2000). Some children, however, are at substantially greater risk than others for not developing secure relationships with parents during infancy, because of their difficult temperaments, for example (Chess & Thomas, 1987; Thomas & Chess, 1986). Even in those cases, intervention can increase the likelihood of secure attachment and cognitively productive interactions. Parents can be taught to observe their children and be sensitive to them (e.g., Belsky, Rosenberger, & Crnic, 1995; van den Boom, 1994, 1995; van IJzendoorn, Juffer, & Duyvesteyn, 1995). Literacy researchers need to be thinking about how to impact families so that emergent literacy interactions beginning in infancy can be maximally positive.

VYGOTSKY'S THEORY: INTELLECTUAL DEVELOPMENT THROUGH INTERNALIZATION OF INTERPERSONAL INTERACTION SKILLS

People learn from other people. Many researchers are now studying how interpersonal relationships contribute to the development of thinking and learning skills. Lev S. Vygotsky, who lived during the first third of the 20th century in what became the Soviet Union, has been the most influential theorist in this arena.

Inner Speech and Thought

Vygotsky (1962) believed that for adults *inner speech* was an important mechanism involved in thought. Inner speech is very different from outer speech. It is abbreviated and fragmentary, with the meaning of complex thoughts captured in very few words and word fragments. It is speech that supports thought. You can get a feel for what is meant by inner speech by finding a somewhat complicated task to do, one that requires some thinking. Yesterday, for example, I repaired the part of my computer system file that controls the printer. As I worked, I thought to myself, "I wonder if the bundle bits might be damaged," which caused me to run a utilities program on the system files in order to repair any bundle bit damage. When that did not work, I thought to myself much faster than I could say it aloud, "Replace the system file." I did, and the printer function subsequently worked. When I reflected on what had gone on, I realized that my thoughts and inner speech were so intertwined that they were difficult to separate, just as Vygotsky (1962) had claimed.

Some extremely important research in Soviet psychology has focused on when people subvocalize (i.e., use inner speech to mediate performance) and when they do not. Subvocalization occurs when people work on problems that are challenging to them (Sokolov, 1975). For example, Sokolov substantiated that subvocalization occurs during reading, with the intensity of subvocalization varying with the difficulty of the text being read and with the task assigned to the reader (e.g., requiring the reader to attempt to memorize what is being read increases the intensity of subvocalization). Talking to one-self about a task while doing a challenging task is a good thing to do, an essential part of problem solving, according to the Russian perspective.

Development of Inner Speech

An important contribution by Vygotsky was a theory about how inner speech develops during childhood. During the first 2 years of life, thought is nonverbal. Speech plays a limited role in thought during the early stages of language development (i.e., beginning at about age 2). Then, children begin to manifest what has been called *egocentric speech* by developmental psychologists. That is, when preschoolers do things, they often talk to themselves about what they are doing. Vygotsky recognized the emergence of egocentric speech to be an important intellectual advance, with such speech beginning to influence what the child thinks and does. How many times does the parent of a preschooler hear "I'm going to play with X" before she or he goes and plays with X? How many times does a parent hear "I'm running to X" before the child runs to X? Often such utterances come when the preschooler is trying to figure out what to do. Vygotsky carried out studies with preschoolers in which the preschoolers were given tasks that were complicated by some obstacle (e.g., when a colored pencil, or paper, or paint that was needed was missing). When difficulties occurred, the amount of egocentric speech was much greater than when preschoolers did the same tasks without obstacles.

Eventually, overt egocentric speech becomes covert and abbreviated. It can always become overt again if the child encounters a challenging problem. Recall from Chapter 2 that when skilled readers encounter very familiar words, reading of the words is automatic—with little involvement of speech processes; speech processes involving sounding out a word only come into play with difficult words. This is consistent with the general principle advanced by Soviet theorists, such as Vygotsky, that speech is an important part of thinking, especially challenging thinking.

Contemporary literacy researchers are actively studying the development of children's use of speech during thinking. For example, Purdue University literacy researcher Beverly E. Cox (1994) observed self-regulatory speech in preschoolers as they attempted to construct and dictate a short story to an adult who wrote it down. As the children thought about what might be added next to the story, Cox heard them say things like these: "Now, what did I do then?"; "Think about what you say before you say it"; and "That's it . . . I think that's it." Such an observation is consistent with Vygotsky's and other developmental psychologists' observations (e.g., Kohlberg, Yaeger, & Hjertholm, 1968) that preschoolers use audible speech in order to organize their thinking.

Development of Thought in Social Interactions

The prominence of Vygotsky's thinking with respect to development has soared in the past quarter-century, largely because of the translation of a work that proposed an explanation of the developments in thinking that were only described in his previously translated work (1962). In *Mind in Society*, Vygotsky (1978) made the case that interaction with others is a prime mover in the development of children's thinking abilities.

Development of Problem-Solving Skills

Adults often assist children with problems they are confronting. A child might not work through many problems without assistance, but with parental support she or he makes fine progress. What goes on in these interactions is thinking, thinking that involves two heads. Years of participating in such interactions leads to their internalization by the child. That is, thought processes that were once interpersonal become intrapersonal. The most frequently reprinted Vygotsky passage captures this developmental progression:

> Any function in the child's cultural development appears twice, or on two planes. First, it appears on the social plane, and then on the psychological plane. First, it appears between people as an interpsychological category, and then within the child as an intrapsychological category. This is equally true with respect to voluntary attention, logical memory, the formation of concepts, and the development of volition. . . . Social relations or relations among people genetically underlie all higher functions and their relationships. . . . In their private sphere, human beings retain the functions of social interactions. (1978, pp. 163–164)

According to the Vygotskian perspective, cognitive development moves forward most certainly and completely if the child is in a world that provides assistance when the child needs it and can benefit from it. Such a responsive world is not intruding, however; rather, it provides support when the child needs it. When 2- or 3-year-olds can solve a problem themselves, appropriately responsive adults let the 2- and 3-year-olds do so. Any parent of a preschooler knows all too well the phrase "I can do it myself!"; and when the child can, the parent honors that declaration. Of course, there are other tasks that 2- and 3-year-olds cannot perform, no matter how much assistance might be provided. A responsive social environment does not even try to encourage children to do such tasks and, in fact, often discourages attempts at behaviors far outside the range of preschooler competence, as when, for example, a father physically lifts his son from the driver's seat of the car as the youngster urges the father to teach him to drive. (Think back to the research on attachment described earlier, with security of attachment linked to support from adults when children need it.)

Between the two extremes of tasks, the ones children can do autonomously and those they could not possibly do at their age, critical developmental interactions occur. That is, interactions that facilitate development are most likely with tasks that children only can do with adult help. The responsive social world provides assistance on these tasks that are within the child's *zone of proximal development*, according to Vygotskian theory. In fact, the zone is defined as behaviors beyond a child's level of autonomous functioning but within reach if assistance is provided. Children learn how to perform tasks appropriately within their zone by interacting with more competent and responsive others who provide hints and prompts to the child on an as-needed basis.

Thus, the responsive adult directs a child's attention to important dimensions of a problem if the child seems not to be attending to those dimensions on her or his own. Sometimes the adult suggests a strategy to the child. Through doing the task with support, the child eventually can perform the task without assistance, having internalized the kinds of thinking that was previously supported by an adult. Without adult assistance, there are many forms of thinking that the child would not discover, either alone or in interaction with peers.

When adults assist in this fashion, they are said to *scaffold* a child (Wood, Bruner, & Ross, 1976), a metaphoric reference to the scaffold of a building under construction. It is an appropriate metaphor: The scaffolding on a building under construction provides supports when the new building cannot stand on its own. As the new structure is completed and becomes freestanding, the scaffolding is removed. So it is with scaffolded adult–child academic interactions. The adult carefully monitors when enough instructional input has been provided to permit the child to make progress toward an academic goal, and thus the adult provides support only when the child needs it. If a child catches on quickly, the adult's responsive instruction will be less detailed than if the child experiences difficulties with a task.

Development of Language Skills

As they use language during the preschool years, some children receive more scaffolding than do others. Children from low-income families are less likely than middle- and upper-class children to be immersed in supportive communicative interactions (Bernstein, 1965). This is critical, since the development of oral communication skills during the preschool years is logically prerequisite to success in reading and writing (e.g., Snow, 1991). For example, two University of Kansas psychologists (Hart & Risley, 1995) documented a correlation between children's language interactions and their subsequent cognitive development. They observed 42 families carefully for 2 years, beginning when a child in the family was 7–9 months of age. During the observations, the researchers attempted to record everything that went on, using tape recorders and notes. The observations then were carefully coded and analyzed for the types of verbal interactions that occurred.

The outcomes in the study were very clear: There were large differences in the quality of language interactions as a function of social class. More high-quality verbal interactions were observed in professional homes than working-class homes, and more in working-class homes than welfare homes. The higher the socioeconomic level, the more the parents listened to their children, prompted their children to elaborate their verbalizations, told their children what was worth remembering, and taught them how to cope with difficulties. These differences in the quality and quantity of verbal interactions were observed throughout the 2 years of observations, and they were pronounced: Whereas, on average, a child in a professional family experienced 4 million verbal utterances a year, a child in a welfare family experienced only 250,000 utterances.

Based on such striking differences in input, it would be expected that there would be differences in outcomes, and there were. By the time the children were 3 years of age, those from professional homes knew much more vocabulary than did children of working-class parents, who knew more than the children of parents on welfare. However, because there were other differences between the homes of professional, working-class, and welfare families, it was not possible in this study to be certain that the differences in language skills in the children were due to the linguistic interactions they experienced. Nonetheless, when the correlations obtained in this study are combined with evidence from other studies, there is a great deal of support for the conclusion that the quality of a child's verbal interactions is reliably related to linguistic and cognitive development.

In particular, responsive adults spend a great deal of time talking *with* their children about things that happened to the child, assisting the child in learning how to be tellers of their own memories (Nelson & Fivush, 2004). Judith A. Hudson (1990), a psychologist at Rutgers University, analyzed her own daughter Rachel's experiences in talking about the past and how those experiences increased Rachel's ability to describe events in her life. What was particularly critical were her many opportunities to talk about the past with Mom, through extended dialogues about the many things that had happened to Rachel. When Rachel had difficulties in remembering, Mom would prompt her, typically with questions.

Through experiencing such dialogues, Rachel learned how to talk about things that had happened to her. Consistent with the Vygotskian perspective, Hudson (1990) concluded that the important thinking skill of being able to describe events in one's life develops through social interaction. When the child could not structure recall of an event, the mother asked questions, providing a scaffold for the child's recollections. As Rachel became increasingly familiar with what should be told during recall of something that happened in the past and began, in fact, to recall with greater completeness, adult scaffolding in the form of leading questions was reduced. Hudson's description of Rachel's progression from a teller of tales with assistance to an autonomous teller of tales is consistent with a variety of evidence that children's abilities to talk about their past depends on dialoguing experiences with supportive adults (Engel, 1986; Nelson, 1993a, 1993b; Nelson & Fivush, 2004; Pillemer & White, 1989; Ratner, 1980, 1984; Reese, Haden, & Fivush, 1993; Tessler, 1986).

Virtually everyone who thinks about reading believes that success in reading depends on language development (Dickinson, McCabe, & Clark-Chiarelli, 2004). Thus, for the reading-education community, there is obvious significance to the finding that conversational experiences during the preschool years figure greatly in the development of cognitive and communication skills. The work of Hudson and her colleagues seems more significant than that, however. Hudson believes that supportive parent–child dialogic experiences not only promote the development of children's abilities to communicate about the past but also increase their abilities to organize and understand their previous experiences (Nelson, 1996; Nelson & Fivush, 2004). Prior knowledge based on experience is important in comprehending information presented in texts. Since children who have had rich and supportive dialogic experiences have better organized and more complete prior knowledge, they should be advantaged in comprehending what they read over children who have not had such experiences. Children who live in a richly responsive interpersonal world and who thus learn how to communicate with others are going to be cognitively far ahead of agemates who do not.

EMERGENT LITERACY

For the most part, the discussion in this chapter thus far has emphasized general cognitive and language skills that support the development of literacy, with only limited discussion of research directly tapping the development of literacy skills per se. In fact, a great deal of literacy development occurs during the preschool years—so much so that the preschool years are often referred to as the period of emergent literacy by reading theorists and researchers (e.g., Clay, 1966, 1967; Saada-Robert, 2004; Tolchinsky, 2004).

There has been a great deal of research directly focusing on emergent literacy. Literacy development begins before the first birthday, through, for example, experiences with plastic "bathtub" books filled with colorful pictures or from mothers and fathers who read nursery rhymes to their children as they rock them to sleep. These early beginnings expand into a rich array of literacy experiences, from scribbling letters to grandma to experiencing stories on grandma's lap. Environments that support emergent literacy include the following: (1) rich interpersonal experiences with parents, brothers and sisters, and others; (2) physical environments that include literacy materials, from plastic refrigerator letters to storybooks to writing materials; and (3) high positive regard by parents and others for literacy and its development in children (Leichter, 1984; Morrow, 2001; Saada-Robert, 2004; Tolchinsky, 2004).

Put more concretely, in homes in which emergent literacy is fostered, children are exposed to paper-and-pencil activities, letters, and even printed words at an early age. Parents read to their children, and they help children as they attempt to read (e.g., by holding a book upright and pretending to read by recalling the story as they remembered it). Books and other reading materials are prominent in homes supporting emergent literacy (Briggs & Elkind, 1973; Clark, 1976; Durkin, 1966; King & Friesen, 1972; Morrow, 1983; Plessas & Oakes, 1964; Teale, 1978; Yaden, Rowe, & MacGillivray, 2000).

Storybook Reading

One activity that has high potential for fostering emergent literacy is storybook reading (Garton & Pratt, 2004; van Kleeck, Stahl, & Bauer, 2003). There are strong and positive correlations between the amount of storybook reading during the preschool years and subsequent vocabulary and language development, children's interest in reading, and early success in reading (Stahl, 2003; Sulzby & Teale, 1991). Given their apparent power in stimulating children's literacy development, caregiver–child interactions during storybook reading have been studied in some detail.

At its best, storybook reading includes rich discussions and animated conversations between the reader and the child. The adult and child work out the meaning of the text, and they have a lot of fun doing it (Morrow, 2001). There is questioning, both by the adult and the child; there is modeling of dialoguing by the adult, with the child sometimes participating; the adult praises the child's efforts to get meaning from the pictures and print; the adult offers information to the child and responds to the child's reactions to the text; and both the adult and the child relate what is happening in the text to their lives and the world around them (e.g., Applebee & Langer, 1983; Cochran-Smith, 1984; Flood, 1977; Pellegrini, Perlmutter, Galda, & Brody, 1990; Roser & Martinez, 1985; Taylor & Strickland, 1986). A rich history of such interactions is predictive of subsequent success in literacy acquisition by the child (Stahl, 2003; Sulzby & Teale, 1991).

Scaffolding is prominent when storybook reading is going well—when it is engaging to the youngsters. Parents who are good at storybook reading encourage children to respond to readings and participate as much as possible in reading itself. They provide support as children need it, provide input that children can understand (e.g., DeLoache & DeMendoza, 1987). With increasing age through the preschool years, children are attentive to longer sections of text (Heath, 1982; Sulzby & Teale, 1987). As they gain experience reading storybooks, adults have more complex discussions with children about the text (Snow, 1983; Sulzby & Teale, 1987). Children who experience a lot of storybook reading are accustomed to interacting with an adult about story content; they are appropriately attentive during storybook reading, much more so than same-age children who have not experienced storybook reading (Bus & van IJzendoorn, 1988).

Some attention has been paid to differences in style of storybook reading and the effects of such variations on cognitive development. Parents who do not put particularly high value on literacy do not engage their children as much as parents who value literacy—for example, they do not prompt their children to think about potential alternative meanings of the text. They do less to make the text fun and understandable for the child (Bus et al., 2000). Children have better vocabulary development when they interact with adults who are skillful at eliciting verbal interactions from them during reading (e.g., Ninio, 1980; Pellegrini, Galda, Perlmutter, & Jones, 1994). There are also correlations between the degree to which parents elaborate on book content and success on literacy tasks in school (Heath, 1982). In short, not all storybook reading is ideal; the *quality* of the storybook reading very much affects a child's cognitive development.

The correlations between quality of storybook reading and literacy development (Sulzby & Teale, 1991) prompted Grover J. Whitehurst and his colleagues at the State University of New York at Stony Brook (Whitehurst et al., 1988) to study whether it might be possible to improve parental skills during storybook interactions and thus positively affect the development of emergent literacy in children. The parents of 14 children between 1 year and 3 years of age participated in a 1-month intervention designed to improve interactions between parents and children during storybook reading. Parents were taught to ask more open-ended questions and more questions about the functions and attributes of objects in stories as they read with their preschoolers. The parents were also given instruction about how to respond appropriately to their children's comments during story reading and how to expand on what the children had to say. The parents in the treatment group were also taught to reduce the amount of straight reading that they did, as well as to eliminate questions that the child could answer simply by pointing to something in an illustration. Fifteen other children and their parents, who served as control participants in the study, were encouraged to continue reading storybooks as they normally did with their children.

First, the intervention parents were able to learn to interact differently with their children during storybook reading, in ways that increased the quality of interactions between the children and their parents. Although there had been no differences between intervention and control children at the beginning of the study with respect to language variables, there were clear differences favoring the intervention participants at the end of the month of treatment: After the intervention, participants outscored the control subjects on a standardized measure of psycholinguistic ability and on two vocabulary tests. What was most striking in this study was that when the same measures were repeated 9 months later, the intervention subjects still had an advantage over the control participants, although the differences were not as large.

Unfortunately, storybook reading is not always as interactive and as much fun as it could be and probably needs to be in order to be effective in engaging children (Hammett, van Kleeck, & Huberty, 2003). High-quality storybook reading especially is less likely in the homes of lower-class and cultural minority children, and when storybook reading does occur, there often is less of the open-ended questioning and fun that seems critical in storybook reading that promotes language development (e.g., Anderson-Yockel & Haynes, 1994; Bergin, 2001; Bus et al., 2000; Federal Interagency Forum on Child and Family Statistics, 1999; Hammer, 1999, 2001; van Kleeck, 2004). Notably, and much more positively, Whitehurst's group also has produced positive effects with storybook reading when Mexican families have been the intervention targets (Valdez-Menchaca & Whitehurst, 1992) and as part of a comprehensive day care/Head Start intervention (Whitehurst et al., 1994, 1999). The Whitehurst group has also provided other recent demonstrations that interactive storybook reading promotes the language development of socioeconomically disadvantaged children (e.g., Zevenbergen, Whitehurst, & Zevenbergen, 2003). There is great potential for storybook reading to contribute to the literacy development of a wide range of children.

Whitehurst and his associates also have made progress in making their approach cost-effective, developing videotapes that teach mothers how to interact with the preschoolers as they read stories (Arnold, Lonigan, Whitehurst, & Epstein, 1994). Others are also making progress in devising storybook reading interventions. For example, Crain-Thoreson and Dale (1995) taught preschool staff members to interact with children more actively during storybook reading. The targeted students then performed better on a variety of language measures, including a vocabulary test and an analysis of the length and complexity of utterances. Dickinson and Smith (1994) designed a similar intervention that produced similar effects.

In short, by actively engaging preschoolers in discussions as part of story-book reading, adults can promote child language development; presumably, the earlier such experience begins, the better (Lonigan, Anthony, & Burgess, 1995; Stahl, 2003).

Developing Rich Emergent Literacy Knowledge in Preschools

Neuman and Roskos (1997) provided an interesting analysis that made clear just how extensive preschoolers' emergent literacy can be, at least when preschoolers experience an environment rich in emergent literacy learning opportunities. They studied 30 preschoolers who participated in a preschool with three play centers that permitted much emergent literacy activity: a post office, a restaurant, and a doctor's office. The children were observed over the course of 7 months.

What Neuman and Roskos (1997) found was that children learned the names and functions of a number of literacy objects in the play centers, including the following: envelopes, pencil, letter, mailbox, menu, bill, check, insurance card, and eye chart. The preschoolers also learned how to do many literate things, including the following: getting stamps, putting together a letter, addressing it, mailing it, delivering mail, taking a restaurant order, ordering from a menu, reviewing a restaurant bill, exchanging pleasantries over a meal, taking inventory at the restaurant, taking down information, giving prescriptions, signing in at the doctor's office, and describing medical emergency procedures. Neuman and Roskos (1997) also observed the use of some higher-order strategies similar to those used by older children as they read, write, and do things literate. These include seeking information, correcting and giving feedback to others, self-correcting, checking a literacy product against a standard (e.g., checking whether letters in the post office are sorted the way that they should be sorted), and gathering up resources before beginning a task. In short, much literate behavior can be learned in a preschool classroom designed to foster emergent literacy activities. The teacher who designs her or his classroom to include a library center and a post office has created a setting that can support storybook reading, children's writing, and associated literacy activities (Roskos & Neuman, 2001).

In more recent work, Neuman (1999; also Koskinen et al., 2000, and McGill-Franzen, Allington, Yokoi, & Brooks, 1999) studied one type of item that can be provided to children in preschool settings, one that does much to increase literacy interactions for preschoolers. When books are made available to children and their teachers are provided training in using them, children engage in literacy-promoting activities (e.g., looking at the books, sharing books with other children), with language and literacy skills enhanced. In highlighting that books can make a positive difference when they are in a child's world, Neuman made us aware that the absence of books is a reason for concern. In follow-up work, Neuman and Celano (2001) studied the availability of books in the worlds of middle-income and low-income preschoolers, finding many more in middle-class schools and communities. Duke (2000a, 2000b) conducted a similar study at the grade-1 level, obtaining a similar finding. One of the ways that rich parents and the schools serving their offspring spawn emergent literate children is that they provide tangible literature resources at home and during preschool.

Interpretational Controversies Regarding Emergent Literacy Experiences

From infancy, there are opportunities for adults and children to interact together with materials and activities related to reading and writing. Some children are more fortunate than others, participating in many more emergent literacy interactions than other children. The lucky children live in families in which literacy experiences are so common that they are family habits which are naturally extended to new family members, beginning shortly after their arrival from the hospital. That some preschoolers do not have consistent, excellent emergent literacy experiences has stimulated researchers such as Whitehurst, Neuman, and Roskos to begin to study ways of increasing interactions between parents, teachers, and children that promote emergent literacy. Their successes to date fuel enthusiasm for the possibility that many more children could be much better prepared for formal schooling by increasing the quality and quantity of literacy interactions during the preschool years.

In closing this section, however, I must admit that there is some variability in the interpretation of the emergent literacy research. For example, while there is agreement that storybook reading's effects on language and literacy development are not overwhelmingly large, some view the statistical associations produced to date as evidence of the power of storybook reading (Bus, van IJzendoorn, & Pellegrini, 1995; Dunning, Mason, & Stewart, 1994; Lonigan, 1994). That is, despite the many problems of measurement with preschool children (and there are many, not the least of which is the lower reliability of measurements on preschoolers compared to older children), the lack of statistical power in many studies (which reduces the likelihood of finding significant statistical associations), and great variability in the procedures from study to study, some researchers are impressed with the consistency of at least positive associations between activities like storybook reading and growth in emergent literacy. In contrast, other researchers (Scarborough & Dobrich, 1994) have examined exactly the same correlations between storybook reading and emergent literacy and have written them off as small and potentially attributable to other factors, suggesting that perhaps the correlations between storybook reading and language and literacy achievement actually reflect other relationships (e.g., perhaps children more interested in things literate and/or those with higher verbal abilities are more likely to engage in storybook reading than children less interested and/or lower in ability). My own reading of the evidence is that there is much more reason to believe that early literacy interactions are important. I am especially struck by experimental work such as that carried out by Whitehurst and his associates. Still, there is a need for much more research.

One possibility is that emergent literacy experiences may not be equally positive for all children. For example, in the studies of Bus and van IJzendoorn (e.g., 1988, 1992, 1995), it is striking that when children interact with parents with whom they are not securely attached, storybook reading is not the happy and engaging event that it can be when securely attached parents and children interact over books. It may very well be that such negative interactions over books may undermine interest in reading (Bus, 1993, 1994). We need to find this out, and then, of course, we must find out how more positive interactions can be encouraged between a preschooler and parent who have yet to develop a trusting relationship, one fostering literacy development.

However positive a child's emergent literacy experiences, they rarely are sufficient for the development of one very important competency associated with successful beginning reading. I take up that competency, phonemic awareness, in the next section.

PHONEMIC AWARENESS AND ITS
DEVELOPMENT THROUGH INSTRUCTION

Even though the language competencies developed during the preschool years are insufficient for the child to become a reader, they are nonetheless important. In fact, there are striking correlations between children's language competencies on entry to kindergarten and success in reading during the primary grades (see Elbro, Borstrøm, & Petersen, 1998; Elbro & Scarborough, 2004; Mann, 2003; Muter & Snowling, 1998; Scarborough, 2001). There has been particularly intense attention to the finding that kindergarten students who lack the language competency known as phonemic awareness often experience subsequent difficulties in learning to read (e.g., Adams, 1990; Blachman, 2000; Pennington, Groisser, & Welsh, 1993; Stanovich, 1986, 1988), although at-risk kindergarten children often have other problems at the phonological level. For example, Elbro et al. (1998) found that kindergarten children who poorly pronounced common words (i.e., they lacked distinct phonological representations of the words) were at greater risk for reading problems at grade 2.

Phonemic awareness is awareness that words are composed of separable sounds (i.e., phonemes) that are blended to produce words. There are a number of tasks that tap phonemic awareness (Adams, 1990; Anthony & Lonigan, 2004; Slocum, O'Connor, & Jenkins, 1993; Stahl & Murray, 1994, 1998; Wagner, Torgesen, Laughon, Simmons, & Rashotte, 1993). There are some data-based differences of opinion among the various researchers studying phonemic awareness about whether the particular tasks that reflect less and more advanced forms of phonemic awareness and whether the various manifestations of phonemic awareness are best thought of as a single competency or multiple, related competencies (Anthony & Lonigan, 2004; Anthony, Lonigan, Driscoll, Phillips, & Burgess, 2003; Mann & Foy, 2003; Mann & Wimmer, 2002). Nonetheless, Marilyn J. Adams's (1990) conceptualization of phonemic awareness still permits understanding of the various ways phonological awareness can be evident. According to her, the most primitive form is simply having enough of an ear for sounds to remember rhyming words more easily than nonrhyming words. The child with this level of phonemic awareness can recall nursery rhymes with greater ease than the child who lacks this basic form of phonemic awareness (Maclean, Bryant, & Bradley, 1987). At the next level, the child can detect the odd word in a set of words, recognizing, for example, that *sod* is the odd word in the trio *can, dan, sod,* or that *mar* is odd in the set *bat, bax,* and *mar.* At a still higher level of awareness, the child can blend component sounds to form words, for example, when presented the sounds *m, ah* (i.e., short *a*), and *t,* producing the word *mat.* Even more advanced is the ability to segment a word into its sounds; the child at this level of awareness can report that *mat* is composed of the sounds *m, ah,* and *t.* Children at the highest level of awareness can split off individual sounds from intact words: For example, when asked to delete the *m* sound from *mat,* the child says *at.* Thus, phonemic awareness culminates when students can actively manipulate and play around with the sounds that compose words. I emphasize the playfulness in such manipulation, for whenever I have observed classrooms in which children are practicing blending, adding, deleting, and inserting sounds as part of phonemic-awareness instruction, they seem to be having a lot of fun.

Given the various manifestations of phonemic awareness, it should not be surprising that there are a variety of ways to assess it, both with laboratory tasks and with more standardized assessments (Sodoro, Allinder, & Rankin-Erickson, 2002).

One study more than any other focused attention on phonemic awareness. Connie Juel (1988) followed a sample of 54 children as they progressed from grade 1 through grade 4, collecting a variety of reading and related measures as part of the study. The 23 Hispanic children, 14 African Americans, and 13 whites were all enrolled in the same school. One of the most striking findings in the study concerned continuing underachievement in reading: There was an 88% chance that if a child was having difficulty reading in grade 1, the child would still be having difficulty in grade 4. More importantly in this context, however, was that the best predictor of poor reading achievement in grade 1 was phonemic awareness: The more advanced levels of phonemic awareness discussed earlier were required for a child to score highly in Juel's (1988) study. Especially striking, low phonemic awareness in grade 1 was highly predictive of continuing reading difficulties in grade 4. Since Juel's (1988) study, there have been other early language predictors that are more telling about later reading (namely, rudimentary reading skills and letter identification; Elbro & Scarborough, 2004; Scarborough, 2001), although phonemic awareness is a very good predictor of later reading competency averaging across all of the relevant data that are available.

Juel's findings especially stimulated very hard thinking and many additional analyses by a number of researchers about phonemic awareness and how it relates to reading competence. Based on these analyses, it is now known that poor readers at all age levels often are less phonemically aware than same-age good readers (e.g., Pratt & Brady, 1988; Shaywitz, 1996). Children who lack phonemic awareness have a difficult time developing understanding of letter–sound relationships as well as learning to spell (Griffith, 1991; Juel, Griffith, & Gough, 1986). Since Juel's studies, additional and diverse evidence has been produced that poor phonemic awareness at 4–6 years of age is predictive especially of early reading achievement, but also throughout the elementary years (e.g., Badian, 2001; Bowey, 1995, 2002; Goswami, 2002b; Hulme et al., 2002; McBride-Chang & Kail, 2002; Muter, Hulme, Snowling, & Stevenson, 2004; Näslund & Schneider, 1996; Speece, Ritchey, Cooper, Roth, & Schatschneider, 2004; Storch & Whitehurst, 2002; Stuart & Masterson, 1992; Torgesen & Burgess, 1998; Wesseling & Reitsma, 2001; Windfuhr & Snowling, 2001). The evidence that phonemic awareness difficulties in the elementary years are associated with reading difficulties has also been established in studies that demonstrate at least as strong relationships between phonemic awareness and reading ability as other potentially important individual differences (i.e., rapid processing and naming of individual letters and numbers; Cardoso-Martins & Pennington, 2004; Kirby, Parrila, & Pfeiffer, 2003; Parrila, Kirby, & McQuarrie, 2004; Schatschneider, Fletcher, Francis, Carlson, & Foorman, 2004; Sunseth & Bowers, 2002; Swanson, Trainin, Necoechea, & Hammill, 2003; Torgesen, Wagner, Rashotte, Burgess, & Hecht, 1997) and reading ability. At least in some analyses, more advanced forms of phonemic awareness (i.e., the ability to segment words into component sounds) have been more predictive of reading ability than simpler forms (e.g., being able to detect rhymes; Nation & Hulme, 1997).

Lack of phonemic awareness seems to be part of a vicious cycle.

Children who are exposed to a great deal of language and have well-developed vocabularies early in life have greater phonemic awareness, for a well-developed vocabulary provides many opportunities to discriminate words on the basis of sound differences (Dickinson, McCabe, Anastasopoulos, Peisner-Feinberg, & Poe, 2003; Goswami, 2000, 2001; Metsala, 1999). Those with less-rich language experiences know fewer words and are less phonemically aware. Deficiencies in phonemic awareness, in turn, can undermine learning to decode, which in turn undermines reading a wide range of materials and comprehending what is read. The long-term result is less practice in reading and less exposure to information in text, and thus, less development of higher-order reading competencies (e.g., ability to make sense of complex syntax) and world knowledge that can mediate understanding of text (Juel, 1988). This is the rich-getting-richer and the poor-getting-poorer story, what Stanovich (1986) referred to as the Matthew effect in reading.

For the most advanced levels of phonemic awareness to develop, formal instruction in reading seems essential (i.e., only a very small proportion of children develop the advanced levels of phonemic awareness in the absence of such instruction; e.g., Lundberg, 1991). The one emergent literacy experience that is predictive of phonemic awareness is parental teaching of letters and their sounds (Crain-Thoreson & Dale, 1992). Many parents, however, do not engage in such teaching, so that education that impacts phonemic awareness typically must occur in school. Thus, there is a need to provide phonemic awareness instruction to kindergarten and grade-1 children if they are to develop it.

Instruction in Phonemic Awareness

Phonemic awareness can be developed through systematic practice in categorizing words on the basis of common beginning, middle, and end sounds. One of the first instructional studies of the development of phonemic awareness, conducted in Great Britain by Lynette Bradley and Peter E. Bryant (e.g., 1983), continues to be the best known.

An important principle emphasized in Bradley and Bryant's (1983) instruction was that the same word can be categorized in different ways on the basis of sound when it is in different sets of words. Thus, if *hen* is in a group of words that include *hat*, *hill*, *hair*, and *hand*, it would make sense to categorize all of these words together as starting with *h*, especially in contrast to other words starting with another letter (e.g., *b* words such as *bag*, *band*, and *bat*). If *hen* were on a list with *men* and *sun*, however, these three words could be categorized as ones ending in *n*. If *hen* were on a list of words that included *bed* and *leg*, it would be possible to categorize the words as ones with *short e* in the middle.

The instruction in Bradley and Bryant (1983) took place over 40 10-minute sessions spread out over 2 years. During the first 20 sessions, 5- and 6-year-olds who initially lacked phonemic awareness were taught to categorize words on the basis of common sounds, using pictures of the objects (i.e., pictures of a *hen*, *men*, and a *leg*). For example, in one lesson, a set of pictures representing the letter *b* was shown to the child, who named the objects. The child repeated the names, with the teacher urging the child to listen to the sounds. The child then was asked if he or she could hear a sound common to each word. This continued until the child could identify the common sound, with the adult providing help and hints if the child experienced difficulty doing this.

The sound identification task was repeated a number of times during training, with variations (e.g., presentation of *bus*, with the child required to pick out a picture starting with the same sound from an array of pictures; presentation of *bus*, with the direction to pick out pictures starting with a different sound than the one at the beginning of *bus*). Children were then given sets of pictures, asked to group them together on the basis of common sounds, and then required to justify their classifications. "Odd-one-out" was played, in which the child was required to eliminate a word starting with (or ending with or containing) a sound different than the sounds suggested by the other pictures in a set. Many such exercises were given for each sound (e.g., *b*), with the teacher moving on to a new sound only when the child seemed to be proficient with the sound previously introduced. Of course, as new sounds accumulated, the difficulty of tasks increased.

The 20 sessions with pictures were followed by 20 sessions with words, in which a child was required to determine whether words rhymed or began with the same sound (alliteration). After the child was proficient at this task, there were lessons on end sounds (e.g., odd-one-out exercises requiring elimination of the word ending in a sound different than the others). After the child could manage categorizing on the basis of final sounds, there was instruction of categorization based on middle sounds in words.

Pictures yielded to purely aural presentations in this training. Various discrimination exercises eventually gave way to production exercises, so that children had to recall words containing particular sounds in particular positions. In the latter half of the curriculum, children were required to spell words using plastic letters, with the teacher providing help as needed, up to and including spelling the word for the child. Spelling exercises included sets of words sharing common features. Thus, for a set involving *hat*, *cat*, and *rat*, an efficient strategy was simply to change the first plastic letter as each new word was requested. The saliency of many different sound patterns was illustrated with such spelling lists.

This training produced substantial gains in standardized reading performance (i.e., about a year's advantage) relative to a control condition in which children were trained to categorize pictures and words conceptually (e.g., *cat*, *bat*, and *rat* are all animals). The students trained in sound categorization were even further ahead of control participants who had received no supplementary categorization training. Even more striking, however, were the results of a 5-year follow-up. Even though many of the control subjects had received substantial remediation during the 5-year interval following participation in the study, there were still striking reading advantages for students who had experienced the sound categorization training when they were in the primary grades (Bradley, 1989; Bradley & Bryant, 1991).

Since the appearance of the Bradley and Bryant (1983, 1985) study, there have been a number of well-controlled demonstrations that phonemic awareness can be developed in children with discernible effects on reading and learning to read (Ehri et al., 2001; National Reading Panel, 2000). I review here some of the most noteworthy examples of this research in order to deepen reader understanding of instruction that can promote phonemic awareness. Thus, in Lundberg, Frost, and Peterson (1988), classrooms of 6-year-olds were provided daily phonemic awareness training for 8 months (i.e., rhyming exercises; dividing words into syllables; and identifying phonemes, including segmenting words into phonemes and synthesizing phonemes into words). Control classrooms received no such training. Three years later, students in trained classrooms performed better on reading and spelling tasks than did students in control classrooms.

Similarly, Ball and Blachman (1988) provided instruction to 5-year-olds. In the phoneme-awareness condition, kindergarten students met in small groups for 20 minutes, 4 days a week for 7 weeks. Students moved counters to represent the sounds in words, were exposed to letter names and their associated sounds, and performed categorization tasks like the ones used in Bradley and Bryant's work. In the language-activities control condition, students had vocabulary lessons, listened to stories, and practiced semantic categorization activities. They also received instruction in letter names and sounds that was identical to that provided to the phoneme awareness participants. There was also a no-instruction control condition in the study. The phoneme awareness group outperformed the two control groups on a word reading test, even though no word reading had been taught in the phoneme awareness condition. In follow-up studies with kindergarten students, the phoneme awareness treatment again produced superior word recognition and spelling as compared to control performance (Ball & Blachman, 1991; Blachman, 1991; Tangel & Blachman, 1992, 1995).

Lie (1991) taught Norwegian grade-1 students to analyze new words with respect to their phonological structure. This training promoted reading and spelling in grade 2, compared to control students not receiving phonological training. Weaker readers benefited more from the training than did stronger students.

Cunningham (1990) compared two approaches to increasing the phonemic awareness of kindergarten and grade-1 children. One approach was "skill and drill," with emphasis on segmentation and blending of phonemes. In the second approach, there was discussion of the value of decoding and phonemic awareness and how learning to segment and blend phonemes could be applied in reading. This latter approach was metacognitively very rich, providing children with a great deal of information about when, where, and why to use the knowledge of phonemes they were acquiring. Although both forms of instruction were effective, the metacognitively rich instruction was more effective at the grade-1 level; that is consistent with the general perspective developed in this volume that instruction which increases children's awareness of when and where to use cognitive skills should result in more general and effective use of cognitive skills.

I have presented these results of true experimental evaluations of phonemic awareness training in some detail because these studies are very important. In general, regardless of the specific methods used to measure phonemic awareness or the specific comparison conditions (e.g., no-instruction controls or alternative-instruction controls), phonemic awareness instruction has been successful in promoting phonemic awareness (Murray, 1995). As just detailed, such instruction does much more, positively affecting subsequent reading achievement.

From those who are opposed to offering instruction aimed specifically at promoting phonemic awareness, I have heard the objection that there is no causal evidence linking phonemic awareness and improved reading. That claim is simply not true. When there is an experimental manipulation of phonemic awareness instruction (i.e., some children receive it and some do not, with recipients determined by random assignment), there is a basis for making a causal claim about the effects of phonemic awareness instruction on subsequent reading achievement. In addition to the causal studies already discussed, interested readers should also see the work of Byrne and Fielding-Barnsley (1991, 1993, 1995; Byrne, Fielding-Barnsley, & Ashley, 2000), O'Connor, Jenkins, and Slocum (1995), Vellutino and Scanlon (1987), Williams (1980), and Wise and Olson (1995). When all of the relevant data were considered by the National Reading Panel (2000; see also Adams, 2001; Ehri et al., 2001), the case that developing phonemic awareness between 4 and 6 years of age has powerful positive effects on subsequent reading achievement was clear, with the panel concluding that phonemic awareness instruction had a moderate impact on subsequent reading achievement. The clearest effect of phonemic awareness was on the ability to decode words, although there was even some impact on comprehension.

Learning to read is easier and more certain if the child has achieved a high level of phonemic awareness than if the child has not.

Unfortunately, many children do not receive phonemic awareness instruction. Sometimes the argument is made that because whole language involves much work with poetry, children in whole-language kindergartens receive sufficient exposure to tasks requiring phonemic awareness. Recall, however, that awareness of rhyme, which is the aspect of phonemic awareness that would seem to be most stimulated by poetry experiences, is only one form of phonemic awareness, and one of the easiest of the phonemic awareness tasks, at that.

I have also heard the objection that phonemic awareness instruction is boring. Although I know of no formal studies on this point, I have been in many classrooms where phonemic awareness instruction takes place and where the kids really seem to have a ball playing with sounds. In my public lectures, I often ask the kindergarten and grade-1 teachers who offer phonemic awareness instruction to identify themselves and ask them whether such instruction is fun for the students or drudgery. Even before I reveal to them my perception of the situation, teachers who have tried such instruction invariably report that the kids like it. If you need proof that phonemic awareness instruction can be a lot of fun, get hold of either *Daisy's Castle* or *DaisyQuest* (Blue Wave Software, now distributed through the Pro-Ed catalog), two computer programs that develop phonemic awareness in a fantasy context and really do what they claim to do (Barker & Torgesen, 1995; Foster, Erickson, Foster, Brinkman, & Torgesen, 1994). My son Tim delighted in these programs.

In many cases, however, my hunch is that the reason teachers do not concern themselves with developing phonemic awareness is because they do not know how to develop it in children. This surmise is based, in part, on the many questions I receive from the teachers about what phonemic awareness is and how it can be developed in children. There is also a growing data base that teachers lack understanding of phonemic awareness as well as knowledge of how to promote many other beginning reading competencies, with some teachers not aware at all that they are deficient in understanding what should be taught and how to teach it (Bos, Mather, Dickson, Podhajski, & Chard, 2001; Cunningham, Perry, Stanovich, & Stanovich, 2004; Spear-Swerling & Brucker, 2003). Not surprisingly, how much the teacher knows about beginning reading makes a difference in what gets taught in the classroom and ultimately in student achievement, although the relationships typically are not particularly strong ones (McCutchen et al., 2002a, 2002b; Moats & Foorman, 2003). There is a real need to heighten teachers' awareness about how phonemic awareness and other beginning reading competencies can be fostered in students. For the teacher who would like to jump-start his or her knowledge about how to teach phonemic awareness, I strongly recommend Adams, Foorman, Lundberg, and Beeler's (1997) *Phonemic Awareness in Young Children: A Classroom Curriculum.* For a very good overview of much of the evidence-based knowledge pertaining to beginning reading instruction, I recommend Honig, Diamond, Gutlohn, and Mahler's (2000) *Teaching Reading Sourcebook for Kindergarten through Eighth Grade.* The latter is helpful throughout the elementary grades, for the knowledge that teachers need to teach reading shifts dramatically during the primary- and elementary-grade years (Block, Oakar, & Hurt, 2002).

I close this subsection by noting that, despite the evidence that phonemic awareness can be inculcated successfully in isolation, it might be a mistake to do so. Schneider, Roth, and Ennemoser (2000) studied German kindergarten children who were at risk for reading problems because of weak phonological skills. The children subsequently received either instruction in phonemic awareness and letter–sound training or in phonemic awareness alone or in letter–sounds alone. When measured in grades 1 and 2, the differences between conditions were not huge, but there were consistent small differences that favored the combined approach. Fuchs et al. (2001) found comparable effects on acquisition of phonemic awareness from phonemic awareness instruction alone and combined with explicit decoding instruction, but with subsequent advantage on decoding favoring the combined training condition. My intuition is that we need more studies of such combined approaches not only because combined phonemic awareness and phonics instruction might be more powerful (see Bus & van IJzendoorn, 1999) but also because it is more likely to occur in school. Although I have seen many studies of isolated phonemic awareness instruction in the pages of journals, when I see such instruction in school it is usually occurring with phonics instruction.

Development of Phonemic Awareness through Reading

Just as development of phonemic awareness leads to improved reading, so does reading increase phonemic awareness (e.g., Goswami, 2002a; Goswami & Bryant, 1990), beginning in the preschool years (Burgess & Lonigan, 1998). Among others, Wimmer, Landerl, Linortner, and Hummer (1991) and Perfetti (1992; Perfetti, Beck, Bell, & Hughes, 1987) have presented evidence that phonemic awareness is increased by reading, with the implication that reading-induced increases in phonemic awareness in turn influence subsequent development of reading competence. Again, the rich get richer by reading more (see also Silven, Poskiparta, & Niemi, 2004)!

I have heard whole-language enthusiasts who are aware that phonemic awareness does increase through reading argue that that is the proof that instruction aimed specifically at the development of phonemic awareness, such as that detailed in the last subsection, is unnecessary. Consistent with whole-language philosophy, they argue that phonemic awareness will develop from immersing the child in reading. Of course, there is a chicken-and-egg problem here, as the child who is initially low in phonemic awareness experiences more difficulties in learning to decode print (more about this in the next chapter), hence is less able to read than other children and thus benefits less from reading. I'm certain that the phrase is getting boring by now but, again, *the rich get richer*, with children high in phonemic awareness initially learning to read more certainly and thus deriving greater benefits from opportunities to read.

The scientific community has made progress in cracking this chicken-and-egg dilemma, however. The specifics of the analyses are too detailed for presentation here. Suffice it to say that in some analyses phonemic awareness seems to contribute more to learning to read than learning to read contributes to phonemic awareness (Hulme et al., 2002; Nation, Allen, & Hulme, 2001; Wagner, Torgesen, & Rashotte, 1994; Wagner et al., 1997), and in others it is just the opposite (e.g., Carroll, Snowling, Hulme, & Stevenson, 2003; Goswami, 2002a, 2002b). As I make this point, I also keep in mind that reading is very good for the young language learner and reader regardless whether reading is chicken or egg here. Thus, when parents and children read alphabet books together, the child learns about the alphabet and words but also improves in phonemic awareness, and vice versa (Murray, Stahl, & Ivey, 1996). Consistent with the balanced perspective in this book, reading books with children and teaching them skills are complementary activities, with the reciprocity between development of phonemic awareness and reading the best explanation for the patterns of outcomes in at least some studies (e.g., Badian, 2001; Neuhaus & Swank, 2002; Sprenger-Charolles, Siegel, Bechennec, & Serniclaes, 2003).

Phonemic Awareness Instruction and Whole Language

There is another set of data devastating to critics of phonemic awareness instruction. When activities that are explicitly intended to increase phonemic awareness are added to whole-language classrooms, there are discernible benefits. In a study of Australian kindergarten instruction, Jillian M. Castle, Jacquelyn Riach, and Tom Nicholson (1994) manipulated the presence or absence of phonemic awareness instruction for kindergarten students experiencing a whole-language program. They carried out two studies, one focusing on development of spelling skills and the other the development of ability to read words not seen previously. The phonemic awareness instruction involved two 20-minute sessions a week for 10 weeks. Control participants received supplementary instruction that involved development of skills not related to phonemic awareness. Although the effects were not large, there were greater gains in spelling skills and reading of pseudowords (i.e., invented words, which ensured that students had not seen them before) in the phonemic awareness training conditions than in the control conditions.

Although Castle et al. (1994) have offered the most carefully controlled insertion of phonemic awareness instruction into what were certainly whole-language classrooms, there are other studies in which phonemic awareness has been added to classrooms. Thus, Byrne and Fielding-Barnsley (1991, 1993, 1995; Byrne et al., 2000) reported long-term gains from adding phonemic awareness instruction to the preschool experiences of 4-year-olds (i.e., 12 half-hour sessions, once a week). Kindergarten children in the study of Blachman, Ball, Black, and Tangel (1994) had previously experienced instruction that was so incomplete with respect to development of skills that the children knew only two letters on average by the middle of the kindergarten year. Adding 11 weeks of systematic phonemic awareness instruction at the end of the year, however, did have an effect on the quality of children's invented spellings, with the trained children producing spellings much closer to the sound pattern of words than did control participants. The trained children were also much more likely than controls to be able to spell words correctly.

In conclusion, when phonemic awareness instruction is added to educational environments in which little skills instruction is occurring, there are clear benefits for the students receiving it. Although the positive effects of phonemic awareness instruction were not large in the Castle et al. (1994) study, which is also the most easily interpreted of these studies with respect to whole language, they are apparent on several different measures. Moreover, the phonemic awareness instruction in Castle and associates' (1994) investigation was brief compared to other versions of phonemic awareness instruction, so that detection of effects in that experiment are notable. The phonemic awareness instruction in the studies of Byrne and Fielding-Barnsley (1991) and Blachman et al. (1994) was also brief, but it nonetheless produced positive effects, compared to ongoing instruction that was weak in skills training, which further encourages the conclusion that phonemic awareness instruction can be very potent.

Summary

Many kindergarten and grade-1 children lack the awareness that words are streams of sounds that can be disentangled and that sounds can be assembled to produce words. They lack phonemic awareness, a metalinguistic insight that seems to be essential in learning to read. Fortunately, phonemic awareness can be developed through instruction, with clear benefits to subsequent acquisition of reading skills. This is an active area of research, with recent analyses of how teaching students to attend to their articulations of sounds (i.e., mouth movements; Castiglioni-Spalten & Ehri, 2003) improves phonemic awareness and learning to read. There is also recent assessment of how finger-point reading in kindergarten (i.e., pointing to words as the teacher and group reads them) impacts phonemic awareness and other reading processes (Morris, Bloodgood, Lomax, & Perney, 2003; Uhry, 2002). Not surprising, there continues to be research on computer-based approaches to the development of phonemic awareness as well (e.g., Cassady & Smith, 2003/2004).

The associations between phonemic awareness and successfully learning to read have prompted much attention to this particular aspect of literacy development. The result has been increased knowledge about phonemic awareness and its development, so that clear guidance now can be offered to practicing kindergarten teachers about how to develop phonemic awareness in their students. Kindergarten is the right time for such instruction, since phonemic awareness is an important prerequisite to learning to decode, which is typically a key focus of grade-1 reading instruction.

Frequently, I have heard the claim that phonemic awareness can be developed by having children spend a great deal of time listening to and interacting with books that are filled with playfully varied speech sounds—for example, rhymes and alliterations. Indeed, such language exposure probably does promote phonemic awareness somewhat (Fernandez-Fein & Baker, 1997; Goswami, 2001), and hence it is noteworthy that a list of books that could be used in this fashion has been compiled (e.g., Yopp, 1995). At a minimum, lots of such books in kindergarten can provide lots of stimulus for vocabulary development and for students to think about the sounds of words. I also frequently encounter the claim that phonemic awareness will develop if children are allowed to use invented spellings in their writings. In fact, there is no doubt that when children invent spellings they are thinking hard about the constituent sounds of words as well as how those constituent sounds can be represented together as the letters in words (Read, 1971; Richgels, 2001). Associations between invented spelling and phonemic awareness have been observed often (Clarke, 1988; Ehri, 1989; Mann, Tobin, & Wilson, 1987; Treiman, 1985). Although I do not think that wordplay and invented spelling will be enough to develop complete phonemic awareness for many children, there are several good reasons to encourage children to engage in wordplay and attempt to write, including that such activities can promote phonemic awareness.

One reaction that I have heard when arguments are made to improve the instruction given to preschoolers is that gains from instruction during preschool are wiped out later—that they are short-term gains. With respect to instruction in phonemic awareness, that is not entirely true. Phonemic awareness instruction can explain about 12% of word recognition performance in the early primary years; although it explains much less of the variance in reading in the later primary and middle elementary years, the effects are still detectable (Bus & van IJzendoorn, 1999). The decline in the importance of phonological awareness with advancing age probably reflects that phonological awareness is more critical when developing word recognition is the critical competency emphasized in reading instruction (i.e., during kindergarten and grade 1) than later, when higher-order components of reading (e.g., comprehension) are emphasized more (de Jong & van der Leij, 1999).

With respect to academic achievement in general, preschool benefits are not wiped out entirely with advancing age and grade in school. I am impressed with the evidence that high-quality preschool experiences can have very positive impacts on later reading achievement, including reading achievement measured many years after preschool has been completed (Barnett, 2001; Gorey, 2001). Given the positive track record of high-quality early childhood education on later academic achievement, why have I not said more about early childhood education in this book? It is because I do not study early childhood education and do not have the fully informed opinion that I have with respect to elementary schooling, which gets the largest amount of coverage in this volume. That said, when I talk about balanced literacy instruction, I always make the case that the preschool years are critical for literacy development and that educators who wait until kindergarten entrance to intervene in the lives of at-risk children are making a huge mistake. We do know how to design literacy-rich preschool environments that promote children's understanding of print and writing conventions as well as letters and sounds (see Yaden et al., 2000, for a review). Failing to provide rich emergent literacy experiences during the preschool years can leave a child far behind his or her kindergarten classmates; a set of rich emergent literacy experiences, at home and in preschool, can provide long-lasting advantages.

SUMMARY AND CONCLUDING REFLECTIONS

1. Throughout the 20th century, psychologists have studied the significance of the preschool years and the importance of the child's earliest social relationships. Bowlby (1969) and other developmentalists came to understand the importance of a child's developing a trusting relationship with an adult early in life, typically the mother. Such a relationship is a context in which mother and child can explore new things together, including letters of the alphabet, words, and texts.

The interface between socioemotional development in infancy and the preschool years and cognitively oriented interactions with caregivers and others has been actively explored in recent years. The work of a Dutch research group (Bus & van IJzendoorn, 1995) has established that emergent literacy interactions are more certainly productive when mother and child are securely attached, a finding that has attracted great attention and undoubtedly will be followed up in the Netherlands and elsewhere. An important implication of this research is that narrowly targeting literacy is unlikely to be an effective strategy for ensuring the development of literate children. Rather, the message in the Dutch data is that every effort should be made to ensure that mothers are responsive to their babies, for such responsivity is at the heart of secure attachment. Fortunately, researchers are identifying ways to stimulate parents to be more naturally responsive to their children, as parental responsivity is the key to the development of healthy parent–infant attachments.

Secure attachment is important for cognitive development because intellectual skills are developed in interaction with others, a perspective pioneered by Lev S. Vygotsky a half-century ago in the Soviet Union and only now being explored in detail in the West. Vygotsky and other Soviet researchers established the importance of speech in thinking and the organization of thinking; this is particularly important with respect to literacy.

2. Chapters 2 and 3 introduced the phonological processes involved in reading—that is, speech as a mediator of word recognition. The important point at this juncture is that Vygotsky also made the case that the development of problem-solving skills involving speech occurs in interactions with others. According to him and other Soviet researchers, the problem-solving dialogues that young children and adults engage in are internalized. From this perspective, there is very good reason for adults and children to spend time in verbal interaction around problems that are difficult for children, including the problems associated with learning about books.

3. At several points in this chapter, research has been reported in which parents are taught how to interact with their children so that parent–child interactions are healthier and more productive. Even brief interventions produce dramatic shifts in these studies. This work makes clear that parent–child interactions have a plasticity about them: Parents who are not appropriately responsive to their children can learn to be more responsive. This also anticipates a theme that is reiterated throughout this book: Some adult–child interactions are more likely to promote the cognitive development of children than others.

For example, an important characteristic of effective parent–child interactions that has been emphasized in this chapter is that the input must be at an appropriate level for the child. In healthy interactions, the adult does not demand too much or too little, but rather supports the child who is working on new competencies. This observation is consistent with a recurrent theme in the motivation literature that people are most motivated when the goal is not so distant that it cannot be achieved, although achieving it requires some effort. That is, it is very motivating to be working at the boundary of one's competence: When this happens, competence expands. This is a point that has been reiterated repeatedly by theorists studying human motivation (e.g., White, 1959). It will come up again as the nature of effective reading instruction is explored further in the chapters that follow, especially in Chapter 11.

4. That natural parent–child interactions alone are typically not enough to prepare the child for success at beginning reading comes through especially clearly in the research on phonemic awareness. More positively, a great deal has been learned about how adults can interact with children in order to develop their phonemic awareness—and it is not by just immersing children in reading and writing and things literate. Rather, it is through instruction that makes sense in light of our understanding of phonemic awareness that has been developed through careful research.

5. Whitehurst and Lonigan (1998, 2001) defined "outside-in" literacy components as coming from outside the printed word and developing through informal social processes during the preschool years. These include general language competencies, such as knowledge of concepts and the words expressing concepts as well as productive use of syntax. Children learn about story structures from such interactions. They acquire an understanding about the conventions of print, including that books are read from left to right and from top to bottom. In contrast are "inside-out" components of literacy, which are sources of information inside the printed word, permitting the translation of words into sounds. These include knowing the names of letters and letter–sound associations, phonological awareness, and understanding that writing of words involves translating sounds into letters. These skills seem to require more explicit teaching by parents than the outside-in competencies. Children who have preschool experiences promoting both outside-in and inside-out capabilities are better prepared for reading instruction in the primary grades than are children living in a language-impoverished environment (Whitehurst & Lonigan, 1998, 2001). For example, the phonemically aware child is prepared to learn how to sound out words; the child whose comprehension of language is well developed through many language interactions during the preschool years readily understands what was read.

Frijters et al. (2000) provided a very nice demonstration of the value of both inside-out and outside-in experiences. They measured the phonemic awareness of kindergarten children and also took measures of how much storybook reading they experienced. What they found was that phonemic awareness predicted letter-sound and letter-name knowledge and storybook reading was linked to vocabulary development. Inside-out and outside-in competencies are both necessary and are complementary to one another in promoting a child's literacy development in school. Children must learn how to read the words and make meaning from those words.

6. It is surprising that very little research attention is being given to technology and its impact on early literacy development. There is the occasional investigation of Internet impact (e.g., Karchmer, 2001) and various types of interactive media that are computer-driven (e.g., de Jong & Bus, 2002; Ricci & Beal, 2002). The differences produced by these options, as compared to conventional reading, have been rather small. The historic successes of *Sesame Street* (Ball & Bogatz, 1970; Bogatz & Ball, 1971; Fisch, 2004) have been complemented by evaluations of programs such as *Between the Lions*, with generally modest and somewhat inconsistent effects although positive enough to justify continued support of such programming as supportive of beginning literacy development (e.g., Linebarger, Kosanic, Greenwood, & Doku, 2004). Given the expanding presence of electronic products presumably aimed at promoting literacy, there is a great need for additional research in this problem area.

7. Finally, I close this chapter with a reflection on culture and emergent literacy skills. The language experienced by preschoolers in middle-class and working-class homes is very different (Gee, 2001; Heath, 1983; Watson, 2001; Wells, 1981). It is rather easy to make the case that the language and parent–child interactions occurring in middle-class, English-first-language American homes is more congruent with development of both outside-in and inside-out competencies considered in this chapter (Goldenberg, 2001; Goldenberg & Gallimore, 1995; Whitehurst & Lonigan, 1998), although there are surely many children in low-income families who do have high-quality emergent literacy experiences (Anderson & Stokes, 1984; Clark, 1983; Goldenberg & Gallimore, 1995; Goldenberg, Reese, & Gallimore, 1992; Heath, 1983; Paratore, Melzi, & Krol-Sinclair, 1999; Taylor & Dorsey-Gaines, 1988; Teale, 1986). Nonetheless, students from low-income, English-second-language, and some minority homes are at risk for difficulties in beginning reading, for there are great schisms between the home and school cultures for many of these children (Delpit, 1995; Feagans & Haskins, 1986; Ogbu, 1982; Pellegrini, 2001; Steele, 1992; Vernon-Feagans, 1996; Vernon-Feagans, Hammer, Miccio, & Manlove, 2001).

Although we are aware of this problem, that there is little to say about how to solve it based on available research haunted me as I wrote the first edition of this book and bothers me even more as I recognize that there has been little progress on the problem in the years since I first wrote about this topic. Moreover, the progress that has occurred is increasing recognition of the complexity of the issues—for example, increasing awareness that there are many possible mixes of first and second languages in a bilingual child's world (Tabors & Snow, 2001; Vernon-Feagans et al., 2001). We also understand better now than we did a few years ago that cultural groups which value conventional reading are more likely to interact with young children over books and other literacy objects valued in North American/European conventional middle-class cultures (see Bus, 2001), with consistent associations between valuing of reading by adult caregivers and children's verbal and literacy competencies (Sénéchal, LeFevre, Hudson, & Lawson, 1996; Snow, Barnes, Chandler, Goodman, & Hemphill, 1991). In one dramatic analysis after another, there has been just plain less of what are considered positive emergent literacy activities in the homes of groups with high proportions of children experiencing difficulties in reading in conventional schools (e.g., Baker, Serpell, & Sonnenschein, 1995; Hart & Risley, 1995; Laakso, Poikkeus, & Lyytinen, 1999). As I have gone out and given talks about balanced literacy instruction, there are invariably questions about the education of children who arrive at school with very different language experiences than the American ideal. Implicit in these discussions is that the current educational approach with such children is to throw them into conventional instruction and hope for the best. This reflects an enormous gap in our understanding of literacy development through instruction. We need to know much more about the literacy development of many more of the children who enter the contemporary schoolhouse door.

More positively, there was a very bright spot in the research in the past few years from the perspective of this author, albeit from outside the United States. Lesaux and Siegel (2003) studied a large sample of Canadian children who spoke English as a second language. During their kindergarten year, they received extensive systematic instruction in phonemic awareness as part of a program of balanced literacy instruction as conceived in this volume. This was followed by systematic phonics instruction in grade 1, again as part of a balanced program as conceived in this book—that is, skills instruction was systematic and explicit, but holistic reading and writing experiences occurred every day. By second grade, these second-language students were reading English at the level of native English speakers, as indicated on a broad range of reading measures administered to the student, and even outperformed the native speakers on some measures. (And, of course, there had been substantial differences between the second- and first-language students on earlier assessments, before they experienced the balanced instruction.) In short, the type of evidence-based balanced approach favored in this volume received a strong boost from this study. Many of the interventions highlighted in this volume have good track records with at-risk populations, which is an important motivation for developing a balanced mix of the types of instruction covered in the various chapters of this book. Although I could hope for more evidence, the evidence that exists is exciting and should prompt much additional study of the use of balanced literacy instruction with diverse populations . . . even before they hit first grade. Lesaux and Siegel (2003) started their intervention in kindergarten, with a large impact evident by grade 2! We need such impacts replicated again and again in kindergarten and primary-grade classrooms across the country.

REFERENCES

Adams, M. J. (1990). *Beginning to read.* Cambridge, MA: Harvard University Press.

Adams, M. J. (2001). Alphabetic anxiety and explicit, systematic phonics instruction: A cognitive science perspective. In S. B. Neuman & D. K. Dickinson (Eds.), *Handbook of early literacy research* (pp. 66–80). New York: Guilford Press.

Adams, M. J., Foorman, B. R., Lundberg, I., & Beeler, T. (1997). *Phonemic awareness in young children: A classroom curriculum.* Baltimore: Brookes.

Ainsworth, M. D. S. (1967). *Infancy in Uganda: Infant care and the growth of love.* Baltimore: Johns Hopkins University Press.

Anderson, A. B., & Stokes, S. J. (1984). Social and institutional influences on the development and practice of literacy. In H. Goelman, A. Oberg, & F. Smith (Eds.), *Awakening to literacy* (pp. 24–37). Portsmouth, NH: Heinemann.

Anderson-Yockel, J., & Haynes, W. (1994). Joint picture-book reading strategies in working-class African American and white mother–toddler dyads. *Journal of Speech, Language, and Hearing Research, 37,* 583–593.

Anthony, J. L., & Lonigan, C. J. (2004). The nature of phonological awareness: Converging evidence from four studies of preschool and early grade school children. *Journal of Educational Psychology, 96,* 43–55.

Anthony, J. L., Lonigan, C. J., Driscoll, K., Phillips, B. M., & Burgess, S. R. (2003). Phonological sensitivity: A quasi-parallel progression of word structure units and cognitive operations. *Reading Research Quarterly, 38,* 470–487.

Applebee, A. N., & Langer, J. A. (1983). Instructional scaffolding: Reading and writing as natural language activities. *Language Arts, 60,* 168–175.

Arnold, D. H., Lonigan, C. J., Whitehurst, G. J., & Epstein, J. N. (1994). Accelerating language development through picture book reading: Replication and extension to a videotape training format. *Journal of Educational Psychology, 86,* 235–243.

Badian, N. A. (2001). Phonological and orthographic processing: Their roles in reading prediction. *Annals of Dyslexia, 51,* 179–202.

Baker, L., Serpell, R., & Sonnenschein, S. (1995). Opportunities for literacy learning in the homes of urban preschoolers. In L. M. Morrow (Eds.), *Family literacy: Connections in schools and communities* (pp. 236–252). Newark, DE: International Reading Association.

Baker, L., Sonnenschein, S., Serpell, R., Fernandez-Fein, S., & Scher, D. (1994). *Contexts of emergent literacy: Everyday home experiences of urban pre-kindergarten children* (Reading Research Report No. 24). Athens, GA, and College Park, MD: National Reading Research Center.

Ball, E. W., & Blachman, B. A. (1988). Phoneme segmentation training: Effect on reading readiness. *Annals of Dyslexia, 38,* 203–225.

Ball, E. W., & Blachman, B. A. (1991). Does phoneme segmentation training in kindergarten make a difference in early word recognition and developmental spelling? *Reading Research Quarterly, 26,* 49–66.

Ball, S., & Bogatz, G. A. (1970). *The first year of "Sesame Street": An evaluation.* Princeton NJ: Educational Testing Service.

Barker, T. A., & Torgesen, J. K. (1995). The evaluation of computer-assisted instruction in phonological awareness with below average readers. *Journal of Educational Computing Research, 13,* 89–103.

Barnett, W. S. (2001). Preschool education for economically disadvantaged children: Effects on reading achievement and related outcomes. In S. B. Neuman & D. K. Dickinson (Eds.), *Handbook of early literacy research* (pp. 421–443). New York: Guilford Press.

Belsky, J., Rosenberger, K., & Crnic, K. (1995). The origins of attachment security: "Classical" and contextual determinants. In S. Goldberg, R. Muir, & J. Kerr (Eds.), *Attachment theory: Social, developmental, and clinical perspectives* (pp. 153–183). Hillsdale, NJ: Analytic Press.

Bergin, C. (2001). The parent–child relationship during beginning reading. *Journal of Literacy Research, 33,* 681–706.

Bernstein, B. (1965). *Class, codes, and control: Vol. 1. Theoretical studies toward a sociology of language.* London: Routledge & Kegan Paul.

Blachman, B. A. (1991). Phonological awareness: Implications for prereading and early reading instruction. In S. A. Brady & D. P. Shankweiler (Eds.), *Phonological processes in literacy: A tribute to Isabelle Y. Liberman* (pp. 29–36). Hillsdale, NJ: Erlbaum.

Blachman, B. A. (2000). Phonological awareness. In M. L. Kamil, P. B. Mosenthal, P. D. Pearson, & R. Barr (Eds.), *Handbook of reading research* (Vol. 3, pp. 483–502). Mahwah, NJ: Erlbaum.

Blachman, B. [A.], Ball, E., Black, R., & Tangel, D. (1994). Kindergarten teachers develop phoneme awareness in low-income, inner-city classrooms: Does it make a difference? *Reading and Writing, 6,* 1–17.

Block, C. C., Oakar, M., & Hurt, N. (2002). The expertise of literacy teachers: A continuum from preschool to grade 5. *Reading Research Quarterly, 37,* 178–206.

Bogatz, G. A., & Ball, S. (1971). *The second year of "Sesame Street": A continuing evaluation.* Princeton, NJ: Educational Testing Service.

Borkowski, J. G., & Dukewich, T. L. (1996). Environmental covariations and intelligence: How attachment influences self-regulation. In D. K. Detterman (Ed.), *Current topics in human intelligence: Vol. 5. The environment* (pp. 3–15). Norwood, NJ: Ablex.

Bos, C., Mather, N., Dickson, S., Podhajski, B., & Chard, D. (2001). Perceptions and knowledge of preservice and inservice educators about early reading instruction. *Annals of Dyslexia, 51,* 97–120.

Bowey, J. A. (1995). Socioeconomic status differences in preschool phonological sensitivity and first-grade reading achievement. *Journal of Educational Psychology, 87,* 476–487.

Bowey, J. A. (2002). Reflections on onset-rime and phoneme sensitivity as predictors of beginning word reading. *Journal of Experimental Child Psychology, 82,* 29–40.

Bowlby, J. (1969). *Attachment and loss: Vol. 1. Attachment.* New York: Basic Books.

Bradley, L. (1989). Predicting learning disabilities. In J. Dumont & H. Nakken (Eds.), *Learning disabilities: Vol. 2. Cognitive, social, and remedial aspects* (pp. 1–18). Amsterdam: Swets.

Bradley, L., & Bryant, P. E. (1983). Categorizing sounds and learning to read: A causal connection. *Nature, 301,* 419–421.

Bradley, L., & Bryant, P. [E.] (1985). *Rhyme and reason in reading and spelling* (International Academy for Research in Learning Disabilities Series). Ann Arbor: University of Michigan Press.

Bradley, L., & Bryant, P. [E.] (1991). Phonological skills before and after learning to read. In S. A. Brady & D. P. Shankweiler (Eds.), *Phonological processes in literacy: A tribute to Isabelle Y. Liberman* (pp. 37–45). Hillsdale, NJ: Erlbaum.

Briggs, C., & Elkind, D. (1973). Cognitive development in early readers. *Developmental Psychology, 9,* 279–280.

Burgess, S. R., & Lonigan, C. J. (1998). Bidirectional relations of phonological sensitivity and prereading abilities: Evidence from a preschool sample. *Journal of Experimental Child Psychology, 70,* 117–141.

Bus, A. G. (1993). Attachment and emergent literacy. *International Journal of Educational Research, 19,* 573–581.

Bus, A. G. (1994). The role of social context in emergent literacy. In E. M. H. Assink (Ed.), *Literacy acquisition and social context* (pp. 9–24). New York: Harvester Wheatsheaf.

Bus, A. G. (2001). Joint caregiver–child storybook reading: A route to literacy development. In S. B. Neuman & D. K. Dickinson (Eds.), *Handbook of early literacy research* (pp. 179–191). New York: Guilford Press.

Bus, A. G., Leseman, P. P. M., & Keultjes, P. (2000). Joint book reading across cultures: A comparison of Surinamese–Dutch, Turkish–Dutch, and Dutch parent–child dyads. *Journal of Literacy Research, 32,* 53–76.

Bus, A. G., & van IJzendoorn, M. H. (1988). Mother–child interactions, attachment, and emergent literacy: A cross-sectional study. *Child Development, 59,* 1262–1272.

Bus, A. G., & van IJzendoorn, M. H. (1992). Patterns of attachment in frequently and infrequently reading mother–child dyads. *Journal of Genetic Psychology, 153,* 395–403.

Bus, A. G., & van IJzendoorn, M. H. (1995). Mothers reading to their 3-year-olds: The role of mother–child attachment security in becoming literate. *Reading Research Quarterly, 30,* 998–1015.

Bus, A. G., & van IJzendoorn, M. H. (1999). Phonological awareness and early reading: A meta-analysis of experimental training studies. *Journal of Educational Psychology, 91,* 403–414.

Bus, A. G., van IJzendoorn, M. H., & Pellegrini, A. D. (1995). Joint book reading makes for success in learning to read: A meta-analysis on intergenerational transmission of literacy. *Review of Educational Research, 65,* 1–21.

Byrne, B., & Fielding-Barnsley, R. (1991). Evaluation of a program to teach phonemic awareness to young children. *Journal of Educational Psychology, 83,* 451–455.

Byrne, B., & Fielding-Barnsley, R. (1993). Evaluation of a program to teach phonemic awareness to young children: A 1-year follow-up. *Journal of Educational Psychology, 85,* 104–111.

Byrne, B., & Fielding-Barnsley, R. (1995). Evaluation of a program to teach phonemic awareness to young children: A 2- and 3-year follow-up and a new preschool trial. *Journal of Educational Psychology, 87,* 488–503.

Byrne, B., Fielding-Barnsley, R., & Ashley, L. (2000). Effects of preschool phoneme identity training after six years: Outcome level distinguished from rate of response. *Journal of Educational Psychology, 92, 659–667.*

Cardoso-Martins, C., & Pennington, B. F. (2004). The relationship between phoneme awareness and rapid serial naming skills and literacy acquisition: The role of developmental period and reading ability. *Scientific Studies of Reading, 8, 27–52.*

Carroll, J. M., Snowling, M. J., Hulme, C., & Stevenson, J. (2003). The development of phonological awareness in preschool children. *Developmental Psychology, 39,* 913–923.

Cassady, J. C., & Smith, L. L. (2003/2004). The impact of reading-focused integrated learning system on phonological awareness in kindergarten. *Journal of Literacy Research, 35,* 947–964.

Castiglioni-Spalten, M. L., & Ehri, L. C. (2003). Phonemic awareness instruction: Contribution of articulatory segmentation to novice beginners' reading and spelling. *Scientific Studies of Reading, 7,* 25–52.

Castle, J. M., Riach, J., & Nicholson, T. (1994). Getting off to a better start in reading and spelling: The effects of phonemic awareness instruction within a whole language program. *Journal of Educational Psychology, 86,* 350–359.

Chess, S., & Thomas, A. (1987). *Origins and evolution of behavior disorders: From infancy to early adult life.* Cambridge, MA: Harvard University Press.

Clark, M. M. (1976). *Young fluent readers: What can they teach us?* London: Heinemann.

Clark, R. (1983). *Family life and school achievement: Why poor black children succeed or fail.* Chicago: University of Chicago Press.

Clarke, L. K. (1988). Invented versus traditional spelling in first graders' writings: Effects on learning to spell and read. *Research in the Teaching of English, 22,* 281–309.

Clay, M. M. (1966). *Emergent reading behavior.* Unpublished doctoral dissertation. University of Auckland, New Zealand.

Clay, M. M. (1967). The reading behavior of five-year-old children: A research report. *New Zealand Journal of Educational Studies, 2,* 11–31.

Cochran-Smith, M. (1984). *The making of a reader.* Norwood, NJ: Ablex.

Cox, B. E. (1994). Young children's regulatory talk: Evidence of emerging metacognitive control over literary products and processes. In R. B. Ruddell, M. R. Ruddell, & H. Sinder (Eds.), *Theoretical models and processes of reading* (pp. 733–756). Newark, DE: International Reading Association.

Crain-Thoreson, C., & Dale, P. S. (1992). Do early talkers become early readers?: Linguistic precocity, preschool language, and emergent literacy. *Developmental Psychology, 28,* 421–429.

Crain-Thoreson, C., & Dale, P. S. (1995, April). *Parent vs. staff storybook reading as an intervention for language delay.* Paper presented at the biennial meeting of the Society for Research in Child Development, Indianapolis, IN.

Cunningham, A. E. (1990). Explicit versus implicit instruction in phonemic awareness. *Journal of Experimental Child Psychology, 50,* 429–444.

Cunningham, A. E., Perry, K. E., Stanovich, K. E., & Stanovich, P. J. (2004). Disciplinary knowledge of K–3 teachers and their knowledge calibration in the domain of early literacy. *Annals of Dyslexia, 54,* 139–167.

de Jong, P. F., & Bus, A. G. (2002). Quality of book-reading matters for emergent readers: An experiment with the same book in a regular or electronic format. *Journal of Educational Psychology, 94,* 145–155.

de Jong, P. F., & van der Leij, A. (1999). Specific contributions of phonological abilities to early reading acquisition: Results from a Dutch latent variable longitudinal study. *Journal of Educational Psychology, 91,* 450–476.

DeLoache, J. S., & DeMendoza, O. A. P. (1987). Joint picturebook interactions of mothers and 1-year-old children. *British Journal of Developmental Psychology, 5,* 111–123.

Delpit, L. (1995). *Other people's children: Cultural conflict in the classroom.* New York: New Press.

Dickinson, D. K., McCabe, A., Anastasopoulos, L., Peisner-Feinberg, E. S., & Poe, M. D. (2003). The comprehensive language approach to early literacy: The interrelationships among vocabulary, phonological sensitivity, and prior knowledge among preschool-aged children. *Journal of Educational Psychology, 95,* 465–481.

Dickinson, D. K., McCabe, A., & Clark-Chiarelli, N. (2004). Preschool-based prevention of reading disability. In C. A. Stone, E. R. Selliman, B. J. Ehren, & K. Apel (Eds.), *Handbook of language and literacy: Development and disorders* (pp. 209–227). New York: Guilford Press.

Dickinson, D. K., & Smith, M. W. (1994). Long-term effects of preschool teachers' book readings on low-income children's vocabulary and story comprehension. *Reading Research Quarterly, 29,* 104–122.

Duke, N. K. (2000a). For the rich it's richer: Print experiences and environments offered to children in very low- and very high-socioeconomic status first-grade classrooms. *American Educational Research Journal, 37,* 441–478.

Duke, N. K. (2000b). Print environments and experiences offered to first-grade students in very-low- and very-high-SES school districts. *Reading Research Quarterly, 35,* 456–457.

Dunning, D. B., Mason, J. M., & Stewart, J. P. (1994). Reading to preschoolers: A response to Scarborough & Dobrich (1994) and recommendations for future research. *Developmental Review, 14,* 324–339.

Durkin, D. (1966). *Children who read early.* New York: Teachers College Press.

Ehri, L. C. (1989). Movement into word reading and spelling: How spelling contributes to reading. In J. M. Mason (Ed.), *Reading and writing connections* (pp. 65–81). Boston: Allyn & Bacon.

Ehri, L. C., Nunes, S. R., Willows, D. M., Schuster, B. V., Yaghoub-Zadeh, Z., & Shanahan, T. (2001). Phonemic awareness instruction helps children learn to read: Evidence from the National Reading Panel's meta-analysis. *Reading Research Quarterly, 36,* 250–287.

Elbro, C., Borstrøm, I., & Petersen, D. K. (1998). Predicting dyslexia from kindergarten: The importance of distinctiveness of phonological representations of lexical items. *Reading Research Quarterly, 33,* 36–60.

Elbro, C., & Scarborough, H. S. (2004). Early identification. In T. Nunes & P. Bryant

Before Reading Words Begins 133

(Eds.), *Handbook of children's literacy* (pp. 339–359). Dordrecht, The Netherlands: Kluwer Academic.

Engel, S. (1986). *Learning to reminisce: A developmental study of how young children talk about the past.* Unpublished PhD dissertation, City University of New York, Graduate Center.

Erikson, E. (1968). *Identity: Youth and crisis.* New York: Norton.

Fagot, B. I., & Kavanaugh, K. (1993). Parenting during the second year: Effects of children's age, sex, and attachment classification. *Child Development, 64*, 258–271.

Feagans, L., & Haskins, R. (1986). Neighborhood dialogues of black and white 5-year-olds. *Journal of Applied Developmental Psychology, 7*, 181–200.

Federal Interagency Forum on Child and Family Statistics (1999). *America's children: Key national indicators of well-being, 1999.* Washington, DC: U.S. Government Printing Office.

Fernandez-Fein, S., & Baker, L. (1997). Rhyme and alliteration sensitivity and relevant experiences among preschoolers from diverse backgrounds. *Journal of Literacy Research, 29*, 433–459.

Fisch, S. M. (2004). *Children's learning from educational television: Sesame Street and beyond.* Mahwah, NJ: Erlbaum.

Flood, J. (1977). Parental styles in reading episodes with young children. *Reading Teacher, 30*, 864–867.

Foster, K. C., Erickson, G. C., Foster, D. F., Brinkman, D., & Torgesen, J. K. (1994). Computer administered instruction in phonological awareness: Evaluation of the *DaisyQuest* program. *Journal of Research and Development in Education, 27*, 126–137.

Frankel, K. A., & Bates, J. E. (1990). Mother–toddler problem-solving: Antecedents in attachment, home behavior, and temperament. *Child Development, 61*, 810–819.

Frijters, J. C., Barron, R. W., & Brunello, M. (2000). Direct and mediated influences on home literacy and literacy interest on preschoolers' oral vocabulary and early written language skill. *Journal of Educational Psychology, 92*, 466–477.

Fuchs, D., Fuchs, L. S., Thompson, A., Al Otaiba, S., Yen, L., Yang, N. J., Braun, M., & O'Connor, R. E. (2001). Is reading important in reading-readiness programs? A randomized field trial with teachers as program implementers. *Journal of Educational Psychology, 93*, 251–267.

Garton, A. F., & Pratt, C. (2004). Reading stories. In T. Nunes & P. Bryant (Eds.), *Handbook of children's literacy* (pp. 213–228). Dordrecht, The Netherlands: Kluwer Academic.

Gee, J. P. (2001). A sociocultural perspective on early literacy. In S. B. Neuman & D. K. Dickinson (Eds.), *Handbook of early literacy research* (pp. 30–42). New York: Guilford Press.

Goldenberg, C. (2001). Making schools work for low-income families in the 21st century. In S. B. Neuman & D. K. Dickinson (Eds.), *Handbook of early literacy research* (pp. 211–231). New York: Guilford Press.

Goldenberg, C., & Gallimore, R. (1995). Immigrant Latino parents' values and beliefs about their children's education: Continuities and discontinuities across cultures and generations. In P. R. Pintrich & M. Maehr (Eds.), *Advances in motiva-*

tion and achievement: Culture, ethnicity, and motivation (Vol. 9, pp. 183–228). Greenwich, CT: JAI Press.

Goldenberg, C., Reese, L., & Gallimore, R. (1992). Effects of school literacy materials on Latino children's home experiences and early reading achievement. *American Journal of Education, 100,* 497–536.

Gorey, K. M. (2001). Early childhood education: A meta-analytic affirmation of the short- and long-term benefits of educational opportunity. *School Psychology Quarterly, 16,* 9–30.

Goswami, U. (2000). Phonological and lexical processes. In M. Kamil, P. B. Mosenthal, P. D. Pearson, & R. Barr (Eds.), *Handbook of reading research* (Vol. 3, pp. 251–267). Mahwah, NJ: Erlbaum.

Goswami, U. (2001). Early phonological development and the acquisition of literacy. In S. B. Neuman & D. K. Dickinson (Eds.), *Handbook of early literacy research* (pp. 111–125). New York: Guilford Press.

Goswami, U. (2002a). In the beginning was the rhyme? A reflection on Hulme, Hatcher, Nation, Brown, Adams, and Stuart (2002). *Journal of Experimental Child Psychology, 82,* 47–57.

Goswami, U. (2002b). Phonology, reading development, and dyslexia: A cross-linguistic perspective. *Annals of Dyslexia, 52,* 141–163.

Goswami, U., & Bryant, P. E. (1990). *Phonological skills and learning to read.* Hillsdale, NJ: Erlbaum.

Griffith, P. L. (1991). Phonemic awareness helps first graders invent spellings and third graders remember correct spellings. *Journal of Reading Behavior, 23,* 215–233.

Hammer, C. S. (1999). Guiding language development: How African American mothers and their infants structure play. *Journal of Speech and Hearing Research, 42,* 1219–1233.

Hammer, C. S. (2001). Come sit down and let mama read: Book reading interactions between African American mothers and their infants. In J. Harris, A. Kamhi, & K. Pollock (Eds.), *Literacy in African American communities* (pp. 21–44). Mahwah, NJ: Erlbaum.

Hammett, L. A., van Kleeck, A., & Huberty, C. J. (2003). Patterns of parents' extratextual interactions during book sharing with preschool children: A cluster analysis study. *Reading Research Quarterly, 38,* 442–468.

Hart, B., & Risley, T. R. (1995). *Meaningful differences in the everyday experience of young American children.* Baltimore: Brookes.

Heath, S. B. (1982). What no bedtime story means: Narrative skills at home and school. *Language in Society, 11,* 49–76.

Heath, S. B. (1983). *Ways with words.* Cambridge, UK: Cambridge University Press.

Honig, B., Diamond, L., Gutlohn, L., & Mahler, J. (2000). *Teaching reading sourcebook for kindergarten through eighth grade.* Novato, CA: Arena Press.

Hudson, J. A. (1990). Constructive processing in children's event memory. *Developmental Psychology, 26,* 180–187.

Hulme, C., Hatcher, P. J., Nation, K., Brown, A., Adams, J., & Stuart, G. (2002). Phoneme awareness is a better predictor of early reading skill than onset-rime awareness. *Journal of Experimental Child Psychology, 82,* 2–28.

Juel, C. (1988). Learning to read and write: A longitudinal study of 54 children from first through fourth grades. *Journal of Educational Psychology*, *80*, 417–447.

Juel, C., Griffith, P. L., & Gough, P. B. (1986). Acquisition of literacy: A longitudinal study of children in first and second grade. *Journal of Educational Psychology*, *78*, 243–255.

Karchmer, R. A. (2001). The journey ahead: Thirteen teachers report how the Internet influences literacy and literacy instruction in their K–12 classrooms. *Reading Research Quarterly*, *36*, 442–466.

King, E. M., & Friesen, D. T. (1972). Children who read in kindergarten. *Alberta Journal of Educational Research*, *18*, 147–161.

Kirby, J. R., Parrila, R. K., & Pfeiffer, S. L. (2003). Naming speed and phonological awareness as predictors of reading development. *Journal of Educational Psychology*, *95*, 453–464.

Kohlberg, L., Yaeger, J., & Hjertholm, E. (1968). Private speech: Four studies and a review of theories. *Child Development*, *39*, 691–736.

Koskinen, P. S., Blum, I. H., Bisson, S. A., Phillips, S. M., Creamer, T. S., & Baker, T. K. (2000). Book access, shared reading, and audio models: The effects of supporting the literacy learning of linguistically diverse students in school and at home. *Journal of Educational Psychology*, *92*, 23–36.

Laakso, M.-L., Poikkeus, A.-M., & Lyytinen, P. (1999). Shared reading interaction in families with and without genetic risk for dyslexia: Implications for toddlers' language development. *Infant and Child Development*, *8*, 179–195.

Leichter, H. P. (1984). Families as environments for literacy. In H. Goelman, A. Oberg, & F. Smith (Eds.), *Awakening to literacy*. Exeter, NH: Heinemann.

Lesaux, N. K., & Siegel, L. S. (2003). The development of reading in children who speak English as a second language. *Developmental Psychology*, *39*, 1005–1019.

Leseman, P. P. M., & de Jong, P. F. (1998). Home literacy: Opportunity, instruction, cooperation, and social–emotional quality predicting early reading achievement. *Reading Research Quarterly*, *33*, 294–318.

Lie, A. (1991). Effects of a training program for stimulating skills in word analysis in first-grade children. *Reading Research Quarterly*, *26*, 234–250.

Linebarger, D. L., Kosanic, A. Z., Greenwood, C. R., & Doku, N. S. (2004). Effects of viewing the television program *Between the Lions* on the emergent literacy skills of young children. *Journal of Educational Psychology*, *96*, 297–308.

Lonigan, C. J. (1994). Reading to preschoolers exposed: Is the emperor really naked? *Developmental Review*, *14*, 303–323.

Lonigan, C. J., Anthony, J. L., & Burgess, S. R. (1995, April). *Exposure to print and preschool-age children's interest in literacy*. Paper presented at the biennial meeting of the Society for Research in Child Development, Indianapolis, IN.

Lundberg, I. (1991). Phonemic awareness can be developed without reading instruction. In S. A. Brady & D. P. Shankweiler (Eds.), *Phonological processes in literacy: A tribute to Isabelle Y. Liberman* (pp. 47–53). Hillsdale, NJ: Erlbaum.

Lundberg, I., Frost, J., & Peterson, O. (1988). Effects of an extensive program for stimulating phonological awareness in preschool children. *Reading Research Quarterly*, *23*, 263–284.

Maclean, M., Bryant, P., & Bradley, L. (1987). Rhymes, nursery rhymes, and reading in early childhood. *Merrill–Palmer Quarterly, 33*, 255–281.

Main, M., Kaplan, N., & Cassidy, J. (1985). Security in infancy, childhood, and adulthood: A move to the level of representation. In I. Bretherton & E. Waters (Eds.), Growing points of attachment theory and research. *Monographs of the Society for Research in Child Development, 50*(1/2, Serial No. 209), 66–104.

Mann, V. A. (2003). Language processes: Keys to reading disability. In H. L. Swanson, K. R. Harris, & S. Graham (Eds.), *Handbook of learning disabilities* (pp. 213–228). New York: Guilford Press.

Mann, V. A., & Foy, J. G. (2003). Phonological awareness, speech development, and letter knowledge in preschool children. *Annals of Dyslexia, 53*, 149–173.

Mann, V., Tobin, P., & Wilson, R. (1987). Measuring phonological awareness through the invented spellings of kindergarten children. *Merrill–Palmer Quarterly, 32*, 310–318.

Mann, V., & Wimmer, H. (2002). Phoneme awareness and pathways into literacy: A comparison of German and American children. *Reading and Writing, 15*, 653–682.

Matas, L., Arend, R. A., & Sroufe, L. A. (1978). Continuity of adaptation in the second year: The relationship between quality of attachment and later competence. *Child Development, 49*, 547–556.

McBride-Chang, C., & Kail, R. V. (2002). Cross-cultural similarities in the predictors of reading acquisition. *Child Development, 73*, 1392–1407.

McCutchen, D., Abbott, R. D., Green, L. B., Beretvas, N., Cox, S., Potter, N. S., Quiroga, T., & Gray, A. L. (2002a). Beginning literacy: Links among teacher knowledge, teacher practice, and student learning. *Journal of Learning Disabilities, 35*, 69–86.

McCutchen, D., Harry, D. R., Cunningham, A. E., Cox, S., Sidman, S., & Covill, A. E. (2002b). Reading teachers' knowledge of children's literature and English phonology. *Annals of Dyslexia, 52*, 207–228.

McGill-Franzen, A., Allington, R., Yokoi, L., & Brooks, G. (1999). Putting books in the room seems necessary but not sufficient. *Journal of Educational Research, 93*, 67–74.

Metsala, J. L. (1999). Young children's phonological awareness and nonword repetition as a function of vocabulary development. *Journal of Educational Psychology, 91*, 3–19.

Moats, L. C., & Foorman, B. R. (2003). Measuring teachers' content knowledge of language and reading. *Annals of Dyslexia, 53*, 23–45.

Morris, D., Bloodgood, J. W., Lomax, R. G, & Perney, J. (2003). Developmental steps in learning to read: A longitudinal study in kindergarten and first grade. *Reading Research Quarterly, 38*, 302–328.

Morrow, L. M. (1983). Home and school correlates of early interest in literature. *Journal of Educational Research, 76*, 221–230.

Morrow, L. M. (2001). *Literacy development in the early years: Helping children read and write* (4th ed.). Needham Heights, MA: Allyn & Bacon.

Moss, E. (1992). The socioaffective context of joint cognitive activity. In L. T. Winegar & J. Valsiner (Eds.), *Children's development within social context: Vol. 2. Research and methodology* (pp. 117–154). Hillsdale, NJ: Erlbaum.

Moss, E., & St. Laurent, D. (2001). Attachment at school age and academic performance. *Developmental Psychology, 37*, 863–874.

Murray, B. A. (1995, December). *A meta-analysis of phoneme awareness teaching
studies.* Paper presented at the National Reading Conference, New Orleans.

Murray, B. A., Stahl, S. A., & Ivey, M. G. (1996). Developing phoneme awareness
through alphabet books. *Reading and Writing: An Interdisciplinary Journal, 8*,
307–322.

Muter, V., Hulme, C., Snowling, M. J., & Stevenson, J. (2004). Phonemes, rimes,
vocabulary, and grammatical skills as foundations of early reading development: Evidence from a longitudinal study. *Developmental Psychology, 40*,
665–681.

Muter, V., & Snowling, M. (1998). Concurrent and longitudinal predictors of reading: The role of metalinguistic and short-term memory skills. *Reading Research
Quarterly, 33*, 320–335.

Näslund, J. C., & Schneider, W. (1996). Kindergarten letter knowledge, phonological
skills, and memory processes: Relative effects on early literacy. *Journal of Experimental Child Psychology, 62*, 30–59.

Nation, K., Allen, R., & Hulme, C. (2001). The limitations of orthographic analogy in
early reading development: Performance on the clue-word task depends on phonological priming and elementary decoding skill, not the use of orthographic
analogy. *Journal of Experimental Child Psychology, 80*, 75–94.

Nation, K., & Hulme, C. (1997). Phonemic segmentation, not onset-rime segmentation, predicts early reading and spelling skills. *Reading Research Quarterly, 32*,
154–167.

National Reading Panel. (2000). *Teaching children to read: An evidence-based assessment of the scientific research literature on reading and its implication for reading instruction—reports of the subgroups.* Washington, DC: National Institute
of Child Health and Development.

Nelson, K. (1993a). Events, narratives, and memory: What develops? In C. A. Nelson
(Ed.), *Memory and affect in development: Minnesota Symposium on Child Psychology* (Vol. 26, pp. 1–24). Hillsdale, NJ: Erlbaum.

Nelson, K. (1993b). Explaining the emergence of autobiographical memory in early
childhood. In A. F. Collins, S. E. Gathercole, M. A. Conway, & P. E. Morris
(Eds.), *Theories of memory* (pp. 355–385). Hillsdale, NJ: Erlbaum.

Nelson, K. (1996). *Language in cognitive development: The emergence of the mediated mind.* New York: Cambridge University Press.

Nelson, K., & Fivush, R. (2004). The emergence of autobiographical memory: A social cultural developmental memory. *Psychological Review, 111*, 486–511.

Neuhaus, G. F., & Swank, P. R. (2002). Understanding the relations between RAN letter subtest components and word reading in first-grade students. *Journal of
Learning Disabilities, 35*, 158–174.

Neuman, S. B. (1999). Books make a difference: A study of access to literacy. *Reading
Research Quarterly, 34*, 286–311.

Neuman, S. B., & Celano, D. (2001). Access to print in low-income and middle-
income communities: An ecological study of four neighborhoods. *Reading Research Quarterly, 36*, 8–26.

Neuman, S. B., & Roskos, K. (1997). Literacy knowledge in practice: Contexts of participation for young writers and readers. *Reading Research Quarterly*, 32, 10–32.

Ninio, A. (1980). Picture-book reading in mother–infant dyads belonging to two subgroups in Israel. *Child Development*, 51, 587–590.

O'Connor, R. E., Jenkins, J. R., & Slocum, T. A. (1995). Transfer among phonological tasks in kindergarten: Essential instructional content. *Journal of Educational Psychology*, 87, 202–217.

Ogbu, J. U. (1982). Societal forces as a context of ghetto children's school failure. In L. Feagans & D. C. Farran (Eds.), *The language of children reared in poverty* (pp. 117–138). New York: Academic Press.

Paratore, J., Melzi, G., & Krol-Sinclair, B. (1999). *What should we expect of family literacy?: Experiences of Latino children whose parents participate in an intergenerational literacy project.* Newark, DE: International Reading Association.

Parrila, R., Kirby, J. R., & McQuarrie, L. (2004). Articulation rate, naming speed, verbal short-term memory, and phonological awareness: Longitudinal predictors of early reading development? *Scientific Studies of Reading*, 8, 3–26.

Pellegrini, A. D. (2001). Some theoretical and methodological considerations in studying literacy in social context. In S. B. Neuman & D. K. Dickinson (Eds.), *Handbook of early literacy research* (pp. 54–65). New York: Guilford Press.

Pellegrini, A. D., Galda, L., Perlmutter, J., & Jones, I. (1994). *Joint reading between mothers and their Head Start children: Vocabulary development in two text formats* (Reading Research Report No. 13). Athens, GA, and College Park, MD: National Reading Research Center.

Pellegrini, A. D., Perlmutter, J. C., Galda, L., & Brody, G. H. (1990). Joint reading between black Head Start children and their mothers. *Child Development*, 61, 443–453.

Pennington, B. F., Groisser, D., & Welsh, M. C. (1993). Contrasting cognitive deficits in attention deficit hyperactivity disorder versus reading disability. *Developmental Psychology*, 29, 511–523.

Perfetti, C. A. (1992). The representation problem in reading acquisition. In P. B. Gough, L. C. Ehri, & R. Treiman (Eds.), *Reading acquisition* (pp. 145–174). Hillsdale, NJ: Erlbaum.

Perfetti, C. A., Beck, I., Bell, L., & Hughes, C. (1987). Phonemic knowledge and learning to read are reciprocal: A longitudinal study of first grade children. *Merrill–Palmer Quarterly*, 33, 283–319.

Pillemer, D. B., & White, S. H. (1989). Childhood events recalled by children and adults. In H. W. Reese (Ed.), *Advances in child development and behavior* (Vol. 21, pp. 297–340). San Diego: Academic Press.

Plessas, G. P., & Oakes, C. R. (1964). Prereading experiences of selected early readers. *Reading Teacher*, 17, 241–245.

Pratt, A. C., & Brady, S. (1988). Relation of phonological awareness to reading disability in children and adults. *Journal of Educational Psychology*, 80, 319–323.

Ratner, H. H. (1980). The role of social context in memory development. In M. Perlmutter (Ed.), *Children's memory: New directions for child development* (Vol. 10, pp. 47–67). San Francisco: Jossey-Bass.

Ratner, H. H. (1984). Memory demands and the development of young children's memory. *Child Development, 55*, 2173–2191.

Read, C. (1971). Pre-school children's knowledge of English phonology. *Harvard Educational Review, 41*, 1–34.

Reese, E., Haden, C., & Fivush, R. (1993). Mother–child conversations about the past: Relations of style and memory over time. *Cognitive Development, 8*, 141–148.

Ricci, C. M., & Beal, C. R. (2002). The effect of interactive media on children's story memory. *Journal of Educational Psychology, 94*, 138–144.

Richgels, D. J. (2001). Invented spelling, phonemic awareness, and reading and writing instruction. In S. B. Neuman & D. K. Dickinson (Eds.), *Handbook of early literacy research* (pp. 142–155). New York: Guilford Press.

Roser, N., & Martinez, M. (1985). Roles adults play in preschool responses to literature. *Language Arts, 62*, 485–490.

Roskos, K., & Neuman, S. B. (2001). Environment and its influences for early literacy teaching and learning. In S. B. Neuman & D. K. Dickinson (Eds.), *Handbook of early literacy research* (pp. 281–292). New York: Guilford Press.

Saada-Robert, M. (2004). Early emergent literacy. In T. Nunes & P. Bryant (Eds.), *Handbook of children's literacy* (pp. 575–598). Dordrecht, The Netherlands: Kluwer Academic.

Scarborough, H. S. (2001). Connecting early language and literacy to later reading (dis)abilities: Evidence, theory, and practice. In S. B. Neuman & D. K. Dickinson (Eds.), *Handbook of early literacy research* (pp. 97–110). New York: Guilford Press.

Scarborough, H. S., & Dobrich, W. (1994). On the efficiency of reading to preschoolers. *Developmental Review, 14*, 245–302.

Schaffer, H. R., & Emerson, P. E. (1964). Patterns of response to physical contact in early human behavior. *Journal of Child Psychology and Psychiatry, 5*, 1–13.

Schatschneider, C., Fletcher, J. M., Francis, D. J., Carlson, C. D., & Foorman, B. R. (2004). Kindergarten prediction of reading skills: A longitudinal comparative analysis. *Journal of Educational Psychology, 96*, 265–282.

Schneider, W., Roth, E., & Ennemoser, M. (2000). Training phonological skills and letter knowledge in children at risk for dyslexia: A comparison of three kindergarten intervention programs. *Journal of Educational Psychology, 92*, 284–295.

Sénéchal, M., LeFevre, J. A., Hudson, E., & Lawson, E. P. (1996). Knowledge of story books as a predictor of young children's vocabulary. *Journal of Educational Psychology, 88*, 520–536.

Shaywitz, S. E. (1996). Dyslexia. *Scientific American, 275*(5), 98–104.

Silven, M., Poskiparta, E., & Niemi, P. (2004). The odds of becoming a precocious reader of Finnish. *Journal of Educational Psychology, 96*, 152–164.

Slocum, T. A., O'Connor, R. E., & Jenkins, J. R. (1993). Transfer among phonological manipulation skills. *Journal of Educational Psychology, 85*, 618–630.

Snow, C. E. (1983). Literacy and language: Relationships during the preschool years. *Harvard Educational Review, 53*, 165–189.

Snow, C. E. (1991). The theoretical basis of the Home–School Study of Language and Literacy Development. *Journal of Research in Childhood Education, 6*, 1–8.

Snow, C. E., Barnes, W. S., Chandler, J., Goodman, I. F., & Hemphill, L. (1991). *Un-*

fulfilled expectations: Home and school influences on literacy. Cambridge, MA: Harvard University Press.

Sodoro, J., Allinder, R. M., & Rankin-Erickson, J. L. (2002). Assessment of phonological awareness: Review of methods and tools. *Educational Psychology Review, 14,* 223–260.

Sokolov, A. N. (1975). *Inner speech and thought.* New York: Plenum.

Sonnenschein, S., Baker, L., Serpell, R., Scher, D., Fernandez-Fein, S., & Munsterman, K. A. (1996). *Strands of emergent literacy and their antecedents in the home: Urban preschoolers' early literacy development* (Reading Research Report No. 48). Athens, GA, and College Park, MD: National Reading Research Center.

Spear-Swerling, L., & Brucker, P. O. (2003). Teachers' acquisition of knowledge about English word structure. *Annals of Dyslexia, 53,* 72–103.

Speece, D. L., Ritchey, K. D., Cooper, D. H., Roth, F. P., & Schatschneider, C. (2004). Growth in early reading skills from kindergarten to third grade. *Contemporary Educational Psychology, 29,* 312–332.

Sprenger-Charolles, L., Siegel, L. S., Bechennec, D., & Serniclaes, W. (2003). Development of phonological processing in reading aloud, in silent reading, and in spelling: A four-year longitudinal study. *Journal of Experimental Child Psychology, 84,* 194–217.

Storch, S. A., & Whitehurst, G. J. (2002). Oral language and code-related precursors to reading: Evidence from a longitudinal structural model. *Developmental Psychology, 38,* 934–947.

Sroufe, L. A. (1996). *Emotional development: The organization of emotional life in the early years.* Cambridge, UK: Cambridge University Press.

Stahl, S. A. (2003). What do we expect storybook reading to do? How storybook reading impacts word recognition. In A. van Kleeck, S. A. Stahl, & E. B. Bauer (Eds.), *On reading books to children: Parents and teachers* (pp. 363–383). Mahwah, NJ: Erlbaum.

Stahl, S. A., & Murray, B. A. (1994). Defining phonological awareness and its relationship to early reading. *Journal of Educational Psychology, 86,* 221–234.

Stahl, S. A., & Murray, B. A. (1998). Issues involved in defining phonological awareness and its relation to early reading. In J. Metsala & L. Ehri (Eds.), *Word recognition in beginning reading* (pp. 65–87). Mahwah, NJ: Erlbaum.

Stanovich, K. E. (1986). Matthew effects in reading: Some consequences of individual differences in the acquisition of literacy. *Reading Research Quarterly, 21,* 360–407.

Stanovich, K. E. (1988). Explaining the differences between the dyslexic and the garden-variety poor reader: The phonological-core variable-difference model. *Journal of Learning Disabilities, 21,* 590–604.

Steele, C. M. (1992). Race and the schooling of black Americans. *Atlantic Monthly, 269,* 67–78.

Stuart, M., & Masterson, J. (1992). Patterns of reading and spelling in 10-year-old children related to prereading phonological abilities. *Journal of Experimental Child Psychology, 54,* 168–187.

Sulzby, E., & Teale, W. (1987). *Young children's storybook reading: Longitudinal study of parent–child instruction and children's independent functioning* (Final Report to the Spencer Foundation). Ann Arbor: University of Michigan Press.

Sulzby, E., & Teale, W. (1991). Emergent literacy. In R. Barr, M. L. Kamil, P. B. Mosenthal, & P. D. Pearson (Eds.), *Handbook of reading research* (Vol. 2, pp. 727–758). New York: Longman.

Sunseth, K., & Bowers, P. G. (2002). Rapid naming and phonemic awareness: Contributions to reading, spelling, and orthographic knowledge. *Scientific Studies of Reading, 6,* 401–429.

Swanson, H. L., Trainin, G., Necoechea, D. M., & Hammill, D. M. (2003). Rapid naming, phonological awareness, and reading: A meta-analysis of the correlation evidence. *Review of Educational Research, 73,* 407–441.

Tabors, P. O., & Snow, C. E. (2001). Young bilingual children and early literacy development. In S. B. Neuman & D. K. Dickinson (Eds.), *Handbook of early literacy research* (pp. 159–178). New York: Guilford Press.

Tangel, D. M., & Blachman, B. A. (1992). Effect of phoneme awareness instruction on kindergarten children's invented spellings. *Journal of Reading Behavior, 24,* 233–261.

Tangel, D. M., & Blachman, B. A. (1995). Effect of phoneme awareness instruction on the invented spelling of first-grade children: A one-year follow-up. *Journal of Reading Behavior, 27,* 153–185.

Taylor, D., & Dorsey-Gaines, C. (1988). *Growing up literate: Learning from inner-city families.* Portsmouth, NH: Heinemann.

Taylor, D., & Strickland, D. (1986). *Family storybook reading.* Exeter, NH: Heinemann.

Teale, W. H. (1978). Positive environments for learning to read: What studies of early readers tell us. *Language Arts, 55,* 922–932.

Teale, W. (1986). Home background and young children's literacy development. In W. H. Teale & E. Sulzby (Eds.), *Emergent literacy: Writing and reading* (pp. 173–206). Norwood, NJ: Ablex.

Tessler, M. (1986). *Mother–child talk in a museum: The socialization of a memory.* New York: City University of New York, Graduate Center.

Thomas, A., & Chess, S. (1986). The New York Longitudinal Study: From infancy to early adult life. In R. Plomin & J. Dunn (Eds.), *The study of temperament: Changes, continuities, and challenges.* Hillsdale, NJ: Erlbaum.

Tolchinsky, L. (2004). Childhood conceptions of literacy. In T. Nunes & P. Bryant (Eds.), *Handbook of children's literacy* (pp. 11–29). Dordrecht, The Netherlands: Kluwer Academic.

Torgesen, J. K., & Burgess, S. R. (1998). Consistency of reading-related phonological processes throughout early childhood. In J. Metsala & L. Ehri (Eds.), *Word recognition in beginning reading* (161–188). Mahwah, NJ: Erlbaum.

Torgesen, J. K., Wagner, R. K., Rashotte, C. A., Burgess, S., & Hecht, S. (1997). Contributions of phonological awareness and rapid automatic naming ability to the growth of word-reading skills in second- and fifth-grade children. *Scientific Studies of Reading, 1,* 151–185.

Treiman, R. (1985). Phonemic analysis, spelling, and reading. In T. H. Carr (Ed.), *New directions for child development: The development of reading skills* (pp. 5–18). San Francisco: Jossey-Bass.

Uhry, J. K. (2002). Finger-point reading in kindergarten: The role of phonemic awareness, one-to-one correspondence, and rapid serial naming. *Scientific Studies of Reading, 6,* 319–342.

Valdez-Menchaca, M. C., & Whitehurst, G. J. (1992). Accelerating language development through picture book reading: A systematic extension to Mexican day care. *Developmental Psychology, 28,* 1106–1114.

van den Boom, D. C. (1994). The influence of temperament and mothering on attachment and exploration: An experimental manipulation of sensitive responsiveness among lower-class mothers and irritable infants. *Child Development, 65,* 1457–1477.

van den Boom, D. C. (1995). Do first-year intervention effects endure? Follow-up during toddlerhood of a sample of Dutch irritable infants. *Child Development, 66,* 1798–1816.

van IJzendoorn, M. H., Juffer, F., & Duyvesteyn, M. G. C. (1995). Breaking the intergenerational cycle of insecure attachment: A review of the effects of attachment-based interventions on maternal sensitivity and infant security. *Journal of Child Psychology and Psychiatry, 36,* 225–248.

van Kleeck, A. (2004). Fostering preliteracy development via storybook-sharing interactions: The cultural context of mainstream family practices. In C. A. Stone, E. R. Silliman, B. J. Ehren, & K. Apel (Eds.), *Handbook of language and literacy: Development and disorders* (pp. 175–208). New York: Guilford Press.

van Kleeck, A., Stahl, S. A., & Bauer, E. B. (2003). *On reading books to children: Parents and teachers.* Mahwah, NJ: Erlbaum.

Vellutino, F. R., & Scanlon, D. M. (1987). Phonological coding, phonological awareness, and reading ability: Evidence from a longitudinal and experimental study. *Merrill–Palmer Quarterly, 33,* 321–363.

Vernon-Feagans, L. (1996). *Children's talk in communities and classrooms.* Cambridge, MA: Blackwell.

Vernon-Feagans, L., Hammer, C. S., Miccio, A., & Manlove, E. (2001). Early language and literacy skills in low-income African American and Hispanic children. In S. B. Neuman & D. K. Dickinson (Eds.), *Handbook of early literacy research* (pp. 192–210). New York: Guilford Press.

Vygotsky, L. S. (1962). *Thought and language.* Cambridge, MA: MIT Press.

Vygotsky, L. S. (1978). *Mind in society: The development of higher psychological processes.* Cambridge, MA: Harvard University Press.

Wagner, R. K., Torgesen, J. K., Laughon, P., Simmons, K., & Rashotte, C. A. (1993). Development of young readers' phonological processing abilities. *Journal of Educational Psychology, 85,* 83–103.

Wagner, R. K., Torgesen, J. K., & Rashotte, C. A. (1994). The development of reading-related phonological processing abilities: New evidence of bi-directional causality from a latent variable longitudinal study. *Developmental Psychology, 30,* 73–87.

Wagner, R. K., Torgesen, J. K., Rashotte, C. A., Hecht, S. A., Barker, T. A., Burgess, S. R., Donahue, J., & Garon, T. (1997). Changing causal relations between phonological processing abilities and word-level reading as children develop from beginning to fluent readers: A five-year longitudinal study. *Developmental Psychology, 33,* 468–479.

Watson, R. (2001). Literacy and oral language: Implications for early literacy acquisition. In S. B. Neuman & D. K. Dickinson (Eds.), *Handbook of early literacy research* (pp. 43–53). New York: Guilford Press.

Wells, G. (1981). *Learning through interaction*. Cambridge, UK: Cambridge University Press.

Wesseling, R., & Reitsma, P. (2001). Preschool phonological representations and development of reading skills. *Annals of Dyslexia, 51*, 203–229.

White, R. W. (1959). Motivation reconsidered: The concept of competence. *Psychological Review, 66*, 297–333.

Whitehurst, G. J., Epstein, J. N., Angell, A. L., Payne, A. C., Crone, D. A., & Fischel, J. E. (1994). Outcomes of an emergent literacy intervention in Head Start. *Journal of Educational Psychology, 86*, 542–555.

Whitehurst, G. J., Falco, F. L., Lonigan, C. J., Fischel, J. E., DeBaryshe, B. D., Valdez-Menchaca, M. C., & Caulfield, M. (1988). Accelerating language development through picturebook reading. *Developmental Psychology, 24*, 552–559.

Whitehurst, G. J., & Lonigan, C. J. (1998). Child development and emergent literacy. *Child Development, 69*, 848–872.

Whitehurst, G. J., & Lonigan, C. J. (2001). Emergent literacy: Development from prereaders to readers. In S. B. Neuman & D. K. Dickinson (Eds.), *Handbook of early literacy research* (pp. 11–29). New York: Guilford Press.

Whitehurst, G. J., Zevenbergen, A. A., Crone, D. A., Schultz, M. D., Velting, O. N., & Fischel, J. E. (1999). Outcomes of an emergent literacy intervention from Head Start through second grade. *Journal of Educational Psychology, 91*, 261–272.

Williams, J. P. (1980). Teaching decoding with an emphasis on phoneme analysis and phoneme blending. *Journal of Educational Psychology, 72*, 1–15.

Wimmer, H., Landerl, K., Linortner, R., & Hummer, P. (1991). The relationship of phonemic awareness to reading acquisition: More consequence than precondition but still important. *Cognition, 40*, 219–249.

Windfuhr, K. L., & Snowling, M. J. (2001). The relationship between paired associate learning and phonological skills in normally developing readers. *Journal of Experimental Child Psychology, 80*, 160–173.

Wise, B. W., & Olson, R. K. (1995). Computer-based phonological awareness and reading instruction. *Annals of Dyslexia, 45*, 99–122.

Wood, S. S., Bruner, J. S., & Ross, G. (1976). The role of tutoring in problem solving. *Journal of Child Psychology and Psychiatry, 17*, 89–100.

Yaden, D. B., Jr., Rowe, D. W., & MacGillivray, L. (2000). Emergent literacy: A matter (polyphony) of perspectives. In M. L. Kamil, P. B. Mosenthal, P. D. Pearson, & R. Barr (Eds.), *Handbook of reading research* (Vol. 3, pp. 425–454). Mahwah, NJ: Erlbaum.

Yopp, H. K. (1995). Read-aloud books for developing phonemic awareness: An annotated bibliography. *Reading Teacher, 48*(6), 538–543.

Zevenbergen, A. A., Whitehurst, G. J., & Zevenbergen, J. A. (2003). Effects of a shared-reading intervention on the inclusion of evaluative devices in narratives of children from low-income families. *Journal of Applied Developmental Psychology, 24*, 1–15.

CHAPTER 5

Learning to
Recognize Words

In this chapter I take up a topic that is at the center of the current debate about beginning reading instruction and has been the focal point of debates about beginning reading for a very long time (Chall, 1967): How should children be taught to recognize words as part of beginning reading instruction? For readers who have read Jeanne S. Chall's classic *Learning to Read: The Great Debate* (1967), there will be a sense of *déjà vu* about much of this chapter, for in general Chall's conclusions from that book have endured. Today, more than ever, there is support for Chall's endorsement of code-emphasis (i.e., phonics-instructional) approaches to beginning reading over meaning-emphasis approaches that play down the need for explicit (i.e., synthetic, systematic) decoding instruction. A great deal of research has taken place since Chall's book first appeared in 1967, and even since its update (Chall, 1983), with much of the data supportive of Chall's positions. (For example, recall the word-level research reviewed in Chapter 2, documenting that very good readers sound out words, and the work reviewed in Chapter 3, making clear that for many struggling beginning readers their problem is that they cannot sound out words.) To be sure, new understanding has emerged from research since 1967, but I contend that most of those new findings are compatible with Chall's (1967) conclusions.

Nonetheless, many teachers identifying with the whole-language approach have resisted explicit, systematic teaching of decoding. I believe that one reason is that they have been convinced through the prominent whole-language texts (see Chapter 1) that recognition of words is not as Chall depicted it. A main motivation for this chapter is to inform the teaching community about the types of word recognition instruction that are supported by research evidence.

In this chapter, I review first the progress made in understanding the developmental progression from not being able to read words at all to skillful reading of words. The remainder of the chapter is organized around the two main approaches to teaching word recognition that have been most supported in scientific analyses to date: teaching students to sound out words and teaching them to decode new words by analogy to words they already know—that is, by using familiar parts of words, parts of words encountered in previously mastered words. I believe that these approaches are complementary. The evidence in support of these two approaches contrasts with the lack of support for word recognition that is focused more on semantic–contextual cues than graphemic–phonemic cues, the approach to word recognition favored in the whole-language texts reviewed in Chapter 1.

NATURAL DEVELOPMENT OF WORD RECOGNITION SKILLS

There is more than one way to recognize a word, with some more sophisticated than others (see Ehri, 1991, which informs much of what follows, for elaborate discussion of this point; also Ehri & Snowling, 2004; Siegel, 2003). In general, the more sophisticated a word recognition process, the later it appears in children's development of word recognition skills.

Logographic Reading

Many American 3-year-olds can "read" the trademark signs for McDonald's, Burger King, and Dunkin' Donuts. They are doing logographic reading (sometimes referred to as visual cue reading; e.g., Ehri, 1991), which involves using only salient visual characteristics of a display that includes a word to recognize the word rather than relying on letter–sound correspondences. There is an association for these children between the distinctive visual cues and the word. Thus, this generation of children often can read the word "Apple" on a computer or the same word on television when it is accompanied by the company's multicolored apple with a bite out of it; the word *Jell-O* has a memorable shape; *STOP* is read correctly by some children so long as it is in the middle of a red hexagon; many 5-year-olds can read the words *SCHOOL BUS* on the back of a large yellow vehicle; and what 4- to 5-year-old has trouble decoding Walt Disney's signature, even though it is written in script?

University of Texas psychologist Phillip B. Gough (reported in Gough, Juel, & Griffith, 1992) presented 4- to 5-year-olds with four words to read, one on each of four flashcards. One of the flashcards had a blue thumbprint on it. The participants went through the deck of cards until they could say each word given its card. Then, came the interesting part. Could the children say the word that had been presented with the blue thumbprint if they were shown the word on a clean card devoid of the thumbprint? No. Could they say the word if they were shown just the blue thumbprint? Yes. Gough et al. (1992) refer to this as selective association, which is another name for logographic reading or visual cue reading. Regardless of what it is called, it is the same process, and preschoolers typically can do it.

Although logographic reading is not real reading, it may play a role in facilitating real reading later on. Cronin, Farrell, and Delaney (1995) had children attempt to read logographs in context (e.g., "McDonald's" in the context of its logo, "Stop" on a stop sign). Some logos could be read by the children whereas others could not (e.g., "Zellers" on the Zellers sign). Then, the children were taught the same words as sight words. In general, words that children could read in the context of a logo were learned more quickly than words not read in the context of a logo. There were a variety of controls in the study, which led to the conclusion that learning to read a word in the context of a logo permitted transfer to learning to read the word outside of its logo context. Something was learned by the preschoolers in Cronin et al. (1995) about the words per se on logos!

Alphabetic Reading

Traditional decoding instruction emphasizes sounding out words using letter–sound relations. This mechanism is operative in both reading and writing well before the time when children know *all* of the letter–sound correspondences (e.g., Ehri & Wilce, 1985; Huba, 1984). For example, pre-schoolers who know some letter–sound correspondences use what they know to attempt invented spellings of familiar words. When readers know some letter–sound relationships, they also are capable of doing what Ehri (1991) refers to as phonetic cue reading, which is "reading" a word based on only a few of its letters. Ehri (1991) contrasts such phonetic cue reading with logographic reading, using the following example:

> Logographic readers might remember how to read *yellow* by the "two sticks" in the middle (Seymour & Elder, 1986). In contrast, phonetic cue readers might see the two *l*'s in *yellow*, hear their name in the pronunciation, and use this information to connect the spelling to the word in memory. (p. 391)

Certainly, however, such reading has its hazards. If the same letter cues are used for several words or if a cue used to decode some word is experienced in a new word, there may be mix-ups. For example, it is not uncommon for a child to misread a word as another similar word sharing common letters that is known to the child (e.g., *yellow* read for *pillow*; Ehri's [1991] interpretation of Seymour & Elder's [1986] data; Ehri & Wilce, 1987a, 1987b). And, of course, phonetic cue readers have a devil of a time if asked to learn a set of words that share letters (e.g., *pots, post, spot, stop*; Gilbert, Spring, & Sassenrath, 1977).

At some point after phonetic cue reading begins, a child comes to understand the alphabetic principle—that "all twenty-six of those strange little symbols that comprise the alphabet are worth learning and discriminating one from the other because [they stand] for . . . the sounds that occur in spoken words" (Adams, 1990, p. 245). Once this realization occurs, there are a number of specific decoding "rules" that must be acquired if the child is to read using the complete alphabet. Some are easy, for they require learning only one piece of information: The letter *b* is pronounced the same regardless of context, as are *d, f, l, n, r, v,* and *z*. Some letters are pronounced differently depending on other letters in the word; the most common example is that vowels are long if there is a final *e* in a syllable and short if there is not. Another example is that *c* is pronounced differently if followed by an *e* or an *i* than if followed by an *a, o,* or *u* (e.g., compare the pronunciation of the *c* sounds in *celestial, city, cat, cot,* and *cut*). In general, conditional rules (i.e., involving consideration of more than one letter to determine the sound of a particular letter) are acquired later than rules involving one letter–sound association (e.g., Venezky & Johnson, 1973). Eventually, young readers learn all of the letter–sound relationships, although there is much complex information to acquire (e.g., Gough et al., 1992):

> For only a minority of the letters (*b, d, f, l, n, r, v, z*) is it possible to identify the [sound] it represents. For the other 18, at least one additional letter must be identified before the identity of the word's first [sound] can be determined; in some cases, at least four more letters are required (compare *chord* and *chore*). The vast majority of the letter–sound correspondences of . . . English . . . are context dependent. (Gough et al., 1992, p. 39)

In addition to learning the letter–sound associations, the beginning reader must learn how to use them to decode words, mapping the individual sounds represented by the letters of a word and blending the sounds. At first, such reading is only accomplished with very great effort. Indeed, it is a matter of years before it becomes very fluent and effortless. Long before that, however, individual words can be identified with relatively little effort.

Sight-Word Reading

I doubt that anyone reading this text has had to sound out a single word in this chapter, except perhaps for unfamiliar proper names such as Ehri. Every word in this text is in readers' sight vocabularies. There probably was a time, however, when you would have sounded out each and every word in this chapter. Conducting many trials of successfully sounding out a word, however, increases the connections between the letter patterns defining the word and the word in memory (Adams, 1990, Chap. 9; Ehri, 1980, 1984, 1987, 1992).

Thus, on initial exposure to a word like *frog*, a child sounds the word out. Such sounding out begins a process in which the connections between each letter and adjacent letters are strengthened (e.g., between *fr-* and *-og*, as are connections defining the entire sequence of letters and letter combinations in the word (strengthening of the connection between *fr-* and *-og*). Eventually the spelling is represented in memory as a unit consisting of *frog*. By repeated reading, there is also a strengthening of the connections between this visual stimulus and the conceptual understanding in long-term memory that defines a frog, so that eventually even the briefest exposure to the word *frog* elicits thoughts of a green, jumpy thing. For many beginning readers, there is rapid sight-word development of commonly encountered words (for more discussion of the development of such automatic word recognition, see Chapter 6).

Reading by Analogy to Known Words

Eventually, letter strings that occur in many different words are perceived as wholes (e.g., repeated co-occurrence of *i*, *n*, and *g* results eventually in *-ing* being perceived as a unit; Stanovich & West, 1989). Prefixes and suffixes are obvious examples, but there are other recurring combinations, many of which are root words (e.g., *-take, mal-, ben-, do-*). When such familiar letter patterns are encountered, it is not necessary to decode alphabetically. Rather, there is a direct connection with the sound sequence in memory.

When words can be read by sight and recurring letter chunks can be processed as wholes, what LaBerge and Samuels (1974; also Samuels, Schermer, & Reinking, 1992) dubbed as automatic reading, there are tremendous advantages for the reader. According to automaticity theory, two processes must occur for a reader to understand a word: (1) The word must be decoded. (2) What is decoded must be comprehended. Both decoding and comprehension require use of short-term memory, that extremely limited resource that can be thought of as one's conscious attentional capacity.

With only 7 ± 2 slots in short-term memory (at best), decoding operations and comprehension processes compete for only a little bit of capacity.

Alphabetic decoding requires a great deal of attention on the part of the reader. Walk into many grade-1 classrooms on any morning, and there will be children during round-robin reading who will have all of their mental energy and attention devoted to the task of sounding out the words when it is their turn to read. If all of their attentional capacity is consumed by decoding, there is nothing left over for comprehension. The result is that words may be pronounced but not understood. One solution for the slow alphabetic decoder might be to decode first and then comprehend. The cost of this is enormous: Because decoding and comprehending are done in sequence, the phonological representation of the word must be held in short-term memory, which involves further reduction of capacity that is needed for comprehension. No matter how the alphabetic reader approaches the task, there is strain on short-term capacity.

Automatic sight-word reading and automatic recognition of commonly encountered word chunks (e.g., prefixes, suffixes, root words, frequently encountered combinations of letters such as -ake and -op), in contrast, require little effort or attention, and thus there is substantial mental capacity left over for comprehension (e.g., Baron, 1977). With experience in reading comes faster, more accurate, and less effortful reading (e.g., Horn & Manis, 1987). A paradox of slow, high-effort, alphabetic reading is that it is less certain to result in accurate decoding than fast, low-effort, automatic decoding via sight words and word chunks.

Once readers know a variety of word chunks, they are in a position to exploit the principle that words with the same spelling pattern often sound the same. Thus, a child who knows how to pronounce *beak* could make a good guess at *peak* the first time it is encountered simply by decoding by analogy (i.e., "This is like *beak*, only it starts with a *p*!"). That same *beak*-word knower would have a fighting chance with *bean*, *bead*, and *beat* as well, using the analogy strategy. Adams (1990, pp. 210–211) provides the example of good readers quickly pronouncing the little-used word *kail* to rhyme with *ail*, *bail*, *tail*, *Gail*, and *hail*. Each time a word with -*ail* in it is encountered and pronounced with the long *a* sound, the association between -*ail* and the long *a* sound is strengthened. Thus, when *kail* is encountered by someone who has had many exposures to the -*ail* and long *a* association, there is automatic activation of *kail* and it is pronounced correctly almost without thinking.

For the most part, analogy has been considered an advanced strategy used only by adults or by children who have been reading awhile, with Australian researcher H. G. Marsh and colleagues especially strong advocates of this position (e.g., Marsh, Desberg, & Cooper, 1977; Marsh, Friedman, Desberg, & Saterdahl, 1981; Marsh, Friedman, Welch, & Desberg, 1981). The case is made later in this chapter (and continued in Chapter 6), however, that children can be taught to decode by analogy well before they might do so on their own.

Summary and Comment

There can be little doubt that when children are immersed in the world of language and print, there is some natural development of their word-reading skills. The holistic and insensitive visual pattern matching that is logographic reading is only the start of a process that becomes the processing of every single letter and the construction of knowledge about commonly occurring letter patterns. That children naturally learn to sound out words and decode by analogy based on frequently encountered word chunks highlights that the instructional recommendations in this chapter only involve systematic elaboration and intensification of powerful natural learning processes. When all of the learning to read is left to children's natural discovery of letter–sound associations and development of knowledge of word chunks, however, reading development is slower and less certain than it can be when children are taught to sound out words and/or decode by analogy. That is why the best-informed reading researchers and educators focus so much attention on teaching beginning readers to decode, increasingly using the methods detailed in the remainder of this chapter (see also Lovett, Barron, & Benson, 2003; O'Connor & Bell, 2004).

TEACHING STUDENTS TO SOUND OUT WORDS

Many children can be taught to decode words by focusing on the sounds associated with individual letters and letter combinations and blending those sounds to produce a reading of the word. Once the word is read, the child will recognize it. Thus, once a child decodes "dog" by sounding it out, the child recognizes a word he or she has been hearing and using for several years. Since the child who is learning to read knows the meaning of many of the words in books appropriate for beginning readers, understanding of the word once it is decoded is likely.

The criticality of phonemic awareness as a beginning reading competency becomes obvious in the context of the sounding-out strategy. As you will recall from Chapter 4, phonemic awareness is the realization that words are composed of sounds. It would make no sense to a child lacking this insight to attend to the letters of a word and attempt to sound it out! That is, before instruction about sounding out a word can make any sense, it is essential that the child understand that words are amalgams of sounds.

In fact, there is research support for the claim that learning to decode depends on phonemic awareness. One study that is cited frequently regarding this point was conducted in Australia by Tunmer, Herriman, and Nesdale (1988), who observed that the first graders who were most certain to make progress in learning to decode were those who possessed phonemic awareness and knew the names of letters. Another frequently cited study making the same point was reported by Fox and Routh (1975), who found that 4-year-olds who could segment words into constituent phonemes benefited from decoding instruction involving the segmentation of words into constituent letters, the mapping of letters to sounds, and the blending of sounds. Four-year-olds who could not segment words into constituent phonemes did not benefit from such decoding instruction.

Beyond phonemic awareness, however, the child who is to sound out words needs to know more. A particularly important prerequisite to acquisition of decoding skills is knowledge of the associations between letters and the sounds they make.

Letter–Sound Associations

There is much that can be taught about letters. In recent generations, something that has been known by many, although not all, young children by the time they enter kindergarten is the names of letters. In part, this is due to intentional educational efforts by our society to teach the alphabet to all preschoolers, perhaps most prominently through *Sesame Street* (e.g., Anderson & Collins, 1988; Ball & Bogatz, 1970; Bogatz & Ball, 1971; Mielke, 2001; Zill, 2001). *Sesame Street* makes contributions to the development of literacy over and above family interactions and other sources of stimulation (e.g., Rice, Huston, Truglio, & Wright, 1990). This television program does much to get preschoolers off to a good start. Perhaps even more impressive, the benefits of watching *Sesame Street* can be detected many years later, when graduates of the *Street* are adolescents (Huston, Anderson, Wright, Linebarger, & Schmitt, 2001; Wright, Huston, Scantlin, & Kotler, 2001).

Knowing letter names is not sufficient knowledge for learning to decode, however. Learning to analyze a printed word into component sounds followed by blending of those sounds requires knowledge of the letter–sound associations. Young readers need to learn about both the long and short vowel sounds as well as the sounds associated with the consonants. That is, they need to know various ways that *g* can sound when encountered in a word, as well as all the other consonants of the alphabet. Such instruction highlights that some letters sound the same regardless of the letters around them in a word (i.e., *b*, *d*, *l*, *n*, *r*, *v*, and *z* make the same sound regardless of the letter context in which they are embedded). Other letters sound different depending on context, for example, *c* is pronounced differently in *cut* than in *city*. Of course, the long vowel sounds occur when there is a final silent *e* in a syllable but often are short when there is no final *e*. In addition to learning the sounds associated with individual letters, good phonics instruction also covers the consonant digraphs (*sh*, *ch*, *th*, and *wh*) and the common consonant blends (e.g., *dr*, *bl*, *sk*, *sch*, and *tw*). In general, a lot of teaching about consonants and vowels and the sounds they make must take place if children are to learn how to decode words. There is some debate about exactly how many sounds there are in English, with a number between 43 and 46 most typically mentioned.

There is certainly a lot for children to learn when they are acquiring the associations between letters and sounds. The most common way of dealing with the very great memory demand is for the letter–sound associations to be taught over a long period of time, with many repetitions and many examples in the context of exercises and games involving letters and their sounds. (P. M. Cunningham, 1995, and Fox, 1996, are filled with suggestions about activities that build knowledge of letter–sound associations.) Of course, such activities are typically in the context of real reading and writing, which also permit many opportunities for use and review of the letter–sound associations.

Some researchers and educators who are aware of the memory demands involved in learning the initial letter–sound associations have gone further, however. Ehri, Deffner, and Wilce (1984) created a set of pictorial memory aids for learning letter–sound associations (see Figure 5.1). Thus, for each consonant sound, children are presented a mnemonic picture that integrates the physical letter and a word beginning with the sound associated with the letter. Can you see the *h* in the picture of a house in the top portion of Figure 5.1? How about a *v* in the picture of a vase of flowers? I had a little trouble seeing the *y* in yak, but found the picture of a yak with a decidedly y-shaped head to be very memorable. The *w* in the wings of the butterfly took me a second to see at first, but now I almost always think of *w* when I see butterfly wings—even on real butterflies! Ditto for the *g* in glasses.

Ehri and colleagues' (1984) approach is based on the well-established fact that even very young children can remember picture mnemonics (Pressley, 1977). Rather than simply assuming that this approach is effective because mnemonics generally work for young children, Ehri et al. (1984) conducted a well-controlled experiment demonstrating clearly that picture mnemonics really did increase the rate at which children learned letter–sound associations.

Unfortunately, Ehri et al. (1984) never made their materials available commercially. Thus, individual classroom teachers who wish to use the picture–mnemonic approach are going to have to produce their own picture

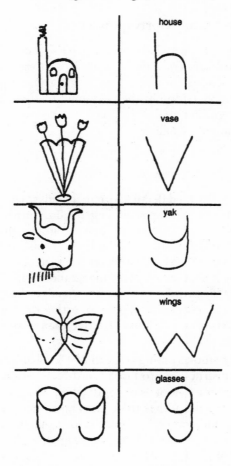

FIGURE 5.1. Mnemonic–pictorial aids for learning letter–sound associations. From Ehri, Deffner, and Wilce (1984). Copyright 1984 by the American Psychological Association. Reprinted by permission.

mnemonics. I have not tried it but have talked to some teachers who have, and they tell me that with a little imagination it is possible to produce memorable mnemonic pictures for all of the letter–sound associations in English.

Learning the letter–sound associations, which confers some intellectual power, is no small achievement. For example, Byrne and Fielding-Barnsley (1990, 1991) determined that preschoolers with phonemic awareness who also knew the letter–sound associations were very adept at decoding unfamiliar words compared to other preschoolers. Even so, there is much to be said for also teaching young readers how to blend the sounds of letters.

Blending Letter–Sound Correspondences

I suspect that as long as there have been teachers teaching students to read, there have been teachers teaching students to analyze words into component sounds and blend the sounds. This instructional approach and its effectiveness is well understood at the beginning of the 21st century largely because of a distinguished mid-20th-century analysis of beginning reading carried out by Jeanne S. Chall.

Chall's (1967, 1983) Analyses and Summaries

Chall (1967, 1983) provided detailed original analyses and reviews of other analyses of the effectiveness of beginning reading instruction. One of the major conclusions of her review was that programs that included "synthetic phonics" instruction (sometimes referred to as systematic or explicit phonics instruction), in which the students are systematically taught letter–sound associations and how to blend the sounds made by letters to pronounce and recognize words, were more effective than other programs. There was a great diversity of findings supporting the conclusion that synthetic phonics instruction was more effective than alternatives.

   • In reviewing studies dating back to 1912, Chall found evidence that synthetic phonics instruction produced word recognition and oral reading during grade 1 superior to look–say approaches, which emphasize students learning words as wholes rather than learning to decode via phonics. Although vocabulary and comprehension tended to be better in grade 1 with the look–say approach, students receiving synthetic phonics measures did better by the end of grade 2. Although look–say students seemed to read faster than did synthetic phonics students, it was at the price of less accuracy.
   • Chall also found studies contrasting synthetic phonics instruction with what she termed intrinsic phonics instruction (sometimes referred to as analytic or implicit phonics). Intrinsic phonics teaching involves analyzing the sounds of known sight words, although word analysis is played down in favor of semantic–contextual and picture cues as means for word recognition. (Notably, intrinsic phonics instruction seems to be closest to the phonics instruction that whole-language theorists claim to do as part of whole-language teaching.) Although these comparisons dated back to 1926, in fact, interest in the issue of whether synthetic or intrinsic phonics produced better readers was especially pronounced in the decade preceding Chall's (1967) text, largely because the most popular reading textbook series of the day used an intrinsic phonics approach. (That is what was going on in many classrooms that used Dick-and-Jane readers: Students learned

to read whole words; once the whole words were acquired, they were analyzed into constituent sounds as part of instruction.)

Studies comparing the intrinsic phonics approach with the synthetic
phonics approach produced clear results. Oral word recognition was better
for students taught with synthetic phonics than for students taught with intrinsic phonics. Spelling tended to be better for students instructed with systematic phonics, with this superiority holding across the elementary grades.
Also, at least during the primary grades, the performance of synthetic phonics
students on standardized vocabulary tests exceeded the performance of intrinsic phonics students. Although not quite as pronounced, the same pattern was observed for standardized comprehension.

• In analyzing the studies up through 1965, Chall (1967) found evidence that synthetic phonics was effective relative to alternatives for the
broad range of abilities, from low IQ to high IQ. Synthetic phonics seemed
to be especially beneficial for low-IQ students, with Chall speculating that
approaches which involve a great deal of induction, such as intrinsic phonics,
might be too difficult for low-IQ students.

• In 1965–1966, the U.S. Office of Education conducted the *Comparative First Grade Studies*, which involved 27 comparative studies of the
various methods used to teach grade-1 reading. Several analyses of these
data resulted in the conclusion that code-based approaches to beginning
reading instruction produced primary-grade reading superior to that produced by other methods, particularly meaning-based methods of the day—
the look–say, intrinsic phonics approaches (Chall, 1983; Guthrie & Tyler,
1975).

• When Head Start was extended into the elementary grades as Follow Through, several Follow Through models were tried. The outcomes
produced by them were then contrasted in formal studies. Variations of
Follow Through that included systematic phonics instruction (which involved direct instruction of phonics in a basal instructional program) produced a better performance on primary-level standardized tests than did
alternative approaches (Abt Associates, 1977; Kennedy, 1978; Stallings,
1975). Chall (1983) interpreted these results as clear evidence favoring systematic phonics for children who are at risk for school failure because they
are living in poverty.

• Beginning in 1967, a number of laboratory studies of phonics instruction were carried out. In general, the critical dependent variable in
these studies was ability to read words not seen before. Both teaching letter–
sound associations and teaching of blending proved potent in these comparisons (Chall, 1983, Table I-1, p. 14).

• From the appearance of Chall's *Learning to Read: The Great Debate* (1967) through the publication of the updated edition of the book
(1983), there were a number of studies conducted in classrooms explicitly

contrasting systematic, direct, synthetic phonics instruction with less systematic, indirect, implicit phonics instruction. Across a variety of measures of word recognition, oral reading, comprehension, vocabulary, and spelling, when there was a difference (and often there was), it favored direct, synthetic phonics instruction over indirect, intrinsic approaches (Chall, 1983, Table I-2, pp. 18–20).

Adams's (1990) Analysis and Summary

The next really important book appraising the effectiveness of systematic phonics instruction was Marilyn Adams's (1990) *Beginning to Read*. She reviewed Chall's data analyses and conclusions for a new generation of readers. Beyond that, she also reviewed theory and evidence produced since Chall's book that was supportive of the case for systematic decoding instruction. For example, Adams (1990, Chap. 11) reviewed how modern basal programs cover phonics versus how they should do so based on contemporary evidence.

Adams also made the case that explicit decoding instruction is now understood to involve a number of different acquisitions:

• Adams reviewed the evidence that kindergarten and grade-1 students often need to be taught the alphabetic principle: "One wants the students to understand that all twenty-six of those strange little symbols that comprise the alphabet are worth learning and discriminating one from the other because each stands for one of the sounds that occur in spoken words" (p. 245).

• Adams established for her readers that students need to learn the physical representation of each letter. That is, they need to acquire the distinctive features of letters (Gibson, Gibson, Pick, & Osser, 1962; Gibson & Levin, 1975). In doing so, they learn the difference between *P* and *R* as a single feature (i.e., the left-to-right downward diagonal in *R*) as well as the difference between *P* and *B* and *R* and *B* as single features (i.e., there is a fat rightward bulge in the bottom half of *B* that does not occur in *P* or *R*).

• Adams overviewed why students must learn the specific sounds that are associated with each letter and the common letter combinations in English (see Table 5.1, later in this chapter), taking up the pros and cons of various orders of teaching the letter–sound correspondences (e.g., short versus long vowels first, consonants before vowels).

• Adams contended that students need much practice in learning to blend sounds, since reading a word consists both of analyzing the letter–sound correspondences and blending those correspondences to pronounce a word.

• Adams reviewed as well the case for teaching phonics rules such as these: "When there are two vowels side by side, the long sound of the first one is heard and the second is usually silent"; "Words having double *ee* usually have the long *e* sound"; and "The two letters *ow* make the long *o* sound." She made a compelling case for not relying exclusively on phonics rules: First, none of the rules is entirely reliable. Second, learning the rules in no way can substitute for the complicated network of understandings about letter–sound correspondences that develops through learning the letter–sound correspondences and blending them to sound out words.

• Adams was emphatic that beginning reading instruction involves a great deal of reading words in real texts. Reading of actual texts makes clear to students why they are learning to decode individual words, and it should include many opportunities to apply the decoding skills being learned. Success in reading during the primary years depends on a heavy dose of reading texts that contain the letter–sound associations and combinations that the child's reading program teaches—that is, a heavy dose of so-called decodable texts (Juel & Roper/Schneider, 1985).

Thus, Adams's (1990) endorsement of the reading of texts from the beginning of reading instruction seems superficially consistent with whole-language recommendations. The texts Adams favors, however, are ones emphasizing the graphemic–phonemic elements that the child knows at some level already (i.e., through instruction). Reading of such decodable texts is not favored by whole-language theorists who want children to read authentic children's literature, which often includes many letter–sound combinations unfamiliar to the child. Indeed, the whole-language theorists have succeeded in nearly eradicating decodable texts from American classrooms. Even basal reading programs had far fewer decodable texts during the whole-language era than they did in earlier eras, reflecting the response of many basal publishers to make their materials as consistent as possible with whole-language principles (Hoffman et al., 1993). As such, the texts are much less consistent with the characteristics of excellent reading instructional materials based on the ideas developed in Adams (1990).

In short, Adams (1990) provided a powerful review of the evidence supporting the systematic teaching of phonics in beginning reading instruction, as well as a review of the scientific evidence supporting up-to-date phonics instruction. Adams also argued for such instruction on the basis of recent analyses of expert reading. She presented much evidence of letter- and word-level processing when skilled readers read.

In doing so, Adams (1990) explained to her readers how one of the foundational conclusions of the whole-language movement was simply not supported by data. That hypothesis, advanced first by Frank Smith and Kenneth S. Goodman (Goodman, 1972; Smith, 1971, 1973, 2004; Smith & Goodman, 1971), was that recognizing words in written context (i.e., in sentences, paragraphs, chapters, and/or whole texts) involves the coordinated use of semantic–contextual information (i.e., the meaning of the text up until a difficult-to-recognize word is encountered), syntactic–contextual information (i.e., the syntactic role of the difficult-to-recognize word as reflected by its position in a sentence), and graphemic–phonemic cues (i.e., as represented by the letter sequence defining the word).

According to Smith and Goodman, readers know a great deal about language, about the meanings of words and the words that might appear in particular meaningful contexts. They also know a great deal about syntactic constraints and the syntactic roles that particular words can play in sentences. When encountering unknown words, according to Goodman (1967), readers engage in a "psycholinguistic guessing game," combining semantic, syntactic, and graphemic–phonemic cues in order to make a stab at the word.

The greatest problem with this hypothesis, as Adams (1990) detailed, is that it is not consistent with the data on skilled reading generated in the past several decades. For example, many different analyses have confirmed that skilled readers sound out words that they do not know (e.g., Barron, 1986; Patterson & Coltheart, 1987; Perfetti, Bell, & Delaney, 1988). Moreover, according to the psycholinguistic guessing-game thinking, eye movements should reveal that many words are being skipped over by the eyes. Certainly, there could be no way that individual letters could be processed given the speed of eye movements and the relatively large amount of time needed to process letters, at least as Smith (1978, Chap. 2) conceived of the literature on eye movement and letter-level processing available at the time that he wrote his book.

In fact, the analyses of eye movements produced in the past two decades have made clear that most words are looked at during reading and that the individual letters in the words are processed (McConkie, Zola, Blanchard, & Wolverton, 1982; Rayner, Inhoff, Morrison, Slowiaczek, & Bertera, 1981; see Chapter 2 of this volume). Moreover, it is weaker readers rather than good readers who rely on context cues and, in so doing, often misread words (e.g., Nicholson, 1991; Nicholson, Lillas, & Rzoska, 1988; Rayner & Pollatsek, 1989; Stanovich, 1980, 1986; Waterman & Lewandowski, 1993).

Even though Adams's (1990) book made the case that good readers rely principally on word- and letter-level cues to read words, basal publishers and others during the whole language era abandoned materials that supported the development of word- and letter-level skills. Even though it is poor readers who rely on semantic–contextual and syntactic–contextual cues, largely because they are not proficient at using graphemic–phonemic cues to decode text, basal publishers and others succumbed to the pressure from whole-language proponents to include many more predictable texts,

texts that encourage and permit guessing of words on the basis of semantic and syntactic cues (Hoffman et al., 1993). That this is questionable has been further substantiated by research since Adams (1990).

Recent Research

Since Adams's (1990) book, there have been additional analyses supportive of the direct teaching of synthetic phonics, contrary to the most important assumptions of the whole-language approach as represented in the writings of Kenneth S. Goodman, Constance Weaver, and like-minded curriculum specialists. There are four studies (Foorman, Francis, Novy, & Liberman, 1991; Lovett, Ransby, Hardwick, Johns, & Donaldson, 1989; Lovett et al., 1994; Nicholson, 1991), in particular, that were very telling in turning around thinking about how word recognition should be taught.

Nicholson (1991) directly confronted one of the pieces of evidence most frequently cited in support of the whole-language approach to word recognition. In a study conducted by Goodman (1965), students in grades 1–3 first read lists of words. Then, the children were presented the same words to read in meaningful text. The students made many more errors when they read the words out of context (i.e., when the words were in lists) than they did when the words were read in context. This, of course, is consistent with the hypothesis that reading will be facilitated when semantic–contextual and syntactic–contextual cues are present (i.e., when words are read as part of a text) compared to when words are read devoid of context cues (i.e., when words are read on lists). This finding has been used repeatedly to defend the whole-language practice of teaching students to recognize words by analyzing syntactic, graphemic–phonemic, and especially semantic cues.

Nicholson (1991) detected several very serious shortcomings in the Goodman (1965) study, however. First, no attention was paid in the Goodman (1965) investigation to the patterns of performance by good and poor readers. In addition, the participants always read the lists followed by reading of the words in context, and thus there was the possibility that the improved performance in moving from list reading to reading in context might reflect some type of practice effect (i.e., the words in context had been seen before, on the lists).

In Nicholson (1991), students once again were asked to process words in lists and in context. In this study, however, the list–context order was manipulated such that some participants read the lists first and others read the words in context first. Moreover, there was systematic analysis of reading as a function of the grade of participants and their reading abilities relative to other students (i.e., good, average, weak). The outcomes in this study were anything but consistent with Goodman's (1965) results:

- Some readers did benefit from reading the words in the sentence context—namely, poor readers at each age level and average 6- and 7-year-olds.
- In contrast, a positive effect on reading was obtained in sentence context for good 6-year-old readers and average 8-year-olds only when reading words in sentence contexts followed reading words in lists, consistent with the practice effect explanation of the original Goodman (1965) finding.
- There was no positive effect derived from reading words in context for good 7- and 8-year-old readers. Indeed, when the 8-year-old good readers did sentence-context reading first, they did better on reading of the words in list format.

In short, Nicholson's (1991) results are consistent with the conclusion that semantic contexts aid weaker younger readers but are not helpful for better older readers. Thus, teaching children to attend to semantic–contextual cues is teaching them to use an immature strategy associated with poorer reading. In contrast, good readers can read based on graphemic–phonemic cues alone.

The other analyses produced in the late 1980s and early 1990s that were considered as supportive of Chall's (1967, 1983) and Adams's (1990) conclusions were instructional studies (e.g., Foorman et al., 1991; Lovett et al., 1989; Lovett et al., 1994). These studies provided supportive evidence of the importance of synthetic phonics instruction as conceived of by Chall (1967)—that is, instruction focusing on letter–sound associations and the blending of letters and sounds to produce words.

Foorman et al. (1991) examined the reading development of grade-1 students enrolled in one of two types of programs: Half the students were experiencing instruction driven by a basal series that emphasized reading words in meaningful context; the meaningful-context cues were emphasized as critical in deciding what an unknown word might be, and relatively little instruction was given in sounding out words in order to recognize them. The other half of the students were enrolled in a program emphasizing letter–sound associations and the blending of sounds to produce whole words. The students experiencing the two programs were matched for socioeconomic status, with the participants all coming from lower-middle-class to middle-class populations in an urban area. By the end of the year, students who were enrolled in the classes experiencing synthetic phonics instruction were reading and spelling words better than the participants in the classrooms emphasizing the use of semantic context cues during decoding.

In a more recent study complementing Foorman et al. (1991), Foorman, Francis, Fletcher, and Schatschneider (1998) examined three types of instruction delivered to Title 1 students in grades 1 and 2. One group received a heavy dose of synthetic phonics instruction with lots of practice with decodable texts (i.e., texts written to emphasize practice in sounding out skills). A second group received synthetic phonics instruction but in the context of a program emphasizing more reading of real literature. A third group received analytic phonics with emphasis on reading of real literature. With respect to word recognition, the best outcomes at the end of a year of instruction were observed in the group receiving synthetic phonics and decodable text. Although other measures (e.g., comprehension) descriptively favored this group as well, the effects on other measures were not as striking as on word recognition.

Maureen W. Lovett and her associates focused their attention on students experiencing extreme difficulties in learning to read. The participating students in that work were so far behind in reading that they had been referred to the Hospital for Sick Children (in Toronto, Canada), Lovett's home institution, for potential diagnosis and treatment. Lovett et al. (1989) succeeded in improving the decoding of very weak readers between ages 9 and 13 through intensive instruction in letter–sound analyses and blending (i.e., tutoring in very small groups of children), which also improved student performance on a measure of standardized reading comprehension. Lovett et al. (1994) also succeeded in teaching such students to decode using phonological analysis and blending, and again performance on a standardized comprehension measure showed improvement compared to a control condition. What is especially impressive in these studies was how well controlled they were, with control participants also enrolled in treatment conditions to evaluate placebo effects. When these results are combined with those of some other analyses (e.g., Francis, Shaywitz, Stuebing, Shaywitz, & Fletcher, 1996; Shaywitz, Escobar, Shaywitz, Fletcher, & Makuch, 1992), there is substantial evidence that many children who fall behind in beginning reading are not qualitatively different from other readers, but rather require intense, systematic decoding instruction in order to learn to read. Confidence in the instructional conclusions offered by Lovett's group is heightened by the fact that other research teams have also reported that students who experience difficulties in learning to read benefit from intensive systematic phonics instruction (e.g., Alexander, Anderson, Heilman, Voeller, & Torgesen, 1991; Blachman et al., 2004; R. S. Johnston & Watson, 1997; Lesaux & Siegel, 2003; Manis, Custodio, & Szeszulski, 1993; Olson, Wise, Johnson, & Ring, 1997; Torgesen & Burgess, 1998; Torgesen, Wagner, & Rashotte, 1997; Torgesen et al., 1996, 1999; Vellutino et al., 1996).

The National Reading Panel (2000; Ehri, Nunes, Stahl, & Willows, 2001) systematically reviewed all of the available experimental data pertaining to phonics instruction and concluded that phonics instruction had clear and positive effects on word recognition, especially at the kindergarten and grade-1 levels, and especially with young struggling readers. The panel concluded that the effects on comprehension were also positive but not as pronounced. An especially important finding was that the panel did not find important differences in the effectiveness of various approaches to phonics (see also Stahl, Duffy-Hester, & Stahl, 1998). Yes, they detected trends favoring the synthetic phonics approach that Chall (1967) so favored—but not dramatically great differences in favor of synthetic phonics over other approaches.

This is important, for I have seen much phonics instruction that is not purely synthetic phonics. Moreover, there are several phonics products that claim to be the most effective approach to phonics instruction based on research, claims that fall apart when all of the evidence is considered rather than the evidence highlighted by such program proponents (see Stahl, 2001, for additional commentary). The fact that diverse approaches to phonics work increases confidence that one-size-fits-all thinking is not correct with respect to phonics instruction, and that there is room for substantial variation in the way phonics is taught to children, with the caveat that such instruction needs to be extensive and systematic.

The research-substantiated success of phonics has also led to a change in the types of books beginning readers are being asked to read. There are fewer real storybooks to read and more books that are constructed to include the letter and sound combinations the child already knows (i.e., decodable books, with such memorable text as "Fat Pat sat on the mat and put the hat on the cat"; Hoffman, Sailors, & Patterson, 2002). This is so despite the fact that the little research done on this issue provides inconsistent support for this conclusion (Jenkins, Peyton, Sanders, & Vadasy, 2004; Menon & Hiebert, 2005)! Not every instructional practice advocated by phonics supporters enjoys widespread research support, although the instructional practices they favor are being adopted much more widely than they were a decade ago.

I close this section by explicitly addressing a claim I have sometimes heard from opponents of explicit decoding instruction (i.e., synthetic or systematic phonics). They say, "All right, so some kids who are experiencing difficulties learning to read do need it, but it really does no good for other students." There are a number of ways to challenge that claim, but I prefer to cite a recent analysis by Fielding-Barnsley (1997). Her study included 32 children who came to kindergarten extremely well prepared for beginning reading. Their preschool experiences had brought them to a high level of phonemic awareness and high alphabetic knowledge. Half of the children in the study were taught 10 words at the beginning of kindergarten, with the instruction emphasizing sounding out the words and highlighting word parts (e.g., the common part of *pam* and *am*). The 10 words were the following: *am, pam, sat, mat, splat, pal, lap, slam, lamp,* and *tam.* The other children learned the words using a whole-word approach. (Remember the approach that predominated in the Dick-and-Jane readers.) In both conditions, the teaching took place over about 6 weeks, with a few minutes a day devoted to teaching of the words.

There were dramatic differences favoring the students who had been taught using decoding as opposed to the whole-word approach. First, the decoding-instructed students read and wrote the taught words better than did the whole-word-instructed students. There were even more dramatic effects, however, with respect to reading novel words that included the letters and word parts of the words taught (e.g., *at, pat, sam, tap*), as well as pseudowords (e.g., *ap, lat, tal*). The students taught using decoding instruction greatly outperformed the whole-word-instructed students. Decoding instruction prepares students to tackle words they have never seen before, even when they are well prepared for beginning reading.

That said, there are now appearing credible analyses that an emphasis on word-level skills instruction might not be in the best interests of children entering first grade with good skills already in place. For example, they make less progress in the first-grade year than in the kindergarten year, perhaps reflecting that they have already learned what is taught and tested in grade 1 (Leppänen, Niemi, Aunola, & Nurmi, 2004). In addition, there have been at least two analyses in the United States where students entering first grade with strong word-level skills grew more in their reading if they experienced a curriculum that was richer in the reading of literature and other holistic activities than in explicit decoding instruction (with explicit decoding instruction better suited for readers with weak entering reading skills; Connor, Morrison, & Katch, 2004; Juel & Minden-Cupp, 2000). Based on such analyses, the case for providing extensive and explicit decoding instruction to weaker readers remains intact, but the same instructional recommendation does not necessarily follow for first graders entering with strong word-level skills.

Summary

There has been a great deal of research in the past several decades on the positive effects of teaching early reading competencies. The case is strong that explicit efforts to teach the alphabet, letter–sound associations, and sounding out of words (i.e., analysis of words into component sounds which are then blended) make a positive impact on progress in early reading. In contrast to the consistently positive evidence associated with synthetic phonics approaches, there has been less support for intrinsic phonics approaches (sometimes referred to as analytic phonics or whole-word approaches) or for the approaches to decoding favored in whole-language teaching (i.e., ones involving emphasis on analysis of semantic–contextual and syntactic–contextual cues). Indeed, perhaps the most disturbing conclusion that comes from this research is that teaching children to decode by giving primacy to semantic–contextual and syntactic–contextual cues over graphemic–phonemic cues is equivalent to teaching them to read the way weak readers read!

The work on synthetic phonics instruction conducted throughout the 20th century has succeeded in clarifying what works and what does not work in developing word recognition skills. Every primary teacher and individual responsible for the education of primary-grades children needs to think hard about the research evidence that was covered in this section. As I say that, I also feel some regret that so much of the recent research attention on explicit decoding instruction (often delivered as intensive tutoring) has focused on students experiencing difficulties in learning to read. The good news is that such instruction does improve the reading of many students who have had difficulties learning to read with regular classroom instruction. One piece of bad news is that not much is known about how modern versions of synthetic phonics work with normally achieving and above-average students. Another is that such instruction is not revealing about how explicit phonics instruction can occur within the context of other elements of literacy instruction. To be fair to many dedicated whole-language teachers who are not so extreme in their views, many try very hard and succeed in balancing skills instruction and holistic reading and writing. What they do not do is embrace any decontextualized teaching of phonics. Later in this chapter and in Chapter 8, I discuss further how some teachers are balancing explicit skills instruction and immersion in whole-language activities, such as writing and reading of literature.

I must emphasize, however, that in fairness as well to Chall (1967, 1983) and Adams (1990), the point must be made that they have been in favor of balanced instruction all along. They made many clear statements in their books about the need for synthetic phonics instruction in a much larger program involving a great deal of reading of various types. It was never only phonics *or* only whole language (or any other alternative) with either of these careful thinkers. That reductionistic dichotomy came about as extreme whole-language advocates attempted to make a case for their approach. As will become obvious in Chapter 8, there have been many calls for balancing of skills instruction and whole-language instruction. I think that my friend Lesley M. Morrow, a reading professor at Rutgers, was the first to refer to balanced instruction as the radical middle. It has become that because of the polemics of recent years, but the truth is that Chall defined the radical middle more than 30 years ago. Part of that radical middle is teaching students to get beyond the individual sounds of words to reading letter combinations and chunks that occur often in words, taken up next.

TEACHING STUDENTS TO READ NEW WORDS BY ANALOGY TO KNOWN WORDS

Recall from the discussion of skilled reading in Chapter 2 that good readers know and use word parts to decode unfamiliar words. Moreover, as reviewed earlier in this chapter, as children encounter common root words, prefixes, and suffixes again and again, they come to treat such word parts as wholes, no longer requiring letter-by-letter analysis and sounding out in order to recognize and pronounce them (e.g., Calhoon & Leslie, 2002; Ehri, 1992; Leslie & Calhoon, 1995). Indeed, even a few exposures to a word chunk are probably enough for beginning readers to begin to learn the chunk as a chunk (Share, 1999)—or perhaps even one (Share, 2004). This process probably begins in first grade (Savage & Stuart, 1998; Sprenger-Charolles, Siegel, & Bonnet, 1998) so that by the middle elementary grades there are clear differences between good and poor readers in their use of word chunks (e.g., Bowey & Hansen, 1994; Bowey & Underwood, 1996; Leslie & Calhoon, 1995): It is likely that good readers process words more at the level of frequently encountered word chunks than as single phonemes much of the time (Booth, Perfetti, & MacWhinney, 1999; Scarborough, 1995) and that poor readers cannot do so, lacking knowledge and awareness of morphemes relative to good readers (Casalis, Colé, & Sopo, 2004; Nagy, Berninger, Abbott, Vaughan, & Vermeulen, 2003). There is even some evidence that there are differences in word-part awareness and knowledge during kindergarten and grade 1 that are predictive of reading competence during the primary and later elementary years (Badian, 1993, 1994, 1995; Carlisle, 1994; A. E. Cunningham & Stanovich, 1993). For example, early competence in selecting the exact match of a short word (e.g., *drop*) from among four possibilities (i.e., *droq, drop, borq, brop*) is predictive of reading comprehension in the later elementary grades (Badian, 1995).

That commonly encountered word chunks are used to decode by good readers, and increasingly by children as they increase in reading skill, has suggested to some that word chunks should be highlighted and taught to children in beginning reading. After all, by age 4, children can detect the separate syllables in multisyllable words (Liberman, Shankweiler, Fisher, & Carter, 1974). They can also detect the onsets and rhyming parts (i.e., *rimes*, defined as a vowel with subsequent consonants; e.g., *-at* in *bat, cat,* and *hat*) of words. Thus, they can detect the rime *-ealth* in *health, stealth,* and *wealth*, identifying as well the onset sounds of *h-*, *st-*, and *w-*

(Goswami, 1998). Beyond detecting onsets and rimes, 5- and 6-year-olds can decode new words by analogy to rhyming words, at least when the rhyming relationship is very obvious. Thus, if a 5-year-old sees the word *beak*, and hears it pronounced with the word remaining in full view, he or she often can decode words like *peak*, *weak*, and *speak* (Bowey, Vaughan, & Hansen, 1998; Goswami, 1986, 1988, 1999; Wang & Gaffney, 1998). As children's reading improves over the course of the first year of reading instruction, they are able to use parts of rimes (e.g., the *-ea* in *-eak*) in a similar fashion (Goswami, 1993, 1998).

Teaching Word Families

How can children be taught to use word parts for decoding? One way is to teach "word families." It is not at all unusual to observe a group of grade-1 children constructing a list of all the words they can think of that end in *-ade*, *-eeze*, or *-isk*. In many classrooms, once the teacher and students have constructed such a list on a big piece of paper, the list joins a display of other lists of word families based on word endings. Endings appearing in 10 or more English words are contained in Table 5.1. Most of the word family endings are rimes—they require only a beginning consonant sound to make a word. Some, however, end in a vowel sound, such as *-aw* or *-ay*. Thus, it is more accurate to say that the word family endings in Table 5.1 are phonograms rather than rimes (Fry, Kress, & Fountoukidis, 1993). The word endings that occur most frequently are the ones learned first by students (Calhoon & Leslie, 2002; Leslie & Calhoon, 1995) and that logically seem like likely candidates to be emphasized in instruction.

When I have observed the word family approach in primary-level classrooms, it is almost always in the context of very strong synthetic phonics instruction. That makes a great deal of sense since good readers do blend individual sounds and word parts they know (i.e., root words, phonograms, prefixes, and suffixes). A little thought to the task of generating all the words that end with *-ade* (*bade*, *fade*, *jade*, *made*, *wade*, *blade*, *glade*, *grade*, *shade*, *spade*, *trade*), for example, will make it obvious that to construct such a list, as well as to be able to say the words on the list, requires knowledge not only of the rime but also of the sounds made by the onsets, as well as understanding of blending. Thus, it is not surprising that only children who already have some knowledge of phonological decoding skills are able to decode by analogy (Ehri & Robbins, 1992; Peterson & Haines, 1992) or at a minimum know a good many letter–sound associations (Walton, 1995). When encountering a word that shares a rime with another word known by the child, the young reader using the analogy strategy sound outs the phonemic onset and blends it with the rime (Bruck & Treiman, 1992).

TABLE 5.1. Common Word Families in English

-ab	-amp	-ear (short *e*)	-ick	-it	-ow (*know*)
-ace	-ank	-eat	-id	-ob	-ow (*cow*)
-ack	-ap	-ed	-ide	-ock	-ub
-ad	-ar	-ee	-ies	-od	-uck
-ade	-are	-eed	-ig	-og	-uff
-ag	-ark	-eek	-ight	-oke	-ug
-ail	-ash	-eep	-ile	-old	-um
-ain	-at	-eet	-ill	-one	-ump
-ake	-ate	-ell	-im	-ong	-ung
-ale	-ave	-end	-ime	-oop	-unk
-all	-aw	-ent	-in	-op	-ush
-am	-ay	-ess	-ine	-ope	-ust
-ame	-aze	-est	-ing	-ore	-ut
-an	-eak	-et	-ink	-orn	-y
-ane	-eal	-ew	-int	-ot	
-ang	-eam	-ice	-ip	-out	

Note. Based on List 47 in Fry et al. (1993).

Decoding by Analogy*

The best developed decoding-by-analogy program that I have encountered was developed at Benchmark School, a school serving children who have difficulties in learning to read in the context of regular schooling. The program was devised by the school's instructional leader, Irene W. Gaskins, in collaboration with Professors Linnea C. Ehri (Graduate Center, City University of New York), Patricia M. Cunningham (Wake Forest University), and Richard C. Anderson (University of Illinois). They dubbed their approach the "Word ID" program (R. W. Gaskins, Gaskins, Anderson, & Schommer, 1994; R. W. Gaskins, Gaskins, & Gaskins, 1991, 1992).

At the heart of the program are 120 key words that capture the key spelling patterns associated with the six English-language vowels. In addition, there also are key words for the two sounds of *g* (e.g., *girl, giraffe*) and the two sounds of *c* (e.g., *can, city*). Some word parts that always sound the same (e.g., *-tion*) are taught as wholes. All of the key words in the program are summarized in Table 5.2.

Thus, to decode the word *dispatcher*, the Word ID user would learn to identify a key word for each syllable of the word. For the first syllable, *dis-*, the key word *this* could be used, since the vowel *i* is followed by a consonant. For the second syllable, *-patch-*, the key word could be *cat*, since the *a*

---

*The entire Word ID program can be purchased from Benchmark School (2107 North Providence, Media, PA 19063).

TABLE 5.2. Benchmark School Word Identification/Vocabulary Development Program: Key Patterns

a	e	i	o	u	y
grab	he	hi	go	club	my
place	speak	mice	boat	truck	baby
black	scream	kick	job	glue	gym
had	year	did	clock	bug	
made	treat	slide	frog	drum	
flag	red	knife	broke	jump	
snail	see	pig	old	fun	
rain	bleed	right	from	skunk	
make	queen	like	on	up	
talk	sleep	smile	phone	us	
all	sweet	will	long	use	
am	tell	swim	zoo	but	
name	them	time	good		
champ	ten	in	food		
can	end	find	look		
and	tent	vine	school		
map	her	king	stop		
car	yes	think	for		
shark	nest	ship	more		
smart	let	squirt	corn		
smash	flew	this	nose		
has		wish	not		
ask		it	could		
cat		write	round		
skate		five	your		
brave		give	scout		
saw			cow		
day			glow		
			down		
			boy		

g			g = i	
girl	grab		gym	
go	dragon		giraffe	
bug	glow			

c = k			c = s	
can	club		city	excitement
corn	discover		princess	centipede

an i mals	drag on
con test	ex cite ment
crea ture	pres i dent
choc o late	ques tion
dis cover	re port
thank ful	un happy
va ca tion	

Note. Reprinted by permission of the Benchmark School and Irene Gaskins.

in -*patch*- is followed by a consonant. For the final syllable (-*er*), *her* would apply. Thus, the student, who is also learning the simple consonant–sound associations of English plus the digraphs and consonant blends, would know the sequence of vowel sounds and would then be able to sound out the word. Thus, rather than *this-cat-her* being pronounced, the student would sound out the word *dispatcher*.

Because students are taught to self-verbalize their thinking as they apply the strategy, consistent with an approach to strategy teaching that often works with children (Meichenbaum, 1977), you might hear something like the following from a young Benchmark student confronted with a word like *dispatcher*:

> I can tell by looking at this word that it has three vowel sounds, therefore I know it will have three chunks. The three common English parts I see in this word are divided here. The spelling pattern, or the vowel and what comes after it, in the first chunk is -*is*. The word that I know with the same spelling pattern is *this*. The spelling pattern or the vowel and what comes after it in the second chunk is -*at*. The word I know with the same spelling pattern is *cat*. The spelling pattern for the third chunk is -*er* with the word I know with this spelling pattern being *her*. The word is *dispatcher*. (adapted from R. W. Gaskins et al., 1995, p. 343)

Similarly, when Benchmark students are presented a word like *caterpillar*, they can sound out an approximate pronunciation through analogy with the component words *cat*, *her*, *will*, and *car*.

The program extends over several years at Benchmark. First, a variety of exercises are used to develop student understanding of the spelling patterns in the key words. Five new key words are introduced at a time, with 5 days of lessons aimed at developing mastery of the words, including practice using the key words to decode other words. After the key words are mastered, lessons in their use continue. During these lessons, teachers model use of the key words to decode. Students review words learned previously in the Word ID program, and they practice decoding new words—with many exercises included in the instruction to produce overlearning of the key words and decoding using them. I have watched many Benchmark students use the Word ID approach: By the middle elementary grades, most of the students can use the memorized key words with ease to decode multisyllable words they have not encountered previously.

What is especially striking, however, is that from the introduction of the program to children in their first year at Benchmark, Word ID lessons do much more than teach children to decode. When key words are introduced, children learn the meanings of the key words, which are also used as part of story writing. The lessons include reading of patterned books. Students hear and read good literature every day they are enrolled at Benchmark. The Benchmark approach is anything but a decoding skill-only approach; rather, Word ID is embedded in ongoing instruction and used to empower children so that they can participate fully in writing and in reading of real literature, with more about the Benchmark approach presented later in Chapter 9.

The development and evaluation of the program has a fascinating history (see R. W. Gaskins et al., 1995), beginning with Irene W. Gaskins's analyses of the particular reading problems of students at the Benchmark School. This led to an initial version of the program, which was tried in a few classrooms at the school. With evidence of improved decoding, spelling, and vocabulary development in those classrooms, the approach was extended. Across-school implementation, however, did not mean that the approach was employed completely and faithfully in every Benchmark classroom. The natural classroom variations in the implementation of the program permitted an important evaluation of it. Richard C. Anderson and his then-student colleague Marlene Schommer analyzed reading achievement as a function of complete implementation of the program and found a striking relationship: The more teachers spent time encouraging and assisting students in the use of the Word ID approach as they read, the better the reading in the classroom. That is, simply providing the Word ID lessons was not as powerful as supplementing the lessons with a great deal of support in applying the lessons. Take note of this finding, for there is plenty of evidence in the chapters that follow that a key ingredient in effective beginning reading instruction is such scaffolding (Wood, Bruner, & Ross, 1976) of student performance—that teachers who provide support as their students attempt to use skills taught in formal lessons are especially effective teachers.

Many reading researchers believe that an especially good measure of decoding ability is pseudoword reading—that is, being able to read letter combinations that have the structural characteristics of real words but are not real words. Such words could not be known by the reader through previous exposure but must be decoded. Anderson and Schommer found that the greater the implementation of the Word ID program in a Benchmark program, the better the students' reading of pseudowords.

The Benchmark faculty and the external university faculty monitored difficulties with the program, refining it until it could be taught efficiently in the classroom and be used efficiently by students. The program became especially well known when it was featured in a videotape produced and distributed by the Center for the Study of Reading at the University of Illinois. Although I. W. Gaskins and her colleagues never published the program commercially, they have made it available to any school district that wants it for the cost of reproducing the materials. They have had many takers. Regardless of where I talk in the United States, I am frequently asked about the Word ID program.

Such visibility caught the attention of some prominent reading education researchers who were particularly interested in the impact of decoding-by-analogy approaches, especially compared to synthetic phonics approaches. Greaney, Tunmer, and Chapman (1997) produced evidence that decoding-by-analogy training improved the reading of primary-level struggling readers. Although some short-term comparisons favored sounding out of words over decoding by analogy (Bruck & Treiman, 1992; Wise, Olson, & Treiman, 1990), in other studies Word ID and synthetic phonics instruction have produced roughly comparable gains in the decoding skills of beginning readers (DeWitz, 1993; Lovett et al., 1994; Walton, Walton, & Felton, 2001). Lovett and colleagues' (1994) study was especially notable because it involved teaching students who experienced a great deal of previous difficulties in learning to read—much like Benchmark students. In Walton and associates' (2001) study, although there was little difference between teaching grade-1 children to decode with analogies versus sounding out of words, there were some subtle advantages for students taught to use analogies (e.g., learning to decode with analogies increased sounding-out skills, but learning to sound out did not enhance decoding-by-analogy skills).

In short, the results of decoding by analogy are consistent: Children can do it (see also Ehri & Robbins, 1992; Peterson & Haines, 1992). This holds true even for students who have experienced previous difficulties in reading who now must read long and complex words (e.g., van Daal, Reitsma, & van der Leu, 1994). In fact, Irene W. Gaskins (2000) has developed a more advanced version of the Word ID approach. This version is intended for grade 5 and above, with the focus on decoding of longer words. The program includes voluminous direct instruction about many features of words, including accents and common roots.

In closing this discussion of the decoding-by-analogy approach, I emphasize that such instruction at Benchmark occurs in the context of a very balanced literacy instructional program, one filled with reading of fine literature, writing, and comprehension strategies instruction (see Chapter 8). Given this balanced mix, Leslie and Allen (1999) offered an interesting analysis. They devised a tutoring approach involving decoding-by-analogy instruction, with the intervention also including instruction in the use of multiple decoding cues, teaching of sight words, comprehension instruction, extensive reading and sharing of reading, and parental involvement in reading instruction. There were clear positive effects with struggling readers, as compared to uninstructed students. Balanced literacy mixes that include decoding-by-analogy instruction are defensible based on the available data.

The Need for Decoding-by-Analogy Instruction

If children can learn to read either with synthetic phonics or word analogy, is there really a need for both approaches? For a very long time, reading clinicians have believed that there are some children who experience difficulties with letter-by-letter analysis and blending but who are able to learn whole words and syllables. Indeed, Irene W. Gaskins's initial motivation for developing the Word ID approach was her perception that many of the Benchmark students really struggled with synthetic phonics. On the other hand, clinicians have also believed that there are children who are quite good at analyzing the individual sounds of words and blending them but who fail to develop word-chunk and sight-word knowledge. Those children are better at decoding using a synthetic phonics approach rather than an analogy approach (Berninger, 1995).

In support of this possibility, there now is evidence that some primary-level students rely more on synthetic phonics to decode whereas others are more reliant on a decoding-by-analogy approach (Berninger, Yates, & Lester, 1991; Freebody & Byrne, 1988). That is, some weaker readers learn to recognize words more easily if they are presented as wholes without making their phonemic composition salient (Wise, 1992). Others do better with phonics approaches than by using instruction emphasizing analogies (Levy, Bourassa, & Horn, 1999).

Employing only one approach (analogies or sounding out) to the exclusion of the other is probably the wrong way to think about most children's development as readers. Good readers do analyze and blend individual sounds, but they also make use of word chunks (Berninger, 1994, Chap. 4; Ehri, 1992). Although the dynamics are not completely understood, good readers deduce word-chunk regularities as they sound out words; moreover, they learn more about the sounds of individual letters and letter combinations while experiencing those sounds as part of word chunks (e.g., Thompson, Cottrell, & Fletcher-Flinn, 1996).

Given all this, what makes most sense for beginning reading instruction is to encourage children to analyze and blend individual sounds while teaching them to make use of word parts during decoding. Although I have seen very good teachers who take this approach, I must admit that at this time it is not well understood how to obtain the advantages of synthetic phonics instruction *and* analogy instruction. Irene W. Gaskins, Ehri, and the Benchmark School faculty have adapted their instruction to combine the synthetic phonics and analogy approaches to decoding instruction, consistent with the evidence that decoding by analogy works best when children also can use phonics cues (Ehri, 1998).

Thus, as Benchmark students learn their key words, they are being taught how to analyze the key words into individual sounds. The key words are used to provide a great deal of instruction about the key letter–sound associations and letter combinations that commonly occur in English. The students spend a great deal of time stretching out the pronunciations of the key words in order to hear their constituent sounds. They are taught to look at the visual patterns in words and to be sensitive that some letter patterns occur in a number of words.

In short, as the Word ID program has matured, it has come to include more about sounding out words, blending the ideas from phonics and decoding by analogy approaches (I. W. Gaskins, Ehri, Cress, O'Hara, & Donnelly, 1997). (As is discussed in Chapter 8, one of the most prominent approaches to tutoring primary students experiencing reading difficulties, Reading Recovery®, also teaches students both to attend to word chunks and to sound out words.)

My own intuition, consistent with the direction of Gaskins and her Benchmark colleagues, is that decoding instruction will work best if there is flexibility, especially for children who might really have problems with synthetic phonics or with using analogies to decode words. Thus, what I envision in the future is phonics instruction teaching not only analysis and blending of sounds of words but also teaching big chunks of words that do not need to be analyzed and blended every time. By providing lots of opportunities for students to experience the major recurring word parts (i.e., frequent letter patterns, such as phonograms, prefixes, and suffixes), they should come to be automatically recognized.

Lovett et al. (2000) provided support for this intuition of mine. The participants in the study were 6- to 13-year-olds with severe reading difficulties. They received 70 hours of intervention. Some received both instruction in the sounding out of words and Word ID-type instruction. Other participants were taught only to sound out words, while others received only Word ID-type instruction. Controls experienced math tutoring with some classroom survival skills training. At the end of instruction, word recognition was clearly better for the participants receiving the combined sounding-out and Word ID-type training. Confidence in Lovett et al.'s (2000) finding is increased by a recent constructive replication study: Walton and Walton (2002) also demonstrated that instruction combining sounding-out and Word ID-type instruction produces superior reading, as compared to either type of training alone.

Much more work needs to be done on the effects produced by teaching struggling readers both to use sounding-out strategies and Word ID approaches. If the reading clinicians are right—and I'm betting that they are, based on the available evidence—flexibility in decoding instruction is especially important for students who might experience difficulties with either analyzing and blending or decoding analogically using word chunks alone. For students experiencing the former problem, instruction should focus more on the word chunks and use of analogies to decode words. For students experiencing the latter problem, downplaying word families and word chunks in favor of analyzing and blending would make sense. In short, what is needed is decoding instruction that accommodates individual differences in students rather than one-size-fits-all instruction. Working out the specifics of such instruction is going to be challenging but, I suspect, will pay off in improved beginning reading instruction. That primary-grade classrooms can involve a fluid mixing of diverse approaches to instruction is a point made vividly in the next section.

PHONICS IN WHOLE-LANGUAGE FIRST-GRADE CLASSROOMS

In Chapter 1, I introduced a study by Dahl, Scharer, Lawson, and Grogan (1999), who studied phonics instruction in eight grade-1 classrooms nominated by whole-language teacher organizations in Ohio. I return to that study now to make the point that word recognition skills can be taught explicitly in whole-language classrooms, with many opportunities for that to occur—in other words, that skills and whole-language approaches can be blended.

Over the course of a school year, the researchers made many observations in the classrooms, typically during reading and writing. The researchers were particularly focusing on the phonics instruction that occurred in these classes. A first finding was that the researchers observed plenty of phonics instruction. It occurred during read-alouds, with the teacher discussing letter–sound relationships in words in stories. Students often made word collections and then grouped the words they knew on the basis of letter–sound features (e.g., same first letter, rhyme, etc.). During guided and shared reading, teachers taught strategies for decoding unknown words. Phonics skills instruction was prominent as teachers listened to students read individually. During writing, there was much encouragement of students to sound out words they were writing. There were word analysis games ("I Spy," requiring students to find particular words in a text) and exercises (e.g., sorting word cards on the basis of letter–sound patterns, discussing patterns in dictated words).

A second finding was that the observers saw lots of instruction intended to develop sound and letter-level skills. They saw much encouragement of phonemic awareness (i.e., teachers prompting students to hear the sounds in words, for example, by stretching the individual sounds of a word out during its pronunciation). There was lots of phonics, focusing on the sounds produced by both vowels and consonants. There was lots of practice blending sounds, too, as well as plenty of attention to root words, affixes, compound words, contractions, and homonyms. In short, everything that was supposed to be in phonics instruction was found by Dahl et al. (1999).

A third important finding was that the phonics instruction decidedly focused on teaching students to be strategic, with students encouraged to use a number of decoding strategies in interaction. They were encouraged to use the onset sound of a word to decode as well as to pay attention to the sentence meaning as they attempted to decode. There was much encouragement of stretching out the sounds of words both during reading and writing (i.e., stretching the intended word out and transcribing sound by sound). During writing, students were encouraged to reread what they read, making certain that words as written contained every sound in them. Students were encouraged to look for familiar patterns in words to aid decoding (e.g., vowel digraphs, soft and hard *c* or *g*). The teachers sometimes asked students to focus on how their mouth is shaped when making certain sounds to cue awareness of a letter–sound relationship. Sometimes the teachers encouraged students to point to each sound in a word as the word was read to emphasize how the sounds and letters connected. The teachers pointed out exceptional words as such. In addition to these strategies, students were encouraged to use resources available in the room to facilitate decoding (e.g., the word wall, dictionaries, other students).

The teachers were keenly aware of the progress of individual students, with minilessons serving a dual purpose of teaching and assessment, so that instruction was tailored to students' needs. As teachers sized up the needs of the children, they planned specific lessons for small groups of children and used large groups to make points that needed to be made to all the children. The teachers in this study taught with awareness of their students' needs.

Did the students learn much about reading in these classrooms? They sure did, as documented through several different instruments sensitive to growth of word knowledge. There were substantial gains for readers at all entry levels.

I am impressed with the gains documented in Dahl and associates' (1999) investigation. I've seen classrooms where skills and holistic literacy experiences intermix well, as will become even more obvious in the chapters ahead. Moreover, there have been very credible indications of real literacy growth in such classrooms, which goes far in motivating this book on balanced literacy instruction. That said, I have also been in classrooms of teachers who identify with whole language and who are very resistant to skills instruction, using only a very few of the tactics documented by Dahl et al. (1999). There is real variety out there among teachers who call themselves whole-language instructors. I think that the teachers described by Dahl et al. (1999) are balanced teachers, and I urge the readers of this book to examine this article for a very stimulating review of what balanced grade-1 teaching can be like among teachers who identify themselves as whole-language teachers.

To the credit of the whole-language educator community, they have responded to the work of Dahl and her associates and teachers who are attempting to balance skills and whole-language components with significant resources that detail how phonics can be taught in whole-language classrooms. I urge educators of beginning readers to spend some time with these resources. They include Moustafa's *Beyond Traditional Phonics* (1997) and *Whole to Part Phonics: How Children Learn to Read and Spell* (1998); Dahl, Scharer, Lawson, and Grogan's *Rethinking Phonics: Making the Best Teaching Decisions* (2001); and Pinnell, Fountas, Giacobbe, and Fountas's *Word Matters: Teaching Phonics and Spelling in the Reading/Writing Classroom* (1998).

CONCLUDING COMMENTS

The goal of reading is not to decode words but to understand the messages conveyed in the text. When readers are not skilled in word recognition, however, comprehension is low. A consistent characteristic of poor readers is that they have difficulties in decoding words, with this factor more than any other accounting for their low comprehension (e.g., Ehrlich, Kurtz-Costes, & Loridant, 1993). There is very good reason for researcher attention to word-level processes and identification of instructional methods to increase word recognition. Arguments that development of word recognition skills should not be prominent in beginning reading instruction must ignore a great deal of data to the contrary.

Among scholars who have carefully and respectfully studied all of the evidence on early word recognition, there is agreement at least with respect to the key conclusions that are the focus of this chapter. There is a consensus among scientifically oriented reading researchers that teaching children to sound out words and to use commonly encountered word chunks (e.g., root words, prefixes, suffixes) makes more sense than teaching them to orient to meaning-related cues in order to recognize words. There is little support for emphasis on approaches to word recognition that make word recognition more a psycholinguistic guessing game based on semantic context clues (e.g., Goodman, 1967) than the analyzing and blending of the component parts of words.

Vygotskian Nature of Learning to Recognize Words

I like to think about word recognition instruction in Vygotskian terms (see Chapter 4). When adults and children work together to sound out words and decode words by recognizing word chunks, they probably are engaging in the early stages of an internalization process, one in which the child learns how to use speech to decode words. One of Lev S. Vygotsky's main messages is that the mind develops in interactions with others, interactions involving a lot of dialogue in which adults and children work on problems together. Learning to read should likewise develop in interaction with others, so that reading strategies that the adult scaffolds dialogically, such as those involved in decoding, will potentially be internalized by the child. (The tutoring provided by the likes of Lovett and her associates, Vellutino and his colleagues, and at Benchmark School reveals substantial scaffolding of students in the Vygotskian sense of the term.)

According to Vygotsky and the other Russian researchers, inner speech, including the inner speech that mediates word recognition, has its origins in social interactions between children and adults wherein adults introduce children to the most important problem-solving strategies that they need to acquire. When an adult models the sounding out of words and then assists the child who at first must sound out words with great effort, it is the beginning of an internalization process, one that is decidedly social. In this way, the adult passes on to another generation a powerful set of tools that humans invented in order to read print.

Challenges to Implementing Evidence-Based Word Recognition Instruction

Will the information presented in this chapter be translated into general practice in the near future? I hope so, but there are challenges ahead. One of the greatest difficulties is that many primary-grade teachers probably do not understand enough about phonics or commonly encountered word chunks to effectively implement either a synthetic phonics program or a decoding-by-analogy approach (Stahl et al., 1998). For example, Scarborough, Ehri, Olson, and Fowler (1998) observed that teachers in training could not reliably identify the phonemes in words, consistent with less than complete knowledge about many aspects of beginning reading (Bos, Mather, Dickson, Podhajski, & Chard, 2001; Cunningham, Perry, Stanovich, & Stanovich, 2004; McCutchen et al., 2002a, 2002b; Moats & Foorman, 2003; Spear-Swerling & Brucker, 2003). If teachers are to develop phonemic awareness and teach phonics to students, they must understand phonemic awareness and phonics well. In my work with beginning teachers, it is clear to me that many are intimidated when asked to teach phonics or other systematic approaches to word recognition.

Of course, one reason that knowledge of word recognition processes is so low is that teacher education programs have not been teaching the information about language that teachers need to know. When whole word programs predominated in the marketplace, there was little incentive to offer teacher education students instruction in synthetic phonics. With the rise of the whole-language approach, there was exceptionally active opposition to teaching beginning teachers about phonics, as detailed in Chapter 1. I cannot tell you how many teachers have told me that they would like to incorporate more word-level skills, such as sounding out and teaching decoding by analogy, but they simply do not know how to begin.

Even when teachers are willing to teach word-level skills, the materials available to them often are not very informative about decoding instruction at its best. Quite frankly, many phonics programs I have seen are dreadful (although there are unambiguous and distinguished exceptions to this general point)—not much more than a collection of skill sheets and drills, providing little information to teachers about the skills that should be developed. There are two trade books on the market that I especially like as starting points for the teacher who wants to improve decoding instruction in her or his classroom. Teachers have told me that they have found these two references useful in understanding the word recognition process and how word recognition can be taught: One is Patricia M. Cunningham's *Phonics They Use: Words for Reading and Writing* (1995), and the other is Barbara J. Fox's *Strategies for Word Identification: Phonics from a New Perspective* (1996). In addition, the best of the tutoring resources also provide a great deal of information about teaching word recognition. These include *The Howard Street Tutoring Manual: Teaching At-Risk Readers in the Primary Grades* by Darrell Morris (1999); *Book Buddies: Guidelines for Volunteer Tutors of Emergent and Early Readers* by Francine R. Johnston, Marcia Invernizzi, and Connie Juel (1998); and *Word Journeys: Assessment-Guided Phonics, Spelling, and Vocabulary Instruction* by Kathy Ganske (2000). I cannot resist adding at this point that, beyond reading the tutoring manuals, teachers can get involved in such tutoring, and when they do they can do a lot of good (e.g., Morris, Tyner, & Perney, 2000; Santa & Høien, 1999). In fact, teachers seem to learn a lot about teaching reading by participating as tutors in programs like *Book Buddies* (Broaddus & Bloodgood, 1999).

They also can learn a lot about reading by using a high-quality comprehensive program. I make this point because such programs were highly criticized during the whole-language era. The best such programs have teacher's manuals that are filled with lots of information about how to teach the various components of reading as well as why these components make sense. One of my frankest admissions is that I did not understand reading instruction nearly so well before I read one such program in its entirety in the late 1980s. That same program today is even a better read, with the few programs that compete well in the contemporary market featuring teacher's manuals that are very up to date. If you are hired in a district that adopts such a program, I urge you to embrace it and resolve to learn all you can from teaching the program and spending time with the explanatory materials in the manual. It will be worth it. I still learn much from time spent with these resources.

Whole Language Today

As the evidence accumulated in favor of the instruction documented in this chapter, whole-language opposition to systematic phonics instruction seemed to intensify in the mid- to late 1990s. The case made by opponents of the word recognition instruction summarized in this chapter was that if children are systematically taught how to recognize words outside the context of reading of real literature, somehow the benefits of whole-language learning would be lost. To their credit, some whole-language proponents offered much advice about how phonics could be taught in the context of experiencing real literature, as determined by the needs of the child, in contrast to being taught as a decontextualized skill in advance of reading of real texts (e.g., Church, 1996; Goodman, 1993; Routman, 1996). These authors did point the way—at least for some teachers—to ways of doing instruction so that extensive teaching of phonics and holistic literacy experiences coexist and complement each other. Exceptionally effective primary teachers balance systematic skills instruction, including word recognition, with immersion in real literature and student writing, as described, for example, by Dahl et al. (1999), which was reviewed earlier in this chapter. With every passing year, there are more and more resources available about how to balance skills instruction and whole language, and I urge readers of this book who plan to continue as whole-language teachers to look for such resources and benefit from them. I urge all teachers to consider as well that for those children entering grade 1 with strong beginning reading skills, there is increasing evidence that such an approach promotes their growth as readers better than does an explicit emphasis on decoding (Connor et al., 2004; Juel & Minden-Cupp, 2000). In most grade-1 classrooms, there are probably children who benefit more from explicit decoding instruction and others who benefit more from a high-quality whole-language approach.

In fact, the recent evidence produced by Connor et al. (2004) bolsters that last conclusion considerably. They found that students who entered grade 1 with weak decoding skills, in fact, experienced the most reading growth if they experienced a classroom strong in explicit decoding instruction. In contrast, for students who entered grade 1 with strong decoding skills, the amount of explicit decoding instruction they received did not seem to matter. For students entering with low knowledge of vocabulary, their decoding improved more in a classroom with greater explicit decoding instruction than in classrooms with less explicit decoding instruction, but they also benefited over the course of a year by increasing opportunities for holistic reading and writing. Students entering with strong vocabulary skills benefited the most from holistic instruction across the year. In short, students differ with respect to how much explicit decoding instruction they need—with the weaker readers benefiting more from decoding instruction, and the stronger readers benefiting more from holistic reading and writing.

I add, in defense of whole-language enthusiasts who have consistently feared decontextualized, systematic phonics instruction, that enthusiasm for phonics has often resulted in instruction that only covers lower-order word recognition skills (i.e., in contrast to higher-order comprehension and composition skills), with such instruction differentially aimed at those children who are at risk, including cultural-minority children (Allington, 1991; Au, 2001; Fitzgerald, 1995). Much of the resistance to systematic phonics instruction stems from the fear that such teaching can take over the beginning reading curriculum, with it certainly the case that there are primary-level classrooms where there is little time left in the morning schedule after word-level skills instruction is completed! No one should read this chapter and conclude there is support here for such instruction. This book is about balanced literacy instruction, with such balance including prominent skills instruction and prominent holistic reading and writing experiences for all children, and for some children (i.e., strong beginning readers) probably a mix that is more intensely holistic than aimed at coverage of basic word recognition skills.

Nature of Excellent Phonics Instruction

That there are only small differences in effectiveness between the various phonics approaches (Ehri et al., 2001; National Reading Panel, 2000; Stahl et al., 1998) does not mean that we do not know what constitutes excellent phonics instruction. After reviewing the literature on phonics instruction, Stahl et al. (1998) developed a sensible set of conclusions about what is part of excellent phonics instruction:

- Good phonics instruction develops the alphabetic principle, the understanding that letters in words represent specific sounds.
- Good phonics instruction develops phonological (phonemic) awareness.
- Good phonics instruction develops a thorough grounding in the letters—that is, automatic recognition of the form of each letter (e.g., there is no confusion between p and q).
- Good phonics instruction should not emphasize rules (which often are filled with exceptions—e.g., "When two vowels go walking, the first does the talking" works 45% of the time; Clymer, 1963), depend on worksheets, dominate instruction, or be boring.

- Good phonics instruction involves a great deal of practice in reading words—words in isolation and in texts—and writing words.
- Good phonics instruction results in automatic word recognition. Skilled reading is not sounding out words; it involves recognizing words effortlessly!
- Good phonics instruction is only one part of reading instruction.

Research to Get Beyond Synthetic Phonics and Knowing Only about Word Recognition in the Primary Grades

A problem with the list of ideas about developing word recognition just presented, however, is that it is derived mostly from studies of synthetic phonics and wholly from studies of primary-grade readers to the exclusion of everyone else. Fortunately, since the publication of the National Reading Panel (2000) report, there has been a spurt of research on other methods of phonics instruction and at other age levels, especially through true experimentation, the methodology favored by the panel.

For example, the intense approach to beginning word recognition that is the Orton–Gillingham approach—which is a multisensory method emphasizing much attention to sounds, including how they are produced by the mouth—was evaluated with at-risk grade 1 students by Joshi, Dahlgren, and Boulware-Gooden (2002). Students experienced Orton–Gillingham in grade 1, and control participants received a basal-driven grade-1 curriculum. At the end of the year, beginning reading was better among readers receiving Orton–Gillingham. We need more true experimental work on Orton–Gillingham as well as some of the other more extensive skills programs such as Lindamood–Bell, especially since these programs enjoy many teacher practitioners and widespread use. We need to know more about how they work with their intended populations—troubled readers—as well as their potential benefits in regular education with a broad range of readers.

Some specific word recognition practices are being evaluated as well. For example, McCandliss, Beck, Sandak, and Perfetti (2003) worked with children who had difficulties learning to read in grade 1. The children participated in an intervention called Word Building for 20 50-minute sessions. (There were also no-intervention control participants.) The centerpiece of Word Building was exercises emphasizing that words change by altering one letter, which also impacts the sound of the word. Thus, *sat* can become *sap* by changing the last letter; *sap* becomes *tap* with a change of the first letter; change the middle letter, and *tap* becomes *top*; add an *s* at the beginning of the word to make *stop*. Such Word Building was complemented by flashcard reading of the words encountered during Word Building and reading of sentences containing the practiced words, with student–teacher discussions of the meanings of the sentences. The intervention worked well, producing much-improved reading of words and even some transfer benefit to a passage comprehension measure. There are many such specific practices that could and should be evaluated in experiments, for they are included in many phonics programs.

Beyond the elementary school, investigators have been studying the effects of word recognition instruction emphasizing sounding out by paying attention to word parts as well as the individual letter sounds in the words and word parts (something akin to the type of instruction studied by Lovett). Such instruction has improved the reading skills, principally word reading, of struggling adolescent readers (Bhattacharya & Ehri, 2004; Penney, 2002).

In short, there is a lot of experimentation still occurring with respect to beginning word reading skills and a great deal of work that could be done. Word recognition should be a prominent area of research for some time to come. I would urge scientists interested in word recognition to look hard at the interventions now being wide deployed and ask "What is untested here?" The answer is *much*, which provides great opportunity for more and new inquiry.

SUMMARY AND CONCLUDING REFLECTIONS

1. Ehri (e.g., 1991) has proposed a general developmental progression in learning to recognize words. Preschoolers can first recognize logographs before they can do alphabetic reading, which begins even before the child knows all the letter–sound associations. Experience in sounding out particular words results in frequently encountered words becoming sight words, no longer requiring alphabetic decoding. Letter strings that occur frequently in words, including root words, phonograms, prefixes, and suffixes, come to be perceived as units, no longer needing to be sounded out when encountered in a new word. At this point, new words can often be decoded by analogy to words known by the reader (e.g., knowing *beak*, the child can read *peak*).

2. There is a great deal of support for the efficacy of systematic phonics instruction. Chall's (1967) book is a summary of the first wave of evidence, which has continued to accumulate since its publication. Synthetic phonics instruction, the approach most favored by Chall, involves learning the letter–sound associations and blending the sounds specified by a word's letters in order to produce the word. The success in using synthetic phonics to teach beginning readers to recognize words contrasts at least slightly with lower success rates for analytic phonics ap-

proaches involving less systematic instruction of phonics (i.e., on an as-needed basis).

3. An alternative to emphasizing the decoding and blending of individual sounds is to teach students to decode by analogy. This approach requires teaching students a large number of word parts that then can be used to read by analogy. Both traditional "word family" approaches and the Benchmark School Word ID program involve decoding by analogy.

4. Good readers decode by analysis and blending and also by analogy, and thus there is hard thinking going on about how to teach beginning readers to use both approaches. A possibility is that each approach is better for some readers. Effective decoding instruction should be flexible enough to permit students to use the approach or approaches that work for them.

5. In contrast to the substantial database in favor of systematic phonics instruction and the growing database in support of decoding by analogy, there is very little support for teaching students to decode by orienting primarily to semantic–contextual and syntactic–contextual cues, as opposed to graphemic–phonemic cues. That is, there is very little research support for the type of decoding favored by whole-language enthusiasts.

6. More positively, there are whole-language teachers who do a great deal of word recognition instruction in context, with documented growth in word recognition skills in their classrooms.

7. Even so, research on how to teach decoding is an extremely active area of research at present, and, if anything, there is a need for more activity in this area. For example, one important hypothesis that deserves a great deal of attention is that a very effective way to teach decoding is to teach students to attend to letter-level phonological cues first, blending individual letter sounds and word parts, and then to check their decoding by determining its sensibility in light of semantic–contextual and syntactic–contextual cues. The case will be made in the chapters ahead that such teaching can be part of balanced literacy instruction. It provides a place for the skills approach to word recognition and the semantic–contextual ideas favored by the whole-language theorists. More than that, it provides places for the various components that are sensible, suggesting an articulation that presumably is at the heart of effective word recognition (Gough et al., 1992).

8. The emphasis on letter-, sound-, and word-level approaches in this chapter should not be construed to mean that such instruction would ever be sufficient to produce readers. Rather, word recognition is a critical component in a complicated mix of components. There is a lot of research ahead in the chapters that follow on word recognition processes and every other process in reading.

REFERENCES

Abt Associates. (1977). *Education as experimentation: A planned variation model: Volume IV-B. Effects of follow through models.* Cambridge, MA: Abt Books.

Adams, M. J. (1990). *Beginning to read.* Cambridge, MA: Harvard University Press.

Alexander, A., Anderson, H., Heilman, P. C., Voeller, K. S., & Torgesen, J. K. (1991). Phonological awareness training and remediation of analytic decoding deficits in a group of severe dyslexics. *Annals of Dyslexia, 41,* 193–206.

Allington, R. L. (1991). Children who find learning to read difficult: School responses to diversity. In E. H. Hiebert (Ed.), *Literacy for a diverse society: Perspectives, practices, and policies* (pp. 237–252). New York: Teachers College Press.

Anderson, D. R., & Collins, P. A. (1988). *The impact on children's education: Television's influence on cognitive development* (Office of Research Working Paper No. 2). Washington, DC: U.S. Department of Education, Office of Educational Research and Improvement.

Au, K. H. (2001). A multicultural perspective on policies for improving literacy achievement: Equity and excellence. In S. B. Neuman & D. K. Dickinson (Eds.), *Handbook of early literacy research* (pp. 835–851). New York: Guilford Press.

Badian, N. A. (1993). Phonemic awareness, naming, visual symbol processing, and reading. *Reading and Writing: An Interdisciplinary Journal, 5,* 87–100.

Badian, N. A. (1994). Preschool prediction: Orthographic and phonological skills, and reading. *Annals of Dyslexia, 44,* 3–25.

Badian, N. A. (1995). Predicting reading ability over the long term: The changing roles of letter naming, phonological awareness and orthographic processing. *Annals of Dyslexia, 45,* 79–96.

Ball, S., & Bogatz, G. A. (1970). *The first year of "Sesame Street": An evaluation.* Princeton, NJ: Educational Testing Service.

Baron, J. (1977). Mechanisms for pronouncing printed words: Use and acquisition. In D. LaBerge & S. J. Samuels (Eds.), *Basic processes in reading: Perception and comprehension* (pp. 175–216). Hillsdale, NJ: Erlbaum.

Barron, R. W. (1986). Word recognition in early reading: A review of the direct and indirect access hypotheses. *Cognition, 24,* 93–119.

Berninger, V. W. (1994). *Reading and writing acquisition: A developmental neuropsychological perspective.* Madison, WI: Brown & Benchmark.

Berninger, V. W. (1995). Has the phonological recoding model of reading acquisition and reading disability led us astray? *Issues in Education: Contributions from Educational Psychology, 1,* 59–63.

Berninger, V. W., Yates, C., & Lester, K. (1991). Multiple orthographic codes in reading and writing acquisition. *Reading and Writing: An Interdisciplinary Journal, 3,* 115–149.

Bhattacharya, A., & Ehri, L. C. (2004). Graphosyllabic analysis helps adolescent struggling readers read and spell words. *Journal of Learning Disabilities, 37,* 331–348.

Blachman, B. A., Schatschneider, C., Fletcher, J. M., Francis, D. J., Clonan, S. M., Shaywitz, B. A., & Shaywitz, S. E. (2004). Effects of intensive reading remediation for second and third graders and a 1-year follow-up. *Journal of Educational Psychology, 96*, 444–461.

Bogatz, G. A., & Ball, S. (1971). *The second year of "Sesame Street": A continuing evaluation.* Princeton, NJ: Educational Testing Service.

Booth, J. R., Perfetti, C. A., & MacWhinney, B. (1999). Quick, automatic, and general activation of orthographic and phonological representations in young readers. *Developmental Psychology, 35*, 3–19.

Bos, C., Mather, N., Dickson, S., Podhajski, B., & Chard, D. (2001). Perceptions and knowledge of preservice and inservice educators about early reading instruction. *Annals of Dyslexia, 51*, 97–120.

Bowey, J. A., & Hansen, J. (1994). The development of orthographic rimes as units of word recognition. *Journal of Experimental Child Psychology, 58*, 465–488.

Bowey, J. A., & Underwood, N. (1996). Further evidence that orthographic rime usage in nonword reading increases with word-level reading proficiency. *Journal of Experimental Child Psychology, 63*, 526–562.

Bowey, J. A., Vaughan, L., & Hansen, J. (1998). Beginning readers' use of orthographic analogies in word reading. *Journal of Experimental Child Psychology, 68*, 108–133.

Broaddus, K., & Bloodgood, J. W. (1999). "We're supposed to already know how to teach reading": Teacher change to support struggling readers. *Reading Research Quarterly, 34*, 426–451.

Bruck, M., & Treiman, R. (1992). Learning to pronounce words: The limits of analogies. *Reading Research Quarterly, 27*, 374–398.

Byrne, B., & Fielding-Barnsley, R. (1990). Acquiring the alphabetic principle: A case for teaching recognition of phoneme identity. *Journal of Educational Psychology, 82*, 805–812.

Byrne, B., & Fielding-Barnsley, R. (1991). Evaluation of a program to teach phonemic awareness to young children. *Journal of Educational Psychology, 83*, 451–455.

Calhoon, J. A., & Leslie, L. (2002). A longitudinal study of the effects of word frequency and rime-neighborhood size on beginning readers' rime reading accuracy in words and nonwords. *Journal of Literacy Research, 34*, 39–58.

Carlisle, J. F. (1994). Morphological awareness and early reading achievement. In L. B. Feldman (Ed.), *Morphological aspects of language processing* (pp. 189–209). Hillsdale, NJ: Erlbaum.

Casalis, S., Colé, P., & Sopo, D. (2004). Morphological awareness in developmental dyslexia. *Annals of Dyslexia, 54*, 114–138.

Chall, J. S. (1967). *Learning to read: The great debate.* New York: McGraw-Hill.

Chall, J. S. (1983). *Learning to read: The great debate* (updated ed.). New York: McGraw-Hill.

Church, S. M. (1996). *The future of whole language: Reconstruction or self-destruction?* Portsmouth, NH: Heinemann.

Clymer, T. (1963). The utility of phonic generalizations in the primary grades. *The Reading Teacher, 16*, 252–258.

Connor, C. D., Morrison, F. J., & Katch, L. E. (2004). Beyond the reading wars: Exploring the effect of child-instruction interactions on growth in early reading. *Scientific Studies of Reading, 8*, 305–336.

Cronin, V., Farrell, D., & Delaney, M. (1995, April). *Environmental print facilitates word reading.* Paper presented at the biennial meeting of the Society for Research in Child Development, Indianapolis, IN.

Cunningham, A. E., Perry, K. E., Stanovich, K. E., & Stanovich, P. J. (2004). Disciplinary knowledge of K–3 teachers and their knowledge calibration in the domain of early literacy. *Annals of Dyslexia, 54,* 139–167.

Cunningham, A. E., & Stanovich, K. E. (1993). Children's literacy environments and early word recognition skills. *Reading and Writing: An Interdisciplinary Journal, 5,* 193–204.

Cunningham, P. M. (1995). *Phonics they use: Words for reading and writing* (2nd ed.). New York: HarperCollins.

Dahl, K. L., Scharer, P. L., Lawson, L. L., & Grogan, P. R. (1999). Phonics instruction and student achievement in whole language first-grade classrooms. *Reading Research Quarterly, 34,* 312–341.

Dahl, K. L., Scharer, P. L., Lawson, L. L., & Grogan, P. R. (2001). *Rethinking phonics: Making the best teaching decisions.* Portsmouth, NH: Heinemann.

DeWitz, P. (1993, May). *Comparing an analogy and phonics approach to word recognition.* Paper presented at the Edmund Hardcastle Henderson Roundtable in Reading, Charlottesville, VA.

Ehri, L. C. (1980). The development of orthographic images. In U. Frith (Ed.), *Cognitive processes in spelling* (pp. 311–338). London: Academic Press.

Ehri, L. C. (1984). How orthography alters spoken language competencies in children learning to read and spell. In J. Downing & R. Valtin (Eds.), *Language awareness and learning to read* (pp. 119–147). New York: Springer-Verlag.

Ehri, L. C. (1987). Learning to read and spell words. *Journal of Reading Behavior, 19,* 5–31.

Ehri, L. C. (1991). Development of the ability to read words. In R. Barr, M. L. Kamil, P. B. Mosenthal, & P. D. Pearson (Eds.), *Handbook of reading research* (Vol. 2, pp. 383–417). New York: Longman.

Ehri, L. C. (1992). Reconceptualizing the development of sight word reading and its relationship to recoding. In P. B. Gough, L. C. Ehri, & R. Treiman (Eds.), *Reading acquisition* (pp. 107–143). Hillsdale, NJ: Erlbaum.

Ehri, L. C. (1998). Grapheme–phoneme knowledge is essential for learning to read words in English. In J. L. Metsala & L. C. Ehri (Eds.), *Word recognition in beginning literacy* (pp. 3–40). Mahwah, NJ: Erlbaum.

Ehri, L. C., Deffner, N. D., & Wilce, L. S. (1984). Pictorial mnemonics for phonics. *Journal of Educational Psychology, 76,* 880–893.

Ehri, L. C., Nunes, S. R., Stahl, S. A., & Willows, D. M. (2001). Systematic phonics instruction helps students learn to read: Evidence from the National Reading Panel's meta-analysis. *Review of Educational Research, 71,* 393–448.

Ehri, L. C., & Robbins, C. (1992). Beginners need some decoding skill to read words by analogy. *Reading Research Quarterly, 27,* 12–27.

Ehri, L. C., & Snowling, M. J. (2004). Developmental variation in word recognition. In C. A. Stone, E. R. Silliman, B. J. Ehren, & K. Apel (Eds.), *Handbook of language and literacy: Development and disorders* (pp. 433–460). New York: Guilford Press.

Ehri, L. C., & Wilce, L. S. (1985). Movement into reading: Is the first stage of printed word learning visual or phonetic? *Reading Research Quarterly, 20,* 163–179.

Ehri, L. C., & Wilce, L. S. (1987a). Cipher versus cue reading: An experiment in decoding acquisition. *Journal of Educational Psychology, 79*, 3–13.

Ehri, L. C., & Wilce, L. S. (1987b). Does learning to spell help beginners learn to read words? *Reading Research Quarterly, 18*, 47–65.

Ehrlich, M.-F., Kurtz-Costes, B., & Loridant, C. (1993). Cognitive and motivational determinants of reading comprehension in good and poor readers. *Journal of Reading Behavior, 25*, 365–381.

Fielding-Barnsley, R. (1997). Explicit instruction in decoding benefits children high in phonemic awareness and alphabet knowledge. *Scientific Studies of Reading, 1*, 85–98.

Fitzgerald, J. (1995). English-as-a-second language learners' cognitive reading processes: A review of research. *Journal of Reading Behavior, 27*, 115–152.

Foorman, B. R., Francis, D. J., Fletcher, J. M., & Schatschneider, C. (1998). The role of instruction in learning to read: Preventing reading failure in at-risk children. *Journal of Educational Psychology, 90*, 37–55.

Foorman, B., Francis, D., Novy, D., & Liberman, D. (1991). How letter–sound instruction mediates progress in first-grade reading and spelling. *Journal of Educational Psychology, 83*, 456–469.

Fox, B. J. (1996). *Strategies for word identification: Phonics from a new perspective.* Englewood Cliffs, NJ: Prentice-Hall.

Fox, B. [J.], & Routh, D. K. (1975). Analyzing spoken language into words, syllables, and phonemes: A developmental study. *Journal of Psycholinguistic Research, 4*, 331–342.

Francis, D. J., Shaywitz, S. E., Stuebing, K. K., Shaywitz, B. A., & Fletcher, J. M. (1996). Developmental lag versus deficit models of reading disability: A longitudinal, individual growth curves analysis. *Journal of Educational Psychology, 88*, 3–17.

Freebody, P., & Byrne, B. (1988). Word-reading strategies in elementary school children: Relations to comprehension, reading time, and phonemic awareness. *Reading Research Quarterly, 23*, 441–453.

Fry, E. B., Kress, J. E., & Fountoukidis, D. L. (1993). *The reading teacher's book of lists.* Englewood Cliffs, NJ: Prentice-Hall.

Ganske, K. (2000). *Word journeys: Assessment-guided phonics, spelling, and vocabulary instruction.* New York: Guilford Press.

Gaskins, I. W. (2000). *Word detectives program: 5th grade and above.* Media, PA: Benchmark Press.

Gaskins, I. W., Ehri, L. C., Cress, C., O'Hara, C., & Donnelly, K. (1997). Procedures for word learning: Making discoveries about words. *Reading Teacher, 50*, 312–327.

Gaskins, R. W., Gaskins, I. W., Anderson, R. C., & Schommer, M. (1995). The reciprocal relationship between research and development: An example involving a decoding strand for poor readers. *Journal of Reading Behavior, 27*, 337–377.

Gaskins, R. W., Gaskins, J. C., & Gaskins, I. W. (1991). A decoding program for poor readers—and the rest of the class, too! *Language Arts, 68*, 213–225.

Gaskins, R. W., Gaskins, J. C., & Gaskins, I. W. (1992). Using what you know to figure out what you don't know: An analogy approach to decoding. *Reading and Writing Quarterly, 8*, 197–221.

Gibson, E. J., Gibson, J. J., Pick, A. D., & Osser, H. A. (1962). A developmental study of the discrimination of letter-like forms. *Journal of Comparative and Physiological Psychology, 55,* 897–906.

Gibson, E. J., & Levin, H. (1975). *The psychology of reading.* Cambridge, MA: MIT Press.

Gilbert, N., Spring, C., & Sassenrath, J. (1977). Effects of overlearning and similarity on transfer in word recognition. *Perceptual and Motor Skills, 44,* 591–598.

Goodman, K. S. (1965). A linguistic study of cues and miscues in reading. *Elementary English, 42,* 639–642.

Goodman, K. S. (1967). Reading: A psycholinguistic guessing game. *Journal of the Reading Specialist, 6,* 126–135.

Goodman, K. S. (1972). Orthography in a theory of reading instruction. *Elementary English, 49,* 1254–1261.

Goodman, K. S. (1993). *Phonics phacts.* Portsmouth, NH: Heinemann.

Goswami, U. (1986). Children's use of analogy in learning to read: A developmental study. *Journal of Experimental Child Psychology, 42,* 73–83.

Goswami, U. (1988). Orthographic analogies and reading development. *Quarterly Journal of Experimental Psychology, 40,* 239–268.

Goswami, U. (1993). Toward an interactive analogy model of reading development: Decoding vowel graphemes in beginning reading. *Journal of Experimental Child Psychology, 56,* 443–475.

Goswami, U. (1998). The role of analogies in the development of word recognition. In J. Metsala & L. Ehri (Eds.), *Word recognition in beginning reading* (pp. 41–63). Mahwah, NJ: Erlbaum.

Goswami, U. (1999). Orthographic analogies and phonological priming: A comment on Bowey, Vaughan, & Hansen (1998). *Journal of Experimental Child Psychology, 72,* 210–219.

Gough, P. B., Juel, C., & Griffith, P. L. (1992). Reading, spelling, and the orthographic cipher. In P. B. Gough, L. C. Ehri, & R. Treiman (Eds.), *Reading acquisition* (pp. 35–48). Hillsdale, NJ: Erlbaum.

Greaney, K. T., Tunmer, W. E., & Chapman, J. W. (1997). Effects of rime-based orthographic analogy training on the word recognition skills of children with reading disability. *Journal of Educational Psychology, 89,* 645–651.

Guthrie, J. T., & Tyler, S. J. (1975). Cognition and instruction of poor readers. *Journal of Reading Behavior, 10,* 57–78.

Hoffman, J. V., McCarthey, S. J., Abbott, J., Christian, C., Corman, L., Curry, C., Dressman, M., Elliot, B., Maherne, D., & Stahle, D. (1993). *So what's new in the new basals?: A focus on first grade* (Reading Research Report No. 6). Athens, GA, and College Park, MD: National Reading Research Center.

Hoffman, J. V., Sailors, M., & Patterson, E. U. (2002). Decodable texts for beginning reading instruction: The year 2000 basals. *Journal of Literacy Research, 34,* 269–298.

Horn, C. C., & Manis, F. R. (1987). Development of automatic and speeded reading of printed words. *Journal of Experimental Child Psychology, 44,* 92–108.

Huba, M. E. (1984). The relationship between linguistic awareness in prereaders and two types of experimental instruction. *Reading World, 23,* 347–363.

Huston, A. C., Anderson, D. R., Wright, J. C., Linebarger, D. L., & Schmitt, K. L.

(2001). *Sesame Street* viewers as adolescents: The recontact study. In S. M. Fisch & R. T. Truglio (Eds.), *"G" is for growing: Thirty years of research on children and Sesame Street* (pp. 131–143). Mahwah, NJ: Erlbaum.

Jenkins, J. R., Peyton, J. A., Sanders, E. A., & Vadasy, P. F. (2004). Effects of reading decodable texts in supplemental first-grade tutoring. *Scientific Studies of Reading, 8,* 53–85.

Johnston, F. R., Invernizzi, M., & Juel, C. (1998). *Book buddies: Guidelines for volunteer tutors of emergent and early readers.* New York: Guilford Press.

Johnston, R. S., & Watson, J. (1997). Developing reading, spelling, and phonemic awareness skills in primary school children. *Reading, 31,* 37–40.

Joshi, R. M., Dahlgren, M., & Boulware-Gooden, R. (2002). Teaching reading in an inner city school through a multi-sensory teaching approach. *Annals of Dyslexia, 52,* 229–242.

Juel, C., & Minden-Cupp, C. (2000). Learning to read words: Linguistic units and instructional strategies. *Reading Research Quarterly, 35,* 458–492.

Juel, C., & Roper/Schneider, D. (1985). The influence of basal readers on first grade reading. *Reading Research Quarterly, 20,* 134–152.

Kennedy, M. M. (1978). Findings from the Follow Through planned variation study. *Educational Researcher, 7*(6), 3–11.

LaBerge, D., & Samuels, S. J. (1974). Toward a theory of automatic information processing in reading. *Cognitive Psychology, 6,* 293–323.

Leppänen, U., Niemi, P., Aunola, K., & Nurmi, J.-E. (2004). Development of reading skills among preschool and primary school pupils. *Reading Research Quarterly, 39,* 72–93.

Lesaux, N. K., & Siegel, L. S. (2003). The development of reading in children who speak English as a second language. *Developmental Psychology, 39,* 1005–1019.

Leslie, L., & Allen, L. (1999). Factors that predict success in an early literacy intervention project. *Reading Research Quarterly, 34,* 404–424.

Leslie, L., & Calhoon, A. (1995). Factors affecting children's reading of rimes: Reading ability, word frequency, and rime-neighborhood size. *Journal of Educational Psychology, 87,* 576–586.

Levy, B. A., Bourassa, D. C., & Horn, C. (1999). Fast and slow namers: Benefits of segmentation and whole word training. *Journal of Experimental Child Psychology, 73,* 115–138.

Liberman, I. Y., Shankweiler, D., Fisher, F. W., & Carter, B. (1974). Reading and the awareness of linguistic segments. *Journal of Experimental Child Psychology, 18,* 201–212.

Lovett, M. W., Barron, R. W., & Benson, N. J. (2003). Effective remediation of word identification and decoding difficulties in school-age children with reading disabilities. In H. L. Swanson, K. R. Harris, & S. Graham (Eds.), *Handbook of learning disabilities* (pp. 273–292). New York: Guilford Press.

Lovett, M. W., Borden, S. L., DeLuca, T., Lacerenza, L., Benson, N. J., & Brackstone, D. (1994). Treating the core deficits of developmental dyslexia: Evidence of transfer of learning after phonologically- and strategy-based reading training programs. *Developmental Psychology, 30,* 805–822.

Lovett, M. W., Lacerenza, L., Borden, S. L., Frijters, J. C., Steinbach, K. A., & De

Palma, M. (2000). Components of effective remediation for developmental reading disabilities: Combining phonological and strategy-based instruction to improve outcomes. *Journal of Educational Psychology, 92,* 263–283.

Lovett, M. W., Ransby, M. J., Hardwick, N., Johns, M. S., & Donaldson, S. A. (1989). Can dyslexia be treated?: Treatment-specific and generalized treatment effects in dyslexic children's response to remediation. *Brain and Language, 37,* 90–121.

Manis, F. R., Custodio, R., & Szeszulski, P. A. (1993). Development of phonological and orthographic skill: A 2-year longitudinal study of dyslexic children. *Journal of Experimental Child Psychology, 56,* 64–86.

Marsh, H. G., Desberg, P., & Cooper, J. (1977). Developmental strategies in reading. *Journal of Reading Behavior, 9,* 391–394.

Marsh, H. G., Friedman, M., Desberg, P., & Saterdahl, K. (1981). Comparison of reading and spelling strategies in normal and reading-disabled children. In M. P. Friedman, J. P. Das, & N. O'Connor (Eds.), *Intelligence and learning* (pp. 363–367). New York: Plenum.

Marsh, H. G., Friedman, M., Welch, V., & Desberg, P. (1981). A cognitive–developmental theory of reading acquisition. In G. E. MacKinnon & T. G. Waller (Eds.), *Reading research: Advances in theory and practice* (Vol. 3, pp. 199–221). New York: Academic Press.

McCandliss, B., Beck, I. L., Sandak, R., & Perfetti, C. (2003). Focusing attention on decoding for children with poor reading skills: Design and preliminary tests of the word building intervention. *Scientific Studies of Reading, 7,* 75–104.

McConkie, G. W., Zola, D., Blanchard, H. E., & Wolverton, G. S. (1982). Perceiving words during reading: Lack of facilitation from prior peripheral exposure. *Perception and Psychophysics, 32,* 271–281.

McCutchen, D., Abbott, R. D., Green, L. B., Beretvas, N., Cox, S., Potter, N. S., Quiroga, T., & Gray, A. L. (2002a). Beginning literacy: Links among teacher knowledge, teacher practice, and student learning. *Journal of Learning Disabilities, 35,* 69–86.

McCutchen, D., Harry, D. R., Cunningham, A. E., Cox, S., Sidman, S., & Covill, A. E. (2002b). Reading teachers' knowledge of children's literature and English phonology *Annals of Dyslexia, 52,* 207–228.

Meichenbaum, D. (1977). *Cognitive behavior modification.* New York: Plenum.

Menon, S., & Hiebert, E. H. (2005). A comparison of first graders' reading with little books or literature-based basal anthologies. *Reading Research Quarterly, 40,* 12–38.

Mielke, K. W. (2001). A review of research on the educational and social impact of *Sesame Street.* In S. M. Fisch & R. T. Truglio (Eds.), *"G" is for growing: Thirty years of research on children and Sesame Street* (pp. 83–95). Mahwah, NJ: Erlbaum.

Moats, L. C., & Foorman, B. R. (2003). Measuring teachers' content knowledge of language and reading. *Annals of Dyslexia, 53,* 23–45.

Morris, D. (1999). *The Howard Street tutoring manual: Teaching at-risk readers in the primary grades.* New York: Guilford Press.

Morris, D., Tyner, B., & Perney, J. (2000). Early steps: Replicating the effects of a first-grade reading intervention program. *Journal of Educational Psychology, 92,* 681–693.

Moustafa, M. (1997). *Beyond traditional phonics*. Portsmouth, NH: Heinemann.

Moustafa, M. (1998). *Whole to part phonics: How children learn to read and spell.* Portsmouth, NH: Heinemann.

Nagy, W., Berninger, V., Abbott, R., Vaughan, K., & Vermeulen, K. (2003). Relationship of morphology and other language skills to literacy skills in at-risk second-grade readers and at-risk fourth-grade writers. *Journal of Educational Psychology, 95,* 730–742.

National Reading Panel. (2000). *Teaching children to read: An evidence-based assessment of the scientific research literature on reading and its implications for reading instruction.* Washington, DC: National Institute of Child Health and Development.

Nicholson, T. (1991). Do children read words better in context or in lists?: A classic study revisited. *Journal of Educational Psychology, 83,* 444–450.

Nicholson, T., Lillas, C., & Rzoska, A. (1988). Have we been misled by miscues? *Reading Teacher, 42,* 6–10.

O'Connor, R. E., & Bell. K. M. (2004). Teaching students with reading disability to read words. In C. A. Stone, E. R. Silliman, B. J. Ehren, & K. Apel (Eds.), *Handbook of language and literacy: Development and disorders* (pp. 481–498). New York: Guilford Press.

Olson, R. K., Wise, B., Johnson, M., & Ring, J. (1997). The etiology and remediation of phonologically based word recognition and spelling disabilities: Are phonological deficits the "hole" story? In B. Blachman (Ed.), *Foundations of reading acquisition* (pp. 305–326). Mahwah, NJ: Erlbaum.

Patterson, K. E., & Coltheart, V. (1987). Phonological processes in reading: A tutorial review. In M. Coltheart (Ed.), *Attention and performance XII: Vol. 12. The psychology of reading* (pp. 421–447). London: Erlbaum.

Penney, C. G. (2002). Teaching decoding skills to poor readers in high school. *Journal of Literacy Research, 34,* 99–118.

Perfetti, C. A., Bell, L. C., & Delaney, S. M. (1988). Automatical (prelexical) phonetic activation in silent word reading: Evidence from backward masking. *Journal of Memory and Language, 27,* 1–22.

Peterson, M. E., & Haines, L. P. (1992). Orthographic analogy training with kindergarten children: Effects of analogy use, phonemic segmentation, and letter–sound knowledge. *Journal of Reading Behavior, 24,* 109–127.

Pinnell, G. S., Fountas, I. C., Giacobbe, M. E., & Fountas, A. C. (1998). *Word matters: Teaching phonics and spelling in the reading/writing classroom.* Portsmouth, NH: Heinemann.

Pressley, M. (1977). Imagery and children's learning: Putting the picture in developmental perspective. *Review of Educational Research, 47,* 586–622.

Rayner, K., Inhoff, A. W., Morrison, R. E., Slowiaczek, M. L., & Bertera, J. H. (1981). *Journal of Experimental Psychology: Human Perception and Performance, 7,* 167–179.

Rayner, K., & Pollatsek, A. (1989). *The psychology of reading.* Englewood Cliffs, NJ: Prentice-Hall.

Rice, M. L., Huston, A. C., Truglio, R., & Wright, J. (1990). Words from "Sesame Street": Learning vocabulary from viewing. *Developmental Psychology, 26,* 421–428.

Routman, R. (1996). *Literacy at the crossroads.* Portsmouth, NH: Heinemann.

Samuels, S. J., Schermer, N., & Reinking, D. (1992). Reading fluency: Techniques for making decoding automatic. In S. J. Samuels & A. E. Farstrup (Eds.), *What research has to say about reading instruction* (pp. 124–144). Newark, DE: International Reading Association.

Santa, C. M., & Høien, T. (1999). The assessment of Early Steps: A program for early intervention of reading problems. *Reading Research Quarterly, 34,* 54–79.

Savage, R., & Stuart, M. (1998). Sublexical inferences in beginning reading: Medial vowel digraphs as functional units of transfer. *Journal of Experimental Child Psychology, 69,* 85–108.

Scarborough, H. S. (1995, April). *The fate of phonemic awareness beyond the elementary school years.* Paper presented at the biennial meeting of the Society for Research in Child Development, Indianapolis, IN.

Scarborough, H. S., Ehri, L. C., Olson, R. K., & Fowler, A. E. (1998). The fate of phonemic awareness beyond the elementary school years. *Scientific Studies of Reading, 2,* 115–142.

Seymour, P. H. K., & Elder, L. (1986). Beginning reading without phonology. *Cognitive Neuropsychology, 3,* 1–36.

Share, D. L. (1999). Phonological recoding and orthographic learning: A direct test of the self-teaching hypothesis. *Journal of Experimental Child Psychology, 72,* 95–129.

Share, D. L. (2004). Orthographic learning at a glance: On the time course and developmental onset of self-teaching. *Journal of Experimental Child Psychology, 87,* 267–298.

Shaywitz, S. E., Escobar, M. D., Shaywitz, B. A., Fletcher, J. M., & Makuch, R. (1992). Evidence that dyslexia may represent the lower tail of a normal distribution of reading ability. *New England Journal of Medicine, 326,* 145–150.

Siegel, L. S. (2003). Basic cognitive processes and reading disabilities. In H. L. Swanson, K. R. Harris, & S. Graham (Eds.), *Handbook of learning disabilities* (pp. 158–181). New York: Guilford Press.

Smith, F. (1971). *Understanding reading: A psycholinguistic analysis of reading and learning to read.* New York: Holt, Rinehart & Winston.

Smith, F. (1973). *Psycholinguistics and reading.* New York: Holt, Rinehart & Winston.

Smith, F. (1978). *Reading without nonsense.* New York: Teachers College Press.

Smith, F. (2004). *Understanding reading: A psycholinguistic analysis of reading and learning to read.* Mahwah, NJ: Erlbaum.

Smith, F., & Goodman, K. S. (1971). On the psycholinguistic method of teaching reading. *Elementary School Journal, 71,* 177–181.

Spear-Swerling, L., & Brucker, P. O. (2003). Teachers' acquisition of knowledge about English word structure. *Annals of Dyslexia, 53,* 72–103.

Sprenger-Charolles, L., Siegel, L. S., & Bonnet, P. (1998). Reading and spelling acquisition in French: The role of phonological mediation and orthographic factors. *Journal of Experimental Child Psychology, 68,* 134–165.

Stahl, S. A. (2001). Teaching phonics and phonological awareness. In S. B. Neuman & D. K. Dickinson (Eds.), *Handbook of early literacy research* (pp. 333–347). New York: Guilford Press.

Stahl, S. A., Duffy-Hester, A. M., & Stahl, K. A. D. (1998). Everything you wanted to know about phonics (but were afraid to ask). *Reading Research Quarterly, 33,* 338–355.

Stallings, J. (1975). Implementation and child effects of teaching practices in Follow Through classrooms. *Monographs of the Society for Research in Child Development, 40*(7/8, Serial No. 163).

Stanovich, K. E. (1980). Toward an interactive compensatory model of individual differences in the development of reading fluency. *Reading Research Quarterly, 16,* 32–71.

Stanovich, K. [E.] (1986). Matthew effects in reading: Some consequences of individual differences in the acquisition of literacy. *Reading Research Quarterly, 21,* 360–407.

Stanovich, K. E., & West, R. F. (1989). Exposure to print and orthographic processing. *Reading Research Quarterly, 24,* 402–433.

Thompson, G. B., Cottrell, D. S., & Fletcher-Flinn, C. M. (1996). Sublexical orthographic–phonological relations early in the acquisition of reading: The knowledge sources account. *Journal of Experimental Child Psychology, 62,* 190–222.

Torgesen, J. K., & Burgess, S. R. (1998). Consistency of reading-related phonological processes throughout early childhood. In J. Metsala & L. Ehri (Eds.), *Word recognition in beginning reading* (pp. 161–188). Mahwah, NJ: Erlbaum.

Torgesen, J. K., Wagner, R. K., & Rashotte, C. A. (1997). Prevention and remediation of severe reading disabilities: Keeping the end in mind. *Scientific Studies of Reading, 1,* 217–234.

Torgesen, J. K., Wagner, R. K., Rashotte, C. A., Alexander, A., Lindamood, P. C., Rose, E., & Conway, T. (1996). *Prevention and remediation of phonologically based reading disabilities.* Paper presented at the Spectrum of Developmental Disabilities XVIII: Dyslexia, Baltimore, MD.

Torgesen, J. K., Wagner, R. K., Rashotte, C. A., Rose, E., Lindamood, P., Conway, T., & Garvan, C. (1999). Preventing reading failure in young children with phonological processing disabilities: Group and individual responses to instruction. *Journal of Educational Psychology, 91,* 579–593.

Tunmer, W. E., Herriman, M. L., & Nesdale, A. R. (1988). Metalinguistic abilities and beginning reading. *Reading Research Quarterly, 23,* 134–158.

van Daal, V. H. P., Reitsma, P., & van der Leu, A. (1994). Processing units in word reading by disabled readers. *Journal of Experimental Child Psychology, 57,* 180–210.

Vellutino, F. R., Scanlon, D. M., Sipay, E. R., Small, S. G., Pratt, A., Chen, R., & Denckla, M. B. (1996). Cognitive profiles of difficult-to-remediate and readily remediated poor readers: Early intervention as a vehicle for distinguishing between cognitive and experiential deficits as a basic cause of specific reading disability. *Journal of Educational Psychology, 88,* 601–638.

Venezky, R. L., & Johnson, D. (1973). Development of two letter–sound patterns in grade one through three. *Journal of Educational Psychology, 64,* 109–115.

Walton, P. D. (1995). Rhyming ability, phoneme identity, letter–sound knowledge, and the use of orthographic analogy by prereaders. *Journal of Educational Psychology, 87,* 587–597.

Walton, P. D., & Walton, L. M. (2002). Beginning reading by teaching in rime analogy: Effects on phonological skills, letter-sound knowledge, working memory, and word-reading strategies. *Scientific Studies of Reading, 6,* 79–115.

Walton, P. D., Walton, L. M., & Felton, K. (2001). Teaching rime analogy or letter recoding reading strategies to prereaders: Effects on prereading skills and word reading. *Journal of Educational Psychology, 93,* 160–180.

Wang, C.-C., & Gaffney, J. S. (1998). First graders' use of analogy in word reading. *Journal of Literacy Research, 30,* 389–403.

Waterman, B., & Lewandowski, L. (1993). Phonologic and semantic processing in reading-disabled and nondisabled males at two age levels. *Journal of Experimental Child Psychology, 55,* 87–103.

Wise, B. W. (1992). Whole words and decoding for short-term learning: Comparisons on a "talking-computer" system. *Journal of Experimental Child Psychology, 54,* 147–167.

Wise, B. W., Olson, R. K., & Treiman, R. (1990). Subsyllabic units in computerized reading instruction: Onset–rime versus postvowel segmentation. *Journal of Experimental Child Psychology, 49,* 1–19.

Wood, S. S., Bruner, J. S., & Ross, G. (1976). The role of tutoring in problem solving. *Journal of Child Psychology and Psychiatry, 17,* 89–100.

Wright, J. C., Huston, A. C., Scantlin, R., & Kotler, J. (2001). The Early Window Project: *Sesame Street* prepares children for school. In S. M. Fisch & R. T. Truglio (Eds.), *"G" is for growing: Thirty years of research on children and Sesame Street* (pp. 97–114). Mahwah, NJ: Erlbaum.

Zill, N. (2001). Does *Sesame Street* enhance school readiness?: Evidence from a national survey of children. In S. M. Fisch & R. T. Truglio (Eds.), *"G" is for growing: Thirty years of research on children and Sesame Street* (pp. 115–130). Mahwah, NJ: Erlbaum.

CHAPTER 6

Fluency

with Lauren Fingeret

Fluent reading refers to accurate and fast reading at the word level, with good prosody (i.e., the reading has expression consistent with mature reading; Stahl, 2004). What we emphasize, however, is that by far the most important function of reading, in our view, is comprehension. Accurate, fast, and even prosodic reading that does not result in the reader's understanding the text is not good enough, though in some cases such word-level fluency may be necessary for attaining comprehension.

Measures of fluency often involve asking readers to read a passage for a set period of time, usually aloud, perhaps for a minute or so. Fluent readers read quickly and with few accuracy errors. When we have administered such measures, we often notice that readers do not pause to think about what they are reading. In fact, the only activity they exhibit is reading the words quickly and accurately, and, although often it is not scored on fluency measures, we feel better if the reading is with good expression (i.e., is prosodic).

Such an emphasis on fluent reading bothers us, for we know, based on many studies of good comprehenders, that the best readers do not read texts straight through, but rather are very reflective as they read (Pressley & Afflerbach, 1995). Excellent comprehenders overview text and scan it. They relate their prior knowledge to ideas in the text. They notice when they are confused or need to reread, and they do so. They construct images in their mind's eye reflecting the content of the text. Good readers summarize, and they interpret, often with intense feeling,

195

rejecting or embracing the ideas of an author. Such reflective reading, actually, can be pretty slow.

Last evening, one author of this chapter (M. P.) read a poem, having no problem with reading the words but pausing to reflect on every word and line, rereading and rethinking the author's intended meaning throughout the reading. There were only 300 words in the poem, and yet it took 5 minutes to read it. An adult reading at 60 words a minute would raise red flags on most fluency measures, although the first author does not have a fluency problem. Nevertheless, fluency at the word level, as operationalized as reading accurately and quickly, is necessary so that the reader can choose to slow down and employ the comprehension strategies described above (i.e., there is enough available cognitive capacity when word-level reading is fluent to permit the decision to use the comprehension strategies and execute them). The criterion we should want in reading education is readers who are fluent at the word level but who constructively respond to text, constructing meaning and reacting to text all along the way, which involves skillful use of the comprehension strategies used by the best readers (Pressley & Afflerbach, 1995) and consistent relating of relevant prior knowledge to the ideas in the text (Anderson & Pearson, 1984). Such reading is slower than the racing through of text that is sometimes accepted as evidence of fluent reading, but the slowness is due to thinking about the ideas in the text, with our view that *truly* fluent readers can and do think hard about what they are reading.

We recognize that our perspective is a minority perspective and must respectfully integrate other data and thinking on fluency. Thus, in this chapter, we discuss the theory, research, and classroom practices that should be on the mind of the researcher community as we attempt to understand better the nature of fluent reading, how it can be promoted, and whether fluent reading is a realistic, or even necessary, possibility for all readers. In the end, however, we will come back to a strong pitch for comprehension to be the measure that matters most in reading.

A FLURRY OF THEORIES, DATA, AND INSTRUCTIONAL PRACTICES

At this point, we must provide a warning. What follows is a flurry of individual theoretical, research, and practice directions that we have on our mind as we think about fluency. The work should be on the minds of everyone concerned with development of fluent reading. As a flurry, at times you might feel lost in a snowstorm. Once this storm ends, in a concluding section of the chapter, we will survey the landscape and how the various bits and pieces fit together and, to continue the analogy, try to begin to clear a path. This path will sum to our best thoughts about what might be tried by practitioners right now with regularly developing and struggling readers, as well as our thinking about where researchers interested in fluency could and should focus.

We enter the flurry with the first scientific article on fluent reading that the first author encountered, provided as a preprint to him by David LaBerge during his new-graduate student week at the University of Minnesota in the fall of 1973. This article is, without a doubt, the most influential theoretical perspective on fluency ever produced and continues to be cited in virtually every scholarly paper on fluency. It was published at a time when thinking about reading was shifting, with the article becoming a primary causal force in the shift.

LaBerge and Samuels (1974)

LaBerge and Samuels (1974) appeared at a time when George Miller's (1956) insight that human consciousness has limited attentional capacity was being fully appreciated as pertaining to all conscious life, not just the laboratory list learning tasks that had spawned it. Scholars interested in human attention, in particular, realized that what people could attend to at any one moment was very limited (Kahnemann, 1973). A complex activity like reading has to be accomplished within the limits of such limited attention, meaning that picking up information from the letters of words to recognizing the parts of words sufficiently to sound out the whole word to comprehending the word all must happen within limited attentional capacity. The only way a word can be comprehended, given this limitation, was that some parts of the task had to be automatic. So, according to LaBerge and Samuels (1974), the mature reader automatically recognizes letters and whole words (i.e., the sight words) and even makes associations from the sounded-out words to their meanings with little attention expended.

Less mature readers expend much capacity. For the prereading child, all of the attentional capacity might be consumed discriminating one letter from another. For the child who has mastered the letters and their sound associations to the point of automaticity, blending the sounds might take up a great deal of capacity, with the result that the child might read all the words in a sentence and still have no idea what the sentence means. The transition from effortful to effortless, error-free, automatic performance at each stage depends on practice in doing the task. Practice does make perfect from this perspective, in the sense that both accuracy and speed increase and attentional capacity demands decrease. Consistent with the basic learning analyses of the time, LaBerge and Samuels (1974) posited that distributed practice (i.e., practice of a task over days and weeks and over various texts and tasks) was better than mass practice (i.e., much drilling in a short period of time with a specific type of text). Given the predominance of the behaviorists in the decades just prior to LaBerge and Samuels's (1974) analysis, LaBerge and Samuels appreciated that feedback during practice helped learning, that affirmations of correct responses would strengthen associations (e.g., between a letter and its sound, between a root word as a visual stimulus and its correct pronunciation), and that negative feedback could weaken errant responses. Because of practice, letter features came to be recognized as whole letters among prereaders; root words composed of individual letters came to be recognized as wholes in grade 1; root words sounded out with effort in grade 1 came to be recognized at first glance by grade 2; meanings of words that are first brought to mind by the reader sounding out the word (i.e., the meaning of boat comes to mind after the young reader says boat) eventually come to mind from simply seeing the word even in the absence of a conscious articulation of the meaning. In short, throughout learning to read, effortful and inaccurate processes are replaced with almost effortless and more accurate processes. As that occurs, preschoolers who could not recognize a single letter will, over time, become fluent readers of whole words and eventually longer texts.

Overall, LaBerge and Samuels's (1974) work represented a brilliant integration of the theoretical perspectives of the time, resulting in a series of experiments, briefly summarized in the article, that supported their framework. Reading the piece today, there is only one really strange component and one possible concern. There was a lot of attention to visual analysis and perceptual learning of letters, mirroring the psychology of the day, as reflected in the most visible psychology of reading published in the decade of the 1970s (Gibson & Levin, 1975), with a number of Gibson students at Minnesota at the time probably providing stimulus for LaBerge and Samuels (1974) to include visual perceptual learning as a focal point. At the same time, a series of analyses were being conducted in other places to evaluate the role of visual versus verbal factors in reading disability. At the end of the decade, Frank Vellutino (1979) would summarize the evidence, making the case that the assumption of many that reading disabilities represented a visual impairment was wrong. Reading disabilities were much more about verbal impairments. Ever since publication of Vellutino's book, that perspective has prevailed, a central by-product being that understanding the psychology of language, especially at the word level, is the key to understanding reading, both disabled reading and skilled reading. In the next section, we turn our attention to that overarching perspective, which must be understood to encompass much of contemporary thinking about fluency.

Before we do that, however, we feel compelled to mention another possible problem with LaBerge and Samuels, one already touched upon in the introduction that we will revisit at length later in the chapter. The goal of reading is comprehension, and fluency, at best, can be valued only as a means to that end. When LaBerge and Samuels developed their theory of automatic information processing, or automaticity theory, they *placed* a premium on speed (and accuracy) in oral reading that may have extended beyond the natural pace characteristic of effortless reading. It is possible that this has led to a widespread overemphasis on oral reading speed in instruction and assessment, to the potential detriment of comprehension. As we conduct oral reading assessments on young readers, for example, we notice they read as quickly as possible with little attention to detail. This is so common among young readers that it seems entirely likely that an implicit, if not also explicit, goal of early reading instruction is to get children to read rapidly, while probably ignoring comprehension measures. As we move further away from a simple view of reading (e.g., Gough & Tunmer, 1986), which would have children learn to read rapidly so they can hear and then understand what they are reading, we may begin to question the extent to which we should be emphasizing the goal of speed in our instruction and assessments at all. Instead, we wonder if focusing more on comprehension strategies, even at a young age, would help to decrease the phenomenon of children reading as fast as they can to finish a passage. This issue should not be confused with problems some children have with speed of processing, which will be addressed later in the chapter, and at this time we present this theory only as another addition to the flurry of possibilities for further inquiry.

Reading Is about Verbal Processing—in Particular, Phonological Processing of Words

You already have read about the contributions that Jean Chall and Marilyn Adams made to reading instruction, primarily by emphasizing phonemic awareness and phonics (see Chapter 5). Even with the advent of whole language, Chall and Adams's phonics-based approach reemerged as the dominant approach, especially as the National Institute of Child Health and Human Development (NICHD) became interested in this research and began to fund it heavily. The result of this interest from the NICHD was a substantial body of work in the next few years in which struggling beginning readers were provided several years of intensive, systematic synthetic phonics instruction.

Such instruction did increase these children's word recognition abilities (i.e., their accuracy), putting them within sight of the decoding accuracy of the general population of readers by the late elementary grades. It did not produce fluent reading (see Torgesen, 2004, for a review; also, Torgesen, Rashotte, & Alexander, 2001), with these students reading much more slowly in the later elementary grades than the general population of readers. More positively, however, when students who are at risk for reading failure, but who have not yet evidenced any, are provided systematic phonics instruction in kindergarten and grade 1, the result in the later elementary grades for these students is reading that is almost as fluent (i.e., fast) as the general population of late elementary readers (Torgesen, 2004). There seem to be two important implications here. There is nothing in these data to suggest that for most readers phonologically based instruction in kindergarten and grade-1 somehow interferes with the development of fluency. That said, for really troubled beginning readers, phonics is not going to be enough to assure fluent reading. To its credit, based on research, the NICHD has concluded that more than phonics is required for fluency to develop. This was made clear in the fluency section of the National Reading Panel (2000) report, which will be taken up shortly. First, however, NICHD-sponsored work has provided some strong hints about why the most troubled readers do not become fluent readers.

Brain Imagery Research

NICHD has been a major sponsor of research intended to map brain functioning in both normal and dyslexic child and adult readers. There now exist brain imaging techniques that permit the detection of more and less active areas of the brain as people read (see Shaywitz & Shaywitz, 2004, for a review, which is the basis for this subsection; also Goswami, 2004, for an overview of neuroimaging research conducted in the area of language and comprehension over the past 15 years, see Gernsbacher & Kaschak, 2003).

One important finding is that normal mature readers, especially, activate a set of three sites on the left side of the brain more reliably than readers with dyslexia (Shaywitz et al., 2002). One area that is especially active is the parieto-temporal region, with healthy functioning of this region associated with the ability to phonologically analyze words (i.e., sound out words). This region is about three-quarters of the way toward the back of the brain and two-thirds of the way toward the top of the brain. A second very active region in normal functioning is the occipito-temporal region, which is near the back of the brain and the bottom of the cortex. The healthy functioning of this region is important in recognizing words as wholes, that is, as sight words, rather than sounding out. The third region, Broca's area, is closer to the front of the brain and functions in the analysis of spoken words. In good readers, these three areas work well in coordination, with the result that readers recognize familiar words automatically without sounding them out and can quickly and accurately sound out less familiar words.

Good readers probably are not born with these left-side areas especially active during verbal processing. For example, Turkelbaum, Gareau, Flowers, Zeffiro, and Eden (2003) reported in a cross-sectional developmental study that activity in these areas increased with age, that is, as children learned to read. What was also very interesting was that, with development, activation of areas on the right side of the brain decreased. Brain activation in response to words probably changes as people learn to read, a hypothesis that deserves serious additional study and is receiving it.

In general, the left-brain functioning of readers with dyslexia is different. The parieto-temporal region, in particular, seems impaired. Often, the Broca's area (and some other areas) will be more active in such readers, suggesting that these regions are somehow compensating for the lack of function in the parieto-temporal region, but since these regions are not quite matched to task, word recognition is slow at best and less accurate than in normal readers. Some adults who were dyslexic as children have, somehow, somewhat compensated for it as adults (Shaywitz et al., 2003). They recognize familiar words well. Interestingly, these compensating readers have more pronounced activity in the occipito-temporal region than do adults with dyslexia who do not recognize familiar words, That is, the compensated adults with dyslexia have more pronounced activity in the area of the brain responsible for recognizing words as wholes than in the area responsible for sounding words out. Because these compensated readers also seem to have more connection between the functioning of the occipito-temporal region and regions of the brain responsible for short-term memory than other readers (including normal readers), it seems likely that they have somehow memorized the sight words. In contrast, in normal readers, there are stronger connections between the parieto-temporal and occipito-temporal regions, suggesting that the fluent reading of familiar words in normal individuals may be caused by repeated sounding out of words rather than rote memorization. The normal reader first sounds out the word and over repeated encounters comes to recognize the word as a sight word. There is some evidence in young readers of active functioning of the parieto-temporal region preceding the active functioning of the occipito-temporal region, as beginning readers who are good at sounding out begin to develop sight vocabulary.

Consider additionally the childhood dyslexics who seem to compensate as adults. Their reading is still not fluent, because they have trouble with unfamiliar words. They still cannot sound out words, with the brain imagery data confirming that there is less than optimal functioning in their parieto-temporal regions (see Shaywitz et al., 2003, for the original data on this fascinating study that we consider potentially very important as thinking about reading education proceeds). Shaywitz et al.'s (2003) observation that fluent reading depends on automatic recognition of high-frequency words and skilled sounding out of lower-frequency words is consistent with other recent analyses (Compton, Appleton, & Hosp, 2004).

In short, the message in recent brain research is that there are probably some individuals with brain differences that preclude them from becoming fluent readers. Even if they come to memorize many familiar words and recognize them on sight, the unfamiliar words will disrupt their reading. Many children with dyslexia grow up to be adults with dyslexia, with no compensating capacity ever developing that permits them to recognize even very familiar words automatically. One important point is that general intelligence should be considered, with Shaywitz et al. (2003) observing that, as a group, adults who had learned to compensate were slightly above-average in intelligence and those who failed to memorize sight words were slightly below-average in intelligence. We may add that the compensating readers did about as well as nonimpaired adults on a comprehension measure and better than the noncompensating adult dyslexics, which suggests that, even if the compensation from memorizing familiar words does not produce as fluent reading as occurs in normal adult readers, it can still improve comprehension. This should be considered a hypothesis, however, rather than accepted on the basis of one study. It is a very important hypothesis, however, one that should be a priority for future study in the immediate future.

Not surprisingly, the NICHD scientists doing brain imagery work are interested in phonologically based reading interventions—specifically, whether experiencing these interventions produces changes in brain activation in areas associated with normal reading. Shaywitz et al. (2004) reported an interesting initial study supportive of the possibility that the phonologically based interventions favored by NICHD and in recent federal legislation (e.g., No Child Left Behind; hereafter, NCLB) may, in fact, stimulate the development of the brain regions associated with skilled reading. That is, they asked whether brain activation in the left-side areas associated with skilled reading was more likely in students receiving such instruction than those not receiving such instruction. Children who, at the end of first or second grade, were performing below the 25th percentile on standardized tests of word recognition and word attack skills were the participants in the study. Students receiving the phonologically based intervention received systematic phonics instruction for the school year, including reading of decodable books, complemented by reading of trade books as decoding skill increased. Other students who were below the 25th percentile on word-level skills experienced the regular school reading curriculum in grade 2 or 3, which varied from school to school, but did not focus on phonological skills. After the year of intervention, the students who received the phonological intervention were reading better than those who did not receive the intervention, with better word recognition and slightly faster reading as well as very slightly better comprehension. That said, the phonological students remained far behind same-age normal readers.

Brain images during reading were also recorded at the beginning and end of the year of the intervention. The most striking result was that by the end of the year of intervention the phonologically treated students had brain images resembling nonimpaired agemates. In particular, there was normal activation in the areas of the brain associated with sounding out words. The disabled readers receiving regular reading instruction had less pronounced brain activation in the areas associated with skilled reading. Brain imaging data were also collected on participants receiving the phonological intervention a year after intervention concluded. Encouragingly, there was now more activity in the occipito-temporal region, the area that appears to mediate recognition of words as wholes. The hypothesis that phonologically based interventions may have effects beyond teaching students how to sound out words gains additional credence with the results of this study, although much additional study still needs to occur. In particular, mapping out the long-term effects of phonologically based interventions in the primary grades, both on behavioral data (i.e., accurate reading of words, fluency, and comprehension) and brain functioning, would be instructive. The brain imagery data are merely suggestive at this point, hardly definitive, and inconclusive with respect to the development of fluency.

Of course, as this discussion continues, it will be clear that there is a need for much more research with respect to fluency, even with respect to interventions that have been around a long time. That is clear from reviewing the outcomes reported in the National Reading Panel (NRP) report (2000), which will be taken up later. First, we review briefly the evidence that speed of processing might be a biologically based difference between children, which has implications for whether fluency can developed through experience.

Speed of Processing

There is a lot of evidence that many weak readers are slow at sounding out words. They can decode accurately but do so slowly (e.g., Bowers & Swanson, 1991; Hogaboam & Perfetti, 1978; Lovett, 1984; Vukovic, Wilson, & Nash, 2004; Wolf & Bowers, 1999; Wolf, Bowers, & Biddle, 2000; Wolf, Pfeil, Lotz, & Biddle, 1994). For example, recently a group at the University of Kansas has been studying the possibility that an important individual difference in reading-disabled students is that they process verbal material in general more slowly than other children. In fact, in their work to date they have found support for that possibility, with speed of processing of verbal material predictive of reading achievement over and above phonological processes in their analyses of second and fourth graders

(Catts, Gillispie, Leonard, Kail, & Miller, 2002; see also Denckla, 1972; Denckla & Rudel, 1976; Levy, Bourassa, & Horn, 1999; McBride-Chang & Kail, 2002; Scarborough, 2001; Vukovic et al., 2004).

Recall from LaBerge and Samuels's (1974) model that more rapid processing is also less capacity demanding. Given that the speed of processing difference between individuals tends to be stable and related to a variety of intellectual outcomes (Baker, Vernon, & Ho, 1991; Jensen, 1987, 1993), there is good reason to ask whether slow thinking that impairs fluent reading can be overcome through experiences, with the possibility that it cannot be overcome because it is a genetically determined individual difference. This may account for why reading disabilities detected in childhood predict reading disabilities in adulthood (Jensen, 1987) and why children who are slow verbal processors and at risk for later reading difficulties can be spotted even before they begin to read (e.g., McDougall, Hulme, Ellis, & Monk, 1994; Torgesen & Davis, 1996; Vellutino, Scanlon, & Spearing, 1995).

National Reading Panel (2000)

We have already examined the NRP report and its findings in the areas of phonemic awareness and phonics, and we know that those areas are favored heavily by the NRP and NICHD, who funded the report (NRP, 2000). But what about fluency? The NRP found clear support for the conclusion that reading fluency can be increased through repeated oral reading with feedback and guidance. That is, both accuracy in reading and speed of reading can be increased. The procedures for doing so are a real "mulligan stew," however, as described by Stahl (2004). They vary in how much repeated reading occurs in the intervention as well as according to whether an adult assists reading, an adult tutors the child, or the child reads along with the audiotapes. Moreover, the NRP did not attempt to differentiate among the alternative procedures for increasing fluency in respect to their relative efficaciousness.

Kuhn and Stahl (2003) looked again at the studies included in the NRP and broadened the criterion a bit so that more than just experimental and quasi-experimental studies were included in their analyses as well as more than studies that provided enough quantitative information to be included in a meta-analysis. Their analyses of the studies examined by NRP and the additional investigations highlighted some important points.

1. Kuhn and Stahl (2003) concluded that adult assistance was quite important with respect to increasing fluency, with simple repeated reading by the child much less certain to produce a positive outcome, as compared to repeated reading with adult assistance.

2. Kuhn and Stahl (2003) also noted that there was no difference in fluency or other reading outcomes between repeated reading of same text and the same amount of time spent reading a variety of texts (Homan, Klesius, & Hite, 1993; Mathes & Fuchs, 1993; Rashotte & Torgesen, 1985; von Bon, Boksebeld, Font Freide, & van den Hurk, 1991).

3. Assistance during repeated reading promoted both fluency and comprehension.

4. There was more evidence in favor of having readers confront somewhat challenging rather than easy texts as they experience fluency instruction.

5. Although most of the research on fluency instruction has been carried out with one-to-one tutoring, there are promising whole-group approaches (Rasinski, Padak, Linek, & Sturtevant, 1994; Stahl, Huebach, & Cramond, 1997) that deserve closer evaluation.

6. All that said, the fluency instruction evaluated to date certainly is not enabling weak readers to catch up to regularly achieving readers, in terms of fluency!

In short, there is support for developing phonemic awareness, teaching phonics, and encouraging fluency through repeated reading with guidance and feedback. As additional analyses on these topics are occurring, it seems likely that, based on evidence, more can probably be done to improve reading and fluency than the NRP concluded. In general, a broad instructional agenda makes sense with respect to increasing fluency and comprehension in struggling readers.

Developing Sight Word and Vocabulary Knowledge

Given the emphasis on reading at the word level in the most popular conceptions of fluent reading, it makes sense to us for all concerned with reading education to be thinking about what words students are learning to read. Returning to LaBerge and Samuels's (1974) framework, it is essential that readers both decode words automatically and access the meanings of the words automatically (i.e., once the word is read, they know what it means). Considering the millions of words in the English language—the unabridged *Oxford English Dictionary* (Simpson & Weiner, 1989), for example, taking up some 20 volumes—how can this happen? It can happen because readers do not need to know all of the words in the dictionary!

Consider first an historically prominent reading fluency intervention. Edward W. Dolch (1939, 1945; 1941, 1951, 1960) believed that children should be taught the words most often encountered in text as sight words, words they should recognize automatically. Through his research, he identified 220 words that made up between 50 and 75% of texts children read, with most being function words (e.g., *the*, *a*), conjunctions, pronouns, prepositions, and common verbs. He also identified 95 nouns that commonly occurred in texts read by children. Both of these lists were part of a larger list of the 1,000 most commonly encountered words.

Dolch had a view of reading and reading instruction that was far ahead of his time (see Pressley, 2005)—here we can cover only those elements most pertinent to our discussion. Although he believed that much learning of sight words could occur in a decontextualized fashion, Dolch also developed many literary stories to enable students to encounter the selected words in context. For struggling readers, in particular, Dolch felt that these stories should be read orally by students with substantial feedback from the teacher, including feedback about how to sound out the words (i.e., the stories contained related words that could be comprehended through phonics skills, which Dolch believed in teaching explicitly). Dolch was emphatic that reading stories was not about reading words but rather about getting meaning from text, often very personalized meanings informed by students' prior knowledge. Dolch's approach emphasized motivation and was filled with practices that are now known to motivate students, based on substantial research (see Pintrich & Schunk, 2002). He advocated texts that were somewhat challenging and believed in providing lots of praise, practicing reading skills in the context of games, and maintaining cooperative classrooms rather than ones emphasizing competition among students.

Dolch lived in an era when experimental research was relatively uncommon and little understood as a means of evaluating curriculum, with Campbell and Stanley's (1966) classic monograph on experimentation appearing several years after the final edition of Dolch's best-known textbook. Thus, Dolch's ideas about instruction have never been subjected to widespread evaluation. What *has* been studied is whether intensive, short-term teaching of sight words in a decontextualized fashion, in fact, improves subsequent reading of text containing those words. Although the data are mixed on that subject (Fleisher, Jenkins, & Pany, 1979; Levy, Abello, & Lysynchuk, 1997), what Dolch actually proposed was the *long-term* teaching of sight words and the reading of real stories containing the words, which, for the 220 most common words and 95 most common nouns, was easily accomplished. Such learning of words and reading of text should occur in a very balanced reading instructional program that extends across the school day, according to Dolch.

Dolch's idea of making certain that students know a core set of commonly encountered words makes even more sense today in light of some recent research. Much is now being learned about just what words K–12 students really need to know, the basic vocabulary of children and adolescents.

Biemiller and Slonim (2001) provided the most recent useful input in this effort. They performed analyses to identify words understood by 80% of children at each grade level (i.e., most children know the meanings of these words). Very importantly, they were focusing on root words (e.g., *fish*, from which *fishing*, *fishy*, and *fished* are derived). By the end of grade 2, children know about 5,000 root words. After that, through grade 12, students gain about 1,000 words a year to a total of about 15,000 words. In short, Biemiller and Slonim (2001) have identified the words that children at each grade level need to understand. While certainly more than Dolch's basic 1,000 words, their list stops short of being an overwhelming number of words. Since many of these words are not especially high-frequency words in English or in texts children encounter, teachers can prioritize further which words should be targeted for sight word development and students' ready access to their meanings.

It is a truism that reading is not just about decoding words. Even the simplest view of reading (e.g., Gough & Tunmer, 1986) posits that reading involves decoding the words and then comprehending them, largely by listening to one's own interpretation of the words. Hence, reading comprehension is viewed as determined by a combination of word recognition skills and listening comprehension abilities. In an important study, Catts, Hogan, Adlof, and Barth (2003) assessed the word recognition, listening comprehension, and reading comprehension skills of a group of students, who ranged widely in reading ability, when they were in second, fourth, and eighth grades. Word recognition was much more predictive of reading comprehension at grade 2 than at grade 4, and again more predictive at grade 4 than at grade 8, where it accounted for a *negligible* portion of the variance in reading comprehension. The researchers also examined the weakest readers at each of the grade levels. Word recognition difficulties were more prominently associated with poor reading when students were younger than when they were older. With increasing age, listening comprehension problems became progressively more prominent in students' reading problems. Based on these data, there is more reason to be concerned about word recognition with younger as compared to older students, but for poor readers word recognition problems are still obvious in grade 8. At all grade levels, however, reading comprehension reflected a balancing of word recognition and listening comprehension skills. The need for balanced development of skills was apparent in these analyses, consistent with the message in research of the past decade that a balancing of factors is essential in effective reading instruction.

Another important hypothesis is that developing word recognition skills to the point of fluency should increase comprehension, although comprehension gains have not always been obtained when readers have learned new words to the point of automatic recognition of them (e.g., Fleisher et al., 1979; Samuels, Dahl, & Archwamety, 1974; Yuill & Oakhill, 1988, 1991). Tan and Nicholson (1997) offered an especially important set of data, however, in support of the position that word recognition fluency improves comprehension.

The participants in Tan and Nicholson's (1997) study were 7- to 10-year-old weaker readers. In the critical training condition of the study, participants practiced recognizing target words until they could read each word without hesitation. As word recognition fluency was developed, there was also some attention to the meaning of the trained words. In contrast, in the control condition, training focused only on word meanings rather than on word recognition, consisting of discussions between the experimenter and the student about the meanings of target words. In fact, in this control condition, the students did not even see the words during training but only heard them.

Following training, all participants in the Tan and Nicholson (1997) study read a passage containing the target words, with 12 comprehension questions following the reading. There were both literal questions and ones requiring readers to make inferences in order to respond to them. The most important result was that the trained participants answered more comprehension questions than did control participants, despite the fact that, if anything, the control condition developed understanding of the target words better. Breznitz (1997a, 1997b) provided another set of analyses confirming that more rapid automatic decoding improves comprehension, probably by freeing up short-term capacity for comprehension.

Prosody

Although fluent reading is characterized as fast, accurate, and prosodic, there has been relatively little attention to the role of prosody in fluent reading. On the one hand, reading prosody may be a by-product of fluent, skilled reading, naturally resulting once decoding becomes automatic enough to free up sufficient attention to permit reasonably good comprehension of what is read (Gough & Tunmer, 1986; Kuhn & Stahl, 2003). On the other hand, it could be that prosody increases reading skill—for example, comprehension—in which case it should be taught to readers like other skills that increase understanding of text. So far, however, although rereading tends to produce increases in prosody, other approaches (e.g., prosodic modeling by a teacher) have not had much impact on prosodic reading (see especially Young, Bowers, & MacKinnon, 1996).

Schwanenflugel, Hamilton, Kuhn, Wisenbaker, and Stahl (2004) provided an especially analytical evaluation of reading fluency and prosodic issues in the reading of grade-2 and -3 students. What they found was that the automatic decoding of words was strongly related to prosody and comprehension. In contrast, prosody was not powerfully related to comprehension, either as a cause or effect of understanding what had been read (although there was a slight positive relationship between prosody and comprehension, consistent with other data; e.g., Kitzen, 2001). The most likely hypothesis based on these data is that for many children prosodic reading is a by-product of becoming fluent at the word level (see also Bear, 1992) but is not strongly associated with comprehension either as a cause or an effect.

Assessment of Fluency

Fluent reading is most often measured in terms of the number of words read accurately in a set period of time. Although there are ways to measure prosody (Schwanenflugel et al., 2004), there has been far less attention to its assessment. In the past several years, a set of measures known as the Dynamic Indicators of Basic Early Literacy Skills (DIBELS; see dibels.uoregon.edu) has been widely deployed at the primary-grade levels and now at the upper elementary level. Basically, this is one more measure that involves measuring the speed of accurate reading (i.e., how many words of grade-level text can be read in a minute). It has been developed in the recent past, and hence there has not been nearly enough psychometric evaluation as is needed to understand the measure well (Rathvon, 2004). Even so, it is being used widely because it has been deemed an excellent assessment by the federal clearinghouse evaluating beginning reading assessments (idea.uoregon.edu/assessment).

As this chapter is being written, Katherine Hilden, Rebecca Shankland, Holly Lang, and Michael Pressley at Michigan State University are analyzing data on the third-grade version of DIBELS. One very important finding in this investigation, as noted earlier, is that children often can read with great speed and accuracy and yet recall few of the ideas in the text they have read. This raises real issues. Nobody should be interested in or promoting fast reading with low comprehension. Yet, given the emphasis on DIBELS testing in many schools, including its use as a preferred measure in many sites receiving federal reading instruction dollars, there is reason to reexamine the validity of this assessment with respect to skilled reading. We emphasize that we do not endorse assessments that reward fast reading without regard to comprehension.

Comprehension Strategies Instruction

Weak readers can become better readers through the teaching of comprehension strategies. The work of Brown, Pressley, Van Meter, and Schuder

(1996) and Anderson (1992) is especially powerful evidence of this. In the former study, weak second-grade readers were taught a small repertoire of comprehension strategies over the course of a school year of instruction, with huge gains in reading achievement at the end of the year. In the latter study, weak readers in grades 6 through 9 were provided similar instruction, with similar large gains in reading achievement. In both studies, there were positive effects across a variety of measures. Many of the children in both of these studies were far from being fluent readers at the word level. Using the comprehension strategies very much seemed to make up for the lack of fluency.

Of course, there is also a bonus in learning to use comprehension strategies. Students get more out of reading, which, if they are reading quality material, increases their knowledge of the world, with such richer world knowledge empowering future comprehension of topically related texts (Anderson & Pearson, 1984). So, by teaching comprehension strategies that permit students to read books with worthwhile content, there is the potential to do much for literacy development, even of students who are not as fluent as their classmates.

Balanced Reading Instruction Is Better

Chapter 8 in this book describes what effective primary teachers actually do to promote literacy. The chief approach to fluency was to encourage extensive reading, with weaker readers having more opportunities than other students to read individually with adults who provided support and feedback. In general, in these classrooms the teacher found ways to provide additional support to the students who needed it most, with the result that every student in the class made progress. An important characteristic of these classrooms was that they were massively motivating, often employing more than 40 different approaches to motivate engagement and never engaging in teaching that potentially could undermine student engagement (Pressley et al., 2003).

As an exercise to make the point that balance is an idea that keeps coming up in the reading intervention literature, review this chapter. How many times was a balance of instruction advocated? Without even looking back, you know the answer is "Quite a few!"

Summary

So what can be made from this flurry of theory, research, and practices with respect to developing fluent readers as well as considering future research on fluency? First of all, the case does seem strong that, for some readers, explicit teaching of word recognition skills through phonics instruction works to inculcate sounding-out capabilities and is a stepping-stone to fluent reading. For many such children, the instruction probably does impact the appropriate brain centers. For other children, however, phonics instruction either is not successful or produces only slow decoding of words. When it is not successful at all, comprehension almost certainly is undermined. You cannot get above-word-level meaning from text without reading the words. For the slow decoders, sounding out words takes up so much cognitive capacity that little is left over for higher-order comprehension, consistent with LaBerge and Samuels's (1974) conception of short-term memory as a potential bottleneck in the cognitive system supporting reading.

The reports of compensating readers who seem to learn high-frequency words so they can recognize them immediately prompts us to think that for some readers something other than phonics is needed. Better reading in such students, if not fully fluent reading, might be produced by assuring that students who experience great difficulties in learning to sound out words might be able to learn sight words as unanalyzed wholes. This, in fact, is an idea that has been around for a long time, most prominently in the work of Dolch. That the Dolch approach has never been validated in experiments is unfortunate. Research on that approach to teaching reading should be a high priority, especially with students who do not become proficient in phonics after great efforts are made to teach them how to sound out words. We emphasize that, in arguing for more work on Dolch's approach, we favor the broad and balanced approach to teaching detailed in Dolch's writing. We do not advocate just a flashcard approach but rather instruction that provides many opportunities for students to practice reading, including the Dolch words in meaningful, connected text. That would include much opportunity for the student to experience oral reading of texts with teacher guidance and feedback. In doing research on the hypothesis that some dysfluent readers would benefit from the teaching of whole words, that work should probably get beyond the original Dolch words. We know more than ever before what words students of various grade levels should be acquiring, with high frequency words that age- and grade-mates are acquiring potentially a very good guide for choosing words to develop as sight words in struggling beginning readers.

There is much more work on fluency as fast and accurate decoding than there is work on prosody. That prosody is at best weakly correlated with comprehension suggests that developing prosody should not be a priority element of instruction. That said, because prosody is a hallmark of skilled reading, there should be some attention to it in readers who do not read with expression. For such work to proceed in an informed way, there needs to be much more research on instruction that promotes prosody. This is a topic that has hardly been touched.

We remain committed to the hypothesis that skills such as fluency are best developed through instruction that balances skills instruction and holistic reading and writing. Pressley and associates have produced much evidence that such instruction works better for students, especially weaker readers. Overly focusing on just a few skills (e.g., phonological decoding instruction, fast and accurate decoding to the point of fluency at the word level) was never observed in the very best elementary classrooms they have studied.

The overarching focus on kindergarten through grade-3 levels during the NCLB era cannot be legitimately rationalized. That there are many poor adult readers makes clear that the need for reading instruction extends far beyond the primary years. More positively, when supplementary instruction continues past the primary grades, so does academic growth in at-risk populations (Campbell & Ramey, 1994). There is going to be no quick fix to the development of fluency or any advanced literacy skill in populations that are slow to develop with respect to literacy.

Additionally, focusing solely on students with reading disabilities cannot be rationally defended. What results from such misguided preoccupation is a literature that has nothing to say about how to develop reading, let alone fluency, in average and above-average readers. Even more surprising, there is almost nothing in the fluency literature that is relevant to teaching readers whose key difficulty is that they have lower-than-average general intelligence. (Note that most of the research literature on learning disabilities concerns children of at least average intelligence who are weak in one academic area, such as reading.) As new research on reading fluency or reading in general develops, much more attention must be paid to the full spectrum of learners.

To return to where we began, the major goal of reading is to understand. Reading fast and accurately means little if comprehension remains low. Future research on the development of fluency should always include assessments of comprehension. There is a lot of research ahead—if for no other reason than that the connections between fluency and comprehension hypothesized by LaBerge and Samuels (1974) some 30 years ago have not been explored in depth. Indeed, far too few of the studies that were read to inform this chapter did not even include measures of comprehension! We need more research on fluency in general as well as more encompassing work than has been the case in the past, especially connecting fluency with comprehension.

Finally, what should each reading practitioner do on Monday morning? As this chapter is being written, Pressley, Gaskins, Solic, and Collins (2005) are completing a study of the Benchmark School, one of the premier schools in the world in terms of evidence-based instruction for students with reading disabilities. Students enter the school after a year or two of reading failure. After 4–7 years at the school, most students leave as competent readers, although many are not fluent in the sense of being able to read all the words in the text with high speed and accuracy. How is this improvement accomplished? Yes, there is systematic teaching of decoding, lots of repeated oral reading with feedback, and lots of emphasis on sight vocabulary. The particular mix a student receives depends largely on how he or she responds to instruction. That level of customization can happen because of the close monitoring that occurs at the school. In addition, the school never loses track of the goal that students should understand what they read in text and should use text productively in higher-order literacy tasks, such as composing written work. There is much teaching of comprehension strategies and writing strategies. By the end of the middle school years at the school, many Benchmark students are very strategic and constructively responsive as they read, even if they can't sound out every word quickly. They get much from the text and can use what they get. Thus, the Benchmark students are proof positive that fully fluent reading in the sense of every word being read accurately and quickly is not absolutely necessary. Even if word-level fluency is beyond the capacities of some children, there remains the hope that they can learn to get much out of text and be functionally literate through the teaching of higher-order literacy competencies, beginning with comprehension strategies. And, of course, the more they comprehend, the more they will develop prior knowledge that will permit them to better understand topically related texts in the future. So, what should reading practitioners be doing on Monday mornings? The answer is: balancing instruction in all the components that contribute to skilled reading.

SUMMARY AND CONCLUDING REFLECTIONS

1. Fluency research and practice remain a flurry of theories rather than one cohesive picture about what fluency is and how we should be teaching its subject matter in classrooms.

2. LaBerge and Samuels's famous 1974 article explained the importance of automaticity for emergent readers. Until immature readers become able to recognize and decode words effortlessly, much of their cognition is tied to identifying words; as word recognition becomes effortless, their attention becomes freed up for comprehension.

3. Systematic phonics instruction can be helpful in promoting fluency in some at-risk readers. It should not, however, be viewed as a panacea for all struggling readers.

4. There has been a lot of activity in the area of brain imagery research recently, and it has yielded some potentially significant findings. Normal mature readers utilize three regions on the left side of the brain, the parieto-temporal region, occipito-temporal region, and Broca's area. Dyslexics, by contrast, often show impairment in these left-side regions.

5. A slow speed in verbal processing can impair fluency for some readers. This process impairs the speed of decoding, even though it is not rooted in phonological ability.

6. Fluency can be developed in the classroom with repeated readings and teacher feedback. In effective primary-level classrooms (Pressley et al., 2003), a main approach to fluency is to give struggling readers ample opportunity to read with a lot of feedback and support from teachers.

7. An important area for future research and possibly instruction is developing sight word recognition and vocabulary knowledge. Edward Dolch, a true visionary in reading instruction, developed a system of sight word instruction embedded in a holistic reading program that should be further explored through experimental research. Additionally, we have a clearer sense than ever of which vocabulary words young children should know, owing to the work of Biemiller and Slonim (2001).

8. Prosodic reading is most likely a by-product of becoming fluent, but is probably neither a cause nor an effect of strong comprehension. That said, it definitely is better for readers to read with expression than without it.

9. New questions are being raised about how properly to assess fluency as well as its relationship to comprehension.

10. As always, comprehension is the chief goal in reading instruction, while fluency may be merely one means to that end. As such, teaching comprehension strategies can help students to make gains in comprehension even when they are dysfluent readers (Anderson, 1992; Brown, Pressley, Van Meter, & Schuder, 1996).

REFERENCES

Anderson, R. C., & Pearson, P. D. (1984). A schema-theoretic view of basic processes in reading. In P. D. Pearson (Ed.), *Handbook of reading research* (pp. 255–291). New York: Longman.

Anderson, V. (1992). A teacher development project in transactional strategy instruction for teachers of severely reading-disabled adolescents. *Teaching and Teacher Education, 8,* 391–403.

Baker, L. A., Vernon, P. A., & Ho, H.-Z. (1991). The genetic correlation between intelligence and speed of information processing. *Behavior Genetics, 21,* 351–67.

Bear, D. R. (1992). The prosody of oral reading and stages of word knowledge. In D.

R. Bear & S. Templeton (Eds.), *Development of orthographic knowledge and the foundations of literacy: A memorial festschrift for Edmund H. Henderson* (pp. 137–189). Hillsdale, NJ: Erlbaum.

Biemiller, A., & Slonim, N. (2001). Estimating root word vocabulary growth in normative and advantaged populations: Evidence for a common sequence of vocabulary acquisition. *Journal of Educational Psychology, 93,* 498–520.

Bowers, P. G., & Swanson, L. B. (1991). Naming speed deficits in reading disability: Multiple measures of a single process. *Journal of Experimental Child Psychology, 51,* 195–219.

Breznitz, Z. (1997a). Effects of accelerated reading rate on memory for text among dyslexic readers. *Journal of Educational Psychology, 89,* 289–297.

Breznitz, Z. (1997b). Enhancing the reading of dyslexic children by reading acceleration and auditory masking. *Journal of Educational Psychology, 89,* 103–113.

Brown, R., Pressley, M., Van Meter, P., & Schuder, T. (1996). A quasi-experimental validation of transactional strategies instruction with low-achieving second grade readers. *Journal of Educational Psychology, 88,* 18–37.

Campbell, D. T., & Stanley, J. C. (1966). *Experimental and quasi-experimental designs for research.* Chicago: Rand-McNally.

Campbell, F. A., & Ramey, C. T. (1994). Effects of early intervention on intellectual and academic achievement: A follow-up study of children from low-income families. *Child Development, 65,* 684–698.

Catts, H. W., Gillispie, M., Leonard, L. B., Kail, R. V., & Miller, C. A. (2002). The role of speed of processing, rapid naming, and phonological awareness in reading achievement. *Learning Disabilities Quarterly, 35,* 510–525.

Catts, H. W., Hogan, T. P., Adlof, S. M., & Barth, A. E. (2003). *The simple view of reading: Changes over time.* Presented at the annual meeting of the Society for the Scientific Study of Reading, Boulder, CO.

Compton, D. L., Appleton, A. C., & Hosp, M. K. (2004). Exploring the relationship between text-leveling systems and reading accuracy and fluency in second-grade students who are average and poor decoders. *Learning Disabilities Research and Practice, 19,* 176–184.

Denckla, M. B. (1972). Color naming deficits in dyslexic boys. *Cortex, 8,* 164–176.

Denckla, M. B., & Rudel, R. G. (1976). Rapid automatized naming (R.A.N.): Dyslexia differentiated from other learning disabilities. *Neuropsychologica, 14,* 471–476.

Dolch, E. W. (1939, 1945). *A manual for remedial reading* (1st and 2nd eds.). Champaign, IL: Garrard Press.

Dolch, E. W. (1941, 1951, 1960). *Teaching primary reading* (1st, 2nd, and 3rd eds.). Champaign, IL: Garrard Press.

Fleisher, L. S., Jenkins, J. R., & Pany, D. (1979). Effects on poor readers comprehension of training in rapid decoding. *Reading Research Quarterly, 15,* 30–48.

Gernsbacher, M. A., & Kaschak, M. P. (2003). Neuroimaging studies of language and comprehension. *Annual Review of Psychology, 54,* 91–114.

Gibson, E. J., & Levin, H. (1975). *The psychology of reading.* Cambridge, MA: MIT Press.

Goswami, U. (2004). Neuroscience and education. *British Journal of Educational Psychology, 74,* 1–14.

Gough, P. B., & Tunmer, W. E. (1986). Decoding, reading, and reading disability. *Remedial and Special Education, 7,* 6–10.

Hogaboam, T. W., & Perfetti, C. A. (1978). Reading skill and the role of verbal experience in decoding. *Journal of Educational Psychology, 70,* 717–729.

Homan, S., Klesius, P., & Hite, S. (1993). Effects of repeated readings and nonrepetitive strategies on students; fluency and comprehension. *Journal of Educational Research, 87,* 94–99.

Jensen, A. R. (1987). Mental chronometry in the study of learning disabilities. *Mental Retardation and Learning Disability Bulletin, 15,* 67–88.

Jensen, A. R. (1993). Why is reaction time correlated with psychometric g? *Current Directions in Psychological Science, 2,* 53–56.

Kahnemann, D. (1973). *Attention and effort.* Englewood Cliffs, NJ: Prentice-Hall.

Kitzen, K. R. (2001). Prosodic sensitivity, morphological ability, and reading ability in young adults without childhood histories of reading difficulty. *Dissertation Abstracts International, 62*(2-A), 460.

Kuhn, M. R., & Stahl, S. A. (2003). Fluency: A review of developmental and remedial practices. *Journal of Educational Psychology, 95,* 3–21.

LaBerge, D., & Samuels, S. J. (1974). Toward a theory of automatic information processing in reading. *Cognitive Psychology, 6,* 293–323.

Levy, B. A., Abello, B., & Lysynchuk, L. (1997). Transfer from word training to reading in context: Gains in reading fluency and comprehension. *Learning Disabilities Quarterly, 20,* 173–188.

Levy, B. A., Bourassa, D. C., & Horn, C. (1999). Fast and slow namers: Benefits of segmentation and whole word training. *Journal of Experimental Child Psychology, 73,* 115–138.

Lovett, M. W. (1984). A developmental perspective on reading dysfunction: Accuracy and rate criteria in the subtyping of dyslexic children. *Brain and Language, 22,* 67–91.

Mathes, P. G., & Fuchs, L. S. (1993). Peer-mediated reading instruction on special education resource rooms. *Learning Disabilities Research and Practice, 8,* 233–243.

McBride-Chang, C., & Kail, R. V. (2002). Cross-cultural similarities in the predictors of reading acquisition. *Child Development, 73,* 1392–1407.

McDougall, S., Hulme, C., Ellis, A., & Monk, A. (1994). Learning to read: The role of short-term memory and phonological skills. *Journal of Experimental Child Psychology, 58,* 112–133.

Miller, G. A. (1956). The magical number seven, plus-or-minus two: Some limits on our capacity for processing information. *Psychological Review, 63,* 81–97.

National Reading Panel. (2000). *Report of the national reading panel: Teaching children to read: An evidence-based assessment of the scientific research literature on reading and its implications for reading instruction: Reports of the subgroups.* Washington, DC: National Institute of Child Health & Human Development, National Institutes of Health.

Pintrich, P. R., & Schunk, D. H. (2002). *Motivation in education: Theory, research, and applications* (2nd ed.). Englewood Cliffs, NJ: Prentice-Hall.

Pressley, M. (2005). *Dolch professional development guide.* Columbus, OH: SRA.

Pressley, M., & Afflerbach, P. (1995). *Verbal protocols of reading: The nature of constructively responsive reading.* Hillsdale, NJ: Erlbaum.

Pressley, M., Gaskins, I. W., Solic, K., & Collins, S. (2005). *A case study of Benchmark School: How a school produces high achievement in students who previously failed.* East Lansing, MI: Michigan State University, Department of Teacher Education.

Pressley, M., Roehrig, A., Raphael, L., Dolezal, S., Bohn, K., Mohan, L., Wharton-McDonald, R., & Bogner, K. (2003). Teaching processes in elementary and secondary education. In W. M. Reynolds & G. E. Miller (Eds.), *Handbook of psychology: Vol. 7. Educational psychology* (pp. 153–175). New York: Wiley.

Rashotte, C. A., & Torgeson, J. K. (1985). Repeated reading and reading fluency in learning disabled children. *Reading Research Quarterly, 20,* 180–188.

Rasinski, T. V., Padak, N., Linek, W., & Sturtevant, B. (1994). Effects of fluency development on urban second-grade readers. *Journal of Educational Research, 87,* 158–165.

Rathvon, N. (2004). *Early reading assessment: A practitioner's handbook.* New York: Guilford Press.

Samuels, S. J., Dahl, P., & Archwamety, T. (1974). Effect of hypothesis/test training on reading skill. *Journal of Educational Psychology, 66,* 835–844.

Scarborough, H. S. (2001). Connecting early language and literacy to later reading(dis)abilities: Evidence, theory, and practice. In S. B. Neuman & D. K. Dickinson (Eds.), *Handbook of early literacy research* (pp. 97–110). New York: Guilford Press.

Schwanenflugel, P. J., Hamilton, A. M., Kuhn, M. R., Wisenbaker, J. M., & Stahl, S. A. (2004). Becoming a fluent reader: Reading skill and prosodic features in the oral reading of young readers. *Journal of Educational Psychology, 96,* 119–129.

Shaywitz, B. A., Shaywitz, S. E., Blachman, B. A., Pugh, K. R., Fulbright, R. K., Skudlarski, P., Mencl, W. E., Constable, R. T., Holahan, J. M., Marchione, K. E., Fletcher, J. M., Lyon, G. R., & Gores, J. C. (2004). Development of left occipitotemporal systems for skilled reading in children after a phonologically-based intervention. *Biological Psychiatry, 55,* 926–933.

Shaywitz, B. A., Shaywitz, S. E., Pugh, K. R., Mencl, W. E., Fulbright, R. K., Skudlarski, P., Constable, R. T., Marchione, K. E., Fletcher, J. M., Lyon, G. R., & Gore, J. C. (2002). Disruption of posterior brain systems for reading in children with developmental dyslexia. *Biological Psychiatry, 52,* 101–110.

Shaywitz, S. E., & Shaywitz, B. A. (2004). Neurobiologic basis for reading and reading disability. In P. McCardle & V. Chhabra (Eds.), *The voice of evidence in reading research* (pp. 417–442). Baltimore: Brookes.

Shaywitz, S. E., Shaywitz, B. A., Fulbright, R. K., Skudlarski, P., Mencl, W. E., Constable, R. T., Pugh, K. R., Holahan, J. M., Marchione, K. E., Fletcher, J. M., Lyon, G. R., & Gore, J. C. (2003). Neural systems for compensation and persistence: Young adult outcome of childhood reading disability. *Biological Psychiatry, 54,* 25–33.

Simpson, J. A., & Weiner, E. S. (Eds.). (1989). *The Oxford English dictionary* (2nd ed.). Oxford, UK: Oxford University Press.

Stahl, S. A. (2004). What do we know about fluency? Findings of the National Reading Panel. In P. McCardle & V. Chhabra (Eds.), *The voice of evidence in reading research* (pp. 187–211). Baltimore: Brookes.

Stahl, S., Heubach, K., & Cramond, B. (1997). *Fluency-oriented reading instruction.* Athens, GA, and Washington, DC: National Reading Research Center and U.S. Department of Education, Office of Educational Research and Improvement, Educational Resources Information Center.

Tan, A., & Nicholson, T. (1997). Flashcards revisited: Training poor readers to read words faster improves their comprehension of text. *Journal of Educational Psychology, 89,* 276–288.

Torgesen, J. K. (2004). Lessons learning from research on interventions for students who have difficulties learning to read. In P. McCardle & V. Chhabra (Eds.), *The voice of evidence in reading research* (pp. 355–382). Baltimore: Brookes.

Torgesen, J. K., & Davis, C. (1996). Individual difference variables that predict response to training in phonological awareness. *Journal of Experimental Child Psychology, 63,* 1–21.

Torgesen, J. K., Rashotte, C. A., & Alexander, A. W. (2001). Principles of fluency instruction in reading: Relationships with established empirical outcomes. In M. Wolf (Ed.), *Dyslexia, fluency, and the brain* (pp. 333–355). Timonium, MD: York Press.

Turkelbaum, P. E., Gareau, L., Flowers, D. L., Zeffiro, T. A., & Eden, G. F. (2003). Development of neural mechanisms in reading. *Nature Neuroscience, 6,* 767–773.

Vellutino, F. R. (1979). *Dyslexia: Theory and research.* Cambridge, MA: MIT Press.

Vellutino, F. R., Scanlon, D. M., & Spearing, D. (1995). Semantic and phonological coding in poor and normal readers. *Journal of Experimental Child Psychology, 59,* 76–123.

von Bon, W. H. J., Boksebeld, L. M., Font Freide, T. A. M., & van den Hurk, A. J. M. (1991). A comparison of three methods of reading-while-listening. *Journal of Learning Disabilities, 24,* 471–476.

Vukovic, R. K., Wilson, A. M., & Nash, K. K. (2004). Naming speed deficits in adults with reading disabilities: A test of the double-deficit hypothesis. *Journal of Learning Disabilities, 37,* 440–450.

Wolf, M., & Bowers, P. G. (1999). The double-deficit hypothesis for the developmental dyslexias. *Journal of Educational Psychology, 91,* 415–438.

Wolf, M., Bowers, P. G., & Biddle, K. (2000). Naming-speed processes, timing, and reading: A conceptual review. *Journal of Learning Disabilities, 33,* 387–407.

Wolf, M., Pfeil, C., Lotz, R., & Biddle, K. (1994). Towards a more universal understanding of the developmental dyslexias: The contribution of orthographic factors. In V. W. Berninger (Ed.), *The varieties of orthographic knowledge: I. Theoretical and developmental issues* (pp. 137–171). Dordrecht, The Netherlands: Kluwer Academic.

Young, A. R., Bowers, P. G., & MacKinnon, G. E. (1996). Effects of prosodic modeling and repeated reading on poor readers' fluency and comprehension. *Applied Psycholinguistics, 17,* 49–84.

Yuill, N., & Oakhill, J. (1988). Effects of inference awareness training on poor comprehension. *Applied Cognitive Psychology, 2,* 23–45.

Yuill, N., & Oakhill, J. (1991). *Children's problems in reading comprehension.* Cambridge, UK: Cambridge University Press.

Lauren Fingeret, MA, is a doctoral student in the Department of Teacher Education, Michigan State University, East Lansing, Michigan.

CHAPTER 7

Vocabulary

with LAUREL DISNEY
and KENDRA ANDERSON

This chapter takes up how children naturalistically learn vocabulary and how they can be taught other vocabulary that they do not learn naturalistically. Since the passage of the Reading First program as part of the No Child Left Behind Act of 2001 (2002), the teaching of vocabulary has been much on the minds of educators as one of the five elements of evidence-based reading instruction, along with phonemic awareness, phonics, fluency, and comprehension. Hence, there was something of an obligation to include a chapter on the topic in this revision of the book, although there was no vocabulary chapter in the previous editions. That decision not to include vocabulary reflected simply that vocabulary instruction does not have a huge impact on reading as far as can be determined from instructional studies. That said, there is one consistent relationship in the research literature pertaining to vocabulary that is suggestive: People with larger vocabularies tend to comprehend better (Cunningham & Stanovich, 1997; Davis, 1944, 1968; Singer, 1965; Spearitt, 1972; Thurstone, 1946). Bear in mind that does not imply that increasing a reader's vocabulary will improve his or her comprehension much. Indeed, there is considerable doubt about that. It very well could be that the correlation between vocabulary knowledge and comprehension reflects a third variable at work—most likely, that both reflect general intelligence.

NATURALISTIC LEARNING OF VOCABULARY

By early adulthood, many individuals have learned 15,000 or more root words (i.e., words that are the bases for families of words, such as *child*, which is the root word for *children*, *child-like*, and *childish*; Biemiller & Slonim, 2001). Most vocabulary words are learned incidentally in context (Sternberg, 1987). Given that only a few hundred words a year appear to be taught directly in school, the only way to explain the learning of so many words is that people acquire them by interacting with others, listening to radio and television, and reading—acquiring words incidentally as they do other tasks. There have been a number of analyses of such contextual learning in the past quarter-century, with the naturalistic acquisition of vocabulary now reasonably well understood (McGregor, 2004).

Family Conversations

Without a doubt, in recent years, the most talked about correlational study having anything to do with vocabulary acquisition was Hart and Risley's (1995) *Meaningful Differences in the Everyday Experiences of Young American Children*. The authors observed 42 families for over 2 years, beginning when each participating child was 6–9 months old. The sample included families from upper, middle, and lower socioeconomic classes. A major interest was the language the children experienced at home, with the most prominent finding in the book being that the amount and quality of language the child experienced varied dramatically as a function of social class. The less affluent the family, the less that was said to the child. The less affluent the family, the less complex was the language directed at the child. The less affluent the family, the more discouraging were the messages the child received (i.e., lower-class children heard a high proportion of prohibitions relative to more socioeconomically advantaged children). Very importantly, there was a clear relationship between the quantity and quality of input and the child's vocabulary development. At 3 years of age, the upper-class children had much more extensive vocabularies than the middle- and lower-class children. For example, the upper-class child with the smallest vocabulary knew more words than the lower-class child with the best developed vocabulary. Who was reading better 6 years later, at age 9? The children who experienced the most language in the first 3 years of life were, with the parent's language interactive style the very strongest predictor of later reading achievement (i.e., accounting for 59% of the variance).

There are other strong correlations in the research literature between amount and quality of language experienced early in life and later language development in general as well as vocabulary development in particular (see also Huttenlocher, Vasilyeva, Cymerman, & Levine, 2001; Naigles &

Hoff-Ginsberg, 1998; Pearson, Fernandez, Lewedeg, & Oller, 1997). A reasonable possibility is that early language interactions are causally important in vocabulary development and subsequent reading achievement. From 2 to 3 years of age, children can import words into their language if they experience them, with incidental learning more likely when children experience a word multiple times and over several days (Schwartz & Terrell, 1983). Such repetition only occurs when children engage in consistent, extensive, and rich verbal interactions with more linguistically mature people. These correlational data provide strong impetus for encouraging parents to surround their children with language, although these are only correlational data. Later in the chapter, however, we will review data that make clear that when language enrichment is manipulated in an experiment, vocabulary development follows the enrichment, making the causal connection between language experience and exposure and subsequent vocabulary development.

Fast Mapping

Children come biologically prepared to learn language (e.g., Chomsky, 1957). One of the most powerful demonstrations of this readiness to acquire language is their "fast mapping" of meanings of words encountered in language.

Carey and Bartlett (1978) asked some preschoolers to do them a favor—"Bring me the chromium tray; not the blue one, the chromium one"—with the request in the context of two available trays, one blue and the other olive. Tested 1 week and 6 weeks later, some of the children receiving this request knew that chromium was a color (i.e., when given a group of names and asked to identify the colors, *chromium* was identified as a color), and others even knew it was olive. They had learned something about the meaning of the word through just one incidental learning opportunity. Moreover, when preschoolers learn a new term via fast mapping, they generalize the term. For example, they recognize another instance of the object, even if it differs in irrelevant features (e.g., size; Behrend, Scofield, & Kleinknecht, 2001; Kleinknecht, Behrend, & Scofield, 1999; Waxman and Booth, 2000). But, perhaps the most dramatic demonstrations have been with 2-year-olds who sometimes fast map vocabulary meanings (Heibeck & Markman, 1987; Markson, 1999) and with demonstration that incidental fast mapping impacts vocabulary learning as much as attempts to teach meanings directly to young children (Jaswal & Markman, 2003). Although others had noted previously the power of single or a few incidental learning opportunities on children's vocabulary acquisition (e.g., Brown, 1957), Carey and Bartlett's (1978) conceptualization and description of such learning as fast mapping focused attention on this phenomenon more than earlier demonstrations of it. Although there is far from complete understanding of fast mapping (P. Bloom, 2000, Chap. 2), that fast mapping occurs makes obvious that incidental learning is a powerful mechanism in vocabulary development. Rich vocabulary environments permit many fast mapping opportunities as well as opportunities to think about repeated words multiple times.

Children Drawing Attention to Objects That Can Be Named

Lois Bloom and her colleagues have provided evidence that children very much are determinants of what gets talked about when young word learners and adults interact. Caregivers tend to name and talk about objects that children are attending to, with the children definitely making clear to caregivers what it is in the environment that interests them and commands their attention. That is, they let adults know what they want to talk about. In turn, what caregivers talk about influences the words that children learn (Bloom, Margulis, Tinker, & Fujita, 1996; Bloom & Tinker, 2001). For a review of all the evidence that children are very much active players in their own incidental vocabulary development, see L. Bloom (2000).

Children Participate in High-Quality Lessons

Although there has been a great deal of attention to vocabulary learning in context during the preschool years, vocabulary learning continues throughout childhood (Biemiller & Slonim, 2001). One way that vocabulary learning can occur is through high-quality curricular events. Consider what happened when Carlisle, Fleming, and Gudbrandsen (2000) provided a high-quality science unit, although vocabulary learning definitely was not the focal point of the study unit but rather an incidental outcome of students participating in the unit.

Carlisle et al. (2000), in fact, found some incidental acquisition of words covered in the unit. (There were control conditions to assess whether learning of words pertaining to the science unit exceeded acquisition of new words in general over a month, which it did.) Even so, there was certainly room for more learning, with knowledge of the vocabulary in the unit far from perfect at the end of the unit of study.

Carlisle et al. (2000) included lots of interesting additional assessments, for instance, establishing that students who began the unit with greater understanding of vocabulary pertaining to the topic of the unit learned more vocabulary incidentally during instruction than students who started the unit with little prior knowledge. What vocabulary a student learns incidentally during content instruction depends both on exposure to vocabulary and the student's previous knowledge about the topic of instruction.

More generally, during the past decade, Pressley and his colleagues have studied the characteristics of very effective and less effective primary-grade classrooms (e.g., Bogner, Raphael, & Pressley, 2002; Dolezal, Welsh, Pressley, & Vincent, 2003; Morrow, Tracey, Woo, & Pressley, 1999; Pressley, Allington, Wharton-McDonald, Block, & Morrow, 2001; Pressley, Dolezal, et al., 2003; Pressley, Roehrig, et al., 2003; Pressley, Wharton-McDonald, Allington, et al., 2001; Pressley, Wharton-McDonald, & Mistretta, 1998; Pressley, Wharton-McDonald, Raphael, Bogner, & Roehrig, 2001; Wharton-McDonald, Pressley, & Hampston, 1998; see Chapter 8 of this volume). As this book is being completed, the Pressley group is completing analyses of extensions of this work to middle schools. Excellent teachers teach vocabulary opportunistically. When a word comes up that is an important word for students to know and the students do not know it, that becomes a teachable moment for excellent teachers. That group has noted as well that excellent teachers do not talk down to their classes but, rather, consistently use mature vocabulary, providing opportunities for students to experience incidental learning of mature vocabulary in context. High-quality lessons include many opportunities for student vocabulary development.

Reservations about Incidental Vocabulary Learning from Context

When Sternberg (1987) offered the conclusion that most vocabulary is learned from context, there were definitely data that made clear that learning from context was anything but certain. For example, it was known that often learners failed to infer correctly the meanings of novel words encountered in texts (e.g., Daalen-Kapteijns & Elshout-Mohr, 1981; McKeown, 1985; Nicholson & Whyte, 1992; Schatz & Baldwin, 1986). Even so, Sternberg (1987) inspired additional evaluations of incidental vocabulary learning from context. Swanburn and de Glopper (1999) reviewed these evaluations and concluded that readers often do learn vocabulary from context, but such learning is anything but certain. They estimated that about 15% of novel vocabulary encountered in text is learned to some extent. Maybe readers do not get the whole meaning, but they get at least some of it, just as fast mapping preschoolers do not get the whole meaning of words they hear one or two times, but fast map some of the meaning (Carey & Bartlett, 1978). At a 15% rate, children require seven or so encounters with a word for there to be a high probability of learning the word from context.

More negatively, there now has been plenty of research making clear that when readers attempt to derive the meanings of words that are encountered in context (i.e., in sentences, paragraphs, stories), they often get them wrong (for a review, see Fukkink & de Glopper, 1998). Why? Sometimes the reader lacks the prior knowledge to make sense of the clues to a word's meaning that are in a text. In addition, verbal contexts surrounding vocabulary words can be rich in clues to meaning or sparse in them, and such differences make a difference in whether people learn the meanings of unfamiliar words and use them sensibly (see Nist & Olejnik, 1995, for a telling empirical analysis). Unfortunately, we do not yet know how to determine which contexts have enough information for most learners to be able to figure out the meaning of a word versus not.

In short, there are perils of leaving the learning of definitions to incidental learning from context. Fortunately, there are intentional approaches to teaching vocabulary that result more certainly in vocabulary being learned than incidental learning approaches, which is the focus of the remainder of this chapter.

HOW CAN VOCABULARY BE TAUGHT?

There are a variety of ways to teach vocabulary, some incredibly simple and others more complicated. In general, this discussion will proceed from the simpler approaches to ones that are more encompassing. For greater in-depth coverage of many of these topics, see, in particular, Baumann and Kame'enui (2004).

Providing Definitions

In Pany, Jenkins, and Schreck (1982), a range of children were asked to learn the meanings of vocabulary words—from average grade-4 children to students in grades 4 and 5 described as learning-disabled to grade-4 students who were considered at risk because of low economic status. The participants in the study were to learn the meanings of vocabulary words, with the words presented and then memory of meanings tested a few minutes later. There were recall measures in the study, recognition of synonyms from distractors (i.e., multiple-choice questions), and items requiring that the learner determine whether the taught words were used correctly in context.

The key independent variable was how the vocabulary words were presented. In the *meanings from context* condition, the vocabulary words appeared in a two-sentence context from which the meaning of the target word could be inferred. In the *meanings given* condition, the student read a sentence containing the word, and then the experimenter told the student the meaning of the word and provided another sentence example in which the word was used. In the *meanings practiced* condition, the experimenter provided a synonym for the target word and the students repeated the synonyms twice. Then, there was an undemanding control condition. Participants in that condition were presented only the vocabulary words—they were not provided the meanings of the words during study. As undemanding as it was, that control condition permitted an important conclusion. Just providing a definition of a word improves learning, for performances in both the *meanings given* and *meanings practiced* conditions were much better than in this undemanding control condition.

Another very important finding, however, was that performances in the *meanings from context* condition were generally not much better than in the undemanding no meaning exposure control condition, consistent with a main conclusion of the first section of this chapter: learning vocabulary meanings incidentally from context is anything but certain. That was despite the fact that the contexts were rigged in Pany et al. (1982) so that inferring the meanings should have been easy (i.e., the first sentence contained the target vocabulary word and the second contained an explicit synonym). Even though children sometimes learn word meanings from context, as they seem to do when they fast map, such learning was not as certain or great as when the meaning was provided in the Pany et al. (1982) study.

Since Pany et al. (1982), there have been several studies in which the meanings of unfamiliar words were explained when the words were encountered, with performance in such conditions contrasted with reading of the text in the absence of vocabulary explanations. Providing explanations has produced generally large effects on vocabulary learning (Brabham & Lynch-Brown, 2002; Brett, Rothlein, & Hurley, 1996; Elley, 1989; Penno, Wilkinson, & Moore, 2002). That said, providing definitions to students does not guarantee that they will really understand completely the meanings of the words defined.

Hence, as long as there have been dictionaries, teachers have been sending students to them to look up the meanings of words. Confidence that this practice produces understanding of the words looked up was shattered by Miller and Gildea's (1987) article. They asked children in grades 5 and 6 to read dictionary definitions for words they did not know and then write meaningful sentences containing the words. The children wrote many sentences that those authors referred to as mystifying, including the following examples (Miller & Gildea, 1987, p. 98):

> Me and my parents *correlate*, because without them, I wouldn't be here.
> I was *meticulous* about falling off the cliff.
> The *redress* for getting well when you're sick is to stay in bed.
> I *relegated* my pen pal's letter to her house.
> That news is very *tenet*.

Moreover, it did not help if the definition was accompanied by a model sentence. Consider *usurp*, which loosely means *take*, accompanied by the illustrative sentence "The king's brother tried to *usurp* the throne." Children's own sentences for *usurp* still missed the meaning, however. In all of the following children's generated sentences, the word *take* or a variation of it would make sense, but not the word *usurp*:

> The blue chair was *usurped* from the room.
> Don't try to *usurp* the tape from the store.
> The thief tried to *usurp* the money from the safe.

Yes, like the participants in Pany et al. (1982) who were provided the definitions of new words, Miller and Gildea's (1987) participants got something out of the definitional information. But the bottom line from Miller and Gildea (1987) was that providing definitions alone or with examples of words used in context is a teaching strategy fraught with difficulties.

There are better and worse dictionary definitions (i.e., clearer and more complete definitions versus more vague and incomplete definitions). There needs to be systematic study about what difference the quality of a dictionary definition makes (although see Scott & Nagy, 1997), for dictionaries are omnipresent in reading instruction. It is high time that we find out whether and which dictionaries result in the most certain learning for students.

Teaching Students to Make Intentional Contextual Analyses of Unfamiliar Words Encountered in Text

In the studies of learning in context considered thus far, students have been left to their own devices to figure out the words. Students can be taught to make contextual analyses, however.

Sternberg (1987) and his colleagues recognized two types of contextual clues that could facilitate vocabulary learning that learners could be taught to analyze. One was external context cues (i.e., meaning cues in the text surrounding a new vocabulary word). The second was internal context clues—prefixes, suffixes, and stems (Sternberg & Powell, 1983; Sternberg, Powell, & Kaye, 1983). Sternberg's theoretical analysis of vocabulary learning from contexts stimulated researchers to study such teaching.

By 1998, Kuhn and Stahl (1998) identified 14 studies in which students had been taught to use external semantic context clues, with clear evidence that, compared to no-instruction controls, students taught to use external semantic contexts, in fact, are better at figuring out the definitions of words. (See also Fukkink & de Glopper, 1998, who also meta-analyzed the studies in which students were taught to use context clues, concluding that such instruction had a moderate impact on students' abilities to figure out meanings.) That said, Kuhn and Stahl (1998) detected an interesting twist that is very important. In four of the studies, control participants simply practiced figuring out the meanings of words in text in the absence of instruction. They improved as much as participants taught specific context analyses strategies. Just being prompted to figure out the meanings of words in context and given a little practice at it is as powerful as much more elaborate instruction (i.e., instruction providing detailed information about the various types of semantic context cues).

What about analysis of internal context clues (i.e., word parts)? The clearly interpretable database on the value of teaching internal cue analysis is thin and equivocal (see Baumann, Kame'enui, & Ash, 2003, for a review). That said, Levin, Carney, and Pressley (1988) demonstrated that if undergraduates are taught word components (i.e., the meanings of prefixes, suffixes, stems), they can use them to figure out the meanings of previously unknown words. The effects in that study were clear and large, although the conditions in the study were such that it was saliently obvious to apply the root word knowledge that was just taught. Graves and Hammond (1980) reported a similar finding with grade-7 students, demonstrating that seventh graders could generalize knowledge of prefixes taught in the context of one set of vocabulary words to new vocabulary words that included the prefixes. Wysocki and Jenkins (1987) found that fourth-, sixth-, and eighth-grade students could transfer knowledge of suffixes to new lists, although the effects were only large with generously liberal scoring of the inferred definitions by the students. In short, there is at least some evidence that teaching morphemes (i.e., the smallest units of meaning—prefixes, suffixes, root words) can improve children's and adults' skills at inferring the meanings of words. That said, we have yet to see a study where this effect is general, that is, obtained when it was not fairly obvious that what was previously learned could and should be used to infer the meanings of new words. Thus, there is need for more study of teaching students to use internal context clues to infer meanings of words, with enough positive data to encourage the hypothesis that such teaching can increase the learning of vocabulary.

One set of recent investigations of intentional contextual analyses caught our attention more than others as we reviewed this literature. Baumann and his associates (Baumann et al., 2002; Baumann, Edwards, Boland, Olejnik, & Kame'enui, 2003) studied the effects of teaching morphemic (i.e., internal) and semantic contextual (i.e., external) analyses to grade-5 students. In one study, instruction occurred over 2 months, in the other over 12 50-minute lessons. In the most ambitious instructional conditions of the experiments, students were taught to use both the morphemic analysis procedures and semantic contextual analysis procedures. The morphemic lessons focused on teaching students to use root words, prefixes, and suffixes to learn the meanings of new vocabulary words encountered in readings, with 15 specific prefixes and 5 specific suffixes taught. The semantic context instruction emphasized reading carefully the sentences around a novel word to determine the word's meaning, with instruction about how context sometimes includes definitional clues, actual synonyms for novel words, information about the opposite meaning of the word, and examples if the novel word is a general concept. The participants were taught that clues to meaning are often spread over several surrounding sentences.

In general, the lessons were well planned, including a lot of practice in using the morphemic and semantic context strategies. The participants were also provided an overarching scheme for applying the morphemic and semantic context strategies they had learned, one emphasizing the critical metacognitive information about when and where the morphemic and semantic context strategies should be used. The fifth graders were explicitly instructed to do as follows:

> When you come to a word and you don't know what it means, use:
>
> 1. CONTEXT CLUES: Read the sentences around the word to see if there are clues to its meaning.
> 2. WORD-PART CLUES: See if you can break the word into a root word, prefix, or suffix to help figure out its meaning.
> 3. CONTEXT CLUES: Read the sentences around the word again to see if you have figured out its meaning. (Edwards, Font, Baumann, & Boland, 2004, p. 170)

There were some clear effects among the specific findings in these studies. Teaching the morphemic and semantic context strategies promoted learning of the words in the texts that were read by the students during the study (see also Tomesen & Aarnoutse, 1998). Also, there was some evidence that the fifth graders were able to transfer the skills they learned to determine the meanings of words in novel texts, although the effects were moderate-sized at best and more often small to nonexistent. There was no evidence, however, that the teaching of these skills increased comprehension of what was read. Teaching ways to enhance vocabulary acquisition does not guarantee more general effects on reading.

Repeating To-Be-Learned Words and Their Meanings

A final finding in Pany et al.'s (1982) study (i.e., the study with the very undemanding control) that deserves mention is that if practicing the word and its meaning does not make definition learning perfect, it makes it better as compared to a single presentation of the meaning. The general point that frequency of exposure to specific vocabulary words increased the learning of them was definitely clear by the mid-1980s (Stahl & Fairbanks, 1986). Moreover, there continued to be demonstrations that repeated presentations of vocabulary improves acquisition relative to a single presentation (e.g., Leung, 1992; Penno et al., 2002; Senechal, 1997), with repetition most effective if the reencounters are spread over a period of time (e.g., days rather than all within 1 day; Childers & Tomasello, 2002). That is, Thorndike's (1911) views on repetition—that learning increases with repeated exposure—are valid with respect to learning vocabulary meanings.

Talking with Children about Objects That Interest Them

Valdez-Menchaca and Whitehurst (1988) studied a second-language learning situation, with English-speaking children learning Spanish. In the experimental situation, adults labeled a toy in Spanish when the child expressed interest in it. Controls heard the same labels, but not at a time when they seemed to be intrigued by the toy. The children who heard the labels when they were interested in particular toys were more likely to use the words in their later speech, although both groups of children learned the meanings of the words. In matters of vocabulary acquisition, as in many aspects of learning, children's interest matters, with learning more certain when teachers teach to children's interests (Hidi, 1990).

Reading with Children

Parents and teachers can increase children's vocabulary by reading with them. The more that parents interact with children over books, the better developed is children's language (e.g., Ninio, 1980; Payne, Whitehurst, & Angell, 1994; for reviews, see Bus, Van IJzendoorn, & Pelligrini, 1995, and Scarborough & Dobrich, 1994). Most impressive, there are some very well controlled experimental evaluations that parents and teachers of preschool and primary-grade children can be taught to interact with children over picture books in ways that increase emergent language skills, including vocabulary development (e.g., Arnold, Lonigan, Whitehurst, & Epstein, 1994; Brabham & Lynch-Brown, 2002; Dickinson & Smith, 1994; Leung, 1992; Lonigan & Whitehurst, 1998; Robbins & Ehri, 1994; Senechal & Cornell, 1993; Valdez-Menchaca & Whitehurst, 1992; Whitehurst et al., 1988, 1999; Whitehurst, Arnold, et al., 1994; Whitehurst, Epstein, et al., 1994; Zevenbergen, Whitehurst, & Zevenbergen, 2003). In short, high-quality book reading by adults and children causes increases in children's language competence, including their vocabulary development. (See Chapter 4 for additional discussion of this point.)

Encouraging Viewing of Informational Television

Young children watch television. They can watch *Sesame Street* and other informative television (i.e., the stuff on PBS and other educationally oriented channels), or they can watch a steady diet of cartoons, situation comedies, and other mainstays of commercial television. It makes a difference with respect to vocabulary development, with vocabulary development more extensive if preschoolers watch informational rather than entertainment television. A secondary benefit is that children who get hooked on informational television during the early preschool years are more likely to choose to view better programming during the later preschool years (Wright et al., 2001).

Providing Rich Vocabulary Instruction

Beck, Perfetti, and McKeown (1982) and McKeown, Beck, Omanson, and Perfetti (1983) taught about 100 vocabulary words to elementary students over a semester. These words were taught using what Beck and her colleagues refer to as a rich instructional approach (see Beck, McKeown, & Omanson, 1987; McKeown & Beck, 2004; see also Dole, Sloan, & Trathen, 1995). Such an approach requires the learners to use and think about the to-be-learned vocabulary in many ways, for example, making decisions about whether and when a word is used in a context correctly and making decisions requiring students to make distinctions about subsets of the words that were related in meaning. There were many encounters with each taught word over the months of instruction, with McKeown, Beck, Omanson, and Pople (1985) providing a very analytical demonstration that more frequent encounters with a vocabulary word as part of rich instruction definitely make a difference in how well it is learned. Also, as part of the Beck and McKeown approach, students often were required to explain their thinking as they worked with the words they were learning. In short, Beck and McKeown emphasized long-term instruction of vocabulary that stimulated student thoughtfulness. Carlo et al. (2004) also provided a demonstration that similarly rich vocabulary instruction can benefit English second-language learners who are learning English vocabulary and to about the same extent as English native speakers.

Beck, McKeown, and their associates provided the most visible studies confirming that rich teaching of vocabulary increases comprehension of text containing taught vocabulary, with more general effects on comprehension smaller (for a review, see Stahl & Fairbanks, 1986; also Wixson, 1986). Their work permitted an optimist to see the glass half-full (see also Kame'enui, Carnine, & Freschli, 1982)—at least comprehension improved if the texts contained the words taught—or a pessimist to see the glass as half-empty—comprehension did not improve much more generally from teaching vocabulary words, most emphatically on standardized assessments of comprehension. In the two decades since Beck's research, we are aware of no work that changes that two-edged conclusion.

One tactic to take, given the classic Beck and McKeown outcome, is to teach words that students will encounter in text. Given that only a few hundred vocabulary words can be taught in school each year, the question arises: Which words should be taught? Beck, McKeown, and Kucan (2002) have proposed an intriguing hypothesis that takes into account that children should be taught words they will encounter and the number of words they can be taught is limited. First, do not worry about teaching the words that children know already as a function of living in the world. Also, do not bother teaching words that are very low-frequency in the language, perhaps because they are very domain-specific (e.g., *isotope*, unless, of course, you are teaching chemistry). What should be taught are high-frequency words that occur across a number of domains but are not known by many students (e.g., at the elementary level, teach *coincidence*, *absurd*, *industrious*, *fortunate*). Beck et al. (2002) refer to these as Tier 2 words, referring to well-known words as Tier 1 and low-frequency words as Tier 3. As far as we know, however, Beck et al.'s (2002) position is an untested hypothesis, although one that seems testable to us and should be tested. See as well the earlier discussion of Biemiller and Slonim's 2001 work. They have identified the 15,000 or so root words that should be known by the end of high school, with that group developing normative data for the entire period of K–12 schooling, which should permit more intelligent decision making in the near future about which words to emphasize for vocabulary instruction at particular grade levels.

SUMMARY AND CONCLUDING REFLECTIONS

1. To increase vocabulary development, surround the child with vocabulary rich language. That metamessage comes through repeatedly in this chapter. Talk with the child during storybook reading and during formal vocabulary instruction, prompting the child to think about the to-be-learned vocabulary words in many, many ways. Flood the classroom with vocabulary-rich talk during formal lessons and informal interactions. The talk and the vocabulary in the world that the child experiences matters most.

2. If you accept the goal proposed by Biemiller and Slonim (2001) of 15,000 root words known by the end of high school, many of which are learned naturalistically, the task of vocabulary instruction can seem manageable. Our calculation is that perhaps 5,000 or so root words (and certainly not as many as 10,000 root words) require formal instruction, as-

suming the child has reasonably rich language interactions during the schooling years (i.e., many of the root words are learned incidentally through verbal interactions and encounters). That 5,000 figure translates to teaching two to four root words a school day, a goal that should be within the reach of most teachers. Educators need to pay much attention in the near future to the specific words that need to be taught and make certain that students are acquiring the vocabulary that occurs most frequently in the world. Biemiller and Slonim (2001) and Beck et al. (2002) are pointing to an important research direction.

3. As we urge more systematic attention to and teaching of vocabulary, we also note that, in the analyses to date, when vocabulary acquisition has generally had an impact on reading (e.g., through increased reading comprehension), the impact has not been large. Passages containing words taught are understood a little better; other impacts are often quite small, often not detectable—or at least not detected in the studies we reviewed in writing this chapter.

One possibility is that in the research to date there has not been extensive consideration of the many ways that knowing vocabulary can improve literacy, with comprehension most frequently studied as an indicator of the general impact of learning vocabulary. For example, more extensive vocabulary impact might occur in and be detected in students' writing and speaking. Vocabulary acquisition might also influence aspects of comprehension besides text comprehension—for example, in understanding comments in conversations or on television. In short, we do not believe that researchers have exhaustively considered the benefits of vocabulary acquisition on literacy. Until there is a lot more evidence that vocabulary has only modest impact on literacy, we remain optimistic that there might be future evaluations that will substantiate that vocabulary teaching makes differences that are worth the instructional investment. We will urge that students be taught to pay attention to unfamiliar vocabulary words when they encounter them and to try to figure out what the words mean. We know, based on the research reviewed here, that students can learn to do that, and now is the time to figure out what happens when students do, in fact, pay attention to novel words and try to figure them out—especially when they are provided many opportunities to experience high-quality talk and texts, talk and texts filled with the words that literate folks know.

REFERENCES

Arnold, D. H., Lonigan, C. J., Whitehurst, G. J., & Epstein, J. N. (1994). Accelerating language development through picture book reading: Replication and extension to a videotape training format. *Journal of Educational Psychology*, 86, 235–243.
Baumann, J. F., Edwards, E. C., Boland, E. M., Olejnik, S., & Kame'enui, E. J. (2003).

Vocabulary tricks: Effects of instruction in morphology on fifth-grade students' ability to derive and infer word meanings. *American Educational Research Journal, 40,* 447–494.

Baumann, J. F., Edwards, E. C., Font, G., Tereshinski, C. A., Kame'enui, E. J., & Olejnik, S. F. (2002). Teaching morphemic and contextual analysis to fifth-grade students. *Reading Research Quarterly, 37,* 150–176.

Baumann, J. F., & Kame'enui, E. (Eds.). (2004). *Vocabulary instruction: Research to practice.* New York: Guilford Press.

Baumann, J. F., Kame'enui, E. J., & Ash, G. E. (2003). Research on vocabulary instruction: Voltaire redux. In J. Flood, D. Lapp, J. R. Squire, & J. M. Jensen (Eds.), *Handbook of research on teaching the English language arts* (pp. 752–785). Mahwah, NJ: Erlbaum.

Beck, I. L., McKeown, M. G., & Kucan, L. (2002). *Bringing words to life: Robust vocabulary instruction.* New York: Guilford Press.

Beck, I. L., McKeown, M. G., & Omanson, R. C. (1987). The effects and uses of diverse vocabulary instructional techniques. In M. G. McKeown & M. E. Curtis (Eds.), *The nature of vocabulary acquisition* (pp. 147–163). Hillsdale, NJ: Erlbaum.

Beck, I. L., Perfetti, C. A., & McKeown, M. G. (1982). Effects of long-term vocabulary instruction on lexical access and reading comprehension. *Journal of Educational Psychology, 74,* 506–521.

Behrend, D. A., Scofield, J., & Kleinknecht, E. E. (2001). Beyond fast mapping: Young children's extensions of novel words and novel facts. *Developmental Psychology, 37,* 698–705.

Biemiller, A., & Slonim, N. (2001). Estimating root word vocabulary growth in normative and advantaged populations: Evidence for a common sequence of vocabulary acquisition. *Journal of Educational Psychology, 93,* 498–520.

Bloom, L. (2000). The intentionality model of word learning: How to learn a word, any word. In R. M. Golinkoff, K. Hirsh-Pasek, L. Bloom, L. B. Smith, A. L. Woodward, N. Akhtar, M. Tomasello, & G. Hollich (Eds.), *Becoming a word learner: A debate on lexical acquisition* (pp. 19–50). New York: Oxford University Press.

Bloom, L., Margulis, C., Tinker, E., & Fujita, N. (1996). Early conversations and word learning: Contributions from child and adult. *Child Development, 67,* 3154–3175.

Bloom, L., & Tinker, E. (2001). The intentionality model and language acquisition. *Monographs of the Society for Research in Child Development, 66* (Serial No. 267), i–viii, 1–91.

Bloom, P. (2000). *How children learn the meanings of words.* Cambridge, MA: MIT Press.

Bogner, K., Raphael, L. M., & Pressley, M. (2002). How grade-1 teachers motivate literate activity by their students. *Scientific Studies of Reading, 6,* 135–165.

Brabham, E. G., & Lynch-Brown, C. (2002). Effect of teachers' reading-aloud styles on vocabulary acquisition and comprehension of students in the early elementary grades. *Journal of Educational Psychology, 94,* 465–473.

Brett, A., Rothlein, L., & Hurley, M. (1996). Vocabulary acquisition from listening to stories and explanations of target words. *The Elementary School Journal, 96,* 415–422.

Brown, R. W. (1957). Linguistic determinism and the parts of speech. *Journal of Abnormal and Social Psychology, 55,* 1–5.

Bus, A. G., van IJzendoorn, M. H., & Pellegrini, A. D. (1995). Joint book reading makes for success in learning to read: A meta-analysis on intergenerational transmission of literacy. *Review of Educational Research, 65,* 1–21.

Carey, S., & Bartlett, E. (1978). Acquiring a single new word. *Papers and Reports on Child Language Development, 15,* 17–29.

Carlisle, J. F., Fleming, J. E., & Gudbrandsen, B. (2000). Incidental word learning in science classes. *Contemporary Educational Psychology, 25,* 184–211.

Carlo, M. S., August, D., McLaughlin, B., Snow, C. E., Dressler, C., Lippman, D. N., Lively, T. J., & White, C. E. (2004). Closing the gap: Addressing the vocabulary needs of English-language learners in bilingual and mainstream classrooms. *Reading Research Quarterly, 39,* 188–215.

Childers, J. B., & Tomasello, M. (2002). Two-year-olds learn novel nouns, verbs, and conventional actions from massed or distributed exposures. *Developmental Psychology, 38,* 967–978.

Chomsky, N. (1957). *Syntactic structures.* The Hague: Mouton.

Cunningham, A. E., & Stanovich, K. E. (1997). Early reading acquisition and its relation to reading experience and ability 10 years later. *Developmental Psychology, 33,* 934–945.

Daalen-Kapteijns, M. M. van, & Elshout-Mohr, M. (1981). The acquisition of word meanings as a cognitive verbal process. *Journal of Verbal Learning and Verbal Behavior, 20,* 386–399.

Davis, F. B. (1944). Fundamental factors in reading comprehension. *Psychometrica, 9,* 185–197.

Davis, F. B. (1968). Research in comprehension in reading. *Reading Research Quarterly, 3,* 499–545.

Dickinson, D. K., & Smith, M. W. (1994). Long-term effects of preschool teachers' book readings on low-income children's vocabulary and story comprehension. *Reading Research Quarterly, 29,* 104–122.

Dole, J. A., Sloan, C., & Trathen, W. (1995). Teaching vocabulary within the context of literature. *Journal of Reading, 38,* 452–460.

Dolezal, S. E., Welsh, L. M., Pressley, M., & Vincent, M. (2003). How nine third-grade teachers motivate student academic engagement. *Elementary School Journal, 103,* 239–267.

Edwards, E. C., Font, G., Baumann, J. F., & Boland, E. (2004). Unlocking word meanings: Strategies and guidelines for teaching morphemic and contextual analysis. In J. F. Baumann & E. J. Kame'enui (Eds.), *Vocabulary instruction: Research to practice* (pp. 159–176). New York: Guilford Press.

Elley, W. B. (1989). Vocabulary acquisition from listening to stories. *Reading Research Quarterly, 24,* 174–187.

Fukkink, R. G., & de Glopper, K. (1998). Effects of instruction in deriving word meaning from context: A meta-analysis. *Review of Educational Research, 68,* 450–469.

Graves, M. F., & Hammond, H. K. (1980). A validated procedure for teaching prefixes and its effect on students' ability to assign meaning to novel words. In M. L. Kamil & J. Moe (Eds.), *Perspective on reading research and instruction: Twenty-ninth yearbook of the National Reading Conference* (Vol. 29, pp. 184–188). Washington, DC: National Reading Conference.

Hart, B., & Risley, T. R. (1995). *Meaningful differences in the everyday experience of young American children.* Baltimore: Brookes.

Heibeck, T. H., & Markman, E. M. (1987). Word learning in children: An examination of fast mapping. *Child Development, 58,* 1021–1034.

Hidi, S. (1990). Interest and its contribution as a mental resource for learning. *Review of Educational Research, 60,* 549–571.

Huttenlocher, J., Vasilyeva, M., Cymerman, E., & Levine, S. (2001). Language input and child syntax. *Cognitive Psychology, 45,* 337–374.

Jaswal, V. K., & Markman, E. M. (2003). The relative strengths of indirect and direct word learning. *Developmental Psychology, 39,* 745–760.

Kame'enui, E., Carnine, D., & Freschl, R. (1982). Effects of text construction and instructional procedures for teaching word meanings on comprehension and recall. *Reading Research Quarterly, 17,* 367–388.

Kleinknecht, E. E., Behrend, D. A., & Scofield, J. M. (1999, March). *What's so special about word learning, anyway?* Paper presented at the biennial meeting of the Society for Research in Child Development, Albuquerque, NM.

Kuhn, M. R., & Stahl, S. A. (1998). Teaching children to learn word meanings from context: A synthesis and some questions. *Journal of Literacy Research, 30,* 119–138.

Leung, C. B. (1992). Effects of word-related variables on vocabulary growth repeated read-aloud events. In C. K. Kinzer & D. J. Leu (Eds.), *Literacy research, theory, and practice: Views from many perspectives: Forty-first yearbook of the National Reading Conference* (pp. 491–498). Chicago, IL: National Reading Conference.

Levin, J. R., Carney, R. N., & Pressley, M. (1988). Facilitating vocabulary inferring through root word instruction. *Contemporary Educational Psychology, 13,* 316–322.

Lonigan, C. J., & Whitehurst, G. J. (1998). Relative efficacy of parent and teacher involvement in a shared-reading intervention for preschool children from low-income backgrounds. *Early Childhood Research Quarterly, 13,* 263–290.

Markson, L. (1999). *Mechanisms of word learning in children: Insights from fast mapping.* Unpublished doctoral dissertation, University of Arizona, Tucson.

McGregor, K. K. (2004). Developmental dependencies between lexical semantics and reading. In C. A. Stone, E. R. Silliman, B. J. Ehren, & K. Apel (Eds.), *Handbook of language and literacy: Development and disorders* (pp. 302–317). New York: Guilford Press.

McKeown, M. G. (1985). The acquisition of word meaning from context by children of high and low ability. *Reading Research Quarterly, 20,* 482–496.

McKeown, M. G., & Beck, I. L. (2004). Direct and rich vocabulary instruction. In J. F. Baumann & E. J. Kame'enui (Eds.), *Vocabulary instruction: Research to practice* (pp. 13–27). New York: Guilford Press.

McKeown, M. G., Beck, I. L., Omanson, R. C., & Perfetti, C. A. (1983). The effects of long-term vocabulary instruction on reading comprehension: A replication. *Journal of Reading Behavior, 15,* 3–18.

McKeown, M. G., Beck, I. L., Omanson, R. C., & Pople, M. T. (1985). Some effects on the nature and frequency of vocabulary instruction on the knowledge and use of words. *Reading Research Quarterly, 20,* 522–535.

Miller, G. A., & Gildea, P. M. (1987). How children learn words. *Scientific American, 252*(3), 94–99.

Morrow, L. M., Tracey, D. H., Woo, D. G., & Pressley, M. (1999). Characteristics of exemplary first-grade literacy instruction. *Reading Teacher, 52,* 462–476.

Naigles, L., & Hoff-Ginsberg, E. (1995). Input to verb learning: Evidence for the plausibility of syntactic bootstrapping. *Developmental Psychology, 5,* 827–837.

Nicholson, T., & Whyte, B. (1992). Matthew effects in learning new words while listening to stories. In C. K. Kinzer & D. J. Leu (Eds.), *Literacy research, theory, and practice: Views from many perspectives: Forty-first yearbook of the National Reading Conference* (pp. 499–503). Chicago, IL: National Reading Conference.

Ninio, A. (1980). Picture-book reading in mother–infant dyads belonging to two subgroups in Israel. *Child Development, 51,* 587–590.

Nist, S. L., & Olejnik, S. (1995). The role of context and dictionary definitions on varying levels of word knowledge. *Reading Research Quarterly, 30,* 172–193.

No Child Left Behind Act of 2001. (2002). Public Law 107-110.

Pany, D., Jenkins, J. R., & Schreck, J. (1982). Vocabulary instruction: Effects on word knowledge and reading comprehension. *Learning Disability Quarterly, 5,* 202–215.

Payne, A. C., Whitehurst, G. J., & Angell, A. L. (1994). The role of home literacy environment in the development of language ability in preschool children from low-income families. *Early Childhood Research Quarterly, 9,* 427–440.

Pearson, B. Z., Fernandez, S. C., Lewedeg, V., & Oller, D. K. (1997). The relation of input factors to lexical learning by bilingual infants. *Appled Psycholinguistics, 18,* 41–58.

Penno, J. F., Wilkinson, I. A. G., & Moore, D. W. (2002). Vocabulary acquisition from teacher explanation and repeated listening to stories: Do they overcome the Matthew effect? *Journal of Educational Psychology, 94,* 23–33.

Pressley, M., Allington, R., Wharton-McDonald, R., Block, C. C., & Morrow, L.M. (2001). *Learning to read: Lessons from exemplary first grades.* New York: Guilford Press.

Pressley, M., Dolezal, S. E., Raphael, L. M., Welsh, L. M., Roehrig, A. D., & Bogner, K. (2003). *Motivating primary-grade students.* New York: Guilford Press.

Pressley, M., Roehrig, A., Raphael, L., Dolezal, S., Bohn, K., Mohan, L., Wharton-McDonald, R., & Bogner, K. (2003). Teaching processes in elementary and secondary education. In W. M. Reynolds & G. E. Miller (Eds.), *Comprehensive handbook of psychology: Vol. 7. Educational psychology* (pp. 153–175). New York: Wiley.

Pressley, M., Wharton-McDonald, R., Allington, R., Block, C. C., Morrow, L., Tracey, D., Baker, K., Brooks, G., Cronin, J., Nelson, E., & Woo, D. (2001). A study of effective grade-1 literacy instruction. *Scientific Studies of Reading, 5,* 35–58.

Pressley, M., Wharton-McDonald, R., & Mistretta, J. (1998). Effective beginning literacy instruction: Dialectical, scaffolded, and contextualized. In J. L. Metsala &

L. C. Ehri (Eds.), *Word recognition in beginning literacy* (pp. 357–373). Mahwah, NJ: Erlbaum.

Pressley, M., Wharton-McDonald, R., Raphael, L. M., Bogner, K., & Roehrig, A. D. (2001). Exemplary first grade teaching. In B. M Taylor & P. D. Pearson (Eds.), *Teaching reading: Effective schools and accomplished teachers* (pp. 73–88). Mahwah, NJ: Erlbaum.

Robbins, C., & Ehri, L. C. (1994). Reading storybooks to kindergartners helps them learn new vocabulary words. *Journal of Educational Psychology, 86*, 54–64.

Scarborough, H. S., & Dobrich, W. (1994). On the efficiency of reading to preschoolers. *Developmental Review, 14*, 245–302.

Schatz, E. K., & Baldwin, R. S. (1986). Context clues are unreliable predictors of word meanings. *Reading Research Quarterly, 21*, 439–453.

Schwartz, R. G., & Terrell, B. Y. (1983). The role of input frequency in lexical acquisition. *Journal of Child Language, 10*, 57–64.

Scott, J., & Nagy, W. (1997). Understanding the definitions of unfamiliar verbs. *Reading Research Quarterly, 32*, 184–200.

Senechal, M. (1997). The differential effect of storybook reading on preschoolers' acquisition of expressive and receptive vocabulary. *Journal of Child Language, 24*, 123–138.

Senechal, M., & Cornell, E. H. (1993). Vocabulary acquisition through shared reading experiences. *Reading Research Quarterly, 28*, 360–374.

Singer, H. A. (1965). A developmental model of speed of reading in grades 3 through 6. *Reading Research Quarterly, 1*, 29–49.

Spearitt, D. (1972). Identification of subskills of reading comprehension by maximum likelihood factor analysis. *Reading Research Quarterly, 8*, 92–111.

Stahl, S. A., & Fairbanks, M. M. (1986). The effects of vocabulary instruction: A model-based meta-analysis. *Review of Educational Research, 56*, 72–110.

Sternberg, R. J. (1987). Most vocabulary is learned from context. In M. G. McKeown & M. E. Curtis (Eds.), *The nature of vocabulary acquisition*. Hillsdale, NJ: Erlbaum.

Sternberg, R. J., & Powell, J. S. (1983). Comprehending verbal comprehension. *American Psychologist, 38*, 878–893.

Sternberg, R. J., Powell, J. S., & Kaye, D. B. (1983). Teaching vocabulary-building skills: A contextual approach. In A. C. Wilkinson (Ed.), *Classroom computers and cognitive science* (pp. 121–143). New York: Academic Press.

Swanburn, M. S. L., & de Glopper, K. (1999). Incidental word learning while reading: A meta-analysis. *Review of Educational Research, 69*, 261–285.

Thorndike, E. L. (1911). *Animal intelligence*. New York: Macmillan.

Thurstone, L. L. (1946). A note on a reanalysis of Davis' reading texts. *Psychometrica, 11*, 185–188.

Tomesen, M., & Aarnoutsee, C. (1998). Effects of an instructional programme for deriving word meanings. *Educational Studies, 24*, 107–128.

Valdez-Menchaca, M. C., & Whitehurst, G. J. (1988). The effects of incidental teaching on vocabulary acquisition by young children. *Child Development, 59*, 1451–1459.

Valdez-Menchaca, M. C., & Whitehurst, G. J. (1992). Accelerating language development through picture book reading: A systematic extension to Mexican day care. *Developmental Psychology, 28*, 1106–1114.

Waxman, S. R., & Booth, A. E. (2000). Principles that are invoked in the acquisition of words, but not facts. *Cognition, 77,* B33–B43.

Wharton-McDonald, R., Pressley, M., & Hampston, J. M. (1998). Literacy instruction in nine first-grade classrooms: Teacher characteristics and student achievement. *Elementary School Journal, 99,* 101–128.

Whitehurst, G. J., Arnold, D. S., Epstein, J. N., Angel, A. L., Smith, M., & Fischel, J. E. (1994). A picture book reading intervention in day care and home for children from low-income families. *Developmental Psychology, 30,* 679–689.

Whitehurst, G. J., Epstein, J. N., Angel, A. L., Payne, A. C., Crone, D. A., & Fischel, J. E. (1994). Outcomes of an emergent literacy intervention in Head Start. *Journal of Educational Psychology, 86,* 542–555.

Whitehurst, G. J., Falco, F. L., Lonigan, C. J., Fischel, J. E., DeBaryshe, B. D., Valdez-Menchaca, M. C., & Caulfield, M. (1988). Accelerating language development through picture book reading. *Developmental Psychology, 24,* 552–559.

Whitehurst, G. J., Zevenbergen, A. A., Crone, D. A., Schultz, M. D., Velting, O. N., & Fischel, J. E. (1999). Outcomes of an emergent literacy intervention from Head Start through second grade. *Journal of Educational Psychology, 91,* 261–272.

Wixson, K. K. (1986). Vocabulary instruction and children's comprehension of basal stories. *Reading Research Quarterly, 21,* 317–329.

Wright, J. C., Huston, A. C., Murphy, K. C., St. Peters, M., Piaton, M., Santlin, R., & Kotler, J. (2001). The relations of early television viewing to school readiness and vocabulary of children from low-income families: The Early Window Project. *Child Development, 72,* 1347–1366.

Wysocki, K., & Jenkins, J. R. (1987). Deriving word meanings through morphological generalization. *Reading Research Quarterly, 22,* 66–81.

Zevenbergen, A. A., Whitehurst, G. J., & Zevenbergen, J. A. (2003). Effects of a shared-reading intervention on the inclusion of evaluative devices in narratives of children from low-income families. *Journal of Applied Developmental Psychology, 24,* 1–15.

Laurel Disney, MS, is a doctoral student in the Department of Teacher Education at Michigan State University, East Lansing, Michigan, and Director of the Reading Clinic at Michigan Career and Technical Institute, Plainwell, Michigan.

Kendra Anderson, EdS, is a school psychologist for the Portage, Michigan public schools.

CHAPTER 8

Expert Primary-Level Teaching of Literacy Is Balanced Teaching

with RUTH WHARTON-MCDONALD
and JENNIFER MISTRETTA HAMPSTON

In the early 1990s, we spent a great deal of time thinking about the fact that we see many children experience difficulties in elementary reading as early as grade 1. Although not all of the research summarized in the previous chapters was available in the early 1990s, enough did exist for us to understand that the development of both phonemic awareness and decoding skills was key in beginning reading. We were also aware, however, that many teachers were committed to whole language and they believed it was affecting competencies beyond the word level. We had been in enough primary-level classrooms filled with literature and writing to know that there was much that was attractive about such instruction. Moreover, we had seen classrooms that seemed to be doing quite a bit of word-level skills instruction while immersing children in literature and rich language arts experiences. We had enough memories then of lots of students seeming to read fairly well in these classrooms to know that success in learning to read was common in the 1990s. Unfortunately, there were also visits to grade-1 classrooms in which students were struggling. We decided that we wanted to know what distinguished the more successful primary classrooms from the less successful ones we had seen, believing that such knowledge was essential to have a fully informed opinion about what should be occurring in elementary language-arts classrooms.

As cognitively oriented researchers, we were aware that cognitive psychologists had devoted much effort to understanding how professionals do what they do, investigating radiologists reading X-rays and airline pilots dealing with emergencies, among others (Chi, Glaser, & Farr, 1988; Ericsson & Smith, 1991; Hoffmann, 1992). The typical tactic in such research was to compare expert professionals to novice professionals. Awareness of this literature stimulated an important insight in the summer of 1992, as one of us (M. P.) reflected on the various texts he had been reading about what primary-level reading instruction should be like.

Most of his reading that summer was in books considered foundational by the whole-language educator community, volumes chock full of pedagogical suggestions. What occurred to him as he read them, however, was that, for the most part, the various recommendations were being made at something of a distance from primary-level teaching. Professors of education wrote these books. As someone who knew many professors of education, and who knew the expert–novice studies, M. P.'s gut reaction was that to ask professors of curriculum and instruction about how to teach elementary reading was somewhat akin to asking airline executives and aeronautical engineers how to fly a plane. In the case of flying, such a strategy would result in a lot of information about what could go on in the cockpit, but much of it would be wrong and many important nuances would be missing. Expert pilots have what is known as conditional knowledge: They know very well about when to make which decisions during a flight, with years of experience resulting in very detailed understanding about when particular tactics work and when others should be tried. Nobody else, including airline executives and aeronautical engineers, has access to such information, which develops only through years of experience flying an airplane.

It seemed to M. P. that the education professors writing the whole-language texts knew a great deal about instructional theory and certainly affected instruction through their research, writing, and influence on teacher education, but nonetheless they had little if any experience in the pilot's seat of American education. They were not the ones who planned and executed days and weeks and months of primary-grade experiences for students, and hence they were in less-than-an-ideal position to know how curriculum and pedagogy mix. That perspective could only be gained by being in primary classrooms for long periods of time.

Based on these reflections and experiences, it seemed to us that to know the nature of effective primary-level reading instruction, the best bet was to study and interact with effective primary-level teachers. We have done much of that since 1992 to develop an informed perspective on what should be occurring in elementary classrooms in order to maximize the likelihood that students learn to read.

A SURVEY STUDY OF OUTSTANDING PRIMARY-LEVEL READING TEACHERS

In order to get a running start in the pursuit of an understanding of outstanding primary-level teaching, Pressley and his associates Joan Rankin and Linda Yokoi (1996) decided to attempt to gather a great deal of data in a fairly short time. To do this, they selected a sample of elementary language-arts supervisors throughout the United States and asked them to identify their very best kindergarten, grade-1, and grade-2 teachers, ones who were exceptional in promoting literacy achievement in students. Once these exceptional teachers were nominated, they were contacted by mail and simply asked to describe in an open-ended fashion the 10 most important elements of their teaching. When all of the responses to this question were cataloged, the list came to more than 400 individual practices that the teachers claimed occurred as part of their teaching. It was clear at this point in the study that primary-level classrooms are very busy places!

Pressley et al. (1996) did not stop there, however. For each of the elements of instruction specified in response to the open-ended query, they developed a question that could be responded to on a quantitative scale, with all of the questions then placed on a questionnaire. Consider the following sample questions, all of which appeared on the questionnaire:

> Do you use "big books?" (Answered on a "never" to "several times a day" scale.)
>
> After a story, do you ask students "comprehension questions"? (Answered on a "not at all" to "all stories" scale.)
>
> What percentage of the material read by your students is outstanding children's literature? . . . written at a "controlled" reading level? . . . written to provide practice in phonetic elements and/or patterns? . . . high-interest, low-vocabulary materials?
>
> Which of the following extension activities do you use regularly, occasionally, or never? arts/crafts with print attached, cooking activities, dramatics or puppet plays, drawing or illustrating stories, movement activities, field trips, games?
>
> Are home/parents involved in your reading instruction for good readers? . . . average readers? . . . weaker readers?

The questionnaire was then mailed to the teachers who had responded to the open-ended question. Most of them responded once again. The teachers described their classrooms, indicating in their responses that their classrooms involved a complex articulation of components.

Literate Environment

Virtually all of the teachers reported that they identified, at least to some extent, with whole-language and language experience approaches. They reported that they attempted to create a literate environment in the classroom, including in-class library, display of student work, and display of chart stories and poems. These classrooms were portrayed as rich with stories being told, read, and reread. Learning centers dedicated to development of listening, reading, and writing were typical.

The teachers reported daily practice of reading and writing, with limited practice of skills in isolation, such as with worksheets or workbooks. Even so, the teachers also reported that they made certain that skills not yet mastered by their students—including phonics, letter recognition, and spelling—were experienced repeatedly by students, often in the context of other reading and writing activities.

The teachers reported that they overtly modeled literacy skills and strategies, as well as positive attitudes toward literacy. They expressed concern with the individual literacy achievement of students, monitoring student needs, giving minilessons and reteaching as needed. Reading and writing were portrayed as individually guided on a student-by-student basis.

Many different types of reading were reported as occurring in these classrooms, including students reading along with the teacher, echo and choral reading, shared reading, students reading aloud with others, daily silent reading, student rereading of books and stories, and reading homework (e.g., teachers sending books home and asking parents to listen to their children read). Many different types of material were read, including outstanding children's literature, big books, chart poems and stories, picture books, and patterned and predictable books. Reading often included author studies, involving the reading of several books by distinguished children's authors and illustrators. The teachers reported limited reading of basal readers, other materials at a controlled reading levels, chapter books, and expository materials.

The teachers indicated that literacy instruction was integrated with the rest of the curriculum. As part of this, extension experiences were reported as common, including arts and crafts, illustrating activities, and games. In short, these expert teachers presented their classrooms as places in which literacy development occurred throughout the day, connected both to formal curriculum and less formal activities.

Teaching of Reading

There was a lot of concern with the development of reading skills, not only in context, when such instruction was needed and made sense, as favored in whole language, but also using decontextualized approaches (e.g., games, spelling tests). The teachers reported developing many particular competencies as part of their reading instruction, including skills prerequisite to reading (e.g., auditory and visual discrimination; attending and listening skills), concepts of print (e.g., concept of a word, parts of a book), letter recognition, the alphabetic principle (i.e., letters code the sounds in words), letter–sound associations, punctuation, decoding strategies (using context and picture cues, sounding out words using letter–sound knowledge), sight words and vocabulary, spelling, text elements (e.g., cause-and-effect relations, theme/main idea, character analysis), comprehension strategies (especially prediction and visualization), and critical thinking skills (including brainstorming, categorization, and recalling details).

Writing

Consistent with the whole-language identification of these teachers, a great deal of writing was also reported. The teachers reported that they employed story and journal writing. Writing occurred in response to pictures, wordless picture books, and stories. Shared writing activities were implemented, including the class dictating stories to the teacher, who served as a scribe. The teachers also reported encouraging students to write at home.

Teachers taught the writing process, including planning, making drafts, and revising. Once it was revised, students often published their writing in these classrooms, sometimes on the computer.

Writing was viewed as connected to reading in a number of ways. An important one was through students reading aloud to classmates and the teacher the stories they had written.

Qualitatively Similar Instruction Regardless of Ability

The teachers were emphatic that the same types of materials and activities were experienced by all students regardless of ability. Yes, the teachers claimed to be more explicit and extensive in their teaching of some prereading, letter-level, and word-level skills with weaker readers. That is, they seemed to believe, contrary to whole-language philosophy, that weaker students would not develop the skills needed to be literate simply through immersion in the literate environment that was their classroom. Consistent with this concern, the teachers reported providing more guidance during reading and writing instruction with weaker readers than with good ones. In a follow-up questionnaire study (Rankin-Erickson & Pressley, 2000), primary-level special educators reported commitment to providing much direct instruction and support of reading and writing skills. That is, in two different studies, primary-level educators claimed that explicit instruction in skills is very good for weaker students. Even so, they thought that all readers needed to be taught the same skills and that all readers should experience good literature and composing experiences.

Motivation

The teachers were clearly concerned with motivating their students to do literate things. In general, their perspective on motivation was consistent with standard whole-language thinking. They reported attempting to motivate literacy by reducing risks for students attempting literate activities, setting an exciting mood, and encouraging students to believe they can be readers and writers.

Grade-Level Shifts in Teaching

By including kindergarten, grade-1, and grade-2 teachers, it was possible for us to have a window on grade-level shifts during the primary years in effective literacy instruction. Not surprisingly, some instructional practices were reported as decreasing with increasing grade level and others were reported as increasing when moving from kindergarten to grade 2.

Practices Decreasing with Advancing Grade Level

With advancing grade level, the teachers reported fewer signs and labels in their classrooms and less use of learning centers. Letter-recognition drills and singing of the alphabet song occurred less often. So did teaching *focusing* on the alphabetic principle, letter–sound associations, and simple concepts of print (e.g., concept of a "letter," directions of print). There was less teacher rereading of stories, shared big book reading, and reading of chart stories and poems with advancing grade level. Picture, patterned, and controlled-reading-level books declined in frequency of use. Writing together (e.g., students dictating stories to teachers) declined. There were fewer parent conferences.

Practices Increasing with Advancing Grade Level

With increasing grade level, there was more round-robin reading reported and more reading aloud in general by individual students. There was also more silent reading of, for example, chapter books. Basal readers were reported as more frequent as students advanced through the primary years.

Consistent with whole language, increased emphasis on using syntactic cues to decode was reported. On the other hand, so was increased teaching of phonics rules, sounding out, and orthographic analysis for decoding. Sight-word and spelling drills increased, as did spelling tests. There was more teaching of vocabulary. The teaching of comprehension strategies increased with advancing grade, including teaching students to activate prior knowledge, generate questions during reading, find main ideas, and summarize. Teaching of critical thinking skills increased, including webbing and identification of causes and effects. There was more writing of stories and more writing in response to reading. Punctuation was emphasized more during writing. The writing process was emphasized more as well, with greater planning, revising, and publishing. Writing portfolios were reported as increasing in saliency with increasing grade level.

Accountability

The teachers reported extensive monitoring of their students, including comprehension checks (e.g., questions following a reading, student retelling of stories heard or read, student retelling with story strips or pictures), writing portfolios, and reading portfolios. The teachers also reported regular conferences with parents and frequent communications with the student's home as part of accountability.

Summary

The teachers in this study, who had been identified as effective by their supervisors, reported school days packed with all types of reading and writing. Most critically, from the perspective of this book, great balance was reported in the instruction offered to students. Consistent with the recommendation of a number of educators and theorists (e.g., Adams, 1990; Cazden, 1992; Delpit, 1986, 1988; Duffy, 1991; Fisher & Hiebert, 1990; McCaslin, 1989; Pressley, 1994; Stahl, McKenna, & Pagnucco, 1994), the teachers in this study depicted their classrooms as integrating the attractive features of whole language with explicit skills instruction. For example, although they claimed to be immersing students in literacy experiences, they also reported extensive and explicit teaching through modeling, explanation, and minilesson reexplanations, especially with respect to decoding and other skills (e.g., punctuation mechanics, comprehension strategies). Explicit teaching of letter-level and decoding skills, as well as elementary writing skills, was reported as especially frequent for students experiencing difficulties in learning to read and write.

There were many reasons for confidence in the survey data. One was that there was little variability in the opinions offered. Another was that the data were orderly in ways that would be expected (Harris & Sipay, 1990) if the teachers were being honest in their reports. Thus, teachers who claimed to be exclusively whole language were, in fact, less likely to endorse practices not endorsed by pure whole-language theorists, such as out-of-context decoding instruction. Also, there were reported decreases in instructional practices that should decrease between kindergarten and grade 2 (e.g., letter-level skills), and there were reported increases in instructional practices that should increase between kindergarten and grade 2 (e.g., spelling).

Even though such data were closer to actual teaching than the musings of a curriculum professor sitting at her or his word processor, nonetheless they were further removed from actual teaching than desirable. Thus, we followed the survey with studies of grade-1 teaching that involved observation. The survey study was a good starting point, however. Nothing that follows in this chapter contradicts the reports provided by the effective teachers who responded in the survey research.

STUDIES OF OUTSTANDING GRADE-1 TEACHING

There was much research on effective elementary schools in the last quarter of the 20th century (Edmonds, 1979; Firestone, 1991), with particular attention to "outlier" schools, institutions that are exceptionally effective given their context (e.g., schools producing high achievement in lower-socioeconomic urban neighborhoods). A consistent pattern emerged across case analyses of such schools. Outlier schools have the following characteristics (Firestone, 1991):

1. They have strong administrative leadership.
2. There are high expectations for all children.
3. They are safe and orderly environments without being overly rigid.
4. The top priority is student acquisition of basic school skills, with willingness to divert resources from other activities to support development of basic school skills in students.
5. Student progress is carefully monitored.

Scholars at the Center for the Improvement of Early Reading Achievement (based at the University of Michigan and Michigan State University) carried out studies in the effective schools tradition, ones aimed at identifying the characteristics of elementary schools that are especially effective in stimulating literacy development of students. Taylor, Pearson, Clark, and Walpole (2000) studied 14 schools across the United States, with each having a high proportion of students living in poverty. In each of these schools, two teachers at each grade level (kindergarten through grade 3) were observed, with achievement in classrooms carefully analyzed. In particular, word-level measures (word recognition accuracy and fluency) and comprehension measures were taken at both the beginning and end of the school year.

Based on improvements in reading performance over the school year, the researchers classified the schools as most, moderately, or least effective in promoting student literacy. The most effective schools included more small-group instruction, more coaching (i.e., scaffolding) by teachers, teaching of phonics but with an emphasis on application during real reading, more higher-order questioning (i.e., questions requiring inferences and integration), greater outreach to parents, and more independent reading. There was greater balancing of skills and holistic instruction (i.e., reading of complete texts, composition writing) in effective schools, and greater student engagement (i.e., students spent more time productively reading and writing).

An Important Classroom-Level Analysis

Michael S. Knapp and Associates (1995) studied the instruction and achievement in 140 elementary classrooms serving students living in poverty in three states. They found that reading achievement was most striking in classrooms in which meaning-making was emphasized. In these classrooms, there were many opportunities to read.

Reading and writing were integrated activities (e.g., students wrote in response to what they read). Students and teachers often discussed stories and books that were being read. The focus was on the deeper meanings in the text rather than on literal recall, and discrete skills were taught in the context of reading and writing of real texts. Sadly, only about 30% of the classrooms observed had this meaning orientation with respect to reading instruction. Also sad is that teachers who emphasized meaning in reading did not necessarily do so in writing or mathematics. That is, teaching for meaning in reading seemed to be a specialized orientation or competency rather than to reflect a general curricular emphasis on meaning. Those who took such a meaning approach were something of risk takers, however, for they worked in the contexts of school districts emphasizing skill competencies as evidence of reading achievement in students. Their gamble to do balanced literacy instruction paid off, however, in higher student achievement.

A Study of Outstanding Grade-1 Teaching in Upstate New York

Several years ago, following the survey work, we decided that the best way to understand effective grade-1 instruction would be to watch some of it (Wharton-McDonald, Pressley, & Hampston, 1998; Wharton-McDonald et al., 1997). Our first challenge in studying outstanding grade-1 teachers was to find them! To do so, we asked language-arts supervisors in the Albany, New York, area to nominate exceptionally effective grade-1 teachers. To be able to determine what was unique about outstanding teaching, we also asked the supervisors to identify teachers who were more typical of the grade-1 teachers in their district. The supervisors made a case for each teacher's participation based on observations of teaching, indications of students' literacy achievement (e.g., reading test achievement, written products), and parental feedback. In autumn 1994, we began to observe 10 teachers, 5 considered outstanding by their supervisors and 5 considered more typical. (One nominated outstanding teacher dropped out during the course of the study for personal reasons, resulting in 9 teachers in the final study.)

Although we respected the supervisors' judgments, we were also determined to find out for ourselves during the course of the study which of the teachers produced exceptional achievement. Thus, as our observation progressed, we were particularly attentive to possible indications of achievement. In the end, three types of information were identified as measures of the effectiveness of teaching:

1. Every 10–15 minutes, the observer would look around the classroom and calculate the percentage of students attentively engaged in academic activities. The classrooms varied with respect to this dimension: Some were characterized by consistently high engagement, even when the teacher was not present or attending to the class, whereas others were more variable in engagement.

2. Reading level was defined by the difficulty levels of books that students were reading at the end of the year. There was wide variation between the classes by the end of the year, ranging from ones in which most students seemed to be working regularly with texts that were at or above grade level to others in which many students were regularly reading books intended for early or middle grade-1 reading.

3. Writing was appraised by examining the stories and essays that children wrote. In some classrooms, typical end-of-the-year compositions were several pages long, reflecting knowledge of a variety of writing conventions, good spelling, and appropriate punctuation. The writing in these classrooms often reflected real coherence in expression, with a single topic

developed over the pages of writing. At the other extreme were classrooms in which end-of-year writing typically was less than a page long—usually two to three sentences. In these classrooms, topical development and mechanics typically were much less impressive.

By the conclusion of the study, which involved at least 10 observations of each teacher and two in-depth interviews of each participant, the researchers agreed that there were really three clusters of teachers. In three classrooms, student engagement was typically high, reading levels were at or above grade level, and writing was relatively coherent and sophisticated. Three classrooms were at the other extreme, with much more variable, and often low, engagement and more modest indications of reading and writing achievement. Three classrooms were in the middle.

The researchers developed a model of each teacher's teaching. Then, they compared and contrasted the nine teachers to develop an understanding of aspects of instruction that were common across classrooms as well as aspects of instruction that distinguished the three best teachers from the other six.

Commonalities in Instruction across Classrooms

The nine classrooms, in fact, did have much in common, with the following characteristics observed in at least seven of them:

- They were positive places, led by caring teachers.
- There was little competition.
- There were classroom routines, and thus much of the time students knew what they were supposed to be doing.
- There were a variety of teaching configurations—whole- and small-group instruction, cooperative learning, and independent work.
- Teachers mixed direct skills instruction (i.e., of decoding, punctuation, capitalization, spelling) and whole-language-type activities. Skills instruction was sometimes accompanied by worksheets, coexisting with whole-language practices, such as the extensive use of trade books, the teacher modeling a love of reading, and process writing.
- All teachers recognized the importance of parental participation in children's literacy development.

In summary—particularly important in the context of this book—there was some balancing of skills instruction and whole-language activities in all of the classrooms we observed.

Unique Characteristics of the Three Outstanding Teachers

As indicated earlier, student engagement was consistently high in the three best classrooms, compared to the much more variable engagement in the other six. There were a number of aspects of the teaching that contributed to this difference in student involvement:

• The best teachers in the sample were masterful classroom managers. They were so good, in fact, that classroom management was hardly noticeable. In the best classrooms, students were busy and appeared to be happy, with virtually no misbehavior observed. The worst that happened in these classrooms was off-taskedness, which typically ended quickly as the teacher moved in to get the student back on task, quietly and positively.

• The top three teachers were also skillful managers of the human resources available to them. Thus, resource teachers who "pushed in" to these classrooms were always busy providing instruction and assistance to students. In contrast, resource teachers often were underused by the more typical teachers—for example, they would spend a great deal of time on the periphery of the classroom with nothing to do as the classroom teacher conducted a whole-group lesson.

• There was a high density of instruction in the best classrooms—that is, there was always something to keep the children engaged. Mornings in the best classrooms seemed jam-packed as compared to a more relaxed pace in the other classrooms.

• Activities connected with one another. Reading materials connected to writing topics, and literacy instruction tied in with content instruction. For example, one of the outstanding teachers integrated her lessons on nutrition, a required part of the grade-1 science curriculum for the district, with readings of works such as Judith Barrett's *Cloudy with a Chance of Meatballs* (1978), which motivated the writing of menus in the style of the children's book.

• In the best classrooms, the activities were consistently academically rich, in comparison to academically vacuous activities that were often observed in other classrooms. For example, in one of the more typical classrooms there was a great deal of copying. In another of the more typical classrooms, much of the literacy instruction was devoted to "sharing" discussions not related to what the children were reading or to other academic content.

• In general, there was more going on—in terms of both activities and objectives covered—in the more outstanding classrooms than in the typical classrooms.

• The classrooms with outstanding teachers were filled with the message that students can and will learn. These teachers were determined that their students would develop as readers and writers. In contrast, there was more willingness by the more typical teachers to believe that lack of student progress simply reflected the students' lack of readiness to read and write.

• In the outstanding classrooms, every student was reinforced for her or his achievements. Each of the three best teachers beamed at the progress being made by weak students in particular.

• Literacy instruction in the top three classrooms was exceptionally well balanced with respect to the elements of whole language—reading of outstanding literature, writing—and the explicit teaching of skills. Reading, writing, and skills instruction were very well integrated in these classrooms. Although there were lessons dedicated specifically to certain skills, the skills instruction observed in the three best classrooms in this study was anything but decontextualized. The skills lessons were filled with reminders about how the skills related to the children's writing and reading. Moreover, the children had many opportunities to use the skills as they read and wrote. As one of the outstanding teachers described it, teaching beginning reading "is a fine balance between immersing the child in whole language and teaching through . . .. sounds, going back to using skills. . . . If you don't have a balance, it's kind of like trying to fit a square through a circle. It doesn't work. You don't connect with everyone if you don't use a variety of [teaching] strategies." In contrast to the integrated, balanced approach displayed by teachers in the top group, the other teachers tended to present instruction that was either heavily skills-based or heavily whole-language, or they attempted to combine the two approaches but did so in a disjointed or inconsistent way. Thus, one teacher in the middle group whose instruction was heavily influenced by the whole-language philosophy also had a weekly spelling program based on basic decoding skills. Students learned to spell word families and practiced words each week but were not necessarily expected to be responsible for spelling words correctly when they wrote stories or compositions in their journals.

There were several more typical classrooms in which the teachers were determined to be as consistent as possible with whole language, including the downplaying of skills instruction. These classrooms just did not work as well as the three best classrooms: Boredom was often very easy to detect, and end-of-the-year achievement in reading and writing was not as apparent. We also observed two classrooms in which skills were paramount. These classrooms did not work either, as boredom was easy to spot, and reading and writing achievement in these classrooms was not even close to the end-of-the-year performances we observed in the best classrooms.

• One of the reasons that the students were busy, happy, and learning in the three best classrooms was that they received help as they needed it.

The three best teachers were exceptionally active in scaffolding students' learning (Wood, Bruner, & Ross, 1976), providing hints and prompts when students faltered, whether during whole-group instruction or one-on-one interactions. Students received assistance as they attempted to read challenging texts and as they drafted and revised what they wrote. The assistance often involved prompting students to use the skills they were learning. For example, on the day before Valentine's Day, one teacher managed to insert minilessons on shapes and phonemic awareness as she introduced an art project:

TEACHER: I think of things when I think of Valentine's Day, too, and I write them down. What shape did I write them on? (*Students are quiet.*) Is it a square? A circle? A rectangle? A triangle? What shape is it?

STUDENT 1: A heart.

TEACHER: Can anyone try to spell "heart"?

STUDENT 2: H-E-A-R-T.

TEACHER: My goodness. If I wanted to use my sounds to spell heart, what would I start with?

STUDENT 3: H.

TEACHER: And what would it end with?

STUDENT 3: T.

TEACHER: So right away, you know some of the letters in "heart."

• Given many such opportunistic reviews, it was clear that the best teachers viewed skill development as they viewed all of reading and writing— as involving long-term construction of knowledge about how to read and write. At the same time, these teachers were not so committed to developmental educational models that they did not use worksheets or provide practice opportunities for some skills.

• The instruction and help that was given to children in the best classrooms did not make the children dependent on the teachers, however. Rather, self-regulation was most common in the three best classrooms. Students in these classrooms often worked independently or with other children. The best teachers developed students who could do much of what was required of them without adult assistance. The children were engaged in productive learning, regardless of whether the teacher saliently monitored them.

• The best teachers were highly aware both of their practices and of the purposes driving those practices. There was nothing haphazard about literacy instruction in these classes. This was in contrast to some of the other teachers, who justified some frequently observed activities as giving the children something to do while the teacher worked with small groups. Busy work was just not a concept in the thinking of the outstanding teachers.

The observers were struck that, despite the commonalities between the outstanding classrooms (summarized in Table 8.1), every classroom in this study had its own personality, including the three classes headed by the best teachers. Thus, it is tough to illustrate outstanding teaching by describing the work of any one outstanding teacher. Still, we think that by considering in greater detail the teaching of one outstanding teacher, the complexity of an outstanding grade-1 class will be made clearer.

Andy's Teaching

One of the three outstanding teachers observed by Wharton-McDonald et al. (1998) was a middle-aged male named Andy. He typically wore a sports shirt and jeans, rarely wearing a tie. His principal described him as looking like "a giant teddy bear," an accurate characterization except no teddy bear was ever so animated, ever so aware of the strengths and needs of the children in his care, nor ever so able to build on student strengths as he addressed their needs. Andy's classroom was an extremely attractive world. One student said it all when he said to himself one day, "I wish I lived here." Andy never criticized students. Typical was the following type of remark when things got a little out of hand: "I hear productive talk, but how about a little softer." He always intervened positively to get students back on task or to correct behavior. Thus, when a student was off-task during an observation, Andy said, "Kenny, why don't you read your essay with Mark?" Kenny and Mark then read together with enthusiasm, with Mark providing revision feedback to Kenny. (All students' names are changed here to protect their privacy.)

When other adults entered the classroom, nothing stopped. Andy effi-

---

TABLE 8.1. Distinguishing Characteristics of the Best Teachers in the Wharton-McDonald, Pressley, and Hampston (1998) Study

- Masterful classroom management
- High density of instruction and activity
- Reading, writing, and other instruction well integrated
- Good balancing of whole language and explicit skills instruction
- High expectations that students would learn
- Extensive use of scaffolding
- Consistent encouragement of self-regulation

ciently and quickly dealt with outside adults, never missing a step in his teaching as he did so. Attention to students more to the exclusion of visiting adults was a characteristic of all three of the best teachers, whereas more typical teachers were much more willing to attend to visiting adults. Interestingly, when the outstanding teachers did divert their attention to visitors, their students just kept at their work. In contrast, students in the other classrooms in the study were more likely to go off-task if the teacher's attention was diverted from them.

Student engagement was invariably high in Andy's class, with students attentive during their whole-group and small-group lessons and working hard when on their own. The students started reading and writing on their own as soon as they arrived in the classroom. Moreover, their time was mostly spent on actual reading and writing, with very little time devoted to activities such as illustrating stories they had written. In other classrooms in this study, we observed much more art, often involving time-consuming, difficult-to-manage materials such as paste or silhouette tracings. Such difficult-to-manage materials never entered Andy's classroom. In short, time was spent well largely because the students managed themselves, with the environment set up so that their attentions were not diverted to solving low-level problems like getting enough paste.

Why were Andy's students so self-regulated? Andy strongly encouraged self-regulation, regularly praising students for making decisions and taking responsibility. There were lots of comments like "Some of you already had the words in alphabetical order before I told you to do so. Good." Each group of desks had a bin of easy-reading books, with students making their own choices about which ones to read. On their own, students selected books from the "Reading Is Fundamental" project that were related to ongoing themes in the class. Andy taught his students to read "inside your heads." He encouraged students to monitor whether what they were reading was making sense and to reread a passage when it did not. Before writing, Andy urged students to attend to mechanics themselves, although mechanics were, in fact, checked by the teacher as part of his monitoring of writing. The classroom included a checking chart so that students could begin to check their own writing and begin revision rather than wait for the teacher. Students practiced a variety of simple thinking skills—comparing, contrasting, and summarizing. These skills occurred in the context of other activities. For example, students were encouraged to plan, an important critical thinking skill, as part of their end-of-basal projects.

Although students were good at working on their own, there also was a lot of cooperation in this classroom, with kids checking each other's work and helping one another work through difficult materials. Andy assigned weaker readers to stronger partner readers. Children worked together on important projects. Students helped one another, just as they often were helped by Andy.

Andy provided extensive scaffolding for students when they experienced difficulties, inserting many minilessons appropriate to the problems of particular students. Tasks given to students were always within their reach, at least with scaffolding: Andy is a *master* hinter. He monitored what his students were understanding during group discussions and provided helpful prompts to assist in their understanding of elusive concepts. For example, when group members were having difficulty differentiating the habitats of ducks and chickens, Andy pondered aloud to himself, "I wonder if it might have something to do with water." Andy checked on his students individually as they worked at their seats, providing help as needed. For example, when a student had difficulties with spelling a word during writing, Andy prompted the student to think about the sounds in the word. There were lots of comments like "Shawn, is that the way we used those letters when we did the other words? Think about it." Shawn went on to spell the word correctly.

Andy first sought out students most likely to be having problems. The weaker kids were never scapegoated, however. Rather, Andy went out of his way to maintain their participation in the class in ways that were decidedly honorable. For example, when it was time for students to read their essays aloud to the class, the weaker students sat at a table near Andy so he could support their reading. The table had several other seats, each of which was occupied only by bidding from other members of the class. Sitting near Andy was seen as special for the students in his class, with no stigma ever attached to any student who spent time interacting with the teacher.

Excellent literature was extremely important in Andy's class, with student writing typically involving responses to high-quality stories and trade books. If one wanted to make an edited tape of outstanding literature experiences, it could be done using footage from Andy's classroom. Consistent with whole language, there was extensive reading of trade books, with much attention to and discussion of distinguished children's authors (e.g., the author of the month). *Weekly Reader* was read. There were many types of reading, from choral reading aloud to partner reading to silent reading.

There was plenty of discussion of what had been read. Andy asked a lot of questions not simply to assess students' knowledge of a reading but to begin conversations. In these discussions, students did a lot of explaining, with Andy constantly using follow-up questions to draw out students' conceptions of things. Andy's subsequent questions typically reflected consideration of previous answers, sending the message that what the students said about the reading was important. Yes, Andy often elaborated on the students' ideas, but the students' voices and ideas were always honored.

Consistent with whole language, there was lots of writing, with clear reading–writing connections in Andy's classroom (e.g., rewrite in your own words a story just heard). This writing instruction covered macrostructural characteristics of stories—for example, clear emphasis on having a beginning, middle, and ending—and a title. It involved writing and revision as a function of conferencing with the teacher. There was also some peer conferencing, with students responding in writing to what they read by following four steps: read, think, tell neighbor, write.

Anything but consistent with whole language, however, Andy's class included systematic coverage of a basal. He liberally used stories from other basal readers as well, especially when they related to content themes. That Andy was not married to whole-language philosophy comes through in many other ways as well. In this classroom, skills instruction intelligently complemented the reading of authentic literature and student writing. There was extensive phonics instruction, both in formal lessons and on-line as part of minilessons. Simple phonics rules were taught (such as that the "bossy final *e*" caused the vowel preceding it to say its name). This occurred in the context of spelling instruction with, for example, lists of words that exemplified particular phonics principles. During the reading of a story, there was often discussion of words with particular characteristics (e.g., a word with a "short *o*" sound). During small-group lessons, there often were word analysis activities, such as finding the little words in big words. Workbook pages sometimes complemented instruction when Andy believed the students could benefit from such work.

Andy consciously stimulated students to think as they did skill activities, often requiring explanations from them. There were lots of exchanges like this one during a whole-group alphabetizing activity:

ANDY: Why did you put *whale* before *woman?*

TOMMY: Both start with a *w* but I used the second letter—*h* comes before *o*, so *whale* before *woman.*

ANDY: That's right. . . Your group has been learning how to alphabetize using the second letter. . . . This one is tricky because one letter in it can have two different sounds.

EDDY: Huge (*pronounced correctly*).

ANDY: Why is it tricky?

EDDY: Because *g* can have a hard *g* or a soft *g* sound.

ANDY: That's right. Sometimes *g* can say (*makes hard* g *sound*) and sometimes (*makes soft* g *sound*). So that's why this word needs a little extra practice.

Andy and his students talked a lot about what was in the books they were reading, how the ideas in their readings related to other ideas being covered in the curriculum, and how to use basic reading skills. There was dialoguing all day in this classroom.

There also was explicit attention to vocabulary development in Andy's classroom. Consistent with the thinking of whole-language advocates, new vocabulary words encountered in stories were discussed by Andy and the students. These discussions were supplemented, however, with many sight words posted around the room. There were sight-word drills. Resource teachers provided more explicit and extensive instruction to weaker students.

There were strong ties across the curriculum, with the gardening theme in the spring, for example, being represented in reading, writing, and a class science activity—as well as in students' self-selected reading from sources such as the "Reading Is Fundamental" books. Easy reading of books about plants continued long after the unit on gardening was completed. Such integration was observed with respect to other themes as well, including the hatching of chickens in the late spring as the students' entrée to sex education. Literature, science, and values came together dynamically as students read about chickens and discussed the biology that permitted the birth of 12 chickens in their classroom. Students wrote on their own about the incubation process, but they also worked together to prepare a news story celebrating their 100% hatching success. Given the detailed student planning that went into the construction of the hatching process and the monitoring of the eggs—just as good readers and writers check to make certain everything is right—the hatching success was unsurprising. Connections were everywhere in Andy's teaching, creating an exciting classroom. We will remember for a long time the students who just had to share what they had written about the hatching chickens because they were so proud of the hatching project and what they wrote about it.

Andy fostered a strong *home–school* connection through homework (e.g., spelling) that he carefully monitored. Students were encouraged to take home challenging stories to read with a parent in the evening. When students talked about doing something academic with a parent, Andy noted and praised it publicly. Before vacation breaks, Andy sent home a packet of homework and a letter to parents to encourage them to work with their students over the break, including writing in their journals.

Although Andy was superb at adjusting his teaching in reaction to student needs, the magnificent orchestration that was a day in Andy's classroom did not simply happen. Andy did a lot of *planning*, with the result a rich classroom day.

Weeks and months of such days paid off, for at the end of the year every student was writing at least three sentences in response to writing assignments, and most of the students were writing a full page or more. Their ideas were well connected in most compositions and were related to topical coverage in the class. Their printing was excellent, as was capitalization and punctuation. The students' writing reflected understanding of line and page conventions. There were some invented spellings, but many words were spelled correctly.

By June, all students except one were reading end-of-grade-1-level material. Most students in the class had read through all of the grade-1 basal readers covered systematically in the class and seemed comfortable in doing so. Quite a few students were reading second-grade trade books and in middle second-grade basal readers.

As we watched Andy's teaching in the context of visiting the more typical classrooms in the Wharton-McDonald et al. (1998) study, we could not help but think how fortunate his students were. What a difference it made for those children to experience Andy's classroom versus one of the more typical ones in the sample. As we thought about that, we also kept in the forefront of our minds that in soliciting classrooms for the study we had emphasized to language-arts supervisors that we did not want any weak grade-1 classrooms, that what we were interested in was outstanding classrooms and others that were solid grade-1 experiences. We had emphasized to the language-arts supervisors that the typical classrooms should be ones that the school district would certainly be comfortable in showing to the public. Thus, the contrast between what happened in Andy's class and what happened in the weakest of the classrooms in the sample we studied probably underestimates the full range of experience of grade-1 students. Many children in American grade-1 classrooms do not get what Andy's students get; many do not even get close!

A National Follow-Up

A shortcoming of Wharton-McDonald et al. (1998) was that the study was conducted entirely in upstate New York. Would excellent grade-1 instruction look about the same across the nation? Pressley, Allington, Wharton-McDonald, Block, and Morrow (2001; also Pressley, Wharton-McDonald, et al., 2001) took up that question, observing grade-1 instruction in upstate New York; urban New Jersey; Dallas–Fort Worth; Madison, Wisconsin; and rural northern California. In each locale, they identified grade-1 classrooms that were effective and ones that were more typical, using about the same criteria as applied in Wharton-McDonald et al. (1998). Although it took a book-length presentation to summarize their results, Pressley, Allington, et al. (2001) found what Pressley, Wharton-McDonald, et al. (2001) reported. Effective grade-1 teachers teach very differently from ineffective ones. Pressley, Allington, et al. (2001) made the case that many more skills are covered during each hour of instruction in the effective classrooms. Word recognition instruction was richer, more often involving the teaching of multiple strategies (i.e., phonics, identifying word parts, looking at the whole word, using picture clues, using semantic context information, using syntactic cues). Effective teachers were more likely to teach effective comprehension strategies (e.g., making predictions, mental imagery, summarizing, looking for the parts of a story). Effective teachers scaffolded much more extensively, very much being academic coaches to their students. The writing process was emphasized more in the effective classrooms, including many prompts to plan, draft, and revise. Teachers demanded more use of writing conventions, such as capitalizing, using punctuation, and correct spelling of high-frequency words. The tasks that students were assigned were very academic (e.g., involving a lot of writing and a little artwork, in contrast to tasks in more typical classrooms involving a lot of artwork and a little writing). In effective classrooms, students' writing was everywhere, including in big books the students wrote and displayed proudly.

No one could review the case studies in Pressley, Allington, and associates' (2001) book and come away without the impression that attractive and effective grade-1 instruction does include extensive teaching of skills, much reading of excellent literature, a great deal of student composition, precise matching of task demands to student competencies, extensive encouragement of student self-regulation, and frequent connections across the curriculum. Moreover, these classrooms were very attractive student-centered worlds. Teachers were positive and reinforcing, with the day carefully managed. Cooperation abounded. The kids loved being in these classrooms.

Concluding Comments

When Pressley et al.'s (1996) survey study, summarized earlier in this chapter, was reviewed for publication, one of the criticisms of it was that the list of instructional practices cited by the respondents was simply too long to be credible. The observations made by Wharton-McDonald et al. (1998) and Pressley, Allington, et al. (2001; also, Pressley, Wharton-McDonald, et al., 2001) confirmed, however, that most of the instructional practices cited in the survey do occur in the classrooms of competent first-grade literacy teachers—most critically, in the best of grade-1 classrooms, in the most effective of first grades. One way to think about instruction is with respect to its elements. This was the focus of the survey and the descriptions provided in this section. There is another way to think about the complicated nature of grade-1 instruction, however, that is also revealing about how the outstanding classrooms compare to the more typical classrooms, namely: Focus on the students.

The children who enter grade 1 are vastly different in their preparation for the instruction they will encounter there. Some enter with a history of rich emergent literacy experiences, and hence they have very well developed language and communication competencies as compared to less fortunate classmates. Some enter with advanced phonemic awareness, able to manipulate sounds in words up to and including the demands required by Pig Latin! Others, however, have much more rudimentary phonemic awareness, perhaps understanding that some words rhyme but little more. Sometimes there are children who are not even that far along in the development of phonemic awareness. The elements of instruction that occur in the grade-1 classroom must meet the needs of all of these children, and that is no small task.

A key mechanism for teaching students in grade 1 so as to be sensitive to their individual needs is for the teacher to monitor students and provide scaffolding. Sometimes the scaffolding is in the form of differentiating task demands for students. For example, we certainly observed occasions when excellent teachers encouraged the best writers to compose a couple of pages about a topic but in the next instant stroked one of the weakest writers for producing a couple of sentences. More often the scaffolding consisted of reminding students about how skills they were learning might help in a particular situation. By providing more frequent and intense scaffolding for students who were struggling, the excellent teachers were able to run classrooms in which all students experienced pretty much the same curriculum while receiving instruction appropriate to their needs and progress. The best teachers made scaffolding a centerpiece of the instructional day and were always helping their students learn.

In contrast, scaffolding was not as prominent or frequent in the other, more typical, classrooms. Indeed, the needs of the students did not seem to be as prominent in many of these classrooms, with the teachers more often focused on their curriculum than on the students. For example, there were extreme whole-language teachers who talked to us a great deal about whole language, both during the formal interviews and on the run. In many ways, they seemed to believe that dedication to whole language would result in their students being readers and writers. We also observed greater attention to outside adults in the more typical classrooms, with teachers often diverting their attention from their students to deal with adults who came to the door or entered the classroom for some reason. In contrast, the excellent teachers rarely missed a beat in teaching their students as they dealt with the outside adult with a quick aside. The best classrooms we observed were as decidedly student-centered as they were balanced with respect to skills and whole-language instruction.

Since the first edition of this book, we have often been asked about whether balanced instruction is appropriate for cultural-minority students.

When the question is asked, it often is accompanied by reference to some educational theorist who emphasizes either skills instruction (e.g., Delpit, 1986, 1995) or whole-language teaching (Hudelson, 1993). Such questions often are accompanied by reminders of demonstrations that there often are mismatches between school practices and the languages, styles, and preferences of students from cultural minorities (Cazden, 1988; Cazden, John, & Hymes, 1972; Edwards & Davis, 1997; Heath, 1983; McCarthey, 1997; Ogbu, 1999; Philips, 1983; Snow, 1983; Valdés, 1996; Vernon-Feagans, 1996; Vogt, Jordan, & Tharp, 1987), mismatches between what is known about the world by majority-culture teachers and what is known by minority-culture students (e.g., Bloome, Harris, & Ludlum, 1991). Those asking these questions often believe that cultural accommodation can improve achievement, pointing to well-known examples of cultural accommodation in literacy instruction (e.g., the Kamehameha Early Education Program [KEEP] at Kamehameha Schools in Hawaii; Au & Mason, 1981/82), unaware that there is really not much evidence confirming that cultural accommodation increases the achievement of cultural minority children (Goldenberg, 2001).

Nowadays, when we respond to questions about whether balance makes sense for cultural-minority children, children living in poverty, or other at-risk groups, we refer to a chapter written by Dorothy S. Strickland (2001). She summarized the evidence that at-risk African American children need consistent high-quality instruction, beginning early in their schooling: They need classrooms that ensure that lots of time is devoted to educational tasks, and they need schools making connections to parents as partners in the education of their children. Strickland recommends strongly that such children work with materials and tasks that are well matched to their current competencies, and she urges extensive and appropriate skills instruction while they do so. The good teacher monitors students carefully and is determined to ensure the growth of every child in his or her charge (Wilkinson, 1998). Strickland's envisionment includes plenty of holistic experiences as well, however. In short, Strickland reads the evidence that at-risk cultural-minority students benefit from instruction that sounds much like the balanced literacy instruction emphasized in this chapter. As we read her advisement, we recalled how many of the best of the balanced teachers studied by us have been teaching many at-risk kids. Balanced literacy instruction is a model that makes sense for students from cultural minorities—indeed, for students of all sorts who are at risk of school failure. For a recent and extremely analytical example of the good such balance can achieve, take a look at D'Angiulli, Siegel, and Maggi's (2004) recent demonstration of benefits extending from kindergarten through grade 5 for students at risk of reading failure because of low socioeconomic status as well as English second-language students (see also Lesaux & Siegel, 2003).

As we urge such balance, which requires a great deal of monitoring and individualization of instruction, we are keenly aware that cultural minorities and at-risk children often do not experience classroom worlds where such attention is possible, both in this country (Kozol, 1992) and elsewhere (Wilkinson, 1998). When it is recognized that there are mismatches between school and home worlds for many at-risk students, which can require massive efforts on the part of educators to understand and accommodate, it is really depressing that the most needy are often those least provided with resources by the educational system. That said, we are impressed that some of the best teachers we have studied served in settings that were undersupplied with resources, with children who had great needs. Great teachers can create great engagement even when the odds are against them.

In closing this discussion, we cannot help but emphasize the nature of the academic engagement that was so manifest in the best classrooms observed in the studies summarized in this section. The balanced instructional approach probably had something to do with it, but we attribute a great deal of the academic engagement to the excellent teachers' management skills. Their whole-group lessons were always well planned, and materials were ready to use when they were needed. This contrasted with the hunt for materials that was so often observed in more typical classrooms. Perhaps even more critical, however, was that students in the best classrooms were asked to do tasks that were much more academic than anything else. For example, in all classrooms in the studies conducted by us, writing often was accompanied by art activities. In the more typical classrooms, the art often required more time and effort than the writing: Students spent long amounts of time getting paste out of the paste jar and agonizing to cut out some weird shape (e.g., a cup with a handle with a finger hole, a silhouette of George Washington). This was never the case in the outstanding classrooms, where students were not given complicated tasks when art accompanied writing. Students' time was better spent—on the writing! We also emphasize in closing that students in the best classrooms typically wrote about what they had read, and they read further to develop their writing topics—all of which often was connected to social studies or science content. Concepts encountered on one day were related to concepts encountered on other days. Cross-curricular connections could not be missed during any visit to one of the best classrooms observed in the work carried out by our colleagues and us.

Even in the best classrooms, however, there are students who experience extreme difficulties. Increasingly in America's primary grades, when reading is not going well, it has meant providing children with a particular form of instructional intervention, taken up next.

READING RECOVERY®

Many grade-1 students make little progress in learning how to read and are at long-term risk for academic difficulties. An important program aimed at such children was developed by New Zealand educator Marie M. Clay (e.g., 1985). It involves daily one-teacher, one-child sessions for 10–20 weeks, with each session lasting approximately 30–40 minutes. The goal is to help these students catch up with their peers. The starting assumption is that students may be learning too narrow a range of strategies for dealing with print and may not be flexible in their use of the strategies they have acquired. For example, students may attempt to sound out every word when in fact a variety of strategies (see the earlier discussion in this chapter) can be applied during the identification of words in texts.

Much of Reading Recovery consists of teaching students strategies defined by Clay (1985; also Pinnell, 1989) as the processes required for reading, including the following:

- Reading left to right on a page
- Using a return sweep rather than a slow return from the right-hand side of the page to the left-hand side
- Monitoring whether what is being read makes sense
- Using cross-checks on meaning-making processes, as illustrated by the following quotation:

  A reader might use one kind of information to predict a word but will check that prediction by using another source of information. For example, glancing at a picture of the Billy Goats Gruff going across a bridge, a young reader might predict the word "water" in the text. Checking the print, however, the reader might notice that the word "stream" is not visually consistent with that prediction. This cross-checking may lead to a self-correction or other indication from the child of an awareness of a discrepancy. (Pinnell, 1989, p. 166)

- Searching for cues to meaning from pictures, language structures, and visual cues in print
- Rereading when meaning is unclear
- Self-correction rather than waiting for teacher correction of errors

The emphasis on strategies in Reading Recovery comes through in quotations such as the following:

Attention of teacher and child must be on strategies or operations—mental activities initiated by the child to get messages from a text. If the teacher becomes involved in teaching items rather than strategies—particular letter–sound correspondences or sight vocabulary words, for example, rather than the strategy of checking a word that would make sense in the context against the information in the print—the prospect of accelerated learning is seriously threatened. Letter–sound correspondences and spelling patterns are learned, but in the course of reading and, especially, writing meaningful text, RR [Reading Recovery] teachers praise children for generative strategies, not for items learned. (Clay & Cazden, 1990, p. 208)

There is a common structure to each Reading Recovery lesson:

1. First the child rereads two or more short, familiar books.
2. Then the child reads a book introduced the day before, while the teacher keeps track of errors that are made. (This provides baseline information; the goal is to have the child eventually reading the book with 90% accuracy on subsequent days as part of step 1.)
3. The child does a letter-identification exercise, which involves plastic letters that attach to a metal board. (Once children know letters, this step is deleted or other decoding or vocabulary teaching is substituted.)
4. The child composes and writes out a story.
5. The child reassembles the story after the teacher cuts it into pieces.
6. A new book is introduced and read by the child.

There is a great deal of teacher monitoring throughout the Reading Recovery process to ensure that the child's particular problems are the focus of instruction, with the child's reading extensively observed and assessed before instruction even begins (Marks et al., 1994). The interaction that goes on around composing and reading of the new books is definitely scaffolded, with the student receiving hints and support as needed (Clay & Cazden, 1990). For example, during writing, the teacher calls attention to the sounds of words and spelling patterns by urging the student to listen carefully to words that will be written, prompting the child to write out a new word several times so that it will be memorable, praising progress, and so on. Consistent with Clay's (1991) perspective that reading instruction should develop inner control (i.e., internalized use of strategies taught to children), such support is phased out as the child is able to function independently (Wong et al., 1994), but additional support is provided following success with earlier texts and tasks as more challenging ones are presented. Conceptually, we find Clay's (1991) description of reading instruction as the development of inner control to be appealing: It is similar to other ideas about internalization of cognitive processes such as those offered by Vygotsky (1978).

We also are taken by Clay's positions on the importance of visual processing of words and attention to word sounds and parts. Clay (1991) argues for teaching children to attend carefully to words, analyzing the words into parts that can be sounded out, but also emphasizes that the decodings that result should be cross-checked with other information (i.e., syntactic and semantic–contextual cues) to determine whether the word as decoded makes sense. As indicated above, Clay has an appealing idea about how multiple cues can be used and coordinated, but there is a real need for research carefully evaluating her ideas about word recognition.

That said, there is a lot of teaching of phonics in the approach (Stahl, 2001). The Reading Recovery student attempts to sound out words during writing, with the teacher always making certain that the final writing is in conventional spelling. There is much use of what are known as Elkonin (1973) boxes, with one box for each sound of a word, with the child eventually putting the letters in the boxes to denote the sounds in a word—for example, the letters c, a, and t in each of three boxes for the three sounds in cat.

Reading Recovery teachers have students make and break words, using plastic letters to do so. Thus, the word cat is broken into c and at, and then transformed into bat, fat, mat, and rat (i.e., the student makes these words by adding initial consonants to the at chunk). An important part of Reading Recovery is using letter- and sound-level clues to sound out words during reading; an important part of writing is to "stretch out" their sounds and map letters to the stretched out sounds to write words. We find all of these mechanisms really compelling when we have watched them in practice, as have other well-informed observers (e.g., Adams, 1990). That is, kids do seem to be learning a lot about the reading and writing of words. We are hopeful that someone soon will really analyze well the benefits of these Reading Recovery activities on children's reading and writing of words. It is essential research to understand Reading Recovery effects.

Why Are Educators Enthusiastic about Reading Recovery?

Extremely visible evaluations of Reading Recovery were conducted in both New Zealand and Ohio, and were publicized by Reading Recovery enthusiasts (see Forbes & Briggs, 2003; Pinnell, 1989; Swartz & Klein, 1997). The claim made in these resources compiled by Reading Recovery advocates was that most Reading Recovery students catch up with their classmates; more impressively, 2 or 3 years later, Reading Recovery enthusiasts reported that their students were reading pretty much like other students.

In truth, sorting out the effects of Reading Recovery has proven a great challenge because of the diverse designs and measures employed to evaluate the approach, including designs that have not always been particularly good ones. D'Agostino and Murphy (2004) carried out what is the most analytical meta-analysis to Reading Recovery effects we have encountered, one including a great deal of the existing data and, of course, more up to date than some previous analyses we reference subsequently as this discussion of Reading Recovery proceeds. In general, they found positive effects for the program. We take this as the best outsider summary of the evidence to date (i.e., one produced by individuals not strongly identified with Reading Recovery), although the effects were more pronounced on measures specifically tailored to Reading Recovery than more standardized measures. On the whole, however, this review provided substantial reason to believe that Reading Recovery is effective in promoting the early reading achievement of many struggling readers.

The Ohio group has been extremely active in training new Reading Recovery teachers, sending them back to their school districts to promote the approach. Those trained Reading Recovery teachers typically have convinced their districts to invest heavily in the development of new Reading Recovery teachers and to use the Reading Recovery approach. Such a corps of dedicated professionals has done much to advance the Reading Recovery cause.

What Are the Concerns about Reading Recovery?

Critics point to the cost of one-to-one tutoring for a third to half of a school year. A typical Reading Recovery teaching load is four students at a time, meaning that the teacher will deal with 12 students a year. This typically works out to some $3,000 to $4,000 per student who receives Reading Recovery, which is, of course, in addition to the costs of the student's regular education. Doubts are especially intense when less expensive approaches to one-to-one tutoring, such as parental tutoring, also seem to have the potential to encourage inner-controlled reading in primary students who are experiencing difficulties (e.g., Mudre & McCormick, 1989). There have been many demonstrations that volunteers (e.g., college students) can effectively tutor beginning readers (Baker, Gersten, & Keating, 2000; Elbaum, Vaughn, Hughes, & Moody, 2000; Fitzgerald, 2001; Invernizzi, Juel, & Rosemary, 1997; Leslie & Allen, 1999; Wasik, 1998). Some of the scientists validating the effects of volunteer tutors have gone one step further, providing manuals that detail how to do beginning-reading tutoring. We strongly recommend these resources to those who want to develop tutoring programs involving volunteers (Johnston, Invernizzi, & Juel, 1998; Morris, 1999; Morrow & Woo, 2000).

The costs of Reading Recovery might be more palatable if it consistently delivered what its enthusiasts claim—that most Reading Recovery students leave the program at grade level and stay at grade level for the remainder of their education. Well-respected analysts of early-reading instruction, however, as we alluded to earlier, have raised the specter that the long-term positive effects of Reading Recovery may not be as great or as certain as enthusiasts would like to claim (Chapman, Tunmer, & Prochnow, 2001; Hiebert, 1994; Shanahan & Barr, 1995). Quite frankly, we would have been shocked if it were otherwise: Typically, when at-risk children receive educational interventions, the treatment effect is most pronounced immediately after the intervention has ended (e.g., effects of cognitive stimulation of at-risk infants during the first 3 years of life [Brooks-Gunn et al., 1995]; effects of Head Start on IQ [Cicarelli, Evans, & Schiller, 1969]). In general, the best approach for keeping on track students who are at risk for academic difficulties is to provide consistent supplementary instruction to them (e.g., Campbell & Ramey, 1994). Reading interventions are somewhat analogous to sustained medical treatments, because being at risk for intellectual difficulties is a chronic condition, not a temporary state. To date, there is no quick and easy inoculation to prevent academic disabilities.

Finally, Reading Recovery enthusiasts represent their approach as the best way to remediate reading difficulties. That claim is rather easily challenged, with a variety of one-to-one tutoring approaches, especially at the primary levels, also producing striking positive effects on early reading (see Shanahan & Barr, 1995; Slavin, Karweit, & Wasik, 1994; Wasik & Slavin, 1993). Some of the most convincing studies were those conducted by Lovett and her associates (Lovett, Ransby, Hardwick, Johns, & Donaldson, 1989; Lovett et al., 1994; see Chapter 5 of this volume) and the work of Vellutino et al. (1996; see Chapter 3 of this volume). Work on intense decoding instruction also has determined that Reading Recovery has greater impact if it includes even more explicit decoding instruction than often occurs during Reading Recovery. For example, Iversen and Tunmer (1993) produced quicker improvement when Reading Recovery was complemented with more explicit instruction about phonology and decoding than when students experienced only Reading Recovery that placed greater emphasis on decoding using word parts, followed by checking through use of semantic–contextual cues. A complementary finding is that success in Reading Recovery and in subsequent reading instruction is greater for students with better phonological processing skills (Chapman et al., 2001).

In addition to the possibility that other one-to-one approaches produce benefits that are similar to, or even greater than, those associated with Reading Recovery, there is growing evidence that small-group tutoring, which is much less expensive than one-to-one tutoring, can also be very effective at the primary level (e.g., Hiebert, Colt, Catto, & Gury, 1992), including, for example, the Word ID Program that has been developed at the Benchmark School (Gaskins, Gaskins, Anderson, & Schommer, 1995; Gaskins, Gaskins, & Gaskins, 1991, 1992; see Chapter 5 of this volume).

Not surprisingly, given the attention during Reading Recovery to letter- and sound-level cues, some who identify with whole-language-type perspectives have responded to Reading Recovery unfavorably, contending that the program addresses only a small part of what literacy development should be (e.g., Barnes, 1996; Dudley-Marling & Murphy, 1997). Enthusiastic Reading Recovery teachers have responded that Reading Recovery lessons are only part of the child's day, part of the balance of instruction the child is receiving, albeit a very important part for the child experiencing reading failure in the primary years (Browne, Fitts, McLaughlin, McNamara, & Williams, 1996). Personally, we find the case that benefits can be derived from individual tutoring such as occurs in Reading Recovery to be more convincing than arguments that there is something wrong with a few minutes of daily instruction that is highly structured and more attentive to the basic skills of reading than other more abstract goals (e.g., emphasizing children's interpretations of what they read, honoring interpretations based on the diversity of sociocultural experiences that children bring to the classroom). Those who criticize the structure of Reading Recovery lessons miss one of the most striking features of Reading Recovery lessons, which we have observed personally: Reading Recovery students seem to get a charge out of the lessons. Although it may be hard for some whole-language enthusiasts to accept that there can be joy for children in anything except immersion in literature and unstructured and undemanding opportunities to compose, experiencing success in Reading Recovery lessons seems to be a source of joy for students. Our perceptions on this point are shared by others who have a great deal of experience in Reading Recovery (Browne et al., 1996).

In summary, there is support for one-to-one tutoring when beginning reading goes awry, whether that tutoring is Reading Recovery or an alternative involving intense emphasis on the most challenging of early-reading competencies, which typically is learning to decode. There are no magic bullets, including Reading Recovery, that cure all problems in learning to read, however, although work on Reading Recovery has been revealing about what can be helpful in early-reading remediation. Work on Reading Recovery also has stimulated the development of alternatives. More positively, much more is known now about beginning reading and how to inculcate it than was known even a decade ago. Reading research is paying off in the American school place and not just through tutoring gains.

Even so, developing a Reading Recovery teacher is a big investment for a school district, for a year of training is required. This is especially risky because sometimes the financial resources that support tutorial remediation like Reading Recovery dry up. When that happens, Reading Recovery teachers often return to regular classroom teaching, importing their Reading Recovery skills to that setting. Roehrig, Pressley, and Sloup (2001) documented the classroom teaching of former Reading Recovery teachers. Ten primary-level teachers were observed over the course of 2 years. Teachers with more training and experience in Reading Recovery used the instructional practices and taught the strategies emphasized in Reading Recovery in their regular classroom instruction, with their instruction seeming like the instruction of the exemplary teachers discussed earlier in this chapter. In particular, the literacy instruction of these teachers was a complex balance of direct instruction, often in the form of minilessons and in the context of authentic reading and writing activities, with the teachers being particularly sensitive to the competencies of each student and the scaffolding necessary for the development of self-regulation. Karyn Beach was one of the teachers observed in the Roehrig et al. (2001) investigation. Visits to Ms. Beach's classroom made obvious that Reading Recovery principles are compatible with balanced literacy instruction in a very effective classroom setting.

Karyn Beach's Teaching

Karyn Beach serves a school with decidedly underprivileged children. Some students arrive at her grade 1 with language skills far below the 6-year-old level; others are not emotionally prepared for school, actively rejecting the teacher and participation in school activities.

The enduring image of Ms. Beach's classroom is one of high student engagement with high-intensity instruction. She provides a great deal of direct instruction, followed up with a great deal of scaffolding of the skills being taught in the class. Something that is very salient in her classroom is that she has incorporated many of the techniques of Reading Recovery into her teaching. Thus, consistent with Reading Recovery, Ms. Beach orients students to analyze words into parts, students reread books for mastery, and students write in response to books they have read.

What is also apparent, however, is that the students are immersed in excellent literature, that the skills instruction is not at the sacrifice of good literature. Ms. Beach is especially adept at including great children's literature in her curriculum, consistent with her belief that excellent literature is one of the most important components in reading instruction. The children are always hearing and reading stories such as "Stone Soup," "The Gingerbread Boy," and "Gunnywolf."

The engagement is also due to Ms. Beach's active encouragement of self-regulation. During her interview, she told about how she spends a great deal of time at the beginning of the year laying the foundations for self-regulation during the year. She lets the students know that she has a strong expectation that they will be working in her classroom. Ms. Beach makes certain the students know the choices they can make when they have finished assignments, especially making certain they know what should occur at each of the classroom's academic centers. We observed lots of positive feedback to students when they were self-regulated. Thus, when students who previously came to school sleepy arrived at school alert, they heard about it ("You must have gotten more sleep. I like that"). Ms. Beach consistently reminds students to go back and reread to correct mistakes, reinforcing them when they do so ("I like how you reread there. Good readers catch mistakes and reread to correct them"). Students are reminded often to get organized before they respond and to plan. Ms. Beach has a way of encouraging risk taking and yet demanding excellence. Thus, when a student is faltering when risk taking, it is not uncommon to hear a comment like "No big deal when you make a mistake. Just do it over." Alternatively, when a student falls short on something that Ms. Beach knows he or she can do, there is a different reaction ("I only have time for the right way. Otherwise I won't call you up to the board again"). Ms. Beach consistently encourages students to give others a chance to "get it," but she sends the message that getting it is not as important as trying to get it ("I don't expect you to be perfect, but I expect you to try hard"). When students do show self-regulation, they often are praised ("You made the right decision"). She reinforces students for ignoring distractions. There is simply no doubt that the encouragement of self-regulation and self-control pays off in this classroom. In general, students do know what they are to do and do it, perhaps most apparent during centers, when students simply work without much need for attention from Ms. Beach. Although she engages the class with much direct instruction and she engages many individual students with scaffolding when they need it, the students also engage themselves much of the time.

Students in Ms. Beach's class succeed. Ms. Beach is masterful at giving the students tasks that are a little bit challenging for them but not over their heads. What is especially obvious is that she makes certain that students are reading books that are challenging but not overwhelming to them. Students who especially need support have aides working with them, with the aides sometimes providing scaffolding to other students when they flounder a bit. Ms. Beach is excellent at monitoring student progress as they do the tasks that are part of their school day, frequently interjecting just the right amount of support a student needs to make progress.

Daily Schedule

Ms. Beach's class gets settled quickly, with the whole class coming in and getting to work at their desks. Every morning, the class works on word-level skills for 15 minutes. Thus, on one day Robin was covering long *e* and the various spelling patterns that could include long *e* (i.e., *e, ee, ea, ei*). The students took turns coming to the board, each of them generating a word having one of the long *e* spelling patterns. This activity was in anticipation of a worksheet on long *e* spellings, one that also used words connected to a thematic unit on healthy foods currently being explored in the class. The students worked on this sheet when they were not in their small reading group, with small reading groups meeting immediately after this morning meeting of the whole group concluded. On the next day, the whole-group lesson following the morning meeting was dedicated to the sounds made by *y*, with students once again generating words containing the different sounds of *y*.

Small groups of between two and five students then meet with Ms. Beach, each for about 15–20 minutes. Reading groups engage in round-robin reading of stories. During one round-robin reading, Ms. Beach cued students to use word analysis strategies they were learning to decode unfamiliar words. Thus, when a student had trouble with "unhappy," Ms. Beach cued the student to notice the *un* chunk, which the group had taken up previously. Throughout round-robin reading, Ms. Beach was cuing all students to look at the words as other students were reading. Sometimes she would ask questions about the words, ones connecting with word-level lessons in the class (e.g., "Hey, that word makes the long *e* sound! What letters in it do that?").

Ms. Beach also asked questions to determine whether students understood the story, with their answers sometimes resulting in prompting of comprehension strategies (e.g., "If you can't remember, go back and reread"). There was writing connected to the stories read—for example, a few comprehension questions, each of which required one-sentence written answers. If the students attempted such questions as seat work, their writing would be reviewed during the group lesson, with Ms. Beach offering revision suggestions. The writing permitted more word analysis work, with Ms. Beach cuing students to sound out words they wanted to include in their writing. Thus, a student who wanted to write *cut* was encouraged to "stretch out" the middle sound in order to identify the vowel in the word.

After recess, language arts sometimes continued. For example, the class had a word wall, consistent with Reading Recovery, and there were activities that occurred in conjunction with the word wall. Thus, we observed a lesson during which Ms. Beach gave students hints about words on the word wall (e.g., "Rhymes with *took* and begins with *l*), with the students' task being to write down the appropriate word. On many days, the after-morning-recess period was taken up with center activities, with a half-dozen centers in the classroom. These were very academically demanding and complementary to other activities in the class. Thus, the computer center often involved listening to and/or reading a classic children's story presented by computer; the spelling center activity sometimes involved making as many words as possible from a given set of letters. In short, literacy activities and instruction continued after recess until lunch.

After lunch, there often would be 15 minutes of Drop Everything and Read (DEAR) time, sometimes followed by teacher or student reading of a story to the entire group. Again, this was never passive, with Ms. Beach opportunistically sneaking lessons into the discussion. Thus, when a youngster who was reading a story to the group had difficulty with a word, decoded it, and then confirmed it by referring to the picture, Ms. Beach identified for the group the child's processing and praised it.

The day almost always included a big block of time for mathematics instruction and activities, with this sometimes scheduled for the afternoon and sometimes for the morning. Science instruction more typically occurred in the afternoon, with it often the case that literacy activities occurred in conjunction with science. For example, there was frequent teacher reading and teacher-led discussion of books related to science themes.

Types of Reading

We often observed Ms. Beach reading stories to the students, with discussion of the authors and illustrators. She includes author studies in her curriculum. For example, in April, there was a Pat Hutchins bin that contained a number of Hutchins's books, many of which were read by Ms. Beach and the class. The librarian in the school also reads stories to the students during their frequent visits to the library, again with discussion of authors and illustrators. The librarian-read story was followed by student selection and student reading of books in the library, books that could be and were borrowed by students. What struck us was the degree of engagement in actual reading by Ms. Beach's class when they were in the library, in striking contrast to a number of other occasions when we passed by the library during visits by other classes. Ms. Beach's class also has an extensive number of books on tape, with a listening center that students visit regularly. She has set up the listening center to encourage students to read along as they listen to the tape of a book, with students knowing they are to do this.

Students do a lot of reading in this class. There is round-robin reading during the small reading group, with stories read several times. Students do buddy readings. Often individual students read stories to the whole class assembled at the rug. Some students in the class read with volunteers after school. The children in Reading Recovery read in the context of their Reading Recovery lessons. Consistent with that approach, Reading Recovery students take home the books they are reading at school and read with parents. That occurs as part of regular classroom reading as well, however, with students taking home books read in the reading group to read with their parents.

Although the classroom has many trade books, Ms. Beach also uses basals, selectively covering the literature in the anthologies. Ms. Beach is extremely savvy in her use of such resources—for example, having students read the "Gunnywolf" story in the basal and comparing it to the *Gunnywolf* book that they read. We observed the students do a play, a version of "The Princess and the Pea" that was included in one basal, a basal that Ms. Beach held on to simply for that one piece of literature that worked so well in her class.

Finally, there is opportunistic reading, with Ms. Beach designing the classroom day for many such opportunities. These range from reading of the morning calendar to reading of math problems to reading of whatever comes up. Sometimes the students read individually, and sometimes there is choral reading. The point is that reading occurs all of the time in this class, with Ms. Beach never letting an opportunity for literate behavior pass by without engaging students themselves in the activity.

Writing

The students in this class do a great deal of writing. Most salient is that students are asked to write in response to many of the stories they read. The minimum requirement for such responses is one sentence, although we observed many occasions when students wrote several sentences. They do other writing as well—for example, with respect to thematic units. There certainly is a process orientation in the class, with Ms. Beach consistently urging students to plan before they write. Moreover, there is lots of revising following some conferencing with the teacher.

More salient, however, is Ms. Beach's insistence on good mechanics and good spelling. Students receive a great deal of instruction about capitalization and punctuation, and they are consistently urged to use what they know. As an excellent scaffolder of student writing, the urgings are often in the forms of hints ("Hm.m . . . What do sentences begin with?" or "Do we put capitals in the middle of words?"). When students use the conventions they know, Ms. Beach's consistent reinforcement of achievement is apparent, with many remarks such as "You remembered the period at the end." Spelling matters in writing in Ms. Beach's class, with her consistently urging students to spell words correctly. When she believes a student knows a word, she encourages the student to sound the word out. Sometimes she cues students to check the word wall for a word they want to use, and, of course, she encourages students to use dictionaries. Neatness also matters, with Ms. Beach consistently reinforcing students for neatness, including proper spacing of letters and words in writing.

Does Ms. Beach's attention to both higher-order writing processes (i.e., planning, drafting, and revising) and mechanics make a difference? The writing in her class was striking with respect to appropriate use of conventions, correct spellings, and neatness. Moreover, we saw many examples of student compositions that included several coherent sentences. Yes, there was a great deal of scaffolding of writing and much reinforcement of writing, but the efforts really seemed to be paying off in very good writing in the class. Ms. Beach reported that she expected that by the end of the year students would be able to write three-sentence stories, ones with a beginning, middle, and end. Most of the students had met her goal, consistent with our observations of the writing in the class, including a careful study of student compositions produced during one week in May.

Teaching of Skills

The teaching of skills is prominent in Ms. Beach's class, with every type of skill that can be covered in grade-1 language arts being covered in this classroom. Early in our observations (in January), we observed Ms. Beach reinstructing students about how to write particular letters, reminding them of previous instruction of the letters. There were also reminders about letter–sound associations as well as principled discussions of the letter–sound associations. For example, when she had students recall the vowels during a morning message period, she also had them explain why y sometimes was a vowel and sometimes was not a vowel.

Perhaps most salient was the cuing of decoding strategies, ones consistent with the Reading Recovery approach that drove the language-arts instruction in this classroom. The students were cued to find the base words by framing out (with their fingers) prefixes and suffixes, with the terms base word, prefix, and suffix frequently used in the class. There was lots of discussion of prefixes and suffixes (e.g., minilessons on -ed when a past tense verb was encountered in the text). Students were urged consistently to pay attention to the parts of words (i.e., to letter combinations that recur in words, such as the blends, e.g., bl-, st-).

There was a lot of work in reading group with plastic letters, using them to show students the parts of words and how parts of words are combined to form full words. There were exercises in which students generated all of the words they could containing particular orthographs (e.g., -an, -at, -en, -ow). We observed activities in class in which students used letters in pocket charts to form words (e.g., one such lesson was aimed at generating words in the pocket chart that ended in the -op sound), with such activities sometimes linked to homework assignments. There were many comments and on-line instructions relating to the beginning, middle, and ending sounds of words.

Ms. Beach did all she could to rouse the students' senses in support of word analysis and attention to the constituent sounds and parts of words. Students were constantly being reminded to look at words. Students were taught to tap out the number of sounds in words as they attempted to spell them and to "stretch out" words in order to hear their sounds as they attempted to spell words. Students also were urged to get their mouths ready to say the sounds represented by the letters in words.

Ms. Beach's teaching of word-level skills got well beyond the teaching of decoding and spelling. An important part of Reading Recovery is building a sight vocabulary, with the highest-frequency words in primary reading placed on a word wall. Some of these high-frequency words were also included on spelling tests, with students preparing for a spelling test every third week. Of course, the meanings of these words were also discussed a great deal, as were the meanings of unfamiliar words whenever they were encountered. Indeed, with all of the emphasis on decoding, there was also much emphasis on meaning (e.g., when meaningful word parts, such as prefixes or suffixes, were encountered, their meanings were taken up). We were struck that discussion of vocabulary often tended to be quite extensive; for instance, during a reading on nutrition, several words encountered in the text were discussed extensively (e.g., *protein*, *starch*, *calcium*, *teeth*, *vitamins*). During formal spelling lessons, students wrote the words out and spelled them aloud for the group, but they also generated sentences using the words appropriately. Decoding and spelling instruction was thoroughly interwoven with the development of a rich vocabulary.

Skills instruction also occurred above the word level. As discussed previously, there was much skills instruction as part of writing. In addition, Ms. Beach presented a great deal of information about the composition of texts as part of reading, with her consistently going over the parts of a book when she read to the children and frequently discussing the parts of a story.

In short, Ms. Beach's class is rich with skills instruction. Reading and writing skills instruction are intermingled throughout the day, with these skills consistently used in the service of higher-order literacy goals—reading of real stories and books and writing of sentences and stories.

Opportunistic Teaching

Ms. Beach teaches and reteaches whenever the need and opportunity arises and masterfully creates opportunities to teach. Thus, if there is a word in a story that contains an orthograph the students know, she might provide a minilesson on the orthograph, perhaps asking students whether the word contains any chunk that is familiar. The vocabulary instruction in the class is so rich because Ms. Beach is alert to unfamiliar words in the texts that the students are reading and is skilled at working in minidiscussions of new words. Morning calendar is structured so that there are opportunities to practice math skills, spelling, and reading. When somebody misreads something, it is an opportunity for Ms. Beach to remind everyone about how important it is for a text to make sense and that, if it does not make sense, rereading is in order. We emphasize, however, that such a minilesson on sense making is simply an example of the opportunistic reading instruction that occurs all day, every day. There were so many days that we sat in awe of all of the occasions that Ms. Beach could turn into instructional moments.

Across-Curricular Connections

Like many elementary teachers, Ms. Beach uses themes to drive instruction, with thematic units lasting from 1 to 6 weeks, with most units lasting a week or two. The current theme in the class is always apparent from books that are being read, posters, and student projects. There is substantial cross-curricular integration possible based on the themes. For example, the unit on penguins permitted reading and writing about penguins but also geography lessons about where penguins live. In addition, Ms. Beach developed a math exercise around penguins, with students measuring the height of penguins of various types and making quantitative comparisons between the penguins. We observed similar integration on several occasions, for example, with respect to units on Martin Luther King and pandas. Because the themes could inspire art activities, there were academic–art connections. Because the themes occurred over several days and weeks, there were many connections across days of instruction. Reading and writing connections occur routinely, with students always writing at least a sentence in response to books read in the reading group. Reading and listening connections were also routine, with students able to listen to stories in the listening center and on the computer, with text versions of all such stories available to students. The computer, in fact, permitted numerous connections, with reading and writing programs used often, programs that often covered social studies and science content.

The words students were learning were encountered and worked with in a number of contexts—for example, with the teacher flagging "word wall" words when they occurred in a text. There were word games included in the centers (e.g., make as many words as possible from the letters in the word *penguin*). Letter- and word-level lessons were followed by worksheets sometimes. Word-level experiences could even be connected with mathematics, as when students counted the number of words they wrote in 5 minutes. Sometimes a large number of words relating to the thematic unit were assembled during a group meeting, read, and discussed.

The most important knowledge and skills are encountered and repeated many times. There are many opportunities for overlearning, but because the content and skills are encountered in different contexts and during a variety of tasks, the class is anything but boring. Indeed, despite all of the repetition, there was not a feeling of repetition. A bonus of Ms. Beach's continuous probing of critical ideas and skills was that it made for much student success, with students knowing answers to her questions.

Ms. Beach works with aides and special education teachers to ensure that the instruction provided by others is matched to the classroom curriculum, so that there is not a fragmenting of the curriculum for the students most in need. Moreover, there is homework and communications to parents about homework so that there can be continuity between what is going on in the classroom and what is going on at home with respect to academic development. About once a week, Ms. Beach sends home a book that the student has been reading in the class so that there can be additional practice at home, practice that also informs the parents about the student's reading progress and needs. In addition, Ms. Beach sends disciplinary communications home to parents, again to increase connection and continuity between what is going on in the classroom and what needs to go on at home. Connections were everywhere in Ms. Beach's class.

Scaffolding

Ms. Beach and her assistants are sensitive to occasions when students are experiencing difficulties in completing their work, with Ms. Beach and the aides then intervening to scaffold. This keeps the students on task and reduces their frustrations. Ms. Beach asks lots of questions, for example, easy comprehension questions as students read aloud in group, with these permitting assessment of whether students are understanding the reading. More questions are directed to the students most at risk. That is, the students who can go it alone are permitted to do so, although Ms. Beach still monitors them and moves to provide assistance to them when it is really needed. The scaffolding by the classroom aides parallels her scaffolding, with them assigned to the most needy students but also intervening from time to time with other students.

Summary

Karyn Beach's classroom experience is intense and coherent. The first lessons of the day are in anticipation of work later in the day; the thematic unit is represented in reading and writing, but also typically in social studies, science, and art. The word-level work that is so salient in Ms. Beach's class is successful largely because there is so much distributed practice of the word-level concepts. Whenever there is a chance during the day to think about word chunks in challenging words or how the sounds in words are mapped to letters and blended, she takes advantage of the opportunity. If there is a "word wall" word encountered in a text, she and the students note it. Moreover, there is nothing dull about these activities for her students. They certainly seem to have internalized the various principles covered by Ms. Beach. For example, we administered a standardized reading test to some of her students. It was striking how readily the students were sounding out difficult words, definitely confident they could figure out the words on the test.

The rich skills curriculum, much of which is driven by Ms. Beach's knowledge of Reading Recovery, is certainly not at the expense of the reading of excellent literature and composing. We always looked forward to the visits to Karyn's classroom. We would get there early and have a chance to chat, and quite a few times stayed after school to talk. There was no doubt we were in the presence of an extremely reflective teacher, one who thought a great deal about her curriculum and her students. Despite unambiguous excellence in her teaching, we were also struck that Ms. Beach never assumed she was doing well but rather seemed always to be thinking about how she could do better. In fact, that motivated her to learn Reading Recovery and then to import it into her classroom. The Reading Recovery training dollars seemed like dollars well spent, in Ms. Beach's case.

CONCLUDING REFLECTIONS

One criticism of the research highlighted in this chapter is that when others have looked at teachers who are supposed to be outstanding (e.g., Wendler, Samuels, & Moore, 1989), they have failed to find much difference in those classrooms. Why are our results so different? We think the reason is that the criteria in our observational studies are so high in order for a teacher to be deemed an outstanding teacher. Achievement, defined as consistent academic engagement that translates into superior reading and writing by the end of the academic year, must be clear in the classroom.

Balance Is a Commonplace Idea

The radical middle proposed here is only radical in contrast to the extreme whole-language and phonics positions that have defined the recent debates about beginning-reading instruction. There are a number of scholars before us (e.g., Adams, 1990; Cazden, 1992; Chall, 1967, 1983; Delpit, 1986; Duffy, 1991; Fisher & Hiebert, 1990; McCaslin, 1989) who have proposed that the most sensible beginning-reading curriculum should be a balance of skills development and authentic reading and writing. The unique contribution of the work of our group is in demonstrating that that is really what good teachers do. It has been heartening in recent years when other scholars we respect offer a similar conclusion based on their own analyses of primary classrooms (e.g., Juel & Minden-Cupp's [2000] analyses of more and less effective grade-1 classrooms).

It has not been lost on us that the current work is offensive to both extremist sides of the recent great debates about beginning reading. The first time we presented the Wharton-McDonald et al. (1998) data at a professional conference, one prominent whole-language advocate stormed out of the session, and we later received reports that the individual had characterized the results of the study as "dangerous." On the other side, after we discussed these results with a state school board, several members of the audience were agitated that there was not a phonics-first tone in our conclusions. There can be no doubt that, based largely on the types of data summarized in this chapter, we came to the conclusion that both sides in the great reading debate of the 1990s were wrong, that excellent elementary instruction is much more than the beginning reading instruction that either of the extreme groups holds dear.

As we were conducting the studies described in this chapter, one of us (M. P.) was working on an edited book on balanced elementary-literacy instruction (McIntyre & Pressley, 1996). In that volume, a variety of individuals in elementary language-arts instruction articulated visions of balance, always based on teachers they had studied. In all cases, both skills instruction and whole-language instruction were occurring in classrooms. One could not miss, however, that some of the chapters included much more emphasis on up-front, systematic coverage of skills (akin to synthetic phonics as Chall [1967, 1983] defined it, in the case of beginning reading), and others emphasized much more instruction on an as-needed basis (akin to implicit phonics as Chall [1967, 1983] defined it, or analytic phonics). As a result, Pressley (1996) concluded that the jury was still out on the exact nature of balancing what works.

Was that conclusion a cop-out? We don't think so. When Chall's (1967, 1983) analyses are examined, it is clear that there is great variability in classrooms offering both synthetic and analytic phonics instruction. In some classrooms, analytic phonics works pretty well; indeed, one of the three outstanding teachers observed in the Wharton-McDonald et al. (1998) study seemed more like an analytic phonics teacher than a synthetic phonics teacher, with most of her teaching of letter–sound associations and blending contexted in lessons focusing on literature and writing. We suspect that there are some really talented analytic phonics teachers who are consistently and busily monitoring their students for the skills instruction they need and providing it many times a day. However, the great variability within the analytic phonics classrooms means that sometimes analytic phonics instruction does not work. Even so, having seen some really unbalanced skills-instruction classrooms in which engagement was very low, we know that synthetic phonics alone does not lead to high reading achievement. In light of all of these data, we believe that the key to high achievement in decoding is extensive coverage of skills (and, at the primary level, decoding skills in particular) and scaffolding of student applications of those skills. That said, synthetic phonics generally produces a slightly better outcome than analytic phonics. Thus, if one is not already an extremely skilled analytic phonics teacher, it makes more sense to attempt synthetic phonics than analytic phonics. We feel especially strongly about this in light of our examination of phonics packages that have been designed to be used in the context of a balanced program. The best of them are synthetic phonics programs.

No matter how good the phonics instruction is, however, we emphasize that phonics instruction alone will not be enough to produce excellent literacy in students. The whole-language components stimulate elements of literacy development not affected by decoding instruction alone, such as vocabulary development, writing competence, and positive attitudes toward reading and writing (e.g., Freppon, 1991; Graham & Harris, 1994; Morrow, 1990, 1991, 1992; Morrow, O'Connor, & Smith, 1990; Neuman & Roskos, 1990, 1992; Robbins & Ehri, 1994). It makes good sense based on the various empirical analyses now available to develop primary-level instruction that is rich in both skills instruction and whole-language immersion.

Technology and the Promise of Richer Home–School Connections in Excellent Teaching

We did not fail to notice that most of the primary classrooms that we observed were attempting to connect with the home, to stimulate activities in the home that would complement what was going on in school. Moreover, the teachers that seemed exemplary also had exemplary communications and interactions with the parents of their students. There is growing evidence that increasing literacy activities at home can make a difference in literacy acquisition. For example, Morrow and Young (1997) carried out an experiment in which families in the treatment condition were encouraged to carry out at home literacy activities mirroring those occurring in their primary-level students' classrooms during the day. The families were urged to do more storybook and magazine reading, vocabulary development based on words in the home environment, and journal writing with children. The inner-city African American and Latino children in the treated condition were reading and writing better at the end of the study than were control students. Jordan, Snow, and Porche (2001) evaluated a similar program, observing substantial language gains among children in the program. Yes, parents can learn how to interact productively with their children over literacy (see Goldenberg, 2001, for a review).

The possibilities for stimulating literacy interactions at home seem especially great when it is recognized that there is a media explosion occurring that provides possibilities at home that were not possible previously. For example, all new television sets in the United States have the capacity for captioning, so that children can now watch captioned television, something that improves reading and vocabulary development (Koolstra, van der Voort, & van der Kamp, 1997; Koskinen, Wilson, Gambrell, & Neuman, 1993). In addition, with the increasing availability of children's books on tape and other types of electronic books, there are many more opportunities to stimulate children to listen to books at home, including listening as they read (Koskinen et al., 1995). Also, with more and more homes having access to computers, there are opportunities for children increasingly to experience electronic texts in a sophisticated computer environment. There is no end to the types of interactions that children might be able to experience with electronic texts, including texts that talk, texts that permit immediate elaboration of ideas currently on the screen, and texts that can be cut and pasted easily (Reinking, 1994). As electronic wizardry becomes cheaper, the ways that literacy development at home and school can connect will expand greatly.

Long-Term Effectiveness of Early Intervention

A major question for many educational decision makers is whether early reading interventions—Reading Recovery and others—really pay off in the long term. Hiebert and Taylor (2000) reviewed the relevant literature and came to a set of compelling conclusions. They found that such interventions did help many students, with program effects still apparent several years after the intervention was over. That the programs improved struggling students' reading did not mean that the kids' reading problems necessarily were fixed, however! Often, the program participants remained behind agemates in reading and would struggle with reading tasks in later grades. What is needed is not one shot of intervention but rather continuing intervention for such children. There are no magic bullets or quick fixes for the many children who struggle to learn to read. One of the main motivations for developing the comprehension instruction detailed in the next chapter was the fact that so many children in the upper-elementary and middle school grades continue to struggle to understand what they read (Palincsar & Brown, 1984).

Teacher Education

Finally, we have systematically observed outstanding teachers in order to have some idea about what competencies need to be developed in beginning teachers. Although our thinking on this point is not yet complete, there are definitely some notions that seem undeniable. The education of excellent primary-level teachers should be balanced to include much of whole-language philosophy and methods, but other important traditions as well. Beyond simply teaching potential primary teachers about phonics, we think it makes sense to give them an excellent overview of the contemporary linguistics that supports language-skills instruction. Young teachers need to know about the English language system of sounds as well as child language development, including descriptions and explanations of grammatical development. They also need background in cognitive development and cognition and instruction, since those disciplines are doing much to define contemporary primary-level literacy instruction. For example, the cognitive developmentalists and psychologists have clarified the nature of phonemic awareness and its significance in development (see Chapter 4). Process writing has been much informed by information-processing analysis of the composition process as involving planning, drafting, and revising (Pressley with McCormick, 1995a; also 1995b, Chap. 15; see also Chapter 10 in this book). Beyond the exhortations of the whole-language theorists for teachers to use fine literature in their classrooms, teachers need to have an extensive background in and an understanding of the excellent children's literature that exists.

And what in whole language should be eliminated? First, we should eliminate all the antiskills sentiment and the argument against systematic skills instruction and decontextualized skills practice. There is just no support for these positions; indeed, there is a good deal of evidence to the contrary. For example, there is plenty of evidence that synthetic phonics instruction does work. That good teachers are able to balance whole language and skills is more than enough evidence that skills instruction and whole-language instruction are not logically incompatible. Second, the inaccurate psycholinguistic arguments in whole language should be dispensed with. Arguments that reading and writing develop analogously to oral language are not supportable based on what is now known about reading and writing, and such arguments should be dropped. No one with an informed understanding about the development of reading and writing believes that they develop as oral language does. Whereas learning to read and write are conscious, intentional processes, oral language development is for the most part anything but intentional. Oral language typically is acquired from immersion in a speaking community, whereas reading and writing simply do not develop that way. Third, the political analyses should go. If conservatives favor skills instruction in the elementary curriculum, they certainly are not alone.

In recent decades, it has been fashionable for colleges and universities to dispense with elementary education as a major in favor of having students major in an arts-and-sciences area, assigning education courses needed for certification as a supplement. One reason for this is that the traditional elementary education curriculum involves many methods courses, which are viewed by many in academia as academically undemanding. We think it is time to rethink the possibility of elementary education as a major, this time emphasizing the conceptual knowledge that an elementary teacher needs to have in order to understand excellent elementary curricula. We can imagine an elementary education curriculum that would include courses in cognitive and social development, cognition and instruction, educational psychology (especially those aspects relevant to classroom management and assessment), linguistics, and children's literature. We would also want to see courses that cover the conceptual foundations of elementary arithmetic, social studies, and science. Having reviewed the literatures related to all of these areas (see Pressley with McCormick, 1995a, 1995b), we can state with some confidence that there is much in the conceptual realm that the aspiring elementary teacher could learn.

The capstone for such an education would be an internship in the classroom of a really outstanding teacher. For the most part, student teaching in the past has sent potential teachers out to classrooms that have not been selected for excellence but rather for willingness to admit student teachers. It seems to us that a much better alternative would be to use the knowledge that is now being developed about outstanding elementary teaching to identify those teachers who should be shepherding the next generation into the profession.

One objection to this might be that there are not nearly enough really excellent elementary teachers to handle the very great demand for student teaching experience. One solution is paradoxical, given the teacher shortages that exist across the country, namely: Train fewer teachers. With a half-dozen or so teachers now being trained in order to produce one career teacher (Goodlad, 1994), there is tremendous waste of time and effort in the system. Rather than training so many potential teachers, become more selective about who should be allowed to become a teacher. One possibility that we find appealing is to select individuals for teacher training in the way that professional sports teams select athletes: An individual gets a shot at the pros only after demonstrating some talent in the amateur ranks. We need to think about the many ways that young people could demonstrate potential talent for teaching before they are admitted to teacher education. Perhaps a strong track record as a child care worker or a tutor or camp counselor would be telling. How talent might be spotted early and used as a basis for selection for teacher education seems to us to be something that should be researched carefully.

In the end, there will be excellent primary-level education in American classrooms when there are excellent primary-level teachers delivering such instruction. We suspect that there are some personal individual differences that predispose a person to be a good primary-level teacher, probably including high energy as well as great commitment to children. But good elementary instruction is more than that. It requires extensive knowledge about the nature of language, modern conceptions of learning to read and write, and thorough understanding of children's literature and other primary-level content. Such knowledge can be taught in teacher education programs. When it is, teachers leave their undergraduate years knowing that teaching is largely about supporting child learners as they construct understandings of reading and writing. The good primary-level teacher understands that his or her lessons are only a start in the knowledge construction process—for example, with a great deal of scaffolding required before students come to own the skills (e.g., word-recognition competencies) that are at the heart of learning to read.

SUMMARY

1. Outstanding primary-level literacy teachers (defined by their positive effects on the literacy achievement of their students) balance elements of whole language (e.g., immersion in authentic literature and writing experiences) and systematic skills instruction. Excellent primary-level literacy education involves the complex articulation of many specific elements, often including both use of skills in context and decontextualized skills experiences.

2. Outstanding primary-level literacy instruction is engaging, as a simple metric reveals: Every 10 or 15 minutes, calculate the proportion of students who are academically engaged—doing something involving reading, writing, or closely related activities. In effective classrooms, most students are so engaged much of the time.

3. Explicit teaching of skills is the beginning of a constructivist process for young learners. It gives them a good start, but it is only that. As children attempt to use and adapt knowledge they are taught (e.g., of letter–sound associations), their understanding of it deepens. The opportunities to apply skills during real reading and writing provide especially rich constructivist experiences, which is why balancing of whole-language and skills teaching makes so much sense as compared to either extreme anti-skills-instruction whole-language or skills-instruction-first approaches.

4. The balanced approach advocated here is consistent with the thinking of many research-oriented scholars in reading.

5. Many students who experience difficulties in learning to read in the grade-1 classroom can benefit from programs like Reading Recovery. Even so, students whose reading improves as a function of intensive tutoring may require much more support if they are to continue to succeed in school. Teachers trained in Reading Recovery can use what they learned to transform their regular classroom teaching so that this approach provides generalizable professional development, not narrow training of tutoring skills.

REFERENCES

Adams, M. J. (1990). *Beginning to read.* Cambridge, MA: Harvard University Press.

Au, K., & Mason, J. (1981/82). Social organizational factors in learning to read: The balance of rights hypothesis. *Reading Research Quarterly, 17,* 115–152.

Baker, S., Gersten, R., & Keating, T. (2000). When less may be more: A 2-year longitudinal evaluation of a volunteer tutoring program requiring minimal training. *Reading Research Quarterly, 35,* 454–519.

Barnes, B. L. (1996). But teacher you went right on: A perspective on Reading Recovery. *Reading Teacher, 50,* 284–292.

Barrett, J. (1978). *Cloudy with a chance of meatballs.* New York: Macmillan.

Bloome, D., Harris, O., & Ludlum, D. (1991). Reading and writing as sociocultural activities: Politics and pedagogy in the classroom. *Topics in Language Disorders, 11,* 14–27.

Brooks-Gunn, J., McCarton, C. M., Casey, P. H., McCormick, M. C., Bauer, C. R., Bernbaum, J. C., Tyson, J., Swanson, M., Bennett, F. C., Scott, D. T., Tanascia, J., & Meinert, C. L. (1995). Early intervention in low-birth-weight premature infants: Results through age 5 years from the Infant Health and Development Program. *Journal of the American Medical Association, 272*(16), 1257–1262.

Browne, A., Fitts, M., McLaughlin, B., McNamara, M. J., & Williams, J. (1996). Teaching and learning in Reading Recovery: Response to "But teacher you went right on." *Reading Teacher, 50,* 294–300.

Campbell, F. A., & Ramey, C. T. (1994). Effects of early intervention on intellectual and academic achievement: A follow-up study of children from low-income families. *Child Development, 65,* 684–698.

Cazden, C. B. (1988). *Classroom discourse: The language of teaching.* Portsmouth, NH: Heinemann.

Cazden, C. (1992). *Whole language plus: Essays on literacy in the United States and New Zealand.* New York: Teachers College Press.

Cazden, C. B., John, V. P., & Hymes, D. (Eds.) (1972). *Functions of language in the classroom.* Prospect Heights, IL: Waveland Press.

Chall, J. S. (1967). *Learning to read: The great debate.* New York: McGraw-Hill.

Chall, J. S. (1983). *Learning to read: The great debate* (updated ed.). New York: McGraw-Hill.

Chapman, J. W., Tunmer, W. E., & Prochnow, J. E. (2001). Does success in the Reading Recovery program depend on developing proficiency in phonological-processing skills? A longitudinal study in a whole language instructional context. *Scientific Studies of Reading, 5,* 141–176.

Chi, M. T. H., Glaser, R., & Farr, M. J. (Eds.). (1988). *The nature of expertise.* Hillsdale, NJ: Erlbaum.

Cicarelli, V., Evans, I. W., & Schiller, T. S. (1969). *The impact of Head Start: An evaluation of the effects of Head Start on children's cognitive and affective development.* Athens: Westinghouse Learning Corporation, Ohio University.

Clay, M. M. (1985). *The early detection of reading difficulties: A diagnostic survey with recovery procedure.* Portsmouth, NH: Heinemann.

Clay, M. M. (1991). *Becoming literate: The construction of inner control.* Portsmouth, NH: Heinemann.

Clay, M. M., & Cazden, C. B. (1990). A Vygotskian interpretation of Reading Recovery. In L. C. Moll (Ed.), *Vygotsky and education: Instructional implications and applications of sociohistorical psychology* (pp. 206–222). Cambridge, UK: Cambridge University Press.

D'Agostino, J. V., & Murphy, J. A. (2004). A meta-analysis of Reading Recovery in United States schools. *Educational Evaluation and Policy Analysis, 26,* 23–38.

D'Angiulli, A., Siegel, L. S., & Maggi, S. (2004). Literacy instruction, SES, and word-reading achievement in English-language learners and children with English as a first language. *Learning Disabilities Research and Practice, 19,* 202–213.

Delpit, L. D. (1986). Skills and other dilemmas of a progressive black educator. *Harvard Educational Review, 56,* 379–385.

Delpit, L. D. (1988). The silenced dialogue: Power and pedagogy in educating other people's children. *Harvard Educational Review, 58,* 280–298.

Delpit, L. D. (1995). *Other people's children: Cultural conflict in the classroom.* New York: New Press.

Dudley-Marling, C., & Murphy, S. (1997). A political critique of remedial reading programs: The example of Reading Recovery. *Reading Teacher, 50,* 460–468.

Duffy, G. G. (1991). What counts in teacher education?: Dilemmas in educating empowered teachers. In J. Zutell & S. McCormick (Eds.), *Learner factors/teacher factors: Issues in literacy research and instruction—Fortieth yearbook of the National Reading Conference* (pp. 1–18). Chicago: National Reading Conference.

Edmonds, R. R. (1979). Effective schools for the urban poor. *Educational Leadership, 37,* 15–24.

Edwards, B., & Davis, B. (1997). Learning from classroom questions and answers: Teachers' uncertainties about children's language. *Journal of Literacy Research, 29,* 471–505.

Elbaum, B., Vaughn, S., Hughes, M. T., & Moody, S. W. (2000). How effective are one-to-one tutoring programs in reading for elementary students at risk for reading failure?: A meta-analysis of the intervention research. *Journal of Educational Psychology, 92,* 605–619.

Elkonin, D. B. (1973). U.S.S.R. In J. Downing (Ed.), *Comparative reading* (pp. 551–579). New York: Macmillan.

Ericsson, K. A., & Smith, J. (Eds.). (1991). *Toward a general theory of expertise.* Cambridge, UK: Cambridge University Press.

Firestone, W. A. (1991). Educators, researchers, and the effective schools movement. In J. R. Bliss, W. A. Firestone, & C. E. Richards (Eds.), *Rethinking effective schools research and practice* (pp. 12–27). Englewood Cliffs, NJ: Prentice-Hall.

Fisher, C. W., & Hiebert, E. H. (1990). Characteristics of tasks in two approaches to literacy instruction. *Elementary School Journal, 91,* 3–18.

Fitzgerald, J. (2001). Can minimally trained college student volunteers help young at-risk children to read better? *Reading Research Quarterly, 36,* 28–47.

Forbes, S., & Briggs, C. (2003). *Research in Reading Recovery* (Vol. 2). Portsmouth, NH: Heinemann.

Freppon, P. A. (1991). Children's concepts of the nature and purpose of reading in different instructional settings. *Journal of Reading Behavior, 23,* 139–163.

Gaskins, R. W., Gaskins, I. W., Anderson, R. C., & Schommer, M. (1995). The reciprocal relationship between research and development: An example involving a decoding strand for poor readers. *Journal of Reading Behavior, 27,* 337–377.

Gaskins, R. W., Gaskins, J. C., & Gaskins, I. W. (1991). A decoding program for poor readers—and the rest of the class, too! *Language Arts, 68,* 213–225.

Gaskins, R. W., Gaskins, J. C., & Gaskins, I. W. (1992). Using what you know to figure out what you don't know: An analogy approach to decoding. *Reading and Writing Quarterly, 8,* 197–221.

Goldenberg, C. (2001). Making schools work for low-income families in the 21st century. In S. B. Neuman & D. K. Dickinson (Eds.), *Handbook of early literacy research* (pp. 211–231). New York: Guilford Press.

Goodlad, J. F. (1994). *Teachers for our nation's schools.* San Francisco: Jossey-Bass.

Graham, S., & Harris, K. R. (1994). The effects of whole language on children's writing: A review of literature. *Educational Psychologist, 29,* 187–192.

Harris, A. J., & Sipay, E. R. (1990). *How to increase reading ability: A guide to developmental and remedial methods.* New York: Longman.

Heath, S. B. (1983). *Ways with words.* New York: Cambridge University Press.

Hiebert, E. H. (1994). Reading Recovery in the United States: What difference does it make to an age cohort? *Educational Researcher, 23*(9), 15–25.

Hiebert, E. H., Colt, J., Catto, S., & Gury, E. (1992). Reading and writing of first-grade students in a restructured Chapter 1 program. *American Educational Research Journal, 29,* 545–572.

Hiebert, E. H., & Taylor, B. M. (2000). Beginning reading instruction: Research on early interventions. In M. L. Kamil, P. B. Mosenthal, P. D. Pearson, & R. Barr (Eds.), *Handbook of reading research* (Vol. 3, pp. 455–482). Mahwah, NJ: Erlbaum.

Hoffmann, R. R. (1992). *The psychology of expertise: Cognitive research and empirical AI.* New York: Springer-Verlag.

Hudelson, S. (1993). Literacy development of second language children. In F. Genesee (Ed.), *Educating second language children: The whole child, the whole curriculum, and the whole community* (pp. 129–158). Cambridge, UK: Cambridge University Press.

Invernizzi, M., Juel, C., & Rosemary, C. A. (1997). A community tutorial that works. *The Reading Teacher, 50,* 304–311.

Iversen, S., & Tunmer, W. E. (1993). Phonological processing skills and the reading recovery program. *Journal of Educational Psychology, 85,* 112–120.

Johnston, F. R., Invernizzi, M., & Juel, C. (1998). *Book buddies: Guidelines for volunteer tutors of emergent and early readers.* New York: Guilford Press.

Jordan, G. E., Snow, C. E., & Porche, M. V. (2000). Project EASE: The effect of a family literacy project on kindergarten students' early literacy skills. *Reading Research Quarterly, 35,* 524–546.

Juel, C., & Minden-Cupp, C. (2000). Learning to read words: Linguistic units and instructional strategies. *Reading Research Quarterly, 35,* 458–492.

Knapp, M. S., & Associates. (1995). *Teaching for meaning in high-poverty classrooms.* New York: Teachers College Press.

Koolstra, C. M., van der Voort, T. H. A., & van der Kamp, L. J. T. (1997). Television's impact on children's reading comprehension and decoding skills: A 3-year panel study. *Reading Research Quarterly, 32,* 128–152.

Koskinen, P. S., Blum, I. H., Tennant, N., Parker, E. M., Straub, M., & Curry, C. (1995). *Have you heard any good books lately?: Encouraging shared reading at home with books and audiotapes* (Instructional Resource No. 15). Athens, GA, and College Park, MD: National Reading Research Center.

Koskinen, P. S., Wilson, R. M., Gambrell, L. B., & Neuman, S. B. (1993). *Captioned video and vocabulary learning: An innovative practice in literacy instruction* (Instructional Resource No. 3). Athens, GA, and College Park, MD: National Reading Research Center.

Kozol, J. (1992). *Savage inequalities: Children in America's schools.* New York: Harperperennial Library.

Lesaux, N. K., & Siegel, L. S. (2003). The development of reading in children who speak English as a second language. *Developmental Psychology, 39,* 1005–1019.

Leslie, L., & Allen, L. (1999). Factors that predict success in an early literacy intervention project. *Reading Research Quarterly, 34,* 404–424.

Lovett, M. W., Borden, S. L., DeLuca, T., Lacerenza, L., Benson, N. J., & Brackstone, D. (1994). Treating the core deficits of developmental dyslexia: Evidence of transfer of learning after phonologically- and strategy-based reading training programs. *Developmental Psychology, 30,* 805–822.

Lovett, M. W., Ransby, M. J., Hardwick, N., Johns, M. S., & Donaldson, S. A. (1989). Can dyslexia be treated?: Treatment-specific and generalized treatment effects in dyslexic children's response to remediation. *Brain and Language, 37,* 90–121.

Marks, T. A., O'Flahaven, J. F., Pennington, L., Sutton, C., Leeds, S., & Steiner-O'Malley, J. (1994). *A study of two first-grade teachers "roaming around the known" with their students* (Reading Research Report No. 9). Athens, GA, and College Park, MD: National Reading Research Center.

McCarthey, S. J. (1997). Connecting home and school literacy practices in classrooms with diverse populations. *Journal of Literacy Research, 29,* 145–182.

McCaslin, M. M. (1989). Whole language: Theory, instruction, and future implementation. *Elementary School Journal, 90,* 223–229.

McIntyre, E., & Pressley, M. (Eds.). (1996). *Balanced instruction: Strategies and skills in whole language.* Norwood, MA: Christopher-Gordon.

Morris, D. (1999). *The Howard Street tutoring manual.* New York: Guilford Press.

Morrow, L. M. (1990). Preparing the classroom environment to promote literacy during play. *Early Childhood Research Quarterly, 5,* 537–554.

Morrow, L. M. (1991). Relationships among physical designs of play centers, teachers' emphasis on literacy in play, and children's literacy behaviors during play. In J. Zutell & S. McCormick (Eds.), *Learner factors/teacher factors: Issues in literacy research and instruction—Fortieth yearbook of the National Reading Conference* (pp. 127–140). Chicago: National Reading Conference.

Morrow, L. M. (1992). The impact of a literature-based program on literacy achievement, use of literature, and attitudes of children from minority backgrounds. *Reading Research Quarterly, 27,* 251–275.

Morrow, L. M., O'Connor, E. M., & Smith, J. K. (1990). Effects of a story reading program on the literacy development of at-risk kindergarten children. *Journal of Reading Behavior, 22,* 255–275.

Morrow, L. M., & Woo, D. G. (2000). *Tutoring programs for struggling readers: The America Reads challenge.* New York: Guilford Press.

Morrow, L. M., & Young, J. (1997). Parent, teacher, and child participation in a collaborative family literacy program: The effects of attitude, motivation, and literacy achievement. *Journal of Educational Psychology, 89,* 736–742.

Mudre, L. H., & McCormick, S. (1989). Effects of meaning-focused cues on underachieving readers' context use, self-corrections, and literal comprehension. *Reading Research Quarterly, 24,* 89–113.

Neuman, S. B., & Roskos, K. (1990). The influence of literacy-enriched play settings on preschoolers' engagement with written language. In J. Zutell & S. McCormick (Eds.), *Literacy theory and research: Analyses from multiple paradigms* (pp. 179–188). Chicago: National Reading Conference.

Neuman, S. B., & Roskos, K. (1992). Literacy objects as cultural tools: Effects on children's literacy behaviors in play. *Reading Research Quarterly, 27,* 203–225.

Ogbu, J. U. (1999). Beyond language: Ebonics, proper English, and identity in Black-American speech community. *American Educational Research Journal, 36,* 147–184.

Palincsar, A. S., & Brown, A. L. (1984). Reciprocal teaching of comprehension-fostering and comprehension-monitoring activities. *Cognition and Instruction, 1,* 117–175.

Philips, S. (1983). *The invisible culture: Communication in the classroom and community on the Warm Springs Indian Reservation.* White Plains, NY: Longman.

Pinnell, G. S. (1989). Reading recovery: Helping at-risk children learn to read. *Elementary School Journal, 90,* 161–183.

Pressley, M. (1994). Commentary on the ERIC whole language debate. In C. B. Smith (Moderator), *Whole language: The debate* (pp. 155–178). Bloomington, IN: ERIC/REC.

Pressley, M. (1996). Concluding reflections. In E. McIntyre & M. Pressley (Eds.), *Balanced instruction: Strategies and skills in whole language* (pp. 277–286). Norwood, MA: Christopher-Gordon.

Pressley, M., Allington, R. L., Wharton-McDonald, R., Block, C. C., & Morrow, L. M. (2001). *Learning to read: Lessons from exemplary first-grade classrooms.* New York: Guilford Press.

Pressley, M., with McCormick, C. B. (1995a). *Advanced educational psychology for educators, researchers, and policymakers.* New York: HarperCollins.

Pressley, M., with McCormick, C. B. (1995b). *Cognition, teaching, and assessment.* New York: HarperCollins.

Pressley, M., Rankin, J., & Yokoi, L. (1996). A survey of instructional practices of primary teachers nominated as effective in promoting literacy. *Elementary School Journal, 96,* 363–384.

Pressley, M., Wharton-McDonald, R., Allington, R., Block, C. C., Morrow, L., Tracey, D., Baker, K., Brooks, G., Cronin, J., Nelson, E., & Woo, D. (2001). A study of effective grade-1 literacy instruction. *Scientific Studies of Reading, 5,* 35–58.

Rankin-Erickson, J. L., & Pressley, M. (2000). A survey of instructional practices of special education teachers nominated as effective teachers of literacy. *Learning Disabilities Research and Practice, 15,* 206–225.

Reinking, D. (1994). *Electronic literacy* (Perspectives in Reading Research No. 4). Athens, GA, and College Park, MD: National Reading Research Center.

Robbins, C., & Ehri, L. C. (1994). Reading storybooks to kindergartners helps them learn new vocabulary words. *Journal of Educational Psychology, 86,* 54–64.

Roehrig, A. D., Pressley, M., & Sloup, M. (2001). Reading strategy instruction in regular primary-level classrooms by teachers trained in Reading Recovery. *Reading and Writing Quarterly, 17,* 323–348.

Shanahan, T., & Barr, R. (1995). Reading Recovery: An independent evaluation of the effects of an early instructional intervention for at-risk learners. *Reading Research Quarterly, 30,* 958–996.

Slavin, R. E., Karweit, N. L., & Wasik, B. A. (1994). *Preventing early school failure: Research, policy, and practice.* Boston: Allyn & Bacon.

Snow, C. E. (1983). Literacy and language: Relationships during the preschool years. *Harvard Educational Review, 53,* 165–189.

Stahl, S. A. (2001). Teaching phonics and phonological awareness. In S. B. Neuman & D. K. Dickinson (Eds.), *Handbook of early literacy research* (pp. 333–347). New York: Guilford Press.

Stahl, S. A., McKenna, M. C., & Pagnucco, J. R. (1994). The effects of whole language instruction: An update and reappraisal. *Educational Psychologist, 29,* 175–186.

Strickland, D. S. (2001). Early intervention for African American children considered to be at risk. In S. B. Neuman & D. K. Dickinson (Eds.), *Handbook of early literacy research* (pp. 322–332). New York: Guilford Press.

Swartz, S. L., & Klein, A. F. (1997). *Research in Reading Recovery.* Portsmouth, NH: Heinemann.

Taylor, B. M., Pearson, P. D., Clark, K., & Walpole, S. (2000). Effective schools and accomplished teachers: Lessons from primary-grade reading instruction in low-income schools. *Elementary School Journal, 101,* 121–165.

Valdés, G. (1996). *Con respeto: Bridging the distances between culturally diverse families and schools.* New York: Teachers College Press.

Vellutino, F. R., Scanlon, D. M., Sipay, E. R., Small, S. G., Pratt, A., Chen, R., & Denckla, M. B. (1996). Cognitive profiles of difficult-to-remediate and readily remediated poor readers: Early intervention as a vehicle for distinguishing between cognitive and experiential deficits as a basic cause of specific reading disability. *Journal of Educational Psychology, 88,* 601–638.

Vernon-Feagans, L. (1996). *Children's talk in communities and classrooms.* Cambridge, MA: Blackwell.

Vogt, L., Jordan, C., & Tharp, R. (1987). Explaining school failure, producing school success: Two cases. *Anthropology and Education Quarterly, 18,* 276–286.

Vygotsky, L. S. (1978). *Mind in society: The development of higher psychological processes.* Cambridge, MA: Harvard University Press.

Wasik, B. A. (1998). Volunteer tutoring programs in reading: A review. *Reading Research Quarterly, 33,* 266–292.

Wasik, B. A., & Slavin, R. E. (1993). Preventing early reading failure with one-to-one tutoring: A review of five programs. *Reading Research Quarterly, 28,* 178–200.

Wendler, D., Samuels, S. J., & Moore, V. K. (1989). The comprehension instruction of award-winning teachers, teachers with master's degrees, and other teachers. *Reading Research Quarterly, 24,* 382–401.

Wharton-McDonald, R., Pressley, M., & Hampston, J. M. (1998). Outstanding literacy instruction in first grade: Teacher practices and student achievement. *Elementary School Journal, 99,* 101–128.

Wharton-McDonald, R., Pressley, M., Rankin, J., Mistretta, J., Yokoi, L., & Ettenberger, S. (1997). Effective primary-grades literacy instruction = balanced literacy instruction. *Reading Teacher, 50,* 518–521.

Wilkinson, I. A. G. (1998). Dealing with diversity: Achievement gaps in reading literacy among New Zealand students. *Reading Research Quarterly, 33,* 144–167.

Wong, S., Groth, L., O'Flahaven, J., Gale, S., Kelley, G., Leeds, S., Regetz, J., & Steiner-O'Malley, J. (1994). *Characteristic teacher–student interaction in Reading Recovery lessons.* College Park, MD: National Reading Research Center.

Wood, S. S., Bruner, J. S., & Ross, G. (1976). The role of tutoring in problem solving. *Journal of Child Psychology and Psychiatry, 17,* 89–100.

Ruth Wharton-McDonald, PhD, is Associate Professor and Associate Chair in the Department of Education, University of New Hampshire, Durham, New Hampshire.

Jennifer Mistretta Hampston, PhD, was Assistant Professor in the Department of Psychology, Youngstown State University, Youngstown, Ohio.

CHAPTER 9

The Need for Increased Comprehension Instruction

with RUTH WHARTON-MCDONALD

Some readers might be wondering how they could be so far along in a book dedicated to elementary literacy instruction with so little yet said about anything beyond grade 3. One of the main reasons for this is that intense researcher interest in emergent literacy and the renewed great debates about the nature of beginning reading have led to much more research attention to the preschool and primary grades in recent years. Nonetheless, there is good reason to think about the upper elementary grades and to worry about the instruction that is occurring there. In particular, much more could be done to promote comprehension abilities in elementary students, with that often thought as more of an upper elementary goal than a primary-grades goal. By the end of this chapter, we hope it is clear that we do not agree that comprehension as a reading goal should be put off until the middle and upper elementary grades, but we recognize that it often is, and thus, we begin this chapter with a discussion of what goes on in the upper-elementary grades.

THE NATURE OF LITERACY INSTRUCTION IN GRADES 4 AND 5

In 1995–1996, we and some colleagues (Pressley, Wharton-McDonald, Hampston, & Echevarria, 1998) decided to study the nature of literacy instruction in grades 4 and 5, because they are often the final 2 years of elementary school. We carried out the grade-4 and -5 study much as we had conducted the observational study of grade-1 instruction reported in Chapter 8. We observed 10 classrooms in upstate New York over the course of a year, all of which were selected by the participating school districts as very solid classrooms. In addition to the observations, two in-depth interviews with each teacher were conducted to clarify the instruction that was observed and to gain understanding of the teacher's intentions in teaching the way she or he did.

Background

We expected to find quite complex instruction in the upper grades:

1. The grade-1 study had made it clear that literacy teaching is a complex articulation of components. It made sense that instruction at the upper end of the elementary years would be at least as complex.

2. In addition, however, we had conducted a survey of grade-5 teachers from across the nation who were nominated as outstanding in the promotion of literacy achievement in their classrooms (Pressley, Yokoi, Rankin, Wharton-McDonald, & Hampston, 1997). The methodology for that survey was much like the methodology in the primary-grade survey: The teachers first responded to a few open-ended questions about the elements of their teaching, and then the elements mentioned by the teachers were examined in a quantitative questionnaire requiring teachers to indicate the frequency of each element of instruction in their classroom.

Consistent with the results obtained at the primary level, the sample of nominated outstanding grade-5 teachers reported that their instruction balanced many components, including whole-language experiences and skills instruction. The various components that entered into the instructional mix included the following:

- Extensive reading at the heart of language-arts instruction
- Diverse grouping patterns (e.g., whole-group instruction, small-group instruction, cooperative learning experiences, individual reading)
- Teaching of both word-level and higher-order (e.g., comprehension, critical thinking) skills and processes
- Development of student background knowledge
- Regular instruction in writing, including lower-order mechanical skills and higher-order composition skills (e.g., planning, drafting, revising as a process)

- Extensive evaluation of literacy competencies, using diverse assessments
- Integration of literacy and content-area instruction
- Efforts to promote student motivation for reading and writing

As was the case at the primary level, we felt that even though the survey was informative about some of the diversity of experience in the upper elementary grades, it did not provide the type of in-depth understanding that comes from getting to know a number of individual classrooms. It did, however, sensitize us somewhat to what we should be looking for in the classrooms in the observational study.

Results of the Observational Study

What emerged from the observational study was a much more complicated set of results than came out of the survey research. Basically, we observed some practices that were common across classrooms, but we also observed many dimensions of difference. In what follows, we detail both and comment on several other findings that were very important and somewhat unexpected.

Commonalities across Classrooms

There were some instructional practices that we observed in at least 8 of 10 classrooms. Because virtually all of these practices were also represented on the survey of exceptionally strong grade-5 teachers from across the nation, we suspect that the following can be found in some way, shape, or form in most grade-4 and -5 classrooms in the United States:

- Some class discussions driven by teacher questioning, with student responses evaluated by the teacher
- Literature-driven reading instruction
- Direct instruction in specific skills
- One-to-one miniconferences with students
- Reading of trade books—in particular, novels
- Opportunities for students to select reading materials
- Teacher read-alouds
- Expressed belief in the importance of reading comprehension at this level of instruction
- Teacher activation of students' prior knowledge
- Exercises emphasizing reading comprehension
- Independent reading time

- Writing of connected text on at least a weekly basis
- Use of the writing process model and instruction in its components (i.e., planning, drafting, and revising long compositions)
- Connections between reading, writing, and content-area coverage (e.g., readings related to a social studies theme inspiring writing of stories related to the theme)
- Use of procedural facilitators for writing assignments (e.g., worksheets reminding students of the parts of a story)
- Teaching of writing mechanics
- Use of computers for writing of final drafts
- Worksheets (teacher-made and commercial)
- Book projects
- Spelling exercises and tests
- Explicit vocabulary instruction
- Homework

In short, in keeping with the grade-5 survey, which reported a balancing of whole-language (i.e., reading of literature, writing) and skills-instruction components, we observed such balancing in the classrooms in upstate New York. Even so, our sense as we watched these classrooms was that they were very different from one another, with the differences at the grade-4 and -5 level much more pronounced than the differences we had observed in primary-level classrooms.

Dimensions of Difference

Because we became aware very early in the study that the classrooms we were watching differed dramatically from one another, we were sensitive throughout most of the study to the many differences that existed. In the end, the differences could be clustered in five groups, pertaining to differences in classroom management, reading, writing, word-level skills, and student academic engagement.

The teachers varied tremendously in their *class management.* For example, in some classes, every day was pretty much the same, whereas there was much day-to-day and week-to-week variability at the other extreme. Some teachers used classic behavior management tactics well, and others used them hardly at all. Grouping varied from predominantly whole-group to predominantly individualized instruction, with just about everything in between also observed. An exceptionally important dimension of difference among classrooms was the extent to which student progress was monitored and responded to in an appropriate fashion. Some teachers were very aware of their students and provided assignments that matched student needs and competencies, whereas others were less concerned with such monitoring and tailoring of work. The classrooms also varied in the extent to which they were driven by concern with external standards (e.g., preparing for state tests) versus concern for student improvement. In addition, whereas some classrooms included a high density of activity, others were relaxed. Homework varied from skills practice to authentic reading and writing.

There were substantial differences in the *amount of reading* in each class and *variability in types of reading* (e.g., Did the teacher cover all of the main genres?), although much reading of novels was observed. There were many different ways that reading could connect with the content-area curriculum, from well-planned units relating to important curricular themes to generally haphazard comments made by the teacher relating ideas in current readings to social studies and science concepts.

There was great variability as to how much *writing* occurred, from being the focus of literacy instruction to being quite a small part of it. Students in most classes did narrative writing. Although planning, drafting, and revising occurred in all classes, the classes varied in the extent of their commitment to the process, from consistent use of and great reflection on planning, drafting, and revising to much more implicit use of the writing process. There were differences in how mechanics were covered as well, from substantial reflection on rhetorical devices used by authors of works the students were reading to coverage of mechanics on worksheets.

There was great variation between classrooms in the extent to which *word-level skills* were emphasized. The amount of vocabulary instruction varied from class to class (e.g., in some classes there were published lists with tests, whereas others focused on discussion of words encountered in readings). Spelling instruction and tests occurred in all classrooms, although the sources of the words varied (e.g., published lists, words encountered in reading), as did the amount of drilling and the extent to which spelling and vocabulary instruction were connected (i.e., from being completely independent to vocabulary words being the spelling words).

Student engagement varied considerably from classroom to classroom, as defined by the percentage of students typically involved in academic activities. In some classes, engagement was usually high. In others, it was much more variable.

Different Core Emphases

Each classroom had at its core some particular emphases around which the curriculum was organized and presented. These core sets of activities, while observed in every classroom, differed somewhat from one classroom to the next. The most common emphases included reading of trade books and writing, which were related through thematic connections, although (as summarized in Table 9.1) each classroom really did have a unique orientation.

Instruction That Was Not Happening

In some classrooms, there were aspects of the instruction that we found to be very disturbing. For example, we observed explicit comprehension instruction only rarely, despite a great deal of research in the past two decades on how to promote children's comprehension of what they read (Almasi, 2003; Blachowicz & Ogle, 2001; Gersten, Fuchs, Williams, & Baker, 2001; Pearson & Fielding, 1991). Indeed, the situation seemed to be much as Durkin (1978/79) described it more than 20 years ago, with a great deal of *testing* of comprehension but very little *teaching* of it. (See the next section of this chapter if you are not familiar with Durkin's work.)

A twist on this situation, however, was that the comprehension tasks now being given to students did seem to be informed by the comprehension

TABLE 9.1. Central Emphases for Each Classroom in the Pressley et al. (1998) Study of Grade-4 and -5 Classrooms

1. Trade book reading and process writing, with thematic connections; reader response to literature; encourages self-regulation including through use of modified reciprocal teaching as students respond to literature in small groups.

2. Reader response to novels consistent with a current theme; writing process instruction with emphasis on self-regulated writing, reading, and studying.

3. Reading of trade books, with connections to writing; heavy emphasis on process writing and self-regulation of reading, writing, and behavior.

4. Basal reading and teacher question-driven discussion of basal selections; isolated skills instruction; quiet seatwork.

5. Content strongly emphasized, including current events; heavy emphasis on vocabulary acquisition and acquisition of factual knowledge; process writing; explicit skills instruction; whole-group teacher question-driven discussions and individual seatwork.

6. Cooperative exploration; theme-driven instruction; lots of reading of trade books; skills instruction, which is not tied to current theme or readings.

7. Reading–writing–content integration, with many activities relating to trade books currently being read by class; extensive discussions driven by teacher questions.

8. Reading trade books; skills instruction with worksheets.

9. Process writing; reading of trade books; reading–writing–content instruction connections.

10. Teacher reading of literature to class; student reading of trade books; writing with process instruction and teaching of mechanics; clear reading–writing–content connections.

process research of the past two decades. It was not uncommon, for example, for students to be asked to respond to short-answer questions requiring them to summarize what they had read, identify confusing points in a text, construct questions pertaining to a text, or predict what might be next in a text. That is, they were asked to respond to questions constructed around the cognitive processes involved in skilled comprehension (i.e., summarizing, monitoring confusion, self-questioning, predicting based on prior knowledge). However, there was little evidence that students were being taught to self-regulate comprehension processes *as* they read, and in some classrooms there was no evidence that they were being taught the active comprehension processes validated in the past two decades—for example, being asked to write down images that occurred to them as they read a story without a hint to the students that they could actively generate images as they read as a comprehension strategy. More generally, students were prompted to generate the types of ideas that might occur to strategic readers as they read, but they were not actually taught the strategies themselves, how to use them, or the utility of the strategies.

It also was striking how little teaching of self-regulation occurred. Rather than teaching students how to become self-regulated learners, the teachers seemed to expect that the behaviors would develop naturally if students were given enough assignments (e.g., workbook sheets) that prompted them to generate the kinds of thoughts generated by strategic readers as they read (i.e., that required them to report questions, images, or summaries that occurred to them as they read). There is, of course, no evidence that we are aware of that such prompting leads to anything like active, self-regulated use of comprehension strategies.

Summary

The 10 grade-4 and -5 classrooms observed by Pressley et al. (1998) varied greatly. In general, the teachers heading these classrooms tended to emphasize a few aspects of literacy development in their classroom, with the core instructional emphases varying from classroom to classroom. Despite the great variability between classrooms, it was possible to find some commonalities. An important commonality was a mixture of literature and whole writing experiences and skills instruction, consistent with the balance model developed in this book.

That there was balance is not to say that we felt the instruction we observed was as good as it could be. Specifically, self-regulation was actively encouraged in only a few of the classrooms, and the lack of comprehension process instruction was especially striking, given the widespread assumption that development of comprehension skills should be a key activity in the upper-elementary grades (e.g., Chall, 1983; Harris & Sipay, 1990).

FOUNDATIONS OF MODERN
COMPREHENSION INSTRUCTION

Since 1990, when Marilyn J. Adams's *Beginning to Read* reviewed in detail the letter-level and word-level processing skills that young readers must acquire, reading researchers and educators have focused their attention on the processes surrounding children's acquisition of decoding skills. One reason was that the dominant approach to beginning reading education in the United States in the 1990s, whole language (e.g., Weaver, 1994), had been suspected of not developing decoding skills in students (Smith, 1994). Even so, regardless of whether instructional orientation is whole-language or skills inculcation, there is a broad base of agreement that the most important goal of reading education should be to develop readers who can *derive meaning* from texts. One of the reasons that researchers have focused on word recognition is because of the belief of some reading researchers and educators that word decoding is *the* bottleneck in the meaning-getting process. Of course, when children cannot decode at all, there is no chance of comprehension. When they can decode only with effort, decoding competes with comprehension efforts for the limited attention capacity available for the processing of text (i.e., the 7 ± 2 chunks of short-term memory; Miller, 1956), so that effortful decoding consumes capacity that might otherwise be used to understand text. With increasing automaticity of decoding, there is a freeing-up of capacity, which permits greater comprehension of what is being read (LaBerge & Samuels, 1974). According to the LaBerge and Samuels model, if decoding is automatized, comprehension at the word level is more or less taken care of (see Chapter 6 on fluency). Although we agree that word-level comprehension is facilitated by automatic decoding, there is no doubt that comprehension beyond the word level requires much, much more.

There has been a great deal of research in the past two decades on how to increase the reading comprehension of elementary-level students, selectively discussed below. Most of this work is concerned with teaching students to use comprehension strategies. In the following subsections we explore the various reasons that researchers focused on the teaching of comprehension strategies as a means to improve comprehension. This work on strategies instruction did not occur in a vacuum; rather, it reflected many converging efforts (see also Pressley & Hilden, 2006).

Awareness of the Need for Comprehension Instruction

In a landmark study, Dolores Durkin (1978/79) raised the consciousness of the reading education community about the need for comprehension instruction. She observed grade-3 through -6 classrooms and students, watching for comprehension instruction during reading and social studies but seeing little of it. Instead of teaching students how to comprehend, teachers were assessing comprehension, asking students questions about material they had just read. Durkin's study did much to stimulate researchers to study comprehension as a process and identify ways to increase it.

Study Skills Instruction as the Norm

In the 1970s, the conventional way of thinking about increasing comprehension was through study skills instruction. Such instruction often boiled down to the teaching of strategies, such as reflecting on prior knowledge related to a reading, restudying difficult portions of passages, visualizing, and summarizing (Forrest-Pressley & Gilles, 1983). One of the most systematic and well-known approaches was the SQ3R approach (Robinson, 1946), involving *s*urvey of the text, *q*uestion generation in advance of reading based on text headers, *r*eading, *r*eciting the text, and *r*eviewing. The problem with all of the study skills approaches was that there was little or no evidence that they really worked (e.g., Tierney, Readence, & Dishner, 1980). That is, there was no convincing proof that the great effort required to execute SQ3R paid off in equivalent benefits (Johns & McNamara, 1980). Although the study skills developers had not done the research and development required to hone their procedures so that they worked well (i.e., provided substantial benefits for the effort expended), the study strategies approaches made it sensible to think about teaching strategies as a way to increase comprehension.

Theories of Meaning Representation That Stimulated Research on Specific Types of Strategies Instruction

In the late 1970s and early 1980s, there was much new theorizing about how meaning is represented in the mind and how mental representations of meaning determine comprehension of complex ideas such as those represented in text. The various representational theories stimulated hypotheses about the nature of effective comprehension strategies instruction.

For example, Walter Kintsch of the University of Colorado and his associate T. A. van Dijk (1978; also van Dijk & Kintsch, 1983) developed a theory about how skilled readers construct representations of the main ideas of text (macropropositions, to use their terminology). Their work inspired studies on teaching students how to summarize texts in order to make them more memorable, producing quite a bit of evidence that elementary students could generate good summaries (e.g., Doctorow, Wittrock, & Marks, 1978; Taylor, 1982).

Canadian cognitive psychologist Allan Paivio (e.g., 1971, 1986; Clark

& Paivio, 1991) proposed that knowledge is composed of complex associative networks of verbal and imaginal representations. This led to work on how children could be induced to construct mental images that would increase their memories of text content through dual imagery and verbal coding (Levin, 1973; Pressley, 1976). In general, when children were taught to construct mental images representing the content of texts, there was increased memory (e.g., as tested by literal, short-answer questions) and understanding (e.g., as tested by questions tapping inferences that could be made during reading of the text), as compared to when same-age students read as usual (Pressley, 1977).

Several theorists proposed that stories have conventional structures: a beginning, including information about the time, setting, and characters in the story; an initiating event, setting a goal or leading to a problem; a series of attempts to achieve the goal or overcome the problem; achievement of the goal or resolution of the problem; and character reactions to the resolution (e.g., Mandler, 1984; Stein & Glenn, 1979). Children, especially weak readers, can be taught to attend to story grammar elements as they read, leading to increases in their comprehension and memory of stories (e.g., Short & Ryan, 1984).

Without a doubt, the most prominent representational theory among reading researchers and educators during the late 1970s and early 1980s was schema theory, as specified by Richard Anderson and David Pearson (1984) at the Center for the Study of Reading. A schema integrates a number of commonly co-occurring concepts into an orderly representation. For example, the schema for the christening of a ship includes its purpose—to bless the ship. It includes information about where it is done (i.e., in dry dock), by whom (i.e., a celebrity), and when it occurs (i.e., just before the launching of a new ship). The christening action is also represented (i.e., breaking a bottle of champagne that is suspended from a rope). Schema activation can dramatically affect comprehension, inferences, attention allocation, and memory of what is read. Thus, schema theorists advocated encouraging students to activate, in several ways, their prior knowledge while reading, by making predictions about text content before reading, relating information encountered in text to prior knowledge, and asking themselves questions about the reasons for the relations specified in text (Anderson & Pearson, 1984).

In summary, representational theorists in the 1970s and early 1980s believed that if children failed to understand and remember text, the problem might have been that they were not constructing complete representations of the ideas coded in the text. Their solution was to encourage students to construct fuller representations through instruction, using strategies for enhancing mental representations of texts—strategies that could be applied before, during, and after reading (Levin & Pressley, 1981), to construct summaries, images, story grammar representations, and specific instantiations of schemata capturing the ideas in text.

Verbal Protocols of Skilled Reading

As discussed in Chapter 2, many verbal protocol studies of reading were carried out in the 1970s and 1980s. It became apparent in these think-aloud studies that skilled readers used cognitive strategies as they read, including strategies favored by the representational theories—summarizing, constructing images, attending to story grammar elements, and relating to prior knowledge including schematic knowledge (Pressley & Afflerbach, 1995). This work made apparent that teaching students to use comprehension strategies was to teach them to read as exceptionally skilled readers do.

Emergence of Metacognitive Theory

An approach known as metacognitive theory was developed in the 1970s. Metacognition is cognition about cognition (Flavell, 1977). It plays an important regulatory role in cognition: Knowing that one can retain more of what one reads by creating a summary of it is important metacognitive knowledge—conditional knowledge (Paris, Lipson, & Wixson, 1983) about summarization. Such knowledge can inform a student how to proceed when confronted with a text containing ideas that must be remembered. That is, metacognition increases the likelihood of long-term appropriate use of strategies (for reviews, see Pressley, Borkowski, & O'Sullivan, 1984, 1985).

Both Flavell (1977) and Flavell and Wellman (1977) offered analyses of how metacognition might regulate cognitive strategies in various task situations. That many strategies were definitely teachable became well established during this era as well (Pressley, Heisel, McCormick, & Nakamura, 1982), although it also became obvious that long-term use of taught strategies only occurred when strategies instruction was metacognitively embellished (e.g., information about the usefulness of a trained strategy was included in instruction; e.g., Borkowski, Levers, & Gruenenfelder, 1976; Cavanaugh & Borkowski, 1979; Kennedy & Miller, 1976). Metacognitive theory, implicating strategies as critical in effective thinking, was thriving, borne out by the first analyses and tests of it.

Vygotskian Theories about the Development of Internalized Cognitive Competence

Lev S. Vygotsky's (1978) theory of cognitive development became prominent in the late 1970s and early 1980s. Recall from Chapters 4 and 8

Vygotsky's view that interactions between adults and children that are critical to cognitive development occur with tasks that are within the child's *zone of proximal development,* tasks which the child can do only with assistance. Vygotsky's perspective on the zone did much to stimulate developmentally oriented researchers and educators to embrace the teaching of cognitive skills that are not fully developed in children but that could develop with adult support—such as comprehension strategies. In particular, developmentalists felt that development of cognitive skills might be consistent with Vygotsky's (1962) theory that skills once acquired from others and used come to be internalized as self-directed inner speech.

One prominent developmentalist who thought this was Donald Meichenbaum (e.g., 1977), who formulated a position about how adults could interact with children to encourage their acquisition and autonomous use of new cognitive skills. Like Vygotsky (1962), Meichenbaum believed that self-speech began as interpersonal overt speech between adults and children, the adult role being highly directive at first but gradually fading as children increasingly internalized directive speech. By the mid-1970s, there were a number of American analyses suggesting that the development of self-directive speech plays an important role in the development of children's self-regulation (e.g., Kohlberg, Yaeger, & Hjertholm, 1968; Patterson & Mischel, 1976; Wozniak, 1972).

Thus, in the late 1960s and early 1970s, Meichenbaum hypothesized that children could learn a variety of cognitive skills if they were taught simultaneously to use self-speech to direct their use of the cognitive skills they were acquiring (e.g., Meichenbaum & Goodman, 1969). Meichenbaum's general approach can be illustrated by a study by Bommarito and Meichenbaum (reported by Meichenbaum & Asarnow, 1979). They taught comprehension strategies to middle-school students who could decode but were experiencing difficulties understanding what they read. Instruction began with an adult modeling self-verbalized regulation of comprehension strategies: looking for the main idea, attending to the sequence of important events in a story, and attending to how characters in a story feel and why they feel the way they do, among other components.

The students saw the adult read and heard the following verbalizations: Well, I've learned three big things to keep in mind before I read a story and while I read it. One is to ask myself what the main idea of the story is. What is the story about? A second is to learn important details of the story as I go along. The order of the main events or their sequence is an especially important detail. A third is to know how the characters feel and why. So, get the main idea. Watch sequences. And learn how the characters feel and why. . . . While I'm reading I should pause now and then. I should think of what I'm doing. And I should listen to what I'm saying to myself. Am I saying the right things? Remember, don't worry about mistakes. Just try again. Keep cool, calm, and relaxed. Be proud of yourself when you succeed. Have a blast. (Meichenbaum & Asarnow, 1979, pp. 17–18)

By the end of six training sessions, the students were self-verbalizing covertly, as control was gradually transferred to them over the course of the sessions. Did the self-verbalization instruction affect reading comprehension? Yes: There was greater pretest-to-posttest gain on a standardized comprehension test among these students than for control condition participants. That is, the researchers concluded that adults could advance the cognitive development of children through scaffolded teaching of important cognitive processes.

Reader-Response Theory

Thus far, we have made the case that in the late 1970s and early 1980s there were lots of pieces of cognitive psychology supporting the teaching of comprehension strategies. For comprehension instruction to make sense and be acceptable to the reading-education community, most of whom do not identify principally with cognitive psychology, it had to be consistent with traditions embraced by reading educators. As it turned out, teaching of comprehension strategies was consistent with an exceptionally important language-arts perspective.

Language-arts educator Louise M. Rosenblatt (1938) made the then-radical proposal that the meaning of a text will vary somewhat from reader to reader. Like Vygotsky, Rosenblatt would be discovered anew in the late 1970s, in her case with the 1978 publication of her book *The Reader, the Text, the Poem.* The reader-response theory defined by that book had an enormous impact on the language-arts education community. It legitimized the teaching of active and interpretive reading.

According to reader-response theory, interpretive variability occurs because the meaning of a text involves a transaction between a reader, who has particular perspectives and prior knowledge, and a text, which can affect different readers in different ways (e.g., Beach & Hynds, 1991; Rosenblatt, 1978). Readers sometimes form impressions of characters in stories, and frequently relate their personal and cultural experiences to events encountered in the text. As part of responding to the text, readers sometimes explain events in a text to themselves. Often they form vivid images. In short, language-arts theorists and educators viewed as reader responses the processes that psychologists considered to be comprehension strategies. Reader response has been acceptable to the language-arts community since the late 1970s. This means that the cognitive psychologists and the language-arts specialists had the same idea of prompting student readers to be more active as they read.

Reciprocal Teaching

By the late 1970s and early 1980s the stage was set for research on teaching elementary students to use comprehension strategies as they read. The diverse elements in this mixture came together at the University of Illinois, Center for the Study of Reading. The Center was the intellectual home of Dolores Durkin, whose work established the need for comprehension strategies instruction. A great deal of important work was carried out there. Several young scholars at the Center would put together a summary of study skills (Tierney et al., 1980). Important work on individual comprehension strategies was conducted there, including work on summarization (A. L. Brown & Day, 1983), imagery (R. C. Anderson & Hidde, 1971), and prior knowledge activation (R. C. Anderson & Pearson, 1984). Reader response was known to the Center group if for no other reason than that the National Council of Teachers of English was headquartered at the University of Illinois, with scholars such as Alan Purves frequently interacting with the Center group.

The scholars who would bring it all together, however, would be Annemarie S. Palincsar and Ann L. Brown. Their landmark study of reciprocal teaching (1984) had a great impact on interest in comprehension strategies instruction.

Reciprocal teaching (Palincsar & Brown, 1984) involves teaching comprehension strategies in the context of a reading group. Students are taught to make predictions when reading, question themselves about the ideas in the text, seek clarifications when confused, and summarize content. The adult teacher initially explains and models these strategies for students but quickly transfers responsibility to the members of the group, with individual students taking turns leading the reading group.

During a reciprocal teaching lesson, one student is assigned the role of group leader, supervising the group's generation of predictions, questions, and summaries as reading proceeds. The group leader also solicits points that need to be clarified and either provides clarifications or elicits them from other group members. The group interactions are cooperative, and the adult teacher provides support on an as-needed basis only. That is, the adult teacher provides scaffolding: enough support so that the group makes progress, but not so much support as to stifle students' active self-direction of their reading and comprehension.

A. L. Brown and Palincsar (1989) summarized a typical discussion of a text in a reciprocal teaching group:

> The dialogue leader begins the discussion by asking a question on the main content and ends by summarizing the gist. If there is disagreement, the group rereads and discusses potential candidates for question and sum-

mary statements until they reach consensus. Summarizing provides a means by which the group can monitor its progress, noting points of agreement and disagreement. Particularly valuable is the fact that summarizing at the end of a period of discussion helps students establish where they are for tackling a new segment of text. Attempts to clarify any comprehension problems that might arise are also an integral part of the discussion. And, finally, the leader asks for predictions about future content. Throughout, the adult teacher provides guidance and feedback tailored to the needs of the current discussion and his or her respondents. (p. 413)

Reciprocal teaching is chock-full of good things, according to cognitive views of learning and development (A. L. Brown & Palincsar, 1989). First of all, students are presented with multiple models of cognitive processing. The teacher models and explains. Every day the group comes together and executes a sequence of strategies well matched to the processes required to understand text; thus, peers in the group are continuously modeling reasoning about text. With respect to the learning of content, students are led to make the types of elaborations and inferences that should facilitate learning of the text—that is, predictions, inferences required as part of question generation and elaboration, and summarization. The discussions permit various points of view to be aired and require students to justify and back up their claims. These discussions permit review and commentary about the strategies being learned and the content being covered. Thus, reciprocal teaching offers opportunities to learn new content and to learn how to process new content.

A major assumption of reciprocal teaching is that, through participation, students eventually internalize use of the four strategies practiced in the group. That is, the processing that was once carried out between persons in the group will come to be carried out within the individual students, consistent with the Vygotskian perspective that individual cognitive development develops from participation in social groups.

Reciprocal teaching has shortcomings, however (Hacker & Tenent, 2002; Marks et al., 1993). Many reciprocal teaching lessons involve a preponderance of literal questions and little in the way of evidence that students are monitoring their comprehension. This is obvious from a lack of clarification questions in many reciprocal teaching lessons. Because reciprocal teaching emphasizes a gradual reduction of teacher support, there are often long pauses in lessons, with students fumbling because the teacher is uncertain whether to enter into the conversation and provide input. With respect to performance on standardized comprehension tests, the effects of reciprocal teaching are not particularly striking, with an average effect size of 0.3 SD, although it is more successful when reciprocal teaching includes more direct instruction of the four comprehension strategies (Rosenshine &

Meister, 1994). Contemporary comprehension strategies instruction can involve more direct explanation than reciprocal teaching, as will be apparent in the next section.

Summary

By the middle 1980s, the stage was set for direct teaching of comprehension strategies, beginning with explanation and modeling of the strategies, with students practicing the strategies with teacher assistance as needed until the strategies were internalized. The profession understood the need for such instruction and had experienced something like it during the study skills era, albeit with different strategies rather than the ones inspired by the substantial basic research on text representations that occurred in the 1970s and early 1980s. There was evidence that good readers used cognitive strategies as they read—including, prominently, the text representational strategies and responsively interpreted text, and were plenty metacognitive as they did so, highly aware of why they were doing what they were doing. Both Vygotskian theory and reciprocal teaching had popularized the notion of internalization, with the latter specifically addressing internalization of comprehension strategies.

DIRECT EXPLANATION OF COMPREHENSION STRATEGIES AND MORE: TRANSACTIONAL COMPREHENSION STRATEGIES INSTRUCTION

In 1984, Michigan State University researchers Laura R. Roehler and Gerald G. Duffy proposed an important model of teaching that begins with teacher explanations. At the heart of it is a process that they referred to as mental modeling, which is showing students what a strategy is and how to apply a strategy by thinking aloud (Duffy & Roehler, 1989). For example, the teacher introducing mental imagery as a comprehension strategy using Roehler and Duffy's (1984) approach might tell students about how good readers sometimes make pictures in their heads that are consistent with the ideas in a story. Then, the teacher might begin to read a story aloud to the students, stopping from time to time to explain the images she or he is constructing of what is going on in the story. Students would then try the strategy, monitored by the teacher, who would provide additional explanations and modeling as needed. Feedback and instruction are reduced as students become more and more comfortable with the strategic process being taught. The information provided to students during practice depends very much on the particular problems the students encounter and the particular ways that their understanding is deficient. Reinstruction and reexplanations occur, as well as follow-up mental modeling. The teacher responds to specific student needs, sometimes offering an elaboration of student understanding up until that point. That is, instruction is scaffolded, according to the Duffy and Roehler approach.

Duffy et al. (1987) produced an extremely well-designed study of the effects of direct-explanation strategy instruction on grade-3 reading, with 10 groups of weak readers assigned randomly to the direct explanation condition and 10 control groups receiving their usual instruction. Duffy et al. (1987) taught grade-3 teachers to explain directly the strategies, skills, and processes that are part of skilled grade-3 reading as the study continued over the course of an entire academic year. The teachers were taught first to explain a strategy, skill, or process and then to mentally model use of it for students. Then came guided student practice, in which the students initially carried out the processing overtly so that the teacher could monitor their use of the new strategy. Assistance was reduced as students became more proficient. Teachers encouraged transfer of strategies by reviewing when and where the strategies being learned might be used. Teachers cued use of the new strategies when students encountered situations where the strategies might be applied profitably, regardless of when these occasions arose (i.e., scaffolding continued throughout the school day). Cuing and prompting continued until students autonomously applied the strategies they were taught.

By the end of the year, students in the direct-explanation condition outperformed control students on standardized measures of reading, including a measure of reading achievement given the year after the direct-explanation intervention had been administered. These results had a profound effect on the reading education community. Direct explanation as defined by Duffy et al. (1987) was subsequently used by many educators as a starting point as they implemented comprehension strategies instruction in their own schools. Direct explanation continues to this day to be an important model of reading skills instruction, including of comprehension skills (Duffy, 2003).

Descriptive Studies of Transactional Comprehension Strategies Instruction

The Pressley research group studied several places where teaching of comprehension strategies was developed and implemented in light of the Roehler and Duffy (1984) model. Because the instruction we studied involved so much more than direct explanation, a different term was needed to describe it, one more inclusive of all that occurs during such teaching. In particular, we wanted a summary term that better captured the dynamic give-and-take between teachers and students that typifies classrooms employing strategies instruction. The descriptive label "transactional strategies instruction" thus seemed appropriate from three different perspectives.

Recall Rosenblatt's (1978) reader-response position that meaning is not in the text alone or in the reader's head alone but rather is constructed by readers as they consider text content in light of their previous knowledge and experiences. Such meaning construction, termed transactional by Rosenblatt, was certainly emphasized in the instruction described here, as students were encouraged to use strategies such as prediction, visualization, and summarization to create personalized interpretations and understanding of text.

The term "transactional" was also appropriate for a second reason, however. Most comprehension strategies instruction occurred in small reading groups involving a teacher and students reading texts together, applying comprehension strategies as they did so. In the developmental psychology literature (e.g., Bell, 1968), the term transactional is used to refer to interactions in which the child's actions in part determine the behaviors of adults in the child's world. Consistent with that use of the term transactional, teachers' reactions in the instruction detailed here were determined largely by the reactions of the students. Teachers responded to student interpretations and difficulties: If a student offered a good summary, the teacher might prompt elaboration of the summary. If the student's summary was difficult for the teacher to understand, she or he might prompt rereading or reconsideration of the text. What happened in transactional strategies instructional groups was determined largely by the reactions of students to teachers and to other students. Such conversations about literature make a great deal of sense, for children's comprehension about ideas in a text increase when they have conversations about literature with peers and teachers (Applebee, Langer, Nystrand, & Gamoran, 2003; Van den Branden, 2000).

The strategies instruction described in what follows was transactional in yet a third sense. Organizational psychologists (e.g., Hutchins, 1991) in particular have been concerned with the types of solutions produced during group problem solving as compared with individual problem solving: Groups invariably produce interpretations that no one individual in the group would have produced. Group interpretations following this pattern were prominent during the comprehension strategies instruction we watched. The group used the strategies they were learning as interpretational tools, producing impressive interpretations of texts.

To summarize, there were three senses in which the classroom strategies instruction we observed was transactional:

1. Meaning was determined by heads employing strategies as they processed the text.
2. How one head reacted was largely determined by what other heads in the group were doing, thinking, and saying.

3. The meaning that emerged as teachers and students together used strategies to read and comprehend a text was the product of all of the heads in the group.

Instruction was transactional in all of these senses largely because of extremely intelligent teacher assistance to students during strategies instruction and practice. That is, direct explanation of strategies and teacher modeling were followed by sensitive teacher scaffolding of strategies use as students worked in small groups.

Benchmark School Studies

Pressley's initial studies on comprehension strategies instruction were conducted at the Benchmark School in Media, Pennsylvania, which is dedicated to the education of high-ability students who experience difficulties learning to read during the first 2 years of schooling. Even though the Benchmark students are at great risk for long-term school failure, most emerge after 4–7 years well prepared to return to regular education. Virtually all Benchmark graduates complete high school, and many attend college. Because much of the Benchmark approach involves teaching students to use cognitive strategies to accomplish reading and other literacy tasks, the school seemed like a perfect place to do an initial investigation of effective strategies instruction: Reading strategies are taught in primary through middle school, with students encouraged to use them across the curriculum.

One study was an interview study of the faculty (Pressley, Gaskins, Cunicelli, et al., 1991). The 31 academic teachers at Benchmark were asked 150 questions about their instruction, each requiring an objective answer (e.g., a response on a Likert scale) but also permitting any additional input the responding teacher might wish to provide. The questions had been generated after extensive observations at the school, intended to tap the most important instructional issues surrounding the comprehension strategies instruction being offered at the school. Up to 5 hours of face-to-face interviews permitted ample opportunity for teachers to provide detailed explanations, based on their extensive experience, of what they believed about strategies instruction as well as why they believed it.

Generalizing across the 31 teachers, we found that there were many points of agreement, including the following:

• The Benchmark teachers strongly endorsed direct explanation and modeling as essential components of effective strategies instruction. Many observations at Benchmark confirmed that such explanations were used during small- and large-group instruction and as part of one-to-one tutoring and reinstruction. Teachers reported that their initial explanations and modeling were more complete than later explanations and modeling, although the faculty members, especially the more experienced ones, were emphatic that explanations and modeling should continue for a long time after introduction of strategies.

• Extensive practice in use of strategies was endorsed by the teachers, as was extensive guidance and feedback in response to student needs during such practice. Even so, the teachers admitted that it is often difficult to diagnose the specific problems experienced by students, and it is a challenge to devise remediation. The teachers were aware that students did not learn strategies quickly: Facile use of strategies across a wide range of tasks and materials occurred only after extensive practice, which included struggling to adapt strategies to a wide range of academic problems.

• Teaching of strategies and their application was reported as occurring across the curriculum, consistent with our frequent observations of Benchmark teachers encouraging use of strategies in many different contexts.

• The teachers considered it essential to provide extensive information to students about when and where to apply the strategies they were learning, as well as information about the learning benefits produced by use of strategies.

• The teachers recognized that transfer of the newly acquired strategies to new academic tasks and contents was anything but automatic; rather, it required extensive teaching about when strategies might be applied as well as practice applying strategies across a number of situations.

• The teachers were emphatic that only a few strategies could be introduced at a time. In accordance with this, in-depth instruction of strategies over months and years was the preferred approach to teaching at Benchmark. The teachers' view was that students developed strategic repertoires over the course of their years in the school—strategies instruction was definitely not seen as a quick fix.

• Although cognitive in their orientation, the teachers also recognized the need for explicit reinforcement of student efforts and successes in applying strategies and accomplishing difficult academic tasks. Feedback to students was considered essential. It was seen as especially important to follow students' success with positive feedback as a means of keeping them motivated. The teachers were well aware that their students had already experienced several years of school failure and believed that Benchmark students' successes needed to be rewarded in order to offset the damage produced by the previous failures. (See Chapter 11 for more on motivation, and, in particular, at the Benchmark School.)

• The Benchmark teachers believed they should develop students who were habitually reflective and good planners. Strategies instruction was seen as a way of accomplishing this higher-order goal.

Pressley, Gaskins, Cunicelli, et al. (1991) presented the same questions that had been given to the Benchmark teachers to a sample of nine nationally known researchers in strategies instruction, distinguished investigators who had extensive hands-on experience in implementing long-term strategies instruction at their home institutions. What was striking was the high congruence between the responses of the Benchmark teachers and this researcher sample. Extensive experience with strategies instruction seems to produce perceptions of it that are consistent with the thinking of the Benchmark teachers.

Two additional studies at the school provided even more detailed understanding of how Benchmark teachers do what they do. One was a case study of the instruction in one Benchmark classroom during the spring semester of 1990 (Pressley, Gaskins, Wile, Cunicelli, & Sheridan, 1991). The focal strategy taught there was the generation of an outline of the major ideas in each text, which would include information about causes and effects coded in the text, temporal sequences, comparative and contrasting information, and simple descriptions. Teaching of these strategies was thoroughly integrated with the teaching of content, with focal strategies instruction occurring during reading, writing, and social studies as teachers and students interacted to create maps. For example, semantic maps were generated by students as they planned writing assignments as part of social studies. Social studies homework often required semantic mapping.

Consistent with teachers' claims in the interview study, explanations and modeling of the semantic mapping strategy were more extensive and explicit early in the instruction. After several months, given a one-line direction from the teacher (e.g., "Make a map of what's in this text"), students often began to map the meaning of a text. The teachers provided assistance to students on an as-needed basis, often giving gentle hints about how specific relationships in a text might be represented in a semantic map.

Instruction in other strategies did not stop when semantic mapping was introduced. Rather, teachers modeled and explained use of semantic mapping in conjunction with other strategies. For example, the strategies of activating prior knowledge, predicting, seeking clarification, and summarizing were all prompted frequently during lessons intended primarily to provide new information about semantic mapping as a strategy.

We had an important insight at Benchmark School that cognitive strategies were being taught as methods to encourage interpretations, which we define as the construction of personally significant understanding. For example, the teachers observed in the Pressley, Gaskins, Wile, et al. (1991) case study taught their students that no two semantic maps should be alike and that each student's map should reflect reactions to the content of the text.

Interpretive activities were especially apparent in analyses of Benchmark classroom dialogues produced by Gaskins, Anderson, Pressley, Cunicelli, and Satlow (1993), who studied the strategy instruction lessons of six teachers at Benchmark. Three lessons were analyzed for each teacher in Gaskins et al. (1993): one when a new focal strategy was introduced, the second somewhat later, and a third considerably later than that. The discourse in these classrooms was markedly different from the discourse in conventional classrooms in typical schools: Many repeated cycles consisting of a teacher asking a question, a student responding to it, and the teacher evaluating the response (i.e., "IRE" cycles involving teacher *initiation*, student *response*, and teacher *evaluation*), ordinarily observed in many classroom studies (see Cazden, 1988; Mehan, 1979), were not found in the Benchmark data. Instead, the teachers engaged in interactive dialogues with their students 88% of the time in what Gaskins et al. (1993) referred to as process–content cycles: The teacher used content as a vehicle to stimulate application and discussion of strategies. When students made comments during discussions, Benchmark teachers did not attempt to evaluate their responses but rather encouraged the students to elaborate on them—encouraging students to process the content further using strategies. The goal was to encourage student understanding of content through strategic processing. Thus, a teacher might ask a student to summarize a passage. Once the summary was offered, the teacher might ask the student if any images came to mind while he or she was reading the text, or encourage the student to liven up the summary by relating it to prior knowledge (e.g., "Do you think most people would ask Bob Cratchet to work on Christmas Eve?"; "Do your parents have to work on Christmas Eve?").

An extremely important finding in the Gaskins et al. (1993) investigation was the identification of events that occurred often in many lessons:

- Students were provided instruction about how to carry out the strategies.
- Teachers modeled the focal strategies (and sometimes use of other strategies as well).
- Students practiced strategies, with teacher guidance and assistance provided on an as-needed basis.
- The focal strategy for a lesson and the focal curriculum content for the day were identified for students early in the lesson.
- Information was presented about why the focal strategy (and sometimes nonfocal strategies as well) was important; often teachers provided anecdotal information about how strategies had helped them.
- Information about when and where strategies apply was conveyed to students.

In summary, when Benchmark teachers were interviewed, when they were observed, and when their discourse was analyzed thoroughly, it was easy to discern direct explanations about and modeling of strategies, followed by student practice that was guided and assisted by teachers, who carefully monitored student attempts to use strategies, offering help when needed. Elementary content coverage was not displaced in favor of strategies instruction; rather, strategies were applied as students learned elementary content.

A Comprehension Strategies Instructional Program in a Maryland County

As it turned out, the Benchmark School was not the only place where such instruction took place. We extensively studied comprehension strategies programs that were developed and implemented in one Maryland county school district. The comprehension instruction in that county occurred around high-quality texts, often in reading groups small enough to encourage exchanges between all students about interpretations of text, imaginal reactions to content, and summaries. When strategies were initially introduced (i.e., in grade 1 or 2), lessons often focused on individual strategies. For example, there were several weeks of students making predictions, predictions, and more predictions followed by weeks of students visualizing, visualizing, and visualizing. Once students were familiar with the strategies, the lessons emphasized coordinated use of strategies, although this required a great deal of teacher prompting, which continued for months and sometimes years. Eventually, by the third year of participation in such instruction, students could meet in groups and carry out strategic processes in a self-directed fashion—that is, teacher prompting and cuing were much less pronounced than they had been in previous years. El-Dinary, Pressley, and Schuder (1992; also Pressley, El-Dinary, et al., 1992) summarized the comprehension instruction they observed in this Maryland county:

- Students were provided instruction about how to carry out the strategies emphasized in curriculum. Usually this was reexplanation of strategic processes that were somewhat familiar to the students, amounting to a recasting of the strategies in new terms.
- Teachers modeled use of the comprehension strategies that were taught.
- Students practiced strategies, with teacher guidance and assistance provided on an as-needed basis. Prompts were often in the form of questions suggesting additional strategic processing or possible ways to extend or expand an interpretation.
- Information was presented about why the focal strategy (and some-

times nonfocal strategies as well) was important. Teachers often provided anecdotal information about how strategies had helped them.

- Students were often required to model and explain use of the comprehension strategies.
- Information about when and where strategies could be applied was conveyed to students. The positive effects of strategies were continuously pointed out to them.
- Sophisticated processing vocabulary (e.g., terms like "predictions," "clarifications," "validation of predictions," and "summaries") were used frequently.
- Flexibility in strategy use was apparent, with teachers emphasizing how different students might apply strategies in different ways to the same content.
- Teachers sent the message that student thought processes mattered.

Of course, these behaviors were apparent at Benchmark as well. Both settings had developed strategies instruction involving a great deal of direct explanation and mental modeling, consistent with Roehler and Duffy's (1984) recommendations. In both settings, students and teachers talked aloud a great deal about their thinking processes (i.e., did mental modeling). They shared their interpretations of texts in an open and generally relaxed group context. Coordination of strategies was emphasized in both programs, with students engaging in years of practice in such coordination.

Concluding Comment

In these two settings, educators who were aware of the comprehension strategies research literature selected from that literature the strategies and methods that made the most sense to them in light of their years of experience. They were particularly impressed with the work of Gerald G. Duffy, Laura R. Roehler, and their associates (e.g., Duffy et al., 1987; Duffy, Roehler, & Herrmann, 1988) on direct explanation of strategic processes. Duffy and Roehler's perspective on direct explanation, including mental modeling and subsequent guided practice of students, is the most influential to date about how to teach strategic processes in classrooms.

Explaining strategies to students, showing them how to use strategies, and helping them as they attempt to apply strategies as part of in-school practice seemed sensible to these educators. The transactional strategies instruction described here evolved as teachers worked with it. Credit the educators with this intervention, which really does affect student achievement, although previous basic and applied theory and research provided great impetus for and guidance during its development.

Validation of Transactional Strategies Instruction

There have been three studies conducted in which transactional strategies instruction has been evaluated in a carefully controlled fashion. Taken together, their outcomes support the conclusion that transactional strategies instruction can promote reading instruction beginning in grade 2 and continuing into high school.

R. Brown, Pressley, Van Meter, and Schuder (1996)

The study of R. Brown et al. (1996) was a year-long quasi-experimental investigation of the effects of transactional strategies instruction on grade-2 children's reading. Five grade-2 classrooms receiving transactional strategies instruction were matched with grade-2 classrooms taught by teachers who were well regarded as language-arts teachers but who were not using a strategies instruction approach. In each classroom, a group of readers who were low-achieving at the beginning of grade 2 was identified. The changes in reading achievement in these students were carefully studied by R. Brown et al. (1996).

In the fall, the weak students in the strategies instruction classrooms and the weak readers in the control classrooms did not differ on standardized measures of reading comprehension and word attack skills. By the spring, however, there were clear differences on these measures, favoring the transactional strategies instruction classrooms. In addition, there were differences favoring the strategies-instructed students on strategies-use measures as well as interpretive measures (i.e., strategies-instructed students made more diverse and richer interpretations of what they read than did controls).

One of the most compelling differences between R. Brown and colleagues' (1996) transactional strategies-instructed students and control students was a demonstration that the students who had learned strategies acquired more content from their daily lessons. We emphasize as well that it was not that the control students did not improve over the course of the year; they did, but students experiencing transactional strategies instruction improved significantly more.

Cathy Collins (1991)

Cathy Collins (1991) improved comprehension in grade-5 and -6 students by providing a semester (3 days a week) of comprehension strategies lessons. Her students were taught to predict what will happen in the story, seek clarification when uncertain, look for patterns and principles in arguments presented in the text, analyze decision making that occurs during text processing, solve problems (including the use of backward reasoning and visualization), summarize, adapt ideas in the text (including rearranging parts of ideas in it), and negotiate interpretations of texts in groups. Although the strategies-instructed students did not differ from controls before the intervention with respect to standardized comprehension performance, there was a 3-SD difference between treated and control conditions on the posttest, a very large effect for the treatment.

Valerie Anderson (1992)

Valerie Anderson (1992; see also V. Anderson & Roit, 1993) conducted a 3-month experimental investigation of the effects of transactional strategies instruction on reading-disabled students in grades 6 through 11. Students were taught comprehension strategies in small groups, with nine groups of transactional strategies students and seven control groups. Although both strategies-instructed and control students made gains on standardized comprehension measures during the study, the gains were greater in the trained group. V. Anderson (1992) also collected a variety of qualitative data supporting the conclusion that reading for meaning improved in the strategies-instructed condition. For example, strategies instruction increased students' willingness to read and attempt to understand difficult material, collaborate with classmates to discover meanings in text, and react to and elaborate upon text.

Concluding Comment

Doing research on long-term interventions such as transactional strategies instruction is very difficult, requiring that researchers make careful measurements in a number of classrooms over a long period of time. As far as policymakers are concerned, however, the gold standard is that an educational intervention make a difference with respect to performance on standardized tests. What was striking in these validations was that a semester to a year of transactional strategies instruction made a definitive impact on standardized tests but also made differences that were captured by other measures. What is also striking is that others besides the originators of transactional strategies instruction approaches are finding ways to adapt the procedures to new contexts and contents with clear improvements in student comprehension, although not always as striking as in the original validation studies (e.g., Klingner, Vaughn, Arguelles, Hughes, & Leftwich, 2004; Klingner, Vaughn, & Schumm, 1998; Mason, 2004).

Having spent a great deal of time in classrooms in which transactional strategies instruction occurs, and in many other classrooms as well, we can say without hesitation that daily life is very different in classrooms based on the transactional strategies instruction model than it is in other class-rooms. Most noticeable is that there is really intelligent discussion of readings occurring in the transactional strategies instruction classes, with the students using the strategies they are learning in conversations about readings. In these conversations, they make predictions about what will happen in the story. They talk about the parts of readings that are confusing and about ways to overcome those confusions. The children offer summaries of what they read, permitting differences in interpretation. The students in these classrooms have come to expect differences, since they know that the meaning of a text is a function of both what is in the text and what the reader knew before reading the text.

In the typical classroom, which does not include strategy instruction, most talk occurs in a participation structure in which the teacher asks questions and the students answer them (e.g., Mehan, 1979). That definitely does not occur in transactional strategies instruction classrooms. There, the students have learned how to talk about a text without being prompted by the teacher to do so. The teacher never prompts students by saying, "Now, it's time for a prediction," or "Can someone think of a good question to ask about this part of the story?" Rather, if the teacher needs to prompt at all, he or she merely prompts the students to be active, asking students to decide for themselves what they should be doing to understand the text. Prompts like "What might you do here?" or "I was wondering how you were thinking about this portion of the text" are common. The teacher prompts students to choose to think, with the students learning that thinking about text involves making predictions based on prior knowledge and what has happened so far in the text, constructing mental images, generating questions and looking for answers, seeking clarifications when confused, and constructing summaries and interpretations about the ideas in the text. There is considerable evidence that the opportunities to participate in such student-driven dialogues are highly motivating to students, enabling them to think of plenty of questions to ask about the text and plenty of ways to relate to one another about the ideas in texts being read (e.g., Almasi & Gambrell, 1994). Such discussions about the content of the text—that is, negotiations about text meanings—have great potential for increasing the comprehension of the individuals in the group (Van den Branden, 2000).

Transactional strategies instruction is about the development of self-regulation, developing students who, on their own, use the comprehension strategies that excellent readers use. Return to Chapter 2 and review the comprehension processes used by excellent readers. Those processes—prediction, questioning, making images, seeking clarification, and constructing summaries—are exactly the processes that are taught as strategies by transactional strategies instruction teachers. Exceptionally skilled readers use these on their own, and thus the transactional strategies instruction teacher does not want to be cuing students to use any specific strategy. Rather, the transactional strategies instruction teacher consistently sends the message that students should be active during reading, choosing their own activities and strategies. If self-regulation is anything, it is choosing to be cognitively active, and transactional strategies instruction is all about teaching students to choose active reading over passive reading and to decide for themselves which strategic processes to use when they confront challenging texts.

Before leaving this discussion of transactional strategies instruction, we feel that we must reflect a bit more on its predecessor, reciprocal teaching, covered earlier in the chapter. When teachers try to implement reciprocal teaching, they often transform it dramatically—to the point that it looks like transactional strategies instruction (Hacker & Tenent, 2002; Marks et al., 1993), with an entire volume summary now available about how reciprocal teaching can be used more flexibly in the classroom than the original version (Oczkus, 2003). Thus, one route to transactional strategies instruction can be by starting with reciprocal teaching of prediction, clarification, questioning, and summarization, with the goal of flexible use of these strategies by students kept in the forefront of the implementing teacher's mind. In short, reciprocal teaching seems like one way to start developing transactional strategies instruction.

Concerning the way strategies instruction stimulates cognitive activity, we cannot resist the temptation to point out that even when very insensitive analyses are employed, as when national data bases of questionnaire data are analyzed, there are clear relationships between cognitive strategies instruction and the reported frequency of reading (Guthrie, Schafer, Wang, & Afflerbach, 1993). Even more intriguing is evidence in the Guthrie et al. (1993) analysis that part of the reason for the increased reading when comprehension strategies are taught is that it leads to more dialogue about what was read. There is plenty of reason to teach comprehension strategies in elementary school, and we suspect that there will be more evidence documenting that students receiving such instruction read better, read more, talk more, and talk more intelligently about what they read.

BALANCED COMPREHENSION INSTRUCTION IS MORE THAN COMPREHENSION STRATEGIES INSTRUCTION

This chapter has focused on comprehension strategies instruction because a great deal of comprehension instructional work has been about strategies. Certainly, comprehension strategies are very, very important. However, balanced comprehension instruction is much more, with comprehension instruction not beginning in the middle and upper elementary grades but much earlier. Yes, there is probably going to be more comprehension instruction in the middle and upper elementary grades, as implied up until this point in the chapter, but that is not to say that concerns about developing comprehension should be absent from the primary grades.

Decoding with Fluency and Comprehension

There are those who assume that if children can decode words in the books they are reading, that will go far in permitting understanding of the messages in texts (Gough & Tunmer, 1986). From this perspective, word-level decoding is a critical bottleneck in the comprehension process: If the reader cannot decode a word, she or he cannot comprehend it (e.g., Adams, 1990; Metsala & Ehri, 1998). Of course, there is some truth to this position. Not being able to read words at all seriously impairs comprehension! Indeed, not being able to decode fluently (Chapter 6) impairs comprehension, for both word recognition and comprehension occur within short-term memory (i.e., consciousness), which is limited in its capacity (Miller, 1956). Hence, word recognition and higher-order comprehension processes compete for the short-term capacity that is available during reading. The more effort required to decode a word, the less capacity that is left over to comprehend it and the larger messages in the text (LaBerge & Samuels, 1974). In general, the more completely developed decoding processes are during the elementary years, the better the understanding of words and connected text (Gough & Tunmer, 1986; Rupley, Willson, & Nichols, 1998; Shankweiler et al., 1999).

When teachers develop word recognition fluency, they are teaching students to improve comprehension. In fact, this is the main motivation for emphasizing fluency as the goal of word recognition instruction. Much has been said in this book about the teaching of word recognition processes as part of balanced literacy instruction, with the point made emphatically that many struggling readers can learn to recognize words through explicit decoding instruction. A critical research issue is to determine whether struggling readers can learn to recognize words to the point of fluency, as discussed in some detail in Chapter 6. In most studies of word recognition considered in this book, the criterion was word recognition accuracy rather than fluency. Yes, struggling readers can be taught to sound out words, but such sounding out is effortful. Being able to sound out words with effort will not produce fluent readers who have high comprehension. Every primary-level teacher has experienced the child who can sound out word after word, sentence after sentence, and paragraph after paragraph but has no clue at the end of a reading about what was read. Those children are accurate decoders. Comprehension requires more. It requires word recognition fluency.

Good readers not only understand what they read, they also know when they are *not understanding what they read*—that is, they monitor their comprehension. Comprehension monitoring is critical, for awareness of a failure to understand prompts the good reader to reread the text and try to make sense out of it. An important finding in recent years is that with increasing skill in decoding the comprehension monitoring of grade-1 students improves as well (Kinnunen, Vaurus, & Niemi, 1998). Skilled decoding goes far in promoting skilled reading.

Using Semantic Context Cues to Understand Word Meanings

As discussed earlier in this book, relying on semantic context cues (e.g., pictures, overall meaning of a text) as primary in word recognition is a mistake. Good readers rely on the letters of a word and word parts to recognize a word! Once the word is recognized, it is important for readers to use picture and semantic context cues to determine the meaning of the decoded word, however. In English, as in most languages, most words have multiple meanings. The only way to know which one applies when a word is sounded out is to pay attention to context cues (Gough, 1983, 1984; Isakson & Miller, 1976). Thus, when a good reader reads "I'll stamp at the post office," she or he gets a mental image of someone placing postage stamps on letters rather than an image of a person stamping feet in a public place. Such a good reader would get a very different image for the sentence "I'll stamp at the pep rally." Context determines the meaning of particular words. This is the reason that many approaches aimed at the improvement of beginning reading, such as Reading Recovery, teach students to pay attention to whether the word that has been sounded out makes sense in the context being read (Clay, 1991). An important component in balanced comprehension instruction is teaching students to pay attention to semantic context cues to help understand what they read, including making decisions about the particular meaning of a word intended by the author of a text.

Vocabulary

There has been some debate about whether it makes sense to teach vocabulary explicitly, although there is a very clear and positive association between the extent of a reader's vocabulary and his or her comprehension skills (e.g., R. C. Anderson & Freebody, 1981; Becker, 1977; Blachowicz & Fisher, 2000; Nagy, Anderson, & Herman, 1987). The main argument against teaching of vocabulary is that the task is overwhelming. That is, a good reader knows more than 100,000 words, and there is no way so many words can be taught (Nagy & Anderson, 1984). Recall from Chapter 7, however, that by the end of high school a student should be expected to know only about 15,000 root words, which certainly is a more manageable number than 100,000 words (i.e., many of the remaining 85,000 are derived from the root words; e.g., Biemiller & Slonim, 2001; d'Anna, Zechmeister, & Hall, 1991). Another concern is that, because children often do not understand the meaning of words fully from exposure to their formal definitions in the dictionary (see Chapter 7), much of their meaning can be acquired only by encountering words in rich contexts (Miller & Gildea, 1987).

Those holding the view that explicit teaching of vocabulary is futile take comfort in the fact that humans seem to have considerable capacity to acquire vocabulary incidentally (i.e., from encountering words in speech and reading; Nagy & Scott, 2000; Sternberg, 1987; see Chapter 7 of this volume). Leaving vocabulary development to incidental learning, however, is leaving much to chance. When readers encounter a new word in the text, often they do not infer its meaning correctly (Miller & Gildea, 1987; again, Chapter 7 of this volume). For example, Harmon (1998) observed that the fourth graders in his study were about as likely to infer a word's meaning from the context as to make an *incorrect* inference. At best, learning vocabulary meanings from text encounters is a slow and uncertain process for elementary students (Schwanenflugel, Stahl, & McFalls, 1997). This is because inferring word meanings from context depends on extensive knowledge of language as well as understanding of the situation being described in the text and coordination of a number of strategies (Harmon, 1998; Nagy & Scott, 2000). Such a result also depends on prior knowledge, for children who know a lot about a particular topic are more likely than less knowledgeable children to infer the meaning of unfamiliar words related to the topic when they are encountered in context (Carlisle, Fleming, & Gudbrandsen, 2000). As always, the rich are more likely to get richer!

The main reason to teach vocabulary to children, however, is that when children are taught vocabulary their comprehension does increase, at least of passages containing the taught words (e.g., Beck, Perfetti, & McKeown, 1982; McKeown, Beck, Omanson, & Perfetti, 1983; McKeown, Beck, Omanson, & Pople, 1985). Hence, we emphasize in this volume that a comprehension development program should include the teaching of the words that students most need to know. An adequate vocabulary is only some of the knowledge a young reader needs, however.

World Knowledge

During the late 1970s and early 1980s, the group at the Center for the Study of Reading, University of Illinois, spearheaded research on the criticality of background knowledge to reading comprehension (e.g., R. C. Anderson & Pearson, 1984). Specifically, they found that what readers knew about the topic of a text before reading it very much influenced the messages they took away from reading that text. An important hypothesis emerging from this work is that students' reading comprehension can be improved by developing their world knowledge. One of the most visible proponents for this position is E. D. Hirsch, Jr. (1987), who has advanced the position that there is a core of knowledge that literate people know. Once acquired, this core knowledge permits spectacular reading feats. For example, one explanation of President John F. Kennedy's ability to read foreign policy documents at 2,000 words per minute with reasonable comprehension is that he knew a lot about foreign policy. A demonstration we have done several times in educational psychology classes that we teach is to take a brand-new, still-in-the-shrink-wrap educational psychology textbook into a class, have the students open the package, and then, as the students do some other activity, we read—actually, skim—the entire text in about 15 minutes. Then, we give the text to several members of the class who follow along as we summarize the book from memory. Sometimes, we ask the students to quiz us additionally. Usually, we answer correctly the questions they ask. The reason we can comprehend so much so quickly is that educational psychology is an area in which our prior knowledge is very well developed.

Hirsch and his associates have developed an entire elementary curriculum based on their conception of core knowledge, with the curriculum specifying knowledge that should be acquired in each of the elementary grades. Although the evaluations of it are not as complete or analytical as we would like, in initial evaluations the core knowledge approach has been boosting language-arts performance in schools where it has been tried (Datnow, Borman, & Stringfield, 2000). Of course, if we go back to the Illinois Center for the Study of Reading theory and data, it makes a great deal of sense that developing core knowledge should increase comprehension. From this perspective, teachers should be doing all possible to make certain that students not only read extensively but also read material filled with worthwhile information.

Beyond having world knowledge, students need to be taught to use the knowledge they possess as they try to make sense of newly encountered texts. One of the really important findings produced by reading researchers in recent years is that skilled thinkers often do not make inferences unless understanding of the text demands them (McKoon & Ratcliff, 1992). That is, when reading a text, good readers typically make prior-knowledge-based inferences only when they are absolutely required to understand the ideas in the text. Another important discovery in the past two decades, however, is that if readers are encouraged to relate what they already know about a topic to a new reading about that topic, their understanding and memory of the text can improve dramatically.

In particular, one way to encourage readers to relate their world knowledge to what they read is to teach them to ask "why" questions as they go through a text. That is, fact-filled text can be rendered much more memorable by encouraging students to ask themselves why the facts in the text make sense. Wood, Pressley, and Winne (1990, Experiment 2) provided a clear demonstration that children in grades 4–8 can benefit from asking themselves "why" questions about facts presented in a connected text. The children studied in Wood et al. (1990, Experiment 2) were asked to learn elementary science content pertaining to different types of animals. For each animal, they read a paragraph specifying the physical characteristics of the animal's home as well as its diet, sleeping habits, preferred habitat, and predators. Some students were instructed to ask themselves why each fact in the text made sense (e.g., for the facts related to skunks, "Why do skunks eat corn?"; "Why do owls prey on skunks?"; "Why is the skunk away from 3 A.M. until dawn?") and to attempt to answer such "why" questions based on prior knowledge as they read. These students remembered much more of what was presented in the text than did control students, who read and studied the text as they normally would.

Such "why" questioning produces large effects on learning and can be used profitably by elementary and middle school students to learn material in factually dense text (Pressley, Wood, et al., 1992). It does so by orienting readers to prior knowledge that can render the facts in a text more sensible, and hence more comprehensible and memorable (Martin & Pressley, 1991). We think it is worthwhile to teach students to get in the habit of trying to figure out why new ideas presented in a text make sense.

Although relating one's prior knowledge to the ideas in a text can increase comprehension, it also has the potential sometimes to undermine comprehension. In fact, one of the ways that weak readers undermine their comprehension is by relating prior knowledge to texts they are reading that is not directly relevant to the most important ideas in the text, making unwarranted and unnecessary inferences as they do so (e.g., Williams, 1993, 2002).

Williams and her colleagues (see Williams, 2002, 2003) have preliminary data about a teaching approach intended to encourage readers with learning disabilities to relate relevant prior knowledge to what they read. The students experience a series of lessons involving activities that make salient that attending to the ideas actually presented in a text is what reading for understanding is about. During each lesson, there is a discussion about a text that will be read during the session, with the teacher talking extensively with the students about the theme of the upcoming story and the importance of the theme in understanding a story. Then, the teacher and students read the story aloud, with the teacher asking questions during the reading intended to orient the students to the thematic ideas of the story. These are questions requiring students to use their prior knowledge—for example, to make predictions about what is going to happen next in a story and to explain the basis for those predictions. After reading the story, there is a discussion involving five main questions, each of which requires processing of the main ideas in the story that was read: Who is the main character? What did he or she do? What happened? Was this good or bad? Why was this good or bad? The students learn to state the main theme of a story in a standard form: "The (main character) should (should not) have _____." For example, "Goldilocks should not have made herself so much at home in the bears' house." Students are then asked to think about when the theme of the story would apply, answering these questions: "To whom would this theme apply?" and "When would it apply?" Students with learning disabilities do, in fact, orient more to the big ideas of stories after experiencing this training, using appropriate prior knowledge to understand what they are reading, with some evidence that this type of training can be effective with at-risk students in as early as grades 2 and 3 (Wilder & Williams, 2001; Williams et al., 2002).

In summary, it makes sense to do all possible to encourage students to develop worthwhile world knowledge through reading and other experiences (e.g., some television experiences are filled with information that literate people know, and other television experiences are not). Contemporary reading series typically include stories and expository texts that are carefully chosen to include material that is worthwhile for the child to read, reflecting the understanding that an important shortcoming of the old-style "Dick-and-Jane" approach is that the stories did not expose children to information they could use subsequently to understand other texts and situations that might be encountered. Having knowledge is one thing; using it another. I always tell audiences that, if they are considering a reading series, look at the themes for the units and the readings within units. If the themes are not about important literary topics, science, social studies, or values, reject the series categorically. With more and more of the elementary school day being ceded to language arts, it is more essential now than ever that language-arts thematic units cover important content.

That readers often do not relate what they are reading to what they already know has prompted research about how to encourage more extensive use of prior knowledge by young readers. One way of doing so is to encourage readers to be asking themselves why the ideas in a text are sensible and to figure out why what is being presented in that text makes sense based on what the reader already knows. With children who have learning disabilities, more complete instruction might be necessary, such as the teaching devised by Williams and her associates, which involves a teacher modeling, explaining, and supporting orientation to the major thematic messages in texts. Such instruction demands that readers make predictions as they read, with predicting always requiring that readers relate what they have encountered in the text with what they already know in order to gauge what might happen next in the reading.

Processing Diverse Texts

Elementary reading instruction is filled with the disproportionate reading of stories, relative to other types of text. For example, Nell K. Duke (2000) found first-grade instruction flooded with narratives, with only 3.6 minutes per day of exposure to informational texts! In contrast, balanced reading instruction should involve substantial exposure to a variety of texts. Because so much of secondary content reading is expository, it makes sense to make certain that elementary students practice comprehension strategies with nonfiction informational texts (Almasi, 2003; Ogle & Blachowicz, 2002), and, of course, good reading series are increasing the amount of expository reading in their thematic units.

In addition, with every passing year, the number of texts available on the Internet increases. At a minimum, elementary school students need to have practice working with such texts, although much research is required before the unique comprehension demands of such texts are understood (Spires & Estes, 2002).

Diverse Text Tasks

The prototypical text task for elementary students is to read a selection so that they can answer questions about it. Sometimes the questions are printed after the text and require a written response. Sometimes teachers ask the questions. Balanced comprehension instruction is going to include asking students to do more than answer questions after reading. There are many other ways to assess comprehension, including ones that require readers to use the ideas encountered in text (e.g., "Write an essay integrating ideas in the text"; Flower et al., 1990). Balanced comprehension instruction will include teaching students how to find information they want in a text (Dreher, 2002; Reynolds & Symons, 2001; Symons, MacLatchy-Gaudet, Stone, & Reynolds, 2001) and using that information once found.

Reader-response theory (Rosenblatt, 1978) had made us very much aware that people read not simply to be informed but also for enjoyment. Good readers often respond affectively to texts (see Pressley & Afflerbach, 1995). A strength of the transactional strategies instructional approach favored in this chapter is that teachers do model their affective responses to what they read, and students share with one another their interpretations and responses to texts. Balanced reading instruction should be aimed at developing not only readers who learn from a text but readers who interpret and respond to the messages in that text. Good readers must learn how to do diverse things with text and react in diverse ways.

Summary

Balanced reading comprehension instruction involves multiple components, as does all balanced reading instruction. Students' word-level processes must be honed, with word recognition developed to the point of fluency and development of extensive vocabulary.

Extensive reading of worthwhile books is a critical part of balanced reading instruction (e.g., Guthrie, Wigfield, Metsala, & Cox, 1999), for example, promoting fluency. Reading the good stuff promotes growth of vocabulary and other world knowledge. Readers are most likely to get the most out of the good stuff if they use sophisticated comprehension strategies as they read. A main message of this chapter is that such comprehension strategies can be taught, with the new twist in this section being that one strategy that should be included in the mix is relating what is being read to prior knowledge.

Often, reading educators do not worry much about comprehension in kindergarten and grade 1, focusing instead on word recognition. Balanced comprehension instruction can and should begin in the early primary years (Pressley, El-Dinary, et al., 1992), with development of word recognition skills part of the comprehension instructional balance. That many college students do not use the most sophisticated of comprehension strategies (e.g., Cordón & Day, 1996), however, makes obvious that there needs to be much thinking about how comprehension instruction can be more universal and more effective in the elementary schoolplace.

Having thought about comprehension instruction throughout our research careers, we found ourselves depressed in 1998, the year the first edition of this book appeared. One reason was that so much of the reaction to the book focused entirely on what it had to say about the phonics versus whole-language debate and beginning reading. There was hardly a mention about what the book had to say about comprehension instruction. (One reason for a considerably longer comprehension chapter in the second edition and this, the third edition, is an attempt to draw greater attention to comprehension.) A second reason for our concern about comprehension instruction in 1998 was that a report from the National Research Council on reading instruction appeared, *Preventing Reading Difficulties in Young Children* (Snow, Burns, & Griffin, 1998). Much was said about word-level processes in that volume, and little was said about higher-order comprehension strategies, with the exception that reciprocal teaching received a prominent mention, perhaps reflecting that one of the developers of reciprocal teaching was on the National Research Council panel. Third, near the end of 1998, we attended the National Reading Conference. The then co-directors of the Center for the Improvement of Early Reading Achievement (CIERA, based at the University of Michigan) approached us to let us know that they were seeing in grade-4 classrooms what we had seen (Pressley et al., 1998)—very little comprehension instruction (subsequently published in Taylor, Pearson, Clark, & Walpole, 2000). By the end of 1998, we felt that there was a real need for greater attention to teaching students how to comprehend.

As we revised this chapter for this third edition, we felt that others also believe as we do that comprehension instruction needs much attention. In early 2001, RAND released a report intended to encourage a much greater federal research agenda with respect to comprehension. *Reading for Understanding: Towards an R&D Program in Reading Comprehension* (RAND Reading Study Group, 2001; see also Sweet & Snow, 2003) called for increased study of all the directions in comprehension instruction covered in this chapter. It also called for work on teacher education and professional development that might stimulate more comprehension instruction in schools. More recently, the Carnegie Corporation of New York has also urged expansion of attention to comprehension instruction beginning in the upper elementary grades (Biancarosa & Snow, 2004).

We very much believe that educating teachers about the nature of comprehension is critical if better comprehension instruction is to occur in schools, and hence the next section is concerned with an important hypothesis about how to jump-start the teaching of comprehension in elementary schools, one that begins with professional development of the teachers themselves.

MOSAIC OF THOUGHT AND TEACHERS REFLECTING ON THEIR OWN COMPREHENSION

Ellin O. Keene and Susan Zimmermann (1997) in their *Mosaic of Thought: Teaching Comprehension in a Reader's Workshop* took an interesting perspective. They felt that an important first step to being a good teacher of comprehension strategies is to become a user of comprehension strategies! They argued that teachers benefit from learning about comprehension strategies and attempting to use the strategies in their own reading. In particular, by using comprehension strategies, the teachers come to understand the positive effects of using comprehension strategies.

We think this is an important insight because teachers often resist teaching comprehension strategies. A particularly illuminating analysis was provided by Pamela Beard El-Dinary in her dissertation study (see Pressley & El-Dinary, 1997). She studied seven teachers as they attempted to become transactional strategies instruction teachers over the course of a school year. What became apparent early in the year was that learning to be a strategies instruction teacher was very challenging. For example, some of the teachers felt that transactional strategies instruction conflicted with their own beliefs about reading and teaching of reading. Some felt it conflicted with the whole-language methods they learned in their teacher education courses (i.e., strategies instruction seemed too teacher-directed). Some teachers felt that comprehension strategies instruction and use of comprehension strategies during reading group sessions took too much time, with the result that students were not reading nearly as many books and stories in reading groups. Also, there were teachers who had problems with the many interpretations emanating from reading group discussions that were strategies-driven: Some permitted any interpretation that emerged, regardless of whether it seemed consistent with the reading, and others seemed uncomfortable with anything except standard interpretations. By the end of the year of observations, only two of the seven teachers were committed comprehension strategies instruction teachers. Pressley and El-Dinary's (1997) work made clear that comprehension strategies instruction, or at least the transactional strategies instructional approach, is not for every teacher.

Keene and Zimmermann's (1997) book is intended to be used by groups of teachers to learn about comprehension strategies, one strategy at a time, with teachers trying the strategies out and sharing their experiences with one another. Unfortunately, Keene and Zimmermann (1997) do not provide a clear test of their proposal: that teachers can learn to be strategic by following their text, concomitantly become committed to being comprehension strategies teachers, and then teach students to use comprehension strategies so that their reading improves. Even so, we are impressed by the number of teachers who have told us about their positive experiences with the approach advocated by Keene and Zimmermann (1997). We hope there is a definitive test soon.

There needs to be such a test, for it is additionally obvious to us, based on work more recent than Pressley and El-Dinary's (1997) study, that learning to be a comprehension strategies instruction teacher is painfully difficult for many teachers. In the last year, Hilden and Pressley (in press) studied two middle school groups as teachers attempted to improve their reading comprehension instruction through professional development (monthly or more frequent meetings, book groups, and coaching by staff members). While many teachers improved their instruction over the course of a year, each teacher had a set of challenges. For example, some struggled with classroom management issues when working with small groups that they had not previously faced when teaching whole-class lessons. Also, many of the teachers had to radically change the way they thought about reading comprehension before they could even begin to teach it differently! That is, comprehension strategies instruction was difficult for some teachers to understand, as it was very different from anything they had taught previously.

Many teachers were not confident that they could teach comprehension strategies. These teachers often worried they would fail and had difficulty seeing how the approach would fit with the rest of the curriculum. In contrast, some teachers dropped out of the professional development program within the first month at one site, because they felt that they already knew enough of about how to teach reading comprehension effectively in their classrooms, even though observations of their teaching did not confirm this. Finally, some teachers saw the students as a challenge. At one of the middle schools, the teachers complained that their students thought the goal of reading was only to read fast rather than to understand and appreciate a piece of literature, whereas other teachers feared their weaker students would not be able to carry out the strategies. However daunting these challenges, many of the teachers felt the goal of improving comprehension instruction was well worth their time, effort, and thought. We note that other researchers have also reported considerable challenges in coaching teachers to undertake competent and confident teaching of comprehension strategies (e.g., Deshler & Schumaker, 1993; Klingner et al., 2004; Klingner, Vaughn, Hughes, & Arguelles, 1999; Pressley & El-Dinary, 1997).

Since the first edition of this volume, several other valuable resources for teachers who wish to improve their comprehension instruction have appeared. Miller's *Reading with Meaning: Teaching Comprehension in the Primary Grades* (2002), Blachowicz and Ogle's *Reading Comprehension: Strategies for Independent Learners* (2001), and Harvey and Goudvis's *Strategies That Work: Teaching Comprehension to Enhance Understanding* (2000) deserve serious study by any teacher who wants to teach comprehension strategies. All three volumes have much to say that is relevant to balanced comprehension instruction, as considered in the last section of this chapter, although the Blachowicz and Ogle (2001) volume seemed most comprehensive to us.

As we recommend such volumes, we also point out that the effective strategies instruction that has been validated (and reviewed in this chapter) is pretty simple—direct teacher explanations and modeling followed by scaffolding of a few strategies. Such instruction typically has not included all the bells and whistles showing up in the many how-to-do-comprehension strategies-instruction manuals entering the marketplace, bells and whistles inferred from teacher experiences by the authors of these manuals. Our predilection is for teachers to try the simple version and look to these volumes for suggestions very selectively—remembering always that comprehension strategies instruction is about students using strategies on their own, not about the completion of worksheets or worksheet proxies of any kinds (e.g., written reports of predictions, images, questions, clarifications, summaries occurring during reading). Such proxies fill these manuals! Make your comprehension instruction about students practicing the strategies as mental processes, modeling for other students as they do so, talking together about the strategies being used during actual reading.

WHAT SHOULD STUDENTS BE READING?

We have little doubt what students should be reading. Beginning reading students should be reading real literature and informational texts, along with some decodable texts. Whenever we visit classrooms where achievement is clearly high, the students often are reading authentic books consistent with the whole-language perspective that literature-based instruction is best (Morrow & Gambrell, 2000, 2001). Nonetheless, many schools still use basal programs, but today's basal programs are filled with real literature and informational readings. These basal resources also come with decodable books, with many teachers adding even more decodables in their classroom libraries over and above the ones that come with any program. Indeed, it is very hard to be in a primary-grade classroom where students are not reading a mix of trade books and decodables, with the decodables fading into the background as students become better at recognizing words.

During the past several years, we have acquired copies of all of the Scott Foresman readers of the 1950s and 1960s, the much-maligned Dick-and-Jane books, although Dick and Jane were players only in the first year and a half of schooling. They disappeared during the first semester of second grade. Real literature constituted many of the stories in the readers from grade 2 onward. For example, that first-semester second-grade reader included a unit of folk tales. Subsequent volumes included many more folk tales but also stories by well-known American authors as well as a number of selections that connected to major historical themes. Even so, very little was made of the literature, as compared to current standards. For example, there were no author studies. Although the teacher's manuals often encouraged discussion of alternative interpretations of stories, that certainly was not a main emphasis in the pedagogy. The hallmark of the "Dick-and-Jane" era was that words were introduced gradually, with students not encountering stories filled with unfamiliar vocabulary. In contrast, a hallmark of most trade books is that they often include vocabulary that their readers probably did not encounter before and may not encounter again for some time. At least in the primary-grade classrooms we inhabited in the 1950s through 1970s, there were lots of trade books being read by many children, so Dick and Jane was not the whole story.

We note especially that many contemporary primary classrooms have bins and bins of books that are rated using a scheme from Reading Recovery. Good teachers everywhere are encouraging students to move through the bins to progressively more complex books. What an absolutely great way to assure that all the children in a primary classroom are reading within their own zone of proximal development!

The various types of books that can be included in the primary-level classroom are inspiring new debates (Hiebert & Martin, 2001), however. For example, how many times must a child encounter a word in order to learn it as a sight word? Assuming that the answer is somewhere between 5 and 50, doesn't that mean the child should be reading quite a few books filled with repeated words—quite a few leveled books? Does it make sense to ask a child to read a book containing words that include sounds not already covered during systematic phonics instruction—a trade book? That said, there are reasons for concern about reading so many decodables. If the child came away with little worthwhile world knowledge from reading about Dick and Jane's neighborhood, think about the little bit of knowledge that follows from reading about how "Pat and Mat sat on a fat cat" and about why "Ted's bed is red." So, there is a probable downside. In addition, since the goal is reading real books—not decodables—shouldn't students be spending time working on decoding words in real texts?

Although we agree with Elfrieda H. Hiebert (Hiebert & Martin, 2001), who believes there is a need for a great deal of research on the consequences of various mixes of text types, we have been impressed with the best controlled test to date of the effects of reading decodables versus other types of texts on young children's reading—with no difference in reading outcomes detected in that experiment as a function of the type of text read (Jenkins, Peyton, Sanders, & Vadasy, 2004). Reading of both real literature and not-so-real literature that is definitely within reach of the child's word recognition skills (Hiebert & Martin, 2001) is an American tradition, regardless of the supposed reading program emphasis. We expect primary students to continue to read a mix of book types for the foreseeable future.

CONCLUDING REFLECTIONS

We have spent a great deal of time in elementary classrooms during the past 8 years. Most classrooms we have seen have included a great deal of teacher direction and student passivity. There is very little teaching of students to be self-regulated comprehenders. There is a great deal of reading, the implicit theory being that if children simply read, read, and read some more, they will become skilled comprehenders. Massive reading does increase fluency, and thus there is something to be said for having students read a great deal in order to increase comprehension. But simply reading more does not accomplish the whole job of developing a self-regulated comprehender.

Good comprehension is not just word-level processing. It involves abstracting the big ideas in a text—the macrostructure, as Kintsch and van Dijk (1978) refer to it. Sometimes good readers construct images capturing the big ideas expressed in a text as well as the critical details. The ideas expressed in the text are understood in terms of and related to prior knowledge by the skilled reader. There is no reason to believe that elementary students naturally discover that they should use such processes to understand a text. Indeed, quite the contrary: There is substantial evidence that many students can make it to college without learning the active comprehension processes used by skilled readers (Pressley & Afflerbach, 1995). More positively, there is substantial evidence that elementary students can learn to comprehend actively: They can learn to predict, question, make mental images, seek to clarify confusions, and summarize as they read.

Consider some of the grade-4, -5, and -6 classrooms we have studied in recent years that were headed by teachers who decided to emphasize comprehension and to teach their students to use comprehension strategies consistently. All of the evidence pertaining to the effectiveness of this approach is positive. Beyond the numbers, however, there is a real excitement in classes in which comprehension processing is being taught. By the end of the year, small groups of children will be using the strategies while they do pair reading. When individual children retell stories they have read, it is not just a spitting back of information in the text; rather, it is interpretive, reflecting the cognitive activities that occurred during reading.

Why is such instruction not more common? For one thing, many teachers do not understand comprehension as active reading—nor as active predicting, questioning, imagining, seeking clarifications, summarizing, and interpreting. One of the most interesting reflections that we have heard again and again from teachers who have become teachers of comprehension strategies is that they did not really know how to read actively until they learned about the comprehension strategies model and began to teach students to use such comprehension strategies.

Another reason that this form of teaching is not more common is that it leads to classroom interactions that are very different from the norm. In typical classrooms, teachers control most interactions, asking questions that students then answer. The goal with comprehension strategies instruction, however, is to teach students to take over their own reading and thinking. When teachers and students read texts together, the teacher is not asking questions but rather participating in a real conversation. The students make predictions, talk about the questions that occur to them as they read, report the images they get during reading, discuss parts of the text that are hard to understand, and generate interpretations, including summary interpretations. After the early stages of comprehension strategies instruction—that is, after the teacher is no longer introducing the strategies—the teacher's role in the conversation is limited to prompting students to be active in deciding how they might process the text at this point. Throughout classroom life, the teacher is also supposed to model strategies use to make clear to students how the comprehension strategies the students are learning can be usefully adapted across many different types of reading. Such mental modeling is not always easy for many teachers (e.g., Hilden & Pressley, in press; Pressley & El-Dinary, 1997).

A final reason that comprehension strategies teaching is not more widespread is that constructivist educators, including many whole-language types, send the message that processes that are taught rather than discovered are not natural strategies. Our reply is that the explanations and mental modeling the teacher provides are just a starting point, and that students actively discover much about the usefulness and adaptability of comprehension strategies as they attempt to use them. From our perspective, good teaching is constructivist in that it sets students to exploring in productive directions. As students in transactional strategies instruction classrooms use strategies together, there is plenty of constructive discovery going on (Pressley, Harris, & Marks, 1992). Long-term strategies use seems to result in individual students internalizing active cognitive processing during reading; the proof of the pudding is better reading when measured in a number of ways across studies. There is much to be said for encouraging many more teachers to define their elementary classrooms as ones in which students learn to use comprehension strategies constructively, practicing them with other students with the many types of reading that can be encountered in the elementary curriculum.

Despite the reluctance of the constructivist educators explicitly to teach strategies, researchers who have been impressed with the data to date continue to explore the value of teaching strategies to students, with, for example, new basic research efforts to understand the benefits of teaching young children to construct mental images as they process text (Glenberg, Gutierrez, Levin, Japuntich, & Kaschak, 2004). In addition, given that, with increasing age during the elementary years, there is increasing emphasis on learning from informational texts, it is heartening that there are renewed efforts to determine how to teach students to get the most out of informational texts, with Bonnie J. F. Meyer's group at Penn State leading the way in this endeavor, producing impressive effects (Meyer et al., 2002). In particular, the Penn State group is exploring how to teach students to analyze expository text over the web, a potentially important direction in figuring out how to teach students to do something we have known to be powerful for some time—that is, to use graphic organizers to organize information in an exposition, to pay attention to sequences of events, to make comparisons, to isolate causes and effects, and to analyze problem-and-solution approaches (see, for example, Almasi, 2003, Chap. 5, for a review). In short, researchers are turning their attention to ever more powerful ways to teach the basic comprehension processes, and that probably will permit more powerful insights in the near future about how to teach students to use comprehension strategies more completely.

At this point in the lecture that inspired this book, M. P. would always ask the audience to think back to the expert reading described in Chapter 2 and ask them, "Isn't that what you want for your students?" He would continue:

> "If you start to teach your students to read that way, something wonderful is going to happen to you. You are going to become a more active reader yourself. But there's more! As you read great stories and books with your students, you are going to experience myriad student responses that you never dreamed possible. If you do not believe it, read an article by Rachel Brown and Lynn Coy-Ogan (1993) that discusses the differing interpretations of Maurice Sendak's *Where the Wild Things Are* [1963] offered by three different groups of students in Lynn's classes. Your classroom is going to become more interesting for everyone in it, including you. It will become like the language arts classes in middle school and high school that produce high language arts achievement" (see Applebee et al., 2003).

SUMMARY

1. Similar to the primary grades, instruction in grades 4 and 5 involves a balancing of skills instruction and more authentic reading and writing. Although there are many commonalities across grade-4 and -5 classrooms, there are also many optional emphases, with each classroom seeming to have a core of practices that define its emphasis.

2. Although development of comprehension ability is a widely agreed-upon goal of literacy instruction, it rarely is offered as systematically as it could be in the elementary grades. This is especially striking in the early 21st century, given the many different lines of evidence that support the teaching of comprehension strategies to elementary students.

3. Reciprocal teaching is perhaps the best known of the comprehension-instructional efforts developed and evaluated by researchers. This approach consists of students learning to use predicting, questioning, seeking clarifi-

cation, and summarization by working in small groups, with the members of the group taking turns leading the group through the strategic processes. We think reciprocal teaching was an important first step in teaching students a repertoire of comprehension strategies, but it was no more than that, as more flexible long-term teaching has now been developed and validated by educators and researchers.

4. Transactional strategies instruction begins with teacher explanations and modeling of strategies, with scaffolded student practice in strategies application following over a long period of time. Much of the practice takes place in small reading groups, which involve a great deal of student conversations, rich in student reports of how they are applying strategies in their interpretations of texts being read by the group. Long-term participation in such groups is intended to produce internalization of the strategic processes. To date, the consistently positive effects of transactional strategies instruction demonstrated in validations are consistent with the interpretation that such instruction is producing such internalization. The record of the positive effects of transactional strategies instruction on standardized tests in well-controlled studies is quite striking, but so are the qualitative benefits produced by such instruction.

5. The most common strategies included in transactional strategies instruction are (1) predicting, (2) questioning, (3) constructing mental images representing text content, (4) seeking clarifications, (5) responding to the text based on prior knowledge, (6) summarizing, and (7) interpreting. Young readers who participate in such instruction are being taught to use the comprehension processes reported by exceptionally skilled readers, as detailed in Chapter 2.

6. Balanced reading instruction is also balanced comprehension instruction. It involves the development of word recognition skills, vocabulary, world knowledge (e.g., through extensive reading), and the teaching of comprehension strategies—including strategies that encourage use of prior knowledge, the reading of diverse types of text, and diverse tasks. Although those interested in comprehension have focused more on comprehension strategies instruction than on other ways of developing comprehension competence, good comprehension instruction is much, much more than the teaching of comprehension strategies. There is much more that can be done to increase students' comprehension than what many teachers are now doing.

7. An interesting contemporary hypothesis is that an important first step in becoming a good teacher of comprehension is to become a good comprehender by learning to use the strategies that good comprehenders use. This hypothesis deserves serious study.

8. Young children read diverse text types as part of beginning-reading instruction, typically a mix of real literature and decodables. This is probably a good thing.

REFERENCES

Adams, M. J. (1990). *Beginning to read.* Cambridge, MA: Harvard University Press.

Almasi, J. F. (2003). *Teaching strategic processes in reading.* New York: Guilford Press.

Almasi, J. F., & Gambrell, L. B. (1994). *Sociocognitive conflict in peer-led and teacher-led discussions of literature* (Reading Research Report No. 12). Athens, GA, and College Park, MD: National Reading Research Center.

Anderson, R. C., & Freebody, P. (1981). Vocabulary knowledge. In J. T. Guthrie (Ed.), *Comprehension and teaching: Research reviews* (pp. 77–117). Newark, DE: International Reading Association.

Anderson, R. C., & Hidde, J. L. (1971). Imagery and sentence learning. *Journal of Educational Psychology, 62,* 526–530.

Anderson, R. C., & Pearson, P. D. (1984). A schema-theoretic view of basic processes in reading. In P. D. Pearson (Ed.), *Handbook of reading research* (pp. 255–291). New York: Longman.

Anderson, V. (1992). A teacher development project in transactional strategy instruction for teachers of severely reading-disabled adolescents. *Teaching and Teacher Education, 8,* 391–403.

Anderson, V., & Roit, M. (1993). Planning and implementing collaborative strategy instruction for delayed readers in grades 6–10. *Elementary School Journal, 94,* 121–137.

Applebee, A. N., Langer, J. A., Nystrand, M., & Gamoran, A. (2003). Discussion-based approaches to developing understanding: Classroom instruction and student performance in middle and high school English. *American Educational Research Journal, 40,* 685–730.

Beach, R., & Hynds, S. (1991). Research on response to literature. In R. Barr, M. L. Kamil, P. Mosenthal, & P. D. Pearson (Eds.), *Handbook of reading research* (Vol. 2, pp. 453–489). White Plains, NY: Longman.

Beck, I. L., Perfetti, C. A., & McKeown, M. G. (1982). Effects of long-term vocabulary instruction on lexical access and reading comprehension. *Journal of Educational Psychology, 74,* 506–521.

Becker, W. C. (1977). Teaching reading and language to the disadvantaged: What we have learned from field research. *Harvard Educational Review, 47,* 518–543.

Bell, R. Q. (1968). A reinterpretation of the direction of effects in studies of socialization. *Psychological Review, 75,* 81–95.

Biancarosa, G., & Snow, C. E. (2004). *Reading next—a vision for action and research in middle and high school literacy: A report from Carnegie Corporation of New York.* Washington DC: Alliance for Excellent Education.

Biemiller, A., & Slonim, N. (2001). Estimating root word vocabulary growth in normative and advantaged populations: Evidence for a common sequence of vocabulary acquisition. *Journal of Educational Psychology, 93,* 498–520.

Blachowicz, C. L. Z., & Fisher, P. (2000). Vocabulary instruction. In M. L. Kamil, P. B. Mosenthal, P. D. Pearson, & R. Barr (Eds.), *Handbook of reading research* (Vol. 3, pp. 503–523). Mahwah, NJ: Erlbaum.

Blachowicz, C., & Ogle. D. (2001). *Reading comprehension: Strategies for independent learners*. New York: Guilford Press.

Borkowski, J. G., Levers, S., & Gruenenfelder, T. M. (1976). Transfer of mediational strategies in children: The role of activity and awareness during strategy acquisition. *Child Development, 47,* 779–786.

Brown, A. L., & Day, J. D. (1983). Macrorules for summarizing texts: The development of expertise. *Journal of Verbal Learning and Verbal Behavior, 22,* 1–14.

Brown, A. L., & Palincsar, A. S. (1989). Guided, cooperative learning and individual knowledge acquisition. In L. B. Resnick (Ed.), *Knowing, learning, and instruction: Essays in honor of Robert Glaser* (pp. 393–451). Hillsdale, NJ: Erlbaum.

Brown, R., & Coy-Ogan, L. (1993). The evolution of transactional strategies instruction in one teacher's classroom. *Elementary School Journal, 94,* 221–233.

Brown, R., Pressley, M., Van Meter, P., & Schuder, T. (1996). A quasi-experimental validation of transactional strategies instruction with low-achieving second grade readers. *Journal of Educational Psychology, 88,* 18–37.

Carlisle, J. F., Fleming, J. E., & Gudbrandsen, B. (2000). Incidental word learning in science classes. *Contemporary Educational Psychology, 25,* 184–211.

Cavanaugh, J. C., & Borkowski, J. G. (1979). The metamemory–memory "connection": Effects of strategy training and maintenance. *Journal of General Psychology, 101,* 161–174.

Cazden, C. B. (1988). *Classroom discourse: The language of teaching and learning.* Portsmouth, NH: Heinemann.

Chall, J. S. (1983). *Stages of reading development.* New York: McGraw-Hill.

Clark, J. M., & Paivio, A. (1991). Dual coding theory and education. *Educational Psychology Review, 3,* 149–210.

Clay, M. M. (1991). *Becoming literate: The construction of inner control.* Portsmouth, NH: Heinemann.

Collins, C. (1991). Reading instruction that increases thinking abilities. *Journal of Reading, 34,* 510–516.

Cordón, L. A., & Day, J. D. (1996). Strategy use on standardized reading comprehension tests. *Journal of Educational Psychology, 88,* 288–295.

d'Anna, C. A., Zechmeister, E. B., & Hall, J. W. (1991). Toward a meaningful definition of vocabulary size. *Journal of Reading Behavior, 23,* 109–122.

Datnow, A., Borman, G., & Stringfield, S. (2000). School reform through a highly specified curriculum: Implementation and effects of the core knowledge sequence. *Elementary School Journal, 101,* 167–191.

Deshler, D. D., & Schumaker, J. B. (1993). Strategy mastery by at-risk students: Not a simple matter. *The Elementary School Journal, 94,* 153–167.

Doctorow, M., Wittrock, M. C., & Marks, C. (1978). Generative processes in reading comprehension. *Journal of Educational Psychology, 70,* 109–118.

Dreher, M. J. (2002). Children searching and using information text: A critical part of comprehension. In C. C. Block & M. Pressley (Eds.), *Comprehension instruction: Research-based best practices* (pp. 289–304). New York: Guilford Press.

Duffy, G. G. (2003). *Explaining reading: A resource for teaching concepts, skills, and strategies.* New York: Guilford Press.

Duffy, G. G., & Roehler, L. R. (1989). Why strategy instruction is so difficult and what we need to do about it. In C. B. McCormick, G. Miller, & M. Pressley

(Eds.), *Cognitive strategy research: From basic research to educational applications* (pp. 133–154). New York: Springer-Verlag.

Duffy, G., Roehler, L., & Herrmann, G. (1988). Modeling mental processes helps poor readers become strategic readers. *Reading Teacher, 41,* 762–767.

Duffy, G. G., Roehler, L. R., Sivan, E., Rackliffe, G., Book, C., Meloth, M., Vavrus, L. G., Wesselman, R., Putnam, J., & Bassiri, D. (1987). Effects of explaining the reasoning associated with using reading strategies. *Reading Research Quarterly, 22,* 347–368.

Duke, N. K. (2000). 3.6 minutes per day: The scarcity of informational texts in first grade. *Reading Research Quarterly, 35,* 202–224.

Durkin, D. (1978/79). What classroom observations reveal about reading comprehension instruction. *Reading Research Quarterly, 15,* 481–533.

El-Dinary, P. B., Pressley, M., & Schuder, T. (1992). Becoming a strategies teacher: An observational and interview study of three teachers learning transactional strategies instruction. In C. Kinzer & D. Leu (Eds.), *Literacy research: Theory and practice: Views from many perspectives. Forty-first yearbook of the National Reading Conference* (pp. 453–462). Chicago: National Reading Conference.

Flavell, J. H. (1977). *Cognitive development.* Englewood Cliffs, NJ: Prentice–Hall.

Flavell, J. H., & Wellman, H. M. (1977). Metamemory. In R. V. Kail & J. W. Hagen (Eds.), *Perspectives on the development of memory and cognition* (pp. 3–33). Hillsdale, NJ: Erlbaum.

Flower, L., Stein, V., Ackerman, J., Kantz, M. J., McCormick, K., & Peck, W. C. (1990). *Reading to write: Exploring a cognitive and social process.* New York: Oxford University Press.

Forrest-Pressley, D. L., & Gilles, L. A. (1983). Children's flexible use of strategies during reading. In M. Pressley & J. R. Levin (Eds.), *Cognitive strategy research: Educational applications* (pp. 133–156). New York: Springer-Verlag.

Gaskins, I. W., Anderson, R. C., Pressley, M., Cunicelli, E. A., & Satlow, E. (1993). Six teachers' dialogue during cognitive process instruction. *Elementary School Journal, 93,* 277–304.

Gersten, R., Fuchs, L. S., Williams, J. P., & Baker, S. (2001). Teaching reading comprehension strategies to students with learning disabilities. *Review of Educational Research, 71,* 279–320.

Glenberg, A. M., Gutierrez, T., Levin, J. R, , Japuntich, A., & Kaschack, M. P. (2004). Activity and imagined activity can enhance young children's reading comprehension. *Journal of Educational Psychology, 96,* 424–436.

Gough, P. B. (1983). Context, form, and interaction. In K. Rayner (Ed.), *Eye movements in reading* (pp. 203–211). New York: Academic Press.

Gough, P. B. (1984). Word recognition. In P. D. Pearson (Ed.), *Handbook of reading research* (pp. 225–254). New York: Longman.

Gough, P. B., & Tunmer, W. E. (1986). Decoding, reading, and reading disability. *Remedial and Special Education, 7,* 6–10.

Guthrie, J. T., Schafer, W., Wang, Y. Y., & Afflerbach, P. (1993). *Influences of instruction on amount of reading: An empirical exploration of social, cognitive, and instructional indicators* (Reading Research Report No. 3). Athens, GA, and College Park, MD: National Reading Research Center.

Guthrie, J. T., Wigfield, A., Metsala, J. L., & Cox, K. E. (1999). Motivational and cognitive predictors of text comprehension and reading amount. *Scientific Studies of Reading, 3,* 231–256.

Hacker, D. J., & Tenent, A. (2002). Implementing reciprocal teaching in the classroom: Overcoming obstacles and making modifications. *Journal of Educational Psychology, 94,* 699–718.

Harmon, J. M. (1998). Constructing word meanings: Strategies and perceptions of four middle school learners. *Journal of Literacy Research, 30,* 561–599.

Harris, A. J., & Sipay, E. R. (1990). *How to increase reading ability: A guide to developmental and remedial methods.* New York: Longman.

Harvey, S., & Goudvis, A. (2000). *Strategies that work: Teaching comprehension to enhance understanding.* York, ME: Stenhouse.

Hiebert, E. H., & Martin, L. A. (2001). The texts of beginning reading instruction. In S. B. Neuman & D. K. Dickinson (Eds.), *Handbook of early literacy research* (pp. 361–376). New York: Guilford Press.

Hilden, K. R., & Pressley, M. (in press). Stories of obstacles and success: Teachers' experiences in professional development of reading comprehension instruction. *Reading and Writing Quarterly.*

Hirsch, E. D., Jr. (1987). *Cultural literacy: What every American needs to know.* Boston: Houghton Mifflin.

Hutchins, E. (1991). The social organization of distributed cognition. In L. Resnick, J. M. Levine, & S. D. Teasley (Eds.), *Perspectives on socially shared cognition* (pp. 283–307). Washington, DC: American Psychological Association.

Isakson, R. L., & Miller, J. W. (1976). Sensitivity to syntactic and semantic cues in good and poor comprehenders. *Journal of Educational Psychology, 68,* 787–792.

Jenkins, J. R., Peyton, J. A., Sanders, E. A., & Vadasy, P. F. (2004). Effects of reading decodable texts in supplemental first-grade tutoring. *Scientific Studies of Reading, 8,* 53–85.

Johns, J. C., & McNamara, L. P. (1980). The SQ3R study technique: A forgotten research target. *Journal of Reading, 23,* 705–708.

Keene, E. O., & Zimmermann, S. (1997). *Mosaic of thought: Teaching comprehension in a reader's workshop.* Portsmouth, NH: Heinemann.

Kennedy, B. A., & Miller, D. J. (1976). Persistent use of verbal rehearsal as a function of information about its value. *Child Development, 47,* 566–569.

Kinnunen, R., Vaurus, M., & Niemi, P. (1998). Comprehension monitoring in beginning readers. *Scientific Studies in Reading, 2,* 353–375.

Kintsch, W., & van Dijk, T. A. (1978). Toward a model of discourse comprehension and production. *Psychological Review, 85,* 363–394.

Klingner, J. K., Vaughn, S., Arguelles, M. E., Hughes, M. T., & Leftwich, S. A. (2004). Collaborative strategic reading: "Real-world" lessons from classroom teachers. *Remedial and Special Education, 25,* 291–302.

Klingner, J. K., Vaughn, S., Hughes, M. T., & Arguelles, M. E., (1999). Sustaining research-based practices in reading: A 3-year follow-up. *Remedial and Special Education, 20,* 263–274.

Klingner, J. K., Vaughn, S., & Schumm, J. S. (1998). Collaborative strategic reading during social studies in heterogeneous fourth-grade classrooms. *Elementary School Journal, 99,* 3–22.

Kohlberg, L., Yaeger, J., & Hjertholm, E. (1968). Private speech: Four studies and a review of theories. *Child Development, 39,* 691–736.

LaBerge, D., & Samuels, S. J. (1974). Toward a theory of automatic information processing in reading. *Cognitive Psychology, 6,* 293–323.

Levin, J. R. (1973). Inducing comprehension in poor readers: A test of a recent model. *Journal of Educational Psychology, 65,* 19–24.

Levin, J. R., & Pressley, M. (1981). Improving children's prose comprehension: Selected strategies that seem to succeed. In C. M. Santa & B. L. Hayes (Eds.), *Children's prose comprehension: Research and practice* (pp. 44–71). Newark, DE: International Reading Association.

Mandler, J. M. (1984). *Stories, scripts, and scenes: Aspects of schema theory.* Hillsdale, NJ: Erlbaum.

Marks, M., Pressley, M., in collaboration with Coley, J. D., Craig, S., Gardner, R., Rose, W., & DePinto, T. (1993). Teachers' adaptations of reciprocal teaching: Progress toward a classroom-compatible version of reciprocal teaching. *Elementary School Journal, 94,* 267–283.

Martin, V. L., & Pressley, M. (1991). Elaborative-interrogation effects depend on the nature of the question. *Journal of Educational Psychology, 83,* 113–119.

Mason, L. H. (2004). Explicit self-regulated strategy development versus reciprocal questioning: Effects on expository reading comprehension among struggling readers. *Journal of Educational Psychology, 96,* 283–296.

McKeown, M. G., Beck, I. L., Omanson, R. C., & Perfetti, C. A. (1983). The effects of long-term vocabulary instruction on reading comprehension: A replication. *Journal of Reading Behavior, 15,* 3–18.

McKeown, M. G., Beck, I. L., Omanson, R. C., & Pople, M. T. (1985). Some effects of the nature and frequency of vocabulary instruction on the knowledge and use of words. *Reading Research Quarterly, 20,* 522–535.

McKoon, G., & Ratcliff, R. (1992). Inference during reading. *Psychological Review, 99,* 440–466.

Mehan, H. (1979). *Social organization in the classroom.* Cambridge, MA: Harvard University Press.

Meichenbaum, D. (1977). *Cognitive behavior modification.* New York: Plenum.

Meichenbaum, D., & Asarnow, J. (1979). Cognitive–behavioral modification and metacognitive development: Implications for the classroom. In P. C. Kendall & S. D. Hollon (Eds.), *Cognitive–behavioral interventions* (pp. 11–35). New York: Academic Press.

Meichenbaum, D., & Goodman, J. (1969). Reflection-impulsivity and verbal control of motor behavior. *Child Development, 40,* 785–797.

Metsala, J., & Ehri, L. (Eds.). (1998). *Word recognition in beginning reading.* Mahwah, NJ: Erlbaum.

Meyer, J. F., Middlemiss, W., Theodorou, E., Brezinski, K. L., McDougall, J., & Bartlett, B. J. (2002). Effects of structure strategy instruction delivered to fifth grade children using the Internet with and without the aid of older adult tutors. *Journal of Educational Psychology, 94,* 486–519.

Miller, D. (2002). *Reading with meaning: Teaching comprehension in the primary grades.* York, ME: Stenhouse.

Miller, G. A. (1956). The magical number seven, plus-or-minus two: Some limits on our capacity for processing information. *Psychological Review, 63*, 81–97.

Miller, G. A., & Gildea, P. (1987). How children learn words. *Scientific American, 257*(3), 94–99.

Morrow, L. M., & Gambrell, L. B. (2000). Literature-based reading instruction. In M. L. Kamil, P. B. Mosenthal, P. D. Pearson, & R. Barr (Eds.), *Handbook of reading research* (Vol. 3, pp. 563–586). Mahwah, NJ: Erlbaum.

Morrow, L. M., & Gambrell, L. B. (2001). Literature-based instruction in the early years. In S. B. Neuman & D. K. Dickinson (Eds.), *Handbook of early literacy research* (pp. 348–360). New York: Guilford Press.

Nagy, W., & Anderson, R. (1984). How many words are there in printed school English? *Reading Research Quarterly, 19*, 304–330.

Nagy, W., Anderson, R., & Herman, P. (1987). Learning word meanings from context during normal reading. *American Educational Research Journal, 24*, 237–270.

Nagy, W. E., & Scott, J. A. (2000). Vocabulary processes. In M. Kamil, P. B. Mosenthal, P. D. Pearson, & R. Barr (Eds.) (2000). *Handbook of reading research* (Vol. 3, pp. 269–284). Mahwah, NJ: Erlbaum.

Oczkus, L. D. (2003). *Reciprocal teaching at work: Strategies for improving reading comprehension.* Newark, DE: International Reading Association.

Ogle, D., & Blachowicz, C. L. Z. (2002). Beyond literature circles: Helping students to comprehend informational texts. In C. C. Block & M. Pressley (Eds.), *Comprehension instruction: Research-based best practices* (pp. 259–274). New York: Guilford Press.

Paivio, A. (1971). *Imagery and verbal processes.* New York: Holt, Rinehart & Winston.

Paivio, A. (1986). *Mental representations: A dual-coding approach.* New York: Oxford University Press.

Palincsar, A. S., & Brown, A. L. (1984). Reciprocal teaching of comprehension-fostering and monitoring activities. *Cognition and Instruction, 1*, 117–175.

Paris, S. G., Lipson, M. Y., & Wixson, K. K. (1983). Becoming a strategic reader. *Contemporary Educational Psychology, 8*, 293–316.

Patterson, C. J., & Mischel, W. (1976). Effects of temptation-inhibiting and task-facilitating plans on self-control. *Journal of Personality and Social Psychology, 33*, 209–217.

Pearson, P. D., & Fielding, L. (1991). Comprehension instruction. In R. Barr, M. L. Kamil, P. B. Mosenthal, & P. D. Pearson (Eds.), *Handbook of reading research* (Vol. 2, pp. 815–860). New York: Longman.

Pressley, G. M. (1976). Mental imagery helps eight-year-olds remember what they read. *Journal of Educational Psychology, 68*, 355–359.

Pressley, M. (1977). Imagery and children's learning: Putting the picture in developmental perspective. *Review of Educational Research, 47*, 586–622.

Pressley, M., & Afflerbach, P. (1995). *Verbal protocols of reading: The nature of constructively responsive reading.* Hillsdale, NJ: Erlbaum.

Pressley, M., Borkowski, J. G., & O'Sullivan, J. T. (1984). Memory strategy instruction is made of this: Metamemory and durable strategy use. *Educational Psychologist, 19*, 94–107.

Pressley, M., Borkowski, J. G., & O'Sullivan, J. T. (1985). Children's metamemory and the teaching of memory strategies. In D. L. Forrest-Pressley, G. E. MacKinnon, & T. G. Waller (Eds.), *Metacognition, cognition, and human performance* (pp. 111–153). New York: Academic Press.

Pressley, M., & El-Dinary, P. B. (1997). What we know about translating comprehension strategies instruction research into practice. *Journal of Learning Disabilities, 30,* 486–488.

Pressley, M., El-Dinary, P. B., Gaskins, I., Schuder, T., Bergman, J., Almasi, L., & Brown, R. (1992). Beyond direct explanation: Transactional instruction of reading comprehension strategies. *Elementary School Journal, 92,* 511–554.

Pressley, M., Gaskins, I. W., Cunicelli, E. A., Burdick, N. J., Schaub-Matt, M., Lee, D. S., & Powell, N. (1991). Strategy instruction at Benchmark School: A faculty interview study. *Learning Disability Quarterly, 14,* 19–48.

Pressley, M., Gaskins, I. W., Wile, D., Cunicelli, B., & Sheridan, J. (1991). Teaching literacy strategies across the curriculum: A case study at Benchmark School. In J. Zutell & S. McCormick (Eds.), *Learner factors/teacher factors: Issues in literacy research and instruction: Fortieth yearbook of the National Reading Conference* (pp. 219–228). Chicago: National Reading Conference.

Pressley, M., Harris, K. R., & Marks, M. B. (1992). But good strategy instructors are constructivists!! *Educational Psychology Review, 4,* 1–32.

Pressley, M., Heisel, B. E., McCormick, C. G., & Nakamura, G. V. (1982). Memory strategy instruction with children. In C. J. Brainerd & M. Pressley (Eds.), *Progress in cognitive development research: Vol. 2. Verbal processes in children* (pp. 125–159). New York: Springer-Verlag.

Pressley, M., & Hilden, K. R. (2006). Cognitive strategies. In D. Kuhn & R. Siegler (Eds.), W. Damon & R. Lerner (Series Eds.), *Handbook of child psychology, Vol. 2: Cognition, perception, and language* (6th ed.). Hoboken, NJ: Wiley.

Pressley, M., Wharton-McDonald, R., Hampston, J. M., & Echevarria, M. (1998). The nature of literacy instruction in ten grade-4 and -5 classrooms in upstate New York. *Scientific Studies of Reading, 2,* 159–191.

Pressley, M., Wood, E., Woloshyn, V. E., Martin, V., King, A., & Menke, D. (1992). Encouraging mindful use of prior knowledge: Attempting to construct explanatory answers facilitates learning. *Educational Psychologist, 27,* 91–110.

Pressley, M., Yokoi, L., Rankin, J., Wharton-McDonald, R., & Hampston, J. (1997). A survey of the instructional practices of grade-5 teachers nominated as effective in promoting literacy. *Scientific Studies of Reading, 1,* 145–160.

RAND Reading Study Group. (2001). *Reading for understanding: Towards an R&D program in reading comprehension.* Washington, DC: RAND Education.

Reynolds, P. L., & Symons, S. (2001). Motivational variables and children's text search. *Journal of Educational Psychology, 93,* 14–22.

Robinson, F. P. (1946). *Effective study* (2nd ed.). New York: Harper & Row.

Roehler, L. R., & Duffy, G. G. (1984). Direct explanation of comprehension processes. In G. G. Duffy, L. R. Roehler, & J. Mason (Eds.), *Comprehension instruction: Perspectives and suggestions* (pp. 265–280). New York: Longman.

Rosenblatt, L. M. (1938). *Literature as experience.* New York: Progressive Education Association.

Rosenblatt, L. M. (1978). *The reader, the text, the poem: The transactional theory of the literary work.* Carbondale, IL: Southern Illinois University Press.

Rosenshine, B., & Meister, C. (1994). Reciprocal teaching: A review of nineteen experimental studies. *Review of Educational Research, 64,* 479–530.

Rupley, W. H., Willson, V. L., & Nichols, W. D. (1998). Exploration of the developmental components contributing to elementary school children's reading comprehension. *Scientific Studies of Reading, 2,* 143–158.

Schwanenflugel, P. J., Stahl, S. A., & McFalls, E. L. (1997). Partial word knowledge and vocabulary growth during reading comprehension. *Journal of Literacy Research, 29,* 531–553.

Sendak, M. (1963). *Where the wild things are.* New York: Harper & Row.

Shankweiler, D., Lundquist, E., Katz, L., Stuebing, K. K., Fletcher, J. M., Brady, S., Fowler, A., Dreyer, L. G., Marchione, K. E., Shaywitz, S. E., & Shaywitz, B. A. (1999). Comprehension and decoding: Patterns of association in children with learning difficulties. *Scientific Studies of Reading, 3,* 69–94.

Short, E. J., & Ryan, E. B. (1984). Metacognitive differences between skilled and less-skilled readers: Remediating deficits through story grammar and attribution training. *Journal of Educational Psychology, 76,* 225–235.

Smith, C. B. (Moderator). (1994). *Whole language: The debate.* Bloomington, IN: ERIC/REC.

Snow, C. E., Burns, M. S., & Griffin, P. (1998). *Preventing reading difficulties in young children.* Washington DC: National Academy Press.

Spires, H. A., & Estes, T. H. (2002). Reading in web-based learning environments. In C. C. Block & M. Pressley (Eds.), *Comprehension instruction: Research-based best practices* (pp. 115–125). New York: Guilford Press.

Stein, N. L., & Glenn, C. G. (1979). An analysis of story comprehension in elementary school children. In R. O. Freedle (Eds.), *New directions in discourse processing* (Vol. 2, pp. 53–120). Norwood, NJ: Ablex.

Sternberg, R. J. (1987). Most vocabulary is learned from context. In M. G. McKeown & M. E. Curtis (Eds.), *The nature of vocabulary acquisition* (pp. 89–105). Hillsdale, NJ: Erlbaum.

Sweet, A. P., & Snow, C. E. (2003). *Rethinking reading comprehension.* New York: Guilford Press.

Symons, S., MacLatchy-Gaudet, H., Stone, T. D., & Reynolds, P. L. (2001). Strategy instruction for elementary students searching informational text. *Scientific Studies of Reading, 5,* 1–33.

Taylor, B. M. (1982). Text structure and children's comprehension and memory for expository material. *Journal of Educational Psychology, 74,* 323–340.

Taylor, B. M., Pearson, P. D., Clark, K., & Walpole, S. (2000). Effective schools and accomplished teachers: Lessons about primary-grade reading instruction in low-income schools. *Elementary School Journal, 101,* 121–165.

Tierney, R. J., Readence, J. E., & Dishner, E. K. (Eds.). (1980). *Reading strategies and practices: Guide for improving instruction.* Boston: Allyn & Bacon.

Van den Branden, K. (2000). Does negotiation of meaning promote reading comprehension?: A study of multilingual primary school classes. *Reading Research Quarterly, 35,* 426–443.

van Dijk, T. A., & Kintsch, W. (1983). *Strategies of discourse comprehension.* New York: Academic Press.

Vygotsky, L. S. (1962). *Thought and language.* Cambridge, MA: MIT Press.

Vygotsky, L. S. (1978). *Mind in society: The development of higher psychological processes.* Cambridge, MA: Harvard University Press.

Weaver, C. (1994). *Reading process and practice: From socio-psycholinguistics to whole language.* Portsmouth, NH: Heinemann.

Wilder, A. A., & Williams, J. P. (2001). Students with severe learning disabilities can learn higher-order comprehension skills. *Journal of Educational Psychology, 93,* 268–278.

Williams, J. P. (1993). Comprehension of students with and without learning disabilities: Identification of narrative themes and idiosyncratic text representations. *Journal of Educational Psychology, 85,* 631–641.

Williams, J. P. (2002). Using the theme scheme to improve story comprehension. In C. C. Block & M. Pressley (Eds.), *Comprehension instruction: Research-based best practices* (pp. 126–139). New York: Guilford Press.

Williams, J. P. (2003). Teaching text structure to improve reading comprehension. In H. L. Swanson, K. R. Harris, & S. Graham (Eds.), *Handbook of learning disabilities* (pp. 293–305). New York: Guilford Press.

Williams, J. P., Lauer, K. D., Hall, K. M., Lord, K. M., Gugga, S. S., Bak, S-J., Jacobs, P. R., & deCani, J. S. (2002). Teaching elementary school students to identify story themes. *Journal of Educational Psychology, 94,* 235–248.

Wood, E., Pressley, M., & Winne, P. H. (1990). Elaborative interrogation effects on children's learning of factual content. *Journal of Educational Psychology, 82,* 741–748.

Wozniak, R. (1972). Verbal regulation of motor behavior: Soviet research and non-Soviet replications. *Human Development, 15,* 13–57.

CHAPTER 10

Writing

with MARY M. JUZWIK

WHY WRITING MATTERS FOR READING

Those concerned about reading instruction should also care about writing. As discussed in the preceding two chapters, effective elementary literacy instruction produces strong student writing. The theoretical and empirical connections between reading and writing have been understood for a long time (Fitzgerald & Shanahan, 2000; Shanahan & Tierney, 1990). For example, both involve graphophonics (i.e., processing letters, syllables, words), both require knowledge of syntax, and both require knowledge of the characteristics of text. Given that writing is not included in interventions funded by No Child Left Behind (2002), it is especially notable that early writing experiences during kindergarten positively affect beginning phonological competencies, including phonological awareness (Craig, 2003; Frijters, Barron, & Brunello, 2000; Silva & Martins, 2002). Writing promotes reading development early on and should be part of the primary-grade morning, as it is in the very best primary-grade classrooms (see Chapter 8), and it continues to be associated with skilled reading in the upper elementary grades (e.g., Jenkins, Johnson, & Hileman, 2004).

Writing ability also stands out as an important variable predicting children's overall reading performance (Jenkins et al., 2004) on reading tests designed to elicit higher-order rather than recitation-level responses (e.g., Langer, 1987). Most educators recognize that writing is frequently required on assessments. This means that children's writing skills may mediate outcomes on high-stakes tests in reading as well as other subject areas. Indeed, the importance of writing proficiency for students is increasing. In autumn 2005, both the Scholastic Aptitude Test (SAT) and the American College Test (ACT) added sections requiring students to write an essay, with high point allocations to these sections.

At the same time, the reports by the National Commission on Writing in America's Schools and Colleges (2003), and the *National Assessment of Educational Progress* (Persky, Daane, & Jin, 2003) note emphatically that American students are not writing at adequate levels. At the 4th-, 8th-, and 12th-grade levels, very few students write well. There have also been very credible analyses that children's writing falls short in very specific ways (Harris & Graham, 1992; Langer, 1986; Scardamalia & Bereiter, 1986):

1. Children's writing mechanics—particularly the basics of handwriting and spelling—are often weak and not yet automatic. One result is that their short-term attention gets so consumed by mechanics that there is little capacity left over to devote to planning, drafting, and revising the messages they are trying to create.
2. Children often fail to establish a goal (a message) before attempting to write, although with increasing age there is increased understanding, continuing into high school (Langer, 1986, Chap. 3).
3. They often fail to generate enough content. They neither exhaustively search their own prior knowledge or knowledge sources in the world for content they could put into writing.
4. Children do a lot of "knowledge telling," which means that they write out what they want to say without organizing it in a way that makes the message clear to the intended readers or is especially well fitted to the writing context (Scardamalia & Bereiter, 1986).
5. Children frequently lack a clear vision of rhetorical purpose, audience, and appropriate genre for their writing, problems often linked to instructional contexts and writing assignments.
6. They too rarely revise, not working with the various bits and pieces of information until the message works well.

Despite the evidence in these reports, some myths remain that children have no need to be taught how to write. One example is the romantic myth of the "autonomous writer." Sitting alone in a garret, writing by "inspiration," the writer is thought to emerge with a brilliant finished product. Unfortunately, many students and teachers have been influenced by this notion. They falsely believe that, if they are not "naturally" talented as writers, then they will never be able to be good writers.

Another common myth, going back to Piagetian psychology, is that children before age 7 or 8 are egocentric and cannot take the perspective of others (e.g., a reading audience). However, there is much evidence that children are not quite so egocentric (for reviews, see Brainerd, 1978; Rosenthal & Zimmerman, 1978). Wollman-Bonilla (2001) confronted the egocentrism assumption directly, providing evidence that, at least some of the time, children as young as first graders can be quite sensitive to audience. Wollman-Bonilla examined the "family journals" of four grade-1 students, ranging in ability but representative of their Boston grade-1 classes. She particularly focused on messages written home to family members attempting to persuade them to do something. For such messages to be effective, the child had to provide some context information and make the case that the parent could and should do as the child requested (i.e., basically, these were requests about school, which the child knew firsthand but the parents did not). An egocentric child in the Piagetian sense should not be able to do this. The child would not recognize that the parent does not know what the child knows. Therefore, the child would not realize that the parent needs to be persuaded even if the child is convinced. In fact, the child messages in the Wollman-Bonilla study were filled with information making clear the contexts that motivated the requests (e.g., I have a book order). The child messages also explained why the parent should act (e.g., "I really would like the diary with lock. . . . If we can get it because of our trip to Florida, I won't be dipresst. . . . I could help pay by using my bank money"). Over the course of the year, the messages improved in every way, from better mechanics to greater persuasive impact. As we read the examples in this study, we were reminded of the writing we observed in the primary-grade classrooms of the most effective of primary-grade teachers. Primary-grade students are capable of making much progress in writing when they do interesting writing tasks in a supportive environment.

As we will see in this chapter, writing difficulties can be addressed through instruction. Research has shown that children can write much better if provided instructionally guided opportunities to write in thoughtfully structured classroom environments. As the chapter proceeds, specific approaches for dealing with each of the above shortcomings will be reviewed, with the clear message that children can be very good writers, the types of writers observed in the very best classrooms considered in Chapter 8.

UNDERSTANDING HOW EXPERT WRITERS WRITE

There are currently two main approaches to writing instruction and research: cognitive approaches such as the Carnegie Mellon model and sociocultural approaches. As we will see, both approaches have yielded useful information for primary-grade teachers. However, before the rise of either current approach, composition instruction focused on the form and properties of the written product. This "formalist" approach, standard during 1950 and 1960s, was largely grammatical instruction. (Meckel, 1963; Nystrand, 2005). A great deal of time was spent in elementary, junior high, and high school on the parts of speech, parts of sentences, grammatical terms (e.g., case, number, voice, tense, etc.), diagramming of sentences, and characteristics of well-crafted sentences and paragraphs (e.g., parallelism, explicit pronoun references, placement of modifiers, topic sentences). This general formalist approach to writing instruction was showcased in textbooks such as John Warriner's *Handbook of English* (1948), which went through many printings and was pervasive in elementary and middle school classrooms until as recently as the mid-1990s. This grammar-focused instructional program did little to improve student composition (e.g., Hillocks, 1984).

New ideas about writing and research on writing slowly began to emerge in the late 1950s. Kraus (1959) tested a new approach to writing with college students against then-prominent instructional tactics. In the new approach, students wrote in response to literature. They received feedback about their writing and worked in small peer groups to improve essays, referring to a style and reference manual when it was helpful. This new approach emphasized the act of writing, focused on peer or self-correction and aimed to develop students as self-regulated writers. There were bits and pieces of other evidence suggesting these themes as well (Meckel, 1963). A clear sense was developing that writing could be taught more effectively.

A scientific research base on writing developed during the 1970s. A field devoted to research on the teaching of composition emerged, with early pioneers including former school teacher Janet Emig (1971) and English professor Mina Shaughnessy (1977). Then, in 1980, there was dramatic shift in thinking about how writing should be taught. This shift was strongly influenced by the cognitive revolution in psychology and by the then-existing research. The new approach concentrated on writing as a series of cognitive processes and strategies. Studying expert writers revealed that writing was a complex set of largely cognitive tasks that could be taught, and when taught, writing improved.

A second new approach to writing research followed in the 1980s and 1990s. This sociocultural model was partly a response to underdeveloped areas within the cognitive model, but it was also strongly influenced by developments in other social sciences. It focused on the social and cultural contexts of the writer, of the text, and of language itself. It explored how meaning in writing is shaped by context but how writing can also, in turn, reshape that context. These two different ways of approaching writing research—the cognitive and the sociocultural—will be discussed in greater detail next.

Writing as Cognitive Processes: The Carnegie Mellon Model

Writing instruction was revolutionized with a series of papers published by John R. Hayes and Linda S. Flower, both of Carnegie Mellon University (1980; also Flower & Hayes, 1980). They had spent time listening to skilled writers talk as they wrote. Hayes and Flower found in such data a complex orderliness to the process of skilled writing not acknowledged in formalist models, summarized as the Carnegie Mellon model of writing (see Figure 10.1). Over the years, Hayes and colleagues have revisited and elaborated their model in light of many more protocol analyses of writing. The cognitive processes of planning (including idea generation and organizing), drafting, and revision were at the center of the original 1980 model, and they remain central. By 1996, the characteristics of the writer as a determinant of writing had been thought out much more completely (see Figure 10.2). These factors include the writer's long-term and short-term memory; the writer's affect and motivation; and the immediate task environment (the topic, audience, motivating cues, and the evolving text itself). These aspects of the writer play important roles during the planning, drafting, and revising processes.

Recursive Cognitive Processes

Hayes and Flower (1980) were not the first to conceive of writing as a series of stages (see Rohman, 1965), but they were the first to realize that progression through these stages was not a straightforward linear progression. That is, the writer might plan a little, research a little, organize a little. During organization it might become apparent that more planning and searching for information is in order. After several cycles of searching and organizing, drafting might begin, only to stop because the author discovered that still more research and organization were needed before proceeding. The author might then return to drafting or revising some of the existing draft along the way. Such nonlinear writing is described as being recursive. When expert writers write, they are systematically recursive, moving fluently between the planning, organizing, drafting, and revising processes. Expert writers monitor these activities constantly.

Writers must be recursive, for there is much to monitor when one writes (Flower & Hayes, 1980). All the planning, organizing, drafting, and revising must happen within a writer's short-term memory. Yet, the most salient characteristic of short-term memory is its very limited capacity. The recursive nature of the processes helps compensate for this. By moving back and forth between planning, organizing, drafting, and revising, a manageable amount of information can be held in mind during each moment of writing.

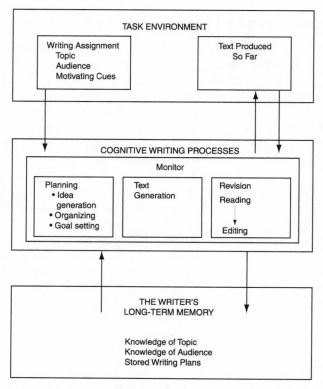

FIGURE 10.1. The Hayes–Flower 1980 model. From Hayes (1996, p. 3). Copyright 1996 by Lawrence Erlbaum Associates. Reprinted by permission.

The Planning Process

Hayes and Flower found that expert writers do extensive planning before they compose a sentence (1980). Writers search their long-term memories for prior knowledge that might be used as ideas in the text. The better developed the author's long-term memory with respect to a topic, the faster the planning is at the outset. In addition, long-term memory can contain information about the audience. Thus, someone writing about a political candidate needs to be aware of whether the text is going to supporters or opponents of the candidate, The contents of the text and its presentation will be affected by the writer's background knowledge of the audience as well as the candidate. In addition, writers typically have writing plans stored in memory, from the sophisticated to the simple. Formalist writing textbooks such as Warriner's (1948) handbook have frequently organized writing into four types of such writing plans—for example, exposition, description, narrative, and argument. These writing plans can go far in as-

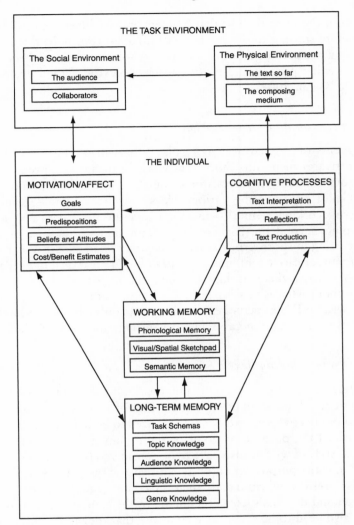

FIGURE 10.2. The Hayes 1996 model. From Hayes (1996, p. 4). Copyright 1996 by Lawrence Erlbaum Associates. Reprinted by permission.

sisting writers in shaping a text, but they can also be limiting when writers simply slot their ideas into a simplistic formula (e.g., the five-paragraph essay; see Johnson, Smagorinsky, Thompson, & Fry, 2003).

   Planning is relatively easy compared to the other processes. It is more time-efficient to try ideas out in one's mind or through rough sketches of arguments than to draft entire texts. Good writers make many notes about what ought to be in the text before they craft a single sentence. Smart writers plan for the same reasons that builders prepare blueprints and building plans before starting to dig the basement. Not surprisingly, this metaphor of building has become relevant for many scholars and researchers examining the writing process and writing instruction (for a good example, see Singer & Bashir, 2004).

Idea Generation and Organization

The contents of long-term memory play a part in writing only when the writer activates them into short-term working memory. Writers also seek ideas from external resources, for example, relevant books and articles. Writers must organize the various ideas they have found—doing so in short-term working memory—and then generate new ideas and insights, often going beyond the background information—with such generation also occurring in short-term working memory. So, an expert writer writing about a murder case might have in front of him a great deal of evidence; on the basis of organizing and thinking about this evidence, he could make inferences about what is missing (e.g., "The prosecutor has everything but a murder weapon!"). Experts begin writing text only after there has been a great deal of information gathering, organizing, and idea generation.

Drafting and Revising Text

In drafting text, authors need to put their individual ideas into words. These individual ideas are typically only part of a larger purpose or argument. To be effective, the individual ideas need to be structured so that they build toward the purpose or point of the argument. The form, arrangement, and style of writing also have to be considered (Flower, 1979; Geisler, 1994). So, if the purpose of an essay is to encourage readers to vote for a particular presidential candidate, then the content must offer reasons why readers should do this, such as the merits of the candidate's record. These reasons also need to be stated in such a way that they make the candidate appealing. The purpose might be accomplished by structuring the ideas as an argument. For example, the essay might say that readers should vote for this candidate because she did X, Y, and Z, and the opponent has never done X, Y, and Z. In sum, the writer plans what he or she will write, then drafts sentences and paragraphs that convey the specific ideas.

The initial written text is unambiguously a draft, with the writer expecting to come back to it to revise. Revision involves making the message clearer. Unlike the formalist conception of writing that emphasized sentence grammar, this approach emphasizes ideas and their structuring as the most critical considerations in writing. Grammar and style are seen as means to an end—the effective making of a main point. Grammar gets more attention in the revision stage than in other stages. Even so, the emphasis is always on revising to make the message clear and convincing.

The 1996 version of the Carnegie Mellon model highlighted the central importance of reading to the writing process. Writers must read source texts to get information, with it being important that these be critical readings (e.g., sizing up the writer's position on issues as a context for what they say in their text). Even more critical, writers must read the text they are writing as it is evolving, continually evaluating it to determine what else needs to be said, what additional information should be found and drafted into a revised text.

A more general concern for the Carnegie Mellon group was problem solving. These researchers came to see skilled writing as a form of problem solving. Both excellent writing and solving of problems of all types require the following:

1. Extensive use of prior knowledge
2. Flexibility
3. Extensive monitoring
4. Deep processing that results in substantial understanding of the task
5. Skillful management of the limited capacity that is short-term memory
6. Making a plan, carrying it out, and revising the plan when there are difficulties

The Task Environment

Hayes and Flower (1980) also recognized that the task environment mattered in what was written. This notion was fuller by 1996 and included the topic, the audience, motivating cues, the evolving text itself, and the composing medium (Hayes, 1996; also Hayes & Nash, 1996). This text is being written in a word-processing environment. Revisions are much easier to accomplish in a word-processing rather than typewriting environment. So, by 1996, the task environment was recognized as having social elements (the audience, collaborators) and physical elements (the text written so far, the composing medium). Even so, the Carnegie Mellon model emphasizes the writer as an individual more than the sociocultural approach to writing.

Sociocultural Research on Writing

Sociocultural researchers of writing challenged the assumption that writing is a top-down process beginning with individual thought and ending with text, a process that might be called "language after the ideational fact"

(Nystrand, 1986). Rather than focusing on a relatively decontextualized individual writer, they explored the dynamics of cultural and dialogic contexts in which writing functioned as a complex social transaction (Bakhtin, 1981, 1986; Bakhtin & Medvedev, 1978; Hymes, 1972; Labov, 1972; Vygotsky, 1962, 1978). Writing was studied as a social process, fundamentally depending on a reciprocal transaction between writers and readers, with meaning at its core (Nystrand, 1986).

Sociological researchers have studied such topics as the effects of writing groups on writing and learning to write (Bruffee, 1984) and the complex and deeply social nature of children's development as writers (Dyson, 1993). Social researchers of writing also examined what the Hayes model calls the "physical environment." For example, how do word processors, emails, and web pages influence the very nature of the writing process? How have they changed our definitions of reading, writing, and text (Haas, 1996)? This body of sociocultural inquiry has widened the vision of what matters about writing and writing instruction, not only for researchers but also for teachers of writing.

It has made clear that culture matters in writing and learning to write. For example, one of us (M. J.) taught elementary- and middle-level Navajo students to become better English-language writers. These students spoke Navajo as their first language. Their out-of-school lives were functionally oriented to many other modes of communication besides written English. Their parents and grandparents had stinging memories of the Bureau of Indian Affair's systematic efforts to strip away Navajo language and traditions from school children. Many of the problems the students encountered with school-based writing were more accurately and usefully seen as cultural conflicts than cognitive problems.

During M. J.'s first year of teaching at a Bureau of Indian Affairs (BIA) boarding school, she paid a home visit to discuss one student's resistance to reading, writing, and to schoolwork more generally. When she explained her concerns, the father responded angrily, pointing across the valley to the stone school buildings: "You people came and took my grandfather's land and tried to take away his language, too. Why do I care if my son is struggling with English or busting up the desks over there? He doesn't need all that to be Navajo!"

As a teacher in this BIA school, M. J. had become part of a much larger cultural and historical story than she had realized upon accepting the job. In order to grasp the nature of this student's struggle with literacy, and particularly with the writing, she as teacher needed first to better understand the cultural dimension of this resistance. She also needed to use that understanding to persuade students that writing in a safe classroom space could provide a means for navigating and exploring conflicting languages and cultures. Over the years spent teaching in that community, she learned to make home visits not so much to share concerns about student's problems but rather to find out what parents wanted for their children and their education and to use family "funds of knowledge" to strengthen her teaching of writing (cf. Moll & Gonzalez, 2004). Educators in multilingual and cross-cultural teaching contexts are likely to find sociocultural theories of writing to be particularly compelling and resonant as they seek to make sense of their own struggles and experiences with teaching children to become more expert writers.

Some sociocultural researchers in the 1980s probed issues of audience and collaboration in writing (e.g., Ede & Lunsford, 1984, 1990), but much of the recent sociocultural work on writing has examined "contexts" of writing in two senses: first, in microecological studies of writing in classrooms and in other "communities of practice" (Wenger, 1998), and secondly, in terms of the institutional, political, and economic contexts of writing. Because of the instructional focus of this book, we concentrate on classrooms as context and look at the work of one important researcher of children's writing.

Anne Dyson's (1993, 1997, 2003) sociocultural research has focused on primary-level children learning to write. In detailed anthropological and linguistic studies, Dyson describes and analyzes the dynamic social processes of children's composing and, more specifically, learning to compose in school. She confirms through longitudinal, observational studies of exemplary teachers that children's literacy does not develop in a neat linear order. This is consistent with Flower and Hayes's notion of recursiveness. Dyson, however, sees children's writing processes as characterized by complex social interactions. These include appropriations of written material from their family and neighborhood social worlds, from popular media (including, for example, video games, sports, and superheroes), and perhaps most significantly from talk and writing of friends and social groups with whom they identify.

For example, Dyson (1997) examined how children communicated with one another as they appropriated superheroes from popular culture into their stories. More generally, Dyson (2003) tracked how a group of first-grade children appropriated from a wide repertoire of textual and other resources—including sports, radio shows, and popular music—as they developed increasing competence at creating multimodal written texts in school. Dyson was able to show that, over time, there were connections among the children's pictures, written language, and talk with friends, documenting that children messily advanced as authors with the help and support of their peers and their teacher. This was exciting for them in part because, during an activity called "Author's Theater," the children performed the stories they had written. Dyson found that the authoring continued as the children cast and acted their superhero stories, even inverting dominant ideologies as they acted the stories. Sometimes X-men showed their feelings and cried in the stories written by children!

Sociocultural researchers have also come to understand the social situation of writers through investigations of "intertextuality" (Bazerman, 1988). "Intertextuality" refers to how a text refers to prior texts, "voices," and genres within a particular system of activity. Stone's (2003) investigation of middle-school children's writing in an after-school program provides an example of inter-textual analysis. The children's writing took place in digital environments such as websites. She traced how children used existing texts—including movies, cartoons, drawings, and other websites—to craft new websites that expressed their individual identities, their cultural affiliations, and their institutional allegiances. One student, for example, created a website that was all about anime. This website appropriated all manner of anime lore and materials from other texts; yet, the student arranged the materials to express her own narrative voice.

Summary

We have now laid out the ways in which writing instruction has been approached during the past 50 years: formalist, cognitive, and sociocultural. Formalist instruction has not stood up well to the scientific scrutiny of expert writers and writing teachers at work. Basic writing research in both the cognitive and the sociocultural domains have yielded a great deal of understanding about what expert writers do, how expert writing can be promoted, and what sorts of environmental factors need to be considered in supporting and developing more expert writing in classrooms. Without a doubt, however, the cognitive approach has resulted in much more writing instructional research than the sociocognitive approach to date. Thus, in what follows, we present an overview of the research on writing instruction, focusing on strategies instruction but also touching on work on structured classroom environments and curricula that support writing development. This section also includes a sampler of some of the most important conclusions about writing instruction that derive from research.

TEACHING WRITING

Young writers can be taught strategies for planning, organizing, drafting, and revising, and when they are taught such strategies in an effective way, their compositions improve. Many of the most striking demonstrations have been with elementary and middle-school writers, particularly students with disabilities, who really were struggling with writing before they were taught strategies.

A Writing Strategies Program That Worked: De La Paz and Graham (2002)

In a controlled trial, De La Paz and Graham (2002) evaluated a form of writing strategies instruction with students in grades 7 and 8. Students in both the strategies instruction condition and the control condition received 6 weeks of instruction. Each group wrote five practice essays. Both groups were informed at the same level of detail about how their essays would be scored The control participants received a great deal of information about the nature of the five-paragraph essay, and the instruction they received focused on mechanics. The teacher of the control group also gave more direction with respect to generation of ideas, sentences, and paragraphs than did the writing strategies teacher.

Before the study began, essays written by students in both groups were comparable in quality. By the end of the instruction, the students receiving strategies instruction were writing better essays. The essays were longer, had more diverse vocabulary, and in every way were higher in quality (i.e., better organized, better use of mechanics, etc.).

The writing strategies instruction that produced this positive outcome was sequenced in four main parts: First, students were given an introduction to good writing and the elements that make for good writing. Students were then taught planning and organizing strategies, drafting strategies, and revision strategies. The following section briefly describes what was taught in each part of the program and how it was taught.

An Introduction to Good Expository Writing

Students were first taught what good expository writing is. As in the control group, teachers also introduced the five-paragraph essay approach, which was required for an upcoming state assessment. The qualities of good writing were taught through the presentation of model essays. The teachers reflected with students on the strengths of these models, highlighting the following:

- The model essays had beginnings, middles, and ends.
- Each essay contained a thesis sentence, as did each paragraph within the essay.
- Transition words were used between sentences and paragraphs.

- Students were asked to identify different types of sentences used in the models.
- Students were asked to reflect on the vocabulary used, including the variety in wording.

Toward the end of instruction, the teacher reviewed these elements of good essays and explained that these would be the criteria used to score the students' essays.

Planning and Organizing Strategies

The teacher's initial introduction to planning strategies extended over several days. Students were provided with a great deal of information about the strategies before having to attempt to use them. Instruction about the planning process highlighted the following:

- Be sure to understand the topic of the essay and the main message to be conveyed.
- List the main ideas to be included in the essay.
- Brainstorm for more ideas for the essay.
- As new ideas are brainstormed, revise the list of main ideas if appropriate. (Notice that planning and revising were taught as being recursive; revising to the plan can occur before a single line of actual essay text is drafted.)
- Decide on the order for the ideas in the essay (i.e., organize the ideas).

After discussion and modeling, students practiced these planning strategies as part of composing five essays. Students were provided prompts to help them write. Thus, they had a brainstorming sheet for planning and organizing their ideas. The teacher provided support as needed, but also permitted students to make progress on their own as much as possible (i.e., use of the strategy was scaffolded).

Drafting Strategies

After students carried out the planning strategies, the teacher explained and modeled the following drafting strategies:

- Rely on the plan to guide writing.
- Write a thesis statement first.
- Compose a thesis paragraph with a thesis statement at its heart. Students were taught that the thesis statement did not have to come

first in the paragraph. The paragraph could begin with a series of questions or an attention-getting comment or even a statement completely opposite to the thesis statement.

After this process and its strategies had been explained, students turned to drafting. As with planning and organizing, they used a planning sheet for their thesis paragraph, prompting them to consider where in the paragraph the thesis statement might be placed. They also received a set of cue cards reminding them what each paragraph should include. As they wrote, students were reminded to stay on topic, follow the organization, and vary vocabulary and sentence types.

Revision Strategies

Throughout the writing process, students participated in small-group conferences with the teacher to reflect on progress for each of the five practice essays as well as the work and revisions that remained. As they reviewed and revised their essays, they were taught to keep all of the criteria in mind:

- Follow the planned organization.
- Keep the essay's goals in mind.
- Vary sentences and vocabulary (e.g., use synonyms rather than repeat words).
- Check transition words as part of the revision.
- Combine short sentences when possible to add variety to the essay.

Throughout the instruction, there was a lot of verbal rehearsal of the strategies, with great effort made to assure that students knew all of the parts of the complex writing strategy they were taught.

The description above is only one version of the writing strategies instruction. There are, however, many other supporting studies. We turn to those now.

Graham's (2005) Meta-Analysis

Graham (2005; see also Graham & Harris, 2003) conducted a meta-analysis of 39 studies of writing strategies instruction. These studies included students from grade 2 through senior year in high school, employed a wide range of particular methods, and measured a variety of writing outcomes, from holistic quality of essays to appropriate use of mechanics. More studies were carried out with students who struggled with writing, but a range of student competencies was included across investigations. Some of the studies focused on one aspect of the writing process (e.g., planning) and others, such as the study just reviewed, covered the entire writing process. Instruction typically occurred over a few weeks to a few months, with some instruction and practice every day during the study, for perhaps 30–50 minutes. That is, the instruction was not so long-term or time-consuming as to be impractical in real school settings.

This review makes clear that teaching students writing processes as well as how to use the processes as strategies (i.e., deliberately, in a controlled fashion) produced consistently positive effects on writing. Just as impressive, the effects of strategies instruction tended to range between large and very large. The effects were often maintained weeks after instruction, and in a number of studies there was evidence of transfer to other writing tasks and settings. There is simply no doubt that student writing can be improved through cognitive strategies instruction. That instruction begins with teacher explanation and modeling of strategies; it proceeds with students trying the strategies themselves, supported by the teacher on an as-needed basis. This body of work is as important as any in the literacy instruction canon and should be studied carefully by anyone concerned with improving student writing. For a primer about the many varieties of planning, drafting, and revision strategies that can be taught to elementary, middle, and high school students, see Harris and Graham (1996) and Graham and Harris (2005).

Structured Classroom Environments Support Writing Development

Sociocultural researchers of writing instruction have directed attention to the structured environments of classrooms. Consistent with the work of Pressley and colleagues (see Chapter 8), Hillock (1984), and Dyson (1993, 1997, 2003) case studies, effective writing teachers create classroom environments that promote "structured writing processes" for children. Instead of the usual insistence that children sit alone at their desks to write silently in solitude, teachers encourage children to write as a social activity. As children craft their writing, friends may sit together in groups and are free to ask one another questions, to engage in unsolicited talk and commentary, and to seek out other forms of support from their peers. Much of the writing in these classrooms is expressive, and children are sanctioned to make sense of their complicated lives and worlds through writing. Narrative and dramatic genres predominate, as do other artistic media such as music and visual art. One teacher studied by Dyson (2003) introduced students to the work of her favorite artists (e.g., Georgia O'Keeffe) and used music to calm students down (classical) or to get them going (jazz). Children read aloud or perform their writing for their peers during Author's Theater. In these ways, teachers strongly encourage the rich communicative potential for writing.

Dyson has advocated "permeable curricula" around writing instruction—teachers encouraging children to appropriate both official and unofficial language in "hybrid" genres. The exemplary teachers studied by Dyson encouraged students to incorporate their interests in sports and in popular figures such as superheroes in their writing projects. In this way, children from a range of class and race backgrounds "get connected" with writing in school. This research also encourages teachers to design assignments and to structure classroom environments that scaffold students in developing an awareness of audience and rhetorical purpose in their writing, such as occurs when students "perform" their writing during Author's Theater (Dyson, 1997).

Working Memory Matters

Consistent with the Carnegie Mellon model, considerable empirical evidence has been generated that writing occurs in short-term working memory. Factors that consume working memory can, in fact, impair writing (Kellogg, 1994, 1996, 2001; McCutchen, 2000). What are factors that can so impede working memory in child writers? If a child has difficulty in spelling or only spells slowly, sounding out a little bit at a time, such struggle consumes working memory and impedes writing (Graham, Berninger, Abbott, Abbott, & Whitaker, 1997; Graham, Harris, & Chorzempa, 2002). Not surprisingly, teaching students directly to spell positively impacts their composition skills (Berninger et al., 2002; Graham et al., 2002). This is consistent with the bulk of the evidence that skill in spelling is most assured when spelling is directly taught rather than left to natural development (Graham, 2000). If a child's handwriting is poor and requires much of the child's attention, working memory is consumed unduly, with the potential to undermine composition quality (Graham et al., 1997; Graham & Harris, 2000; Graham, Harris, & Fink, 2000). The data are compelling that it makes sense to attend to lower-order skills development. Inefficient lower-order skills use can prevent higher-order processes from operating efficiently.

Genre Matters

Researchers in reading (e.g., Duke, 2000) have noted the paucity of literacy teaching through informational genres in elementary literacy instruction. They argue that these often-overlooked genres need to assume a more prominent place in instruction. This is particularly the case since these are the genres of many middle- and secondary-grade textbooks. Literacy researchers also have increasingly started to recognize that genre matters in elementary writing instruction. Often the only genre in which students practice writing in primary classrooms is creative storytelling. But this ability may not adapt well to the task of writing up lab reports or analyzing themes in novels. These latter are the writing tasks and genres that students are likely to encounter as they move up to higher grade levels. Therefore, the best of recent research on writing has accounted for genre in studying other problems and questions in writing and writing instruction. For example, Graham's (2005) meta-analysis on strategy instruction and the teaching of writing controls for the genre categories of narrative and expository writing. Others have noted that both narrative and nonnarrative genres can be used as important tools for disciplinary learning during the elementary years (Kamberelis & Bovino, 1999; Wells, 1996).

Recent research—much of it sociocultural—has also focused more explicitly on genre—for example, comparing the teaching and learning of different written genres and examining genre development in students over time (e.g., Coe, Lingard, & Telenko, 2002; Freedman & Medway, 1994; Russell, 1997). The Sydney school, a group of Australian literacy researchers with a linguistic focus, have extensively theorized how to teach genre (e.g., Cope & Kalantzis, 1993). Kamberelis (1999) conducted an empirical study of the differential working knowledge of different genres (including stories, science reports, and poems) displayed by 54 children in kindergarten, first-, and second-grade classrooms. Children's narrative genre skills were much more developed than their relatively nascent writing in the poem and science genres. This suggests a need for primary literacy teachers and researchers to probe how children might be taught to become competent in writing nonnarrative genres earlier on in their schooling.

Motivation Also Matters in Writing

We explore motivation in reading in detail in Chapter 11. We mention motivation here only as it relates to writing. While primarily cognitive, the model recognized that writer affect matters. When young writers have more elaborated and complete writing goals, it impacts their writing (Ferretti, MacArthur, & Dowdy, 2000). There has also been substantial work documenting that writing skill affects self-efficacy beliefs. By writing well, young people come to believe they are more effective in general. Increased self-efficacy then motivates future writing (Klassen, 2002; Pajares, 2003; Pajares, Britner, & Valiante, 2000). For a review of the evidence that authentic writing tasks can motivate student writing as well as the evidence that a writing-supportive classroom environment matters, see Bruning and

Horn (2000). And, of course, recall the many different mechanisms for motivating academic work in the most effective primary-grade classrooms (see Chapter 8). There are many ways to motivate writing, and this is an area where "whole-language" teacher researchers (e.g., Atwell, 1998) have much to contribute to the more scientifically based literature. It is likely that the teacher who uses a great variety of motivating tactics can succeed in getting students to write more and to write more expertly.

Writing's Influence on Learning

Does writing about content increase learning of content? This topic has not been extensively studied at the elementary level, and most existing research involved writing in the context of elementary mathematics instruction. Yet, there are enough studies to make a tentative conclusion, Writing, in fact, produces a small positive effect in content learning. This is consistent with the small positive effect observed when studies of learning from writing across all grade levels are considered (Bangert-Drowns, Hurley, & Wilkinson, 2004). The effects of writing on content-area learning are definitely promising enough to deserve additional study. The only reservation in this literature is that the effects of learning from writing seemed very weak, even negative at the middle school level. That said, there are only a handful of studies at the middle school level, with some of these involving very short implementation periods (i.e., the majority were 6 weeks or shorter).

Concluding Comment

There is substantial evidence that children need to be taught how to write, with observed deficiencies in higher-order processes, such as planning, drafting, and revising, and lower-order processes, such as handwriting and spelling. The researcher community is responding to the need to know more about children's writing and how to promote it through diverse research. The most extensive research has been conducted in the area of cognitive strategies instruction, with substantial evidence that teaching children to use cognitive strategies as they plan, draft, and revise improves writing. There is also research on the nature of classrooms that promote writing in children, the impact of low-level deficiencies in writing on overall writing performance, how writing impacts reading, the sophistication of young writers with respect to audience, writing in diverse genres, how motivation affects student writing, and content-area learning that occurs during writing. As researchers continue to study these problems, we anticipate that a much fuller conception of writing instruction that works will be possible in future editions of this book.

SUMMARY

1. Formalist approaches to writing that emphasized grammar have yielded to research-oriented cognitive process models and sociocultural models. Both of these newer approaches focus much more on the writer as a message maker than did the formalist approach.

2. The cognitive process models were developed from verbal protocol data collected from skilled writers by scholars. These models emphasize that composing involves recursive planning, drafting, and revising. These cognitive processes are affected by the writer's motivations, the audience, and the environment in which the writing takes place, including the physical medium.

3. Sociocultural writing theorists emphasize context and environment in writing, more than cognitive models. These contexts include the available language resources, the culture of the writer, and the role of social interaction and communication.

4. Children need to be *taught* to write. Both their higher-order skills (i.e., understanding that writing requires planning, drafting, and revising, and how to do it) and lower-level skills (spelling, handwriting) require development. There has been much progress in understanding how the higher-order processes can be taught as strategies.

5. The development of children's writing is an extremely active area of research, with many directions now being studied by literacy scholars.

REFERENCES

Atwell, N. (1998). *In the middle: New understandings about writing, reading, and learning.* Portsmouth, NH: Boynton/Cook.

Bakhtin, M. M. (1981). *The dialogic imagination* (M. Holquist, Ed., C. Emerson & M. Holquist, Trans.). Austin: University of Texas Press. (Original work published 1935).

Bakhtin, M. M. (1986). *Speech genres and other late essays* (C. Emerson & M. Holquist, Eds., V. W. McGee, Trans.). Austin: University of Texas Press. (Original work published 1953).

Bakhtin, M. M., & Medvedev, P. N. (1978). *The formal method in literary scholarship: A critical introduction to sociological poetics* (A. J. Wehrle, Trans.). Baltimore: Johns Hopkins Press.

Bangert-Drowns, R. L., Hurley, M. M., & Wilkinson, B. (2004). The effects of school-based writing to learn interventions on academic achievement: A meta-analysis. *Review of Educational Research, 74,* 29–58.

Bazerman, C. (1988). *Shaping written knowledge: The genre and activity of the experimental article in science.* Madison, WI: University of Wisconsin Press.

Berninger, V. W., Vaughan, K., Abbott, R. W., Begay, K., Coleman, K. R., Curtin, G.,

Hawkins, J. M., & Graham, S. (2002). Teaching spelling and composition alone and together: Implications for the simple view of writing. *Journal of Educational Psychology, 94*, 291–304.

Brainerd, C. J. (1978). *Piaget's theory of intelligence*. Englewood Cliffs, NJ: Prentice-Hall.

Bruffee, K. A. (1984). Collaborative learning and the "conversation of mankind." *College English, 46*(7), 635–652.

Bruning, R., & Horn, C. (2000). Developing motivation to write. *Educational Psychologist, 35*, 25–37.

Cicero. (1986). De oratore. In J. S. Watson (Ed. and Trans.). *On oratory and orators*. Carbondale and Edwardsville: Southern Illinois University Press.

Coe, R. Lingard, L., & Telenko, T. (Eds.). (2002). *The rhetoric and ideology of genres: Strategies for stability and change*. Cresskill, NJ: Hampton.

Cope, B., & Kalantzis, M. (1993). The power of literacy and the literacy of power. In B. Cope & M. Kalantzis (Eds.), *The powers of literacy: A genre approach to teaching writing* (pp. 63–89). Pittsburgh: University of Pittsburgh Press.

Craig, S. A. (2003). The effects of an adapted interactive writing intervention on kindergarten children's phonological awareness, spelling, and early reading development. *Reading Research Quarterly, 38*, 438–440.

De La Paz, S., & Graham, S. (2002). Explicitly teaching strategies, skills, and knowledge: Writing instruction in middle school classrooms. *Journal of Educational Psychology, 94*, 687–698.

Duke, N. (2000). 3.6 minutes per day: The scarcity of informational texts in first grade. *Reading Research Quarterly, 35*(2), 202–224.

Dyson, A. H. (1993). *Social worlds of children learning to write in an urban primary school*. New York: Teachers College Press.

Dyson, A. H. (1997). *Writing superheroes: Contemporary childhood, popular culture, and classroom literacy*. New York: Teachers College Press.

Dyson, A. H. (2003). *The brothers and sisters learn to write: Popular literacies in childhood and school cultures*. New York: Teachers College Press.

Ede, L., & Lunsford, A. (1984). Audience addressed/audience invoked: The role of audience in composition theory and pedagogy. *College Composition and Communication, 35*, 104–154.

Ede, L., & Lunsford, A. A. (Eds.). (1990). *Singular texts/plural authors: Perspectives on collaborative writing*. Carbondale and Edwardsville: Southern Illinois University Press.

Emig, J. (1971). *The composing processes of twelfth graders*. Urbana, IL: National Council of Teachers of English.

Ferretti, R. P., MacArthur, C. A., & Dowdy, N. S. (2000). The effects of an elaborated goal on the persuasive writing of students with learning disabilities and their normally achieving peers. *Journal of Educational Psychology, 92*, 694–702.

Fitzgerald, J., & Shanahan, T. (2000). Reading and writing relations and their development. *Educational Psychologist, 35*, 39–50.

Flower, L. (1979). Writer-based prose: A cognitive basis for problems in writing. *College English, 41*, 19–37.

Flower, L. S., & Hayes, J. R. (1980). The dynamics of composing: Making plans and juggling constraints. In L. W. Gregg & E. R. Steinberg (Eds.), *Cognitive processes in writing* (pp. 31–50). Hillsdale, NJ: Erlbaum.

Freedman, A., & Medway, P. (Eds.). (1994). *Genre and the new rhetoric*. London: Taylor & Francis.

Frijters, J. C., Barron, R. W., & Brunello, M. (2000). Direct and mediated influences on home literacy and literacy interest on prereaders' oral vocabulary and early written language skill. *Journal of Educational Psychology, 92,* 466–477.

Geisler, C. (1994). *Academic literacy and the nature of expertise: Reading, writing, and knowing in academic philosophy*. Hillsdale, NJ: Erlbaum.

Graham, S. (2000). Should the natural learning approach replace spelling instruction. *Journal of Educational Psychology, 92,* 235–247.

Graham, S. (2005). Strategy instruction and the teaching of writing: A meta-analysis. In C. A. MacArthur, S. Graham, & J. Fitzgerald (Eds.), *Handbook of writing research* (pp. 187–207). New York: Guilford Press.

Graham, S., Berninger, V., Abbott, R., Abbott, S., & Whitaker, D. (1997). The role of mechanics in composing of elementary school students: A new methodological approach. *Journal of Educational Psychology, 89,* 170–182.

Graham, S., & Harris, K. R. (2000). The role of self-regulation and transcription skills in writing and writing development. *Educational Psychologist, 35,* 3–12.

Graham, S., & Harris, K. R. (2003). Students with learning disabilities and the process of writing: A meta-analysis of SRSD studies. In H. L. Swanson, K. R. Harris, & S. Graham (Eds.), *Handbook of learning disabilities* (pp. 323–344). New York: Guilford Press.

Graham, S., & Harris, K. (2005). *Writing better: Effective strategies for teaching students with learning difficulties*. Baltimore: Brookes.

Graham, S., Harris, K. R., & Chorzempa, B. F. (2002). Contribution of spelling instruction to the spelling, writing, and reading of poor spellers. *Journal of Educational Psychology, 94,* 669–686.

Graham, S., Harris, K. R., & Fink, B. (2000). Is handwriting causally related to learning to write? Treatment of handwriting problems in beginning writers. *Journal of Educational Psychology, 92,* 620–633.

Haas, C. (1996). *Writing technology: Studies on the materiality of literacy*. Mahwah, NJ: Erlbaum.

Harris, K. R., & Graham, S. (1992). Self-regulated strategy development: A part of the writing process. In M. Pressley, K. R. Harris, & J. T. Guthrie (Eds.), *Promoting academic competence and literacy in school* (pp. 277–309). San Diego: Academic Press.

Harris, K. R., & Graham, S. (1996). *Making the writing process work: Strategies for composition and self-regulation*. Cambridge, MA: Brookline Books.

Hayes, J. (1996). A new framework for understanding cognition and affect in writing. In M. Levy & S. Ransdell (Eds.), *The science of writing: Theories, methods, individual differences, and applications* (pp. 1–27). Mahwah, NJ: Erlbaum.

Hayes, J. R., & Flower, L. S. (1980). Identifying the organization of writing processes. In L. W. Gregg & E. R. Steinberg (Eds.), *Cognitive processes in writing* (pp. 3–30). Hillsdale, NJ: Erlbaum.

Hayes, J. R., & Nash, J. G. (1996). On the nature of planning in writing. In M. Levy &

S. Ransdell (Eds.), *The science of writing: Theories, methods, individual differences, and applications* (pp. 29–55). Mahwah, NJ: Erlbaum.

Hillocks, G. (1984). What works in teaching composition: A meta-analysis of experimental treatment studies. *American Journal of Education, 93,* 133–170.

Hymes, D. (1972). On communicative competence. In J. B. Pride & J. Holmes (Eds.), *Sociolinguisitcs* (pp. 269–293). London: Penguin.

Jenkins, J. R., Johnson, E., & Hileman, J. (2004). When is reading also writing: Sources of individual differences on the new reading performance assessments. *Scientific Studies of Reading, 8,* 125–151.

Johnson, T. S., Smagorinsky, P., Thompson, L., & Fry, P. G. (2003). Learning to teach the five-paragraph theme. *Research in the Teaching of English, 38*(2), 136–176.

Kamberelis, G. (1999). Genre development and learning: Children writing stories, science reports, and poems. *Research in the teaching of English, 33*(4), 403–460.

Kamberelis, G., & Bovino, T. (1999). Cultural artifacts as scaffolds for genre development. *Reading Research Quarterly, 34*(2), 138–170.

Kellogg, R. T. (1994). *The psychology of writing.* New York: Oxford University Press.

Kellogg, R. T. (1996). A model of working memory in writing. In C. M. Levy & S. Ransdell (Eds.), *The science of writing: Theories, methods, individual differences, and applications* (pp. 57–71). Hillsdale, NJ: Erlbaum.

Kellogg, R. T. (2001). Competition for working memory among writing processes. *American Journal of Psychology, 114,* 175–191.

Klassen, R. (2002). Writing in early adolescence: A review of the role of self-efficacy beliefs. *Educational Psychology Review, 14,* 173–203.

Kraus, S. (1959). The teaching of written composition in the public schools: A summary of research. *University of Oregon Curriculum Bulletin, 15*(190).

Labov, W. (1972). *Language in the inner city.* Philadelphia: University of Pennsylvania Press.

Langer, J. A. (1986). *Children reading and writing: Structures and strategies.* Norwood, NJ: Ablex.

Langer, J. A. (1987). A sociocognitive perspective on literacy. In J. A. Langer (Ed.), *Language, literacy, and culture: Issues of society and schooling* (pp. 1–20). Norwood, NJ: Ablex.

McCutchen, D. (2000). Knowledge, processing, and working memory: Implications for a theory of writing. *Educational Psychologist, 35,* 13–23.

Meckel, H. C. (1963). Research on teaching composition and literature. In N. L. Gage (Ed.), *Handbook of research on teaching* (pp. 966–1006). Chicago: Rand McNally.

Moll, L. C., & Gonzalez, N. (2004). Engaging life: A funds-of-knowledge approach to multicultural education. In J. A. Banks & C. A. McGee Banks (Eds.), *Handbook of research on multicultural education* (pp. 699–715). San Francisco: Jossey-Bass.

National Commission on Writing in America's Schools and Colleges. (2003). *The neglected R: The need for a writing revolution.* New York: College Entrance Examination Board.

No Child Left Behind Act of 2001. (2002). Public Law 107-110.

Nystrand, M. (1986). *The structure of written communication: Studies in reciprocity between writers and readers.* Orlando: Academic Press.

Nystrand, M. (2005). The social and historical context of writing research. In C. A. MacArthur, S. Graham, & J. Fitzgerald (Eds.), *Handbook of writing research* (pp. 11–27). New York: Guilford Press.

Pajares, F. (2003). Self-efficacy beliefs, motivation, and achievement in writing: A review of the literature. *Reading and Writing Quarterly, 19,* 139–158.

Pajares, F., Britner, S. L., & Valiante, G. (2000). Relation between achievement goals and self-beliefs of middle school students in writing and science. *Contemporary Educational Psychology, 25,* 406–422.

Persky, H. R., Daane, M. C., & Jin, Y. (2003). *The nation's report card: Writing 2002.* Washington, DC: U.S. Department of Education, Institute of Education Sciences.

Rohman, D. G. (1965). Pre-writing: The stage of discovery in the writing process. *College Composition and Communication, 17,* 2–11.

Rosenthal, T. L., & Zimmerman, B. J. (1978). *Social learning and cognition.* New York: Academic Press.

Russell, D. R. (1997). Rethinking genre in school and society: An activity theory analysis. *Written Communication, 14,* 504–554.

Scardamalia, M., & Bereiter, C. (1986). Research on written composition. In M. C. Wittrock (Ed.), *Handbook of research on teaching* (3rd ed., pp. 778–803). New York: MacMillan.

Shanahan, R., & Tierney, R. J. (1990). Reading–writing connections: The relations among three perspectives. In J. Zutell & S. McCormick (Eds.), *Literacy theory and research: Analyses from multiple paradigms, Thirty-ninth yearbook of the National Reading Conference* (pp. 13–34). Chicago: National Reading Conference.

Shaughnessy, M. (1977). *Errors and expectations.* London: Oxford University Press.

Singer, B. D., & Bashir, A. S. (2004). Developmental variations in writing composition skills. *Handbook of language and literacy development and disorders.* In C. A. Stone, E. R. Silliman, B. J. Ehren, & K. Apel (Eds.). New York: Guilford Press.

Silva, C., & Alves-Martins, M. (2002). Phonological skills and writing of presyllabic children. *Reading Research Quarterly, 37,* 466–483.

Stone, J. C. (2003). *Genre and identity in the borderlands.* Doctoral dissertation, University of Wisconsin, Madison.

Vygotsky, L. S. (1962). *Thought and language.* Cambridge, MA: MIT Press.

Vygotsky, L. S. (1978). *Mind in society.* Cambridge, MA: Harvard University Press.

Warriner, J. E. (1948). *John E. Warriner's handbook of English.* New York: Harcourt.

Wells, G. (1996). Using the tool-kit of discourse in the activity of teaching and learning. *Mind Culture Activity, 3*(2), 74–101.

Wenger, E. (1998). *Communities of practice.* Cambridge, UK: Cambridge University Press.

Wollman-Bonilla, J. E. (2001). Can first-grade writers demonstrate audience awareness? *Reading Research Quarterly, 36,* 184–201.

Mary M. Juzwik, PhD, is Assistant Professor of Language and Literacy in the Department of Teacher Education, Michigan State University, East Lansing, Michigan.

CHAPTER 11

Motivation and Literacy

During the early 1990s, when the National Reading Research Center was established (based at the University of Georgia, in Athens, and the University of Maryland, in College Park), the organizers conducted a national survey of teachers that asked their opinions about the most pressing issues confronting education. One concern was much more prominent than any other in the responses: The teachers were emphatic that maintaining student academic motivation was a major challenge that needed to be addressed by any center concerned with promoting the reading achievement of students. In response to that input from teachers, the National Reading Research Center immediately focused on the promotion of student engagement in literacy (O'Flahavan, Gambrell, Guthrie, Stahl, & Alvermann, 1992).

A great deal about academic motivation was learned during the tenure of the National Reading Research Center. Some of the most important findings related to motivation are covered in this chapter. For example, the Center was able to establish that the main reason that teachers were concerned about motivation was that they recognized that motivation to read is connected to good grades (Sweet, Guthrie, & Ng, 1998). Other important discoveries were the many facets of student motivation that can affect reading (Baker & Wigfield, 1999; Wigfield & Guthrie, 1997; Wigfield, Guthrie, & McGough, 1996; Wigfield, Wilde, Baker, Fernandez-Fein, & Scher, 1996). These include the following:

- *Reading self-efficacy*—Believing that one can read well affects one's commitment to reading.
- *Reading challenge*—How challenging a book is for a reader at a particular competence level can affect whether the book will be read.
- *Reading curiosity*—Students are more likely to read about topics that are interesting to them.
- *Aesthetically enjoyable reading topics*—Some things are read because they are fun to read.
- *Importance of reading*—Recognition that reading is important can affect motivation to read and to be a good reader.
- *Reader recognition*—Being recognized as a good reader can affect motivation to read.
- *Reader grades*—Grades earned for reading can affect motivation to read.
- *Reading competition*—Being a better reader than others can motivate reading and working at becoming an even better reader.
- *Social reasons for reading*—Opportunities to read with family and friends can affect motivation to read.
- *Compliance*—Students sometimes read to fulfill academic obligations (e.g., assignments).
- *Reading work avoidance*—There are factors that certainly reduce the likelihood of reading (e.g., difficult words in text, too-complicated stories).

The Center's work must be reported in the context of many other analyses of student motivation that have been conducted in the past two decades. This research activity, including the work of the National Reading Research Center, permits much more complete understanding of student motivation for reading and the determinants of that motivation than was possible in the past.

It will become clear as this chapter proceeds that academic motivation is a fragile commodity. Although kindergarten and grade-1 children arrive at school expecting to do well, and are enthusiastic about school and academic tasks, expectations often diminish as students go through school. For academic motivation to remain high, students must be successful and perceive that they are successful. Perhaps it is not surprising that students who have a difficult time in school experience declining academic motivation. More surprising is that the policies of most elementary schools are such that most students will experience declining motivation, perceiving that they are not doing well, at least compared to other students.

More positively, much is being learned about how to reengineer school so that high academic motivation is maintained. Some of the most important ideas about how to maintain student motivation will be taken up in the second half of the chapter. When the messages in the latter half of this chapter are combined with the messages in the first half, it will be clear that more is now known about how to keep students motivated than is being done to motivate students in contemporary schools.

THE DECLINE OF ACADEMIC MOTIVATION DURING THE ELEMENTARY YEARS

Humans are born intrinsically motivated to learn and improve their performances. This is transparent to anyone who has watched a child trying to learn to walk. Indeed, developmental psychologists have made a good case that young children have great motivation to explore their world and that such exploration is important in stimulating mental and physical development (White, 1959).

Despite a motivated start on life, motivation often declines during the elementary years (Eccles, 1993; Eccles & Midgley, 1989; Harter, 1990; Meece & Miller, 1999, 2001; Stipek & MacIver, 1989). As children proceed through elementary school, they generally value school less; they are less interested in school and what is studied in school (e.g., Eccles & Midgley, 1989; Eccles et al., 1989; Meece & Miller, 1999, 2001; Wigfield, 1994; Wigfield & Eccles, 1992; Wigfield, Eccles, MacIver, Reuman, & Midgley, 1991).

Academically, kindergarten and grade-1 children believe they can do anything. If you ask them whether they are going to learn to read, they are certain of it (e.g., Entwisle & Hayduk, 1978). Moreover, even after failure, they remain confident that next time they will do better (Clifford, 1975, 1978, 1984; Parsons & Ruble, 1977; Phillips, 1963; Pressley & Ghatala, 1989; Stipek & Hoffman, 1980). Although grade-1 students who experience difficulties in learning to read generally understand that it is a difficult task, confidence in their competence to read remains high (J. W. Chapman & Tunmer, 1995). In contrast, students in grades 5 and 6 are much less confident that they will meet teacher and parent expectations with respect to academic achievement. They are much more aware of their failures than their successes (Kloosterman, 1988). Students in grades 5 and 6 often believe they are doing worse than they are (e.g., Juvonen, 1988). The weaker the student, the more pessimistic the self-appraisal and the less enthusiastic the student is about academic activities (e.g., Renick & Harter, 1989).

Georgia Southern University professor Michael C. McKenna and his associates (McKenna, Ellsworth, & Kear, 1995) have most clearly documented the declines in student attitudes about reading. They surveyed more than 17,000 elementary students in grades 1–6 from across the

United States. The survey contained 10 questions assessing how students felt about reading as a recreational activity (e.g., "How do you feel about spending free time reading?"; "How do you feel about going to a bookstore?"). It also included 10 questions assessing students' academic attitudes about reading (e.g., "How do you feel about reading your school books?"; "How do you feel when it is time for reading class?"). The students provided a rating for each question on a 1 (very negative) to 4 (very positive) scale.

For both boys and girls, for all ethnic and racial groups, and for all ability levels, there were clear declines in the positive attitudes of students toward reading, both recreational and academic. Yes, girls were more positive than boys, and the declines in attitude were not as consistent for high-ability readers as for other students. Even so, what was most striking in the data was that no matter how the researchers looked at them, attitudes toward reading were relatively high in grade 1, with student indifference toward reading the norm by grade 6.

Wigfield et al. (1997) also examined reading motivation across the elementary years. They found a clear decline in interest in reading during the elementary years as well as a clear decline in student perceptions that reading was useful.

Perhaps most disturbing is the fact that by the middle-grade-school years, some children are really down on reading. When Linda B. Gambrell and her National Reading Research Center colleagues (Gambrell, Codling, & Palmer, 1996; Gambrell, Palmer, Codling, & Mazzoni, 1996) administered a reading motivation inventory to grade-3 and grade-5 students, they found nontrivial proportions of children who claimed they would rather clean their rooms than read (17% of respondents), who expected to spend little time reading when they grew up (14%), and who felt that people who read are boring (10%). There is reason for concern when children are so turned off by an activity as important as reading.

Developmental and educational psychologists carried out in-depth analyses of some of the reasons for the declines in positive academic attitudes and motivation during the elementary years. There are several contributing factors, each of which is reviewed in what follows. These factors coalesce so that declining academic motivation with advancing grade level is inevitable for many students, at least given the nature of contemporary schooling.

Developmental Shifts in Attributions about the Causes of Performance

Different people explain their successes and failures in different ways. When some people experience success or failure, they explain the outcome as due to personal effort. That is, a success is attributed to trying hard, while a failure is explained as reflecting lack of effort. Alternatively, successes and failures can be explained in terms of abilities: Such people might reason that "I succeeded because I am naturally smart, being born with a high IQ," or "I cannot read well because I was born with dyslexia." Sometimes people explain successes or failures in terms of task characteristics. For example, a student who did well on a test might believe it was because the test was easy, and a student who did poorly might blame the failure on the test being too difficult. Finally, some believe that what happens to them is determined by luck, with successes due to good luck and failures due to bad luck.

Of all these explanations—effort, ability, task difficulty, and luck—the only one that is under personal control is effort. Thus, if you believe that you succeeded on a task because of high effort, there is reason to exert effort in the future. If you think that your failure reflects insufficient effort, the route to future success is to do more and try harder, and effort attributions are consistently associated with high effort in the future (Weiner, 1979). In contrast, there is nothing a person can do about inherited abilities, the difficulty of tasks, or luck; thus, individuals who believe their academic outcomes depend on ability, task difficulty, or luck have little or no motivation to try hard in the future.

One of the reasons that children's motivations decline is that, as children mature during the grade-school years, the ways that they explain their performance outcomes change. Kindergarten and grade-1 students do not differentiate between effort and ability. Thus, young children typically attribute their successes to effort. Moreover, whenever they exhibit effort, they believe their effort reflects high ability. Thus, if they fail but expended high effort, they leave the task still believing they have high ability because they exerted effort! In short, 6- and 7-year-olds typically believe that they can succeed by trying hard (Nicholls, 1978, 1990).

With increasing age during the elementary years, children differentiate effort and ability. Thus, by the end of the elementary years, children understand that if two people expend the same amount of effort, the one who is more successful probably has higher ability. Moreover, by the end of the grade-school years, students are explaining successes and failures more in terms of ability than effort. Successes are considered to be indications of high ability and failures to be indications of low ability.

Of course, such attributions are much less motivating than the effort attributions of younger children. When a person believes that ability determines performance, there is no motivation for exerting effort, since effort does not matter. That children increasingly believe their failures are due to low ability probably goes far in explaining their decreasing motivation to tackle academic tasks.

Young Students and Their Attributions as They Try to Learn to Read

Learning to decode and recognize words is a very challenging task for some children. Children can make a lot of mistakes along the way. The grade-1 child is not as likely to be discouraged by such mistakes as a child in grade 4 who is struggling to learn decoding. After all, for the grade-1 child, trying hard is what counts. In contrast, the grade-4 child has come to believe that having to try harder on a task that others accomplish with much less effort is a sign of low ability. Thus, for the grade-4 child still struggling with decoding as classmates read with ease, there is plenty of reason to conclude that he or she does not have the ability to read. Such a conclusion would undermine the student's expenditure of effort in learning how to decode. This is one reason that the first grader struggling to read is much more likely to be influenced by teacher and parent urgings to try harder than is an older child. From a motivational perspective, it makes no sense to expect that if children do not learn to read on their own in grades 1 or 2, they will learn later, when they are ready. The motivation to exert the effort to learn to read will never be greater than it is during the primary years. The older the struggling reader, the more the struggle will be interpreted as reflecting low ability, with the child increasingly unmotivated to learn to read.

Children with Learning Disabilities

The role of attributions in motivating academic efforts has been studied, especially in children with learning disabilities. Learning-disabled children are much more likely than their normally achieving classmates to believe that their academic performances are determined by ability and to be very pessimistic about their academic abilities (Brooks, 2001; Elbaum & Vaughn, 2003; Gans, Kenny, & Ghany, 2003; Jacobsen, Lowery, & DuCette, 1986; Pearl, 1982). Yes, there are exceptions: Some learning-disabled children continue to believe that they can do better by trying hard. Continuing to believe that effort matters probably makes a difference for these children. Such low achievers who believe they can control their academic progress through effort, in fact, do achieve at higher levels than low achievers who believe their low achievement reflects low ability (Kistner, Osborne, & LeVerrier, 1988).

Often I speak to groups of special educators, and when I do I always ask the audience the following question: "What if you talk with grade-5 or -6 learning-disabled students about how they are doing in school and ask a student to explain why he or she is having problems in school. What does such a child say?" Every audience provides the same answer: "The kid says, 'It's because I'm stupid.' " Years of school failure result in students concluding that their academic achievement is not controllable, that they do not have the ability to do well academically. They have come to expect academic failure. Developmental studies show that such attributions are very different from the attributions these children made when they were younger, when they believed that effort might help them make progress.

What is going on here? How does a spirited 6-year-old who knows he can learn to read become a 10-year-old who believes that reading is something that he cannot accomplish? (No sexism implied here, for young boys are more likely than young girls to experience difficulties in learning to read.) The child's continued failures lead to negative affect (Covington & Omelich, 1979a) and decreasing expectancies for future success (Covington & Omelich, 1979b). That classmates are experiencing success following their efforts does not help; in fact, it probably intensifies the struggling student's feelings of personal incapacity (Covington, 1987). Learned helplessness—that is, the belief that nothing one does can lead to success—develops in such a situation (Dweck, 1987). Children who struggle to learn to read quickly come to believe that they are not good readers and that reading is difficult and something they do not like (J. W. Chapman, Tunmer, & Prochnow, 2000). Doing nothing can actually be therapeutic for such children, for at least failure following lack of effort does not lead to the conclusion that one is stupid. In that case, learning-disabled children can more easily convince themselves that they do not do well in reading because they are not interested enough to try (Covington & Omelich, 1981, 1984). Is it any surprise that children with reading disabilities often seem passive in school? Trying gets them nowhere; not trying permits an explanation of failure that is not as damaging to their self-esteem as failure following effort.

Recall the argument made in Chapter 3 that children who experience difficulties in learning to decode could and would learn if they were taught using an approach different from the one experienced in school. Failing to make progress in decoding during grade 1 may not seem frustrating to the child because the grade-1 child is so willing to persist. Such willingness to persist wanes as the child matures and comes to understand that she or he is making little progress, eventually interpreting this as an indication of low ability. Not intervening when children are experiencing initial reading difficulties is setting students up for additional failure and diminishing self-esteem. School days filled with failure are school days filled with the lesson that "You are stupid." That the grade-1 child is not much ruffled by failures is no reason not to intervene, for it will not be long before that same child is interpreting failures as indications of a lack of ability. Once children come to the conclusion that they lack ability with respect to reading, there is little or no reason for them to make additional efforts to learn to read, and hence interventions at that point must also be targeted at increasing the child's academic self-esteem. Reading difficulties that might have been addressed in grade 1 through simple decoding instruction become much more serious, now that the once vital child seems helpless. Waiting to intervene makes no sense from the perspective of attribution theory. Early difficulties in learning to read reduce subsequent efforts to learn to read, thus producing more reading problems (Onatsu-Arvilommi & Nurmi, 2000), a cycle that should be stopped as soon as there is any hint of it, if there is going to be any hope of developing a competent, motivated reader.

Other Factors Affecting Attributions

The belief that efforts pay off is affected by histories of success and failure, the former encouraging the students' continuing belief in effort and the latter causing them to doubt their own abilities. Other factors play a role as well. Teachers and parents can encourage effort attributions. They can make children aware of how their personal successes are tied to their efforts (Schunk, 1991). Parents' and teachers' awareness of their power to be persuasive about the role of effort in success is the main reason that effective educational environments (such as the ones considered in previous chapters) and the motivating environments considered later in this chapter always include the repeated message that effort matters.

Teachers and parents can also help to develop in children an understanding of intelligence that is very different from the theory that intelligence is determined by genes and thus unmodifiable. The message can be sent to students that ability is not a fixed entity but, rather, is changeable. Psychologist Carol S. Dweck and her colleagues (e.g., Dweck & Leggett, 1988; Henderson & Dweck, 1990) have proposed that a critical determinant of achievement motivation is whether a person believes that intelligence is fixed biologically and hence neither malleable nor affected by environmental variables. Dweck describes people who believe that intelligence is fixed as possessing an "entity" theory of intelligence: Such people believe intelligence is a thing that one either has in great quantity or does not. In contrast, those who think intelligence is modifiable subscribe to an "incremental" theory of intelligence.

Dweck has found that the particular view of intelligence held by an individual has a powerful impact on his or her achievement behavior. Entity theorists are oriented toward seeking positive evaluations of their abilities and avoiding negative evaluations. Such a perspective can be damaging when negative feedback occurs, as it inevitably does in school. Such students are likely to interpret failures as indications of low intelligence and hence be discouraged by failures. In contrast, incremental theorists are much more oriented toward increasing their abilities, believing that daily efforts lead to small gains, all of which can add up to substantially higher

intelligence when effort persists over the long term. Such students keep trying when obstacles occur because they see obstacles as a natural part of the
learning process.

In short, students who are entity theorists are more likely to experience
negative emotion when confronted with failure, believing that failure signals low ability and allowing that belief to undermine future attempts at
academic tasks. Indeed, the entity theorist may be so motivated to avoid
additional evidence of low ability that she or he will not engage again in a
task that has been associated with failure in the past. Incremental theorists
experience much less negative affect in response to failure, interpreting the
failure as part of the improvement process, which motivates high persistence.

As long as there is success, there is little difference in the behaviors of
entity and incremental theorists. It is when failure occurs that the differences in their outlooks become apparent, with the entity theorists much
more at risk for believing they are helpless when they experience difficulties
during challenging tasks, leading to low persistence and task avoidance. In
contrast, incremental theorists just keep plugging away following a failure.

It is for these reasons that effective classrooms should include the following messages:

- Trying hard fosters achievement and intelligence.
- Failure is a natural part of learning.
- Being best is not what school is about; getting better *is*.

Every teacher and parent can send the messages that people get
smarter by trying hard, that part of getting smart is bouncing back from
failures, and that school is about becoming better, not becoming best.
Given the tendency of children to explain their performances in terms of
ability, there is plenty of reason to do everything possible to encourage students to believe that effort attributions are the way to go when explaining
performance.

Reading Class Is Boring

One final possibility that has to be acknowledged is that many of the tasks
presented to students in the name of reading are, in fact, boring. In many
states, a great deal of time labeled reading instruction is diverted from actual reading to preparation for the tasks on the state reading test, with such
tests heavy on low-level skills (i.e., word recognition, rapid reading of simple text) rather than reading and responding to interesting texts. By sixth
grade, the boredom can be so great that the challenge is for students to put
up with the test preparation without their boredom spilling over into mis-

behavior (Fairbanks & Broughton, 2003). Test preparation is not reading but has the potential for decreasing interest in reading.

Summary

Primary-grade children have much more faith in effort than do students in the later grades. This provides great motivation for accomplishing complicated tasks such as learning to read. When grade-1 children experience frustration, their effort attributions support the expenditure of additional effort. In contrast, older children are more likely to make ability attributions than effort attributions, so that failures are no longer seen as indications of insufficient effort but as indications of low ability. Failures followed by attributions of low ability lead to reduced motivation for the frustrating activity. Thus, grade-1 students are more likely to be motivated to continue with challenging tasks than are grade-3 students.

Worse yet is when the grade-3 student is confronted with a task that is difficult for her or him but was accomplished several years earlier by most other grade-3 children. Thus, the grade-3 student who has not yet learned to read interprets his or her failures to date as strong evidence of a lack of ability to read, undermining attempts to make additional efforts to learn to read. There is no reason to believe, based on attributional theory, that a high motivation to learn to read will be maintained for children who go through grades 1 and 2 without acquiring the basic reading skills that they need.

Researchers have done a good job of establishing the value of encouraging students to continue to make attributions as they did when they were in grade 1 and to believe that academic success depends on effort. Even more generally, psychologists have determined that academic motivation is more likely to be encouraged if students come to believe that intelligence itself is the result of effort rather than the reflection of innate ability. A lot of input about the value of effort is necessary, however, because with increasing grade level the implicit message in the classroom is that effort is not what matters—that there are the smart and the not-so-smart.

Grade-Level Differences in Classroom Reward Structures

Intrinsic academic motivation is killed off by academic failures. An important reason that such failures are more devastating with increasing grade level is that competition between students accelerates during the elementary years.

Competition is a way of life in many classrooms. There is grading on the curve, so that only a very few students can receive the highest grades. Worse yet, grades are often public and salient in the classroom, as when students "call in" their grades as the teacher marks them in the grade book or when students retrieve their papers from the "graded bin." Finding one's own paper in such bins results in exposure to the grades of many other students in the class. Thus, each student in a class knows how she or he is doing relative to others.

Many societal forces support such competitiveness. How many parents respond to their children's report card by asking how "so-and-so" did, followed by remarks about how it would be nice if their son or daughter were like "so-and-so"? Local papers carry news about academic achievements in the school, for example, publishing the names of students earning straight A's.

One result of this obsession with identifying who is smart and, implicitly, who is not, is to undermine the academic motivation of many children. Classroom competition and evaluation foster what John G. Nicholls (1989) referred to as ego involvement. Success in the competitive classroom (especially relative to peers) implies high intellectual capacity (i.e., that one is smart, which is ego-enhancing), while failure implies low capacity (which is ego-diminishing). Since most students will not end up doing "best" in the class, feelings of failure, self-criticism, and negative self-esteem occur often (Ames, 1984). Many students come to expect that they will not earn top grades or be reinforced as much as other students. Such a system has high potential for undermining effort when success is not certain (e.g., with new task demands), for trying and failing leads to feelings of low ability.

One likely reason that there is a clear decline in academic motivation from the early primary to the later elementary grades is that comparative evaluations are less frequent and salient in the early primary years than in the later primary and middle grades (Harter, Whitesell, & Kowalski, 1992; Stipek & Daniels, 1988). With increasing age, children are more aware of the competitiveness in their classrooms (see Harter et al., 1992; also Schmidt, Ollendick, & Stanowicz, 1988) and of the implications of not succeeding. What is certain, based on research (e.g., Wigfield, 1988), is that by the middle elementary years, paying attention to how one does compared to others affects perceptions of one's own competency, expectancies about future success, and thus (potentially) school performance.

Life in Noncompetitive Classrooms

The problems produced by classroom competitiveness are especially apparent when competitive classrooms are compared with ones that are not so competitive. In some classrooms, rather than rewarding students for being better than one another, students are rewarded for doing better than they did previously. They are rewarded for personal improvement on academic tasks. Nicholls referred to such classrooms as fostering task involvement.

Nicholls and his colleague Terri A. Thorkildsen (e.g., 1987) studied 30 grade-5 classrooms ranging in ego and task involvement. They found that work avoidance was much more commonly reported in ego-involved (competitive) classrooms than in task-involved (noncompetitive) classrooms. The students in the task-oriented classrooms believed that success in school depended on interest, effort, and attempting to learn, whereas the students in the ego-involved classrooms believed that success depended on being smarter than other kids and trying to beat out other students. That is, whether grade-5 students continued to believe in effort, as they had when they were younger, or in ability as a determinant of performance depended on the reward structure of the classroom.

Task-oriented classrooms are much more likely to keep students interested in and committed to school than are ego-oriented classrooms (Meece & Miller, 1999; Nicholls, 1989). The problem is that many more classrooms are of the ego-involved type than of the task-involved type. Far too often, the goal is to get better grades than the ones earned by peers rather than to learn (e.g., Ames, 1992; Blumenfeld, 1992). Many other classrooms are structured so as to encourage expectations of failure (i.e., relative to other students) rather than success. This has significant consequences for students.

For example, Susan B. Nolen (1988) assessed whether grade-8 students were task- or ego-oriented youngsters. In addition, Nolen assessed students' use of particular strategies for reading and understanding textbook material. Although both task- and ego-oriented students used superficial strategies for processing text (e.g., reading the whole thing over and over), the task-oriented students were much more likely than the ego-oriented students to endorse and use strategies that involved deeper processing of text (e.g., trying to see how this fits with what they had learned in class). The type of sophisticated reading that should be fostered in students occurred more often in the noncompetitive (non-ego-oriented) classrooms.

Mainstreaming

The effects of classroom competitiveness are also striking when the fate of students with learning difficulties is considered. In recent years, there has been a national movement to eliminate special classrooms for students experiencing academic difficulties and, instead, have them receive their education in regular classrooms. By the middle elementary grades, mainstreaming means placement into a competitive classroom in which failure relative to others is virtually assured for the child with learning difficulties. A similar situation occurs with respect to the education of English-as-a-second-language students. Such students often enter competitive classrooms far behind the other students. The competitive nature of the classrooms guarantees failure relative to other students, with potentially devastating impact on the motivation of the students who were disadvantaged from the outset. Whenever a class includes a mix of abilities and preparation levels, classroom competition virtually guarantees that many students will experience failure, potentially impacting most negatively on the academic self-esteem and motivation of at-risk students.

From a motivational perspective, if school must be competitive, placing at-risk students in classrooms with other at-risk students has advantages. A student may have more positive perceptions about his or her own academic ability and better school performance (measured in some absolute way) if enrolled in a low- rather than a high-ability class, because what one thinks about one's own ability is determined with reference to the students in one's class. Social comparisons with classmates can motivate additional effort (e.g., when one is at the top of a low-ability class) or undermine effort (e.g., when one is near the bottom of a high-ability class; e.g., Marsh, 1987). Of course, better yet for such students would be to place them in noncompetitive classes where they would be given good grades for improving. However, the reality is that most schools in the United States are going to remain competitive for the foreseeable future. If that is the case, mainstreaming has great potential to undermine the motivation of the students who are mainstreamed.

Consequences of Success

So far in this section the concern has been with the negative effects of rewards on those who do not often receive them in classrooms. As it turns out, classroom rewards can undermine the intrinsic motivation of those who receive the rewards. When students receive tangible rewards for activities that are intrinsically interesting to them, their intrinsic interest in the activity can decline. Thus, when teachers begin to reward behaviors that had been intrinsically rewarding, they may undermine students' interest in those activities in the future when rewards are not available. This is known as the overjustification effect, with students coming to believe that they are engaging in rewarded activities for the reward they are receiving rather than because of the intrinsic value of the activity (Lepper, Keavney, & Drake, 1996). Once rewarded, they begin to justify their behavior to themselves, making the case to themselves that they are carrying out the behavior because of the tangible reward. The person who does something in the absence of reward can only explain her or his behavior to her- or himself in terms of personal interest in the activity.

McLoyd (1979) provided an apt demonstration of the overjustification effect with respect to reading. Children read high-interest books, some receiving a reward for doing so. McLoyd observed that when students could read on their own without the possibility of reward, those who had not received rewards for reading did more reading than those who previously received rewards for doing it. There is very good reason to suspect that students who are reading and writing for "points" given by a teacher or for high grades may not be as highly motivated to read in the absence of teacher rewards than they would have been had they participated in instruction in which classroom rewards for performance were not so salient.

I am often asked about the implications of the overjustification effect for reading reward programs such as the one sponsored by Pizza Hut. The answer is that it depends on the kid. For children who are already motivated to read, providing extrinsic rewards has the potential to undermine their intrinsic motivation to read. For children who are not motivated to read, such programs can motivate reading that would not otherwise occur, unless, of course, the number of books read is highly public, with competition between students to read the most books. I urge teachers to use such programs with unmotivated students but to refrain from using tangible incentive programs with students who are already reading for the fun of it and to implement the programs to downplay competition (e.g., the reward is received without public reference to the total number of books read by individual students).

I am also often asked about Accelerated Reader®, a system of providing points to students for reading texts and answering literal questions about the texts to demonstrate comprehension of the material. Based on my reading of studies that have been done, I cannot decide what impact this system has on achievement. With respect to motivation, however, it, at best, has variable impact on motivation and attitudes (Mallette, Henk, & Melnick, 2004; Vollands, Topping, & Evans, 1999). That the approach involves a great deal of public display of achievement data—for example, charts indicating how many books each student has read—certainly has to give one pause from a motivational perspective, with this approach definitely stimulating classroom competition, which is known to undermine academic motivation. If a teacher is going to use this approach, I would urge that efforts be made to keep student reading data private, with students plotting their own progress to note how much they have read but not caught up in comparing their own progress with that of other readers in the class. The more public comparative achievement data, the greater the risk for undermining motivation. Even with such precautions, however, there is not enough research on Accelerated Reader to be confident in any conclusions about it, including its general impact on student motivation to read, especially interest in reading once the student exits the program.

Summary

One of the reasons that, with increasing grade level, children increasingly tend to believe that ability determines achievement is that classrooms are more competitive with advancing grade level. Competitive classrooms foster the attribution that ability is what matters, thus undermining student academic motivation. It does not have to be that way, however: It is possible to structure classrooms so that students are graded on improvement rather than in comparison to other students. In such classrooms, there seems to be greater academic motivation and more sophisticated reading. The problem is that there are too few such classrooms, for the competitive classroom model thrives in contemporary America. The United States generally is a nation of competitive classrooms, which are structured so that most children will experience failure relative to other children (or at least be less successful than many other students in the class).

A further complication is that rewards such as grades can undermine students' intrinsic motivations. Recall from the survey conducted by McKenna et al. (1995) that many children are intrinsically motivated to read in the early grades but that the motivation of even the top students declines. This occurs even though top students are being rewarded with high grades for doing well! Whenever the emphasis on grades is high enough that students can convince themselves that they are reading only to obtain a high grade or other tangible reward, there is danger of undermining whatever intrinsic motivation a student might have (Sweet & Guthrie, 1996).

One of the strengths of primary-grade classrooms is that they are more likely to be organized along cooperative principles. The increasing shift to competitiveness during the later primary (i.e., increasingly in grades 2 and 3 compared to kindergarten and grade 1) and middle elementary years comes at a time when students' thinking abilities mature in ways that increase their notice of their own achievements relative to those of others.

Developmental Differences in Making Social Comparisons

Young children tend not to compare themselves much with others, especially with respect to psychological characteristics such as intelligence, reading ability, or extent of prior knowledge. Yes, preschool children can and do compare the tangible goodies they have with the tangible goodies another child has (Ruble, Boggiano, Feldman, & Loebl, 1980): "I have more orange juice than you." "Do not!" "Do too!" But they do not make much of differences or similarities in performance on academic tasks. Thus, a grade-1 student who feels bad because she or he is having difficulty with two-column addition is unlikely to feel better if the teacher reminds the student that all the other kids in the class are experiencing the same difficulty. With increasing age during the elementary-grade years, students become concerned with their academic standing relative to others (Ruble, 1983). Again, because for most students there will be others around who are doing better, the increasing focus on comparing one's own achievement with that of classmates has increasing potential for leading to negative conclusions about one's own ability. Such conclusions can then translate into reduced motivation to achieve.

Summary

Academic intrinsic motivation declines with increasing grade level. Why? It is probably due to shifts in information-processing abilities and proclivities as well as characteristics of American schooling as an institution.

With respect to information processing, there is an increasing tendency with increasing age during the elementary grades to make achievement comparisons with others. For many children, this means increasing recognition that their performance is not as good as that of other students. There are also developmental shifts in attributional tendencies. Although preschoolers and early-elementary-grade students do not interpret academic difficulties as indications of low ability, the tendency to do so increases with age. The greater the effort required to obtain academic success, the more likely it is to encourage an inference of low ability with increasing grade level. In short, developmental shifts in information processing lead to developmental shifts in expectations about future success and failure.

These shifts favoring student inferences about low ability occur in the context of schooling that increasingly emphasizes competition with increasing grade level. Despite the healthiness of sending the message that intelligence is incremental, school is an institution that often signals that intelligence is fixed, something a student either has or does not have (Ames, 1992). This is very discouraging for many students who do not do well in such a competitive environment. The bad attitudes that many high school students have about school seem very justified, given such an institutional climate. School has shaped them to expect academic failure or at least feelings of less than complete success relative to many classmates.

My view is that changing the motivational structure of schooling should be a high priority in education reform. In the meantime, individual teachers and parents can do their part by repeatedly sending the message to children that effort counts and that an excellent mind is built a little bit at a time through academic effort. Reward children for growth, not for outperforming others. As is elaborated in the rest of this chapter, reading researchers have identified a number of more specific ways to maintain and increase the motivation of children for reading.

INCREASING STUDENT MOTIVATION FOR LITERACY

The research in the past two decades on student motivation has heightened awareness that students often are not motivated to read or to learn to read better. This awareness has energized efforts to identify ways to increase student motivation. Admittedly, most of what is described here has not been researched so thoroughly that any of the recommendations can be given with great confidence. As a whole, however, the research community has identified a variety of methods with the potential for increasing student motivation for reading, each of which is conceptually sensible, if not yet fully validated. Teachers who use the methods described in this section will be on the cutting edge of educational motivation, although I expect that edge to be sharpened somewhat in the next few years as more evaluation data on the various techniques reviewed here accumulate.

The methods described in this section range from individual components of literacy instruction (e.g., interesting materials, attribution retraining) to entire redefinitions of the literacy program (e.g., concept-oriented instruction, whole language). The discussion proceeds from research on individual components to approaches intended to redefine literacy instruction completely.

Appropriately Challenging Texts and Tasks

The data are overwhelming that tasks a little bit beyond the learner's current competence level are motivating (e.g., Brophy, 1987). Tasks that are a little bit challenging cause students to work hard and feel good about what they are doing. In addition to being boring, low-challenging tasks never provide learners with the opportunity to see what they can do, and thus undermine confidence (Miller & Meece, 1999). Recall from previous chapters that effective teachers monitor what children are capable of doing and then nudge them to try something slightly more challenging. Such challenge is at the heart of a healthy motivational outlook.

Attribution Retraining

That the attributions of many low-achieving children are dysfunctional (i.e., the students attribute their failures to uncontrollable ability factors and hence are not motivated to exert academic effort; e.g., Carr, Borkowski, & Maxwell, 1991) has inspired some researchers to attempt to retrain attributional tendencies. Both applied efforts and basic research (e.g., Foersterling, 1985; Stipek & Kowalski, 1989) have documented that attribution retraining can make a substantial difference in the motivation of students who otherwise tend to attribute their poor performances to factors other than effort. Particularly relevant here, John G. Borkowski and his colleagues (e.g., Borkowski, Carr, Rellinger, & Pressley, 1990; Borkowski, Weyhing, & Carr, 1988; Reid & Borkowski, 1987) have provided the most compelling analyses and data about interventions aimed at shifting the attributions of low achievers in order to promote reading comprehension.

Borkowski has recognized that, for low-functioning students, attributing success to effort alone would probably be ineffective. This is consistent with the perspective emphasized throughout this book that strategies, metacognition, and conceptual knowledge also contribute to reading achievement. Thus, Borkowski's group has been teaching students to use strategies to accomplish intellectual tasks at the same time that they persuade students that their successes and failures on academic tasks are due to their own efforts while using appropriate strategies (Clifford, 1984). Borkowski and his colleagues persuade students that, as they learn strategies, they are acquiring tools that will permit them to improve their academic performance, providing a powerful motivation to use the strategies they are acquiring (M. Chapman, Skinner, & Baltes, 1990).

For example, in one study (Carr & Borkowski, 1989), underachieving elementary students were assigned to one of three conditions:

1. In the *strategies + attribution training condition*, children were taught comprehension strategies. They were instructed to self-test while they read in order to determine whether they understood their reading. The students were also taught summarization, topic sentence, and questioning strategies as a means of understanding a text. The attributional part of the training consisted of emphasizing to students that they could understand the text by applying the comprehension strategies—that their comprehension of the text was a function of how they approached it rather than of any inherent comprehension abilities.
2. Participants in the *strategies-only condition* were taught the strategies without the benefit of attributional training.
3. Students in the *control condition* were provided neither strategies instruction nor attributional training.

What a difference the strategies + attributional training made! When tested 3 weeks following the conclusion of the instruction, the strategies + attribution participants were more likely to be using the strategies than other participants in the study, and recall of text was higher in this condition than in the other conditions of the study. In addition, the strategies + attribution subjects were using comprehension strategies in the classroom much more than the students in the other conditions of the study.

Although much more work analyzing the effects of attributional retraining needs to be done in order to understand completely its potential for modifying views of self as learner, many who work with learning-disabled students in particular are already employing attributional retraining with their students. For example, as learning-disabled students are taught comprehension, writing, and memory strategies in a well-known learning-disabilities curriculum created by Donald D. Deshler, Jean B. Schumaker, and their colleagues at the University of Kansas (e.g., Deshler & Schumaker, 1988; Deshler, Schumaker, Harris, & Graham, 1998), there is consistent emphasis on the role of controllable factors, such as the use of strategies, as a determinant of performance. This is because the Kansas group recognizes that the attributions made by learning-disabled students often are dysfunctional (e.g., "I am stupid"). Such attributions, if permitted to persist, have high potential for defeating other instruction, since believing that one is stupid is also believing that there is nothing that can be done about it.

Interesting Texts to Read

Throughout the 20th century, going back at least to John Dewey (1913), it has been recognized that interest matters with students: High interest increases student engagement and learning from text (e.g., Hidi, 1990, 2001; Renninger & Wozniak, 1985; Schiefele, 1992). This insight has prompted many authors and materials developers to attempt to create academic materials that "grab" students' interest.

Richard C. Anderson and his colleagues (e.g., Anderson, Mason, & Shirey, 1984) carried out some of the best-known work on the role of interest in children's reading of texts. Children read sentences that had been rated either as interesting or uninteresting. Interesting sentences were much more certain to be remembered later than were uninteresting sentences, producing a very large effect relative to the size of effects produced by other manipulations (e.g., readability of sentences).

Anderson's group also conducted some extremely detailed analytical studies (e.g., see Anderson, 1982) to determine the mechanisms underlying the interest effect, hypothesizing that more interesting materials were more likely to be attended by students. In fact, that seemed to be the case, with students spending more time reading interesting texts. In addition, interesting texts were so absorbing that readers failed to respond to an external signal (e.g., to press a button in response to a sound heard while they were reading) as quickly as they did when reading uninteresting texts. Even so, greater attention alone did not account for their greater learning of the interesting materials, for when differences in attention and effort were factored out of the learning data (i.e., the amount of time spent reading sentences was controlled statistically), there were still large effects of interest (e.g., Shirey & Reynolds, 1988). Thus, interest can affect directly both attention and learning, but only some of the increases in learning are due to its effect on attention to academic content.

Unfortunately, when Anderson, Shirey, Wilson, and Fielding (1987) analyzed social studies and science textbooks presented to children in school, they found them to be dull. They also determined that authors often attempted to make texts interesting by adding stimulating anecdotes. Texts filled with anecdotes, however, often lack coherence (e.g., Armbruster, 1984). In addition, the reader can completely miss the point of the text even while remembering the anecdotes in it. That is, stimulating information and seductive details can be recalled (e.g., John F. Kennedy and Robert F. Kennedy played touch football on the White House lawn with their children), although there is no learning of either abstract or general points covered in the text (e.g., the Kennedy administration proposed sweeping social reforms; Garner, 1992; Garner, Alexander, Gillingham, Kulikowich, & Brown, 1991; Garner, Gillingham, & White, 1989; Hidi & Baird, 1988; Wade & Adams, 1990).

While there is not much reason to be sanguine that texts can be made more interesting without also being seductive, we should not dismiss the possibility of increasing student interest in what they read. A low-cost way to increase the interest of students is to permit them to choose for themselves what they will read. This is one of the main motivations of whole-language educators to provide students with so much choice. Of course, a problem with letting kids read what they are interested in reading is that classroom libraries and school libraries are mostly filled with books that are of little interest to youngsters (Ivey & Broaddus, 2001; Worthy, Moorman, & Turner, 1999). What grade schoolers want are scary books, comics and cartoons, some popular magazines, sports books, books about drawing, books about cars and trucks, animal books, and funny novels, with only funny novels in abundant supply in schools (Ivey & Broaddus, 2001; Worthy et al., 1999). Some kids can buy what they want to read and do so; others cannot or do not. I think we need to think hard about how to increase access to books and magazines that are attractive to kids as well as how to make really worthwhile readings more attractive to elementary students. I've seen enough classrooms where teachers have gotten the kids turned on to excellent literature to know that it is possible to do so. Balanced literacy teachers know what the good stuff is for kids to be reading and find ways to make certain their students are reading it. Whole language heightened our consciousness about the motivating power of good literature.

Whole Language: Literature and Literature-Based Activities

A consistent claim of whole-language theorists and enthusiasts is that literacy-rich environments are motivating to students. In fact, there is considerable support for their assertion. National Reading Research Center researchers Barbara M. Palmer, Rose Marie Codling, and Linda B. Gambrell (1994) asked grade-3 and grade-5 students from 16 classrooms about the factors that motivated them to read. Forty-eight children varying in their reading ability and motivation to read were interviewed in depth. In many different ways, the students reported that their motivations to read depended on rich literacy environments.

Thus, prior experiences with books were a major motivation for wanting to read, as well as for choosing to read particular books. Children reported wanting to read books after seeing them on the television show *Reading Rainbow* or after hearing a book read by a teacher or parent. Similarly, prior experience with books in a series motivated continued reading of the series. For example, the American Girls series permits the child to learn more about characters that they have learned to like from reading previous books in the series.

Social interactions revolving around books also matter. The participants in the study reported wanting to read books that their friends, parents, and teachers talked about. Remarks such as the following were common:

> My friend Kristin was reading it and told me about it and I said, "Hmmm, that sounds pretty interesting."

> I got interested in it because the other group . . . [was] reading it, so I checked it out of the library. (Palmer et al., 1994, p. 177)

Book access was also reported as important by the children, who reported high motivation to read books they owned and ones available to them in the classroom. Particularly striking was the importance that the students attributed to the classroom library, consistent with the emphasis in whole language that classrooms filled with books motivate literate interactions with them (Fractor, Woodruff, Martinez, & Teale, 1993; Morrow, 1992).

As noted in the last section, a hallmark of the whole-language philosophy (as well as educational motivational theorists; Schraw, Flowerday, & Lehman, 2001) is that literacy instruction should include freedom of choice and will be more motivating if it does. Consistent with the perspective that choice is important in motivating literacy, the children in the Palmer et al. (1994) study reported they were more excited about reading books that they chose to read than ones they were required to read (Spaulding, 1992). My own predilections are to believe the children, for they are closer to their motivations than anyone else. Many social scientists are skeptical of self-reports, however, especially with respect to motivation. They prefer observations of motivated reading. What would be most believable to the social science community would be observations of greater motivation in literacy-rich environments than in more conventional classroom environments. There is in fact some evidence of this type.

Julianne C. Turner's (1995) dissertation study at the University of Michigan was a very thorough comparison of motivation in literacy-rich whole-language grade-1 classrooms versus grade-1 classrooms that emphasized skills. She studied six grade-1 classrooms in a school district that used whole language and six grade-1 classrooms in a similar district that used a basal instructional program. The whole-language classrooms were pretty much consistent with whole language as described in Chapter 1, except that there was quite a bit of teacher explanation about phonics and other skills. This explanation often came in the context of group reading of texts (e.g., big books), however. The basal instructional program included stories and skill work, including ditto worksheets as part of phonics instruction.

One of the most striking outcomes in Turner's (1995) study was that the children in the whole-language classrooms used more learning strategies than did the students in the basal classes. That is, they seemed more engaged with the content, rehearsing it more, elaborating on ideas they encountered, planning more, and monitoring whether they were understanding what they read. Thus, whole language seemed to make a difference. Even so, both types of classrooms afforded opportunities for the types of tasks and situations that Palmer et al. (1994) concluded were motivating. Consistent with Palmer and colleagues' (1994) conclusions, across both types of classrooms, students persisted most in reading when they were involved in activities like partner reading and reading of trade books, in contrast to when they were involved in activities such as worksheets. When children could select texts on their own, they read more. In short, Turner (1995) observed that when the classroom conditions matched those that the children in the Palmer et al. (1994) study claimed were motivating, students seemed more motivated.

Lesley M. Morrow (1992; Morrow & Sharkey, 1993) and her colleagues at Rutgers University, in work sponsored in part by the National Reading Research Center, also explored the motivational consequences of instruction consistent with whole-language principles. She introduced a literature-based reading program into grade-2 classrooms. The program included literacy centers that stimulated a variety of literacy activities (e.g., reading, felt-board enactments of stories, listening to taped stories, writing), teacher-guided literature activities (e.g., reading and telling of stories by teachers, student retelling and rewriting of stories, writing of original stories, book sharing), and independent reading and writing periods that permitted student choice of literacy activities (i.e., reading, writing, listening, enacting, etc.). In the whole-language classrooms, there was a great deal of social, cooperative interaction between students as they engaged in literacy activities.

In contrast, students in control classrooms participated in a traditional basal program supported by workbook exercises. Control instruction included small-group lessons and seatwork. After completing workbook activities, students read library books. Although teachers occasionally read stories to children in the control classrooms, this was not a focus of instruction.

By the end of the intervention, there were clear advantages for the students in the whole-language classrooms. For example, students in these classrooms were better able to retell and rewrite stories that were read to them than were students in control classrooms. Students in the whole-language classrooms outperformed control participants on a listening comprehension test. They also outperformed controls when asked to compose their own stories, using language that was more complex and included more diverse vocabulary than the language of the control participants. Most critical in the context of this chapter on student motivation, the students in the whole-language classrooms read more books and stories outside of school. When the whole-language students talked about their literacy program, they did so with enthusiasm, emphasizing that it was fun.

In summary, there is converging evidence that when classroom life is rich in literature and authentic reading experiences students are more motivated than when instruction is more consistent with traditional skills and drills. Perhaps the most incontrovertible conclusion with respect to instruction filled with social interactions around the reading of real literature is that such experiences enliven classrooms. Whole-language experiences can be very motivating (Bergin & LaFave, 1998).

Running Start (Reading Is Fundamental)

The main idea of the Running Start program, sponsored by the Reading Is Fundamental organization, is that motivation to read will be encouraged by immersing children in books (Gambrell, 1996). The Reading Is Fundamental group emphasizes that children are motivated to read when they can interact with others about what they are reading, when they are exposed to adults and other children who are enthusiastic about reading, and when the adults in their world have high expectations that they can learn to read. Reading Is Fundamental emphasizes that reading is motivating to the extent that children have choice about what they will read and when they will read.

The Running Start program is a 10-week intervention, with grade-1 children challenged to read 21 books (or have the same number of books read to them) during the 10 weeks. At the outset of the program, Reading

Is Fundamental donates a large number (60–80) of new books to the library of participating classrooms. The classroom is organized to support student progress toward the goal of interaction with 21 books over the 10-week period, with reading and book sharing common activities in class. Parents and older children visit classrooms to interact with children over books, sometimes reading to them and sometimes listening to the children read.

Motivation to read is encouraged in multiple ways in Running Start classrooms. Children keep track of their progress toward the 21-book goal using a sticker chart. Bookmarks are used to remind children to read but also serve as rewards for reading. When children meet the 21-book goal, they are given some books to take home and keep.

Linda B. Gambrell's (1996; Gambrell, Codling, et al., 1996; Gambrell & Morrow, 1995) group at the National Reading Research Center evaluated the motivational effects of the Running Start program. Both children and parents across the United States reported being more motivated to read, and to read together, as a function of participating in the program. The work included a quasi-experimental evaluation of the Running Start program with economically deprived urban grade-1 students. In general, compared to control participants who did not experience the Running Start program, the program participants read more on their own and with family members. Importantly, 6 months following the conclusion of the Running Start program, the program participants reported more reading and literacy-related activities (e.g., talking about books with parents) than did control students.

One of the reasons that the Running Start program had the impact that it had was that it transformed the culture of the participating classrooms. The teachers created more elaborate literacy corners in the rooms, and more time was devoted to silent reading. The students and teachers in intervention classrooms talked to one another more about reading and books.

In summary, Reading Is Fundamental, a well-known charitable organization, has long supplied books to children who did not have them. (Remember the Ed Asner commercials soliciting support for Reading Is Fundamental?) The organization has now created a grade-1 intervention designed to increase student motivation to read alone and with parents. Gambrell's group at the National Reading Research Center was able to provide evidence of the program's impact on motivation.

A Community-of-Learners Approach: Concept-Oriented Reading Instruction

Ann L. Brown and her associates pioneered the community-of-learners approach, in which content-area instruction is integrated with literacy instruction (Brown, 1992; Brown et al., 1993; Brown & Campione, 1994; Campione, Shapiro, & Brown, 1995). Rather than superficially covering many topics, communities of learners explore a few issues in great depth during an academic year. When students begin to study a new topic, they generate questions that they want to answer. Students are taught strategies for carrying out research. Much of their time is spent doing collaborative research aimed at answering the questions that they have posed. This research will include library research, but it can also include making field observations or carrying out experiments or any of a variety of activities that might reveal something about the concept that is being explored. Students also learn comprehension strategies that increase their abilities to find and remember the important parts of texts they read as part of their research. Finally, they do a great deal of writing. The overarching goal is for community-of-learners students to acquire strategic and conceptual knowledge that they can use broadly. The group generated considerable evidence that students learn skills that transfer, which are acquired as they attempt to understand concepts that they research and write about (Campione et al., 1995).

John T. Guthrie (1996) and his National Reading Research Center associates (Grant, Guthrie, Bennett, Rice, & McGough, 1993/94; Guthrie et al., 1996) developed a variation of the community-of-learners approach. They are studying literacy instruction that integrates reading, writing, and teaching of science, emphasizing real-world science observations, student self-direction, strategy instruction, and student collaboration and interaction during learning. Guthrie refers to this approach as concept-oriented reading instruction (CORI).

In a year-long evaluation of the approach, grade-3 and grade-5 students observed concrete objects in their natural world as part of an effort to develop conceptual interests that would motivate their study of the phenomena observed. Thus, to begin their study of birds and the environment, students observed bird nests in the wild. This was followed by other concrete experiences, including attempts to build bird nests, observing and recording behaviors at bird feeding stations, and visiting a collection of stuffed birds. Such concrete experiences provided much learning, illustrated by this report from a student after attempting to build a bird nest:

> We built our nest with leaves, grass sticks, and twigs. Mud too. But first we looked for each of these things at the playground. Clay was to stick our nest together because if we didn't have clay our nest would break. We called the clay mud. I learned that it's hard to make a nest unless you really try to. I learned that birds have a hard time making nests but we read a book that helped us learn and I found out that if you try with a group it might be easy. And you might make a lot of friends. (Guthrie et al., 1996, p. 312)

The concrete observations led to the development of students' questions, and to collaborative brainstorming to come up with questions. These questions would motivate additional observations, reading, writing, and discussions. Questions were displayed on the walls of the classroom as a reminder of what students wanted to discover through their research, reading, and writing. This was science instruction that involved making observations, gathering and recording data, recognition of patterns, and development of explanations for these observations and patterns.

In order to answer the questions that students had posed for themselves, they needed to develop their search skills. As part of CORI, students were taught how to search for books and other materials. They learned how to use tables of contents, indexes in books, headings, and pictures in texts in order to narrow their search for relevant information. Students learned to (1) be certain of what they wanted to find out before they searched (i.e., to form a search goal); (2) identify the organization of materials they are searching; (3) extract critical information from sources, constructing summaries and paraphrases of critical material; and (4) abstract across sources, producing syntheses of important ideas and general concepts emerging from the various sources of information. These strategies were taught using teacher and peer modeling followed by teacher scaffolding of these skills as students searched. Of course, because students worked together as they searched, there was also peer scaffolding of skills.

CORI students also learned comprehension strategies, which included identifying the main ideas in texts, looking for critical details, summarizing, comparing between texts, relating illustrations in texts to verbal content, evaluating a book, and reflecting on the point of view expressed in a text. These skills were practiced with narratives and expository pieces, with students learning that topics can be addressed and explored in both fictional and factual writing. Students learned how to take notes about main ideas, details, and so on as well.

Virtually all reading was of authentic literature, with a variety of trade books read as part of units. Thus, as students studied birds, they read *Owl Moon* (Yolen, 1987), *White Bird* (Bulla, 1966), and *Wingman* (Pinkwater, 1975). Students also read poems relating to birds. As they read these texts, students were taught about the importance of imagery during reading and how the story grammar elements (i.e., setting, plot, conflict, resolution) combine as part of a story.

By reading materials related to the thematic topic and searching for answers to critical questions, the students became experts about the topic. This expertise was used by students as they wrote reports relating to the concept, developed stories pertaining to focal concepts, and created visual displays (e.g., bulletin boards). As students carried out these activities, they learned how to tailor their messages to particular audiences and how to express meaning in a variety of ways.

CORI students improve in search and comprehension skills, writing, understanding of focal concepts, comprehension of texts, and interpretation skills (e.g., Guthrie, Anderson, Alao, & Rinehart, 1999; Guthrie et al., 1998). Particularly important here is that the majority of students reported greater motivation to read and participate in literacy activities as the program continued (e.g., Guthrie, Wigfield, & VonSecker, 2000). Moreover, the majority of students reported reading more as the year proceeded.

Since the second edition of this book, Guthrie and his colleagues have continued to evaluate and validate the impact of CORI on student engagement, comprehension, and achievement (e.g., Guthrie, 2004; Guthrie & Cox, 2001; Guthrie et al., 2004). I am increasingly convinced that this approach is effective relative to conventional classroom instruction. At the same time, I do not feel that Guthrie's group has yet conducted rigorous comparisons with alternative methods that can be effective in promoting reading achievement. For example, Guthrie et al. (2004) compared CORI with a condition in which students were only taught comprehension strategies. CORI students did better, and, in fact, the students receiving comprehension strategies instruction were at about the level of students receiving conventional instruction. That is, CORI did better relative to an ineffective version of comprehension strategies instruction. My guess is that the version was ineffective because the comprehension strategies instruction teachers received very brief training in how to teach that way, which is a problem since it is known based on previous work that it takes about a year to become proficient in teaching comprehension strategies (Pressley & El-Dinary, 1997), and when comprehension strategies instruction has worked, it has been with teachers who understand the approach very well (e.g., Brown, Pressley, Van Meter, & Schuder, 1996).

Guthrie has worked with the group at Benchmark School to determine the feasibility of the approach with middle school students who had a history of reading problems (Gaskins et al., 1994). Although there certainly were challenges in implementing the approach with such students, there were clear gains in students' search skills and evidence of improved conceptual understanding, with the students viewing science less as the learning of facts and more as the acquisition of conceptual understanding. Later in this chapter, there will be additional discussion of the many ways that Benchmark School motivates its students, with CORI folded in as part of the multifaceted approach to student motivation that is now in place at the school.

Finally, Swan (2003) has offered a book-length summary about how to implement CORI in elementary schools. This resource is invaluable for teachers who want to attempt to do highly motivating conceptually driven instruction that also impacts literacy development, most particularly aiming to improve student comprehension and understanding of what they read.

Summary

Many researchers are studying the nature of instruction that grabs students' interest, motivating them to read and learn. Although there have been frustrations—for example, interesting texts often prove to be more seductive than informative, as they were intended to be—there have been many more successes than failures. Perhaps most encouraging of all, instructional practices that motivate are enjoying dissemination. Despite justifiable reservations about whole language with respect to the development of basic decoding skills, many whole-language practices are motivating, and they certainly are widely disseminated; also Reading Is Fundamental is reaching more classrooms every year. Even if a school does not adopt these efforts, however, much can be gleaned from the motivational research that can be adopted and adapted in any classroom.

An important point that sometimes gets overlooked in discussions of motivation is that nothing motivates like success! To the extent that educators devise literacy interventions that cause children to succeed in literacy, there will be increased motivation to do things literate. A child's identity and commitment to reading depends greatly on getting good at it; hence, as you reflect on the many recommendations for increasing student motivation, never forget that promoting success in reading goes far in promoting motivation to read (McCarthey, 2001). Moreover, success is more likely with the types of high-quality instruction emphasized in this book.

FLOODING THE CLASSROOM WITH MOTIVATION

In our studies of effective grade-1 classrooms, my colleagues and I had noted that effective teachers did much to motivate their students. This observation motivated us to focus more on the motivational differences between engaging and not-so-engaging grade-1 classrooms. Bogner, Raphael, and Pressley (2002) observed seven grade-1 classrooms over the course of a school year. Two of those classrooms were very engaging in that students were working on reading and writing much of the time, raptly attentive as they did so. The other five teachers who were observed were much less successful in motivating their students to read and write. Inattention and off-task behaviors were much more common in these less engaging classrooms than in the two classrooms that were very engaging.

Teacher Behaviors Encouraging Engagement

The most important finding in this study was that the two very engaging teachers did a great deal to motivate literacy in their classrooms relative to the five teachers who were less engaging. Thus, there were many aspects of their *teaching style* that were motivating, including the following: There was a great deal of cooperative learning in the class, although individual students were held accountable for their work. The two engaging teachers did a lot of scaffolding. There were many connections in the classroom, including to library readings. The engaging teachers encouraged autonomy in their students and gave them choices. The engaging teachers had a gentle and caring manner, with many positive one-to-one interactions, home–school connections, and opportunistic minilessons. The engaging teachers connected with their students personally. They supported appropriate risk taking, made the classroom fun, and encouraged the students to be creative. The two most engaging classrooms were very positive places.

Beyond teaching style, the engaging teachers had great content in their classrooms. The material each child covered was challenging but not overwhelming. The engaging teachers used games in instruction. They worked with the students to produce products that the students were proud of, such as big books written by the class. The engaging teachers favored depth over breadth, often having several readings that connected to current social studies and science units, each of which might last several weeks. There was good literature everywhere in the engaging classrooms.

The engaging teachers also had great communications with their students. They provided concrete examples when covering abstract concepts. The engaging teachers encouraged their students to be curious and created suspense (e.g., "I wonder how Ebenezer is going to react to the ghosts"). The engaging teachers made certain the students knew the learning goals and understood assignments. They provided a lot of praise and feedback, consistently modeling interest and enthusiasm as they did so. The engaging teachers also modeled thinking and problem-solving skills (e.g., how to sound out words, figure out what a word encountered in a text context means). The engaging teachers sent the message consistently that schoolwork was important and deserved intense attention, often expressing confidence that the students were equal to the academic demands of school.

Self-concept development was important in the classrooms taught by the two engaging teachers. These teachers encouraged their students to make effort attributions (i.e., to believe their successes were due to their hard work, to interpret failure as a sign to work harder). The engaging teachers sent the message that people get smarter through their own efforts—for example, by reading a lot.

The engaging teachers had terrific classroom management. In particular, they monitored well. They knew what the whole class was doing all the time, and they were exceptionally aware of who needed help, moving quickly to provide assistance.

Teaching Behaviors Discouraging Engagement

In addition to doing so much proactively to motivate students, there were other things that the exceptionally motivating teachers did not do. In contrast, less engaging teachers undermined student motivation. Consider their *teaching style*: Some teachers encouraged competition between students. They taught in ways that actually encouraged inattentiveness (e.g., encouraging the students to give big cheers when they did something right, which always resulted in several minutes of disruption). Some teachers provided very public grades, which made obvious when students did poorly. Some provided extrinsic rewards for behaviors that the students were intrinsically motivated to do already. In the less engaging classrooms, the *content* was often boring or so easy that students did not have to engage in order to complete it. In the less engaging classrooms, *communications* often were disturbing, with negative feedback common. The *self-concept development* efforts in less engaging classrooms sometimes ran counter to encouraging student effort—for example, encouraging students to believe their successes reflect high ability and failures reflect low ability. Effective *classroom management* was lacking in the less engaging classrooms: There was little monitoring of the class. Teachers often tried to control the class with threats and punishments.

In short, the two engaging teachers simply flooded their students with teaching that encouraged effort and academic commitment while never doing the types of teaching that can discourage student efforts. In contrast, the less effective teachers did much less that positively encouraged academic engagement and, in fact, did quite a bit to discourage academic engagement. Nancy Masters was one of the two very engaging teachers studied by Bogner et al. (2002).

Nancy Masters's Teaching

On a typical day, Nancy Masters used more than 40 different positive motivational mechanisms to inspire and engage her students. Her classroom was filled to overflowing with motivating activities and positive tone. Cooperation was emphasized consistently during both whole-group and small-group instruction. Thus, when students read books with partners, Ms. Masters reminded them that "The point is, you're supposed to *help* your partner." She provided reassurance and interesting scaffolding when students took on challenging activities. Thus, before a test requiring application of phonics skills, Ms. Masters reminded her students of the phonics they had been learning and emphasized that they should apply what they knew about phonics on the upcoming test.

Ms. Masters emphasized depth in her teaching, covering mature and interesting ideas. For example, during Black History Month, not only did students complete detailed group book reports about five prominent African Americans, but also Ms. Masters led a discussion about the Jim Crow laws, one in which the students participated enthusiastically, demonstrating they had learned a great deal about discrimination during the month. During this conversation, Ms. Masters talked about different ways that people can affect social change, covering civil disobedience, disobeying unjust laws, and working within the system to change such laws. She and the first-grade students discussed equality and inequality, with student comments reflecting their grasp of some very difficult concepts.

Nancy Masters's teaching connected across the curriculum and community, between school and home. During the first month of the school year, she took her class to visit the kindergarten room. In doing so, she began to become acquainted with her future students while forging connections across grade levels for the kindergarten and grade-1 students. Her students wrote in their journals about this visit. When they wrote stories a few weeks later, Ms. Masters held out as a carrot another visit to the kindergarten room. She told her grade-1 students, "Maybe we'll show the kindergarten [your stories]." Nancy also pointed out times when students' home experience connected with school. Thus, when a student read the word *little* very quickly, Ms. Masters commented, "Have you been working at home with your mom? I'm so proud of you!" In doing so, she simultaneously emphasized the importance of effort and homework while connecting to the student's home life. Ms. Masters also hosted a career day during which parents talked about and demonstrated their professional skills. After the visits, the students wrote in journals and did an at-home art project about their favorite profession. This special home assignment complemented the regular homework, which consisted of reading 15 minutes a night, doing a short math worksheet, and practicing spelling words.

Nancy Masters gave many opportunistic minilessons. In-class assignments seemed appropriately challenging and engaging (i.e., students could not finish them quickly, and they seemed interested in them). Her emphasis on good literature, the writing process, and comprehension were apparent during every class visit. Also, the class constructed many products, which were tangible evidence of accomplishment, including big books that were displayed prominently in the classroom and discussed often. Ms. Masters promised the class that each student would be able to take home one class-constructed book at the end of the year. She made many across-curriculum connections for her students (e.g., having students use the Internet and the library to find material about Black History Month, material then used in writing an essay).

Ms. Masters expressively communicated with students. As she read to students, she modeled her interest and enthusiasm and reflected her curiosity about what would happen next in a story, often creating a sense of suspense about the events in a reading. When the class received a new basal reader, she opened it and said, "A brand-new book!! It's like a present. I know you want to open it and look inside. Go ahead and look inside. See anything interesting? Anything you've read?"

Ms. Masters provided clear learning objectives and goals. Thus, at the beginning of the school year, she had the students copy stories she had written on the board, explaining they were copying stories so that "You can see what good writing looks like." Similarly, when she taught strategies during writing workshop, Ms. Masters emphasized that use of the strategies would help students write as they needed to write by the end of grade 1.

Nancy Masters emphasized effort attributions. Thus, on the day report cards were distributed to students, she told the students twice that their most important grade was their grade for effort. She and her students often used the term "personal best" to describe how they were doing.

Nancy Masters monitored the students well. She often said, "When I come around, I want to hear you reading or helping your partner or discussing the story." During her walk-arounds, she provided help to students who were struggling.

Of course, Ms. Masters's efforts to motivate her students paid off. There was consistently high engagement in her class. The pace was always quick. The assignments were always interesting. She excited her students about their work. Her students were always engaged in productive work!

Motivational Flooding beyond First Grade

Since Bogner et al. (2002), the Pressley group has carried out comparable studies across the primary grades (Dolezal, Welsh, Pressley, & Vincent, 2003; Pressley et al., 2003) and in sixth-grade middle school settings (Raphael, Pressley, & Mohan, 2005). Essentially, the results obtained at those levels are identical to the grade-1 outcomes. Teachers varied widely in whether they engaged students, with the most engaging teachers being the ones who motivationally flooded their classrooms. In the most engaging classrooms, the teacher was doing something every minute to motivate the class, small groups, or individuals. She or he used many motivational mechanisms to do so, ones making a great deal of sense based on the educational motivational research. In addition, engaging teachers did nothing that had the potential to undermine student motivation. In contrast, less engaging teachers used far fewer positive motivational mechanisms and used them less often, relying much more on tactics that can turn students off (e.g., punishment).

In the past few years, the Pressley group has turned its attention to how whole schools that are very successful in promoting the achievement of at-risk populations accomplish what they accomplish, noting substantial attempts to motivate students in such schools (e.g., Pressley, Raphael, Gallagher, & DiBella, 2004). Their most recent investigation, conducted at Benchmark School, is especially relevant here (Pressley, Gaskins, Solic, & Collins, 2004). Students come to Benchmark after experiencing school failure for one or more years, typically failure to learn to read. Over 1–9 years (the average is 4–7 years), students learn how to read, compose, and experience conceptually focused math, social studies, and science instruction, with much of this content-area instruction consistent with the motivating CORI conception of teaching and learning considered earlier in this chapter. The most important finding here, however, is that in every class and across the school day, there is motivational saturation. Students are consistently encouraged to believe they can determine their own achievement through their efforts and by learning and using the strategies and content taught at the school. There is much praise of achievements, with praise informing the students about what they did right. Grades are downplayed, with grading for improvement the norm. The students are given appropriately challenging tasks, ones just a bit beyond their current levels, matched to individual students. Cooperative learning occurs in every class. The teachers do all that is possible to teach interesting content in interesting ways and succeed in doing so, with many connections made across the curriculum. Discipline is intelligent and reflective, with the centerpiece being reflection on the effects of misbehavior on self and others. Finally, and very importantly, the teachers show great pedagogical care (Goldstein, 1999; Noddings, 1984), with teachers' concerns for students apparent in every class. Benchmark teachers know their students very well, with this deep personal knowledge translating to great teaching commitment and real teacher determination to motivate high achievement and success in students (Worthy & Patterson, 2001). And, of course, both academic engagement and achievement are high at Benchmark, consistent with other educational settings that are perceived as pedagogically caring places—warm and supportive environments—by students (e.g., Skinner, Wellborn, & Connell, 1990; Skinner, Zimmer-Gembeck, & Connell, 1998; Wentzel, 1998).

CONCLUDING REFLECTIONS

Americans are currently barraged with information about how schools are failing. The case typically is made with test scores. Much of the wailing about American students' low and declining test scores is not justified (Berliner & Biddle, 1995). I never lose sleep over test scores. What I do lose sleep over, however, is the documentation of steadily declining academic motivation as students proceed through school. Yes, in part, the declines are artifactual in that kindergarten and grade-1 children are just so darn optimistic and full of enthusiasm, so filled with intrinsic motivation that the only direction they can go is down. Still, there is something wrong when some kids are ready to throw in the towel by the time they are in grade 5 or 6 (or even earlier). Even the best readers are less enthusiastic about reading with every additional year they are in school (McKenna et al., 1995). There is plenty of reason for American educators to be doing everything they possibly can to increase student motivation.

One productive way to think about the motivational research summarized in this chapter is to think about the ideas that emerge that can be used in any elementary classroom. Although the case is not airtight and much research remains to be done before absolutely firm conclusions can be offered, I think there is enough evidence available right now to recommend that every teacher do everything possible to follow these guidelines that relate to student motivation:

• Ensure student success. This can be accomplished by making certain that students are attempting tasks that are within their reach. Tasks are motivating when they are appropriately challenging, rather than too easy or too hard.

• Be a teacher who scaffolds student learning. Be a teacher who monitors when students are having difficulties, and provide enough support so that students are able to make progress.

• Encourage students to attribute their successes to expending appropriate efforts and their failures to lack of effort or failing to deploy effort appropriately (e.g., using a wrong strategy). This principle is as important for good students as it is for weak ones. The good student who attributes successes to high ability is constructing a personal story that provides no motivation for trying hard. The weaker student who believes that failures reflect low ability, which is unchangeable, has no reason to believe that effort will matter.

• A related point: Encourage students to believe that intelligence is not innate and fixed, but rather ever changing. The smart get smarter by learning more, by learning to use the strategies that smart people use and by acquiring in-depth understanding of important concepts, such as those at the heart of science, social studies, and literacy curricula. People who believe the incremental theory of intelligence have much more reason to try hard than do those who take to heart an entity perspective on intelligence, to use Carol S. Dweck's (1987) terminology.

• Failures occur. Encourage students to interpret failures as a natural part of learning. Discourage students from believing that failures reflect low ability. Students are served well when you foster in them the understanding that failures indicate a need to try harder in the future. Teachers should use student failures to diagnose when and how they can scaffold a student.

• Do not permit failures to persist, believing that failure represents a lack of developmental readiness and that the child will quickly acquire the now-difficult-to-acquire skill when he or she is "ready." For example, the grade-1 student who is having difficulties in learning to decode will be discouraged by continued failure. It is better to explore alternative ways of teaching decoding with the struggling student, doing all that is possible to take advantage of the grade-1 student's great faith in effort. Persistent failure to make progress discourages motivation; every effort should be made to prevent students from continuing to fail.

• Do not encourage student competition. Student competition undermines motivation rather than fostering it. In competitive classrooms, many more students are going to feel like losers than winners. Rather than encouraging competition between students, it is better to reward students for improving on their past performances and to send the message consistently that improvement is what matters.

• Encourage student cooperation and interaction over literacy tasks. When students talk about books, they let one another know what is worth reading and what is exciting to read. Students can scaffold each other, for example, by helping each other with difficult words during pair reading. Students' conceptual knowledge develops more completely when they work together in communities of learners, especially when motivation is high in such classroom communities.

• Play down "grades as rewards" for literacy activities, especially activities that are intrinsically motivating for students. When students begin to be artificially rewarded for doing what they like to do, their intrinsic motivation for the activity can decline. In general, the more a classroom encourages working for grades, the more it discourages intrinsic motivation.

• Make certain that students have access to a wide range of interesting books. Classroom libraries seem to be a critically important source of reading material for students, and hence it makes sense to do everything possible to ensure the availability of a rich classroom library.

• As much as possible, permit student choice with respect to what they read and to what topics are the conceptual focus of instruction. Teach children how to find books on the topics that interest them.

• Integrate literacy instruction with content learning. Such integration makes clear to students that the reading and writing skills they are acquiring are useful for learning important ideas, which is especially likely if the conceptual ideas explored as part of science and social studies grab students.

• Favor depth over breadth as much as possible, as is done in communities of learners, choosing a few exceptionally motivating topics as the conceptual focus for the school year.

Not surprisingly, many of these concepts have been encountered in previous chapters. Why? Recall the discussions of excellent teachers presented in Chapters 8 and 9. All of them were very motivating largely because they integrated many of the ideas covered in this chapter into their teaching.

In reviewing what is now known about student motivation, it is clear that there is no evidence whatsoever that any one of these mechanisms is so powerful that it alone is more powerful than the others. Whole-language claims about the power of literature to motivate students must be considered in light of declining motivation for students experiencing frustrations as part of learning to read. Thus, is it reasonable to believe that students in exclusively whole-language environments who are experiencing difficulty in learning how to recognize words will remain motivated because of the presence of literature in their classroom worlds? I doubt it. One of the reasons to like balanced curricula is that the motivational gains of whole language have a better chance of occurring if children have the skills to work successfully on the reading and writing tasks that occur in their classrooms. Nothing motivates an individual like successful accomplishment of interesting and appropriately challenging tasks.

SUMMARY

1. In general, academic motivation declines from the onset of schooling through high school. Declines in enthusiasm for and interest in reading parallel the general developmental declines in academic motivation.

2. There are a variety of psychological developments contributing to declining motivation, including developmental changes in how students react to failures: The younger the child, the greater the chance that she or he believes failure reflects lack of effort rather than lack of ability. Older children are more likely than younger children to make comparisons with others, which undermines motivation for the child experiencing difficulties.

3. There are also structural changes in the school setting that contribute to declining motivation with increasing grade level—most prominently, increasing competition.

4. There are a variety of mechanisms that are being validated in research as positively affecting student motivation. One is the training of students to make effort attributions rather than ability attributions to explain both failures and successes. A variety of mechanisms favored in whole language, such as the choice and reading of excellent literature, seem to promote student motivation to read. (This is just one of a number of reasons to favor much of what is offered in whole language, even if the whole-language perspectives on decoding are in error.) The community-of-learners approach promises to increase depth of conceptual understanding, as it motivates students to engage academically.

5. There has been a lot of progress in understanding academic motivation in the past two decades. It is essential that such work continue and the results of such work be applied to school reform. If taken seriously, the research findings in this chapter have the potential to turn American schooling inside out and upside down. For example, imagine the ramifications of taking seriously the idea that academic competition and competitive grading be eliminated because such competition undermines intrinsic motivation!

6. Skills teaching as part of balanced instruction increases the likelihood of student success with reading, which goes far in motivating reading. Whole-language proponents have done much to increase the variety of literature that children read in school, consistent with their approach to motivational enhancement. A balanced approach takes advantage of multiple motivational mechanisms. In the best cases, children feel successful and thus are motivated to try. When they do try, they find books that are wonderfully interesting to read and are within their reach because of the skills they have been learning. Balanced instruction is a better bet for motivating students than are less complete types of instruction, such as whole-language or skills-emphasis approaches. Recall that a hallmark of excellent instruction as documented in Chapter 8 was that students were highly engaged and motivated, and that this was much more common in balanced classrooms.

7. Some teachers, like Nancy Masters, do succeed in flooding their classrooms with motivation, and it shows! Notably, Ms. Masters also does nothing that undermines her kids' efforts. What we want teachers to get from her example is inspiration—that it is possible to do much to motivate literacy engagement. We've never spent an hour in her classroom when we were not confident that every kid was getting much out of the lessons being taught. We've never spent a moment in her classroom when it was not obvious that every student just loved being there. Effective literacy teachers are loved teachers, living in classroom worlds that make their own lives as fulfilling as the developing lives of their students.

REFERENCES

Ames, C. (1984). Competitive, cooperative, and individualistic goal structures: A motivational analysis. In R. Ames & C. Ames (Eds.), *Research on motivation in education* (Vol. 1, pp. 117–207). New York: Academic Press.

Ames, C. (1992). Classrooms: Goals, structures, and student motivation. *Journal of Educational Psychology, 84,* 261–271.

Anderson, R. C. (1982). Allocation of attention during reading. In A. Flammer & W. Kintsch (Eds.), *Discourse processing* (pp. 292–305). New York: North-Holland.

Anderson, R. C., Mason, J. M., & Shirey, L. (1984). The reading group: An experimental investigation of a labyrinth. *Reading Research Quarterly, 20,* 6–38.

Anderson, R. C., Shirey, L. L., Wilson, P. T., & Fielding, L. G. (1987). Interestingness of children's reading material. In R. E. Snow & M. J. Farr (Eds.), *Aptitude, learning, and instruction: Vol. 3. Cognitive and affective process analyses* (pp. 287–299). Hillsdale, NJ: Erlbaum.

Armbruster, B. B. (1984). The problem of "inconsiderate text." In G. G. Duffy, L. R. Roehler, & J. Mason (Eds.), *Comprehension instruction* (pp. 202–217). New York: Longman.

Baker, L., & Wigfield, A. (1999). Dimensions of children's motivation for reading and their relations to reading activity and reading achievement. *Reading Research Quarterly, 34,* 452–477.

Bergin, D. A., & LaFave, C. (1998). Continuities between motivation research and whole language philosophy of instruction. *Journal of Literacy Research, 30,* 321–356.

Berliner, D. C., & Biddle, B. J. (1995). *The manufactured crisis: Myths, fraud, and the attack on America's public schools.* Reading, MA: Addison-Wesley.

Blumenfeld, P. C. (1992). Classroom learning and motivation: Clarifying and expanding goal theory. *Journal of Educational Psychology, 84,* 272–281.

Bogner, K., Raphael, L. M., & Pressley, M. (2002). How grade-1 teachers motivate literate activity by their students. *Scientific Studies of Reading, 6,* 135–165.

Borkowski, J. G., Carr, M., Rellinger, E. A., & Pressley, M. (1990). Self-regulated strategy use: Interdependence of metacognition, attributions, and self-esteem. In B. F. Jones (Ed.), *Dimensions of thinking: Review of research* (pp. 53–92). Hillsdale, NJ: Erlbaum.

Borkowski, J. G., Weyhing, R. S., & Carr, M. (1988). Effects of attributional retraining on strategy-based reading comprehension in learning-disabled students. *Journal of Educational Psychology, 80,* 46–53.

Brooks, R. B. (2001). Fostering motivation, hope, and resilience in children with learning disorders. *Annals of Dyslexia, 51,* 9–20.

Brophy, J. (1987). On motivating students. In D. Berliner & B. Rosenshine (Eds.), *Talks to teachers* (pp. 201–245). New York: Random House.

Brown, A. L. (1992). Design experiments: Theoretical and methodological challenges in creating complex interventions in classroom settings. *Journal of the Learning Sciences, 2,* 141–178.

Brown, A. L., Ash, D., Rutherford, M., Nakagawa, K., Gordon, A., & Campione, J. C. (1993). Distributed expertise in the classroom. In G. Salomon (Ed.), *Distrib-*

uted cognitions: Psychological and educational considerations (pp. 188–228). New York: Cambridge University Press.

Brown, A. L., & Campione, J. C. (1994). Guided discovery in a community of learners. In K. McGilly (Ed.), *Classroom lessons: Integrating cognitive theory and classroom practice* (pp. 229–270). Cambridge, MA: MIT Press/Bradford Books.

Brown, R., Pressley, M., Van Meter, P., & Schuder, T. (1996). A quasi-experimental validation of transactional strategies instruction with low-achieving second grade readers. *Journal of Educational Psychology, 88*, 18–37.

Bulla, C. R. (1966). *White bird.* New York: Philomel.

Campione, J. C., Shapiro, A. M., & Brown, A. L. (1995). Forms of transfer in a community of learners: Flexible learning and understanding. In A. McKeough, J. Lupart, & A. Marini (Eds.), *Teaching for transfer: Fostering generalization in learning* (pp. 35–68). Hillsdale, NJ: Erlbaum.

Carr, M., & Borkowski, J. G. (1989). Attributional training and the generalization of reading strategies with underachieving children. *Learning and Individual Differences, 1*, 327–341.

Carr, M., Borkowski, J. G., & Maxwell, S. E. (1991). Motivational components of underachievement. *Developmental Psychology, 27*, 108–118.

Chapman, J. W., & Tunmer, W. E. (1995). Development of young children's reading self-concept: An examination of emerging subcomponents and their relationship with reading achievement. *Journal of Educational Psychology, 87*, 154–167.

Chapman, J. W., Tunmer, W. E., & Prochnow, J. E. (2000). Early reading-related skills and performance, reading self-concept, and the development of academic self-concept: A longitudinal study. *Journal of Educational Psychology, 92*, 703–708.

Chapman, M., Skinner, E. A., & Baltes, P. B. (1990). Interpreting correlations between children's perceived control and cognitive performance: Control, agency, or means–ends beliefs? *Developmental Psychology, 26*, 246–253.

Clifford, M. M. (1975). Validity of expectation: A developmental function. *Alberta Journal of Educational Research, 21*, 11–17.

Clifford, M. M. (1978). The effects of quantitative feedback on children's expectations of success. *Journal of Educational Psychology, 48*, 220–226.

Clifford, M. M. (1984). Thoughts on a theory of constructive failure. *Educational Psychologist, 19*, 108–120.

Covington, M. V. (1987). Achievement motivation, self-attributions, and the exceptional learner. In J. D. Day & J. G. Borkowski (Eds.), *Intelligence and exceptionality* (pp. 355–389). Norwood, NJ: Ablex.

Covington, M. V., & Omelich, C. L. (1979a). Effort: The double-edged sword in school achievement. *Journal of Educational Psychology, 71*, 169–182.

Covington, M. V., & Omelich, C. L. (1979b). It's best to be able and virtuous too: Student and teacher evaluative responses to successful effort. *Journal of Educational Psychology, 71*, 688–700.

Covington, M. V., & Omelich, C. L. (1981). As failures mount: Affective and cognitive consequences of ability demotion in the classroom. *Journal of Educational Psychology, 73*, 796–808.

Covington, M. V., & Omelich, C. L. (1984). Task-oriented versus competitive learning structures: Motivational and performance consequences. *Journal of Educational Psychology, 6*, 1038–1050.

Deshler, D. D., & Schumaker, J. B. (1988). An instructional model for teaching students how to learn. In J. L. Graden, J. E. Zins, & M. J. Curtis (Eds.), *Alternative educational delivery systems: Enhancing instructional options for all students* (pp. 391–411). Washington, DC: National Association of School Psychologists.

Deshler, D. D., Schumaker, J., Harris, K. R., & Graham, S. (1998). *Teaching every child every day: Learning in diverse schools and classrooms.* Brookline, MA: Brookline Books.

Dewey, J. (1913). *Interest and effort in education.* Boston: Riverside.

Dolezal, S. E., Welsh, L. M., Pressley, M., & Vincent, M. (2003). How do grade-3 teachers motivate their students? *Elementary School Journal. 103,* 239–267.

Dweck, C. S. (1987, April). *Children's theories of intelligence: Implications for motivation and learning.* Paper presented at the annual meeting of the American Educational Research Association, Washington, DC.

Dweck, C. S., & Leggett, E. L. (1988). A social–cognitive approach to motivation and personality. *Psychological Review, 95,* 256–273.

Eccles, J. S. (1993). School and family effects on the ontogeny of children's interests, self-perceptions, and activity choices. In J. E. Jacobs (Ed.), *Nebraska symposium on motivation: Vol. 40. Developmental perspectives on motivation* (pp. 145–208). Lincoln: University of Nebraska Press.

Eccles, J. S., & Midgley, C. (1989). Stage/environment fit: Developmentally appropriate classrooms for early adolescents. In R. E. Ames & C. Ames (Eds.), *Research on motivation in education* (Vol. 3, pp. 139–186). New York: Academic Press.

Eccles, J., Wigfield, A., Flanagan, C., Miller, C., Reuman, D., & Yee, D. (1989). Self-concepts, domain values, and self-esteem: Relationships and changes in early adolescence. *Journal of Personality, 57,* 283–310.

Elbaum, B., & Vaughn, S. (2003). Self-concept and students with learning disabilities. In H. L. Swanson, K. R. Harris, & S. Graham (Eds.), *Handbook of learning disabilities* (pp. 229–241). New York: Guilford Press.

Entwisle, D., & Hayduk, L. (1978). *Too great expectations: The academic outlook of young children.* Baltimore: Johns Hopkins University Press.

Fairbanks, C. M., & Broughton, M. A. (2003). Literacy lessons: The convergence of expectations, practices, and classroom culture. *Journal of Literacy Research, 34,* 391–428.

Foersterling, F. (1985). Attribution retraining: A review. *Psychological Bulletin, 98,* 495–512.

Fractor, J., Woodruff, M. C., Martinez, M. G., & Teale, W. H. (1993). Let's not miss opportunities to promote voluntary reading: Classroom libraries in the elementary school. *Reading Teacher, 46,* 476–485.

Gambrell, L. B. (1996). Creating classroom cultures that foster reading motivation. *Reading Teacher, 50,* 14–25.

Gambrell, L. B., Codling, R. M., & Palmer, B. M. (1996). *Elementary students' motivation to read* (Research Report). Athens, GA, and College Park, MD: National Reading Research Center.

Gambrell, L. B., & Morrow, L. M. (1995). Creating motivating contexts for literacy learning. In L. Baker, P. Afflerbach, & D. Reinking (Eds.), *Developing engaged readers in home and school communities* (pp. 115–136). Mahwah, NJ: Erlbaum.

Gambrell, L. B., Palmer, B. M., Codling, R. M., & Mazzoni, S. A. (1996). Assessing motivation to read. *Reading Teacher*, *49*, 518–533.

Gans, A. M., Kenny, M. C., & Ghany, D. L. (2003). Comparing the self-concept of students with and without learning disabilities. *Journal of Learning Disabilities*, *36*, 287–295.

Garner, R. (1992). Learning from school texts. *Educational Psychologist*, *27*, 53–63.

Garner, R., Alexander, P. A., Gillingham, M. G., Kulikowich, J. M., & Brown, R. (1991). Interest and learning from text. *American Educational Research Journal*, *28*, 643–660.

Garner, R., Gillingham, M. G., & White, C. S. (1989). Effects of "seductive details" on macroprocessing and microprocessing in adult and children. *Cognition and Instruction*, *6*, 41–57.

Gaskins, I. W., Guthrie, J. T., Satlow, E., Ostertag, J., Six, L., Byrne, J., & Conner, B. (1994). Integrating instruction of science, reading, and writing: Goals, teacher, development, and assessment. *Journal of Research in Science Teaching*, *31*, 1039–1056.

Goldstein, L. S. (1999). The relational zone: The role of caring relationships in the co-construction of mind. *American Educational Research Journal*, *36*, 647–673.

Grant, R., Guthrie, J., Bennett, L., Rice, M. E., & McGough, K. (1993/94). Developing engaged readers through concept-oriented instruction. *Reading Teacher*, *47*, 338–340.

Guthrie, J. T. (1996). Educational contexts for engagement in literacy. *Reading Teacher*, *49*, 432–445.

Guthrie, J. T. (2004). Teaching for literacy engagement. *Journal of Literacy Research*, *36*, 1–30.

Guthrie, J. T., Anderson, E., Alao, S., & Rinehart, J. (1999). Influences of concept-oriented reading instruction on strategy use and conceptual learning from text. *Elementary School Journal*, *99*, 343–366.

Guthrie, J. T., & Cox, K. E. (2001). Classroom conditions for motivation and engagement in reading. *Educational Psychology Review*, *13*, 283–302.

Guthrie, J. T., Van Meter, P., Hancock, G. R., Alao, S., Anderson, E., & McCann, A. (1998). Does concept-oriented reading instruction increase strategy use and conceptual learning from text? *Journal of Educational Psychology*, *90*, 261–278.

Guthrie, J. T., Van Meter, P., McCann, A. D., Wigfield, A., Bennett, L., Poundstone, C. C., Rice, M. E., Faibisch, F. M., Hunt, B., & Mitchell, A. M. (1996). Growth of literacy engagement: Changes in motivations and strategies during concept-oriented reading instruction. *Reading Research Quarterly*, *31*, 306–332.

Guthrie, J. T., Wigfield, A., Barbosa, P., Perencevich, C., Taboada, A., Davis, M. H., Scaffidi, N. T., & Tonks, S. (2004). Increasing reading comprehension and engagement through concept-oriented reading instruction. *Journal of Educational Psychology*, *96*, 403–423.

Guthrie, J. T., Wigfield, A., & VonSecker, C. (2000). Effects of integrated instruction on motivation and strategy use in reading. *Journal of Educational Psychology*, *92*, 331–341.

Harter, S. (1990). Cause, correlates, and the functional role of self-worth: A life-span perspective. In R. J. Sternberg & J. Kolligian (Eds.), *Competence considered* (pp. 67–97). New Haven, CT: Yale University Press.

Harter, S., Whitesell, N. R., & Kowalski, P. (1992). Individual differences in the effects of educational transitions on young adolescents' perceptions of competence and motivational orientation. *American Educational Research Journal, 29,* 777–807.

Henderson, V. L., & Dweck, C. S. (1990). Motivation and achievement. In S. S. Feldman & G. R. Elliott (Eds.), *At the threshold: The developing adolescent* (pp. 308–329). Cambridge, MA: Harvard University Press.

Hidi, S. (1990). Interest and its contribution as a mental resource for learning. *Review of Educational Research, 60,* 549–571.

Hidi, S. (2001). Interest, reading, and learning: Theoretical and practical considerations. *Educational Psychology Review, 13,* 191–209.

Hidi, S., & Baird, W. (1988). Strategies for increasing text-based interest and students' recall of expository text. *Reading Research Quarterly, 23,* 465–483.

Ivey, G., & Broaddus, K. (2001). "Just plain reading": A survey of what makes students want to read in middle school classrooms. *Reading Research Quarterly, 36,* 350–377.

Jacobsen, B., Lowery, B., & DuCette, J. (1986). Attributions of learning-disabled children. *Journal of Educational Psychology, 78,* 59–64.

Juvonen, J. (1988). Outcome and attributional disagreements between students and their teachers. *Journal of Educational Psychology, 80,* 330–336.

Kistner, J. A., Osborne, M., & LeVerrier, L. (1988). Causal attributions of learning-disabled children: Developmental patterns and relation to academic progress. *Journal of Educational Psychology, 80,* 82–89.

Kloosterman, P. (1988). Self-confidence and motivation in mathematics. *Journal of Educational Psychology, 80,* 345–351.

Lepper, M. R., Keavney, M., & Drake, M. (1996). Intrinsic motivation and extrinsic rewards: A commentary on Cameron and Pierce's meta-analysis. *Review of Educational Research, 66,* 5–32.

Mallette, M. H., Henk, W. A., & Melnick, S. A. (2004). The influence of Accelerated Reader on the affective literacy orientations of intermediate grade students. *Journal of Literacy Research, 36,* 73–84.

Marsh, H. W. (1987). The big-fish–little-pond effect on academic self-concept. *Journal of Educational Psychology, 79,* 280–295.

McCarthey, S. J. (2001). Identity construction in elementary readers and writers. *Reading Research Quarterly, 36,* 122–151.

McKenna, M. C., Ellsworth, R. A., & Kear, D. J. (1995). Children's attitudes toward reading: A national survey. *Reading Research Quarterly, 30,* 934–956.

McLoyd, V. C. (1979). The effects of extrinsic rewards of differential value on high and low intrinsic interest. *Child Development, 50,* 1010–1019.

Meece, J. L., & Miller, S. D. (1999). Changes in elementary school children's achievement goals for reading and writing: Results of a longitudinal and an intervention study. *Scientific Studies of Reading, 3,* 207–229.

Meece, J. [L.], & Miller, S. D. (2001). A longitudinal analysis of elementary school students' achievement goals in literacy activities. *Contemporary Educational Psychology, 26,* 454–480.

Miller, S. D., & Meece, J. L. (1999). Third graders' motivational preferences for reading and writing tasks. *Elementary School Journal, 100,* 19–35.

Morrow, L. M. (1992). The impact of a literature-based program on literacy achievement, use of literature, and attitudes of children from minority backgrounds. *Reading Research Quarterly, 27,* 250–275.

Morrow, L. M., & Sharkey, E. A. (1993). Motivating independent reading and writing in the primary grades through social cooperative literacy experiences. *Reading Teacher, 47,* 162–164.

Nicholls, J. G. (1978). The development of the concepts of effort and ability, perception of academic attainment, and the understanding that difficult tasks require more than ability. *Child Development, 49,* 800–814.

Nicholls, J. G. (1989). *The competitive ethos and democratic education.* Cambridge, MA: Harvard University Press.

Nicholls, J. G. (1990). What is ability and why are we mindful of it?: A developmental perspective. In R. Sternberg & J. Kolligian (Eds.), *Competence considered* (pp. 11–40). New Haven, CT: Yale University Press.

Nicholls, J. G., & Thorkildsen, T. A. (1987, October). *Achievement goals and beliefs: Individual and classroom differences.* Paper presented at the annual meeting of the Society for Experimental Social Psychology, Charlottesville, VA.

Noddings, N. (1984). *Caring: A feminine approach to ethics and moral education.* Berkeley: University of California Press.

Nolen, S. B. (1988). Reasons for studying: Motivational orientations and study strategies. *Cognition and Instruction, 5,* 269–287.

O'Flahavan, J., Gambrell, L. B., Guthrie, J., Stahl, S., & Alvermann, D. (1992). Poll results guide activities of research center. *Reading Today, 10,* 12.

Onatsu-Arvilommi, T., & Nurmi, J.-E. (2000). The role of task-avoidant and task-focused behaviors in the development of reading and mathematical skills during the first school year: A cross-lagged longitudinal study. *Journal of Educational Psychology, 92,* 478–491.

Palmer, B. M., Codling, R. M., & Gambrell, L. B. (1994). In their own words: What elementary students have to say about motivation to read. *Reading Teacher, 48,* 176–178.

Parsons, J., & Ruble, D. N. (1977). The development of achievement-related expectancies. *Child Development, 48,* 1075–1079.

Pearl, R. (1982). LD children's attributions for success and failure: A replication with a labeled LD sample. *Learning Disability Quarterly, 5,* 173–176.

Phillips, B. N. (1963). Age changes in accuracy of self-perceptions. *Child Development, 34,* 1041–1046.

Pinkwater, D. (1975). *Wingman.* New York: Bantam-Skylark.

Pressley, M., Dolezal, S. E., Raphael, L. M., Welsh, L. M., Bogner, K., & Roehrig, A. D. (2003). *Motivating primary-grade students.* New York: Guilford Press.

Pressley, M., & El-Dinary, P. B. (1997). What we know about translating comprehension strategies instruction research into practice. *Journal of Learning Disabilities, 30,* 486–488.

Pressley, M., Gaskins, I. W., Solic, K., & Collins, S. (2004). *A portrait of Benchmark School: How a school produces high achievement in students who previously failed* (Technical Report). East Lansing, MI: Michigan State University, Literacy Achievement Research Center.

Pressley, M., & Ghatala, E. S. (1989). Metacognitive benefits of taking a test for children and young adolescents. *Journal of Experimental Child Psychology, 47*, 430–450.

Pressley, M. Raphael, L., Gallagher, J. D., & DiBella, J. (2004). Providence–St. Mel School: How a school that works for African-American students works. *Journal of Educational Psychology, 96*, 216–235.

Raphael, L. M., Pressley, M., & Mohan, L. (2005). *What does motivating and engaging instruction look like in middle school?* (Technical Report). East Lansing, MI: College of Education, Literacy Achievement Research Center.

Reid, M. K., & Borkowski, J. G. (1987). Causal attributions of hyperactive children: Implications for teaching strategies and self-control. *Journal of Educational Psychology, 79*, 296–307.

Renick, M. J., & Harter, S. (1989). Impact of social comparisons on the developing self-perceptions of learning disabled students. *Journal of Educational Psychology, 81*, 631–638.

Renninger, K. A., & Wozniak, R. H. (1985). Effect of interest on attentional shift, recognition, and recall in young children. *Developmental Psychology, 21*, 624–632.

Ruble, D. N. (1983). The development of social-comparison processes and their role in achievement-related self-socialization. In E. T. Higgins, D. N. Ruble, & W. Hartup (Eds.), *Social cognition and social development* (pp. 134–157). New York: Cambridge University Press.

Ruble, D. N., Boggiano, A. K., Feldman, N. S., & Loebl, J. H. (1980). Developmental analysis of the role of social comparison in self-evaluation. *Developmental Psychology, 16*, 105–115.

Schiefele, U. (1992). Topic interest and levels of text comprehension. In K. A. Renninger, S. Hidi, & A. Krapp (Eds.), *The role of interest in learning and development* (pp. 151–182). Hillsdale, NJ: Erlbaum.

Schmidt, C. R., Ollendick, T. H., & Stanowicz, L. B. (1988). Developmental changes in the influence of assigned goals on cooperative and competition. *Developmental Psychology, 24*, 574–579.

Schraw, G., Flowerday, T., & Lehman, S. (2001). Increasing situational interest in the classroom. *Educational Psychology Review, 13*, 211–224.

Schunk, D. H. (1991). Self-efficacy and academic motivation. *Educational Psychologist, 26*, 207–232.

Shirey, L. L., & Reynolds, R. E. (1988). Effect of interest on attention and learning. *Journal of Educational Psychology, 80*, 159–166.

Skinner, E. A., Wellborn, J. G., & Connell, J. P. (1990). What it takes to do well in school and whether I've got it: A process model of perceived control and children's engagement and achievement in school. *Journal of Educational Psychology, 82*, 22–32.

Skinner, E. A., Zimmer-Gembeck, M. J., & Connell, J. P. (1998). Individual differences and the development of perceived control. *Monographs of the Society for Research in Child Development, 63* (2–3), v–220.

Spaulding, C. C. (1992). The motivation to read and write. In J. W. Irwin & M. A. Doyle (Eds.), *Reading/writing connections: Learning from research* (pp. 177–201). Newark, DE: International Reading Association.

Stipek, D. J., & Daniels, D. H. (1988). Declining perceptions of competence: A consequence of changes in the child or in the educational environment? *Journal of Educational Psychology, 80,* 352–356.

Stipek, D. J., & Hoffman, J. M. (1980). Children's achievement-related expectancies as a function of academic performance histories and sex. *Journal of Educational Psychology, 72,* 861–865.

Stipek, D., & Kowalski, P. (1989). Learned helplessness in task-orienting versus performance-orienting test conditions. *Journal of Educational Psychology, 81,* 384–391.

Stipek, D., & MacIver, D. (1989). Developmental change in children's assessment of intellectual competence. *Child Development, 60,* 521–538.

Swan, E. A. (2003). *Concept-oriented reading instruction: Engaging classrooms, lifelong learners.* New York: Guilford Press.

Sweet, A. P., & Guthrie, J. T. (1996). How children's motivations relate to literacy development and instruction. *Reading Teacher, 49,* 660–662.

Sweet, A. P., Guthrie, J. T., & Ng, M. M. (1998). Teacher perceptions and students' regulation of motivation. *Journal of Educational Psychology, 90,* 210–223.

Turner, J. C. (1995). The influence of classroom contexts on young children's motivation for literacy. *Reading Research Quarterly, 30,* 410–441.

Vollands, S. R., Topping, K. J., & Evans, R. M. (1999). Computerized self-assessment of reading comprehension with the Accelerated Reader: Action research. *Reading and Writing Quarterly: Overcoming Learning Disabilities, 15,* 197–211.

Wade, S. E., & Adams, R. B. (1990). Effects of importance and interest on recall of biographic text. *Journal of Reading Behavior, 22,* 331–353.

Weiner, B. (1979). A theory of motivation for some classroom experiences. *Journal of Educational Psychology, 71,* 3–25.

Wentzel, K. R. (1998). Social relationships and motivation in middle school: The role of parents, teachers, and peers. *Journal of Educational Psychology, 90,* 202–209.

White, R. W. (1959). Motivation reconsidered: The concept of competence. *Psychological Review, 66,* 297–333.

Wigfield, A. (1988). Children's attributions for success and failure: Effects of age and attentional focus. *Journal of Educational Psychology, 80,* 76–81.

Wigfield, A. (1994). Expectancy-value theory of achievement motivation: A developmental perspective. *Educational Psychology Review, 6,* 49–78.

Wigfield, A., & Eccles, J. S. (1992). The development of achievement task values: A theoretical analysis. *Developmental Review, 12,* 265–310.

Wigfield, A., Eccles, J. S., MacIver, D., Reuman, D. A., & Midgley, C. (1991). Transitions during early adolescence: Changes in children's domain-specific self-perceptions and general self-esteem across the transition to junior high school. *Developmental Psychology, 27,* 552–565.

Wigfield, A., Eccles, J. S., Yoon, K. S., Harold, R. D., Arbreton, A. J. A., Freedman-Doan, C., & Blumenfeld, P. C. (1997). Change in children's competence beliefs and subjective task values across the elementary school years: A 3-year study. *Journal of Educational Psychology, 89,* 451–469.

Wigfield, A., & Guthrie, J. T. (1997). Relations of children's motivation for reading to the amount and breadth of their reading. *Journal of Educational Psychology, 89,* 420–432.

Wigfield, A., Guthrie, J. T., & McGough, K. (1996). *A questionnaire measure of children's motivation for reading* (Instructional Resource No. 22). Athens, GA, and College Park, MD: National Reading Research Center.

Wigfield, A., Wilde, K., Baker, L., Fernandez-Fein, S., & Scher, D. (1996). *The nature of children's motivation for reading, and their relations to reading frequency and reading performance.* Athens, GA, and College Park, MD: National Reading Research Center.

Worthy, J., Moorman, M., & Turner, M. (1999). What Johnny likes to read is hard to find in school. *Reading Research Quarterly, 34,* 12–27.

Worthy, J., & Patterson, E. (2001). "I can't wait to see Carlos!": Preservice teachers, situation learning, and personal relationships with students. *Journal of Literacy Research, 33,* 303–344.

Yolen, J. (1987). *Owl moon.* New York: Philomel.

CHAPTER 12

Concluding Reflections . . . for the Time Being

The overarching conclusion of this book is that balanced elementary instruction—that is, a balancing of whole-language and skills components—seems more defensible than instruction that is only immersion in reading and writing, on the one hand, or predominantly skills driven, on the other. A great deal of this book is about how good reading involves the learning and use of word recognition and comprehension strategies, the effectiveness of strategies use depending, in part, on the reader's prior knowledge about the world, including knowledge built up through reading. Of course, I'm not the only one talking about these issues!

THREE NATIONAL REPORTS

Since the first edition of this book, there have been three important reports coming out of Washington, DC, all purporting to provide insights about reading instructional practices that are based on research. The conclusions offered in these reports complement the ideas presented in this book but were less emphatic about balancing than I have been here.

National Research Council Report

Preventing Reading Difficulties in Young Children (Snow, Burns, & Griffin, 1998) was published by the National Research Council, reflecting the work of a committee of scholars who had previously contributed distinguished reading and allied research (e.g., work on language development, writing, and literacy). The Snow et al. volume (1998) was a consensus document, with the authors reading the literature and agreeing among themselves about reading instructional practices that are research-defensible. Given that seven members of the committee had studied sound-, letter-, and word-level reading competencies more completely than other aspects of instruction, it was not surprising that Snow et al. (1998) argued extensively in favor of sound-, letter-, and word-level skills in reading instruction. Perhaps one reason that the first edition of the book you have just read was so successful was that its appearance coincided with the publication of Snow et al. (1998), both coming out in the spring of 1998. Many who read Snow et al. (1998) complained that it was too imbalanced in favor of skills instruction, prompting some to seek alternatives.

National Reading Panel Report

From its outset, the National Reading Panel (2000) decided to operate differently than Snow et al. (1998), intentionally limiting its scope, with the publicly admitted motivation for doing so being the overwhelming volume of evidence pertaining to early reading instruction. The panel decided to review only the following topics of instruction: alphabetics (i.e., phonemic awareness instruction, phonics instruction), fluency, comprehension (i.e., vocabulary instruction, text comprehension instruction, teacher preparation, and comprehension strategies instruction), teacher education and reading instruction, and computer technology and reading instruction. Members of the panel also limited their focus to true experiments and quasi-experiments, presumably in response to a congressional demand that the panel adopt rigorous research methodological standards. In order to generate conclusions using meta-analysis, the members' preferred research integration strategy, a number of experimental and/or quasi-experimental comparisons on a topic had to be available. The technique generates an average effect size (i.e., a numerical average of effect sizes observed in all the comparisons conducted to date). In short, the panel circumscribed its mandate, focusing only on particular topics studied many times over in experiments and/or quasi-experiments.

The panel offered some very strong conclusions based on its review of the literature, with the most visible ones being the following:

- Phonemic awareness instruction is effective in promoting early reading (e.g., word reading, comprehension) and spelling skills. The panel concluded that phonemic awareness instruction is effective with first graders and kindergarten students as well as with reading-disabled students in the later elementary grades.

- Systematic phonics instruction improves reading and spelling and to a lesser extent comprehension. Even though Chall (1967) had concluded that synthetic phonics (i.e., instruction teaching students explicitly to convert letters into sounds and blend the sounds) is more effective than other forms of systematic phonics instruction, the panel reported no statistically significant advantage for synthetic phonics instruction over other phonics approaches.

- Guided oral reading (i.e., a teacher listening as a student reads, providing instruction as needed) and repeated reading of texts increase reading fluency during the elementary years.

- A variety of methods of vocabulary instruction make sense, with vocabulary instruction positively impacting reading comprehension.

- Comprehension strategies instruction improves comprehension, with a number of strategies positively affecting understanding of a text, including teaching students to be aware of whether they are comprehending and to deal with miscomprehension when it occurs (e.g., by re-reading); using graphic and semantic organizers to represent text; teaching students to attend to story structure (e.g., "who," "what," "where," "when," and "why" information) as they read; question generation and question answering during reading; and summarization. Teaching students to use a small repertoire of effective strategies (e.g., predicting upcoming text content, seeking clarification when confused, asking questions, constructing mental images representing text content, and summarization) was especially strongly endorsed by the National Reading Panel. Both direct explanation (Duffy et al., 1987) approaches—starting with teacher modeling and explanation of strategies followed by scaffolding teacher practice of the strategies—and transactional strategies instruction (i.e., direct explanation with an emphasis on teacher–student and student–student discussions and interpretations of the text during practice of strategies; Brown, Pressley, Van Meter, & Schuder, 1996; Pressley, El-Dinary, et al., 1992) were supported by the panel.

- Teacher in-service can change teachers' instruction of reading, with impact on student achievement, although much more research is needed to identify particular in-service approaches that are helpful.

- Computer technology has great potential for improving beginning reading achievement, with promising approaches for promoting word recognition, vocabulary development, and comprehension enjoying some support already.

In summary, the panel argued that there is much support for skills-based instruction—instructional development of phonemic awareness, phonics competencies, knowledge of vocabulary, and comprehension strategies. Although there were some comments about teacher development and computer-based reading instruction, the conclusions offered about these topics were less complete and emphatic because there was so little research on those issues that the panel regarded as credible. The message emerging from the panel report was that there is massive scientific evidence in favor of teaching reading skills. A metamessage was that there is much less support for anything besides teaching of isolated skills. Thus, even with respect to the higher-order competency of comprehension, the panel emphasized the many studies about the teaching of individual strategies. In discussing the teaching of the entire complicated processing that sophisticated readers employ when they read challenging texts (Pressley & Afflerbach, 1995), they emphasized that only a very few studies provided telling data.

RAND Report on Comprehension

The RAND Reading Study Group, commissioned by the U.S. Department of Education, consisted of a who's who of scholars in the area of comprehension. They produced *Reading for Understanding: Toward an R&D Program in Reading Comprehension* (RAND Reading Study Group, 2001). This was an exceptionally intelligent discussion of what is known about comprehension instruction and what needs to be known, what is known about preparing teachers to teach comprehension and what needs to be known, as well as what is known about assessing comprehension and what needs to be known. For example, with respect to the issue of what is known about increasing comprehension through instruction, there is commentary on fluency, comprehension strategies instruction, vocabulary instruction, cross-curricular connections, representation of diverse genres in comprehension instruction, motivation as key to instructional success, and how teachers articulate a variety of instructional procedures to develop student comprehension. An overarching point with respect to instruction was that not nearly enough time is devoted to comprehension instruction in contemporary schools. With respect to what needs to be known about comprehension instruction, among other recommendations, the RAND group encouraged more work on comprehension instruction in the context of current curricula, especially with respect to the understanding of weaker readers. The researchers were especially concerned that there be inquiry about how to work comprehension instruction into already busy schedules, especially for low achievers. The RAND group noted the need to know more about how to use assessment to guide comprehension instruction. It was also very concerned that there be more research on promoting comprehension in

English-second-language learners. In short, the RAND group provided a wide-ranging discussion of the many issues surrounding comprehension instruction. This document is must reading in its complete form for all K–12 educators in my view and all concerned with the development of reading competence in K–12 education.

Summary Evaluations

My first reactions to the Snow et al. (1998) and National Reading Panel (2000) reports were that they were very credible, as far as they went. For example, most of the conclusions in these two reports were included in the first edition of this book, and most of the findings were well known to those who had spent time studying the scientific literature on reading instruction. Even though the conclusions of these reports were believable, it also seemed to me that the National Reading Panel, in particular, was unacceptably narrow in its consideration of reading instruction. Even within the panel, there was at least one voice calling for a broader conceptual approach—that of Joanne Yatvin, a reading educator serving a school district in Oregon. The panel's report concluded with her minority view that there were a number of instructional issues that were never even considered for inclusion by the panel that should have been addressed by a body charged to review the research-based knowledge about teaching children to read.

Even if the panel's willingness only to consider experimental and quasi-experimental data is respected, there was plenty covered in the present book that would have made sense to include in the National Reading Panel report. For example, I am impressed by the comparative data establishing that families can be taught to interact productively with their children over literacy tasks (Jordan, Snow, & Porche, 2000; Morrow & Young, 1997). There are very good evaluations establishing that volunteer tutors can make a difference (Baker, Gersten, & Keating, 2000; Elbaum, Vaughn, Hughes, & Moody, 2000; Fitzgerald, 2001; Invernizzi, Juel, & Rosemary, 1997; Wasik, 1998). Given the substantial body of experimental and quasi-experimental data confirming that whole-language practices do have positive impacts on literacy (e.g., Dahl & Freppon, 1995), and given the prevalence of whole-language practices in contemporary schools, it would have made sense to offer some analyses of the research on whole language. In short, many of the elements of balanced instruction that enjoy empirical support were ignored by the National Reading Panel (2000). Although the coverage by Snow et al. (1998) was broader, that report never got beyond commenting on the efficacy of particular components. As the descriptions of the teaching of "Andy," Karyn Beach, and Nancy Masters made clear earlier in this volume (see Chapters 8 and 11), balanced teaching is the orchestration of many components. The reports coming out of Washington have little to say about such orchestration. A decade after writing the first version of this book, and hundreds of observations of balanced teaching later, I am convinced that balanced teaching is best understood by reflecting both on the individual components and about how masterful teachers like Andy, Karyn Beach, and Nancy Masters weave those components together to create their teaching methods. The voices and teaching of such teachers were excluded from the National Reading Panel (2000) report, and that is regrettable from my point of view.

That is not to say that the National Reading Panel had no impact on teaching. In fact, its view of reading went far in informing the Reading First provisions of the No Child Left Behind legislation (2002). That legislation has gone far in stimulating much more skills instruction at the kindergarten through grade-3 levels emphasizing phonemic awareness, phonics, fluency, vocabulary development, and comprehension strategies (Pressley, Duke, & Boling, 2004). The legislation might have had greater impact and benefited more children, however, had it been more broadly informed by a panel more committed to covering completely the evidence that can inform elementary reading instruction.

The RAND Reading Study Group (2001) document is without a doubt the most impressive of the national reports from the perspective of balanced scholarship and its forward look. The other two reports are mostly about what is known; the RAND report is as much about what needs to be known. It is stimulating and informative reading for educators and researchers. That said, I have seen little evidence that the document has had much of an impact. With the endorsement here, I am urging all teachers and teachers-in-training to read the RAND document and act on it.

THREE MODELS OF BEGINNING READING AND EARLY READING INSTRUCTION

Three instructional models were considered in this book. Each continues to be present in contemporary school places.

The Skills-Emphasis Model

According to the skills-emphasis approach, reading depends on the development of a number of particular competencies. Because some competencies are logical prerequisites to others, different competencies are the focus of development and instruction at different grade/age levels.

During the preschool years, or at the latest kindergarten or grade 1, children should be able to differentiate letters from one another as well as know the names of letters and letter–sound associations. Children also need to learn that words are blendings of sounds. Such phonemic awareness depends critically on experiences that emphasize the sounds in words and how those sounds can be manipulated. Without phonemic awareness, instruction to sound out words by mapping the letters to their sounds and blending the letters would make little sense (i.e., the purpose of decoding instruction would not be clear).

At first, letter–sound mapping and blending require much effort and need a great deal of support. With practice, associating component letters to their sounds and blending them become more automatic. In addition, frequently encountered letter combinations come to be perceived automatically as chunks. When familiar chunks are part of unfamiliar words, they come to be much of the basis for sounding out and blending. As initially unfamiliar words are reencountered, recognition of the word as a whole is increasingly automatic. Such automatic recognition requires little if any effort.

The decreasing effort needed for word recognition frees up cognitive capacity for comprehension of the words being read. That is, decoding and comprehension compete for the limited attentional capacity that is available, the 5 ± 2 slots of short-term memory. One reason that comprehension often is low when students are struggling decoders is that all their capacity is being devoted to identifying the words, with little left over for understanding (LaBerge & Samuels, 1974).

Once words are recognized automatically, their meanings are also accessed automatically. One of the ways that psychologists have demonstrated this is with research on the Stroop effect. Tim, my 9-year-old at the time, was so taken with this effect that his grade-4 science project was dedicated to it. Tim presented his friends and some younger children with lists of color words—blue, red, green, yellow, black, purple, orange, and brown. On one list, each word was printed in the color ink that corresponded to it (i.e., "blue" was printed in blue ink, "red" printed in red ink). On the other list, each word was printed in an ink not corresponding to its color (e.g., "blue" was printed in red ink, "red" was printed in blue ink). His friends' task was not to read the words but simply to name the ink colors in the order of presentation. Consistent with classic Stroop results, Tim found that when his grade-4 and -5 friends attempted this task, it was really difficult for them when the color words were printed in an ink other than the color the word stands for. In contrast, kindergarten and grade-1 students had no difficulty reading off the sequence of colored inks, regardless of the meaning of the word. What was happening? The grade-4 and -5 students' reading of words was so automatic that they accessed the meaning of the words even when they were not trying to read them, and this accessing of meaning produced interference when they attempted to say the name of the different-colored ink the word was printed in. Becoming adept at reading words definitely affects comprehension. With the exception of situations like the Stroop task, automaticity of comprehension typically improves performance.

Word-level processes certainly are not all there is to comprehension, however. For example, scholars from a variety of perspectives are exploring how comprehension beyond the word level occurs and can be facilitated (e.g., Lorch & van den Broek, 1997; Pressley, 1997). Good readers process the details in a text, as specified by word-by-word reading of that text, but do not get bogged down in those details as they construct an understanding of the main ideas in the text (e.g., Kintsch & van Dijk, 1978). Good readers are very active in this construction process, selectively attending to informative aspects of the text, explicitly attempting to elaborate upon and remember points in the text that seem particularly relevant to the reader's reason for reading, and responding affectively to ideas encoded in the text.

As previously discussed, skills-development approaches have fared well in scientific evaluations. In particular, instruction aimed at fostering emergent literacy and phonemic awareness skills has proven to affect reading in the long term. Decoding instruction intended to develop sounding-out and blending skills has proven potent, as has instruction directed at developing reader knowledge of orthographs and their utility in word recognition. Comprehension instruction that encourages more active strategic processing of a text really does make a difference in student understanding (e.g., Pressley, El-Dinary, et al., 1992).

As positive as the evaluations have been of instructional development of particular reading competencies, the skills-emphasis approach often does not appeal to educators. It seems mechanistic and reductionistic, especially to educators who are confronting children who seem ready to try to write even though they cannot spell; who are enthralled by stories long before they can read many words well; and who use language that seems quite complex. The skills-emphasis approach especially seems mechanistic and unattractive when presented in publisher products that overemphasize skills, such as published decoding programs that are nothing more than daily worksheets, or when phonics fanatics, as I think of them, literally scream that phonics should be first in grade-1 reading. Such educational hawkers often show little understanding of how literature can be used to develop literacy competencies and enthusiasm for reading, and little knowledge about the important links between writing and the development of reading. Moreover, the phonics-first crowd often seems to assume that if the child learns to decode with phonics everything else will fall into place. According to them, the only bottleneck in learning to read is learning to decode.

The skills-emphasis model does not fail because skills are not critical; it fails because the skills that are the focus of skills-emphasis enthusiasts, especially decoding skills, are not all there is to literacy. The skills-emphasis model is an incomplete model of literacy development, one that does not even acknowledge as important many defensible whole-language practices that are embraced by those who control the American elementary schoolplace— elementary teachers.

The Whole-Language Model

An alternative to the skills-emphasis approach is whole language, which takes the position that instruction focusing on the development of specific skills is essentially wrongheaded. Literate people read whole texts and sometimes write them, too. The message from whole language is that if you want children to become readers of texts, have them read texts; if you want them to be writers, have them write. Holistic reading and writing will foster a deep understanding of the nature and purposes of reading; it will make obvious to the child why letter- and word-level processes, developing as a natural consequence of doing real reading and writing, are important.

In recent years, whole-language advocates have conceded that skills should be taught, but in context. In other words, the child should be taught the skills that she or he in particular needs for holistic reading and writing. Thus, if a teacher notices that a student is having difficulties with writing plurals (e.g., a Latino student who is required to write in English, which uses very different approaches to pluralization than the child's native Spanish), it makes sense to do some explicit teaching of plurals at that point. The reason for such teaching will be obvious to the student in such a context, and the improvements in reading and writing gained from such instruction will also make clear the importance of learning about plurals.

Whole language is premised on a belief that children have powerful language-learning capabilities. The proof of this is that children learn oral language without explicit teaching, simply from immersion in a speaking world. Analogously, it is presumed that children should be able to learn to read and write from immersion in print and print experiences. The flaw in this thinking, however, is that learning to read and write is not much like learning to speak; humans have not evolved to be able to discover how to read and write from immersion in print experiences.

Beyond the conceptual shortcomings of whole language, it has not enjoyed as much validation as alternative approaches, such as the skills-emphasis model. There are several reasons for this:

1. There is a great deal of data that are inconsistent with the fundamental assumptions of the approach, such as demonstrations that only weak readers rely on semantic–contextual cues to decode words.
2. The data that do document positive effects of whole language are

not abundant, perhaps because of antagonism in the whole-language community toward scientific study of whole language.

3. Even though there are data documenting positive effects of whole language on some aspects of literacy development, whole language does not seem as certain to result in adequate decoding competency as other approaches. This is a point of emphasis, since decoding increasingly seems like a critical literacy competency in the current political context.

If the whole-language versus skills-emphasis debate has done nothing else, it has inspired a lot of analyses substantiating how critical being able to decode is for the development of mature literacy. Whole language is attractive in many ways, however. It is extremely child-centered, and educational models that focus on the natural development of children in authentic contexts have a long history of appeal. Nonetheless, its initial specifications were so vague that many teachers could not figure out how to become whole-language teachers. That situation has improved with the publication of many books about educational activities that are consistent with whole-language philosophy. Nonetheless, even a casual reading of these sources makes clear that good whole-language environments demand much of teachers: Excellent whole-language teachers must know literature well, understand the writing process, and be committed to monitoring their students intensively in order to identify the competencies that should be developed, the ones students most need to master in order to read and write.

Because of the scant empirical support for whole language and inattention to the supportive studies that exist, it is being questioned by policymakers everywhere, so that the teacher who uses it often will do so in the face and wake of substantial administrative resistance. Because students in whole language often do not make rapid progress in word-level decoding, parents are often very concerned about their students. For many parents, reading is being able to recognize the words!

Basically, the whole-language model has the same flaw as the skills-emphasis approach: It is an incomplete model of the literacy development process. It is especially incomplete with respect to its specification of a realistic conception of sound-, letter- and word-level learning.

The Balanced Teaching Model

There is much that is attractive about whole language and much that is intuitively sensible. Many teachers have come to the conclusion, however, that children's immersion in literature will be most beneficial if they are armed with the skills necessary to attack the words in books. These teachers also believe that writing is more likely to be rewarding for children if their creative imaginations are assisted by skills (e.g., spelling) that increase their abilities to translate what they can imagine into words on the page. In my own work and that of my closest colleagues, the classrooms where reading and writing seem to be developing best are ones in which there is a lot of coverage of skills and a great deal of teacher support as children apply the skills they are learning to the reading of excellent literature and to writing.

DEVELOPMENT OF LITERACY COMPETENCE

The Appendix to this chapter summarizes much that was covered in this book, laid out along the lines of the ages and stages of development. Much must develop for a person to become a highly skilled reader, which involves efficient processing of individual words during active and selective processing of a text.

Literacy development begins long before the child passes through the schoolhouse gate for the first time. Understanding has increased greatly in the past several decades about how literacy development proceeds early in life. With respect to elementary instruction, which is the focus of this book, plenty has been learned about the value of explicit decoding and comprehension strategies instruction but also about the value of real reading opportunities and daily composition. The most important findings are summarized in the Appendix. The Appendix concludes with a summary of what is known about literacy development beyond the elementary years, as a reminder that literacy development is not a childhood thing but rather a lifespan development.

The complexities reflected in the developmental progression detailed in the Appendix make clear that simplistic notions regarding development and instruction of literacy are not adequate—whether from the whole-language camp or from the skills-first/emphasis enthusiasts. Many simplistic claims about reading instruction continue to be made, however, that are simply wrong. Ten of the most offensive ones are taken up later in this chapter.

The Research That Is Needed

Much, much more research is needed on effective elementary literacy instruction. The great progress to date gives good reason to believe that even greater progress can be made by researchers who are informed by what has been discovered so far.

There are always follow-up studies that are a slight extension of previous work. This section is not about such incrementalism, however. Rather, in this section, I take up some of the big and broad research efforts that are needed with respect to reading education and the development of skilled reading.

More Descriptive Studies of Effective Balanced Teaching

Much can be learned in laboratory-like experiments about how skills can be developed, and the skills-instruction enthusiasts have provided much such work. Much can be learned about the types of literature and writing experiences that are possible by reading the mostly testimonial writing of whole-language teachers, and the whole-language enthusiasts have provided many testimonials. To understand the complex articulation of skills instruction and whole language that represents balanced instruction, however, one must begin with observation of excellent balanced instruction.

Descriptive studies are not as valued in the social sciences as are studies aimed at evaluating predetermined hypotheses about causes and effects. More positively, however, shifts in educational research toward more qualitative methodologies have led to recent enthusiasm for descriptive work. As one who has done a great deal of descriptive research, I see this as a good sign, especially because this work has produced great insights about what really good elementary literacy instruction looks like. Still, much more is needed if sure conclusions are to be drawn from such work and if the generalizability of existing conclusions is to be tested. Then, there is a need for comparative studies informed by the observational work—that is, in situ evaluations of balanced classrooms as compared to other types of instructional environments.

Balanced instruction is more complex than skills approaches or whole language and calls for more complex methodologies to evaluate and elucidate it. That is, scientific work does more than inform scientists: At its best, it also informs practitioners; to achieve that, detailed descriptions are absolutely necessary. People often can learn better from specific concrete examples (i.e., cases) than from abstract descriptions.

Teacher Education Research

Substantial resources need to be devoted to research on teacher education that helps teachers develop into effective literacy educators who can deliver effective balanced instruction. Logically, it seems that such teachers must have in-depth understanding of children's literature, a sophisticated understanding of the linguistic structure of American language and vocabulary, and a good understanding of the cognitive–instructional models that underlie scaffolded instruction and the most effective approaches to process writing (e.g., Harris & Graham, 1994). Teachers must learn how to mix explanations with students' scaffolded participation in reading and writing. Such teaching requires consistent detailed monitoring of students as they read and write, as well as detailed understanding of the reading and writing tasks themselves, in order to envision how students can be encouraged as they attempt those tasks.

Pamela B. El-Dinary and I (e.g., Pressley & El-Dinary, 1997; see also Deshler & Schumaker, 1993; Klingner, Vaughn, Arguelles, Hughes, & Leftwich, 2004; Klingner, Vaughn, Hughes, & Arguelles, 1999) found that it was very challenging for teachers to become balanced comprehension instruction teachers. Complex articulations of components must occur if students are going to learn the decoding and comprehension skills so that they can apply them in real reading and writing. As work on balanced teaching proceeds, it is imperative that the research community be sensitive to the challenging nature of such teaching, making it a priority to conduct research that reveals how teachers can overcome the challenges to becoming maximally effective teachers.

In my view, those education faculty members in colleges and universities who wish to inform young adults about how to be teachers must immerse themselves in elementary schooling. As someone who has done so, I have become adept at spotting those faculty colleagues who are so grounded and those who are not. There is no need for more books by individuals who have not spent extensive time in the school settings they wish to affect. There now exist powerful observational approaches that can inform scholars about complex settings, such as classrooms. It is the scholars who choose to wrap themselves in those methods and devote their days to on-site classroom analyses who deserve the attention of the educator community. I would have never come to the insights about teaching reflected in this volume without those hundreds of mornings and days in elementary classrooms during the past decade and a half.

My work has made very clear that it is hard to be an effective literacy teacher and difficult to learn how to become one. It is high time to evaluate carefully alternative approaches to teacher development.

Longitudinal Research

It is part of my being, as a developmental psychologist by training, to believe in the longitudinal study of development—to believe that much can be learned by following individual children for a number of years. To some extent, there has been longitudinal study of literacy development, but unfortunately such study has often failed to provide the types of comprehensive descriptions of development and explanations of developmental differences that are needed to make one feel confident that much is really known about the children being studied. Thus, there are now a number of studies examining quantitative indicators of phonemic awareness in 4- and 5-year-olds as predictors of standardized test achievement in the elementary grades. I have never felt that I knew much about these children after reading such studies, however. But when more detailed descriptions have been provided (e.g., Snow, Barnes, Chandler, Goodman, & Hemphill, 1991), important insights have emerged on such issues as why schooling becomes more important with increasing age as students progress through it. (Homes of at-risk students are more certain to be able to provide support of primary-level skills than skills developed in later grades.) Snow and colleagues' (1991) work also made clear in vividly concrete ways the discontinuities in the quality of teaching as children progress through school, as well as the consequences of such discontinuities (Pressley & Palmer, 1992).

Such work is really critical, because American students do experience discontinuities in their schooling. The assumption that students receive either whole-language or skills instruction exclusively fails many times because a student can have a whole-language teacher one year and a skills-oriented teacher the next. Is it not possible that, were balanced instruction to become the majority view, instruction might become more continuous from one grade to the next for many more children? I think this possibility is worth exploring. Moreover, the effects of such year-to-year continuity on literacy development should also be evaluated.

Studies of the Language of Instruction

There are major debates in the United States about whether instruction should occur in a child's first language if that language is not English. This is a question that could be evaluated scientifically in well-controlled comparisons. To the extent it has been (e.g., Carlisle & Beeman, 2000), the answer seems to be yes, literacy acquisition goes better when it is in the child's first language before it is in the second language. I am beginning to think that one way that American literacy education is decidedly imbalanced is that English is the language of instruction to the exclusion of all other languages. It might be a very good thing if instruction became more multilingual—for example, enriching students' vocabulary knowledge in their native language through exposure to cognates in other languages (Cunningham & Graham, 2000). For certain, when U.S. schools in some jurisdictions serve children with as many as 90 different first languages, there is a need to think hard about how the language of instruction makes a difference. It is easy to imagine that instruction in the reading skills of several languages would increase understanding of language in general; it is also easy to imagine that holistic reading and writing experiences in several languages might go far in increasing students' knowledge about how to understand and produce meaning in an increasingly multilingual world.

A next frontier for instructional balance is understanding how to do literacy instruction in two or more languages simultaneously, with existing data making clear that this is a powerful approach to literacy instruction (Slavin & Cheung, 2005). As a longtime resident of Canada, I recall my many students who grew up in Québec and who emerged exceptionally literate in two languages. Memories of those students convince me that instruction can be balanced across at least two languages.

Extending Elementary Reading Principles into the Middle School and High School Years

No one could come away from reading this book without appreciating the enormous amount that has been learned during the past two decades about literacy development in the preschool and elementary years. It is striking how much attention has been given to young children's literacy development, however, compared to students in the upper elementary, middle school, and high school years. That really needs to change, because many middle school and high school students need reading instruction.

As a researcher who has principally focused on elementary school, I am proud of the many reforms in American elementary education that are linked to research. In contrast, there has been much less reform in the secondary schools, and often the reform that has occurred is not inspired so much by research as by inspiring visions of high school education, such as Theodore R. Sizer's (e.g., 1996) essential schools. The excitement of change in the local elementary school often is not mirrored by exciting changes in the district's middle school or high school.

Amid the backdrop of little or no research-based change in secondary schools, although see Jetton and Dole (2004), there is one important exception. Some special educators have made enormous progress in developing, validating, and disseminating effective literacy instruction to students with learning disabilities. The most strikingly effective group on this score operates out of the University of Kansas, with Donald D. Deshler and Jean B. Schumaker (e.g., 1988, 1993) providing the conceptual and pragmatic leadership. I cannot tell you how many times I have heard secondary literacy educators react to descriptions of the Kansas work with the appraisal that "All high school students need to learn the comprehension and writing strategies that students with learning disabilities are being taught." There is enough research on literacy-strategies instruction at the secondary level for me to respond confidently that such claims are on target (see Deshler, Schumaker, Harris, & Graham, 1998; Wood, Woloshyn, & Willoughby, 1995).

TEN DUMB AND DANGEROUS CLAIMS ABOUT READING INSTRUCTION

There are many strong claims being made about reading instruction, many of which fly in the face of considerable data. In this section I offer what I consider to be 10 dumb and dangerous claims about reading instruction that are commonplace in contemporary conversations about education. In the manner of David Letterman, I present this as a top-10 countdown. Of course, I am aware that others might order these claims differently, or even have alternative claims that they feel should be on the list. Nonetheless, I think by providing such a list—and briefly reminding readers of the evidence that counters each of these claims—I can provide an effective review of some of the most disturbing beliefs about reading instruction that are not in synchrony with scientific evidence. Here we go:

10. *When otherwise normal students have difficulties in learning to read, there is a biological basis for the problem, and thus, instruction will do little good.* In fact, biological dyslexia is rather rare as compared to reading failures due to lack of appropriate instruction. Many children who experience difficulties in learning to decode, given normal classroom instruction, benefit from more intensive instruction, such as is provided by tutoring.

9. *Students learn to read in the first three grades and read to learn after that.* Even learning to decode is far from complete by the end of grade 3, so there is much learning to read yet to be accomplished. There is also much left to accomplish with respect to comprehension—good reason to continue teaching students to read long after the primary years are completed. In addition, it should be emphasized that even during the height of learning to read—in grades 1 to 3—children are learning while they read if they are reading worthwhile texts.

8. *Teachers who use published reading materials or teach skills are being de-skilled themselves. Moreover, they are in political conspiracy with right-wing elements determined to maintain the social, economic, and political status quo.* These claims, which are embraced by some whole-language enthusiasts, are not true. In fact, when teachers use published programs, they do not follow the prescriptions in the programs blindly; rather, they pick and choose, using the components and activities of the published programs that make sense in their own reading programs. As for the political conspiracy part, there are many very politically liberal people who think that it is a good thing for children to be taught how to read! When I have read the arguments of those who advance the conspiracy theory, I am struck that I can object to almost every claim they make, including the claim that those of us who favor some explicit instruction as part of literacy instruction do not recognize the advantages provided by whole-language experiences. That brings up dumb and dangerous claim number 7 . . .

7. *Whole language does not promote literacy.* Immersion in reading and writing experiences increases understanding of the elements of reading and writing, such as the structural characteristics of stories and other types of writing. Hearing and reading stories increases vocabulary and world knowledge. Invented spelling experiences promote understanding of the sound structure of words. In short, students in whole-language environments make much progress in literacy. What whole language does not pro-

mote sufficiently for many students, however, are letter-level, letter–sound, and word recognition skills, which leads us to number 6 . . .

6. *Children will come to phonemic awareness and discover the letter and sound facts (phonics facts) through immersion in reading and writing alone. Teaching these competencies rather than allowing them to emerge naturally might do some harm; for example, it could decrease children's motivation to read.* Yes, whole-language immersion results in some learning of phonemic awareness and phonics, but much more can be accomplished through more explicit teaching of skills than occurs in whole-language environments. The idea that teaching interferes with natural development is an old one with no credible evidence in support of it. Indeed, with respect to motivation, leaving a child to struggle and experience failures and frustrations has very high potential to undermine motivation to read. That brings up the next dumb claim . . .

5. *If a child experiences difficulties in learning to decode, simply wait and the child will learn to read when ready.* Children who are behind in grade 1 often stay behind. Rather than waiting and hoping that the child catches on to reading, real progress can be made with tutoring that promotes decoding skills in children experiencing difficulties in early reading.

4. *Short-term tutoring for students experiencing reading difficulties can get them on par with other students, and those students will stay on par once tutoring has concluded.* For students experiencing difficulties in school, sustained, long-term excellent instruction is more likely to be successful than short-term instruction. A medical analogy for the short-term instruction approach is an inoculation, with benefits expected for a long time following brief intervention. What works in reading development with students who have difficulties, however, is more akin to continued medical care of a chronic condition.

3. *Students become good comprehenders if they just read, read, and read.* There is substantial evidence that children become much better comprehenders if they are taught to use the active comprehension processes that skilled readers use. As is true for phonemic awareness and word recognition skills, students do not seem to discover sophisticated comprehension strategies through immersion in reading alone.

2. *Students should be taught to give priority to meaning (i.e., semantic–contextual) cues in word recognition.* This is a very dated idea that just has not died because of whole-language theorists' embrace of it, despite analyses making clear that good readers give priority to phonological, letter-combination, and word-chunk cues in word recognition. In addition, instruction that emphasizes sounding out and decoding by analogy promotes word recognition more than does instruction emphasizing semantic contexts. That does not mean that semantic–contextual cues play no role. Such cues permit evaluation of whether an attempted decoding based on

phonological cues is accurate. Such cues also permit readers to decide which of several meanings of a word makes sense in the context, once the word has been decoded.

1. *Skills instruction and whole language are incompatible.* Systematic skills instruction has a good track record, and there are plenty of effective balanced-literacy teachers who carry out systematic instruction of skills, scaffolding student use of skills into real reading and writing. Such teachers are proof that systematic skills instruction can occur in the context of extensive reading of literature and student writing. That adding systematic skills instruction to whole-language environments improves literacy development is also proof of sorts that whatever skills instruction is in whole language is not enough relative to what students could and should receive.

The case for balanced teaching as detailed in this book is a case for optimism that many children can learn to read better than they would if the 10 ideas just reviewed were to prevail in determining who is taught and how. Of course, one of the points of this book is that ideas as dumb and dangerous as these have prevailed in American schools. More optimistically, I hope that this book permits many more teachers, parents, and policymakers to realize that the thinking reviewed in this top-10 list should not continue to affect educational decision making.

BALANCED LITERACY TEACHING COMPARED TO PRACTICE

In December 1995, I participated in a symposium at the National Reading Conference, an organization composed of literacy researchers of various persuasions. My task that day was to be the discussant for a session on balanced reading instruction. The session took place in a jam-packed room, and the crowd spilled into the hallway. The attendance was so great, given the capacity of the room, that the presenter–audience dynamic was quite unusual: It was impossible as a panelist not to know the audience's reaction because the crowd was sitting against the wall behind the presenters, pushed up to the podium, to the left, to the center, and to the right. It was a little tight in the room.

As is typical in discussions about beginning reading, there were strong reactions to the presentations. After all, the audience included extremists committed both to whole language and to direct instruction of decoding skills as the primary objective of beginning-reading instruction. The panelists wanted to emphasize to the audience that it makes sense to forget both the extremes in favor of balance. I could feel the tension between whole-language and skills advocates growing as the meeting progressed, however, and there was potential for a real blowup during my discussion.

I simply could not say directly what I wanted to say without potentially setting off a shouting match, but I was determined to get the message out anyway. Several who were attending that evening subsequently urged me to write up my remarks. I present here the gist of my remarks from that day.

Commentary for a Symposium on Balanced Literacy Instruction

"I come here today not as a literacy researcher but as a candidate for Little League commissioner in my hometown. The reason I am running for the position is because I disagree with the two opposing models of our minor league program in Little League baseball. Some of the parents and managers believe that our minor league program should focus more than anything on the development of baseball skills. They are so adamant that some even believe that the minor leagues should not schedule regular games. The other side of the argument is that our 6- to 9-year-olds should be playing baseball as a game most of the time, for such immersion is how a person learns to play the game. At present, our minor league program is much more this second model than the first, and thus I will talk about my perceptions of that approach first.

"Our 6- to 9-year-olds are playing a lot of baseball games. For some of the kids, this is working just great. Unfortunately, however, many others are not making progress in learning the game. If their understanding of the overall game is developing (i.e., the 6-year-olds know where the bases are and which direction to run, should they hit the ball), their understanding of many fundamental details is lacking. How many of you have seen one of our 8-year-olds who did not realize that she or he could overrun first base? How many times have I seen a 9-year-old who does not know how to approach a hard grounder in the outfield? And when it comes to hitting, we have 8- and 9-year-olds who still do not know how to grip a bat, let alone know that they should be waiting for a pitch in the strike zone.

"I know the argument that, by playing the game, the kids will come to like the game. I have to be honest, however, that I see too many youngsters who are bored stiff because they do not understand the game in which they are immersed. I see too many children in tears because they do not even know what they are doing wrong when they make an error or strike out. They know only that they are not playing well. And, lastly, I am struck that so many children have dropped out of baseball in the minor leagues and will never play in the regular Little League because of what they felt was a bad experience in the minors.

"That is not to say that I favor the other side of this debate. Batting, running, and fielding practice all have their place, but baseball practice after practice without ever playing a game would be a drag. Unless the kids actually use the skills in games, they will never understand why they are learning to overrun first, put their whole body in front of a ground ball, or wait out a pitcher. I remember when I was on a junior high basketball team. The coach ran us through in-and-out weaves of various sorts for practice after practice. Even so, we were totally disorganized in the games. I'll never forget during a half-time screaming session how the light bulbs went on when the coach yelled, 'Why don't you use those weaves we practiced!' Suddenly, we realized that those in-and-out patterns could be used in the game! Skill drills alone just do not result in kids who can play the game.

"As many of you know, I was a member of a few baseball teams. My memory of successful teams was that there was some practice of skills, typically more early in the season than later, and typically more at the start of practice than at the end of it. After the skills practice, however, came the scrimmage game, with the team divided into two squads that played each other. During the scrimmage, the coaches did a lot of teaching, reminding players especially about how the skills they had been practicing transferred to the scrimmage. Thus, if during the scrimmage a runner did not overrun first, the coach might say, 'Remember how we practiced going past first?' If an outfielder approached to the side of a grounder, the coach might suggest, 'Get your body in front of it,' a pointer that would make sense given the earlier drill. What the coach was doing is called scaffolding. The coach knew the kids did not 'get it' completely during the skill instruction and practice. 'Getting it' depends on using the skill in context, and the player is much more likely to 'get it' if given a hint at an appropriate moment than if the moment passes without the coach offering a minilesson.

"Now, some of you whole-baseball coaches and parents are going to respond that the skills-practice part of this balance thing will bore the kids to tears. I don't buy it. I need only reflect on how I bounced a tennis ball against a wall for hours and hours and months and months to get good at picking up grounders. How much time did I spend in my youth throwing high poppers to myself to get accustomed to fielding fly balls? I've even heard from some of you that skills practice will interfere with the kids learning how to play real baseball. My response to that is 'Where's the evidence?' I think you would be hard-pressed to identify a single successful athlete who did not do a lot of skills practice. Swimmers and runners practice leaving the blocks, football linesmen practice with the sleds and tackling dummies, basketball players shoot and shoot and shoot, and major league baseball players spend a lot of time in the batting cage and more time in the field shagging grounders and fly balls. If skills practice interferes with learning to play the real game, there are many professional athletes in every sport who do not show the effects of such interference.

"My position is for a balanced approach to our minor league program, one in which practices involve skills instruction and drills plus scrimmages. The practices would be interwoven with some real games, but real games that are structured so that a lot of scaffolding and mini-lessons can take place. Our minor league games should not be about winning and losing but about learning the game in the exciting and motivating environment that is a six-inning baseball game. There should be a score book, but one that is more than a record of the runs scored: It should be a running record of player accomplishments and weaknesses that the coach can review later to reflect on what needs to be emphasized in future practice sessions. The center of attention has to be the improvement of the players, with every kid getting the help she or he needs and getting stroked for making improvements. That's what a balanced Little League minor league program should be like, in my view."

Balanced Instruction and Student Construction of Knowledge in General

I did not become the Little League commissioner. What I am, though, is an accomplished researcher in the area of children's learning, one who has spent a great deal of time reflecting on the conditions that result in the cognitive development of students. As such, I am well aware of the many suggestions made by constructivists that boil down to "Don't teach—let the child discover." There is a long history of such thinking in education, going back to John Dewey (1933) and continuing with the Piagetians (Inhelder, Sinclair, & Bovet, 1974; Kohlberg & Mayer, 1972) to the present generation of so-called radical constructivists, including the whole-language theorists. There is also a long history of student discovery that does not result in rapid and certain cognitive development (e.g., Schauble, 1990), certainly not as rapid and certain as can occur through instruction (Brainerd, 1978; Mayer, 2004; Shulman & Keislar, 1966; Wittrock, 1966).

In Chapter 11, I made the case that academic achievement is most likely when instruction is matched to student competence. Whatever instruction the teacher provides should be matched to the level of the student's competence—in the student's zone of proximal development, to use the Vygotskian term (Vygotsky, 1978). There should be no illusion, however, that the student will really understand the lesson from the teacher's presentation. My colleague Karen R. Harris and I (Harris & Pressley, 1991; Pressley, Harris, & Marks, 1992) have made the case that when a teacher explains a strategy to a student the student does not really understand it well, but the instruction is a start. If the teacher then places the student in a situation where the strategy can be applied and scaffolds the student's use of the strategy in the situation, more learning will occur. With additional scaffolded practice opportunities, there is more learning still, as the student comes to understand how and when the strategy can be applied and adapted. With increasing experience, there is less need for the teacher to assist the student or even provide a hint that the strategy might be applied. Eventually, the student uses the strategy flexibly and appropriately, coordinating its use with the other strategies and knowledge.

If there is anything that can be learned from Lev S. Vygotsky, it is that cognitive skills and strategies are passed from one generation to the next. Adults guide cognitive development by leading children to think in ways that many children would not discover on their own. (How many parents have taught their children baseball skills that were taught to them by their parents?) There is some explaining in such cross-generational transmissions, but there is much more scaffolding, which is necessary because people do not learn by listening alone but also by doing, which should occur in a realistic context. (How many parents spend much time scaffolding during Little League scrimmages?) Adults who are effective in promoting development do not leave development to the child's discovery of skills. (Even the great Babe Ruth owed his development as a baseball player to a member of a previous generation: Ruth cited Brother Mathias, who taught him baseball at St. Mary's School in Baltimore, as being the greatest person he ever knew.) Discovery learning is the wrong approach to instruction; the case in favor of teaching as scaffolding is much more conceptually compelling, occurring as it does in the evening, when the Little Leaguer is fortunate enough to have an excellent baseball coach, and during the day, if the Little Leaguer is lucky enough to be enrolled in a classroom headed by an effective literacy teacher.

FINAL COMMENTS

Much has been learned about what makes sense in elementary reading instruction. The recent version of the great debate has been posed as skills instruction versus whole language, most frequently at the primary level and as phonics versus whole language.

Whole language is like Little League baseball if players only played games. Their playing of whole games would be substantially impaired by lack of skills. Just as bad, skills emphasis is like Little League baseball if it involved mostly infield, outfield, and batting practice. As good as players experiencing such an approach might be at picking up grounders, running down fly balls, and hitting consistently, they would not be baseball players. They would not know how the components interrelate as part of an entire game. Baseball, like all sports, involves both the development of skills and practice in applying those skills in whole games, played at a level appropriate to the developmental level of the players.

Analogously, reading involves the development of skills but also practice in their application during reading and writing tasks that are appropriately challenging to students. That is why the balanced model of instruction is a better model than either the skills-emphasis approach or the whole-language approach. Balanced instruction involves much more systematic instruction of skills than does any version of whole language, with its emphasis on teaching only when there is demonstrated need. But balance also suggests much more involvement with literature and writing than occurs in many skills-emphasis classrooms.

When students are skilled in reading and writing and their motivation is maintained through appropriately challenging literacy experiences, they read and write more. Lack of skills, which is a danger of whole language, has high potential to undermine long-term motivation for literacy. Lack of exposure to interesting reading and writing experiences, which can characterize skills-emphasis classrooms, also can undermine motivation for literacy experiences, since children, like everyone else, thrive on interesting experiences and are turned off by boredom. Balanced literacy instruction is the best bet for maintaining and even enhancing student motivation to do literate things, providing students with the skills they need to be successful in reading and writing and having them practice those skills by reading interesting books and writing about topics that are important to them.

Before I end the third edition of this book, I feel obligated to address a question often posed to me: Why did I not say more about assessment, a topic so much on the minds of many present-day educational policymakers? One answer is that this is a book about instruction. The other is that assessment has just not been that visible in the excellent classrooms that I have studied with one exception: Excellent teachers are always informally assessing their students, monitoring where each student is and what each student needs. The excellent teacher acts on that monitoring, providing appropriate instruction or direction to each and every student in the room. Although excellent teachers give curriculum-based tests—for example, spelling tests and sight-word fluency assessments—there is very little concern with standardized tests among these teachers. Yes, they give their students practice in filling in bubble sheets in preparation for such tests, but they do not obsess nor do they massively change their curriculum in advance of school- or state-mandated tests. That said, I have heard many of the best teachers I have studied express great reservations about the validity of the standardized assessments forced on them. In short, the excellent balanced teachers I have encountered seem to think like the assessment scholars I most admire (Allington, 2001; Johnston & Rogers, 2001; Murphy, with

Shannon, Johnston, & Hansen, 1998; Paris, 2001; Paris & McEvoy, 2001; Paris & Urdan, 2001). They see great value in informal assessment and do it constantly, but they are not convinced of the validity of many standardized tests (see especially Johnston & Rogers, 2001). They do not view standardized assessments as doing much good for the kids they teach, and they feel that every school day should be filled only with activities that are good for their students' heads and hearts.

That said, I know that the national obsession with assessment is going to continue. As it does, I hope there is some better thinking brought to the enterprise about what should be measured. Jill Fitzgerald (Fitzgerald & Noblit, 2000), a distinguished literacy scholar, decided to teach grade 1 for a year and committed to do it in a balanced fashion, as described in this book. As Jill did so, she came to a number of insights about how the children in her class were growing:

1. Phonological awareness increased.
2. Sight word knowledge increased.
3. Children's matching of letters and sounds improved, as did their knowledge of orthographic patterns in words.
4. Children's word recognition strategies increased and improved, with children using visual–letter cues, syntactic cues, and contextual meaning cues.
5. Their vocabularies expanded.
6. The students came to understand that reading was about understanding and communicating, and as they did so they communicated more about what they learned from reading.
7. They developed a love of reading and wanted to do more reading.
8. They learned to respond to literature emotionally (e.g., loving a story, being scared).
9. One of those emotions was joy in becoming better readers, being able to do something they could not do previously.

These are huge accomplishments, with contemporary standardized assessments only tapping some of them. As this assessment animal matures, I hope new measures are developed that better capture all of these dimensions.

In recent years, much of what has been said about beginning literacy instruction has been nothing more than rancorous and partisan bickering. Alternatively, discussions about beginning literacy can be healthy and lead to additional research on elementary reading instruction that can inform practice. I hope it is the latter—but even if it is not, I am confident that much revealing reading instructional research is yet to come. Thus, the conclusions offered in this third edition are only for the time being, subject to revision in light of new evidence.

APPENDIX

LANDMARKS IN DEVELOPMENT OF LITERACY COMPETENCE (OR, WHAT HAPPENS WHEN)

0-2 Years of Age (Infancy)

• Emergent literacy experiences begin; infants who have rich verbal interactions during infancy are advantaged over those who do not, with language development beginning from birth. For example, vocabulary development is more extensive with rich language interactions.

• A secure parent–child attachment sets the stage for healthier emergent literacy experiences than if attachment is insecure.

• When there is risk of insecure attachment (e.g., because the baby is temperamentally difficult), parents can be taught how to interact with their infants so that there is a greater chance for secure attachment.

• Prior knowledge development is schematic from infancy onward, with the children's schematic knowledge reflective of the experiences they have had (e.g., children have schemata for what happens at fast-food restaurants when they pay many visits to McDonald's and Burger King).

2-5 Years of Age (Preschool Years)

• Many and diverse emergent literacy experiences are possible; readiness for school-based literacy instruction is determined in part by the quality and quantity of emergent literacy experiences.

• Over the long term, rich verbal and cognitive interactions with adults result in internalization of verbal and cognitive skills that are critically relevant to reading. Thus, egocentric speech is more prevalent in early preschool years than in later years, when inner speech predominates.

• When parents are not naturally adept at emergent literacy interactions, often they can be taught to be so, with improvements in children's language the result.

• Learning the names of the alphabetic letters is an important acquisition, as is learning the letter–sound associations. Such learning is acquired in a variety of ways, from interactions with parents to viewing of such programs as *Sesame Street*.

• Word recognition skills begin to develop, with preschoolers, for example, able to read logographs (e.g., McDonald's, as long as the name is on the famous golden arches logo). Four-year-olds can use analogies based on word chunks to some extent to read new words (e.g., if a child is shown the word *bee*, she or he can recognize that *see* is like *bee* in that both include the *-ee* part).

• There are language difficulties and differences apparent in many children who will later be diagnosed as biologically dyslexic.

• The beginnings of phonemic awareness sometimes are stimulated through such parent–child activities as reading of rhymes and playing of rhyming games.

- Children can begin to write, with the first invented spellings often only the first consonant of a word, and one- or two-word stories that the child can expand to many words and sentences as she or he "reads" the story back to another child or an adult.

5–7 Years of Age (Last Year of Preschool and Early Primary Grades)

- Academic motivation is at its highest during the primary years. Students tend to believe they can succeed if they try.
- Complete phonemic awareness typically does not develop through emergent literacy experiences alone, but can be activated through instruction during kindergarten, which can have a positive impact on later learning. The instruction typically involves a variety of activities aimed at student listening for sounds in words and manipulating the various sounds in words. When such phonemic awareness instruction is added to whole-language preschool and kindergarten experiences, there are positive effects on later literacy development.
- Alphabetic reading begins for many children, including approximations to it at first (e.g., reading a word based on only a few salient letters).
- Formal schooling now includes daily reading and composing from the first days of kindergarten. As students gain proficiency in reading and writing words, the diversity of reading and writing activities expands.
- Children can learn to decode through phonics instruction—through synthetic phonics instruction more certainly than analytic phonics instruction. They can also learn to decode through analogy-based approaches. There is no logical reason that phonics and analogy-based approaches cannot be combined, as children learning via phonics can acquire knowledge of word parts as they experience them and children learning by initial focus on word parts can also learn to blend the sounds produced by word chunks with individual sounds (e.g., blending the sounds of s and -ee to pronounce see). There is a lot of evidence that effective decoding instruction involves teaching students how to analyze words with respect to component sounds and how to blend those sounds. As students learn to decode, their automatic sight word skills improve (i.e., words decoded frequently become sight words).
- Although children in classrooms that are exclusively whole language are taught to rely heavily on semantic–contextual cues to decode, such instruction does not produce skilled decoding as reliably as phonics or word-chunk analogy-based approaches.
- Excellent classrooms involve a balancing of whole-language experiences (i.e., reading of real texts, composition) and skills instruction. Teachers scaffold student use of skills during realistic reading and writing. There also is integration of literacy and content-area instruction. There is good reason to suspect that classrooms that are either extremely skills-oriented or extremely anti-skills-oriented (i.e., skills

instruction occurs on an as-needed basis only in the context of reading and writing) are not as effective as more balanced classrooms.

- Some 20–30% of normally intelligent grade-1 students experience difficulties learning to decode. Most of these students can learn to decode with more intensive instruction; a very small percentage are biologically dyslexic, with biologically determined problems in phonological processing and/or perhaps in visual–spatial processing.

- Children can begin to learn writing strategies, specifically, strategies for planning, drafting, and revising, with possibly multiple-page stories by the end of the first grade.

- Vocabulary acquisition continues, with explicit teaching of vocabulary having an impact over and above the incidental learning of vocabulary from immersion in a rich language environment.

7–11 Years of Age (Later Primary and Upper-Elementary Grades)

- Academic motivation tends to decline. This is especially likely the more a student experiences academic failures and frustrations. Students' faith in success with effort declines during the elementary years. Students increasingly view academic frustrations as indications of low ability.

- Classroom competition increases with increasing grade level, with the potential to undermine the motivation of many students, who increasingly notice how they do as compared to others and interpret their relative failures as signaling low ability. Good grades given to good readers are not unambiguously beneficial for them either, having the potential to undermine the intrinsic motivation to read that many good readers bring to the task. That is, good readers can come to justify the reading they are doing as motivated by good grades; in situations where there are no grades for reading, there is no longer an incentive to read (i.e., there is an overjustification effect).

- Effective classrooms emphasize that effort matters, sending the message that trying hard fosters achievement and intelligence, failure is a natural part of learning, and school is more about getting better than being best. Rewarding students for improvement rather than performance relative to others promotes academic motivation.

- With increasing grade level, there is greater variability in the core emphases in classrooms. That is, first-grade classes across the country typically are more similar to each other than to fifth-grade classes in the same school. Some core emphases (e.g., encouragement of comprehension-strategies use) can make a significant positive difference in the development of literacy competence in grades 2 through 5.

- Comprehension strategies can be taught, typically resulting in improved understanding of texts, especially if strategies instruction is long-term and thoroughly integrated across the school day. Many times, however, such skills are not taught as explicitly or extensively as they could be taught. Consequently, students are not as active in their reading as they could be.

• Excellent classrooms report a balancing of whole-language (i.e., reading of real texts, composition activities) and skills instruction. Teachers scaffold use of skills during realistic reading and writing. There also is integration of literary and content-area instruction.

• Reading of novels becomes an important language-arts activity.

• With greater reading, automatic word recognition increases, as does the extent of vocabulary and other knowledge. Those who do a lot of reading become better readers than those who do little reading.

• Students who are struggling with fluency can be impacted by receiving feedback during one-on-one reading with an adult, with such instruction important, for comprehension depends on fluent reading.

• Teaching of vocabulary continues to make sense, with many words for the student to learn.

• Writing emphasizes even more planning, drafting, and revising processes. Conventions and spelling are emphasized increasingly with advancing grade levels.

• Students begin to experience content-area texts, many of which are not interesting. When students have some choice in what they read, motivation is higher.

Beyond the Elementary Years

• Skilled reading is both top-down (e.g., predictions about the upcoming text based on prior knowledge) and bottom-up (e.g., individual letters and words are processed).

• Skilled readers can read at 200–300 words per minute, processing most words, and indeed most letters within words, as they read. Saccadic eye movement is orderly from left to right within each line of text, with fixations on informative words.

• Skilled readers rely more on letter- and word-level graphemic–phonological cues (including recognition of common word parts) for word recognition than do unskilled readers. Unskilled readers attend more to semantic–contextual cues than do skilled readers in attempting to recognize (i.e., decode) a word. Once a word is recognized, however, good readers use semantic–contextual cues to determine the exact meaning of the decoded word in the present context and do so with greater certainty and success than less skilled readers.

• Skilled readers effortlessly recognize many words (i.e., they have large sight vocabularies). Such effortful recognition of sight words frees up short-term cognitive capacity, permitting it to be used for comprehension.

• Skilled readers probably continue to benefit from vocabulary instruction over and above the vocabulary learning that occurs incidentally.

• Good readers remember the gist of what they read, to some extent as an automatic consequence of reading the text. Comprehension and memory of text, however, also are enhanced through the use of a variety of active comprehension strategies, which are enabled, in part, by extensive prior knowledge, permitting construction of bridging inferences.

• For those who did not make progress in learning to write in the elementary grades, planning, drafting, and revising strategies can still be taught with great benefit.

• Reading skills continue to develop well into adulthood.

• Many adults remain unskilled readers, from those who cannot decode at all to many others who cannot do things commonly attributed to skilled readers.

REFERENCES

Allington, R. L. (2001). How to improve high-stakes test scores without really improving. *Issues in Education, 6,* 115–124.

Baker, S., Gersten, R., & Keating, T. (2000). When less may be more: A 2-year longitudinal evaluation of a volunteer tutoring program requiring minimal training. *Reading Research Quarterly, 35,* 494–519.

Brainerd, C. J. (1978). Learning research and Piagetian theory. In L. S. Siegel & C. J. Brainerd (Eds.), *Alternatives to Piaget: Critical essays on the theory* (pp. 69–109). New York: Academic Press.

Brown, R., Pressley, M., Van Meter, P., & Schuder, T. (1996). A quasi-experimental validation of transactional strategies instruction with low-achieving second grade readers. *Journal of Educational Psychology, 88,* 18–37.

Carlisle, J. F., & Beeman, M. M. (2000). The effects of language of instruction on the reading and writing achievement of first-grade Hispanic students. *Scientific Studies of Reading, 4,* 331–353.

Chall, J. S. (1967). *Learning to read: The great debate.* New York: McGraw-Hill.

Cunningham, T. H., & Graham, C. R. (2000). Increasing native English vocabulary recognition through Spanish immersion: Transfer from foreign to first language. *Journal of Educational Psychology, 92,* 37–49.

Dahl, K. L., & Freppon, P. A. (1995). A comparison of inner-city children's interpretations of reading and writing instruction in the early grades in skills-based and whole language classrooms. *Reading Research Quarterly, 30,* 50–74.

Deshler, D. D., & Schumaker, J. B. (1988). An instructional model for teaching students how to learn. In J. L. Graden, J. E. Zins, & M. J. Curtis (Eds.), *Alternative educational delivery systems: Enhancing instructional options for all students* (pp. 391–411). Washington, DC: National Association of School Psychologists.

Deshler, D. D., & Schumaker, J. B. (1993). Strategy mastery by at-risk students: Not a simple matter. *The Elementary School Journal, 94,* 153–167.

Deshler, D. D., Schumaker, J., Harris, K. R., & Graham, S. (1998).*Teaching every child every day: Learning in diverse schools and classrooms.* Brookline, MA: Brookline Books.

Dewey, J. (1933). *How we think: A restatement of the relation of reflective thinking in the education process.* Boston: Heath.

Duffy, G. G., Roehler, L. R., Sivan, E., Rackliff, G., Book, C., Meloth, M., Vavrus, L., Wesselman, R., Putnam, J., & Bassiri, D. (1987). Effects of explaining the reasoning associated with reading strategies. *Reading Research Quarterly, 22,* 347–368.

Elbaum, B., Vaughn, S., Hughes, M. T., & Moody, S. W. (2000). How effective are one-to-one tutoring programs in reading for elementary students at risk for reading failure?: A meta-analysis of the intervention research. *Journal of Educational Psychology, 92,* 605–619.

Fitzgerald, J. (2001). Can minimally trained college student volunteers help young at-risk children to read better? *Reading Research Quarterly, 36,* 28–47.

Fitzgerald, J., & Noblit, G. (2000). Balance in the making: Learning to read in an ethnically diverse first-grade classroom. *Journal of Educational Psychology, 92,* 3–22.

Harris, K. R., & Graham, S. (1994). *Helping young writers master the craft: Strategy instruction and self-regulation in the writing process.* Cambridge, MA: Brookline Books.

Harris, K. R., & Pressley, M. (1991). The nature of cognitive strategy instruction: Interactive strategy construction. *Exceptional Children, 57,* 392–404.

Inhelder, B., Sinclair, H., & Bovet, M. (1974). *Learning and the development of cognition.* Cambridge, MA: Harvard University Press.

Invernizzi, M., Juel, C., & Rosemary, C. A. (1997). A community tutorial that works. *The Reading Teacher, 50,* 304–311.

Jetton, T. L., & Dole, J. A. (Eds.). (2004). *Adolescent literacy research and practice.* New York: Guilford Press.

Johnston, P. H., & Rogers, R. (2001). Early literacy development: The case for "informed assessment." In S. B. Neuman & D. K. Dickinson (Eds.), *Handbook of early literacy research* (pp. 377–389). New York: Guilford Press.

Jordan, G. E., Snow, C. E., & Porche, M. V. (2000). Project EASE: The effect of a family literacy project on kindergarten students' early literacy skills. *Reading Research Quarterly, 35,* 524–546.

Kintsch, W., & van Dijk, T. A. (1978). Toward a model of discourse comprehension and production. *Psychological Review, 85,* 363–394.

Klingner, J. K., Vaughn, S., Arguelles, M. E., Hughes, M. T., & Leftwich, S. A. (2004). Collaborative strategic reading: "Real-world" lessons from classroom teachers. *Remedial and Special Education, 25,* 291–302.

Klingner, J. K., Vaughn, S., Hughes, M. T., & Arguelles, M. E., (1999). Sustaining research-based practices in reading: A 3-year follow-up. *Remedial and Special Education, 20,* 263–274.

Kohlberg, L., & Mayer, R. (1972). Development as the aim of education: The Dewey view. *Harvard Educational Review, 42,* 449–496.

LaBerge, D., & Samuels, S. J. (1974). Toward a theory of automatic information processing in reading. *Cognitive Psychology, 6,* 293–323.

Lorch, R., & van den Broek, P. (1997). Understanding reading comprehension: Current and future contributions of cognitive science. *Contemporary Educational Psychology, 22,* 213–246.

Mayer, R. E. (2004). Should there be a three-strikes rule against pure discovery learning? *American Psychologist, 59,* 14–19.

Morrow, L. M., & Young, J. (1997). Parent, teacher, and child participation in a collaborative family literacy program: The effects of attitude, motivation, and literacy achievement. *Journal of Educational Psychology, 89,* 736–742.

Murphy, S., with Shannon, P., Johnston, P., & Hansen, J. (1998). *Fragile evidence: A critique of reading assessment.* Mahwah, NJ: Erlbaum.

National Reading Panel. (2000). *Teaching children to read: An evidence-based assessment of the scientific research literature on reading and its implications for reading instruction—reports of the subgroups.* Washington, DC: National Institute of Child Health and Development.

No child left behind act of 2001. (2002). Public Law 107-110.

Paris, S. G. (2001). Trojan horse in the schoolyard: The hidden threats in high-stakes testing. *Issues in Education, 6,* 1–16.

Paris, S. G., & McEvoy, A. P. (2001). Harmful and enduring effects of high-stakes testing. *Issues in Education, 6,* 145–159.

Paris, S. G., & Urdan, T. (2001). Policies and practices of high-stakes testing that influence teachers and schools. *Issues in Education, 6,* 83–107.

Pressley, M. (1997). The cognitive science of reading. *Contemporary Educational Psychology, 22,* 247–259.

Pressley, M., & Afflerbach, P. (1995). *Verbal protocols of reading.* Mahwah, NJ: Erlbaum.

Pressley, M., Duke, N. K., & Boling, E. C. (2004). The educational science and scientifically-based instruction we need: Lessons from reading research and policy making. *Harvard Educational Review, 74,* 30–61.

Pressley, M., & El-Dinary, P. B. (1997). What we know about translating comprehension strategies instruction research into practice. *Journal of Learning Disabilities, 30,* 486–488.

Pressley, M., El-Dinary, P. B., Gaskins, I., Schuder, T., Bergman, J. L., Almasi, J., & Brown, R. (1992). Beyond direct explanation: Transactional instruction of reading comprehension strategies. *Elementary School Journal, 92,* 511–554.

Pressley, M., Harris, K. R., & Marks, M. B. (1992). But good strategy instructors are constructivists! *Educational Psychology Review, 4,* 1–32.

Pressley, M., & Palmer, B. (1992). Literacy acquisition at home and school: Review of C. E. Snow, W. S. Barnes, J. Chandler, I. F. Goodman, and L. Hemphill, *Unfulfilled expectations: Home and school influences on literacy. Contemporary Psychology, 37,* 18–19.

RAND Reading Study Group. (2001). *Reading for understanding: Toward an R&D program in reading comprehension.* Santa Monica, CA: RAND.

Schauble, L. (1990). Belief revision in children: The role of prior knowledge and strategies for generating evidence. *Journal of Experimental Child Psychology, 49,* 31–57.

Shulman, L. S., & Keislar, E. R. (Eds.). (1966). *Learning by discovery: A critical appraisal.* Chicago: Rand McNally.

Sizer, T. R. (1996). *Horace's hope: What works for the American high school.* New York: Houghton Mifflin.

Slavin, R. E., & Cheung, A. (2005). A synthesis of research on language of reading instruction for English language learners. *Review of Educational Research, 75,* 247–284.

Snow, C. E., Barnes, W. S., Chandler, J., Goodman, I. F., & Hemphill, L. (1991). *Unfulfilled expectations: Home and school influences on literacy*. Cambridge, MA: Harvard University Press.

Snow, C. E., Burns, M. S., & Griffin, P. (1998*). Preventing reading difficulties in young children*. Washington, DC: National Academy Press.

Vygotsky, L. S. (1978). *Mind in society: The development of higher psychological processes*. Cambridge, MA: Harvard University Press.

Wasik, B. A. (1998). Volunteer tutoring programs in reading: A review. *Reading Research Quarterly, 33*, 266–292.

Wittrock, M. C. (1966). The learning by discovery hypothesis. In L. S. Shulman & E. R. Keislar (Eds.), *Learning by discovery: A critical appraisal* (pp. 33–75). Chicago: Rand McNally.

Wood, E., Woloshyn, V. E., & Willoughby, T. (Eds.). (1995). *Cognitive strategy instruction for middle and high schools*. Cambridge, MA: Brookline Books.

Author Index

Subject Index

"f" following a page number indicates a figure; "t" following a page number indicates a table

461